# PERSPECTIVES IN CARIBBEAN PSYCHOLOGY

Editors

**Frederick W. Hickling**
**Brigitte K. Matthies**
**Kai Morgan**
**Roger C. Gibson**

**CARIMENSA**
University of the West Indies, Mona, Jamaica

Caribbean Institute of Mental Health and Substance Abuse
– CARIMENSA
University of the West Indies
Mona Campus   Kingston 7   Jamaica WI

ISBN    978-976-41-0224-3

Cover background painting by Nicholas Palomino

Cover insert painting by Nicole Bender

Designed and formatted by Cecille Maye-Hemmings

Printed in Jamaica
by Phoenix Printery Ltd

# Contents

# Foreword

> Every person is in some respects
> Like all other persons
> Like some other persons
> Like no other person.

*Author unknown*

The study of human behaviour has a fascination which has spawned the discipline of psychology and generated several theories to explain the commonalities, variations and idiosyncrasies which typify the personalities, opinions, beliefs, attitudes and values which individuals develop and exhibit. The editors of this very impressive volume have brought together a rich collection of articles which make a significant contribution to the psychology literature as they explore, analyse, evaluate and discuss various aspects of the behaviour of Caribbean people as well as internationally practised and culturally relevant interventions when this behaviour is deemed to be pathological. The editors and authors, led by Frederick W. Hickling and Brigitte K. Matthies, must be hailed as trailblazers; they have not only been pioneers in establishing the graduate programme in psychology at the University of the West Indies (UWI), they have also now documented material which will support and enrich both the UWI's and other similar programmes in the Caribbean and beyond.

The volume provides readers with the Caribbean cultural context and framework from which these articles are to be considered in **Part I: Background and Philosophy** and edited by Brigitte K. Matthies and Kai Morgan. Identity and culture as well as survival and psychopathology are issues which are explored, and Morgan and O'Garo's analysis of the historical and cultural influences such as race, religion, family forms and language, which affect the development and expressions of Caribbean identity, sets the stage for the case studies reported by Hickling and emanating from upper, middle and lower social classes as well as from the 'under' class in Jamaican society. The patterns of mental illness revealed by these studies are linked to historic as well as contemporary tensions, based mainly on race and social class. A prominent feature is the incidence of migration as 'escape', as 'coping', and as source of major personal conflict. The web of relationships which contribute to the psychopathology of the Jamaican people is diagrammatically illustrated and encapsulates the multi-faceted nature of the interaction among influences and between these influences and the individual. Central to this web is the family, and a chapter by Ramkissoon et al. is devoted to consideration of this primary source of many of the guiding stimuli affecting behaviour in a community and a society. The wide variations in family structure and arrangements and the challenges, including those which are culturally based, which can hinder the attainment of home-ostasis, or balance, in the family system, are highlighted. The difficulties these present for therapy interventions as well as for assessments are outlined. The resilience of youth and their ability not merely to 'cope with' but to 'triumph over' risk factors which impact on their lives is also a focus, and Robertson-Hickling shares case studies which demonstrate the strong supportive influence and impact of interventions in coming to grips with racial identity and discrimination in both Jamaica and the UK. The cultural diversity of Trinidad and Tobago and the retention and expression of specific 'indigenous' social and cultural behaviours by the different ethnic and cultural groups, form the basis of research and analysis carried out by Maharajh and Kalpoo, who also debate the possibility of misinterpretation and misrepresentation of these behaviours as being patterns of psychological disorder. Two fairly large and interesting studies explore the historic as well as current attachment of a stigma to mental illness, defined as "worthy of disgrace, degradation, fear and social distance", and the detrimental consequences to the mentally ill person – medically, socially and legally – are identified. The authors, Arthur et al., emphasize the importance of education in influencing policy, changing attitudes, reducing the isolation of the mentally ill and improving the quality of life they enjoy.

Brigitte K. Matthies is the editor of **Part II**, which explores the issues of development and the vital importance of early childhood influences, along with the variables which operate in later childhood and adolescence and affect resultant adult functioning, including sexuality. The nature-nurture interaction in the development of the child from conception to birth, and then during early development is explained, while the environmental and cultural influences on physical, socio-emotional growth and cognitive development as well as language acquisition and development are highlighted by Samms-Vaughan. This interaction of the biological with the psychological and social, and the challenges involved in identity-seeking are the subject of the chapter by Brodie-Walker which focuses on adolescents. 'Abnormal' development, expressed in personality disorder, violence and antisocial attitudes and behaviour, is analysed; much of the analysis is research-based and thus provides readers with primary sources of data on a population which has not hitherto been extensively examined. An analysis of the pervasiveness and increasing incidence of Caribbean violence is linked historically to the Caribbean legacy of enslavement and plantation life by Matthies et al., who postulate that the current experience stems from economic and social factors, is manifested in hostility and abuse expressed physically, psychologically and sexually, and affects children, spouses, homosexuals and self through suicide. This proposition is the subject of detailed analysis, and the influence of factors such as music, media and videogames are underscored.

An important chapter by Haynes-Robinson on the evolution of sexual behaviour in the Caribbean provides a 'psychohistoriographic' perspective and takes the reader through a discussion of the sexual norms and behaviours of the Taino Indians to present-day issues of sex and sexuality; from the fluidity and equality of gender roles among the Taino through the emergence of more defined gender roles during colonization by the Spanish and the British to the post-slavery use of sex and sexuality for status and power, giving rise to the development of hegemonic masculinity. Current norms relating to sexuality, including the ongoing rejection of homosexuality, as well as explicit expressions of sexuality through avenues such as calypso, Carnival and Dance Hall are explored. The chapter on the psychological impact of HIV and AIDS by Weller and Khan underlines the value of an interdisciplinary response to a serious health issue and the importance of psychological perspectives in the understanding and treatment of this and similar concerns in a particular cultural setting. Thus, 'new' rather than 'best' practices are discussed and the analysis serves as a catalyst for innovative and culturally relevant responses. These responses may or may not include aspects of indigenous traditional medicine, which constitute an historic and cultural retention in the Caribbean, but which has been regarded as an uncomfortable 'fit' with conventional Western medicine. Recent initiatives in health and wellness which consider the mind/body/spirit/emotion linkage herald recognition of the role of an individual's total lifestyle in the treatment of mental and other illnesses. Case studies from Hickling and James point to the persistence of beliefs in consequences of 'red-eye' (jealousy), 'bad mind' (spite), and 'grudgeful' (envy) and support the argument of the phenomenological implications of these traditional formulations.

The development of metrics which can be used to provide empirical data and informed insights into adult functioning is particularly interesting. Maladaptive behaviours which result in social dysfunction and occupational malfunction are unmasked as personality disorders by Hickling et al. and the unique ways in which these are manifested in the cultural context justify the need to create a Jamaica Personality Disorder Index. The chapter by Tony Ward on neuropsychological assessment – defined as the "application of psychological knowledge to the understanding and remediation of neurological conditions such as head injury, stroke, Alzheimer's disease, etc.", extends the discussion on the use of measurement tools to instruments such as the Wechsler Adult Intelligence Scale and highlights the value of such assessments in the holistic treatment of a range of clients – in schools where children have special learning needs as well as in clinics and hospitals with adult patients who are suffering from neurological and other disorders. Development of an instrument to measure severe psychopathology in the culturally diverse milieu of the Caribbean is outlined in detail by Lambert et al. and elucidates the challenges of constructing culturally relevant, reliable and valid measures using rigorous statistical procedures. Such instruments are vital for explanation and prediction of psychopathology as well as for facilitating research which can advance knowledge and improve treatment.

**Part III** is edited by Frederick Hickling and here the utility and value of the psychology professions, the issues surrounding the possible tensions which can exist in relation to the roles and responsibilities of professionals in this area, and the application of traditional models of psychotherapy in Caribbean settings are reviewed. Psychological assessment, which is widely used by therapists to deepen understanding of their patient-clients in order to inform 'characterological' diagnoses, raises similar challenges for the professional as do other forms of measurement in terms of reliability, validity and cultural relevance. Johnson and Coley stress that experience and professional expertise in the collection and interpretation of data and generation of reports which can inform research and training are vital. A thought-provoking article on the application of traditional psychotherapy models from Johnson et al. clearly communicates the theoretical bases of practice for the clinical psychologist and urges flexibility in the application of these theories. An eclectic and integrated approach is recommended as being the most successful method of facilitating psychological health in the Caribbean milieu. This recommendation is supported by the personal testimonies/narratives of professionals, reported by Hickling et al., which allow for an understanding of the complementary rather than competitive nature of the practice of clinical psychology and psychiatry, and underscore the necessity for professionals in these areas to work together now and in the future. Further evidence of this need is provided by Doorbar through the case studies of psychotherapy culled from over 53 years of one clinical psychologist's practice among patients with differing demographics; these cases vividly demonstrate the variety, the challenges and outcomes of practice. Also highlighted by Shields and Ottey in this section is the value of forensic psychology, which addresses the application of psychological theories and principles within the legal system, its relevance at different levels of the judicial system and for differing purposes. The ethical and other issues associated with these psychologists providing specialist testimony and being the expected 'expert witness' are fully explored. Of special interest in the Caribbean, which has produced a disproportionate number of successful world class athletes, is the chapter on sports psychology by Morgan and Malete, which highlights the importance of including issues such as motivation, competence, self-fficacy, self-confidence and self-esteem which comprise the psychological dimension, to the physiological and biomechanical training for the holistic development of athletes.

Understanding and heeding the cultural context is a common thread throughout the volume. Language, race and the media have been identified as important cultural variables in understanding the psychology of Caribbean people. The investigation of the role of language and race in the development of self-concept among Caribbean children by Carpenter and Devonish not only provides very useful methodological guidelines for research with young children but also yields interesting findings relating to the self-esteem and self-image of Belizean and Jamaican children in middle childhood. The influence and interventions possible in a media-saturated society are outlined by Hickling et al. who point to the media as an agent of negative impact as well as positive change; the former having tremendous cognitive, emotional and behavioural effects; the latter possible through the efforts of media psychologists and the implementation of creative responses.

The chapter by Hickling et al. on therapeutic strategies, aimed at the resocialization and rehabilitation of persons who have to be taken into care, recount the shift from historic custodial philosophy, to an embrace of greater communication and a more egalitarian system than the 'total institution' concept, and the application of therapeutic community principles in Jamaica. The expected resistance to such change and the difficulties associated with this are outlined and fully discussed, along with strategies to overcome such resistance.

This exciting compilation of articles will appeal to a variety of audiences: psychology professionals will welcome the theoretical reviews, the documentation of valuable research and the culturally relevant and contextualized discourse; students will benefit from the comprehensive coverage of issues and the insightful analysis of these issues; and lay persons who have an interest in observing and understanding behaviour will consider this a treasure trove of information. The editors and authors are to be congratulated on not only providing a most valuable resource and accessible reference on a range of vitally important issues, but also stimulating thought and ideas which will guide future research and investigation in Caribbean and cross-cultural psychology.

Elsa Leo-Rhynie, CD, PhD
Professor Emerita
The University of the West Indies

August 2008

# Introduction

Is psychology a 'universal' phenomenon, where 'one size fits all' applies to people and cultures worldwide? We think not. Much of the published knowledge in the field of psychology has emanated from the resource rich nations and scholars of Europe and North America, and much of that work has evolved from and centred on people and cultures of Caucasian origin. Many psychologists and psychiatrists who work in the Caribbean have constantly laboured with psychological concepts and evidence which make little sense to the people whom they serve, and have struggled to apply theories and approaches to their work that defy logic and ignore much of their daily reality. Many of the psychologists and psychiatrists of the Caribbean have been trained in Europe and North America, in alien environments from which they were born and raised, and with different languages and cultures, different ideologies and epistemes that have shaped their world views. There is no doubt that societies – like people – are living, growing and developing organisms, with social values and outlooks that are constantly changing and evolving. Culture is never static, and although constantly being manipulated by the dominant social group of each nation, it is consistently being shaped by beliefs, outlooks and strategies of the minority cultures that exist within these nations.

Is there a Caribbean psychology? We think so. We believe that many of the chapters presented in this book will provide the empirical evidence that this is so. Perspectives in Caribbean Psychology has been written for students of psychology in the Caribbean at every level, and for readers worldwide who share an interest in multicultural psychology. We are convinced that the Caribbean has a unique culture that has significantly influenced the world. The Caribbean has had a unique history of invasion, conquest and domination by an aggressive European culture. The Spanish, the British, the French, the Dutch, the Germans and the North Americans continue to struggle for hegemony and dominance in the more than forty Caribbean island-nations and twenty-five million people who constitute the geographic Caribbean. These European countries have instituted oppressive colonial, dominant social structures over the past five centuries that have been characterized by genocidal eradication of the indigenous populations, the introduction of forced migration and enslavement of African people, and the indenture of hundreds of thousands of poverty-stricken Asians, and the ruthless exploitation of the natural and physical resources of these island-territories. The stark similarity of the tourism culture in most of these island territories is still dominated by European- and North American-owned facilities, even though there has been an attempt in some islands to replace this with local ownership. However, European and North American social and cultural values continue to dominate, and is an ever-present reminder of the continued European-American domination of this region that shapes our language, our thinking and our cultural practices. This book attempts to record the psychological experiences and dynamics that represent the daily struggle with this domination and the unique psychological realities that have emerged in the attempts to come to terms with this reality. It attempts to chronicle the adaptation, cultural retentions, resilience and migratory tenacity that is the hallmark of our Caribbean people at home and in the Diaspora.

The task of marshalling this evidence must be placed in the context of the historical realities of the development of psychology and psychiatry in this region. In the English-speaking Caribbean, psychology has only gained real prominence in the educational tapestry in the past decade, with the development of graduate and postgraduate courses in psychology and clinical psychology at the University of the West Indies (UWI) (Hickling and Matthies, 2003), and other local and regional universities. The fact that psychology is one of the largest undergraduate degrees offered by the UWI, with nearly 700 new students annually reflects the huge demand in the Caribbean to understand what makes us think, feel and behave. The development of postgraduate training programs in clinical psychology at UWI – both at Mona, Jamaica and St. Augustine, Trinidad – since 2003 has already made an indelible mark in the process of this self-understanding, and in the study and documentation of Caribbean psychology. By refocusing the centre of psychology training in the Caribbean, the European and North American epistemological stranglehold on this topic and on our thinking has now been broken. We are now producing our own graduates in this area, most of whom are remaining in the region and enriching the study, research and teaching in Caribbean psychology. We believe that the development of postgraduate clinical psychology by UWI in this decade has been one of the most significant epistemological and ideological events of this region, one that will have far-reaching results and outcomes on the region and the world. This volume is a reflection of that profound impact and will undoubtedly prove to be an invaluable resource for current and future students and practitioners of psychology in the Caribbean Diaspora.

The fact that there have been four editors of this book, two psychiatrists and two psychologists, also reflect a profound shift in the approach to mental health in this region. Traditionally, the bitter rift that has existed between psychiatrists and psychologists in the First World has spilled over into the mental health realities in the English-speaking Caribbean region, with psychiatry itself being the ugly duckling of Medicine, tending to keep psychology out of the regional arena. This one-sided hegemony was broken at the UWI and in the Caribbean in 2002, when a Jamaican psychiatrist and a Jamaican psychologist teamed up to establish the postgraduate programmes in clinical psychology at UWI. This book is a reflection of that unification effort. There has been, and continues to be, significant resistance to the introduction of clinical psychology in Medicine in the region. The divisive tendencies that overwhelm First World mental health have, not unexpectedly, leaked into the Caribbean experience. In spite of this resistance, this book reflects a huge leap in the negation of this resistance.

This book has taken five years to evolve, with the assistance of a grant from the former Principal of UWI, Mona – Professor Kenneth Hall, who on retirement from UWI has become the Governor-General of Jamaica. Our thanks are extended to him and his vision for the need of psychology in the region. The Professor of Psychiatry at UWI Mona then assembled this team of psychiatrists and psychologists to marshal the forces around the Caribbean to make this publication possible. The team devised the structural and conceptual synthesis of the volume, which was divided into three sections – Part I: Background and philosophy, edited by psychologists Brigitte K. Matthies and Kai Morgan; Part II: Applications and interactions of psychology in everyday life, edited by Brigitte K. Matthies; Part III: Roles and tools of the Caribbean psychologist, edited by psychiatrist Frederick W. Hickling. Psychiatrist Roger Gibson had the arduous task of communicating the requirements of the editorial team to the prospective authors, encouraging and cajoling the scholarship to produce each chapter, and to marshal the emerging academic material for peer-review and completion. A team approach to the writing and production of each chapter was encouraged, and it is a tribute to the colleagues across the Caribbean, North America and the UK that the production of the ideas and the translation into the written work have emerged at the highest standard and with a minimum of disagreement or conflict.

The publication of *Perspectives in Caribbean Psychology* is also helping to break new ground and forge new directions in mental health publication in the Caribbean region. The fledgling CARIMENSA Press that has published this volume is a newly developed publishing house dedicated to writings on mental health in the region, and aims to fill the vacuum of mental health publications in the Caribbean and around the world. The CARIMENSA Press is a component of the recently established Caribbean Institute of Mental Health and Substance Abuse (CARIMENSA) located in the Faculty of Medical Science, UWI, Mona. CARIMENSA focuses on the delivery of Cultural Therapy to children, adolescents, and adults at risk in the region. This Institute aims at emancipating the region from the mental slavery that has gripped its people for five centuries. CARIMENSA also focuses on the postgraduate teaching of Cultural Therapy as a novel Caribbean-originating and Caribbean-based method of combating the massive psycho-sociological problems of Caribbean people. Finally, CARIMENSA focuses on the research into mental health issues in Caribbean people, especially in the use of Cultural Therapy to overcome many of these problems, and to synthesize these issues into academic scholarship through the

CARIMENSA Press. The emergence of Perspectives in Caribbean Psychology must be seen from this perspective, in the forging of new directions for mental health in the region and the world and must be seen in tandem with its two previous publications _Dream a World – The Development of Cultural Therapy in Jamaica_, and _Psychohistoriography – A Postcolonial Psychoanalytic and Psychotherapeutic Model_. Certain chapters in the latter book were initially designed for inclusion in _Perspectives in Caribbean Psychology_. However, as the size of the latter book burgeoned beyond seven hundred pages and twenty-four chapters, the editorial decision to publish the chapters on psychohistoriography, a postcolonial Caribbean psychotherapeutic process, in a stand-alone authored volume, was made.

The painting on the front cover has special significance for this book. This painting was created by Nicole Bender, a young Jamaican woman who was one of the pioneer students of the Clinical Psychology M.Sc. programme in 2002 at UWI, Mona. Nicole presented the painting as a gift to Professor Hickling as an artistic compilation and her impressions of the underlying components of one of the fundamental courses in the newly created M.Sc. programme. The course was called 'An Introduction to Caribbean Psychology' and had been designed and taught by Hickling. It traced a historiographic account of Caribbean psychology, with an exhaustive list of required readings of major Caribbean historians, sociologists, anthropologists, psychologists and psychiatrists. Ms. Bender's painting captured the essence of the course, and traced the Caribbean struggle of genocide, colonization, plunder, slavery and indenture, and captured the resilience of the Caribbean people against these monumental odds. Much of this historiography is presented in the book published in 2007 by CARIMENSA, _Psychohistoriography – A Postcolonial Psychoanalytic and Psychotherapeutic Model_, which should be read in parallel with _Perspectives in Caribbean Psychology_.

Several people need to be thanked for providing the pieces of this complex jigsaw puzzle that has resulted in this final outcome – first, the UWI Mona Principal's research team for funding the development of this book; then, the UWI Mona Strategic Transformation Team under the leadership of Professors Alvin Wint and Ken Hall for the seed financing for CARIMENSA and the CARIMENSA Press; third, the Head of Department of Sociology, Psychology and Social Work, Faculty of Social Sciences – Mr. Clement Branche, the Dean of the Faculty of Medical Science – Professor Archibald McDonald, and the present Principal of UWI, Mona – Professor Gordon Shirley, for their continued support of the process. The MSc Clinical Psychology programme and the CHASE Fund have played an important supportive role in the production of this book. The CARIMENSA Press publication team – headed by copy editor and compositor Cecille Maye-Hemmings, and including the indexer Maxine McDonnough, as well as Richard Scholefield of Phoenix Printery – has to be singled out for its painstaking and arduous work in the detailed preparation of this volume of which we are all proud. We wish to thank all of the authors across the globe for their work above and beyond the call of duty, and finally to one of the pioneers in educational psychology in the Caribbean, former Pro Vice-Chancellor and Principal, Professor Emerita Elsa Leo-Rhynie who has written such a rich and exciting foreword.

One Love.

Frederick W. Hickling
Brigitte K. Matthies
Kai Morgan
Roger C. Gibson

## REFERENCES

Hickling, F. W., & Matthies, B. K. (2003). The establishment of a clinical psychology post-graduate programme at the University of the West Indies. *Caribbean Journal of Education* 25 (1): 25-36.

# PART I

## BACKGROUND AND PHILOSOPHY

*Edited by*

Brigitte K. Matthies and Kai Morgan

# 1 Caribbean Identity Issues

*Kai Morgan & Keisha-Gaye N. O'Garo*

## Concept of Identity

The nature of identity has been an ongoing debate within the realm of sociology, psychology, mental health and many other related disciplines for a considerable period. The construct is multifaceted in its definition (characteristics determining who or what a person or thing is), and cultural in its orientation as each culture or subculture must define specifically what those characteristics are. This introduces the concept of a cultural identity and, more distinctively, a Caribbean identity. Some of these general characteristics may include personality, social role, gender and family. According to Mills (1990) and Miller (cited in Barron & Reddock, 2001), this framework encompasses more elements for Africans across the Diaspora, versus other ethnic groups who have not historically endured the impact of slavery. These factors include body image, race, skin colour, physical beauty, education, religion, and community. These factors have been widely explored within both the African-American (Clark & Clark, 1947; Cross, 1991) and the Caribbean contexts (Balutansky & Sourieau, 1998; Barron & Rheddock, 2001; Chevannes, 2002), as key factors in determination of selfhood. Debates and controversy have ranged between the low self-esteem and fragmented identity of African peoples and the fallacy of such a finding. Nevertheless, how these factors began to manifest themselves in Caribbean culture requires a discussion of the historical antecedents.

## EFFACEMENT OF AFRICAN IDENTITY

Slavery was a sophisticated and highly-developed operation that was devised to infiltrate the preservation of the African infrastructure. To ensure control, slave traders imposed division by instilling fear, distrust, and envy. Upon arrival in the New World, many slaves were isolated from their families and tribes, and were placed with other slaves of different linguistic backgrounds, thereby severing communication and limiting opportunities for conspiracy and revolution (Geiss, 1974). Slaves were pitted against each another, based on their skin colour, age, and preferential treatment. Furthermore, to ensure that slaves become lost people, with neither history, past, nor future, slaveholders erased memories of Africa and instilled Eurocentric values and religious beliefs in them. Not only were slaves discouraged from practising their traditional customs and sharing stories from their homeland, but they were normally subjected to horrific atrocities, such as flogging, mutilation, and death, if they were either believed to be or found to be in violation of the rules. The African family was shattered, and with the sanctions of marriage dismantled and internalized as dispensable, the roles of fatherhood and motherhood snatched away, a plethora of orphans was created. Even to the present day, the feeble family infrastructure persists.

The advent of slavery was to have an enormous economic, sociological and psychological impact on Caribbean societies. The slave trade represented the beginning of the loss of African identity and the beginning of psychic fragmentation. Faced with a legacy of pillaging and destruction of fundamental institutions, and concepts of self, the Caribbean community was charged with the awesome task of rebuilding itself.

## EDUCATION AND INFRASTRUCTURE

Before the triangular trade, there were clear modes of development and structure in Africa and in the Caribbean. The original inhabitants of the Caribbean islands, the Tainos (Arawaks), Caribs, and Mayans, had educational and infrastructural systems that were so well developed, and so complex that to this day, their durability and quality can neither be mimicked nor understood by the greatest of architects, archaeologists, or anthropologists (Williams, 1987). The wealth and knowledge that Africans brought to the rest of the world is now a well-documented phenomenon (Williams, 1987). Their knowledge of art, architecture, science,

and religion was so vast that others, seeking world dominance and credibility, and wishing to denigrate the greatness of the African, sought to
pillage, steal and plagiarize their works (Williams, 1987).

Slavery and the triangular trade were clearly money-making ven-
tures. Europeans needed labour for sugar production and there was a significant resource base in Africa and, therefore, this was utilized (Williams,
1994). Above all, it ensured British capitalism and economic wealth.
Needless to say, the education of these slaves and the development of the
economies in which they lived were not items on the priority list. Jamaica
and Belize were known as 'plunder' economies, where there was little
focus on the establishment of educational institutions and infrastructure
for the masses, except for the few elite slave masters, plantation owners
and their families. Belize was a rich source of logwood and mahogany
(Augustine, 1997), while Jamaica was rich in sugar production. The colonial masters sought to exploit the resources of these lands with no future
thoughts of development. In these societies, the plantation owners rarely
occupied the land, but had their overseers manage the properties. These
overseers were usually individuals who were at the bottom of the socioeconomic ladder in Britain and saw moving to the colonies as potentially
status-building. Often they left their families in Britain and sexually
exploited the slave women on the plantation, fathering many mulatto
children and influencing the social structure of the plantation in an inde-
fatigable way (Patterson, 1973). The Caribbean communities of Barbados,
Trinidad, Jamaica and the Leeward Islands have all been defined by sociologists as having fractured, unstable, family lives and structures, resulting from slavery and the plantation system (Higman, 1975).

The Africans brought their knowledge and expertise with them to the
Caribbean, but the process involved in slavery slowly diminished their
value, and inhibited their artistic endeavours. Some of the traditions had
to be practised in secret and others were almost completely abandoned.
This obstructed the slaves' education and the education of their offspring,
limiting their Africentric worldview and its impact on infrastructure and
policy.

Hilliard and Akbar (1998), in their discussion of education, highlight
its important and crucial functions as a vehicle for the transmission of
self-knowledge and identity formation. However, the 'diseducation' and
'miseducation' of Africans in the Americas and the Caribbean have

served to dismantle these functions. Diseducation is defined as the process that occurred during the first generation of slaves, whereby they were disconnected from the naturalness of life and 'miseducated', that is, indoctrinated with the imperialist or colonial views of life, reasoning, community, religion and culture, and trained to operate in a way that goes against their natural inclinations (Hilliard & Akbar, 1998; Woodson, 1990). Miseducation, for example, would be a lion that has been trained to jump through burning hoops. This function is not necessary to his survival and he has been trained in this manner for a totally different purpose, which inevitably serves the trainer and is a handicap to the trainee. As part of our training and miseducation as Black people, we have been indoctrinated within the concept of Cartesian dualism (Akbar, 1990). This concept postulates that the mind and body are separate entities and hardly interrelated in their functioning (Damasio, 1994). Thus, Black people, adhering to this mind-set put forth by the 'great' philosopher René Descartes, begin to operate at the extremes of particular dichotomies, instead of within a balanced system (Akbar, 1990). The most salient of these dichotomies are between

1) the individual and the collective;

2) materialism and spiritualism;

3) rational and emotional;

4) competition and co-operation; and

5) structure and spontaneity.

Akbar (1990) believes that the African mind has been split and that our focus on one end of the dichotomy has resulted in all the social and psychological problems that Africans across the Diaspora face. Our lack of power, poor conflict resolution skills, lack of community spirit, and over-representation in prisons and mental health facilities, are all manifestations of this split mentality – a mentality which is the direct result of being stripped of the functions that education serves in any community, or group of people, in their social and self-development.

Education is the vehicle through which change is ultimately made. Through the miseducation of African people, our identities have gone astray. We have found ourselves in a place where our children do not know their history, and a people without their history, are a lost people.

As previously mentioned, the contributions of Africans have been often ignored. The great accomplishments of Egypt, Ethiopia, and Nubian civilizations were all eradicated and the colonizer was portrayed as a saviour of the primitive race, bringing Christianity and westernization. School curricula are not geared towards the edification of Black people by Black people. In Haiti, French Creole has become the scapegoat for education's poor productivity (cited in Balutansky & Sourieau, 1998), and in Jamaica, the widespread illiteracy is likely due to the lack of cultivating the taste for reading, as opposed to the inability to read (Bryan, 1991). Although the curriculum does entail small facets of the African culture included in History, English Literature, and Religious Education, by and large, the creolization of education has resulted in another facet of our identity in which great attempts have been made to eradicate the African detail of history.

## FAMILY AND COMMUNITY

Slavery in the Caribbean continued on its path of destruction of a race, in its dealings and subjugation of the family structure. Divide and rule principles were utilized to strengthen prejudices, to separate families and to alienate communities. The Africans' upbringing was collectivist in nature, with strong communal ties in a predominantly tribal or village setting, where the extended family consisted not only of blood relatives, but of the neighbourhood, and these played vital roles in raising the children, taking care of the family, and supporting the community as a whole. During the triangular trade, rules of division were enforced, disintegrating the organization of the Black family and community. Women and children were separated from men and sent to different colonies. Upon their arrival in the various colonies, a more deliberate structure was imposed, whereby men and women were often removed from families and transposed to different plantations; individuals and families were stripped of their names, thereby establishing the framework for instability and the destruction of the family as it had always been known (Patterson, 1973). The division not only fragmented collective disposition, but it sowed seeds emphasizing individuality, thereby encouraging competiveness and contention amongst Blacks. This dissension was evident in the hierarchical distinction between house and field slaves and the power differential of having slaves capture and punish other slaves. The social structural dynamics and functioning of plantation life only served to enhance values and morals which were to the detriment of the 'trainees', stripping them of their intuitive understanding of family and community, once again impacting on their sense of self.

The lack of a nuclear family structure, the demoralization of the male – leading to a matriarchal society, abuse, respect for elders and the fact that marriage was not encouraged, are all factors that play very significant roles in our concept of the family today and represent the legacy that slavery left behind. Patterson (1973) speaks of "the ambivalence in the negro mother who saw her children as a burden on one hand and love for them on the other. This led to a combination of extreme cruelty from frustration and great love and affection for her children. This cruelty was partly displaced aggression and hatred for her slave masters."

The nuclear family could hardly exist within the slave context. As such, it was actively discouraged. Even where the family structure was developed, the man could not assert his authority as a husband or father, as his wife or daughter was also someone else's property. The result of this was a complete demoralization of the Negro male, incapable of asserting his authority either as a husband or a father, the object of his affection often beaten, abused and raped before his very eyes. With the female partner often having closer links with the source of all power in the society, the male slave was emasculated. He, therefore, lost all his masculine pride and developed irresponsible parenting and sexual attitudes, which persists even today. Post-slavery, Black women were perceived as less threatening than their male counterparts, and as a result, found employment more easily, making them the primary breadwinners of the family. With these role reversals, the Black family fell prey to enormous strains, fragmenting the relationship between man and woman, father and child, and mother and child. This further negated what had become the remote and unusual concept of an intricate, multi-faceted connection between parents and children as a whole unit.

Not only has slavery infringed on the Black family and the Black man, it has also left its stain on Black women, creating the erroneous misperception that Black women are sexually promiscuous, loose, aggressive, and 'babymaking machines'(Akbar, 2006). During slavery, White men placed White women on pedestals, never considering them as sexual beings. They took out their sexual frustrations and aggression on Black women, thus fostering the idea that Black women were only property used for exploitation and degradation, while their White female counterparts were idealized as pure and untouched. These horrendous acts have stripped away Black women's trust in themselves, in men, and in society as a whole – a distrust which is evident even in contemporary society, when Black men complain that Black women are strong, angry, controlling, crazy, jealous, never satisfied, and demanding.

The bond between mother and child also disintegrated under the enormous pressure of slavery. Upon giving birth, children were snatched out of their mothers' arms, preventing them from performing one of the most intimate, yet essential acts, to ensure that a connection was established with their offspring: bonding. Again, this disconnection fostered the success of slavery. As a result of this inhumane conditioning, many mothers became either abusive or over-protective (Akbar, 2006), taking out their fear, powerlessness, anger, and frustration on those human beings who could not hold control over them.

The bond between father and child is almost non-existent, with an enormous number of children growing up in today's society without fathers playing an active role in their lives. During slavery, Black men were valued for their siring abilities and their physical strength (Akbar, 2006). The ability to procreate many children for production purposes, coupled with the debasement of marriage, created an entrenched behaviour – that persists even today – of sexual conquests with minimal responsibility or commitment to the partner, the children, and the family in its entirety.

## RELIGION

Religion is a key component of the African's understanding of selfhood. According to Mbiti (1975):

> Wherever the African is, there is his religion, he carries it to the fields where he is sowing seeds or harvesting a new crop; he takes it with him to the beer party or to attend a funeral ceremony, and if he is educated, he takes religion with him to the examination room at school or in the university; if he is a politician he takes it to the house of parliament.

Again, this was an institution that was summarily pinpointed as primitive and dangerous, and its practice was prohibited on most, if not all, plantations. The tenets of Christianity were superimposed as the 'way to salvation' and the beginning of westernization as we know it today, planted its roots firmly in the ground. However, Africans have held on to their traditions in many ways, and today the tenets and practices of Obeah, Myalism, Voodoo, Santeria, Pukkumina, Revivalism and Rastafari are a testament to the creolization of religion. Religion became a survival mechanism. However, in many Caribbean countries, the African flavour of religion is seen as denigration. It is, therefore, often marginalized, as in the case of Obeah in Jamaica and Voodoo in Haiti.

Obeah is a witch or wizard that possesses the power to leave his body, fly at night, and cause great harm and/or kill his enemy (Erskine, 1981). There is a sense of mystery and reticence tied to the practice of Obeah, dating back to slavery. Slaves were prohibited from practising Obeah, since it did not conform to the Christian rules and dogma. Nevertheless, many sought the Obeah man for protection against their master and for taking revenge on fellow slaves, since it was forbidden for slaves to fight one another (Erksine, 1981). The Obeah man was viewed as prestigious, and was approached with fear and reverence by slaves. Even today, the Obeah man is sought surreptitiously for his powers to ward off spirits, for purposes of revenge, and to win someone's heart. In Haiti, Voodoo is also alive and strong. Legba is a maimed Haitian God whose roots are in Africa and Greece. Legba's creolization shows the insecurity that counters secure ideologies and dogmas; however, Legba is viewed as a metaphoric challenge to European authority. In Suriname, Winti focuses on personified supernatural beings who can disclose the past, present, and future and cure illness. This practice has also been forbidden, but this has only served to fuel the revolutionary impulse (Balutansky & Sourieau, 1998).

## SKIN COLOUR, PHYSICAL BEAUTY AND BODY IMAGE

Prior to the settlement of Caribbean territories and the institution of slavery, Europeans had maintained negative attitudes about skin colour (Augustine, 1997). This was impacted on by the language where 'white' usually represents all that is pure and good (e.g. virginity, purity), while 'black' connotes evil, dirt and sinister behaviour (Augustine, 1997; Hillman, 1997). This overall attitude of cultural and racial superiority, reinforced by Cartesian dualism, became the basis on which the power and dominance of the Caucasian over the Negro was utilized and justified in slavery. It also formed the premise for colour prejudice, which has lasted throughout the years and exists in both overt and subtle ways in contemporary society (Augustine, 1997). However, Williams (1994), an economist, would disagree with this perspective as he articulated a purely economic, not racial basis for the enslavement of Africans:

> the reason was economic, not racial; it had to do not with the colour of the labourer but with the cheapness of the labour. As compared with Indian and white labour, Negro slavery was eminently superior... The features of the man, his hair, colour and dentrifice, his 'subhuman' characteristics, so widely pleaded, were only the later rationalisations to justify a simple economic fact: that the colonies needed labour and resorted to Negro labour because it was cheapest and best (pp.19-20).

Despite the reasons postulated for slavery, philosophers, economists, sociologists, and psychologists alike can agree that the degradation of the soul which occurred has negatively impacted on Africans across the Diaspora with such devastating depth that we are still dealing with those very real issues today.

With the instilling of 'subhumanness' and the infiltration of inferiority, the acceptance of self as negative and inferior became hallmarks for the mental and emotional enslavement that eventually occurred within people of African descent. Skin colour, body image, and physical beauty all then became subject to the ideals and standards of the Eurocentric worldview.

Nettleford (1965) highlights the importance of race in the discourse on identity and states that, essentially, race is an important determinant in people's assessment of each other. Thus, racial attitudes, especially when accompanied by a 'national schizophrenia' is important. In the Jamaican society, whiteness implies privilege, wealth, position and purity, while 'black' implies manual labour, poverty, low status and ignorance. One of the distinctive features of Caribbean countries is a half-identification or in-betweenness, resulting from those attitudes towards the ranges of colour that can be found in the societies.

Jamaicans are faced with the dilemma of determining who exactly is a 'son of the soil'. To be an authentic 'son of the soil', one should be able to make claim to Arawak ancestry; in a real sense Jamaicans are all immigrants. Similarly, all Caribbean people of African descent are immigrants. Jamaican's peculiar position has been explained as: 'we are neither Africans, though most of us are Black; we are not Anglo-Saxon, though we would have others believe this; we are Jamaicans'. This implies a racial harmony among the Jamaican people that is not boasted of in any other Caribbean country. Racial harmony is what the Jamaican society has always tried to make the world believe exists. However, it is the 'many' in the motto and not the 'one' that gets the focus; in the minds of many Jamaicans there is still the poor Black man, the middle-class, privileged Brown man, and the wealthy White man. The Chinese and Indians have been integrated into the middle-class due to colour of skin, intermarriage and wealth. They were the first set to work in the banking industry when there was a gap in the labour force. The idealization of mixed blood poses a problem for identity, in that the Black majority then cannot be viewed as an aberration, so where exactly are they to be classified and what honour must be paid to them? The 1960 census saw a shifting of the position of the people: the word 'African' became 'Black'.

Stratification based on racial consciousness is not wrong. However, the conditions that apply are that there must be adequate educational opportunities, accessibility to rewards for effort and even rewards for greater effort. This will cause greater social mobility, which is a compensatory responsibility, however, in Jamaica this is a limited facility. We are still enslaved in the social structure born of the plantation system, where things African have been devalued (Nettleford, 1970).

Based on a study of 475 Jamaican adolescents done by Miller (cited in Barron & Reddock, 2001) in 1966, results indicated that though the average Jamaican's body-build coincides with the concept of beauty, his or her colour and facial features do not. The author generally concluded that beauty is associated with Caucasian features, and ugliness with Negroid features. Interestingly, no preference was found among the participants for White-skin colour in their ideal. However, all colour groups studied (which ranged from White and fair to Chinese, dark and Black) expressed preference for fair or light-skinned people. These results are slightly different from reports made by Henriques (1953) and another by Kerr (1952) in the 1940s, in which results showed a preference for white-skinned individuals, suggesting a slight change in conceptualizations and perceptions in Jamaicans. Forty years later, Caribbean people have made many strides and attempts at accepting and loving our African heritage. This can be seen in the selection of beauty queens, the increase in women and men wearing natural hairstyles and sporting dreadlocks (Charles, 2003).

However, the Eurocentric view of beauty continues to be idealized and equated with acceptance, success, power, and respect. According to Wade (1996), skin colour predicts educational attainment, occupation, as well as personal and family income. Those who are light-skinned are likely to attain better economic, vocational, and educational status than their dark-skinned counterparts. As a result, many feel compelled to resort to stripping away their Afrocentric identity, through the usage of skin bleaching agents and getting married to their light-skinned and other racial counterparts to achieve the economic and social benefits. Furthermore, in the past decade there has been evidence that Jamaicans are becoming susceptible to body image disturbances, and even more dangerous, eating disorders. With an increase of media influences and telecommunication access, many individuals, particularly adolescents, are internalizing 'the thin ideal' body. In a study conducted by McGuire et al. (2002), with 18,000 Caribbean adolescents between the ages of 10 and 18, it was found that girls were more likely to diet or exercise as a means of losing weight; whereas boys were more likely to take laxatives, vomit, or use diuretics.

Hence, we see the evidence of how we were stripped of our self-concept of what encompasses beauty, and left confused with the ideal of a thin body, long straight hair and nose and blue-coloured eyes as the standard of outward beauty. This merging of racial and ethnic groups has left Caribbean people with a fused identity which sometimes fosters a low sense of self, but on the positive side, can also enhance one's selfhood.

## RACE

Within the Caribbean, several mixtures of races could occur: the Tainos and Kalinago Indians (original inhabitants from the Western hemisphere), the Whites (settlers and colonizers), the Blacks (slaves) and the Indians and Asians (indentured labourers). These all interbred to produce what is being referred to as Creole. One's status in society was inherently dependent on which races were mixed and furthermore, which race was more apparent in one's physical structure. Thus, the whiter one's complexion was, the more elevated one was in society. This would then define almost everything else in one's sense of self and social life: what type of education could be had; who one's partners could or should be; and how one spoke; to name a few (Balutansky & Sourieau, 1998; Braithwaite, 1971).

Race mixing first began amongst the indigenous peoples of the Caribbean: the Caribs used to capture the Arawak women and take them as their wives, in St. Vincent. Shipwrecked slaves mated with this Carib/Arawak blend and they became known as Garifuna. Some time later, as the British attempted to transport these Garifuna to Jamaica, many died and the remainder were abandoned near the coast of Central America where they continued to intermix with the local Amerindians and established settlements (Balutansky & Sourieau, 1998). This was only the beginning of creolization. The propagation continued within and across the Caribbean islands until today, where there remains a complex amalgam of races and ethnicities, drawn together from the repercussions of slavery, colonialism and migration (Johnson, n.d.). Jamaica is one such amalgam. The Africans brought to the island were vastly diverse, from Yoruba to Asante to Fon to Bantu. But within a context of racial oppression, from this highly pluralistic composition, was born a Black ethnicity, a situation not quite unlike that of other regions of the Diaspora. This Black ethnicity had been well established when an Asian presence was infused into the Black-White Jamaican society. After emancipation, Blacks moved en masse as far away as possible from the plantations, the most enduring reminder of bondage.

In the search for an alternative source of cheap labour, the colonial government set its sights on India and China after efforts directed at Europe, North America and Africa had failed. Between 1845 and 1917, East Indians were brought to Jamaica and Trinidad under the indentureship programme (Johnson, n.d.). Despite great difficulties, the East Indians did form a permanent community in the islands. In an effort to diminish any Indian-African resistance, the colonial government devised deliberate policies to segregate the Indians from the Africans. The African-Jamaicans often displayed the same contempt of White Jamaicans for the Indians, which appeared to be due to the threat they posed to the few opportunities in the economy. On the other hand, Sherlock and Bennett (1997) highlighted in *The Story of the Jamaican People*, that the Indians' fixed caste system, in which skin pigmentation partly determined social status, caused them to view the darker complexioned African-Jamaicans as socially inferior. Even into the twentieth century, some Indians would not allow their children to attend the same schools with Black children. The historical situation in Trinidad is not very different, however, the constellation of Indians and Africans is not as diverse and constitutes a 45%/45% split with the remaining 10 per cent consisting of mixed races, Chinese, Lebanese and Whites. (Lal, n.d.)

The Chinese, the other Asian post-emancipation immigrant group, came a little later than the Indians. As shortages of Black labour on the plantations continued and Indian labour also began to prove unreliable, successive waves of Chinese immigrants were welcomed. Chinese immigration to Jamaica continued into the twentieth century, by which time the established Chinese Jamaicans were beginning to send for relatives through a discernable chain migration process. As a non-English speaking, non-Christian group, they faced similar contempt and bigotry. However, many found their niche in the grocery retail business and were enormously successful. This success elicited resentment from other groups in the society. Reaction to official and unofficial discrimination contributed to the building of a viable and permanent Chinese-Jamaican community.

Also present in the racial, ethnic tapestry were people from the Middle East. The Jewish presence actually began in the Spanish colonial era. Jews first arrived as indentured servants who helped to establish the sugar industry. In spite of initial discrimination against them as a non-Christian group, they made phenomenal progress, moving from the plantations into commerce. As prosperous merchants, they came to exert strong control over the Jamaican economy. This put them on a par with the privileged White planters, who were known to seek financial help from Jewish enterprises. The other groups from the Middle East – Palestinians, Lebanese and Syrians (collectively more commonly referred to simply as 'Syrians') – followed similar economic paths, moving their way up from peddlers to merchants and traders.

At the time of Jamaica's independence (1962), the population consisted of 76.8 per cent Black, 16.9 per cent Mixed, 0.9 per cent White, 0.6 per cent Chinese, 1.7 per cent Indian and 3.1 per cent others. Today (2006), according to the latest census, there are 90.9 per cent Blacks, 7.3 per cent Mixed, 0.2 per cent White, 0.2 per cent Chinese, 1.3 per cent Indian, and 0.1 per cent others (http://www.infoplease.com/ipa/A0107662.html). Although the numerical preponderance of Blacks is glaring, it could not subsume the presence of the other races, whose roles and niches in the society had been firmly carved by the time of independence. In essence, then, the new nation was multiracial, yet always at the bottom echelon of society was the Black race. But from the outset, the architects of Jamaica's nationhood intended to drastically reduce or obliterate racial conscious-ness as an essential, defining trait of the nation. This resolve is encapsu-lated in the motto adopted: "Out of Many, One People." This was meant to be more than rhetoric. It was to be at the heart of the spirit of an ideol-ogy for nationhood (Johnson, n.d.). But does it then portray a falsehood and psychologically de-emphasize the significance of our blackness and thus Afrocentricity? These issues are also raised for other Caribbean islands, as in some islands that mixing was seen as negative and the African contributions were usually ignored or denied. For instance, in Cuba, Trinidad, Barbados, Puerto Rico and Dominica, great preference is given to affiliations of White and Indian heritage (Balutansky & Sourieau, 1998).

## THE CREOLE IDENTITY

"You can send the Indians to India
And the Negroes back to Africa
But will somebody please tell me
Where they sending poor me, poor me?
I'm neither one nor the other-
Six of one, half a dozen of the other,
If they serious 'bout sending back people in tru-
They're going to have to split me in two"

In this refrain sung by the Mighty Dougla (in Trinidad this means a person who is Afro-Indian), the core of the struggle of the Creole is expressed (cited in Nettleford, 1965). 'Creole' was originally a term used to describe the pure descendants of early settlers, then it gradually came to refer to those of mixed heritage. The term allowed one some measure of status and power and signified a level of education and domestication versus, being primitive and uneducated as the pure Negro was (Conde, cited in Balutansky & Sourieau, 1998).

What resulted from the effacement of identity and this major transi-tion is what can be termed the 'creole identity', which is an amalgamation of the conceptualizations of the Black 'I', the Creole 'I', the Jamaican or Trinidadian or Barbadian 'I', and finally, the Caribbean 'I' (Balutansky & Sourieau, 1998). This identity structure is essentially a combination of Eurocentric and Afrocentric worldviews, with regard to a number of different and critical areas of self, including race, language, religion, education, family and sexuality.

The lives and values of Caribbean people have been shaped and controlled by creolization. Lamming said that it is a "continuing psychic experience that has to be dealt with long after the actual colonial situation formally ends". The entire experience of slavery could have a negative impact on the Caribbean psyche, as it resulted in the people being violently dislodged and forced to live in subcultures with no real kinship bonds. Anything that was developed was punished.

## LANGUAGE

Patois, French Creole, and Ebonics are all a testament to the creolization of language, which occurred during slavery across the Diaspora. For example the Garifuna language is made up of 45 per cent Arawak, 25 per cent Carib, 15 per cent French, 10 per cent English and 5 per cent Spanish (Balutansky & Sourieau, 1998) while Jamaican patois is a rich mixture of Twi, English, Kru, Manding, and Kwa (Adams, 1991; Pryce, 1997). However, again, by far the English language or other colonial master's language was associated with the upper echelons of society and it was considered highly unusual to be poor and speak English. In many Caribbean islands, creole language is currently associated with denigration, under-education, and poverty. The Rastafarians in Jamaica, in their bid to liberate their language from hegemony, have used the 'I' to oppose the servile 'me', the possessive 'my' and the objective 'me', as the 'I' identifies man as an individual. Erna Brodber (cited in Baluntansky & Sourieau, 1998) has made the observation that Bajans speak in a manner similar to Black Americans. She related this to the fact that Barbados was not really infused by any other culture other than European and African, which was also the situation in the USA. Once again, the creolization of language is supremely evident across the Caribbean and is part of the concept of identity. Nevertheless, once again, a celebration of creole languages is not evident, and it is often relegated to the bottom, seen as inappropriate and for the 'lesser peoples'.

## SEXUALITY

Prostitution, multiple relationships, young girls with older men, materialism, and sexual abuse are all manifestations of issues arising out of sexuality that can be analysed within the framework of Caribbean identity.

Sexual behaviour and mating patterns were characterized by multiple relationships among the masters and their slaves, resulting in the institutions and the sanctions of marriage being almost unknown, and ridiculed by the slaves. If an overseer sent for a girl, she was obliged to go, and those men whose wives were sent for could not complain without risking being flogged, ostensibly for some other misdemeanour. Girls were introduced to sexual intercourse at an early age and many became mothers before they entered their teens. The pattern was different for the men who began sexual activity at a much later age.

In many instances, rape was unnecessary since the girls gave in to the overwhelming pressures and made the best of the rewards. These connections not only exempted the female from the toils of the field, it also gave her many enviable exemptions in other respects, and in her own eyes, raised her to a fancied superior position among other slaves.

A prosperous male slave was permitted to have one stable relationship with one woman, in conjunction with a series of loose relationships with other 'wives' who were not only changed frequently, but were permitted to have other lovers. This was regarded as quasi-polygyny and quasi-polyandry. Sometimes the man had several wives at the same time and the woman had many husbands successively, so that almost every child had a different father.

These structures are supremely evident in Caribbean societies today.

## Rebuilding African Identity

### RASTAFARI

There can be no discussion of African identity issues without discourse on Rastafari. The Black activist Rastafarian movement has proven to be an antagonist to the multi-racial nationalism, which officially underpins Jamaica's identity. Jamaican society has caused a problem of identity and the Rastafarian seeks to solve it in his mind and rid himself of the hypocrisy in his conscience, so he has taken a new view of the situation. The Negro has no Negroland, the Jamaicans are not from Africa and the only persons who can be classified as indigenous are the Arawaks and the Mulattoes. So the Rastafarian resolves that he is going back to Africa (making Jamaica the Babylon that holds him in captivity). Leonard Howell (Ethiopian World Federation), Archibald Dunkley (King of Kings Missionary Movement), Claudius Henry (African Reform Church) and Joseph Hibbert (Ethiopian Coptic Church) were the first leading proponents of Haile Selassie I as divinity. All of these men, like Marcus Garvey, had in their life experience been privy to the commonalities of Africans in other parts of the Diaspora, with regard to their racial, economic and political oppression (Lake, 1998). However, it was Leonard Howell who galvanized the movement in the early 1930s and laid out the following principles (Barrett, 1977):

1) hatred for the White race;

2) the complete superiority of the Black race;

3) revenge on Whites for their wickedness (these first 3 principles seek to effect a complete reversal of the equally extreme white value system that dominated the Jamaican society);

4) the negation, persecution and humiliation of the government and legal bodies of Jamaica;

5) preparation to go back to Africa;

6) acknowledgement of Emperor Haile Selassie I as the Supreme Being and only ruler of Black people.

It was during this time, when Howell retreated to a commune called the Pinnacle that Rastas began to wear dreadlocks, smoke marijuana and refer to themselves as Nyabingi. Among these practices, RastafarI also advocate certain dietary restrictions, attire and endorse the 'livity' which is a natural way of life.

While the bourgeoisie and elite were consolidating their power and promoting a philosophy which depicted Jamaican society as politically, racially and culturally harmonious, encapsulated in the motto: 'Out of Many, One People', the Rastafarians continued to preach to the poor and disenfranchised about African identity and race consciousness. There were large migrations to the UK at the time by many Jamaicans (seeking fortune) as well as the habitual looking to England by the privileged Jamaicans (for inspiration). What the Rastafarians did was to substitute Ethiopia for the UK and the USA, and chose Africa as the 'spiritual home' – as England had been for many Brown and White Jamaicans, Lebanon for Jamaican Syrians, and China (under Kuomintang) for Jamaican Chinese.

In 1968, the *Twelve Tribes* sect of RastafarI was founded in Trench Town by Vernon Carrington, who became known as Gad. He was originally a member of the Ethiopian World Federation and of a Revivalist church. Though this sect advocates wearing dreadlocks, vegetarian diets, and conservative dress for women, if members choose not to strictly adhere to these rules, they are allowed freedom of choice. The Bible is studied very devoutly and it is only through the Bible that one can achieve true wisdom and knowledge of RastafarI.

The *Nyabingi* sect does not consider Haile Selassie I as God, nor do the members believe in the reincarnation of Jesus Christ, but see him as one among the pantheon of ancestral leaders. In addition to this, they espouse similar doctrine and practices.

The *Bobo Shanti* or the *Ethiopian National Congress* are recognized as the most orthodox of RastafarI of which one of the early leaders was Prince Emmanuel. Like the Nyabingi, they tend to live in groups and adhere to strict religious laws with regard to diet, sex, relationships, dress and so on.

The years that followed a report headed by University of the West Indies, lecturer, Professor Barry Chevannes (1960), saw further confrontations between the wider society and the Rastafarian movement – a hardening of positions on both sides, resulting in violence and truces between police and the 'Cultists'. Some symbolic expressions by the Rastas were: unkempt hair, wearing bright garb, open defiance against the unjust law forbidding the smoking of ganja (marijuana), commitment to Africa, conscious reference to the self as a Black man rather than Negro, yearning for knowledge of the African past, expressions of wrath against an oppressive and what the Rastafarians regarded as 'a continuing colonial society', campaigns against police brutality suffered by the poor (presumably because of their poverty), the mal-administration of justice, and hatred of the 'White-bias' in the society.

However, Rastafarianism could no longer be seriously dismissed as the escapist indulgencies of an economically worthless and lunatic fringe, because educated persons were supporting it. By the late 1960s there was greater acceptance of Rastafarianism by members of the wider society. Attitudes, ideals and even practices were being embraced.

The Rastafarian movement challenges the stability of nationalism and the harmonious multiracial concept that the society believes of itself. The Rastafarian movement was to effectively report the incongruences within the social system that caused the poor to become poorer and the rich more prosperous. So the government started to encourage visits to Jamaica by African dignitaries, which culminated in the historic visit by Haile Selassie I in 1966.

Marcus Garvey is another leader who is revered by Rastafarians far and wide. Hailed as the proponent of the prophecy regarding Haile Selassie's enthronement as the Emperor of Ethiopia ("Look to Africa, when a Black king shall be crowned, for the day of deliverance is at hand..."), coupled with his many endeavours to raise up the mighty race of African peoples across the Diaspora, he is highly respected within the Rastafarian tradition.

The movement, the culture, the religion have evolved and though the commitment to repatriation has lessened, and many are committed to life here in Jamaica, the Rastafarians have shaped the rhetoric on identity indefatigably, through their convictions regarding selfhood, and have guided many youths in this positive way towards an understanding on their Africanness.

## BLACK POWER MOVEMENT

The philosophy and opinions of Marcus Garvey purport: "Power is the only argument that satisfies man. Except the individual, the race or the nation has Power that is exclusive. Hence, it is advisable for the Negro to get power of every kind: Power in education, science, industry, politics, and higher government. That kind of power that will stand out signally, so that other races and nations will see, and if not see then feel." This and other quotes make Marcus Garvey the father of the Jamaican Black Power movement. The embrace of the American importation (Black Power) may serve to blur the fact of the continuity of this search among the uprooted in Jamaica for self-sufficiency and self-respect. In addition, they lay themselves open to the accusation of continuing in colonial fashion – looking outside the Jamaican society for ideas and original thinking.

The Black Power Movement as manifested in the Caribbean called for the Black Caribbean people to create institutions with Black leaders at the helm, who would take decisions in the interest of Black people. When a

Jamaican calls out for "black awareness of his history, cultural heritage as an indispensable aid to self-knowledge, as well as for pride of his racial origin without apology for the colour of his skin, the shape of his nose, and texture of his hair", he is reacting to well known objective factors in his community and in the world at large. Black power seeks to celebrate the Black majority and to give substance to the form of freedom (won in 1938, with the abolition of slavery).

Historically, the Black man in Jamaica has been said to be deprived of his true identity as regarded by the Black Power advocates. He was transformed to the 'small man' and 'a member of the working classes' (by the PNP). Thus, he was organized into Trade Unions, so the word 'slave' was traded for 'worker'. The Black man fails to find satisfaction, as he has no control in his workplace, as he has no ownership of it. The black essence found a way of expression in the middle to late 1950s in the Rastafarian movement.

Black awareness and Black pride came to be seen as a psychology – a state of mind. However, the society still needed to be liberated from its White bias. The value system of the Western world tips the scales in its favour. Too many Jamaicans think (or believe the myth) of White European superiority and Black African backwardness. To demonstrate our disagreement with this myth, Jamaicans have outwardly shown their pride in themselves and their race. The Rastafarians used to wear sandals, knitted caps, sashes of red, green and gold and their hair matted and long. The twentieth century Jamaican of the Black Power Movement followed the examples, with females wearing Afros, and many wearing African dress or daishikis.

To know an African, one has to reconstruct African pre-bondage history (this is one of our weakest aspects of the African past). Concepts of power achievement are based on European canons of historiography with emphasis on crusades, conquests, kings and emperors, political power struggles and political takeovers. The same can be said about the Jamaican and West Indian history. Blacks have been scattered, enslaved, subject to the plantation system, and experienced colonization – these have all thrown up a common framework of suffering and humiliation.

## ISLAM

The impact that Islam has had on Afrocentric thought and ideology is also a discourse that cannot be left out, in the rhetoric on Caribbean identity. The Islamic faith has a long-standing influence on Jamaican culture, dating back to 1494, when Moorish sailors, skilled in sea navigation, played an integral part in the discovery and settlement of Jamaica. However in 1503, the Moors were no longer protected by Royal Pardon from the Spanish Crown, and so were captured and imported to Jamaica as slaves. Approximately 57 per cent of these slaves were from Muslim territories (Afroz, 2003). From these slaves arose a rebellious group, fighting against the atrocities and fleeing from the bondage of slavery. We have come to know them in our history as the Maroons. The Maroons are not only known for their rebellious and resilient nature, but also for their development of intricate infrastructure, such as aqueducts, water wheels, windmills, and the beginning of the sugar cane industry (Afroz, 2003). They provided refuge for many slaves who fled their masters' homes and forced Britain to sign a peace treaty in 1739, recognizing the Maroon community as a separate entity, and one that did not fall under British jurisdiction (Afroz, 2003).

Although many slaves retained their Islamic beliefs and practices, the adverse effects of slavery left many mentally, emotionally, and physically decapitated, thereby triggering a cultural and religious disintegration. It was the arrival of Indian Muslims in the 1850s that caused the resurgence of Islam in Jamaica. Then in 1962 when Jamaica gained independence, many Jamaicans migrated to North America and England. While in the USA, many Jamaicans, particularly those amongst the under-privileged class, were attracted to the Nation of Islam (NOI) group. The NOI group was one of many Islamic groups developed in the USA to ensure economic and social vitality, and cultivate national identity within the Black community. The most appealing attributes of this organization were not only the religious teachings, but also the sociopolitical movement that fostered national identity amongst Blacks, meeting needs, such as safety and equality, that the government failed to protect and uphold.

The Nation of Islam's principles differed greatly from the tradition of Islam. Under the direction of Elijah Muhammed, Blacks were taught that they were the chosen people of Allah and that Whites were evil – resulting in the overturning of entrenched views that Blacks are inferior and

Whites are superior. Elijah Muhammed also supported separation from White American society, in the hope of creating an empire that would nurture social and political elevation within the Black community, leaving Whites powerless (Smith, 1999). These ideologies continue to be fostered and perpetuated even today by Louis Farrakhan, a devoted follower of Elijah Muhammed. However, when those Jamaicans who had been affiliated with the NOI returned to Jamaica and settled in St. Mary, they were met with resistance by the Islamic Association of Jamaica, which was predominately made up of Indian Muslims. The Islamic Association of Jamaica felt strongly that the NOI teachings and principles were not aligned to the principles and teachings of traditional Islam, and so the members were not true Muslim followers.

According to the United State Department's International Religious Freedom Report (2004) there are approximately 15,860 Muslims in the Caribbean with some of the highest populations found in Guyana and Trinidad, 10 per cent and 6 per cent, respectively, followed by Grenada (0.3%), Jamaica (0.2%) and Haiti (0.04%), to name a few. Living in a Christian-dominated country such as Jamaica, poses great risks to the endurance of the Muslim community. In Jamaica, almost 50 per cent are unemployed, with Muslim women being economically worse off (Afroz, 2003). Those who are employed tend to be engaged in private businesses, farming, and working with in government services (Afroz, 2003). Additionally, Afroz (2003) states that the absence of political representation, their small numbers, and the lack of economic power are some reasons why the Muslim population is discriminated against, thereby hindering their history from being incorporated into the educational curriculum and disseminated as an essential core of Caribbean heritage.

## PAN-AFRICANISM

Arising from the historical degradation and cultural diffusion that slavery created and the desire to become a unified and enlightened cultural group, the movement of Pan-Africanism emerged. The overall objective was to foster and maintain strong communal ties with Africa, either through migration to Africa, or by the creation of an African nation that is primarily economically, politically, and culturally driven by Blacks.

The notion is that through worldwide solidarity, Blacks will be able to achieve the political independence, empowerment, and cultural and intellectual consciousness, essential in breaking free from the mental chains that continue to dismantle the Black family and community, as seen even in today's societies.

Based on the history of slavery, it is obvious that division is the most crippling, yet the most effective method of maintaining confusion, power differentials, and discrimination among Black people. Not only has there been friction between light-skinned and dark-skinned individuals, but there has also been friction experienced across cultures. Robert Chrisman (1974) poignantly points out that a Chinese individual is not referred to as Chinese American, although they may be third or fourth generation American. Instead he or she is simply known as Chinese, whereas, the same does not hold true for African descendants: you either consider yourself an African American, a Caribbean/West Indian, or an African. As a result, entrenched stereotypes result, fostering cultural divisions that persist even today. For instance, Caribbean people are perceived as violent drug dealers and weed heads; African Americans are perceived as being lazy and the highest welfare consumers; and Africans as barbaric, with few resources and limited technological advancement.

One cannot speak of Pan-Africanism without mentioning the acclaimed Caribbean predecessors of the movement, including Edward W. Blyden, Marcus Garvey, Claude McKay, and Sylvester Williams, to name a few. Each played a significant role in the establishment of Pan-Africanism, fostering hope and aspirations of Black unity, as well as economic, political and intellectual progression. The Pan-Africanist movement began in the West Indies between 1834 and 1838, when Caribbean people made several trips to West Africa as part of Christian missionary work, creating a conduit of conscious-raising ideas. Although the New World countries did not reap the benefits of Pan-Africanism, it facilitated the decolonization of Africa (Geiss, 1974).

So why wasn't Pan-Africanism successful in fostering unity amongst Blacks, giving us the economical, political, and cultural platform needed to secure the quintessential independence from our former bondage? According to Geiss (1974) for one, Africa was romanticized as the 'lost paradise', with a concoction of images from past experiences merged with idealizations passed from generation to generation. As a result, these romanticized ways of thinking may have prevented many from internalizing a more rational outlook, in establishing communal ties with

Africa and other Black populations around the world. Additionally, many Blacks adopted the perspective from their former slave masters that Africans were primitive savages, and as a result, did not want to associate with nor support the goals of the Pan-Africanist movement.

Although Pan-Africanism was not successful, it fractured the passive acceptance and internalization of the identity that was imposed on Blacks during slavery, and ignited an active pursuit of knowledge together with the creation of the Black identity. The Black identity is the synthesis of the African identity, successfully protected from the ills of slavery, and the New World identity that was internalized, hence the evolution of four distinct groups: the African American, the African Caribbean, the African Hispanic, and the African.

## Toward a Caribbean Identity

The journey to define who we are as a people and a nation has been a long and arduous process. Actually, many would argue that the struggle continues today to overcome more intricate and sophisticated barriers than those in the past, including: the dissemination of messages that continue to teach and reinforce poor self-image; disjointed communities and families; self-hatred; and low self-esteem to name a few in the Black community. These current barriers pose a greater psychological threat to our existence, because they are easily threaded into our way of life, through covert messages in our school and work arenas, communities, society, and even in our homes. Indeed, it is because of these oppressive systems that mental disorders manifest.

Studies have reported that there is an exceedingly high incidence of Blacks in the prison systems and mental health institutions of the metropoles of North America and Europe (Sheehan, Hardie & Watson, 1995; Maden, 1993; O'Hare, Pollard, Mann, & Kent, 1991; Snowden & Cheung, 1990). Facing tremendous psychocultural challenges, including alienation, socioeconomic deprivation, acculturative stress, and difficulties adjusting to a new culture, have made many Caribbean immigrants susceptible to various forms of psychopathology. Racism and discrimination play a primary role in the perception of Blacks by the dominant culture as aggressive, violent, and primitive people. Thus, when Blacks come into contact with mental health providers, medical providers, and officers of the law, they are more likely to be arrested and committed to mental health institutions. Some have conjectured that paranoia is the result of the need to protect the psyche against the brutality of racism and the continuous threat to survival, thereby insulating Blacks from the feeling of powerlessness and of being 'less than human' (Grier & Cobbs, 1968). An example of paranoia is the controversial 'roast breadfruit psychosis'. According to Hickling and Hutchinson (1999), when racial identity confusion arises, it manifests into the roast breadfruit syndrome, where a Black individual sees and identifies him or herself as White. The term of the disorder was coined from the breadfruit, a Caribbean staple, whose green coloured skin turns black when roasted, while the inner portion remains white in colour. It has been posited that by attempting to rationalize one's identity in the midst of facing vast and challenging systemic barriers, psychotic symptomatology is likely to manifest as a result. The symptoms include the great need to be accepted into White society, being ashamed of one's cultural background, and attempting to alter one's physical characteristics to appear White (Hickling & Hutchinson, 1999).

Psychocultural challenges have not only compromised the mental health of Blacks, but also their physical health. It has been suggested that many Blacks have internalized an active way of coping with the vast environmental challenges presented to them on a daily basis, without sufficient psychosocial and socioeconomic resources. Meeting these great demands through sheer hard work and determination, and with very little support, makes it difficult for stressors to be effectively managed. This compromises not only their mental health, but also their physical health (James, Hartnett, & Kalsbeek, 1983; James, 1994). This coping style is known as John Henryism, named after an African American legend who was a steel-driver, known for his extraordinary strength. He was paired against a steel-driving machine, which he successfully defeated. However, due to mental and physical exhaustion, he died shortly after this achievement.

So what makes us resilient as a people, in spite of these everyday systemic challenges that we face? The answer is our strong cultural pride which emanates from our religion, arts, and our strong work ethic, to name a few of the factors that embrace and reinforce positive Caribbean culture. So it is to this amalgamation of influences and ideology that we come, in order to define what it is, and who it is we truly are.

## Unique Caribbean Thought, Expressions, Ideology

In Caribbean culture, amalgamating work with leisure not only aided in the completion of tasks, but it also strengthened communities and fostered the Caribbean identity we are familiar with today. People often make their work less arduous by incorporating singing or a sporting dimension, such as a digging competition, into the task. Music and singing have traditionally been used to preserve history, heritage, and culture. One of the fastest growing music subgenres that continues to impact on the community is dancehall. Dancehall music gained its recognition in the early 1980s, as a medium for discourse on politics, fashion, social and economic deprivation, sex, and violence (Hippolyte, 2004). Through dancehall music, many have found a platform to communicate the thoughts and ideologies of Caribbean people to the world at large, thereby creating the opportunity for the culture to extend beyond the boundaries of their homelands. Dancehall is not the first and only subgenre in the music industry to have such an impact. Ska and reggae are some of the vehicles that have paved the way for dancehall to be as successful and claim the international recognition as it has during the past few years. Music has been and continues to be the quintessential medium of articulating and preserving Caribbean pride and identity, and of transmitting our ideologies and expressions not only internationally, but also from generation to generation.

Carnival is another form of cultural expression that has positive psychological functions and has come to symbolize externalization, catharsis and sexual release. It is a celebration of the culture, the people, and the land, and is one of the essential means for healing and mental liberation. Through celebration, people positively identify with themselves and their culture, thereby increasing their self-esteem and self-worth (Akbar, 2006). It is through collective self-esteem that our culture can continue to thrive and perpetuate positive attributes and expressions to Caribbean people.

Another form of leisure-time activity which occupies pride of place in Caribbean culture is sports. Cricket in one of the most popular sports in Jamaica and it provides an atmosphere primed for celebration of athletic ability and communal support. At the local level, teams from different parishes compete against each other, promoting community identity and cultural pride. Other popular sports include, football, badminton, and track and field.

These are all examples of modes that have nurtured cultural pride and communal self-worth, allowing Caribbean people (even if for a short period of time) to begin to shake off the remnants of slavery and to heal at the individual, family, and the community levels. It is through this communal support and purging, that we have managed to solidify the unity that was fragmented, and has been in danger of being destroyed forever. So while we look back and grieve about the atrocities that our ancestors endured and survived, we appreciate the ideologies and knowledge they have imparted to us, so that we can continue to strive to fulfil our potential.

## REFERENCES

Adams, E. L. (1991) *Understanding Jamaican patois, Jamaican grammar.* Kingston, Jamaica: Kingston Publishers Limited.

Afroz, S. (2003). Invisible yet invincible: The Muslim Ummah in Jamaica. *Journal of Muslim Minority Affairs*, 23 (1), 211-222

Akbar, N. (2006). *Breaking the chains of psychological slavery.* Tallahassee, FL: Mind Productions & Associates.

Augustine, E. W. (1997). *Colorialism in Belize.* Belize City: Angelus P.

Balutansky, K. M., & Sourieau, M. (Eds.) (1998). *Caribbean creolization: Reflections on the cultural dynamics of language, literature, and identity.* Tallahassee, FL: University Press of Florida.

Barrett, L. E. (1977). *The Rastafarians – Dreadlocks of Jamaica.* Kingston, JA: Sangsters.

———. (1997). *The Rastafarians.* Boston, MA: Beacon Press

Braithwaite, E. (1971). *The development of creole society in Jamaica, 1770-1820.* Oxford, UK: Clarendon Press.

Bryan, P. (1991). *The Jamaican people 1880-1902.* London, UK: Macmillan Education Ltd.

Charles, C. A. D., (2003). Skin bleaching, self-hate & black identity in Jamaica. *Journal of Black Studies*, 33 (6), 711-728

Chevannes, B. (1994). *Rastafari roots and ideology.* Syracuse, NY: Syracuse University Press.

Chrisman, R. (1974). Introduction. In R. Chrisman & N. Hare (Eds.), *Pan-Africanism.* New York, NY: Bobbs-Merill Co.

Clark, K. B., & Clark, M. P. (1947). Racial identification and preference in Negro children. In T. M. Newcomb & E. L. Hartley (Eds.), *Reading in social psychology*. New York: Holt.

Cross, W. E. (1991). *Shades of black: Diversity in African-American identity*. Philadelphia, PA: Temple University Press.

Erskine, N. L. (1981). *Decolonizing theology: A Caribbean perspective*. Maryknoll, NY: Orbis Books.

Geiss, I. (1974). *The pan-African movement: A history of pan-Africanism in America, Europe, and Africa*. New York, NY: Africana Publishing Co.

Grier, W. H., & Cobb, P. (1968) *Black rage*. New York: Basic Books.

Hall, D. (1999). *In miserable slavery: Thomas Thistlewood in Jamaica 1750-86*. Kingston, Jamaica: University of the West Indies Press.

Henriques, F. (1952). *Family and colour in Jamaica*. London, England: Eyre & Spottiswoode.

Hickling, F. W., & Hutchinson, G. (1999) The roast breadfruit psychosis. Disturbed racial identification in African-Caribbeans. *Psychiatric Bulletin, 23* (3), 132-134.

Higman, B. W. (1975). The slave family and household in the British West Indies. *Journal of Interdisciplinary History, 6* (2), 261-287.

Hilliard, A. G., & Akbar, N. (1998). *Know thyself*. Tallahassee, FL: Mind Productions & Associates.

Hillman, J. (1997). The seduction of black. In J. Hillman, H. Hogarth, J. Bertoia & C. Boer (Eds.), *Haiti or the psychology of Black*. Woodstock, CT: Spring Publications.

James, S. A. (1994). John Henryism and the health of African Americans. *Cultural and Medical Psychiatry, 18*, 163-182.

James, S. A., Hartnett, S. A., & Kalsbeek, W. D. (1983). John Henryism and blood pressure differences among black men. *Journal of Behavioral Medicine, 6*, 259-278.

Johnson, V. S. Racial frontiers in Jamaica's nonracial nationhood. Retrieved May 20, 2006 from www.education.ucsb.edu/socialjustice/johnson.pdf.

Kerr, M. (1953). *Personality and conflict in Jamaica*. Liverpool, England: Liverpool University Press.

La Guerre, J. G. (1993) A review of race and class in the Caribbean. In J.E. Greene (Ed.), *Race, Class and Gender in the Future of the Caribbean*. Kingston: Institute of Social and Economic Research, University of the West Indies.

Lake, O. (1998). *Rastafari women: Subordination in the midst of liberation theology*. Durham, NC: Carolina Academic Press.

Lal, V. (n.d.) Contemporary electoral politics in Trinidad. Retrieved on April 30, 2007 from www.sscnet.ucla.edu/southasia/Diaspora/politics_trini.html

Maden, T. (1993). Crime, culture, and ethnicity. *International Review of Psychiatry, 5*, 281-290.

McGuire, M. T., Story, M., Neumark-Sztainer, D., Halcon, L., Campbell-Forrester, S., & Blum, R. (2002). Prevalence and correlates of weight-control behaviors among Caribbean adolescent students. _Journal of Adolescent Health_, 31, 208-211

Miller, E. (2001 ). Body image, physical beauty and colour among Jamaican adolescents. In C. Barron & R. Rheddock (Eds.), _Caribbean sociology: Introductory readings_. Kingston, Jamaica: Ian Randle Publishers.

Mills, C. (1998). _Blackness visible_. New York, NY: Cornell University Press.

Nettleford, R. (1965). National identity and attitudes to race in Jamaica. _Race_, 7, 5-51.

———. (1970). _Mirror, mirror: Identity, race and protest in Jamaica_. Kingston, Jamaica: Williams, Collins & Sangster Jamaica Ltd.

O'Hare, W. P., Pollard, K. M., Mann, T. L., & Kent, M. M. (1991). African Americans in the 1990's. _Population Bulletin_, 46, 1-40

Patterson, O. (1973). _The sociology of slavery: An analysis of the origins, development and structure of Negro slave society in Jamaica_. Kingston, Jamaica: Sangster's Book Stores Ltd.

Pryce, J. T. (1997). Similarities between the debates on Ebonics and Jamaican. _Journal of Black Psychology_, 23, 238-241.

Sheehan, J. D., Hardie, T., & Watson, J. P. (1995). Social deprivation, ethnicity and violent incidents on acute psychiatric wards. _Psychiatric Bulletin_, 19, 597-599.

Smith, J. I. (1999). _Islam in America_. New York: NY: Columbia University Press.

Snowden, L. R., & Cheung, F. K. (1990). Use of inpatient mental health services by members of ethnic minority groups. _American Psychologist_, 45, 347-355.

Wade, T. J. (1996). The relationships between skin color and self-perceived global, physical, and sexual attractiveness, and self-esteem for African Americans, _Journal of Black Psychology_, 22 (3), 358-373

Williams, E. (1994). _Capitalism and slavery_. Chapel Hill, NC: North Carolina Press.

Williams, C. (1987). _The destruction of black civilization: Great issues of a race from 4500 B.C. to 2000 A.D._ Chicago, IL: Third World Press.

Woodson, C. (1990). _The mis-education of the Negro_. Trenton, NJ: Africa World Press, Inc.

# 2 Psychopathology of the Jamaican People

*Frederick W. Hickling*

> We who are born of the ocean can never seek solace in river.
>
> *Edward Kamau Braithwaite, 1967*

## Psychopathology of the Elite

The study of the psychopathology of Jamaican upper class patients in the mid 1970s reported in a previous chapter (Hickling et al, 2007) began to open up an understanding of the subjective factors that seem to underlie the complex Jamaican society, and the behaviour crippling the actualization process in this country on an individual and collective level. No doubt, similar psychological contradictions can be demonstrated all across the English-speaking Caribbean. The essential finding of the study was that in spite of the complaints, clinical findings or psychiatric diagnosis, all patients presented with a triad of behaviours, power management problems, psycho-sexual problems and dependency – all of which were often obscured by a primary psychiatric complaint, or psychopathological diagnosis.

Many authors have written of the racial, class and sexual inadequacies of the Jamaican ruling class. Perhaps the most remarkable of these is the account of Englishman, Thomas Thistlewood in Jamaica, 1750-1786, by Douglas Hall (1989). This startling publication of the Thistlewood diaries tells the extraordinary tale of the arrogance of the White ruling class and the distasteful sexual proclivities acted out in daily life in the harsh realities of African slavery. It highlights the sharp contrasts of brutality and care, methods of social control, and the contradictory realities of human relations between master and slave, which existed at that time. This document gives us an insight into the foundations of the Jamaican ruling class – the rights of Englishmen – and the development of the institutions and methods that have shaped the present-day structure of Jamaican society. The case study summarized here, illustrates that the objective reality in Jamaica has not changed considerably over 200 years. This psychiatrist, operating in the Jamaican society over the past three decades, has seen the psychopathology of the Jamaican people and the madness of the Jamaican society at close hand, and has had the opportunity to expose these observations to the rigor of scientific scrutiny.

## Case Study

A White male, born in England, brought to Jamaica at age nine by his parents who worked with the Colonial Civil Service. The eldest son of a rigid, autocratic alcoholic 'busha' and a self-effacing passive, controlling mother, started his own drinking career at the age of 16. By the time he graduated from university he had developed full-blown alcoholic pathology, with a number of admissions to hospital for delirium tremens and severe intoxication, and a number of police arrests for disorderly conduct. He held a number of managerial positions although he had difficulty in keeping a job.

Psychoanalysis revealed gross racial, class, and religious conflicts, and marked sexual inadequacies. He was tormented by homosexual fantasies and guilt, and consumed with the desire to have sex with Black women. His only sexual contact was with Black prostitutes, and he did not have the courage to approach White women for sexual relations. He lived with a working class Black woman, supporting her Black child in exchange for sexual favors. She treated him with scant respect and often abused him publicly for his sexual and other inadequacies. He in turn kept her exclusively isolated from his social contacts, and would not bring any of his friends home.

Migration is a pivotal feature of this psychopathology, this time there being a clear root in Colonial English society, made manifest in Colonial Jamaica. His coping mechanisms were impaired and the resultant psychopathology bizarre. The pathological nature of his family and parental structure is also noted. Thomas Thistlewood and the patient had several things in common. Both were from lower middle-class British backgrounds. Both were White; both migrated to Jamaica; both moved immediately into privileged managerial positions in Jamaica; both acted out racist, sexual inadequacies with Black women; both acted out contradictory behaviours of brutality and caring; both lived within a clear master-servant relationship from a minority ruling class position. Implicit within all of this is the racist superiority complex of the European, so eloquently described by Fanon (1967). Of course the most startling insight of this case is the fact that this complex remains so explicitly unchanged after 200 years.

## Case Study

The next case is that of a 23 year-old White female, US citizen who was brought by her wealthy parents at an early age to settle in the tropical Jamaican paradise. Her early childhood was stormy and traumatic, with an aggressive, alcoholic father and an authoritarian, castrating mother, who were soon divorced. She had been seen by many psychiatrists in the USA and she had had a number of admissions to the 'crazy house' for children. She had exhibited hyperactive, violent episodes as a child, with bizarre temper tantrums and 'acting-out' behaviour. She alternated between living in a community in the USA and another in Jamaica, working in a strip club in the USA for months at a time, and then relaxing and writing in Jamaica for an extended period. She presented with a paranoid psychosis following abuse of multiple drugs, including mainlining on amphetamines, heavy usage of cocaine and alcohol. Her overt lesbian behaviour, addiction to amphetamines and Quaaludes, and her confused and aggressive outbursts continued her childhood dependency on psychotherapeutic assistance.

This case reflects a dialectical relationship with the previous cases. Migration, this time in reverse – from the wealth of the USA to the freedom of paradise found in Jamaica for the transitory American, illustrates the dialectical antipodes of this individual's social behaviour as a psychological response to the socioeconomic system. Thomas-Hope (2006) has described this pattern of migratory behaviour as transnationalism – a phenomenon whereby families develop patterns of migration spanning two or more countries, exploiting the attractiveness of both societies. The pattern of psychopathology of this patient reflects keenly the realities of the contradicting social forces that nurtured and precipitated her maladaptive coping behaviour. This patient was a casualty of the 'freedom of wealth' within the socioeconomic dialectical continuum of the USA–Jamaica sociological environment.

There have been a plethora of studies of the pattern of mental illness in migrant populations over the past 60 years mainly in the USA, Canada, Australia and the UK. The earlier studies almost always found higher rates of disorder among the foreign-born than among the native-born population, particularly with a diagnosis of schizophrenia. Perhaps the most famous was the early study by Odegaard in 1932, which demonstrated higher rates of schizophrenia among Norwegians who had migrated to Minnesota in the USA, than among the native-born US citizens. As the methodological design of these studies continued to improve, it became clear that there was no evidence for the excessive rate of psychopathology in the foreign-born overall. Indeed, some immigrant groups show much better mental health than the natives of the country to which they have migrated (Cochrane & Bal, 1989). One of the few strikingly consistent findings to emerge from these studies, however, is the elevated rate of schizophrenia in the first generation migrants.

Most studies of the psychopathology of immigrant populations have focused on groups of White, Black and other immigrants to countries with a predominantly White population. In a study of the pattern of psychopathology of White immigrants to Jamaica, a predominantly Black country (Hickling, 1996), the hypothesis that was tested was that White immigrants to a predominantly Black country had a different pattern of psychopathology than the native Black population. The case notes of every White foreign-born patient who had been seen in a private psychiatric clinic in Kingston, Jamaica between 1979 and 1990, were examined with a number of demographic and clinical variables being extracted and documented. The author had examined all the patients. These patients were all matched for age, sex and social class with a control group of Jamaican-born patients who had also been seen in the same private clinic over the same period. The controls were not matched for race, as it was impossible to find an equivalent ethnic sample of White Jamaican-born controls from this clinic population. The matching selection was random and blind.

There were 49 White foreign-born patients in the sample, of whom the majority (N = 34, 69%) were female. This represented 3 per cent of the author's total clinic population in the period 1979 to 1990. Of these, 22 (45%) were born in the USA, 19 (39%) were born in the UK, and eight (16%) were born in Europe. The most common diagnosis in both groups was affective disorders, followed closely by anxiety and substance abuse disorders. Schizophrenia represented 20 per cent of the diagnoses in the immigrant group, but this was not significantly different from that of the Jamaican controls. Noting the similar willingness of both groups to seek treatment, there was no statistical difference between the groups in the pattern of diagnosis. This unique finding runs contrary to the consistent finding in the international migration literature of increased rates of schizophrenia in first generation immigrant populations. The study demonstrated that there is not an increased rate of any mental illness in White immigrants to Jamaica, when compared to matched Jamaican controls. The study pointed to a possible reason for this finding, and another possible etiologic perspective on the finding of increased rates of schizophrenia in first generation immigrant populations. The study also demonstrated that the White mentally ill immigrants to Jamaica occupied a significantly higher socio-economic class while living in Jamaica, than their parents did in their country of origin. This indicates that for this cohort of immigrants, migration creates a condition of immediate upward social mobility – a factor which rarely, if ever, occurs for immigrants, whether Black or White, to White First World countries. In this study, although the Jamaican control patients were of significantly higher socioeconomic class than their parents, the parents of the Jamaican controls were of a significantly higher socioeconomic class than the parents of the White immigrant patients to Jamaica, suggesting that the immediate upward social mobility in the White immigrant cohort is a unique factor for that group.

The hypothesis was, therefore, advanced that the political/economic system in Black postcolonial countries like Jamaica protected White immigrants from the social stress of migration, which often causes schizophrenia in migrant groups in predominantly White societies. The hypothesis also suggests that there exists in postcolonial societies like Jamaica, a socio-political structure created by the European ruling class, which allows typical White ruling-class psychopathology to flourish, while providing protection from psychopathological conditions like schizophrenia, which can possibly be induced by significant existing sociological stress. However, the findings also indicated that the ruling class construct was not exclusively a White domain. In fact, the predominant members of the cohort studied (45%) were brown-skinned miscegenates of the Creole society – created by the sexual proclivity of the initial European colonizers – and 28 per cent of the cohort was made up of Black people.

Within the Black patients of this ruling-class group, the predominant psychopathological feature was self-racism, a denial of their own blackness, and hatred and rejection of anything black. Of course, Fanon wrote extensively of this syndrome in Black skins, white masks, which in Jamaica we know as the 'roast breadfruit syndrome'. It is more commonly used in the language of the Black ghetto to describe people who, though black-skinned, see themselves from and identify with a partial or entirely Eurocentric perspective. Hickling and Hutchinson (1999) described this syndrome in African Caribbeans as the 'roast breadfruit psychosis'. The characteristic appearance of a 'roast breadfruit' (black skin, white heart) has aptly lent itself to the neologistically expanding Caribbean dialects to describe Black people who think themselves White. This identity conflict is an extremely common phenomenon in Black postcolonial societies and has been often described in contemporary Black literature. In Afro-America the same phenomenon is called the 'Oreo cookie' syndrome, after the popular chocolate biscuit that has a white marshmallow sandwich filling. In Asian and Polynesian cultures the phenomenon is often described as the 'coconut syndrome', mirroring the fruit that has a brown outer shell and a white inner pulp. In Native American people the phenomenon is called the 'apple' syndrome, for similar reasons. Littlewood and Lipsedge (1989) alluded to the phenomenon in a number of the case studies that they presented. They quote Lugard (1929): "there is no class... which is less welcome to the lay Englishman than the 'Black

White man' who has abandoned his racial integrity and is quick to learn European vices".

The rise of the Black Power movement in the 1960s in the USA, and its spill-over into the Caribbean highlighted intensely the 'roast breadfruits' and the 'Oreo cookies'. The movement attacked the practices of some Black people's attempts to straighten their hair and to bleach their skins with various chemicals and astringents, as well as seeking cosmetic surgery to straighten and diminish their broad African noses and their full African lips. Opprobrium was thrown on Blacks who only dated or married Whites, aspired to live in White neighborhoods, attended White schools and identified only with White music, art and culture. The movement denounced Blacks who tended to denigrate other black-skinned people, and to belittle and deny the existence of a rich Black culture. The Black world was attempting to throw off the yoke of centuries of White colonial oppression and European cultural imperialism.

## Case Study

This case was a brown-skinned young woman, daughter of an upper-middle-class Black Jamaican mother with absent and unknown White father. She started a promiscuous sexual career at an early age and became pregnant by age 13 for a White Jamaican male. By age 23 she presented with a drug-induced paranoid psychosis requiring hospitalization. Trapped by racial and class contradictions and a fragmented family, this young woman dropped out of school, turned to hard-drug abuse, high-class prostitution, lesbianism and finally a psychotic breakdown in an attempt to try to cope with her problems. Psychotherapy revealed an intense hatred and disgust for Black people, and especially poor Black people. By age 35 she had two more children for two different White men. Her psychosis was short-lived (three months), but her racial confusion, sexual proclivity and promiscuity continued. Her ruling-class position continued to provide economic and emotional sustenance.

The Black patients too, had similar presentations. The frightening and sobering realization was the fact that these people from the Jamaican ruling class were all in positions of influence and power. Many of them were actual political and managerial leaders of the country in powerful and influential positions, which affected the day-to-day running and survival of the country, and held dominion over the mass of the Jamaican people. Not only were these people, with their own active psychopathology notwithstanding, custodians of the ruling-class culture that dominated Jamaican society, but they directly controlled the lives of the mass of Jamaican people. The Jamaican middle-class in a spin! Trapped by racial and class contradictions and a fragmented family, this young lady reacted exactly like her White middle-class North American counterpart, turning to drug abuse, social sexual perversions, and finally, a psychotic breakdown in an attempt to cope with her problems. For this lady, Jamaican and US cultures were interchangeable. Trapped by the contradictions of the schizophrenic society, acting out the schizophrenic contradictions in the reality of her life.

**Case Study**

The next case is of a 14-year-old brown-skinned male, born in Jamaica to a wealthy Black father and a White American mother. The parents were divorced when he was age four, and he grew up with a paternal aunt in Jamaica. The patient started giving trouble at home and at school in Jamaica and was sent to the USA to live with his mother. There, his conduct disorder worsened in the harsh racial realities of a Black child of a White woman in the USA. He began abusing alcohol, sniffing cocaine and smoking marijuana as he was introduced to a drug culture in the USA. He also started truanting from school, and getting into trouble with the authorities. In desperation, his family sent him back to Jamaica to the paternal aunt who reported continued conduct disordered behaviours, stealing and rebelliousness toward authority. Psychological assessment revealed a very superior IQ of 140, in a young man displaying hostility to his aunt, to his parents, his relatives and the Jamaican/ American social conditions. He displayed gross racial class conflicts and a love-hate relationship with the American society.

This was an exceptionally bright young man, a product of miscegenation, marital conflict and the wealthy middle-class, subject to the force of social migration, acting out his confusion and hostility in both societies, by displacing his anger and aggression on to his own social living. His natural coping reaction was rebellion and destruction of the societies that spawned him. He was a casualty of social fragmentation, a nidus of rebellion.

The psychiatrist had the task of helping these people back to health, not only as a palliative, but to devise psychotherapeutic strategies to influence their own personal transformation and change. This was the challenge – to negate the pervasive psychopathology that made the ruling-class what it is, to attempt to formulate a new psychological framework negating their class-pathology and to assist in their transformation into a new position.

## Psychopathology of the Poor Classes

In a study of in-patients and out-patients to the psychiatric service of the University Hospital in 1971 (Hickling, 1975), results indicated unequivocally that schizophrenia was the predominant diagnosis of the social classes III, IV and V (using the UK Registrar Generals classification of social class by occupation) – accounting for over 30 per cent of all patients seen from those groupings. Hickling and Rodgers-Johnson (1995) studied the risk factors for schizophrenia in Jamaica, by sampling patients with first contact psychosis from the entire island for the year 1992. Patients presenting for the first time with that condition, using a standardized diagnostic instrument, would be expected to provide a more accurate representation of this condition for class and race. Of the 317 patients identified, 285 (90%) were from the lowest social classes (social classes IV & V). They were predominantly of African origin (98%), and 2 per cent Indian; 89 per cent were Black, and 11 per cent were brown. There were no White patients in the sample and only two from the upper social classes. This was not in keeping with the national population figures for race at that time, which reported a three per cent representation of White people in the population statistics. The predominant clinical manifestations of patients with this condition are auditory and visual hallucinations, disorders of thinking and volition, and delusions, mainly of a paranoid character. Males (65%) were represented twice as often as females. Schizophrenia in Jamaica is confirmed as being a condition of adolescence and young adulthood, with the mean age being 26.381, SD = 8.47. The condition presented in males at an earlier age than in females.

**Case Study**

The next case is of a 16-year-old Black girl born in a rural farming parish to peasant parents. Her mother and father were never married, nor lived together. Both parents migrated from their rural district, her mother to the USA, and her father to the nearby city in search of work. Raised by her maternal grandmother, and after her death, when the patient was age six, by a paternal aunt. She attended the primary school in her district, and by her early teens was having severe conflicts with her aunt. A confrontation arose when the aunt's common-law partner attempted to have sexual relations with the patient. When she refused to comply, they both threw her out of the house with nowhere to go. She then proceeded to make her way to the capital city – Kingston – where she lived from the garbage on the streets for three weeks. Malnourished and exhausted, she was picked up by a man who took her to his home, raped her and threw her out on the streets again. After wandering around the streets for another week she was picked up by the police and brought to the Bellevue Mental Hospital, dirty, dishevelled and with hallucinations, thought disorder and paranoid delusions. A diagnosis of an acute schizophrenic illness was made. Her illness responded very quickly to treatment. She remained within the rehabilitation services of the hospital, mentally well, but with nowhere to go in the community.

This case was selected primarily to illustrate the roots of poverty that characterize the problems of so many Jamaicans, and of most cases of mental illness in this country. The secondary objective was to highlight the family pathology, which is so common, whereby children are reared in a hostile dehumanizing environment by reluctant foster parents. The third objective was to illustrate the coping response of migration used by so many Jamaicans in an attempt to solve economic problems – rural to urban migration, used both by the patient, and her father before her, and external migration to the USA by her mother. It is unusual for a conventionally defined schizophrenic illness to present with such a clear set of stressful antecedents, and it is usually quite difficult to link external stressful events with the genesis of this type of mental response. However, the diagnosis in this case could also have been a Brief Psychotic

Disorder, which would account for the presence of stressful etiologic antecedents.

### Case Study

A 38-year-old Black woman born to rural peasant parents, raised in the country by her maternal grandmother is the other case presented for consideration. She worked in Jamaica for some years as a lowly paid primary school teacher before migrating to the USA with her husband in search of better economic conditions. She was forced to accept a domestic job in the alien, hostile, New York environment, and simultaneously began to experience severe marital conflicts when her husband started having sexual relationships with other women. She developed an acute psychotic illness, showing features of auditory and visual hallucinations, paranoid delusions and violent aggressive behaviour and was admitted to a New York mental hospital. Unable to cope with conditions in the USA, she separated from her husband and returned to Jamaica, where her mental condition continued to deteriorate. She subsequently had seven admissions to the Bellevue Mental Hospital, displaying hostile, violent, abusive and promiscuous behaviour with each of her psychotic episodes.

This case reflects the migration response to economic deprivation, the USA being seen as the nirvana, the land of opportunity, and the panacea of all economic ills. Contrary to her expectations, the patient had been forced to accept menial work, suffered marital disarray and broke down under the pressure of this stressful cultural translation. Returning to Jamaica and further disabused by the social conditions, she sought refuge in illness in the mental hospital. There she continued to hold strongly to her belief that her problems had occurred as a result of Obeah, which had been perpetrated on her by her racist White employers in the USA.

Clear dialectical trends can be seen to be emerging. Black and White people, breaking down psychologically in the socioeconomic conditions of poverty and wealth, and in both instances, transnational migration being the motivational energy, and at the same time being the psychopathological precipitant. All of theses cases were turning up in the microcosm of Jamaica at the same time, from different social classes. The resultant social effect, however, was the same, and the dialectical social causes were also the same.

## Case Study

The next case is of a 38-year-old Black farm labourer, who left his peasant farm holdings and family to seek money in the farm work labour programmes of the southern USA. Picking apples, he fell from a ladder and injured his neck. After spending a few days in the hospital he was sent home to Jamaica with no medical abnormality demonstrated. After months of treatment at the Orthopedic Clinic for a very stiff neck, he was referred for psychiatric evaluation. After a chemical abreaction his neck stiffness disappeared and he revealed the root of his hysterical symptoms. As long as he remained sick, he received three hundred US dollars monthly in medical compensation. This was a small fortune for a Jamaican peasant farmer at that time.

The secondary gain in this case of Dissociative Disorder (NOS) was clearly the financial reward, and pinpoints the pathogenesis of this illness to the socioeconomic realities of a market economy seeking cheap labour sources. The therapist felt extremely contradictory feelings and guilt in the reality that by curing the illness, the patient was being sentenced to poverty.

## Psychopathology of the Middle Classes

This group of Jamaicans did not represent any specific or unique findings. They presented with the same range of psychopathology as found in the elite and poor classes. Caught in the middle, they expressed elite aspirations, while retaining working and peasant-class sensibilities. In this Jamaican context, the contradictions about the shade of skin colouring became paramount, but fewer of this class of patients had as much problem with the 'roast breadfruit syndrome', as the black- and brown-skinned members of the Jamaican elite.

**Case Study**

> Consider the 32-year-old Afro-Chinese woman born to a Chinese
> father, who came to Jamaica from Hong Kong, and an African
> mother. Raised by her father in the Chinese customs in relatively
> well-off circumstances, she looked down on her mother. In her own
> words "I first saw my mother when I was age 12, she was very
> black – I spat at her". She went to live with her mother when her
> father died. Se was 12 years old. Her mother, who lived in condi-
> tions of severe poverty, flogged her mercilessly and treated her as
> an outcast – different from her other children. The patient was an
> extremely beautiful woman, and from the age of 14, she used her
> good looks to manipulate male relationships, and used sex as her
> ticket out of the poverty in which she lived. She sought psychiatric
> treatment after a failed marriage, a suicide attempt, insomnia and
> migraine headaches. She was addicted to diazepam (valium) and
> sleeping pills.

Jamaican people have been migrating to other countries in search of
work and economic advancement since the beginning of the 20th century. First to Panama, to assist in the construction of the Panama Canal, to
other Caribbean and Central American countries such as Cuba, Costa
Rica and Nicaragua, to the USA in the 1920s and 1930s, and then in waves
to the UK in the 1950s and 1960s. Here the migration theme again arises,
but this time with a difference. The miscegenated product of an African
woman and a Chinese father, this lady represents a product of the historical forces of the late 1800s when Chinese, Indian and middle Eastern
migrants arrived in Jamaica looking for work, often as indentured
labourers, in a post-slavery colonized world where jobs were scarce. The
clash of cultures and the inverted racial prejudices produced a woman
whose life mirrored the contradictions of race, sex, class and culture. This
case highlights the psychological effects of miscegenation (the inter-
breeding of races) and misogyny (the hatred of women), both behaviours
engendering strong emotions.

In the power of the miscegenates and the hatred of one's colour, it is
the colour of the lighter-skinned race that most often subordinates and
vilifies the black-skinned contribution. This sets up a hierarchy of prejudice based on skin shade, which had its origin in laws passed by the

British in the late 18th century, linking ownership of property and freedom to the degree of miscegenation (Braithwaite 1971). This represents a powerful negative force in contemporary Jamaican society. Hatred of women in this culture is another powerful negative, often stemming from the hatred of mothers. This misogyny can more clearly be witnessed when we explore the psychopathology in adolescents.

### Case Study

A 25-year-old middle-class female was admitted to hospital with an acute psychosis, presenting with paranoid delusions, auditory hallucinations, thought disorder and bizarre behaviour. Her family reported that she had dropped out of university earlier in the year and went to live in a Rastafari commune with her boyfriend. She had had a baby six months prior to her admission. She responded quickly to treatment, and then reported the difficulties that she experienced with her new baby in the Rastafari commune. She had to live apart from her mate whenever she was menstruating, and was required to carry out domestic activity for him and other members of the commune at a level which she had not been accustomed to in her own home. She was regarded with suspicion as an outsider in the commune, and found a low level of support from her baby's father. Psychotherapy after hospitalization revealed that she was experiencing significant family conflict about racial identity, especially with her father, a Black anglophile professional. She responded to her family's and her own 'roast breadfruit' identity by rejecting 'Babylon', joining the Rastafari movement and growing dreadlocks. Her clinical state settled quickly, she returned to Kingston and to university, and years later she was running a successful professional business without recurrence of her illness. She still has dreadlocks and is a Rastafarian.

'Babylon' is the name given by the Rastafari Movement to the established sociopolitical economic and religious system of the European, which enslaved Africans and brought them to the Americas to work the plantations. Characteristic features of Rastafari include: declaring knowledge of the Emperor Haile Selassie of Ethiopia as the Almighty, the Conquering Lion of the Tribe of Judah, King of Kings, Lord of Lords, the

Alpha and Omega, JAH Rastafari; demanding the Biblical prophecy that Babylon must fall; and asserting that the Black man will return to Africa from the four corners of the world to which he has been scattered; demanding an end of exploitation and upholding the Nyabinghi Order, embodying "death to Black and White oppressors," (Philos, 1935). The Rastafari Movement has become a powerful revolutionary counter-cultural force that has swept across the Caribbean and around the world. Made popular internationally by hypnotic reggae music, and reggae superstars – notably Bob Marley and Peter Tosh, Rastafari represents a new cultural emergence of the Black man with his own symbols. The spectacular colours of the red, gold and green of Africa, the use of marijuana in ritual sacrament, and a religious, social and political philosophy are unique to its existence.

This was the world that had attracted this middle-class Jamaican woman, and which precipitated revolutionary changes in her life to establish an identity of her own, passing through traumatic psychiatric episodes, as she tried to grapple with the form of a new revolutionary culture. Her main conflict was the 'roast breadfruit' psychology, which had shackled her to the economic and ideological world of her parents and the oppressor class and deformed her identity. However her adoption of the Rastafari cultural mores catapulted her into a new series of gender conflicts for which she was psychologically and sociologically unprepared. The Rastafari movement is essentially a male-dominated one, and although the woman is the Queen to her Rastaman, and is allowed to work if she wishes, she is subject to several taboos and rigid restrictions. In certain orders of Rastafari, during menstruation the woman must stay by herself, and cannot cook for her man or participate in any activities with him; oral sex is not permitted and there is controversy about polygamy, although monogamy is the norm for most Rastafari families. Recent participatory research in gender relations in Rastafari concludes that there exists a strong patriarchal emphasis within the 'livity' of Rastafari (Tafari-Ama, 1989), as an attempt of some Rastafari males to subordinate females as a means of making up for their own sense of powerlessness within the present system. It also speaks of the changing roles and the progressive dynamic shifts of women in Rastafari. However, the tendency for a positive emphasis on male responsibility exists within the brethren, which they perceive to be lacking in other social relationships in society. The fact that this young Jamaican woman continues to be a member of the Rastafari movement many years later is a testament to her rejection of her 'roast breadfruit' upbringing and her ability to incorporate a new ideology in sync with her psychological transformation and lifestyle change (Hickling and Griffith, 1994)

This identity problem has been a source of great conflict, and represents the psychological immaturity of the Jamaican people, and the road to be traveled by many. Hickling and Hutchinson (1999) described and characterized the 'roast breadfruit' syndrome as a mechanism for the development of psychotic symptoms in African-Caribbean individuals. In an attempt to rationalize their identity, these individuals have to reject this syndrome and all it means, once confronted with its existence. Hickling and Hutchinson defined the clinical components of this 'roast breadfruit' psychosis together with its antecedents and risk factors, with a view to clarifying the most appropriate therapeutic agenda for its amelioration and to indicate areas for future research.

## Case Study

A 30-year-old Black Jamaican man presented with the first onset of psychotic symptoms and was admitted to the psychiatric ward of the University Hospital of the West Indies, where he received a diagnosis of cannabis-induced psychosis. Over the succeeding five years, he had several re-admissions and received several different diagnostic labels, including schizophrenia, depressive psychosis, manic-depressive psychosis, and paranoid psychosis. He continued to be a heavy user of cannabis and this was believed to contribute to his frequent relapses. His early upbringing had been in deprived socioeconomic circumstances, but the circumstances of his family improved in his teenage years, and he was sent to North America for his university education. He married an affluent White North American woman and returned to Jamaica to set up a commercial business. His social behaviour at this time was illustrative of the 'roast breadfruit' syndrome. Because of his success and his White wife, he was able to enjoy White society, and felt that Black Jamaican culture was primitive and unsophisticated. However, influenced by the 'Black Power' movement of the late 60s and 70s, he began to explore his origins and became increasingly involved with the Rastafarian community. This led to estrangement from his wife and child, and commercial failure. It was in this context that he developed his first psychotic illness. His repeated admissions to hospital were only curtailed by the intervention of psychological therapy, directed specifically at addressing his racial, class, sexual and authority conflicts, with emphasis on his identity as a Black Caribbean man. Since this cultural therapy (Hickling 2007) he has had no further admissions, in spite of continued social use of cannabis. He has grown comfortable and accepting of his Rastafarian beliefs, and has been also been in almost continuous employment.

Many references occur in literature written in the African Diaspora to the problems of race ideology and racial identification. These have been found to occur in people of African descent in Western societies, arising out of their experience of European slavery and colonization (Carter, 1995; Patterson, 1998). The internalization of these feelings of inferiority in some people has contributed to the problems of identity formation. Applying these ideas to the frequently reported increased rates of psychoses among the African and Caribbean populations of Britain, suggests that this may be a factor significant contributor to their psychological distress. Using the cultural analogy of a roast breadfruit (Artocarpus altilis) which is black on the outside but white on the inside, and utilizing the fiction of Toni Morrison (1970), and the more analytically influenced work of psychiatrist, Frantz Fanon (1967) as the frame of reference, Hickling and Hutchinson illustrated the effect of postcolonialism on the mental health of Black people. By identifying a particular form of mental illness which they referred to as the 'roast breadfruit psychosis', positing that the core problem of Black, formerly colonial people living in Britain is that of being constantly confronted with their racial identity in an external environment that is psychosocially and culturally unfavorable. There is internal ambivalence because of the psychic effects of colonization, and from this perspective, they postulated the existence of a 'roast breadfruit' syndrome, which could deteriorate into psychotic and affective symptoms that defy neat nosological characterization.

**Case Study**

A 19-year-old Black Jamaican woman presented to the mental
health services in Germany and was seen at the request of her parents, who had been divorced for a number of years. She had attended an exclusive secondary school in Jamaica, and then spent a year
in Switzerland as an exchange student. Her social behaviour at that
time was illustrative of the 'roast breadfruit' syndrome. On her
return to Jamaica she violently rejected her parents' lifestyle, which
she condemned as being too materialistic, and also began using
cannabis. Within a few months she left for Germany and married a
German gypsy who she had met in Jamaica. After living for two
years in Germany where she had been confronted with her blackness, she began to embrace the Rastafarian philosophy and grew
her hair in dreadlocks. She presented to the psychiatric service in
Germany with what was described as a manic psychosis. Her burning her hair and her scalp in an attempt to remove the dreadlocks
had precipitated the contact. There was no previous or family history of mental illness. On discharge, she discontinued her medication
and became aggressive and violent to the family with whom she
was staying and was then re-admitted to hospital, this time to a
locked ward. Her manic psychosis returned with greater intensity.
The diagnosis remained manic psychosis, but when she continued
to deteriorate, it was thought necessary to involve a Jamaican psychiatrist. When interviewed, she declared she was not crazy, but
that she had discovered that her early upbringing was false, that the
value system of her parents and her friends in Jamaica was too
materialistic. She was declaring her blackness by growing her hair
in dreadlocks as a symbol of her identity, although she denied being
a Rastafarian. She had burnt off her dreadlocks because she had
wanted to die for her beliefs. At the time she was disinhibited and
demonstrated pressure of speech and flight of ideas. She was also
irritable and had paranoid ideas of reference. It became evident that
her psychosis had developed at the time when she was trying to
work through her 'roast breadfruit' syndrome of White cultural
identification in a racially hostile German environment. The burning of her dreadlocks was a further indication of her identity crisis
and racial confusion. She recovered from her acute psychosis and

returned to Jamaica where she underwent cultural therapy, which focused on the ambivalence of her cultural references. She is now asymptotic, is employed, and doing well on psychotropic medication.

These cases illustrate that there are specific issues related to cultural identity that may inform the onset of psychosis in some people of African-Caribbean origin. The pre-morbid state of all four was illustrative of Black people whose racial and cultural identity was of being 'functionally White', and could be classified as having the 'roast breadfruit' syndrome. In each case, there was a personal, social confrontation of the reality of their blackness, in contradiction with their White perception of themselves in the racially threatening communities in North America and Europe. In each case as well, this precipitated a psychotic illness that defied neat, conventional nosological categorization, but fit the nosology of the 'roast breadfruit' psychosis. In all cases also, the behavioural manifestations of the psychosis reflected their own racial confusion. Equally, in all cases, resolution of the problem, and the resulting healing, only occurred when these racial identity issues were addressed in culturally specific psychotherapy.

These paradigms clearly influence presentation, course and treatment of these individuals, and beg for the introduction of not only a culturally sensitive, but also a culturally specific form of therapy. The confrontation of social identity in a White society, where skin colour is the greatest signifier in daily life, and determines the degree of social acceptance, is in itself a considerable stressor. When that colour is intimately associated with social disadvantage, dangerousness and inferiority, the stress only increases. This combination of colour and culture is not unique to Caribbean people, but is especially relevant to them because of their history of being transplanted from Africa involuntarily. Their engagement with European culture was, therefore, forced and unavoidable, and their definitions of social and cultural norms were affected as a result. This may mean that these processes also frame their presentations of psychological distress, particularly when confronted with the ambivalence of ambiguous identity. The consequences of these contradictions for psychiatry are now being recognized worldwide, in multicultural environments. This is the case, especially in First World countries that are expe-

riencing massive migration of non-European people. These contradictions can be resolved only by a complete reframing of nosology and phenomenology, as well as by approaches to treatment that include a greater
awareness of sociocultural issues.

The cases which have been cited in this chapter have come from all
walks of Jamaican society, and have been either in the public mental
health systems, private practice or the prisons. As such, they are a representative cross-section of Jamaican psychopathology in the decades of the
1970s, 80s and 90s. Despite the class background, the racial or religious
statuses of the patients, certain trends and dialectical themes begin to
stand out with startling regularity. The common trend in all of these cases
relates to money and the dialectical relationships of wealth and poverty.
Despite the end of the dialectic continuum to which the patient belonged,
the outcome was the same – namely maladaptive coping responses, leading to a limited spectrum of psychopathology. Impoprtantly, the nature of
psychopathology was flavoured by the cultural setting of the patients. In
the unique crucible of this psychopathologic study, the Jamaican society
offered the psychiatrist patients who were Black, White, rich and poor,
and every conceivable combination of those antipodal conditions. The
poor were in search of wealth, and the wealthy in search of something to
fill their emptiness. This contradictory social forces gave rise to the next
most common social theme or trend, namely migration. Again, this
revealed itself dialectically, occurring from country to city, from an underdeveloped country to a developed country and vice versa – all in search
of economic satisfaction. Migration, in turn, gave rise to the stress of cultural translocation between Jamaica and the USA and the intense class,
racial and economic contradictions present in those situations.

Further analysis of these cases led to greater insight into the coping
responses to social pressure. Racial miscegenation, escape into the world
of drug abuse, a flight into religion – whether Christianity or Obeah,
explosion into the rebellion of the Rastafari counter-culture, or into violent crimes against society, are all features of these responses. Sexual
pathology was common in all cases, always rooted in the male/female
dialectical struggles, either in their parents' lives, and/or their own.
Broken homes; matriarchal mothers; authoritarian, often absent fathers;
upwardly mobile social class motivations; emergence from poverty and

slavery; and an over-representation of European culture – all were found within the matrix of the individual and the social psychopathology.

All of these phenomenological contradictions described exist in a society where economic and social power resides almost exclusively in the purview of the elite. This derives in our post-slavery society from the rights of Englishmen, which were set up and institutionalized in slavery and colonialism, and which concentrated State power and the ruling social organizations in the hands of the elite. However, the remainder of the society, although marginal to this organizational control of power, was not at all powerless, and moved to set up democratic organizations to represent themselves, and to reflect their culture and values. In this regard, trade unions, political parties, and other social and economic organizations have emerged in order to represent the needs of the poorer classes. This notwithstanding, the experience since independence indicates that although some social change has taken place, and social mobility has been achieved by some, the lot and circumstance of the majority of the people have remained essentially the same, and in many respects, may indeed have diminished. The spectre of violence, the decay of the health and social services, the tribalization, patronage, and the economic uncertainty which have emerged have not changed the reality for the majority of the Jamaican people since the imposition of the twin sisters – the impostors: adult suffrage and independence – as a postscript to colonialism and the withdrawal of Britain from political control of the country.

The most common theme to have emerged from the analysis of the Jamaican psychopathology in this post-independence period is the dialectical continuum of the oppressor and the oppressed, seen initially as the colonizer and the colonized, which is inexorably bound to the other themes mentioned before. If all the cases were seen as one whole, there would be seen to emerge an energizing or driving social force, individual life energies being pushed forward by a resultant overall force. This force or power arises from the synthesis of dialectical opposites, locked together in an enormous power-struggle. At the social level, the power-struggle reveals itself as a class struggle – between wealth and poverty, oppressor and the oppressed, the colonizer and the colonized. The evidence reveals that the psychopathology of Jamaican society exists on a spectrum consisting primarily of personality disorder on the elite end, and schizophrenia on the poor end, with a skewed scattering of these conditions across the spectrum. The psychopathology spectrum corresponds to the social structure in a similar fashion described by Mills (1987) as the co-terminal relationship between race and class, as a 'both-and' relationship, rather than an 'either-or' plural relationship as described by Smith (1965). Power management is a critical variable of both these conditions. Intense conflicts, power struggles and psychosexual dysfunction characterize personality disorder on the one hand, while schizophrenia is characterized by a dissociation from power relationship activity – a withdrawal from reality and sexual isolation on the other. Evidence is presented that there exists in the Jamaican society a social structure, which protects the elite from and exposes the poor to schizophrenia.

There is no denying the racial analysis of the oppressor-oppressed continuum. Historically, the oppressors have been all White, and the oppressed, Black, with a variation of miscegenated shades along the spectrum. The colour of the oppressors has changed from white, to brown and in some instances, black. The logic of this analysis predicts, therefore, the intensification of this violence, as long as this oppressor/oppressed dialectic continues. We have taken control of this society since independence, but the promise of a society where everybody has equal access to the means, in an environment and where Black people have economic and political control of their own destiny, has eluded us. The poor and underclass seem only to be left with the exercise of negative power, seen in the escalating violence and murder; the rising crime and mayhem; the workers' strikes, community roadblocks and demonstrations; the ability to be reactive rather than proactive. The evidence presented suggests that as the poor struggle to escape from their debilitating situation, religion, migration and rebellion are used as powerful coping mechanisms. The Jamaican people who have survived 500 years of slavery, colonialism, and oppression have heightened attributes of adaptive aggression; serious problems of managing authority; poor impulse control; and power management difficulties. They also possess a cultural creativity and talent beyond the size of the population and that is far greater, per capita, than the rest of the world. It has been suggested that there exists a social barrier in Jamaican society for actualization of talent and creative ability, which acts like a glass ceiling preventing the majority of Jamaican people from expressing their fullest potential. This sets up a graveyard of champions, which is self-perpetuating and self-limiting.

The evidence presented suggests that the presence of conflict and neglect in child-rearing appears to be a major factor in the resultant psychopathology, and that our women seem to hold the key in the transmission of sound power management principles for successful and healthy interpersonal relationships. Even the acquisition of higher levels of education by the Jamaican people in the latter half of the 20th century reflects a manifestation of the exercise of negative power. Many Jamaicans who have benefited from expensive secondary and tertiary education programmes have migrated to the developed metropoles of North America and Europe, those societies benefiting from our 'brain hemorrhage'. For those Jamaicans who remain, education seems to have become subordinated to the bare necessities of the marketplace, rather than meeting the monumental challenges of social development and nation building. The achievement of academic mediocrity seems to have replaced the achievement of academic and intellectual scholarship, where ignorance and egocentrism seem to have triumphed over knowledge and self-critical development. The falsehoods of psychological denial and rationalization have replaced the harsh truths of incisive analytic thought.

Jamaica's history, which has been well documented by a number of authors, indicate that the Jamaican people have come close to shattering the brittle, but tough, glass ceiling on a number of occasions. These include the Maroon rebellions, the Sam Sharpe rebellion, the Morant Bay rebellion, the 1938 rebellion, and the Walter Rodney uprising in 1968.

Jamaican-born Marcus Garvey, father of modern Pan-Africanism, must take his place as one of the most significant philosophers and political figures of the 20th century. Robert Nesta (Bob) Marley, also a Jamaican, must take his place as one of the most popular and successful musicians of the 20th century, loved and revered for his musical creations by people of every race, and every nation of the world. His revolutionary music was being played and sung during the destruction of the Berlin wall; during the revolutionary insurrection in Tiananmen Square in China; at the front line of every revolution, and in cafés and nightclubs across the world. Rastafari and reggae music have both swept the world as revolutionary, ideological, political, theocratic and musical movements. Both are products of late-20th century Jamaica. The great revolu-

tionary Jamaican leaders have helped to bring insight to these social contradictions existing in Jamaica. However, none of these has succeeded in
shattering the glass ceiling. The historical experience of the Jamaican people indicates that on each of these explosive occasions, the social structure
has simply absorbed and accommodated the collective discontent of the
people and has strengthened the oppressive ceiling with the very energy
and essence of the people's struggles. It is suggested that what was missing in those nodal points of history was a subjective 'overstanding' (to
use a popular Rastafarian neologistic construction) of the glass ceiling, of
the exercise of negative power, and the mobilization of this negative
power which is required for transformation. The sciences of psychology
and psychiatry recognize the existence of objective phenomena in human
behaviour, as well as the subjective expression of these phenomena in
thinking and feeling. The experience of this author over the past 30 years
recognizes that there are cultural and psychotherapeutic tools, which
connect objective with subjective experiences, and when appropriately
manipulated, can successfully mobilize this exercise of negative power.
This can successfully challenge the glass ceiling, and hence can assist in
the transformation of individuals and groups, and ultimately, the transformation of this society.

## Adolescence and Gender Issues

In an unpublished study by this author of 194 Jamaican young people
aged 19 years or less, seen in a Jamaican private psychiatric clinic
between 1975 and 1991, there were 109 males (56%) and 85 females (44%).
They were equally represented in terms of their origin, with 70 per cent
from an urban address, and 30 per cent from a rural address. Of the samples, 66 per cent were between 15 and 19 years old, 25 per cent between
10 and 14, and eight patients fell below the age of 10 years. The majority
(80 – 41%) was from socio-economic class (SEC) III, 62 (32%) from SEC IV,
while SEC II, and I each represented 12 per cent of the sample, with 3%
being from SEC V. Sixty-five per cent of the sample had attained a secondary school education, and another 14 per cent had attended primary
school. The sample was predominantly of African origin and born in
Jamaica (98%); and adolescent crisis was the single highest diagnostic category (28%). The diagnosis of adolescent crisis is equivalent to that of

personality disorder in adults. The diagnosis of personality disorder is not used in patients below the age of 21, as it is considered that the personality is not fully formed before this age. This was followed closely by the diagnosis of schizophrenia (22%), and affective disorder (19%). The diagnosis of schizophrenia was significantly over-represented in males. Significantly more females (p = 0.05) lived with mothers alone. One hundred and thirty-four (69%) of the total sample, with significantly more females (p = 0.05) than males came from homes characterized by separated or divorced parents and parental conflict.

## Case Study

A 21-year-old social class III Black male was brought to the clinic by his father, who reported that his son was experiencing 'stress', that he was hearing voices, and thought that people in the community were talking about him and trying to kill him. The young man had withdrawn from society and kept himself locked away in his room for most of the day and refused to communicate with people. He had no friends, was insecure and felt that there was something wrong with the way he looked. As a result, his schoolwork had deteriorated and he had become a recluse. The young man agreed that what his father had reported was true, except for the fact that he was not hearing voices, but was actually hearing people shouting things about him. He reported that he heard people outside his house shouting to each other: "De bwoy inside is a batty-bwoy. Yu nuh see how him lock up ina de house all day?" (The boy inside is a dirty homosexual. Can't you see how he isolates himself in the house all day?) shouted a female voice. "No, is jus wuckless him wuckless." (No, that is not the explanation. He is simply worthless.) replied the other female voice. "No" replied the first voice "Him is a dutty batty man, an if him don't leave the area we ah go kill him blood claat." (He is a dirty homosexual, and if he does not leave the district we are going to kill him). The young man reported that these voices were real people, and he could not explain why other people could not hear them as he did. He was afraid of their threats, and as a result, had tried to move away from the area, but everywhere he went the voices followed him. In fact when he went on the road he would see people looking at him in a knowing, hostile and disapproving way. He knew that people driving their motorcars on the road would blow their car horns at him in a particular way, which he recognized as a code which communicated to other road users: 'This is a batty bwoy; be careful of him."

The young man reported these hallucinatory and delusional experiences in a clear sensorium. He looked and talked normally and only when he started talking about these bizarre experiences (which was often) would people realize that something was wrong with him. He was the first of two sons, both of whom had grown up in Kingston with their father. Their mother had migrated to the USA when they were infants. She returned to live with them and their father when he was age 10, but had quarreled constantly with their father, and they were divorced soon after. At high school the young man was initially very bright and quite successful, but by third form his scholastic performance deteriorated and he began having a conduct problem. As a result, he was moved from school to school, and his scholastic performance continued to deteriorate. He found it impossible to socialize with people and became more and more reclusive.

The study of Jamaican adolescents identified that schizophrenia and drug abuse were the most common diagnostic categories in adolescent Black males, and that adolescent crisis and affective disorders (depression in particular) were the predominant diagnostic categories in adolescent Black females in Jamaica. It also drew attention to the fact that there was a significant gender difference in psychopathology in Jamaican adolescents. The clinical picture indicates that symptoms of sadness, anger and rage are much more frequent in females than males, and there was a much greater tendency towards psychosis in males than females. Attention must be drawn to the similarity in diagnostic patterns between the high rates of schizophrenia in the poorer classes, and high rates of personality disorder in the Jamaican elite, as was noted earlier. This should be viewed against the background of the similar pattern of diagnoses between male and female adolescents now being discussed. The question to be answered is whether there is a similar causative mechanism between the classes, and between the genders for both of the conditions discussed – both of which seem to fall on opposing ends of a diagnostic dialectic.

The ability to express the emotion of conflict and unhappiness in Jamaican females, an ability that seems to be underdeveloped in males, may represent a protective mechanism against the development of schizophrenia and related conditions. The correlation of intense parental conflict, separation, and divorce suggests major etiologic significance between the development of adolescent psychopathology in Jamaican young people and their inability to handle hostility and conflict in their homes. This study showed that there was a significantly higher rate ($p=0.04$) of absent fathers and divorced and separated parents in the females of this sample than the males, although the rates of both these variables was high for both sexes. The causative factor seems to fall into the spectrum of the ability of the genders and the classes to manage power and, thereby, manage authority.

This power management dynamic also seems to be related to problems of male psychosexual development, poor self-esteem, and identity formation in the development of schizophrenia in Black male adolescents. The adolescent study reported significantly higher levels of homophobia, homosexual fantasies and homosexual activities in male, compared to female adolescents, especially in schizophrenic symptomatology. These factors are correlated with the findings that significantly more female adolescents lived with their mothers alone than their male counterparts. Conversely, significantly more of the adolescent males lived with both mother and father than the females studied. Most of the female patients reported that they had been beaten (physically abused) by their mothers. These findings suggest that high heterosexual activity, adolescent crisis, depression, anger and rage in the female adolescents represent rebellion against mothers who raise their female children in a more hostile, conflictual and punitive manner than their male children. There is a corollary to this as well, namely that female parenting behaviour to male children may be more ambivalent and double binding – hence more schizophrenogenic. Both males and females often reflect the psychological damage in intensely held feelings of misogyny.

The conclusion that is emerging is that the woman seems to be the major agent of psychological acculturation and power management in the Jamaican society, regardless of class. She influences and shapes both male and female growth and change behaviour in the children whom she mothers, and the males with whom she mates and bonds, regardless of class position. Disturbances in this influential power management process seem to be a major influence in the development of psychopathology. It seems that a much greater understanding of this relationship to power will have to be gained, before we will be able to bring about the mechanisms of transformation and change that have been written about in political science. Indeed, the dialectic relationship between the relative lack of female power in a male-dominated social structure has been the major focus of human existence for millennia. This control of the socio-genetic agents of power management being discussed, may indeed hold a key to the dialectics of transformation and change in human society.

## Case Study

A 41-year-old professional brown-skinned Jamaican male, struggling to understand the nature of his difficulties in managing and sustaining a meaningful emotional relationship with women – having just broken off with his girl friend of five years – related in therapy that for the first 13 years of his life, he was very close to his mother. In his words, they were inseparable, and devoted to each other. The relationship changed dramatically when he entered puberty, and he began to reject what she wanted him to do and how she wanted him to conduct his affairs. He related the incident when he was Head Boy of a prestigious secondary school in Kingston, conducting a management meeting with his prefects and his Headmaster walked into the meeting, announcing to him in front of his prefects, that his mother had just phoned to complain that he had not made his bed that morning. The patient reported that his authority rating with his prefects took a steep decline from that point. The anecdote was about the blatant manipulation of raw power by his mother, using the Headmaster as a willing dupe. Twenty-five years later the episode lingered at the surface of this man's psyche as a burning and pervasive insult that had ravaged his learning curve about the management of power and authority, and his relationship with women. The central feature of his personality disorder was his recurrent engagement with the women in his life, in a destructive power-struggle, an unhealthy dependency relationship, and pathological sexual relationships.

This man was making a genuine effort to resolve a problem in the fabric of his life, and had created his own analysis of the dynamics of relationships of mothers with their sons. In his experience, mothers had two types of relations with their sons. On the one hand, there were the mothers who had a war-like relationship with their sons, and on the other, mothers who engulfed and overpowered their sons to the point of emasculation. However, he did not have a clear insight into the fact that both dynamics were not mutually exclusive and could exist, as in his case, within a single relationship. Nor did he recognize that both these dynamics were also related to the cyclical negative relationships that he had with women.

### Case Study

The next case is of a 32-year-old Black female who complained of continued thumb sucking. On examination, it was soon revealed that this was a symptom which defended her from the anger and hostility which she felt about her lowly economic status as a domestic worker, and which she acted out in continuing power struggles with her boyfriend. With no economic relief in view, she contemplated migration to the USA as the most logical panacea, and at a real level, continued to fight and struggle with her mate. She soon revealed that she often precipitated the power struggle with her mate that would always end with him abusing her physically. Finally, she admitted that she received masochistic pleasure from his beating her almost, as it were, to compensate for economic impotence.

This summarizes the oppressive economic society, controlling and shaping the emotional and psychosexual relationships of all its people, psychological and economic manipulative slavery, replacing the state of physical slavery that had been abolished 150 years previously.

## Psychopathology of the Underclass

A mental health professional operating in Jamaica today, is faced with all classes of Jamaican people, from every walk of life, and from every social circumstance. Fifty-five minutes before midnight on the 26th December, 1974, 11 inmates of the St. Catherine District Prison who had all been condemned to hang for murder, slipped through the bars of their cells on "Gibraltar" – the ward for condemned men. They had previously cut the bars with hacksaw blades. Another inmate called out to the warder on duty, demanding a drink of water. As soon as the warder entered Death Row, the 11 men, who had cut their way out of their cells, held him. Two of these men, seeing the main gate of the condemned ward open, bolted for their freedom. This set the stage for an incident, which has been described variously as a 'breakout' by the local newspaper, 'an attempted mass breakout' by the prison authorities, and as a 'demonstration against injustice and oppression' by the condemned men. As a result, a Commission of Inquiry was set up by the Prime Minister, Michael Manley, under the Chairmanship of Dr. Lloyd Barnett, to investigate the circumstance surrounding the incident. A psychiatric team headed by the author, including psychiatrist, Dr Frank Knight and psychologist, Dr Ruth Doorbar, and social workers, Hu Marsh and Earle Fearon, was commissioned to undertake a thorough psycho-sociological examination of all the condemned men on Death Row and to report on the circumstances of the incident and conditions of incarceration (Hickling et al 1976).

In a report to the Commission of Inquiry, the psycho-sociological profiles of the 36 condemned murderers were presented with an analysis of their psychopathology. The study revealed that 16 of the men were born and lived in the rural areas, while an equal number was born and had lived in urban areas. Comparative analyses revealed that the urban men were significantly more involved in adolescent delinquent behaviour, had previous convictions, committed murders using guns, and killed exclusively adult males who were unknown to them. The urban murderers had significantly higher intellectual endowment as measured by the Wechsler Adult Intelligence test. There was a bimodal distribution of the IQ scores of the urban murderers, with an unusual loading in the Superior Range, suggesting that these men were not representatives of an average prison population. The rural murderers also had significantly more anti-social personalities as measured by the Minnesota Multiphasic Personality Inventory and by clinical assessment.

The psychosocial analysis was also revealing. The fathers of the urban men were significantly more skilled or semi-skilled as workers than their rural counterparts, and provided significantly more financial support for their children. The mothers of the urban men had a larger number of consorts for whom they had had children than their rural counterparts. Significantly more urban men were literate and had gone beyond the fourth grade in school. However, both rural and urban condemned men were from very low socioeconomic circumstances. Significantly more urban men had started sexual relations by age 12, and had had more sexual partners and less stable cohabitation patterns than the rural men. On all counts, the urban condemned men were significantly different from the rural men, consequently a simple homogenous grouping labeled as 'murderers' had little meaning in objective reality. The rural group had committed killings related to poor emotional control, in situations where they saw a single person – usually known to them – who threatened their personal welfare. The urban group, on the other hand, had killed, in almost all cases, persons unknown to them. Moreover, with the exception of three victims, they had killed representatives of established society such as policemen, security guards, bank managers, prison warders and businessmen. The murders carried out by this group must be seen as attacks against the establishment, as acts of societal rebellion. Many of the urban killers claimed that they had connections with political gangs connected to one or the other political party. The following is the case study of one of this group of urban rebels.

## Case Study

This was an Afro-Chinese male, born in the ghettos of Kingston, reared by his African mother, never knowing his father. Rebellious from childhood, he was in constant trouble at home and at school as a child. Flogged mercilessly by his mother, he soon became a gang leader connected to one of the local political parties, and was involved in many crimes of armed robbery with violence, eventually being sentenced to hang for murder when he was 17.

Psychological assessment while in prison revealed a keen intelligence, with an IQ in the 'superior range', and an agile, creative mind. Although he openly admitted to us – the psychiatric evaluation team – that he had committed a number of killings, he claimed that he had not killed the man for whose death he had been convicted. He openly and literally identified with the lyrics of one of Bob Marley's songs: "I shot the sheriff, but I did not shoot the deputy". Claiming membership of the Rastafari movement, he contended that his role in life was to fight Babylon in any way, thereby justifying his life of criminal activity. He was paroled from prison, but soon resumed his violent criminal activity, and was subsequently killed in a shoot-out with the police. Crime, violence, and aggression were consciously articulated as rebellion by this ghetto genius. Making no apology for his life and actions, he deliberately set about attacking the established society of private property in his personal rebellion against those whom he perceived as the oppressors. A creative artist, soft spoken philosopher, he was unrelenting in his vicious violent attack against his social captors. He lived by the gun and died by the gun. A self-styled freedom fighter, he epitomized the struggle of the oppressed against the oppressor.

Jamaica has acquired the reputation of being one of the most dangerous, violent societies in the world, with a disastrous effect on investment and development, and an increasing national paranoia. The country had over 800 murders in 1980, a figure which has since risen to over 900 in 1996, and 1674 in 2006, with the problem burgeoning, and no end in sight. After surviving more than 500 years of the oppression of European slavery and colonialism, Jamaican people seem to have developed personality characteristics that highlight adaptive aggression, serious authority management issues, poor impulse control and power management difficulties. In a social environment of marked unequal distribution of wealth, poor educational and economic opportunity, and an apolitical system based on patronage and clientilism, violence that was originally manifested as rebellion against European political, economic and racial exploitation has turned inward, as tribalism and self-destruction, following the attainment of Universal Adult Suffrage under the Westminster system of parliamentary democracy. It is suggested that in this type of environment where crime, migration and entrepreneurial aggression seem to be the surest avenues for social advancement from poverty and the ghetto, such strategies have become the dominant response to the existing oppression, as manifested in present-day Jamaican society.

The verbal reports of the condemned men we examined pointed to the close relationship between these violent activists and both the Jamaica Labour Party and the People's National Party. This illustrates a major issue – the lack of fulfillment of the expectations of the poor and the underclass by institutions such as political parties, which were created to champion the interests of poor people. Thus, political gangs and warfare, along with the growth of garrison constituencies which dominate the present political landscape, are further examples of the exercise of negative power by the poor and the underclass. The two major political parties have promised much and delivered little. They, therefore, have to bear a heavy responsibility for the tribalization and high levels of violence and the unfulfilled expectations of the Jamaican people. In more recent times, the negative power of these political activists has been translated into the spread of criminal drug activities. Led by powerful drug dons, the underclass attempts to deal with the poverty and unfulfilled expectations of their communities, by seizing economic advantage through the drug trade and other criminal activities.

A society – building new relationships between men and women, where fear and anxiety have vanished, and insecurity and frustration are replaced by positive expanding self-assurance, respect and trust, where oppression and exploitation are replaced by a sharing, egalitarian state – needs to be constructed in this generation. The study of individual psychopathology has been the basis on which the science of psychoanalysis and the practice of psychiatry have been built. In recent decades, the study of the social antecedents in the causation of individual psychopathology has led to the elaboration of the wider science of social psychiatry. Further analysis of these cases lead to greater insight into the coping responses to social pressure. Racial miscegenation, escape into the social world of drug abuse, a flight into religion, whether it be Christianity or Obeah, or explosion into the rebellion of the Rastafari counter culture, or violent crimes against society were some of these responses. Sexual pathology was common in all cases, always rooted in the male-female dialectical struggles, either in their own lives, in their parents' lives, or in both. Broken homes; matriarchal mothers; authoritarian, often absent fathers; upwardly mobile social class motivations; emergence from poverty and slavery; and an overrepresentation of a European culture, were all found within the matrix of the individual and the social psychopathology.

From the study of the individual psychopathology of these cases, it is clear that an unseen case study lies hidden within the facts of the 12 – namely the socio-psychopathological framework of the societies that had spawned them. The societies of Jamaica, the USA, England, Africa and Hong Kong, all played a significant role in the genesis of the individual psychopathology. Moreover, these countries have present-day social structures inextricably bound together by the history of colonialism and imperialism of the past 500 years. European 'discovery' of the New World, the rape of the Americas by these colonizers, the development of the slave trade between Africa and the New World fuelled the fledgling capitalist system. This was followed by the breakaway of the USA from the English colonizers in a revolution which energized their industrial revolution, dictating the development of American capitalism, and expressing tangible manifestation in the present-day international capitalist system. Jamaica has a similar history of colonialism, having been stolen from the Arawak Indians by the genocidal Spanish colonizers, captured by the British in 1655, and the present-day society built by the labour of the millions of Africans, brought across the Middle Passage and forced to be slaves. They put up a stiff resistance to slavery by a history of violent struggle. Rebellions in 1834, 1865, and 1938 forced the British colonizers to grant adult suffrage in 1944, and political independence in 1962. But the economy of Jamaica was and is firmly tied into the international capitalist system, with much of the country owned by foreigners in the USA and Britain. And by perusal of the presented case material in this study, it is clear that the interchangeable social conditions in these countries have been the major etiological agents in the pathogenesis of the individual psychopathology.

Figure 1 depicts the dialectic relationship of the individual psychopathology, as revealed by analysis of the presented case studies, and by the social psychopathology of the socioeconomic system in which they lived and attempted to cope.

With the recognition that all dialectic life forces release energies which power the forward movement of social activity and development, and recognizing that working through these dialectic contradictions produces new levels of energy syncretism – which is the essence of the social development of mankind – the following must be concluded from this study: in the actual working through of the dialectical forces represented in the diagram, the people and the societies they form are in the actual process of personal and social transformation. This transformation will create the dialectic synthesis of the new society, as the people continue to work

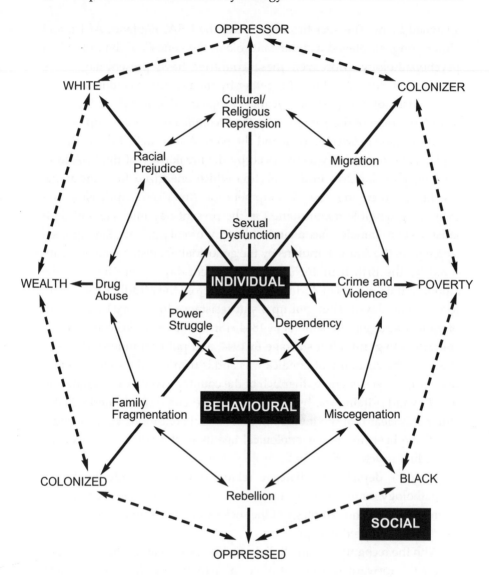

*Figure 1: Dialectical relationship of individual and social psychopathology.*

through their life contradictions. The figure describes three interlocking levels of dialectical contradictions, starting centrally with the individual, and linking in concentric circles with social, and then pathological political constructs. This suggests a dynamic three-dimensional cause-and-effect kaleidoscope governing this psychopathological continuum. Much has been written on this social transformation that is taking place in the world. The political realities of the past decade in Jamaica are a living testament to this. In an attempt to resolve the dialectic contradictions of the rich and the poor, the oppressor and the oppressed, the White and the Black, the Jamaican society underwent a social revolutionary period, which released enormous cultural energies, but intensified the dialectical struggle for power and ownership. Over 1,600 people were killed in Jamaica in 2006 by political violence, and even with the partial cessation of hostilities that followed the elections in 1980, the resolution of the social power struggle is not yet in sight.

With the recognition of the fact that this is an international power-struggle and that this struggle is reflected at the psychological level of the individual, mental health professionals must become even more sharply aware of their role as social therapists. Any successful attempt to relieve personal psychopathology must be reflected by a concomitant change in the social structure, no matter how small. Psychology professionals must concern themselves with much greater insightfulness of the process of individual and social change, and the elucidation of the sciences that connects these processes. Thereafter, we must connect with the people and the society with tangible applications of our skills, for the alleviation of psychological illness. Then, and only then, will we begin to free ourselves from the dialectic social psychopathology that surrounds us, and create a world of egalitarianism, brotherhood and peace. This chapter focuses primarily on the psychopathology of the European-engineered Caribbean social environment without apology, with the recognition that the social re-engineering required as an antidote to this pathology must come from a clear 'overstanding' of its genesis. No doubt the resilience of the Caribbean people that is also described in this volume will also help to point the way for the roadmap of wellness and positive psychology that is the compelling agenda of this generation.

## REFERENCES

Braithwaite, E. (1971). _The development of creole society in Jamaica 1770-1820._ London: Oxford University Press.

Carter, R. T. (1995). _The influence of race and racial identity in psychotherapy. Toward a racially inclusive model._ New York: John Wiley and Sons.

Cochrane, R., & Bal, S. (1989). Mental hospital admission rates of immigrants to England. *Social Psychiatry and Psychiatric Epidemiology* 24,2-11.

Fanon, F. (1967). *The wretched of the earth.* New York: Grove Press.

General Register Office. (1966). *Classification of occupations.* London: H.S.M.O.

Hall, D. (1989). *In miserable slavery: Thomas Thistlewood in Jamaica, 1750-1786.* London: Warwick University Caribbean Studies.

Hickling, F. W. (1975). Psychiatric care in a general hospital unit in Jamaica. *West Indian Medical Journal,* 24: 76–84.

———. (1996). The psychopathology of white mentally ill migrants to Jamaica. *Journal of Molecular and Chemical Neuropathology,* 28: (1-3):261-8.

———. (2007). *Psychohistoriography. A postcolonial psychoanalytic and psycho-thera-peutic model.* Kingston: CARIMENSA, University of the West Indies.

Hickling, F. W., & Griffith, E. E. H. (1994). Clinical perspectives on the Rastafari movement. *Hospital Community Psychiatry,* 45:49-53, January 1994.

Hickling, F. W., & Hutchinson, G. (1998), The roast breadfruit psychosis: A conse-quence of disturbed racial identification in African-Caribbeans. *Psychiatric Bulletin,* 23, 132-134.

Hickling, F. W., Knight, F., Doorbar, R., Marsh, H., & Fearon, E. (1976). *Report of a psycho sociological investigation of the 36 condemned men at the St. Catherine dis-trict prison and the causes of the 26th December demonstration by 26 of those men.* Lloyd Barnett Commission of Enquiry. Kingston: Government of Jamaica.

Hickling, F. W., Martin, J., & Harrisingh, A. (2008). Redefining personality disor-der in Jamaica. In F. W. Hickling, B. Matthies, K. Morgan, & R. Gibson (Eds.), *Perspectives in Caribbean psychology.* Kingston: CARIMENSA, University of the West Indies.

Hickling, F. W., & Rodgers-Johnson, P. (1995). The incidence of first-contact schiz-ophrenia in Jamaica. *British Journal of Psychiatry,* 166, 522-526

Littlewood, R., & Lipsedge, M. (1989). *Aliens and alienists.* London and New York: Routledge.

Lugard, F. D. (1929) *The dual mandate in British Tropical Africa.* Edinburgh: Blackwood.

Morrison, T. (1970). *The bluest eye.* New York: Holt, Rinehart and Winston.

Mills, C. W. (1987). Race and class: Conflicting or reconcilable paradigms. *Social and Economic Studies,* 36 (2), 69-108.

Odegaard, O., (1932). Emigration and insanity: A study of mental disease among Norwegian-born population in Minnesota. *Acta Psychiatrica et Neurologica Scandinavia,* 7 (Suppl. 4).

Patterson, O. (1998). *Rituals of blood. Consequences of slavery in two American cen-turies.* New York: Basic Civitas.

Philos, F. (1935). Secret society to destroy whites. Kingston: *The Jamaica Times,* December 7, 1935.

Smith, M. G. (1965). *The plural society in the British West Indies.* Berkeley: University of California Press.

Tafari-Ama, I. (1989). Analysis of a research project: Gender relations in Rastafari. (Unpublished thesis). The Hague: Institute of Social Studies.

Thomas-Hope, E. (2006). Maximizing migration: Caribbean return movements and the organization of transnational space. Chapter 8. In D. E. Plaza & F. Henry (Eds.), *Returning to the source. The final stage of the Caribbean migration circuit.* Kingston: University of the West Indies Press.

# 3   Resilience

## Secrets of Success in African-Caribbean People

*Hilary Robertson-Hickling*

## Introduction

The concept of resilience has been researched extensively by psychiatrists, psychologists, and educators (Gordon & Coscarelli, 1996; Tugade, 2004). Rutter (1984, 1985, 1990, 1999) is one of the researchers who have contributed much to our understanding of the concept and the interventions necessary to ensure survival in life-threatening and traumatic circumstances in the lives of children. However, a review of the literature has shown that little has been written about the African-Caribbean community.

This chapter examines the concept within the context of the lives of African-Caribbean people in the UK in general, but more specifically in Birmingham, England and in Jamaica where the experiences of forced and free migration, poverty and racism have been part of the history of these communities and continue to have an impact. The cases presented seek to highlight the impact of the risks encountered by different groups of African-Caribbean people in different contexts, and outlines the resilience fostered by such protective factors as supportive parents, teachers and other mentors in the school and community, as well as the individuals' desire to succeed and overcome adversity.

## DEFINING THE CONCEPT

The definition below encompasses many of the difficulties encountered by Black people who have experienced these problems for generations, yet have found the will, individually and collectively, to struggle against, to revolt, to create and to contribute to these societies which are, in fact, hostile to them.

> Resilience or "psychological resilience" is a psychological term which describes the capacity of people to cope with stress and catastrophe. It is also used to indicate a characteristic of resistance to future negative events. The psychological meaning of resilience is often contrasted with risk factors.
>
> (*Wikipedia the Free Encyclopedia*, 2007)

The author extends the definition of resilience above to celebrate the triumph over stress and catastrophe. Resilience is a concept which seems to describe the survival of the descendants of the millions of Africans who crossed the Middle Passage to come to the Americas (Patterson, 1998; Williams, 1984). From North America, through Central America and the Caribbean and throughout South America, it continues to be a struggle to rise above the adversity and many of the psychological scars of slavery and colonialism which still persist in the post-modern era. In spite of these adverse circumstances, Black people have been creative in all facets of life and continue to be optimistic and hopeful about the future. In the plastic and performing arts, as well as in sports, Black people have used the limited access to the platforms of achievement to succeed. In the academic, business and many other sectors, the struggle continues on a daily basis. Even in the USA which has more than 30 million Black people, racism continues to undermine and underestimate their value. This was recently demonstrated in the debacle of Hurricane Katrina in New Orleans, where many African-Americans perished, or lost everything, while aid from the federal and state government came slowly or not at all (*Time Magazine*, 2005).

# Risk and Resilience in Jamaica

Jamaica was a British colony from 1655 to 1962. During this time, the majority of the people of African origin experienced slavery, then after

Emancipation, struggled to become independent landowners, artisans or to make a living in some other honest way. Poverty, inequality and oppression have dogged Jamaica throughout its history, even until today in the post-independence period where globalization now poses challenges. Many Jamaicans have been migrating to seek a better life since the middle of the 19th century. While some remaining in Jamaica have made considerable progress, there are still many Jamaicans who live with poverty, unemployment and an increasing level of violence (Sherlock, 2000).

## COOPERATIVE ASSOCIATION OF STATES FOR SCHOLARSHIPS

Within this context, many people, particularly young people, need opportunities so that they can advance. Programmes like the Cooperative Association of States for Scholarships (CASS) have helped to foster resilience by providing poor, bright students with an opportunity to access tertiary education through scholarships.

In the period 1994–1997 the author was employed by the prestigious Georgetown University to coordinate a scholarship programme for underprivileged adolescents living in Jamaica, a scholarship which would allow them to pursue tertiary education in the USA. This programme was administered by the Cooperative Association of States for Scholarships (CASS), an association that operated in the Caribbean and Latin America. The programme was managed by the Centre for International Education on behalf of the United States Agency for International Development (USAID). In Jamaica, the CASS programme operated out of Connolley House, a private community health and development centre, which provided mental health services to persons, whether ill or healthy. The work of Connolley House helped to restore people to health and also to prevent illness by facilitating individual achievement and organizational health. There was little stigma attached to coming to the psychiatrist at Connolley House as against going to a mental hospital or ward for care. Some of the students selected for CASS had to be assessed by the psychiatrist because of their inappropriate behaviour during the orientation programme. The work with all the clients at Connolley House was conceptual, practical and collaborative and grew from a common understanding of the behaviour of Caribbean people.

This programme provided approximately 250 scholarships for poor, bright students who could not afford to pay for tertiary education in their own countries in Central America and the Caribbean. The Jamaican quota was 25 scholarships and the author was responsible for the recruitment, selection and orientation of the students who would take up tertiary placements at those community colleges in the USA where the scholarships were tenable. As part of the selection process, conducted by the coordinator, there was a panel of persons with expertise in the fields of study, comprising representatives of Georgetown University and programme alumni, with the aim of identifying the candidates who would be adaptable, academically capable and willing to return to make a contribution to their respective communities, in keeping with the agreement with USAID. During the period of the orientation we had to prepare them for the study experience in the USA. This group of Black Jamaicans or African-Caribbean people was specially prepared for life in a country known for its history of racism. The orientation included many aspects of American life, the educational system, the US Constitution, and the laws.

Throughout the process, there were frequent reminders of the strength, resilience and the desire to succeed exemplified by the young people interviewed, who came from schools across Jamaica. These were young people who were providing leadership in their schools, communities and workplaces in spite of significant social or economic obstacles. Their lives were a constant reminder that the majority of Jamaicans had overcome horrendous obstacles for centuries, through forced migration from the continent of their ancestors, through slavery and British colonialism. It had been a history of triumph over adversity (Sherlock, 2000).

One of the outcomes of the CASS programme in Jamaica was the development of the "Secrets of Success" of the scholarship candidates. It was a concept that emerged during the process of interviewing each candidate, when the question was posed: "What is the secret of your success?" Many of these students coming from impoverished urban and rural environments could not conceive of themselves as being successful. Their 'insightlessness' about the possibility of their own resilience and success was reflected in their disbelief at the question. The question forced them to affirm that they had indeed been successful, as they realized that the interviewers clearly considered that their achievement was itself an example of this.

Many of the students acknowledged that it was their faith which had brought them through the financial problems, conflicts in the home, and lack of parental support. Often a relative, a teacher or someone else had helped to sustain them by God's grace. An enduring faith in God had helped to see them through the tribulations and made their dreams come true.

Many expressed the desire to make a difference in their families, schools, communities and country. They explained how the scholarship would enable them to help to develop Jamaica, and to be role models to young people in their communities. They suggested that they could encourage young girls to postpone pregnancy and young boys to avoid involvement in gangs – they could show their peers that something else was possible.

Some expressed excitement at being the first to go to college and explained how this would benefit their families, encourage younger siblings and show their peers what was possible. They were willing to be pioneers, as many of their parents had not been able to go as far as they had, because of early pregnancy, financial or other family problems. They also recounted stories of persistence and perseverance in the face of many odds. They expressed confidence in themselves and a willingness to keep trying in spite of any obstacles facing them. One young man, for instance, had applied three times before he was successful in winning a CASS scholarship.

The desire for acknowledgement and recognition of their efforts, as well as those of their families and of their country has spurred many students to succeed. They were also committed to learning the vocational and professional skills offered by the scholarship and sharing the cross-cultural skills with those whom they would meet in the USA.

These young people demonstrated a strong connection to home, family and nation, which was a sign of belonging (Robertson-Hickling, 1997).

## Secrets of Success in Jamaica – Promoting Resilience

The following case demonstrates the capacity of one young man's strong personal conviction and faith in God, which together with the aid of a supportive teacher, helped him to overcome the odds. Among these odds were poverty and the limited educational opportunities in his immediate community, which resulted in his having to walk several miles to attend extra classes.

## Case 1

A young man from rural Jamaica belonged to a family of nine children. His father was a labourer, who was opposed to his efforts to further his education, and his mother a domestic helper. He went to great lengths to get a primary and then secondary education. Sometimes this required him to walk to school barefoot and without lunch money. His teacher saw that he had ability and encouraged him to apply for one of the CASS scholarships to study food processing. He succeeded on the second attempt to win the scholarship, completed his Associate degree at a college in California, returned to Jamaica to work at an agricultural college and then completed his Bachelor's degree at The College of Agriculture. He is now in charge of the Quality Control Department of a large internationally famous Jamaican food processing company. He has assisted in educating at least two of his siblings and has helped to extend the house of his parents.

This young man has shown resilience in several ways: he persevered with his education, he has been a role model; assisted two siblings, and has helped his parents to extend their house. When the opportunity presented itself, on his return to Jamaica, he went on to complete his Bachelor's degree. The company with which he now works as a manager has promoted him several times.

## Case 2

This case demonstrates how a young woman who is determined to succeed, with the help of a supportive school, teachers and administration will do just that. Her completing CXC's and 'A' Levels was possible with the support of the school that she attended.

A young woman from a low income community in Kingston, Jamaica was very bright and displayed considerable academic potential in her primary school. She was awarded a scholarship to a leading girls' school where she passed 8 CXC subjects and three 'A' Level subjects. Her family was unable to assist her to pursue tertiary education, so she applied for various scholarships, including the CASS scholarship, which she received. Throughout her school life at the primary, secondary and tertiary levels she received the support of her teachers, which she has asserted, was a very important factor in her sucess.

The school can provide a protective environment for young people in adverse circumstances and this was clearly so in the life of this young woman. She had a focus and purpose which gained the support of her teachers and school administration. This coincides with one of Rutter's (1984) findings about the role of the school.

## THE SCHOOL

Whereas Rutter suggests that the school can be a protective factor, the opposite view is held by some researchers in the UK. For example, in the group in Birmingham, school was a place of trauma. Coard (1971), Duncan (1991), Francis (1992), and other researchers agreed on the trauma factor, although they differed in the explanation. Many parents who themselves suffered at the hands of the educational system, continue to have tremendous faith in teachers in the schools to guide their children to achieve their potential. There is a sense of powerlessness expressed by many people about the difficulties that they are experiencing in trying to transform their lives in Britain. Despite the valiant efforts of some members of the earlier generations to address the problems faced by the Black community, many of the problems remain intractable.

The work of Rutter et al (1979) shows that one source of external protective factors can be the *school*. Children in discordant and disadvantaged homes are more likely to demonstrate resilient characteristics if they attend schools that have good academic records and attentive, caring teachers. Schools can provide children with positive experiences that are associated with either success or pleasure. These experiences need not necessarily involve academic success but might be associated with musical achievement, holding positions of responsibility in the school, developing a good relationship with a teacher, or social success among classmates (Rutter, 1984, p. 131).

## Risk and Resilience in Britain

The process of migration is very dynamic and there is a strong migratory culture in the Caribbean. There are now four generations in the African-Caribbean community in the UK, which has implications for the structure of families, and gives rise to other issues such as the return migration to the Caribbean or elsewhere.

> Between 1948 and 1973 approximately 555,000 persons of Caribbean birth migrated to Britain, the majority before the 1962 Immigration Act effectively cut off further migration...Although the Caribbean community in Britain represents less than one percent of the population of Britain, migrants as a percentage of the population of the _home counties_ are large...there has been a significant reduction in the size of the Caribbean communities in the last decade, some of it as a result of death, but mostly due to re and return migration. At the same time, the migrants who arrived in Britain during the 1950s and 1960s are now comfortably in middle-age. Many of their children were born and brought up in Britain. Many are now grandparents. There has been a qualitative change in the structure of the Caribbean community in Britain. At one level it is a stable community with established lineages and network: at another it clearly retains elements of transnational mobility (Chamberlain, 1997, p. 2).

Paradoxically, people have experienced both loss and gain in the process of migration. There is the ambivalence which is described below as the concept of 'Double Jeopardy' (Hickling, 1991), where people have problems in the UK and then encounter problems when they return home after an extended period to find that adjustment is difficult because of changes that have taken place.

> Despite the horrors of their exile in Britain, it would be a mistake to believe that the first generation of Afro-Caribbeans regards their experience of living in Britain as an unmitigated disaster. They experience racism and they occupy in their vast proportion the lowest rung of the social hierarchy of Britain. Nevertheless, in material terms, the overwhelming majority enjoys a standard of living in Britain, which many would not have dreamt of back in the Caribbean (James, 1992, p. 244).

The above case highlights that there are both negative and positive factors in the migration experience. The experiences of significant numbers of the African-Caribbean population in the UK indicate that there are environmental factors which have had a negative impact on the health and well-being of Caribbean people in Britain. (Kareem and Littlewood, 1992) The following statistics show an over-representation of Black people in some of the major institutions such as prison, mental hospitals and under-representation in terms of scholastic and economic achievement.

The African-Caribbean community has to deal with the high rates of incarceration and the problems in the criminal justice system, an example of which is described below:

> In the Criminal Justice System black people are over-represented in the UK prison population where 17% of male prisoners in England and Wales were from ethnic minority groups constituting 6% of the general population. The rates of imprisonment for blacks were 8 times higher than in whites. 51% of blacks over the age of 21 were serving longer sentences of over four years than whites 35%. (Home Office White Paper Cm 3190, 1996).

In terms of the mental health system, the following shocking statistics describe a community which is misunderstood, misdiagnosed and stigmatized:

> In the Mental Health Services, Black/Ethnic Minorities (compared to the 'white' majority community) are more often diagnosed as schizophrenic, and compulsorily detained under the Mental Health Act. In addition they are transferred to locked wards from open wards, are admitted to hospital as 'offender patients' and held by police under Section 136 of the Mental Health Act.[1] They are not referred for psychotherapy, given high doses of medication and sent to psychiatrists by courts (Home Office White Paper Cm3190, 1996).

> In the Education and Schooling System there were a large number of permanent exclusions of black pupils of compulsory school age. African-Caribbean children were excluded 4 times more commonly than white children.[2] (Home Office White Paper Cm3190, 1996)

There is recognition of the paradox of this migratory experience which is important in understanding the ambivalence felt by many African-Caribbean people about Britain. There have been both costs and benefits to the experience, as has been revealed in the lives of many African-Caribbean people, including those persons whose cases follow. This first case was chosen because it provides not only insights into the impact of the risks, but also the possibilities of resilience fostered by the intervention of a culturally appropriate and safe therapy in an organization. The second case was chosen because it exemplifies a person who was exposed to the same risks, but had access to such protective factors as supportive parents and above-average intelligence nurtured by her parents and mentor. These factors have allowed this person to be resilient.

The impact of racism on the development of the identity of African-Caribbean people has been of genuine concern to psychologists, educators, researchers and social workers for decades. Low self-esteem, self-hatred and a negative racial identity have been the characteristics attributed to Black children and adults. A review of the psychological literature shows that there are different perspectives on the identity development question, which have produced contradictory conclusions. One body of research that dominated the psychological literature from the early 1940s and through the 1950s is the Black self-hatred thesis. This thesis suggests that Black people hate themselves as a result of their experiences of racism and oppression which they have internalized.

Another body of research – developed in the USA – focuses on models of psychological nigrescence; i.e. the process an individual goes through in his or her journey toward a secure and confident Black identity (Robinson 1995). Cross (1978) developed a five-stage model of nigrescence as follows: The Pre-Encounter Stage; The Encounter Stage; The Immersion-Emersion Stage; The Internalization Stage; and The Internalization-Commitment Stage.

> At the Pre-Encounter Stage the person's worldview is White orientated (Eurocentric). He or she will even deny that racism exists. Interestingly, this stage transcends class distinctions. At the Encounter Stage the person now experiences or observes a situation that brings him or her to face racism. This experience is so shattering that it forces the individual to re-interpret his or her world. The Immersion-Emersion stage encompasses the most sensational

aspects of Black identity development ... Within this Phase the person struggles to remove all semblance of the old identity while intensifying 'Blackness'. In the Internalisation Stage which follows the individual has now managed to separate the old identified self and the new self, thus moving towards a positive Black identity. In the final stage, Internationalization-Commitment, the person focuses on things other than themselves and their ethnic or racial group (Maxime, 1986, p. 50). (Robinson, 2000, p. 115) notes that:

A vast amount of research in the United States has shown that Black (African-American) children may suffer from racial group identification difficulties due to the effects of discrimination and racism (*see* for example Clark and Clark, 1940; Powell-Hopson and Hopson, 1988).

Earlier studies of Black adolescents in Britain (Mirza 1992; Modood, Beishon, & Virdee 1994) have found that these young people have positive racial identities. However, there is some clinical evidence that a few Black children and adolescents do suffer from severe problems of identity (Small, 1986; Maxime, 1986).

## Failure in School – Promoting Risk

Most of the mentally ill respondents had negative experiences at school in the UK. These ranged from bullying, low levels of expectation from teachers, and underachievement – all of which laid the foundation for low-level menial work when people sought employment. The following case demonstrates the impact of the failure in school which then promotes risk.

### CASE 3  Identifying Risk and Fostering Resilience

This man was a 41-year-old second generation African-Caribbean. He was born in Northampton where he lived until the age of 16. He attended school in Birmingham but did not enjoy the experience as people picked on him. He was a very lonely child and missed a great deal of his schooling because of epilepsy. In secondary school he had no friends, was bullied and teased. He recalls being treated as an "idiot person". He left school at age 16 without qualifications and worked as a welder/solderer for one year. As an adult, he was admitted and assessed at All Saints Hospital with paranoid psychosis. He was then released and during the two-year period when he lived on his own, he gradually began to neglect himself, to the point where it was deemed unsafe for him to continue independent living. He was admitted to Servol Community Trust where he received staff support and started to attend a study programme. He became socially active and was able to travel independently. This had been a successful confidence-building experience and there has been marked improvement in his internal state. Educational courses were put in place to try to correct his verbal communication skills. His domestic living skills and communication skills, coupled with confidence-building, had been targeted, with a view to his returning to semi-independent living.

The person in this case was exposed to all of the risks of racism, the impact of his epileptic condition and his mental illness. Nevertheless, his experience in Servol, where he took part in the Cultural Therapy Programme, demonstrated his resilience. Not only was he undertaking educational courses, but he was also being prepared for semi-independent living. He was overcoming his adversity.

In the following case, Rutter's assertion proved to be true and this woman was able to succeed at school and go on to undertake professional studies as a solicitor.

## Fostering Resilience: 'Secrets of Success'

### Case 4

This woman, in her late thirties, was a very successful solicitor and Councillor with the Birmingham City Council. She was born in Birmingham to Jamaican parents, who have been supportive of her throughout her life, and she always had high expectations. Although she grew up in a maisonette on a council estate in the midst of poverty and squalor, her parents ensured that she spent much time indoors reading and helping to take care of smaller siblings when they came along.

A good student, she also received encouragement from influential teachers at the local primary school, as well as the secondary school where she excelled, and this prepared her for her studies in law. Her mother's love and support had also been fostered through involvement in the church. Her mother was an evangelist and her love was unconditional. Her upbringing was characterized by commitment to community and service to others. This resulted in her preparing myriad forms for friends and family to deal with the bureaucracy that governs every possible aspect of life. As a representative of her family and community, she developed diplomatic skills, which would help her to navigate the corridors of power at all levels, and are now reflected in her political career.

She was encouraged to enter politics by her mentor who was an African-Caribbean woman, the first Black mayor of Birmingham. She also had White male mentors who had seen her leadership potential and encouraged her development. A family woman, now married for more than a decade, she has three children, and like many modern women, tried to maintain and juggle her roles at home, in her career and in politics. She had the type of personality that combined with her legal training to produce a great negotiator. She had set herself clear personal goals, in addition to being encouraged at home, at school and at church. Throughout her adult life she had been a teacher at Saturday School, and had had the capacity to communicate across the divides of race, ethnicity, gender and class.

Resilience is possible for those who are at greatest risk if there are interventions which make it possible for them to try to do new things and achieve new goals. There is a need for organizations which provide culturally safe and appropriate support for persons overcoming mental illness. With the necessary support, persons can repair broken family relationships, regain their self-confidence and learn new skills.

As demonstrated by the second case, success begets success at school, at home and in the community. In spite of the risks to which this woman was exposed, she was able to be resilient and achieve her personal and professional goals and become a leader in the community.

## Phases of the Research

The preliminary phase of the research on the concept of resilience was undertaken between September 1997 and May 1998, when the author was part of an African-Caribbean team which implemented a Cultural Therapy Programme at Servol, the leading Black mental health care provider. The data was collected through participant observation, interviews and focus groups with a group of 20 African-Caribbean persons with severe and enduring mental illness. Their diagnoses are outlined in Table 1.

The characteristics of the persons who were well are outlined in Table 2.

All those referred to in Tables 1 and 2 were African-Caribbean persons who were well and had overcome the adversities in Britain. The thesis examined the quest for healing in the Black British community and looked at mental healthcare in Birmingham, England. The healing was achieved in the face of the ravages of racism and other factors which resulted in privation, poverty and mental illness. The underlying objective of the research was to identify factors that allowed African-Caribbean people to survive and even thrive in the midst of such adversity.

The study was conducted at Servol Community Trust in Birmingham. Servol's administrative office was also the location of the Clubhouse on Dudley Road, which borders an inner city area. The clients were persons who had a severe and enduring mental illness. They lived at four residential facilities belonging to Servol: Strensham Hill, Aston, Gillot Road and a Crisis House on Gillot Road. Servol was located in NHS geographic locality administered by the North Birmingham NHS Mental Health Trust. Servol's partnership with the North Birmingham NHS Mental Health Trust provided a crisis residential home for persons experiencing the acute phase of a mental illness, which prevented them from being admitted to a mental hospital. Servol also offered long-term residential facilities for patients with a severe and enduring mental illness.

Table 1: Characteristics of the respondents with a severe and enduring mental illness

| Respondents | Characteristics | | | | | | |
|---|---|---|---|---|---|---|---|
| | Marital status/age/ gender | Place of birth | Citizenship | No. of Children | Length of time in mental health system | Diagnosis | Highest level of education |
| Case #1 | Single 34 female | UK | British | 3 | 20 years | Psychosis | Secondary * |
| Case #2 | Single 40 female | UK | British | n/a | 20 years | Epilepsy with psychosis | Secondary |
| Case #3 | Single 43 female | UK | British | n/a | 29 years | Schizophrenia | Secondary |
| Case #4 | Single 34 female | UK | British | n/a | 17 years | Paranoid schizophrenia | Secondary |
| Case #5 | Single 33 female | UK | British | n/a | lifelong | Epilepsy with psychosis and intellectual disability | Special needs* |
| Case #6 | Single 41 male | UK | British | n/a | 8 years | Epilepsy with psychosis | Secondary |
| Case #7 | Married (separated) 42 female | UK | British | 3 | 6 years | Puerperal psychosis | Secondary* |
| Case #8 | Single 49 male | Jamaica | British | n/a | 5 years | Paranoid psychosis | University |
| Case #9 | Single 36 male | UK | British | n/a | 21 years | Schizophrenia | College* |
| Case #10 | Single 59 female | St. Kitts | British | 1 | 31 years | Paranoid schizophrenia | Secondary |

Table 1 (Contd.): _Characteristics of the respondents with a severe and enduring mental illness_

| Respondents | Characteristics | | | | | | |
|---|---|---|---|---|---|---|---|
| | Marital status/age/ gender | Place of birth | Citizenship | No. of Children | Length of time in mental health system | Diagnosis | Highest level of education |
| Case #11 | Single 45 female | UK | British | 1 | 10 years | Schizophrenia | Secondary |
| Case #12 | Single 35 male | UK | British | n/a | 19 years | Schizophrenia | Secondary |
| Case #13 | Single 49 male | Jamaica | British | 4 | 4 years | Schizophrenia | Secondary* |
| Case #14 | Single 43 male | Jamaica | British | 3 | 10 years | Schizophreni | Secondary* |
| Case #15 | Single 62 male | Jamaica | British | n/a | 40 years | Manic psychosis | Secondary* |
| Case #16 | Single 43 male | Jamaica | British | n/a | 10 years | Schizophrenia | Secondary* |
| Case #17 | Single 38 male | UK | British | n/a | 15 years | Schizophrenia | Secondary |
| Case #18 | Single 33 female | UK | British | n/a | 10 years | Manic depres- sive psychosis | Secondary |
| Case #19 | Single 42 female | Jamaica | British | 1 | 24 years | Schizophrenia | Secondary |
| Case #20 | Single 35 male | UK | British | 1 | 18 years | Schizophrenia | College |

Table 2: Characteristics of well persons

| Respondents | Marital status/ age/gender | Place of birth | Citizenship | No. of children | Highest level of education outside UK | Highest level of education within UK | Nature of employment |
|---|---|---|---|---|---|---|---|
| 1 | Single 25 male | UK | British/ Jamaican | n/a | Bachelor's | Master's | Lawyer |
| 2 | Single 30 male | UK | British | n/a | n/a | Bachelor's | Youth worker |
| 3 | Single 30 male | Jamaica | American/ Jamaican | n/a | Master's | Incomplete PhD | Engineer |
| 4 | Single 29 male | Jamaica | British/ Jamaican | n/a | Bachelor's | PhD | University lecturer |
| 5 | Single 32 female | Jamaica | British/ Jamaican | 1 | Secondary | Bachelor's | Community worker |
| 6 | Divorced 34 female | Nigeria | British/ Nigerian | 2 | Bachelor's | Master's | Centre manager |
| 7 | Married 32 female | UK | British/ Ugandan | 2 | Bachelor's | Master's | Lawyer |
| 8 | Single 32 female | Trinidad | British/ Trinidad | n/a | Bachelor's | Postgraduate Diploma | Psychologist |
| 9 | Single 34 female | UK | British | 1 | n/a | College Diploma | Clerical officer |
| 10 | Single 34 female | UK | British | 1 | n/a | College Diploma | Receptionist |

## SERVOL AND HAVERSTOCK HOUSE

The members of the African-Caribbean Group with mental illness in Birmingham were managed clinically by the Assertive Outreach Teams of the North Birmingham Mental Health Trust. As a result of the process of deinstitutionalization, these persons were living in community-based residential facilities.

Servol's administrative and client activity centre was easily accessible for the clients. It was a three-storey Victorian House with three large rooms on the top floor. The largest was a meeting room in which the main activities of the Cultural Therapy Programme were conducted. The Director's office, a general office, toilets and a hairdressing salon were located on the first floor. On the ground floor there was a kitchen, a dining room, a lounge where smoking was permitted, and where there was a small tuck-shop. On the walls were posters of African-Caribbean persons and motifs. There was Reggae music playing and the smell of African-Caribbean food being prepared. It was a home away from home for the African-Caribbean clients, staff and visitors.

## INTERVIEWS

The decision to conduct interviews permitted the collection of data from a wide cross-section of individuals that would also facilitate the development of case studies in both the first phase and second phase of data collection.

## CASE STUDIES

The case-study reporting mode augments the interview method, underscoring the qualitative research methodology employed in this study.

## FOCUS GROUPS

In the UK, at each of the focus groups we sat in a circle and a Focus Group Guide was used. The Guide contained the 12 questions that I had prepared on the definition of health and healing, and health and cultural issues in the African-Caribbean community. This stimulated a discussion within the group as the participants answered the questions. The discussions were tape-recorded and then transcribed by computers. The data were subjected to qualitative content analysis, and the themes and sub-hemes identified and analyzed.

The questions appear in the appendix.

## Conclusions

These focus groups provided insights into the impact of racism in the lives of African and African-Caribbean people in the United Kingdom, as well as the strategies that individuals undertook to maintain their health and well-being. Those persons born outside of the UK – in Africa or the Caribbean – possessed a conceptual and experiential framework which enabled them to believe in themselves and have self-confidence. The experience of growing up as part of majority Black populations allowed them to withstand the pressures of life as members of a Black minority in Britain. They had experienced high expectations at home, at school and subsequently at university. They also had other frames of reference and could, therefore, see beyond Britain and see themselves as people with options. This was in sharp contrast to the persons with a chronic and enduring mental illness who, although expressing the wish to travel "home to the Caribbean" or elsewhere, were "stuck" and felt trapped in Britain.

For the participants in the focus groups, health and healing was encouraged by the linkages outside of Britain where they were born, their identities formed, where they had received their education – in some cases up to university level. For those persons born in Britain the converse seemed true, African-Caribbean identity and achievement had been challenged by institutional racism. Many families were trapped in the zones of social exclusion in Britain.

However, there are success stories of African-Caribbean people who were born or have grown up in Britain. They have had families that have helped them to succeed, had positive experiences in school and have benefited from supportive communities. Many have had positive experiences in the church, experiences which have helped them to cope with the difficulties of life. The focus groups provided an opportunity for Africans and African-Caribbean people to discuss some of the areas of conflict and misunderstanding between themselves. The presence of Black people from Africa and the Caribbean in Britain has enabled both groups to challenge their stereotypes of each other, and to develop higher levels of collaboration as they face the challenges of life in Britain.

# Appendix

**Focus Group Guide**

*Topic: Health And Healing In The Black British Community*

1.  Please comment on the following definition of health given by the World Health Organisation in the Alma Ata Declaration in 1974. "Health is a state of complete physical mental and social well-being and not merely the absence of infirmity."

2.  There are six major diseases which affect the community; can you say anything about these diseases and their causes?
    • Certain sexually transmitted diseases
    • Sickle cell anemia
    • Hypertension and stroke
    • Mental illness
    • Diabetes
    • Thalassaemia

3.  Can you suggest ways of preventing any of these diseases?

4.  Can you suggest ways of coping with these diseases?

5.  Are there cures for dealing with them?

6.  Is there a difference between healing and curing these diseases?

7.  Do these diseases affect Black men and women differently?

8.  What is the impact on the family when a member or members of the family are affected?

9.  Where can/do Black people seek help for illness?

10. What can the help givers do?
    • The individual

- The family
- The general practitioner
- The church
- Other help/care givers e.g. One Hundred Black Men

11. Can you describe an icon which represents "a picture of health?"

12. Can you identify a passage, a poem, a song which has healing powers for you?

## NOTES

1. A section of the UK Mental Health Act that authorizes a police officer to remove a person from a public place.
2. *Department for Education and Employment News*, "Minority Ethnic Pupils in Maintained Schools by Local Education Authority Area In England." Jan. 1997 ( Provisional ), 342/97-30th Oct. , 1997.

## REFERENCES

Chamberlain, M. (1997). *Narratives of exile and return*. London and Basingstoke: The Macmillan Press Ltd.

Coard, B. (1971). *How the West Indian child is made educationally subnormal in the British school system*. London: New Beacon Books.

Cross, W. (1991). *Shades of black. Diversity in African–American identity*. Philadelphia: Temple University Press.

Duncan, C. (1991). Black children and pastoral care. In M. Crooks (Ed.), *Beyond the blackboard. Issues for parents, teachers and governors concerning Black children and education*. Birmingham: Hand Print.

Francis, E. (1992). Psychiatric racism. In W. James & C. Harris (Eds.), *Inside Babylon. The Caribbean diaspora in Britain*. London: Verso.

Hickling, F. W. (1991). "Double Jeopardy" The psychopathology of Black mentally-ill returned migrants to Jamaica. *International Journal of Social Psychiatry*, 37, 44-52.

James, W. (1993). Migration, racism and identity formation. The Caribbean experience in Britain. In W. James & C. Harris (Eds.), *Inside Babylon. The Caribbean diaspora in Britain*. London New York: Verso.

Kareem, J., & Littlewood, R. (1992). *Intercultural therapy. Themes, interpretations and practice*. London: Blackwell.

Maxime, J. (2000). *Strangers no more. Transformation through racial justice. A training resource.* Peterborough: The Methodist Church.

Mirza, Heidi, S. (ed.) (1997). *Black British feminism. A reader.* London and New York: Routledge.

Robertson-Hickling, H. (1997). Secrets of success. Unpublished paper.

———. (2006). "The quest for healing in the Black British community. A reflective study on mental healthcare in Birmingham, England." Ph.D Diss. University of Birmingham.

Robinson, L. (1995). *Psychology for social workers. Black perspectives.* New York: Routledge.

———. (1998). *Race, Communications and the caring professions.* Buckingham: Open University Press.

Rutter, M. (1984). Resilient children. Why some disadvantaged children overcome their environments, and how we can help. *Psychology Today,* March, 57-65.

———. (1985). Resilience in the face of adversity: Protective factors and resistance to disorder. *British Journal of Psychiatry,* 147, 598-611.

———. (1990). Psychosocial resilience and protective mechanisms. In J. Rolf, A. Masten, D. Cicchetti, K. Neuchterlein & S. Weintraub (Eds.), *Risk and protective factors in the development of psychopathology.* New York, Cambridge University Press.

———. (1999) Resilence concepts and findings: Implications for family therapy. *Journal of Family Therapy,* 21, 119-144.

Sherlock P., & Bennett, H. (1998). *The story of the Jamaican people.* Kingston: Ian Randle Publishers.

Small, S. (1994). *Racialised barriers. The Black experience in the United States and England in the 1980s.* London & New York: Routledge.

*Time Magazine* September 12, 2005.

Tugade, M. et. al. (2004). Psychological resilience and positive emotional granularity: Examining the benefits of positive emotions on coping and health. *Journal of Personality,* 72, 6.

# 4 Family Life in the Caribbean
## Assessment and Counselling Models

*Marina Ramkissoon, Sharon-Ann Gopaul-McNicol, Barry Davidson, Brigitte K. Matthies, & Orlean Brown Earle*

## Introduction

There is limited research on Caribbean families from psychological perspectives, given the strong sociological and anthropological traditions of the region (Barrow, 1996). The purpose of the present chapter is to highlight issues of Caribbean family life with an emphasis on psychological assessment and treatment. The Caribbean, and particularly the Jamaican context, is described with respect to the meaning of 'family', parenting, family structures and psychological family types.

## Notions of Family in the Caribbean

A family is typically defined as a social pattern or social arrangement in which there are individuals who are specifically related by blood, marriage, and sometimes adoption (Watson and Davidson, 2006). These individuals are linked together in a special type of social relationship and form a group called a family unit. The family usually shares a domestic unit or a household, and a single residential setting. Heather Ricketts (2000) notes, however, that traditional ideas of family are not fully relevant to the Jamaican context. In fact, family forms in the Caribbean have been better described with reference to the influence of slavery and plantation systems, including the popular matrifocal or single-mother family structure and household (Barrow, 1996). Important family members may not always be present in the household, especially fathers. For example, a mother may live at her place of employment, or a father may still live with his own mother. Family members, therefore, do not necessarily share a common food supply or live together in a single residential setting. Non-relatives may have responsibility for parenting, and even the community can act in the parenting role. Merle Hodge (cited in Ricketts, 2000, p.3) also notes that references to 'family' have various meanings: household members, a sexual union, persons who do not share a household, as well as blood and non-blood relatives. Persons who depend on each other economically have also been labeled 'family' in this context (Hodge; in Ricketts, 2000, p.3).

## Family Structures

There is a rich history of Afro-Caribbean family studies. Anthropological studies from the 1940s described the slave-descended Afro-Caribbean family as dysfunctional compared to North American nuclear family models (Brown, 2002). Later research in the 1970s recognized family patterns as functional adaptations to harsh socioeconomic circumstances (Barrow, 1996; Leo-Rhynie, 1993). An example of this is 'shifting families' which are characterized by physical separation of a child or children from one or more primary caregivers, especially, but not limited to birth parents. Many children are shifted because of the migration of their mothers and fathers. Migration is quite popular as a means of socioeconomic mobility, and has been a characteristic of Jamaican families for many years. Many mothers see it as the only means of providing financially for their children, and readily pass on the everyday childrearing to another caregiver. Children who are shifted three or more times are likely to have more caregivers compared to unshifted children, and are likely to be introduced to new caregivers with each additional shift (Ramkissoon, 2006). When the shift involves physical movement of the child rather than caregiver, there may be problems adjusting to a new family, household composition, community and social environment. Studies have shown that increased family instability has negative effects on child adjustment and wellbeing (Ackerman et al., 1999), and this practice has been noted to have negative psychological effects on the children and many experience resentment and feelings of anger towards parents who migrated (Pottinger, 2005).

A recent research report by Watson and Davidson (2006) described the various family forms found in the Caribbean as follows:

1. the **nuclear family** consisting of mother, father and children, where parents were either married or living in a common-law relationship;

2. the **single parent matrifocal family** in which the mother was the only permanent parent figure in the family, the male being usually absent, and there were a number of variations

   - the mother bringing up her children single-handedly
   - the mother having "visiting" relationships with a partner or partners, but having no permanent father figure in the household, or
   - the mother and her children living in a wider descent group, usually with her mother and/or female relatives.

3. the **extended family** with members of a wider descent group called the 'consanguine' family, or those related by blood; usually those members stayed together for several reasons:

   - family property, usually land, was not easily divisible;
   - the entire family valued the children as a new generation to perpetuate the family name and traditions; or
   - the economic and domestic responsibility for childrearing was shared with a wider group.

   In many instances a woman or the mother was the permanent central figure in the extended family, assisted by other relatives. This was sometimes seen as the grandmother family, if the central female parental figure was the grandmother rather than her daughter(s).

4. the **single parent patrifocal family**, now on the increase – this household has no mother figure present; it is usually father and children, or grandfather and children;

5. the **blended or step-family** – a nuclear family in whose home children from a previous marriage or relationship resided as well;

6. the **sibling family** – one in which an elder sister and/or brother was bringing up their younger siblings without either parent figure.

It is important to note that alternative family structures are on the rise in more developed countries. In the USA, for example, the percentage of married couples with children fell from 50 per cent to 36 per cent of all families between 1970 and 1997 (US Census Bureau, 1998).

## Parenting

A recent report from the Planning Institute of Jamaica (Ricketts and Anderson, 2005) illustrates parenting in the current Jamaican context, through an analysis of data collected in a special parenting module of the Survey of Living Conditions in 2004. Data were collected from 1,098 adult primary caregivers and on approximately 2,500 children. About one quarter of the children on which data were collected were classified as 'foster' children since they were living without biological mothers or fathers at the time. The study sought to provide details on how parents defined their roles, their parenting practices and the challenges faced. Two main causal factors were suggested in determining parental readiness and practice: the parents' or caregivers' socio-economic, cultural and structural characteristics, and the stress levels experienced by parents.

Most of the caregivers identified in the study were female (90%) and more female caregivers were in poverty, and responsible for more children than their male counterparts. Many of these female caregivers, poor caregivers, as well as young caregivers and those from rural areas, reported feeling more stressed and a sense of being trapped in the parenting role. Poverty was also related to higher levels of restricted interaction between parent and child, while parents with higher levels of education and younger parents had more interactive parenting styles. High levels of parental stress were associated with physical punishment for children and shouting or quarrelling in the home.

Other notable aspects of parenting in Jamaica, especially in the lower socioeconomic classes, are authoritarianism (Evans and Davies, 1997), poor communication between parents and between parents and child, domestic violence, absent fathers (Chevannes, 1999), migrant caregivers (Crawford-Brown and Rattray, 2001), HIV/AIDS victims, and shifted or foster children (McDonald-Levy, 1998). One critical group often ignored in the literature on parenting involves children at risk: abused and neglected; child labourers; children in extreme poverty; street children; children with disabilities; shifted children; and institutionalized children (Ramkissoon, 2005a). The specific circumstances that breed children at risk do not fit traditional conceptualizations of family units. For instance, shifted children often identified persons not living in their current homes as their primary caregivers. These children were moved from one household to another, and changed primary caregivers over time (Ramkissoon, 2005a). Finally, Caribbean families, especially Afro-Caribbean families, utilize broad social support systems, comprised mostly of female relatives for parenting and material resources (Ricketts, 2000). However, community members and non-relatives are also called upon at times for parenting support (Ramkissoon, 2006). SUMMARY

In summary, both historically and currently, there is much variation in the family structures and household compositions of Afro-Caribbean people. As such, their notions of family are more fluid than fixed, even if they espouse nuclear family ideals. Given these specific features in the meaning of family, parenting and family structures, psychologists and social workers must be careful to adapt strategies for intervention and assessment which may be based on different assumptions. Whether the therapists' approach assumes that these family patterns are dysfunctional or culturally accepted survival strategies, will have implications for how they assess and treat the attendant problems.

## Need for Family Interventions in the Region

One has only to look at the titles of the chapters in this book to realize that Caribbean people are faced with serious problems in their daily lives. Violence, drug use, HIV/AIDS, the legacy of slavery, the stigma of mental illness, poverty and lack of education all serve to create problems in families that may require professional intervention. Even if we accept that a variation in family forms is the norm for the region, this does not make it any easier for individuals to deal with sudden alterations in the composition of their families, e.g. through migration, violent deaths, a visiting partner moving on, etc. In addition, the authoritarian style of parenting that is so common in the region is associated with difficulties in identity formation, in dealing with authority figures, and the reduced flexibility of the family in dealing with developmental changes (e.g. a teenager getting pregnant), and crises (such as loss of a job and subsequent loss of income).

Elsewhere, family interventions typically take the form of family therapy. Family therapy occurs when more than one individual in a family unit is seen by a therapist for treatment. Among these examples might be a couple with relationship difficulties that may also include sexual problems; a parent and his or her adolescent child who are not getting along, and the child has been running away; siblings grieving the loss of their parents in a motor vehicle accident; or an entire family trying to come to terms with a member newly diagnosed with schizophrenia. While some family therapists believe that all influential family members should be involved in the therapy (e.g. Salvador Minuchin and his Structural Model), others believe that successful family work can be done even if only one family member is involved in treatment. They argue that a change in one member will ultimately effect a change in the others (e.g. Murray Bowen and his Transgenerational Model).

However, in general, family therapists firmly believe that problematic behaviour in children is related to issues within their family and that effective treatment requires more than individual work with the child. For example, the child who refuses to go to school could be seen as 'shy' or 'anxious' and be treated as such with play therapy, or medication – but things may not be as simple as that. Perhaps there is spousal abuse in the home and the child feels scared to leave his or her mother alone. Perhaps the mother is depressed and lonely and is comforted by the child's presence and is actually subtly encouraging the child's desire to stay home. Perhaps the child's father is a jealous individual and likes having someone in the home who can report to him on what happens when he is not there, so he too benefits from the child's 'abnormal' behaviour. Clearly, if any or all of these possibilities are true, successful alteration of the child's behaviour will require involvement of the parents in the treatment as well. In fact, it could be argued that a successful intervention with the couple alone could result in a cessation of the behaviour in the 'identified patient', that is, the child.

Family therapists are also particularly interested in developmental stages, as well as gender differences and their influence on family functioning. They recognize that different family members can have conflicting goals related to different developmental stages of life and/or the simple passage of time. An example might include a child trying to assert his or her independence versus the mother trying to keep her 'baby' at home in an effort to cling to her role as mother. Therapists also recognize that gender-based family rules can result in problems within families (e.g. female children can be resentful of the way they are expected to behave in comparison to their male siblings).

While there are few family therapists in the Caribbean, there is no doubt that this specialized form of psychotherapy is needed in the region. In addition, psychologists, social workers, nurses and counsellors are some of the individuals who could benefit from specialized training in family therapy.

## Difficulties Presented in Family Therapy in the Caribbean

*[handwritten annotation: SPIRITUAL RESTLESSNESS]*

Rather than making reference to psychological theorizing about mental illness, people tend to make sense of their world, based on their shared belief systems, – religious as well as cultural. Mental illness is, therefore, more likely to be attributed to some form of spiritual restlessness meted out to the individual via a vengeful spirit, than attributed to dysfunctional cognitive processing (Gopaul-McNicol, 1993). Many people from various Caribbean countries believe in some form of witchcraft that can be 'worked' on someone by an enemy to cause various forms of harm, usually out of envy or revenge. Folk belief says that when a person is 'possessed', a spirit enters the individual's body, so that the behaviour of the person becomes the behaviour of the spirit. It is felt that the more suggestible a person is, the more likely he or she is to become 'possessed'. These folk beliefs are deeply embedded in the culture and can exert a profound influence on people's lives (Reid, Gopaul-McNicol, Gordon, and Beason, 2005). Many children in the school system wear a guard, receive spiritual baths (herbal bath with holy water), and have a priest or minister bless their homes, or even throw salt around the house to protect themselves from these evil forces. These beliefs are accepted by many sectors of society, transcending race, class, age and gender.

It is quite common for people to seek the services of an "obeah man or woman"[1] while simultaneously seeking psychological help, or subsequent to the failure of a spiritual healer to provide a 'cure'. For example, a woman had sought therapy because her sons suddenly began to misbehave "as soon as my mother-in-law had moved into the house." Since her mother-in-law had never accepted her, she attributed the children's misbehaviour to her mother-in-law's "evil eye." She talked openly about her suspicions, assuming that the therapist not only understood, but would be able to help her to exorcise the children. When the role of a psychologist was explained to her, she was very disappointed that this practitioner would not even be able to accompany her to the obeah man or woman. She felt that the problem with her sons was not a psychological one, but a spiritual one. Given the intensity of her belief, and in keeping with the bio-cultural model, it was recommended that she seek the counsel of an obeah man/woman to remove the 'bad spirits', but to resume therapy if the negative behaviours of her sons continued. She was receptive to this idea and more trusting of the psychological treatment process after she had taken the children to the spiritual healer. Her use of psychological services, however, should not be interpreted as an abandonment of her faith in the spiritual healers.

Thus a diagnostician/therapist, who hears a parent say "my child is not conforming because an evil spirit is on him" and then sees the child wearing a chain with a big cross (guard), should neither be alarmed nor think that the family is 'weird'. Similarly, when a woman attributes her husband's infidelity or lack of familial interest to the belief that "someone gave him something to eat that has him 'tottlebey' [term commonly used in Trinidadian vernacular for 'stupid']," she is not imagining something, but is expressing a cultural assessment of her husband's behaviour. The individual who says, "I see the evil spirit in my house" or "the evil spirit talked to me," is not necessarily hallucinating; nor is the individual who says, "God came to me and told me to give up my job, so I did", necessarily delusional. If mental health professionals are not aware of the Caribbean folk systems, they may misdiagnose a patient or devalue or demean folk culturo-logical behaviours.

A major point for therapists in assessing psychiatric problems in Caribbean families is, therefore, to determine the difference between 'being possessed' and true mental illness. In First World countries, Afro-Caribbean migrants are disproportionately represented in the schizophrenic patient population and are more likely to receive medical drugs rather than counselling (Mclean, Campbell and Cornish, 2003). The cultural exclusion felt by these migrants reduces their service-seeking behaviour, and it is possible that even Caribbean-born therapists, especially those trained abroad, may harbour stereotypical perceptions which can affect their diagnosis and treatment of Caribbean patients.

As a result of these issues, getting the family of the 'identified patient' to recognize and accept the role they play in the creation and maintenance of the problem, and getting them to agree to be a part of the treatment can be a challenge. The idea of having everyone come to see the 'doctor', perhaps on a weekly basis for several months, just to talk, is not one that is easily accepted by Caribbean people. Also, issues related to lack of available services, transportation costs and difficulties, long waiting lists and the ability of family members to make themselves available for the therapy, all contribute to the difficulties presented in conducting family therapy in the region.

## Issues Concerning Utilizing Family Therapy Theory in the Caribbean

The General Systems Theory, originally suggested by biologist Ludwig von Bertalanffy in the late 1920s (_see_ von Bertalanffy, 1968), greatly influenced the understanding of family functioning (Gladding, 2006) and the subsequent development of family therapy theory. Today, the General Systems Theory represents a comprehensive effort to create a theoretical model that is relatable to all living systems, and which focuses on the complex interactions of the elements of the system as a major tool in maintaining it, rather than looking at the elements in isolation. By accepting that the family is a living system, and applying the model, psychologists developed a whole new way of conceptualizing psychological problems and of helping people. Aspects of the General Systems Theory that are relevant to the family are the concepts of **organization** and **wholeness** in a system. According to the model, the elements of a system are organized around each other in a predictable fashion. Moreover, the elements once combined, produce a whole that is different from the sum of its parts. All families need organization, and each member needs to know his or her place within the organization. A family without this clarity and organization will not operate effectively and disruptions to family functioning will occur. Families should also be understood as units of interacting members rather than a group of individuals with their own individual problems. The idea is that you will never fully understand how a family functions by studying each member individually.

The concept of **homeostasis** or balance is also relevant – that idea that a system is self-regulating and that, if disrupted, will tend to maintain a balance or equilibrium. It is known that family members have a certain way of interacting with each other and they attempt to return to this way of functioning even when it may not ultimately be in their best interest. For example, the wife of an alcoholic covers for him with his boss when he misses work, helps him through his hangovers and makes sure there is enough beer in the fridge when he comes home, despite the fact that he is abusive towards her when drunk. The functioning of her family may not be ideal, but there is a certain harmony that can be kept if she behaves in that way. The one time her husband tried to stop drinking she was frightened and did not know what to do to keep him happy. She hated the sudden increase in his demands for sex, and their children didn't like the fact that he was at home much more than before, and getting involved in her disciplining of them. In turn, the father found Alcoholics Anonymous "boring and a waste of time", missed his "drinking buddies" and found it hard to deal with his raw emotions at work. They were all relieved when he started drinking again and things went back to 'normal'. Family therapists help families reach homeostasis at a new and more functional level.

All systems have rules and the family is no exception. Some family rules are fairly universal such as "children should obey their parents" and others may be quite specific to that family: "We do not talk about Uncle Mike." Family therapists help families examine and change inflexible or outdated rules that are contributing to family problems. For example, a bedtime rule of 7.00 pm or a rule of no unsupervised visits with friends for a 16-year-old can create rebellious behaviour.

The concept of **feedback loops** is also related to the idea of homeostasis. All systems need to have a regulatory mechanism by which they manage to maintain a steady state, and monitor their efforts to achieve goals. Feedback loops are circular mechanisms that provide information about a system's output back into its input, in order to govern the system (e.g. a thermostat in an air conditioning unit). In the example of the teenager given above, the rebellious behaviour 'output' would be recognized by the system ('input') as a disruption to homeostasis, and if the system is flexible enough, it would be dealt with by changes to the rules (e.g. a later bedtime, or a relaxation of the 'no time with friends without supervision' rule). A period of feedback on the effect of the new rules will follow, and continued adjustments will be made until the system is in balance once more. An unhealthy system might respond to the rebellious behaviour with increased rules (e.g. no use of the phone after 5.00 p.m.) and this attempt to control the situation is likely to backfire with a new output (e.g. lying and sneaking out).

Other aspects of the General Systems Theory that are relevant to the family include **subsystems** (those parts of the system assigned to a particular function), **boundaries** (an invisible line that separates an individual, a subsystem or a system from its surroundings) and the notion of **open or closed systems** (a measure of how easily information flows in and out of a system that is related to adaptation). A typical family subsystem is one responsible for the discipline of the children (called the parental subsystem by proponents of the Structural Model of family therapy). In a healthy family the members of this 'parental' subsystem and their expectations (i.e. rules related to how children should behave and the consequences for misbehaviour) are clear to all members of the family, and followed. Depending on the structure and organization of the family, the members of the 'parental' subsystem could include both parents, one parent, other caregivers including grandparents and aunts, neighbours and even elder siblings. If the parental subsystem does not have flexible boundaries but operates as an open system, then the children will not know what is expected of them, and may ultimately have difficulty dealing with authority figures such as teachers and bosses. Unhealthy parental subsystems include caregivers that are too harsh, or who are uninvolved or ineffectual, and members who are not on the same page in terms of discipline (e.g. one too strict, one too lenient) or who undermine each other out of anger or ignorance.

Almost all family therapy theorists today would agree that their understanding of the families they work with is influenced by systems theory, though the particular aspects of the model they follow may differ. Since family therapy was first practised in the 1950s, many schools of family therapy have developed and their theories remain highly influential. Readers who are particularly interested in family therapy theory and practice are encouraged to take a look at a comprehensive textbook of family therapy (e.g. Goldenberg and Goldenberg, 2007) since a description of all the models cannot be set out here. Many of these models are likely relevant to the practice of family therapy in the Caribbean, as the Caribbean family is also a system – its component parts may be somewhat different from those elsewhere, but its members do interact, influence each other, and there are rules governing the system, and consequences for system disruption. As such, theories that have been developed elsewhere to understand family functioning and guide treatment could be of real benefit here. Naturally, when attempting to make generalizations about human behaviour, societal and cultural differences should be considered. Theories of family functioning, and therapeutic intervention developed for North American or European White populations may assume different ideals or norms from those which would be applicable to working with Caribbean people. Although there is room for universal 'truths', these variations must at least be acknowledged by therapists during assessment and treatment of families of varying ethnicities and social contexts.

## The Circumplex Model of Marital and Family Systems

Olson et al. (1983) developed the highly influential Circumplex Model of Marital and Family Systems based on General Systems Theory. The Circumplex model proposes that the degree of family functioning is dependent on family cohesion and family adaptability. Here, cohesion refers to emotional bonding and formation of coalitions and adaptability refers to the degree of change within the family in terms of roles, rules and power structures in times of stress. Research and assessment using the Olson model frequently suggest that dysfunctional families can be either too high or too low on both dimensions, i.e., a curvilinear relationship (Gladding, 1996). Extremely low cohesion represents a disengaged family, which may either be chaotically disengaged (very high adaptability) or rigidly disengaged (very low adaptability). Similarly, extremely high cohesion may represent a chaotically enmeshed family or a rigidly enmeshed family. Olson's original model classified families into balanced, mid-range and extreme, in terms of functioning. Balanced families, on the other hand, are moderate on both cohesion and adaptability.

The predictive ability of the Olson Circumplex model has been debated (White, 1996) with some suggestion that it cannot sufficiently differentiate between functional and dysfunctional families. Reasons for this include inconsistencies in research methodology involving the use of clinical and non-clinical samples. Both a curvilinear and a linear relationship have been found between the circumplex dimensions and family functioning (Green, Harris, Forte and Robinson, 1991). The Olson model has been modified by others such as White (1996) who suggested family communication as an additional dimension.

Despite the critique, it is logical to propose that, given the variability of family forms in Jamaica, the dimensions of cohesion and adaptability would be useful for classification and assessment of family units. Structurally, families with members spanning several households, as in the case of 'absent' fathers, migrant mothers and shifted children for example, may experience higher levels of chaos and disengagement. Emotional bonding among these family members may also be expectedly low. Watson and Davidson (2006) identified four major family types in the Jamaican context, based on their family counseling experiences:

1. The **traditional family**, controlled by one or two parents, where the parent in control makes the decisions, resolves disagreements, makes the rules, and enforces them. Family members are driven to succeed with this parent's blessing.

2. The **enmeshed family** seems to be closely knit, but is one in which each member is controlled by the rest of the group members. Decisions are rarely reached and disagreements are rarely resolved. Discipline is difficult and sometimes unfair, because rules are unclear, and affection is emotionally seductive and personally damaging. Family members are driven by fear. Incestuous relationships exist, but family secrets are maintained. It is a family that consists of codependent individuals.

3. The **individualistic family** is one in which each member controls him or herself and decisions are clearly self-serving. In this type, disagreements can be deadly as this family resolves conflict by 'might makes right'. Discipline is harsh and is administered by the strongest over the weaker members. Affection is shallow and manipulative, and family members are driven by the desire to dominate. It is convenience that keeps these family members together. The arrangement offers room and board until something better comes along.

4. The **healthy family** is a family where there is unconditional love, forgiveness, empowerment of members and intimacy. It is a satisfying family in which control lies in the hands of the parents until children come of age. In this family, decisions are made using inputs from both parents and children. Disagreements are resolved by negotiation, and discipline is fair because rules are clear and enforced consistently. Affection is genuine and freely expressed. The motivation behind this family is the satisfaction of mutual respect.

Caribbean therapists must consider, however, that culturally, some of the variability in family forms and functioning are accepted as normal. For instance, having a non-resident father does not automatically translate into bad parenting, despite stereotyping (Ramkissoon, 2005b). Similarly, shifting a child to a non-biological caregiver, while the father seeks gainful employment locally and the mother migrates for the same reason has been shown to have positive socio-economic benefits (McDonald-Levy, 1998). Culturally, therefore, unless symptoms of maladaptive behaviour are demonstrated, especially in children in these circumstances, families will not seek 'help' or the see the need for improvement. The therapist should be sensitive to such patterns, where only extreme cases might be identified as problematic. Additionally, different problems may arise out of this cultural variability, with subsequent implications for intervention. Hence, while the Circumplex Model is useful, it is modelled on the nuclear family form as an ideal-type. Whereas low levels of cohesion may reflect dysfunctionality for a typical Western nuclear family, for a child who has been shifted, emotional bonding may be sourced more from the other primary caregivers and host family, rather than the child's biological family. Moreover, adaptability may be high in this case, but the 'chaos' may be viewed as normal and, therefore, not cause harm to the child nor to his or her parents.

## Issues for Assessment of Caribbean Families

Evidence of this cultural variability and the implications for assessment are seen in the work of Lambert, Samms-Vaughan and Schmitt (2005). Validation of psychological measures designed in the USA for Caribbean populations is becoming increasingly popular (_see_ Ramkissoon, 2004; Lambert, Samms-Vaughan, & Schmitt, 2005 for examples). The Family Cohesion and Adaptability Scale (FACES: version 2) is a popular assessment of family functioning, based on the Circumplex Model and normed on White middle-class Midwestern adults (Bagarozzi, 1985; Olson, Sprenkle, & Russell, 1979). Studies in the USA on the validity of the FACES usually reveal two factors: family cohesion and family adaptability. Lambert, Samms-Vaughan and Schmitt (2005) reported that the two-factor structure found for US samples was not replicated in a sample of 1,737 Jamaicans. Confirmatory factor analysis showed a poor data to model fit; and exploratory factor analysis showed two factors: cohesion and distance. The Jamaican model included adaptability items in the cohesion subscale. In other words, cohesion carried a somewhat different meaning in the Jamaican sample and included ideas about sharing chores, participation in decision making and fair use of discipline. The distance factor included items like 'members feel closer to people outside than inside the family', 'difficulty of thinking of things to do as a family', 'members do their own thing' and 'members do things in twos rather than as total family'. Results of the study by Lambert et al. (2005) suggest that the FACES tool may be detecting shifting patterns or the transient status of some family members. The distance factor may represent considerable movement of persons in and out of the home, and a high degree of boundary ambiguity.

In general, assessment is a process intended to elicit a sample of behaviour from a set of tasks within a given domain, in order to make judgements about an individual's probable behaviour relative to that domain. As such, Armour-Thomas and Gopaul-McNicol (1997; 1998) and Gopaul-McNicol and Armour-Thomas (2002) proposed a bio-cultural approach to assessment of Caribbean families. The authors argued that the human mind functions and develops within cultural niches, thereby making inevitable the co-mingling of biological and cultural processes. Although the range of cognitive potentials may be constrained by biological programming, these potentials are culturally channelled along different developmental pathways toward different end states. A fundamental assumption of the bio-cultural perspective is that characteristics of the person (e.g. language, personality, cognition potentials) are reciprocally interactive with specific characteristics within the individual's culture. The authors contend that, as human beings, we are born with capacities to acquire language, to think and feel in complex ways. However, selected attributes within a given culture determine when, how and under what conditions, these potentials develop and are manifested in behaviour. Similarly, the nature and quality of social interactions and other kinds of cultural stimulation determine how well our biologically-derived capacities adapt to the ecologies in which we live and grow. The influence is, therefore, reciprocal or synergistic in that the interplay within and between biological and cultural characteristics results in changes that become the basis for greater and progressively more complex changes in both domains.

A bio-cultural approach to assessment allows for consideration of the specifics of family life in the Jamaican context. Cultural practices and beliefs related to absentee fatherhood, child shifting, corporal punishment, beliefs about the rights of the child and female household headship must be considered when assessing Jamaican families. Gender roles for parenting, gender socialization of boys and girls, together with stereotypes about male-female relationships and interactions also impact on family life. Cultural beliefs about children include 'not sparing the rod and spoiling the child' and 'children must be seen and not heard' (Smith and Mosby, 2003). Women, especially in the lower classes in Jamaica, are stereotyped as untrustworthy, scheming and materialistic, while men are characterized as 'macho', 'gyalists' (multiple partnering), and 'marginal fathers' (Chevannes, 1999).

## Culture, Family and Treatment

Gopaul-McNicol (1993; 1997) has emphasized that treatment with Caribbean families can best be understood via a comprehensive model –

the Multicultural/Multimodal/Multisystems (MULTI-CMS) approach. The theoretical bases for the MULTI-CMS model originated from 15 years of research in working with Caribbean families in the region, the UK, Canada and the USA. Gopaul-McNicol stated that effective therapy with Caribbean families requires from the therapist a flexibility that allows him or her to draw from different systems theories and incorporate them into an overall treatment plan. It requires the therapist to intervene at various levels – individual, family, extended family, church, community, and social services. This approach has been found to be most effective with Caribbean families because it provides a flexible set of guidelines for intervention. This approach also recognizes that within the community, the idea that 'it takes a whole community to raise a child' is fully endorsed by most people. Thus, empowering them to use all of the support systems available to them is crucial to the treatment process. The use of these systems can be implemented at any stage in therapy, but the families must be aware of all potential systems before therapy is terminated, so that they can readily tap into them if the need arises. Encouraging the individual to embrace the support of their extended family and non-blood kin, and of churches, in areas such as child care and education, may help in preventing personal difficulties. In other words, this model seeks to change and empower individuals and a society through interactions with various key systems over an extended period of time. A case study using this model can be found in Gopaul-McNicol (1993).

Unlike many treatment approaches which are based on linear models, the MULTI-CMS model is based on the concept of circularity and is composed of four phases (Gopaul-McNicol, 1993, 1997; Gopaul-McNicol and Brice Baker, 1997, 1998; Gopaul-McNicol and Thomas-Presswood, 1998). Each component of each phase can recur repeatedly at various levels throughout treatment. The therapist must, therefore, be willing and flexible to intervene at whichever phase and whatever level in therapy. With this understanding, the flow of treatment for the Multicultural/Multimodal/Multisystems approach is outlined below. Details of these phases are described elsewhere (Gopaul-McNicol, 1993).

_Phase I. Assessment Process_
    Step 1. Initial assessment
        a. Explaining the process
        b. Establishing trust

Step 2. Gathering information

Step 3. Outlining the goals

*Phase II. Educational Treatment Process*

*Phase III. Psychological Treatment Process*

*Phase IV. Empowerment Treatment Process*

In general, using the MULTI-CMS approach to treatment with Caribbean families, a therapist can explore a broad spectrum of techniques to address the needs of this population. Once we understand the various types of family units that exist in the Caribbean and promote best practices with regard to the types of assessment that we utilize, the authors are confident that, notwithstanding the variety of situations, the region will witness better utilization of psychological services.

## NOTE

1.   The term 'spiritist' is also common in the Caribbean region.

## REFERENCES

Ackerman, B., Kogos, J., Youngstrom, E., Schoff, K., & Izard, C. (1999). Family instability and problem behaviors of children from economically disadvantaged families. *Developmental Psychology*, 35 (1), 258-268.

Armour-Thomas, E., & Gopaul-McNicol, S. (1997). Bio-ecological approach to cognitive assessment. *Cultural Diversity and Mental Health*, 3 (2), 131-144.

———. (1998). *Assessing intelligence: Applying a Bio-Cultural Model.* Thousand Oaks, California: Sage Publications.

Bagarozzi, D. A. (1985). Family measurement techniques: The family coping strategies scale. *American Journal of Family Therapy*, 13 (2), 67-71.

Baptiste, D. A., Hardy, K. V., & Lewis, L. (1997). Clinical practice with Caribbean immigrant families in the United States: the intersection of emigration, immigration, culture and race. In J. L. Roopnarine and J. Brown (Eds.), *Caribbean Families: Diversity among ethnic groups. Vol. 14. Advances in Applied Developmental Psychology.* London, England: Apex Publishing Company, pp. 275-303.

Barrow, C. (1996). *Family in the Caribbean: Themes and perspectives.* Kingston, Jamaica: Ian Randle Publishers.

Brown, J. (2002). Gender and family in the Caribbean. *Sexual Health Exchange*, 4,

Royal Tropical Institute. Available: http://www.kit.nl/exchange/html/2002-4_gender_and_family_in_th.asp

Chevannes, B. (1999). _What we sow and what we reap: Problems in the cultivation of male identity in Jamaica._ Grace Kennedy Foundation Lecture. Kingston, Jamaica: Grace Kennedy Foundation.

Crawford-Brown, C. P. J., & Rattray, J. M. (2001). Parent-child relationships in Caribbean families. In N. Boyd Webb (Ed.), _Culturally diverse parent-child and family relationships: A guide for social workers and other practitioners._ New York, NY: Columbia University Press, pp. 107-130.

Evans, H., & Davies, R. (1997). Overview of issues in childhood socialization in the Caribbean. In J. L. Roopnarine and J. Brown (Eds.), _Caribbean families: Diversity among ethnic groups. Vol. 14. Advances in Applied Developmental Psychology._ London, England: Apex Publishing Company, pp. 1-24.

Gladding, S. T. (2006). _Counseling: A comprehensive profession._ Upper Saddle River, NJ: Prentice Hall.

Goldenberg, H., & Goldenberg, I. (2007). _Family therapy: An overview._ Pacific Grove, CA: Brooks Cole.

Gopaul-McNicol, S. (1993). _Working with West Indian families._ New York, NY: Guilford Press.

———. (1997). _A multicultural/multimodal/multisystems approach to working with culturally different families._ Westport, CT: Praeger Publishers, Greenwood Publishing Group.

Gopaul-McNicol, S., & Armour-Thomas, E. (2002). _Assessment and culture: Psychological tests with minority cultures._ San Diego, CA: Academic Press.

Gopaul-McNicol, S., & Brice-Baker, J. (1997). Caribbean Americans. In S. Friedman (Ed.), _Cultural issues in the treatment of anxiety._ New York, NY: Guilford Press, pp. 81-89.

———. (1998). _Cross-cultural practice: Assessment, treatment and training._ New York, NY: John Wiley and Sons, Inc.

Gopaul-McNicol, S., & Thomas-Presswood, T. (1998). _Working with linguistically and culturally different children: Innovative clinical and educational approaches._ Needham Heights, MA: Allyn and Bacon.

Green, R. G., Harris, R. N., Forte, J. A., & Robinson, M. (1991). Evaluating FACES-III and the Circumplex model: 2440 families. _Family Process,_ 30 (1), 55-73.

Lambert, M., Samms-Vaughan, M., & Schmitt, N. (2005). The family cohesion and adaptability scale II: Is the factor model for Jamaican adults similar to that established for the US Adults? _Caribbean Journal of Psychology,_ 2 (1), 50-70.

Leo-Rhynie, E. (1993). _The Jamaican family: Continuity and change._ Grace Kennedy Foundation Lecture. Kingston, Jamaica: Grace Kennedy Foundation.

McDonald-Levy, B. (1998). Two sides of the same coin: Child fostering and child shifting. M.Sc thesis report, Consortium Graduate School, UWI, Mona.

Mclean, C., Campbell, C., & Cornish, F. (2003). African-Caribbean interactions with mental health services in the UK: Experiences and expectations of exclusion as (re)productive of health inequalities. *Social Science and Medicine*, 56 (3), 657-669.

Olson, D. H., Sprenkle, D. H., & Russell, C. S. (1979). Circumplex model of marital and family systems: I. Cohesion and adaptability dimensions, family types, and clinical applications. *Family Process*, 18 (1), 3-28.

Olson, D. H., McCubbin, H. I., Barnes, H., Lasen, A., Muxen, M., & Wilson, M. (1983). *Families: What makes them work?* Thousand Oaks, CA: Sage Publications.

Pottinger, A. M. (2005). Children's experience of loss by parental migration in inner-city Jamaica. *American Journal of Orthopsychiatry*, 75 (4), 485-496.

Ramkissoon, M. (2004). The validity of the multidimensional scales of perceived self efficacy in Jamaica. *Caribbean Journal of Psychology*, 1 (1), 40-54.

———. (2005a). The impact of the social environment on early childhood development and survival with a focus on gender and on the provisions and facilities for children at risk in the birth-8 age group. Final Report for the Dudley Grant Memorial Trust Resource Centre Upgrading Project. Unpublished report.

———. (2005b). An investigation of the physical and psychological presence of the Jamaican father. Caribbean Childhoods: From Research to Action. *Journal of the Children's Issues Coalition. Vol. 2: Children at Risk*, 17-37.

———. (2006). Descriptions of child shifting in Jamaican children. Unpublished manuscript.

Reid, G., Gopaul-McNicol, S., Gordon, J., & Beason, T. (2005). Cultural factors in diagnosing schizophrenia. In A. Carter-Obayuwana, S. Gopaul-McNicol & D. Louden (Eds.), *Personality assessment and culture*. Lincoln University, Pennsylvania: Lincoln University, Office of Research Development, Planning and Coordination, pp.167-174.

Ricketts, H., (2000). Parenting in Jamaica: A situation assessment and analysis. Prepared for the Coalition of Better Parenting, with support from UNICEF.

Ricketts, H., & Anderson, P. (2005). Parenting in Jamaica. A study conducted on behalf of the Planning Institute of Jamaica. Unpublished report.

Smith, D. E., & Mosby, G. (2003). Jamaican child-rearing practices: The role of corporal punishment. *Adolescence*, 38 (150), 369-381.

US Census Bureau (1998). Household and family characteristics: March 1997, pp. 20-509.

Watson. M., & Davidson, B. (2006). *Healthy families: A Caribbean perspective*. Kingston, Jamaica: Family Life Ministries.

White, F. A. (1996). Family processes as predictors of adolescents' preferences for ascribed sources of moral authority: A proposed model. *Adolescence*, 31 (121), 133-144.

Von Bertalanffy, L. (1968). *General systems theory: Foundations, development, applications*. New York, NY: George Brazillier, Inc.

# 5 The Stigma of Mental Illness in Jamaica

*Carlotta M. Arthur, Frederick W. Hickling, Roger C. Gibson, Hilary Robertson-Hickling, Wendel D. Abel, Tamika Haynes-Robinson, & Rob Whitley*

## Introduction

There is growing interest in the topic of the stigma of mental illness worldwide. A large body of research conducted in Western nations indicates that stigma related to mental illness may be an important factor in seeking mental health treatment, as well as a significant issue in the quality of life for individuals with mental illness and their families (Corrigan, 2004). However, research on the stigma of mental illness in developing nations is quite sparse, and work on this topic in Jamaica and the Caribbean has, until recently, been largely anecdotal.

This chapter will describe two major pieces of work, conducted in the last two years, that examine this issue within the Jamaican context. The first was a large ethnographic qualitative study, designed to explore stigma and the perceptions of mental illness and the mentally ill in Jamaica. Focus groups were conducted in settings throughout the nation with mentally ill participants, their families, caregivers, and community members. This chapter will discuss important themes that were identified from participants' discussions. The second study was a population-based investigation in Jamaica that examined aspects of a quantitative national survey, designed to determine the extent of internalization and entrenchment of stigmatizing attitudes and behaviour in persons who are normally victims of such discrimination, namely, family members of the mentally ill (Gibson et al, in press). This work will then be discussed primarily against the background of the history of psychology in Jamaica and the Caribbean, and the treatment of mental illness in a colonial and postcolonial environment. The development of 'custodialization' and hospital-based treatment and care for the mentally ill will be discussed first. Then, the manner in which community psychology in Jamaica emerged from the postcolonial period will be described. Finally, the process of deinstitutionalization and the development of postcolonial social psychotherapy in dealing with mental illness stigma will be examined.

## Stigma: Definitions and Theories

The concept of stigma first originated from the Greek root meaning a mark or symbol which was used to identify criminals or slaves (Goffman, 1963). As time passed, however, the term was increasingly associated with more external sociological meanings. The result was that the term 'stigma' came to connote deviance or abnormality, which was worthy of disgrace, degradation, fear, and social distance (*see, for example,* Link & Phelan, 2001; 2006). The Western literature suggests that mental illness is broadly considered by many to have these qualities (Corrigan, 2000; 2005). Further, Western media depictions of the mentally ill as unpredictably violent and dangerous, combined with widely held beliefs that mental illness is not 'true' illness as organic disease is, may contribute to the maintenance of mental illness-related stigma in Western societies (Corrigan et al., 2002; Link, Cullen, Frank, et al., 1987; Pompili, Mancinelli, & Tatarelli, 2003).

A number of recent theories have been proposed regarding the cause of stigma. These theories have centred around sociological norms rooted in Western models of economic and political discrimination by a powerful group, versus a less powerful stigmatized sub-group (Link & Phelan, 2001; 2006). Since the publication of Goffman's (1963) pioneering work on stigma, models have been advanced that are useful in understanding how the stigma of mental illness operates in Western societies (*see, for example,* Angermeyer & Matschinger, 2005; Link & Phelan, 2001). One such model was put forward by Link and Phelan (2001; 2006) who proposed that "five interrelated components combine to generate stigma" (2006; p. 528). This multi-component approach is beneficial not only for the understanding of stigma and how it operates, but it also elucidates several levels at which stigma may potentially be addressed.

The first component of the Link and Phelan (2001; 2006) model involves the distinguishing and labelling of differences between groups, typically in an oversimplified manner, e.g., 'mad' vs. 'normal'. The labelled differences are then linked to negative stereotypes, e.g., 'mad' people are 'dangerous.' This negative stereotyping then leads to the third component which involves a cognitive separation of 'us' from 'them.' Indeed, stereotyping may then become the basis for believing and accepting that the negatively stereotyped and labelled groups are so different from others, as to be considered sub-human by some. In the case of the mentally ill, this has significant implications for how others think about and behave toward such persons. Moreover, stigmatized individuals are often discussed as being what they are labelled, e.g., the person is 'a schizophrenic' as opposed to having schizophrenia or being mentally ill (Estroff, Penn, & Toporek, 2004; Link & Phelan, 2001). The fourth component involves not only discrimination against the stigmatized group but also an associated loss of status, which may contribute to discrimination at both the individual and institutional levels. In fact, the perception that a stigmatized person will be devalued and discriminated against by society may be one that is shared and internalized by the stigmatized persons and their families – given that they were socialized in the same society as those doing the stigmatizing. Persons with mental illness and their families may expect fear and rejection, and these expectations may have a significant impact on their attitudes and behaviour (Corrigan et al., 2003). The fifth component is power, including economic, social, and political power. Not only does it take power to impose stigma on others, but the stigmatized group is often stripped or 'robbed' of this critical asset. Although power is seldom directly addressed in discussions of stigma, it is a key component in the social construction of stigma. This is so because power is required to produce recognition of labelled differences within a society, ensure recognition of the negative stereotypes associated with the labelled differences, to ensure and perpetuate separation of the negatively labelled group. Power also controls and limits institutional resources allocated for the use of stigmatized groups. Although the Link and Phelan (2001; 2006) model is a general model of social stigma, it is one of the primary models used in discussions of mental illness-related stigma (*see, for example,* Angermeyer & Matschinger, 2005). A publication by Link, Yang, Phelan, and Collins (2004), expanded the original Link and Phelan (2001) formulation to include emotional reactions from both the standpoint of the society and the stigmatized person.

## NEGATIVE CONSEQUENCES OF MENTAL ILLNESS-RELATED STIGMA

The stigma attached to mental illness can have a profoundly negative effect on multiple facets of the lives of mentally ill person, as well as on the lives of their families and friends (Corrigan & Kleinlein, 2005), and acts to "rob people of rightful life opportunities" (Corrigan, Watson, Warpinski, & Gracia, 2004, p. 17). Areas affected by mental illness stigma include employment, housing, involvement in the criminal and civil justice systems, mental health care access, mental health care provision, and associated policy. Problems and discrimination in employment are issues frequently faced by individuals with mental illness. These persons frequently have difficulty securing and maintaining employment (Corrigan, Larson, Watson, Boyle, & Barr, 2006; Corrigan & Kleinlein, 2005; Stuart, et al., 2006). Housing presents similar problems, as many individuals with mental illness report significant difficulty in acquiring desirable or even adequate housing, following their discharge from in-patient mental health units (Corrigan et al., 2006; Corrigan & Kleinlein, 2005; Forchuk, Nelson, & Hall, 2006). The fact that the stigma of mental illness may extend into the Court and criminal justice systems has been documented in Western nations, with mentally ill offenders having increased difficulty navigating these systems. There is additional stigma attached if such persons are in receipt of a 'forensic' label (Arboleda-Florez, 2003; Brett, 2003). One of the most problematic areas in which stigma may have an impact is in the availability and provision of mental heath care services, with policy often dictating a grossly uneven distribution of resources to mental health care versus other types of medical care (Beinecke, 2005; Bowis, 2005; Corrigan & Kleinlein, 2005).

From the point of view of the individual with mental illness, stigmatization may also be an impediment to receipt of care and compliance with treatment regimens (Phillips, Pearson, Li, Xu, & Yang, 2002). Stigmatization can contribute to decreased self-esteem, reluctance to access mental health treatment services, and reduced social prospects. Indeed, internalization of mental illness by affected individuals is an exceptionally harmful consequence of mental illness-related stigma. The stigmatized individual learns to restrict his or her activities to comply with the social control and isolation demanded by society. Moreover, it has been reported that persons frequently behave in a prejudicial manner even towards their own mentally ill relatives (Lee, Lee, Chiu, & Kleinman, 2005). Finally, stigma may have a negative effect on the course and prognosis of mental disorders (Corrigan & Kleinlein, 2005; Link, Struening, Neese-Todd, Asmussen, & Phelan, 2001).

Recognizing the potentially devastating effects of mental illness stigma, health-related organizations around the globe have launched anti-stigma campaigns (Sartorious, 1997; USDHHS, 2003). In fact, in 2006, Jamaica's Ministry of Health commissioned a population-based survey to examine the knowledge, attitudes and practices of the Jamaican public on issues related to mental health and illness. The goal was to obtain information useful for the development of a comprehensive and culturally appropriate mental health promotion programme that would improve public knowledge and awareness, and ultimately improve the quality of mental health care in Jamaica.

## Mental Illness Stigma Research Internationally

Most of the international research on stigma has been conducted in Western nations. In fact, a review by Link et al. (2004) assessed 123 empirical studies on mental illness stigma. The vast majority of these were conducted in North American and Europe. Several were also conducted in Asia, including the developing nation of India. However, research on mental illness stigma in other developing countries was strikingly absent from the literature reviewed. The ideas explored in Western stigma research are typically of Eurocentric semiotic construction utilized by developed countries to formulate an ideology of stigma towards mental illness. It should not be assumed that results of research conducted in developed countries would generalize in every respect to developing countries.

In addition to research conducted in India (*see, for example,* Sudhir et al., 2004), a few other studies on the stigma of mental illness have been conducted in developing countries around the world (*see, for example,* Shibre et al., 2001; Wig et al., 1989). Such research in the Caribbean is severely limited. De Toledo Piza Peluso and Blay (2004) conducted a review of research in Latin America and the Caribbean and discovered that, in general, attitudes towards the mentally ill were predominantly positive, especially among individuals with a higher educational or socioeconomic level. However, the review included only one study conducted in the Caribbean, in the Commonwealth of Dominica (*see* Kohn, Sharma, Camilleri, & Levav, 2000). A few other studies on mental illness and associated stigma have been conducted in Cuba (*see, for example,* Collinson & Turner, 2002), but these were not large-scale studies designed primarily to examine stigma and elucidate attitudes about mental illness. Clearly, there is a substantial gap in the literature on mental illness stigma in developing countries in general, and in the Caribbean in particular.

## Research on Mental Illness Stigma in Jamaica

Recently, two empirical research studies were conducted in Jamaica that examined perceptions of mental illness and the mentally ill, together with mental illness-related stigma. The goals of this research included improving the understanding of issues related to mental illness and the associated stigma in Jamaica, not only among individuals with mental illness, but also among their families and communities. Another of the research objectives was to begin to fill the gap in the literature on stigma and attitudes towards mental illness and the mentally ill in Jamaica.

### FOCUS GROUP STUDY: PERCEPTIONS OF MENTAL ILLNESS AND THE MENTALLY ILL

The first study was a nation-wide focus group study designed to clarify the perceptions of individuals from a range of backgrounds in Jamaica, in relation to mental illness and the mentally ill. The study also sought to examine whether, in the wake of widespread media campaigns in the 70s to educate Jamaicans about these issues, contemporary Jamaicans would exhibit stigmatizing attitudes and perceptions towards the mentally ill and mental illness.

The aim of this study was to use ethnographic qualitative research methodology to elucidate perceptions of mental illness and the mentally ill among contemporary Jamaicans: patients, families, caregivers of patients, and community members with no previous mental health system involvement. Another of its aims was to elicit information that could be useful in the development of culturally appropriate recommendations, grounded in empirical research and the lived experiences of Jamaicans, to guide public health policy and to improve the provision and utilization of mental health care services in Jamaican communities.

**Methods**

Participants were recruited face-to-face by trained personnel dispatched to numerous sites throughout Jamaica, including Ward 21 of the University Hospital of the West Indies, mental health clinics, and community sites throughout Jamaica. Participants were drawn from persons with mental illness, their family members or caregivers, and community residents with no previous association with the mental health care system in Jamaica, either directly or through a relative. Participants were stratified into groups by gender, age, social class, and where they lived (urban or rural).

Twenty focus group sessions of seven to eight participants each were conducted at sites throughout Jamaica. To promote consistency, moderators participated in a training session on the use of a moderator guide. Focus group sessions were transcribed on-site by trained court-reporters and audio-taped as a back-up. The moderator posed a series of questions to participants including: "What does the word 'stigma' mean?" "Who does stigma apply to?" "Why? And describe these people," "What do you think about people with mental illnesses?" and "What do you think about people who have been to Bellevue or Ward 21" versus a health centre?"

In addition, to gather information regarding participants' perceptions and attitudes using another approach, participants were presented with a vignette:

> A 24-year-old man suddenly begins to preach, starts to look into the sun, and claims to have powers and an ability to control the sun. He also begins to destroy his relatives' home and chop down all the banana trees in the yard. His relatives manage to control him and take him to St. Ann's Bay

Hospital where he is injected, treated and released one week later. Upon release he goes back home embraces his relatives and offers his apologies for his past behaviour.

The moderator posed two additional questions to participants following the vignette: "What is your attitude toward this man?" and "What would be your attitude if he was sent to Kingston and treated at Bellevue?"

Focus group participants who were over the age of 40, who may have been exposed first hand to media campaigns in the 70s to educate Jamaicans about mental illness and the mentally ill, were asked additional questions such as: "Do you remember a radio psychiatry programme in the 1970s?" "If so, do you think it affected your perception of mental illness? How?" and "How did it affect your perception?"

The study team reviewed the transcripts and developed primary codes. Transcripts were then segmented into thematic units and *Atlas.ti* was then used to classify, cross classify, and organize the thematic units with reference made to the transcripts and primary codes.

## SURVEY STUDY: INTERNALIZING STIGMA ASSOCIATED WITH MENTAL ILLNESS

The second study (Gibson et al., in press) described here, examined particular aspects of a large national survey to study the internalization of mental illness stigma among families of those with mental illness (Ostman & Kjellin, 2002). This study utilized a questionnaire that was in development at the University of the West Indies during the time that the focus group study was being conducted, and drew upon the discussion and ideas examined by the focus groups. It tested the hypothesis that a good marker of the extent to which internalization has occurred is the extent to which persons who normally experience stigma (i.e. mentally ill persons and their family members), themselves exhibit stigmatizing behaviour towards other persons with mental illness. This study attempted to determine whether, in Jamaica, there was any difference in the prevalence of stigmatizing behaviour by family members of mentally ill persons, compared with the prevalence of such behaviour by the general population. The areas which were explored in this study depended on the examination of some of the findings of the national survey commissioned by the Jamaican Ministry of Health.

**National Study**

Using a sampling procedure devised by the Statistical Institute of Jamaica (STATIN), this national survey attempted to collect a nationally representative sample of the Jamaican population. One hundred and thirty-seven of the country's 5,300 enumeration districts were randomly selected and within each of these districts, 12 households were randomly selected (_see_ Gibson et al., in press for further details). The survey instrument was a semi-structured interviewer-administered questionnaire. It consisted of 42 questions which were designed to explore sociodemographic variables and various elements of knowledge, attitudes and practices towards mental health and illness.

Specific areas of interest for this study included the presence or absence of a diagnosis of mental illness in respondents and their family members; respondents' feelings about mentally ill family members, and actions taken by respondents when in the presence of someone perceived to be mentally ill.

## RESULTS OF FOCUS GROUP STUDY: PERCEPTIONS OF MENTAL ILLNESS AND THE MENTALLY ILL

Nine primary themes were identified across participants' discussions. These primary themes, which derived mainly from questions to participants, were as follows: 1) definitions and understanding of the concept of 'stigma,' 2) emotional and behavioural responses toward mental illness and the mentally ill, 3) beliefs about causes of mental illness, 4) coping strategies of caregivers and patient's relatives, 5) the mental institution as a cause of stigma, 6) the mental institution as a change agent, 7) public education and understanding about mental illness and stigma, 8) consequences of being mentally ill for the mentally ill person, and 9) responses to the vignette presented during the focus groups. Several sub-themes were identified within each primary theme.

### Definitions and Understanding of Stigma

A few participants were not familiar with the term 'stigma.' Most participants, however, seemed to have a clear grasp of the concept of stigma, as defined by the Link and Phelan (2001; 2006) model, and of what it meant to 'stigmatize' a person who was mentally ill, even if 'stigma' was not their term of choice. This understanding was generally consistent across gender, age, social class, and area of residence (urban or rural).

### Emotional and Behavioural Responses

Many participants reported negative emotional responses, attitudes, and behaviour toward the mentally ill. Again, this cut across demographic characteristics. Participants reported thinking that the mentally ill were dangerous, emotionally weak, and had poor coping skills. They often reported avoiding the mentally ill and the 'mad' in particular, which was a term frequently reserved for severely mentally ill persons.

### Beliefs about Causes of Mental Illness

The most frequently endorsed causes of mental illness included drug use, biological explanations, genetics/heredity, stress, and inability to cope. Participants also endorsed religious/spiritual causes of mental illness, including demon possession and Obeah. There was no clear consensus of opinion on the causes of mental illness, although our *Atlas.ti* codes analysis suggested that drug use, biological explanations, genetics/heredity, stress, religious/spiritual causes, and inability to cope were perhaps the most frequently expressed beliefs.

### Caregiver Coping Strategies

Caregivers and relatives of individuals with mental illness frequently reported that their initial response was to react with shock, sadness, despair – and with constant worry about their mentally ill relatives. Many indicated, however, that their attempts to cope were affected positively by learning more about mental illness and the mentally ill. Participants reported that when they learned that their relatives' bad behaviour and acting out was due to mental illness, they were able to lose their fears; show empathy, support, and caring; and bounce back from the initial shock of the situation.

### The Mental Institution as a Cause of Stigma

Participants expressed strong views about mental health-related institutions, particularly Bellevue, the State mental hospital in Jamaica. Indeed, the stigma was so strong that it extended to the staff and mental health professionals working at Bellevue.

## The Mental Institution as a Change Agent

Some participants indicated that community clinic-based care was preferable. Others felt that Bellevue and Ward 21 were better equipped to treat mental illness effectively. The mental institution was also perceived as having a role in reducing the stigma of mental illness in Jamaica. Some participants recalled the anti-stigma campaigns of the 1970s in Jamaica, including efforts made at Bellevue Hospital.

## Public Education and Understanding about Mental Illness and Stigma

A number of participants indicated that it was their belief that the stigma of mental illness was due to lack of education among the populace about the nature and treatment of mental illness. They suggested that improving public education about these issues would do much to improve public perceptions and behaviour toward the mentally ill.

## Consequences of Mental Illness for the Mentally Ill

Individuals with mental illness reported a range of emotions and thoughts about being mentally ill. Some thought it was a disgrace to be mentally ill; others disagreed and found no shame in it. There was debate among participants about whether or not to disclose publicly that they had a mental illness. Some thought it was best kept secret, while others thought that keeping such a secret would only serve to worsen their mental health. Many participants reported that they disliked taking medication for their illness, indicating that the medication itself was a source of disgrace. Others disagreed and reported that the benefits of the medication outweighed the stigma associated with taking it.

## Responses to the Vignette

Participants reported a diversity of opinions regarding the young man in the vignette. Some reported immediately that they would no longer trust him; others indicated that, as this was the first time he was behaving in that manner, they would give him another chance and take him back into their home. Most reported that they would at least keep an eye on him. Participants expressed a range of beliefs regarding the cause of the young man's behaviour, including drug use, madness, severe stress, and being under the control of another.

## RESULTS OF SURVEY STUDY

Of the 1644 randomly selected households, 1306, or 79.6%, agreed to participate. One important finding was that participants having a mentally ill family member were less likely (57.0%) than others (66.4%) to avoid individuals perceived as mentally ill. In addition, they were significantly more likely to treat such persons with kindness (82.6% vs. 72.8%), to socialize with them (55.5% vs. 44.2%) and felt comfortable with them (33.3% versus 25.3%). Chi square tests demonstrated statistical significance for all these differences ($p<0.05$). Those who reported that they would verbally abuse or physically assault persons perceived to be mentally ill were equally uncommon in respondents with or without mentally ill family members. Respondents with mentally ill family members had overall positive attitudes towards those relatives. However, a sizeable proportion felt afraid of (43.8%) or disgusted by (43.1%) their relatives who fell into this category.

The small number (n= 42) of mentally ill respondents translated into low statistical power for demonstrating differences between the responses of this subgroup with the responses from others. Not surprisingly, no such differences were found.

Contrary to the initial hypothesis, family members of mentally ill persons, although not completely devoid of stigmatizing behaviour, demonstrated this kind of conduct far less than persons without mentally ill family members. The findings allude to some benefit to be gained from having members of the general population engage and interact more with persons with mental illnesses.

## CONVERGENCE OF THE TWO STUDIES

There were areas of convergence between the qualitative focus group study and the quantitative survey study. The survey study appeared to quantify attitudes that were expressed by family members of individuals with mental illness in the focus group study. While a sizeable number of the relatives of mentally ill individuals reported negative feelings of fear and disgust towards them, some had generally positive attitudes. Focus group study participants with mentally ill relatives indicated that their feelings, thoughts, and behaviours toward the mentally ill, although initially negative, had improved since they had learned more about mental illness, as a result of having a mentally ill relative. For example, some relatives reported losing their fear and having increased feelings of sympathy and empathy after learning more about mental illness. Taken together, these results suggest that education about mental illness and contact with the mentally ill can have a significant impact and reduce stigmatizing attitudes and behaviours.

After two centuries of custodially-driven approaches pioneered by European colonialism, where the mentally ill were corralled in custodial institutions and subjected to draconian treatments (Hickling & Gibson 2005) the level of fear and stigma generated by these mental health policies reached its nadir in the local population. Becoming mentally ill during that period generated high levels of anxiety and terror in people, leading to significant family separation, dislocation and the loss of major social privileges. The mentally ill who were certified to the Bellevue Mental Hospital lost their rights to vote and to employment, and the certification practices subjected the mentally ill to become the butt of cruel jokes. For example, the myth that certification to the mental hospital generated a financial increment led to the popular joke that people could become wealthy by turning their friends and relatives in to the officials of the lunatic asylum.

The mental health experience in Jamaica in the latter half of the 20th century is illustrative of the use of postcolonial social psychotherapy in challenging the stigma of mental illness. With the development of a community mental health legal policy (Hickling & Marahajah, 2005) and services (Hickling et al., 2000) which provided an alternative to mental hospitalization, the draconian custodial laws and practices were confronted and challenged by alternative treatment experiences and approaches for the mentally ill. These new community-based practices profoundly and effectively bypassed the terror of the custodial systems, and checkmated the stigma towards mental illness that had been generated by custodialization. A young person who developed a major psychosis, was admitted to a general hospital medical ward (Hickling et al., 2000), and discharged in a recovered state to his or her family within two weeks, was simply regarded by the family and community as having suffered and recovered from a simple nervous condition. This person would be received with welcoming love and rejoicing. However, someone who was admitted to the Bellevue Mental Hospital at a similar time, with a similar psychosis, would be discharged with a high level of stigmatized opprobrium as a mad person, and treated in a completely different manner. The creation of antithetical policies and treatments significantly negated the stigmatized terror of the custodial episteme.

The community mental health process was buttressed by specific campaigns that also worked effectively to reduce the stigma towards mentally illness. The development of radio psychiatry and other techniques that were facilitated by the electronic media (Abel et al., 2005) and the use of sociodrama and cultural therapy in the mental hospital (Hickling, 2005), were techniques that have been called social psychiatric stimulators, aimed at the community, in the transformation of mental illness-related stigma in Jamaica. These techniques met with profound success. This success has been documented by the chapter in this volume (Hickling et al., 2008) that demonstrates the role of the print media in the destigmatization process (Whitley & Hickling, 2007). By simply drawing the attention of the media to the social psychiatric stimulator, the media response would be dramatic and self-perpetuating. The media would pick up on the social psychiatric stimulator, report on the events extensively and then encourage subsequent community discussion and affirmation in the press. The process leads to what we have called 'psychological deinstitutionalization' (Whitley & Hickling, 2007)

## Conclusion

Jamaica conducted a number of pioneering efforts to educate its populace about mental illness and the mentally ill in past years. This work was found to have had a significant impact on the reduction of the stigma of mental illness, and the improvement of attitudes towards the mentally ill (Johansen, 1985; Hickling, 1992). Like recent Western anti-stigma campaigns, this work acknowledged the devastating impact of stigma on the mentally ill and endeavoured to change attitudes and behaviour through education.

The research presented here was designed to reveal attitudes toward mental illness and the mentally ill among Jamaicans residing at home. However, it may also have important implications for Jamaicans residing around the world, in countries such as the UK and the USA. As such, this work may be used as a leverage point for conducting similar research with these groups, particularly in light of the increased interest in members of the African Diaspora in these countries (_see,_ for example, Arthur & Katkin, 2006; Hickling, 2002) and the acknowledged barriers to mental health treatment among them (_see,_ for example, Gary, 2005). Moreover, the study methodologies that we have presented here may be useful for conducting similar stigma research in other developing countries, especially within the Caribbean.

This work also has implications for changes and improvement in health policy in Jamaica, as well as improved communication about access and care for the mentally ill. Perhaps an effective strategy would be to employ a multi-level approach, addressing multiple groups simultaneously, with programmes tailored for each targeted group. For example, anti-stigma education campaigns for the Jamaican public could focus primarily, at least initially, on providing accurate information about mental health and illness in ways that would reach large sections of the public, e.g., via the media (Whitley & Hickling, in press).

The work presented here has begun to fill a gap in the stigma research literature in the Caribbean and Jamaica. Much more work is needed on this topic to fully understand the perceptions and attitudes of Jamaicans towards mental illness and the mentally ill, for example, individuals' attitudes towards psychotherapy. Significant strides have been made in this area in the region, for example, in Jamaica – where several graduate programmes have been instituted at different institutions; and in Barbados and Trinidad – where the field is burgeoning and psychology programmes are also being developed. This will naturally have an impact on people's general attitudes towards mental illness and its treatment. Additionally, more research is needed, not only to determine what types of anti-stigma campaigns would be most effective, but also to identify the best means of using this work to positively impact on policy – thereby improving the quality of life and life opportunities for persons with mental illness and their families.

## REFERENCES

Abel, W., McCallum, M., Hickling, F. W., & Gibson, R. C. (2005). Mental health services and public policy in Jamaica. In F. W. Hickling & E. Sorel (Eds.), _Images of psychiatry: The Caribbean_ (pp. 297-313). Kingston, Jamaica: University of the West Indies.

Angermeyer, M. C, & Matschinger, H. (2005). Labeling-stereotype-discrimination. Aninvestigation of the stigma process. *Social Psychiatry & Psychiatric Epidemiology*, 40, 391-5.

Arboleda-Florez, J. (2003). Integration initiatives for forensic services. *World Psychiatry*. 2 (3), 179-83.

Arthur, C. M., & Katkin, E. S. (2006). Making a case for the examination of ethnicity among Blacks in United States Health Research. *Journal of Health Care for the Poor and Underserved*, 17 (1), 25-36.

Beinecke, R. H. (2005). Stakeholder perspectives on public managed behavioural care in Massachusetts. *Administration and Policy in Mental Health*, 32 (4), 427-438.

Bowis, J. (2005). Politics and psychiatry. *Die Psychiatrie: Grundlagen & Perspektiven*, 2 (2), 96-100.

Brett, A. (2003). Psychiatry, stigma and courts. *Psychiatry, Psychology and Law*, 10 (2), 283-288.

Collinson, S. R., & Turner, T. H. (2002). Not just salsa and cigars: Mental health care in Cuba. *Psychiatric Bulletin*, 26 (5), 185-188.

Corrigan P. W. (2004) How stigma interferes with mental health care. *American Psychologist*, 59 (7), 614-25.

Corrigan, P. W., & Kleinlein, P. (2005). The impact of mental illness stigma. In P. W. Corrigan, (Ed.), *On the stigma of Mental illness: Practical strategies for research and social change* (pp.11-44). Washington, DC: American Psychological Association.

Corrigan, P. W., Larson, J. E., Watson, A. C., Boyle, M., & Barr, L. (2006). Solutions to discrimination in work and housing identified by people with mental illness. *Journal of Nervous and Mental Disease*, 194 (9), 716-718.

Corrigan, P. W., Rowan, D., Green, A., Lundin, R., River, P., Uphoff-Wasowski, K., et al. (2002). Challenging two mental illness stigmas: personal responsibility and dangerousness. *Schizophrenia Bulletin*, 28 (2), 293-309.

Corrigan, P., Thompson, V., Lambert, D., Sangster, Y., Noel, J.G., & Campbell, J. (2003). Perceptions of discrimination among persons with serious mental illness. *Psychiatric Services*, 54, 1105-10.

Corrigan, P. W., Watson, A. C., Warpinski, A. C., & Gracia, G. (2004). Stigmatizing attitudes about mental illness and allocation of resources to mental health services. *Community Mental Health Journal*, 40 (4), 297-307.

de Toledo Piza Peluso, E., & Blay, S. L. (2004). Community perception of mental disorders: A systematic review of Latin American and Caribbean studies. *Social Psychiatry and Psychiatric Epidemiology*, 39 (12), 955-61.

Estroff, S. E., Penn, D. L., & Toporek, J. R. (2004). From stigma to discrimination: An analysis of community efforts to reduce the negative consequences of having a psychiatric disorder and label. *Schizophrenia Bulletin*, 30 (3), 493-509.

Forchuk, C. N., Nelson, G., & Hall, G. B. (2006). 'It's important to be proud of the place you live in': Housing problems and preferences of psychiatric survivors. *Perspectives in Psychiatric Care*, 42 (1), 42-52.

Gary, F. A. (2005). Stigma: Barrier to mental health care among ethnic minorities. *Issues in Mental Health Nursing*, 26, 979-999.

Gibson, R. C., Abel, W. D., White, S., & Hickling, F. W. (In press). Internalizing stigma associated with mental illness: findings from a general population survey in Jamaica. *Revista Panamericana de Salud Publica* (In press).

Goffman E. (1963). *Stigma: Notes on the management of spoiled identity*. Englewood Cliffs, NJ: Prentice Hall.

Goos, C. (2006). Mental health: Facing the challenges, building solutions--Report from the WHO European Ministerial Conference. *Addiction*, 101 (6), 901-902.

Hickling, F. W. (1989). Sociodrama in the rehabilitation of chronic mentally ill patients. *Hospital and Community Psychiatry*, 40 (4), 402-406.

———. (1992). Radio psychiatry and community mental health. *Hospital and Community Psychiatry*, 43 (7), 739-741.

———. (2002). The African Renaissance and the struggle for mental health in the African Diaspora. *Proceedings from The African Diaspora: Psychiatric Issues*, Nov. 17-21, 2002, Boston, MA.

———. (2005). Catalyzing creativity. In F. W. Hickling & E. Sorel (Eds.), *Images of psychiatry: The Caribbean* (pp. 241-271). Kingston, Jamaica: Department of Community Health and Psychiatry, University of the Wes Indies.

Hickling, F. W., & Gibson, R. C. (2005). The history of Caribbean psychiatry. In F. W. Hickling & E. Sorel (Eds.), *Images of psychiatry: The Caribbean* (pp. 15-41). Kingston, Jamaica: University of the West Indies.

Hickling F. W., & Maharajh H. D. (2005) Mental Health Legislation. In F. W. Hickling & E. Sorel (Eds.), *Images of psychiatry: The Caribbean* (pp. 43-74). Kingston, Jamaica: University of the West Indies.

Hickling, F. W., McCallum, M., Nooks, L., & Rodgers-Johnson, P. (2000). Treatment of acute schizophrenia in open general medical wards in Jamaica. *Psychiatric Services*, 51, 659-663.

Hickling, F. W., Thompson, E., Chandler, S., & Matthies, B. (2008). Media psychology in the Caribbean. In F. Hickling, B. Matthies, K. Morgan and R. Gibson (Eds.), *Perspectives in Caribbean psychology*. Kingston, Jamaica: CARIMENSA, University of the West Indies.

Johansen, M. (1985) A questionnaire Survey of a Radio Psychiatry Program in Jamaica. BA thesis (Mass Communications), University of the West Indies, Mona, Jamaica.

Kohn, R., Sharma, D., Camilleri, C. P., & Levav, I. (2000). Attitudes towards mental illness in the Commonwealth of Dominica. *Revista Panamericana de Salud Publica*. 7 (3),148-54.

Khandelwal, S. K., Jhingan, H.P., & Ramesh, S. (2004). India mental health country profile. *International Review of Psychiatry*, 16 (1-2), 126-141.

Lee, S., Lee, M. T., Chiu, M. Y., & Kleinman, A. (2005). Experience of social stigma by people with schizophrenia in Hong Kong. *British Journal of Psychiatry,* 186, 153-7.

Link, B. G., Cullen, F. T., Frank, J. et al. (1987) The social rejection of former mental patients: understanding why labels matter. *American Journal of Sociology,* 92, 1461-1500.

Link, B. G., & Phelan, J. C. (2006). Stigma and its public health implications. *The Lancet,* 367, 528-529.

———. (2001). Conceptualizing stigma. *Annual Review of Sociology,* 27, 363-385.

Link, B. G., Struening, E. L., Neese-Todd, S., Asmussen, S., & Phelan, J. C. (2001). Stigma as a barrier to recovery: The consequences of stigma for the self-esteem of people with mental illnesses. *Psychiatric Services,* 52, 1621-6.

Link, B. G., Yang, L. H., Phelan, J. C., & Collins, P. Y. (2004). Measuring mental illness stigma. *Schizophrenia Bulletin,* 30 (3), 511-541.

Ostman, M., & Kjellin, L. (2002). Stigma by association: psychological factors in relatives of people with mental illness. *British Journal of Psychiatry,* 181, 494-8.

Phillips, M. R., Pearson, V., Li, F., Xu, M., & Yang, L. (2002). Stigma and expressed emotion: a study of people with schizophrenia and their family members in China. *British Journal of Psychiatry,* 181, 488-93.

Pompili, M., Mancinelli I., & Tatarelli R., (2003) Stigma as a cause of suicide. *British Journal of Psychiatry,* 183, 173-174.

Sartorius, N. (1997) Fighting schizophrenia and its stigma. A new World Psychiatric Association educational programme. *British Journal of Psychiatry,* 170, 297.

Shibre, T., Negash, A., Kullgren, G., Kebede, D., Alem, A., Fekadu et al. (2001). Perception of stigma among family members of individuals with schizophrenia and major affective disorders in rural Ethiopia. *Social Psychiatry & Psychiatric Epidemiolgy,* 36 (6), 299-303.

Stuart, H. (2006). Mental illness and employment discrimination. *Current Opinion in Psychiatry,* 19 (5), 522-526.

United States Department of Health and Human Services (1999). *Mental Health: a report of the Surgeon General.* Washington: United States Department of Health and Human Services.
Accessed July 31, 2006 at http://www.surgeongeneral.gov/library/mentalhealtl- i/home.html

United States Department of Health and Human Services (2003). *Substance Abuse and Mental Health Services Administration.* Center for Mental Health Services ADS Center Elimination of Barriers Initiative.
Accessed December 12, 2006 at http://www.stopstigma.samhsa.gov/ebi.htm

Whitley, R., & Hickling, F. W. (In press). Open papers, open minds? Media representations of psychiatric deinstitutionalization in Jamaica. *Transcultural Psychiatry* (In press).

Wig, N. N. (1989). Indian concepts of mental health and their impact on care of the mentally ill. *International Journal of Mental Health,* 18 (3), 71-80.

# 6 Culture and Behaviour

## Recognition of Cultural Behaviours in Trinidad and Tobago

*Hari D. Maharajh & Akleema Kalpoo*

In any established society, notwithstanding its level of development, there exist social and cultural behaviours that are unique to its inhabitants. These behaviours, if not understood as social and cultural manifestations of a complicated system of human interpretation and expression may be mistakenly interpreted as patterns of psychological disorders. Consequently, normal behaviour may be exaggerated in some societies but still falls within the rubric of the pathoplastic effect of culture.

Trinidad and Tobago, not unlike many Caribbean countries, is a plural society resplendent in its cultural diversity. It prides itself with an ethno-historical background of African slavery, Indian indentureship and European migration emerging into a post-emancipation society of open expressions of social commentaries in song, dance and language. It remains today an easy-going society with a style of 'picong' communication which, to the observer, remains strange.

This chapter analyses contemporary behaviours of the migrant groups that have formed this society with references both to the sending and receiving countries, noting that the relics of a culture persist despite cultural changes. A questionnaire survey on the culture of Trinidad and Tobago is undertaken to study the cultural behaviours existing there and to assess the population's awareness, perception and description of these behaviours.

The influences of culture and mental health have been an area of interest of early researchers (Durkheim, 1951; Kraeplin, 1909; Voss, 1915). Later, social scientists viewed psychiatric illness as a form of social deviancy where the individual was regarded as mentally ill because he had broken the local codes of social conduct (Kiev, 1972). This concept of psychiatric disorders as a deviation from social and cultural norms rather than a product of an underlying biological dysfunction has not been accepted by many psychiatrists (Central Statistical Office, 1992). Some are of the opinion that social impairment is insufficient and psychiatric diagnosis should be made only on the basis of mental status, not in terms of cultural behaviour. Today, the tangential progression from behaviour, to rationalization of identity, to syndrome, and then to psychosis remains invariably enigmatic and untenable. However, attempts to bridge this divide have been made through the introduction of a multiaxial system that promotes the application of a bio-psychosocial model (American Psychiatric Association, 2000).

Cultural behaviours can be defined as an adaptive response occurring in organized social groups whose lifestyles, sentiments and interactions have been transgenerationally transmitted. These behaviours are often associated with compensatory processes of rationalization and are sometimes conceptualized in the context of native humour.

Cultural behaviours are different from culture-bound syndromes. The latter is defined as recurrent locality-specific patterns of aberrant behaviour and troubling experiences that may or may not be linked to a particular DSM-IV-TR diagnostic category. These are indigenously considered to be illnesses, or at least afflictions, and most have local names (American Psychiatric Association, 2000). Culture-bound syndromes are thus culturally determined abnormal behaviour patterns that are specific to a particular culture or geographical region. These express core cultural themes, and have a wide range of symbolic meanings – social, moral and psychological (Dein, 1997).

Genuine culture-bound syndromes are not exclusively linked to a particular culture but rather related to a prominent cultural emphasis or to a specific social stress situation (Jilek, 2000; Jilek & Jilek-Aall, 2000). Syndromes have been described with a cultural emphasis on a number of themes.

Many themes are related to fertility and procreation, such as koro in Malay-Indonesian language, Jiryan in India, Dhat syndrome (Jilek, 1986; Jilek & Jilek-Aall, 1977; Paris, 1992; Tseng et al, 1988; Yap, 1965) and suoyang in Madarin-Chinese (Paris, 1992; Yap, 1965; Jilek, 1986; Tseng et al, 1988). Others focus on physical appearance, such as taijin-kuofu among the Japanese (Kirmayer, 1991; Lee, Shin & Oh, 1994), learnt dissociation such as latah and amok in Malay-Indonesia language (Burton-Bradley, 1968, 1975; Murphy, 1973; Pfeiffer, 1994; Simons, 1996; Van Wulfften Palthe, 1991; Westermeyer, 1972, 1973; Winzeler, 1995), and acculturative stress such as brain fag symptoms in African students (Prince, 1960, 1985).

Over the past two decades, Trinidad and Tobago, because of its cultural diversity, has attracted a number of visiting researchers. Littlewood (1985) has described 'tabanca' (lovesick behaviour) as an indigenous conceptualization of depression in rural Trinidad. This, he claims, is an affliction of working class Afro-Caribbean males who aspire to white and middle class values and lifestyles. His views are considered to be a misinterpretation of this cultural phenomenon. Local psychiatrists (Maharajh & Parasaram, 1997; Maharajh, Clarke, & Hutchinson, 1989) have been critical of his findings, stating that he did not take into account the cultural milieu that colours expression of the behaviour and that he was blinkered by his own unconscious cultural assumptions. Eriksen (1990) has described 'liming' in Trinidad as a dignified art of doing nothing, noting that one cannot be recognized as a real Trinidadian unless one masters the art of doing nothing. A British research team (Bhugra, Hilwig, Hossein, et al., 1996), in a socio-political motivated study investigated the incidence of psychosis in Trinidad in response to reports of high incidences amongst the Afro-Caribbean population in Britain. He noted that there was no excess in the incidence of psychosis in Trinidad as reported among the black Caribbean population in the UK.

There is concern about the misinterpretation and misrepresentation of indigenous cultural phenomenon and the utilization of findings and conclusions by foreign researchers. Their interpretations of cultural behaviours as culture-bound syndromes or progressing to chronic insanity (Littlewood, 1985) can be quite misleading and border on assumptions of cultural hegemony.

## Recognizing Cultural Behaviours

In an attempt to recognize cultural behavioural patterns in Trinidad and Tobago, a two-fold approach was implemented, with the aim of

- documenting cultural behaviours that exist in Trinidad and Tobago thereby minimizing interpretation and misrepresentation of these phenomena by those not exposed to the culture

- studying the indigenous population's awareness, perception and description of these behaviours.

A questionnaire survey (n = 536) on the culture of Trinidad and Tobago was undertaken to study the cultural behaviours existing there and to assess the population's awareness, perception and description of these behaviours. In a pilot study, respondents were presented with nine identified behaviours and perceived five of them to be a part of the Trinidadian culture: Liming, Carnival Mentality, Player or Playboy Personality, Tabanca and Obsessional Lateness were identified as existent cultural behaviours.

## A Pilot Project

Cultural behaviours were identified by a pre-study survey of a semi-structured interview designed to identify cultural behavioural patterns of Trinidad and Tobago (Appendix 1). A stratified random sample of 52 respondents were chosen. This sample was representative of the general population with respect to age, sex, ethnicity, social class, marital status and education (Central Statistical Office, 1992).

Behaviour was defined as "the whole way of life of people" and involved both traditional practices handed down from generation to generation, and descriptions of contemporary social behaviours. Interestingly, more than half – 30 respondents (58%) – considered religious or spiritual beliefs and practices as not being part of culture. A total of nine behaviours were identified: Obsessional Lateness, Smartman Syndrome, Liming, Middle-age Indian Woman Syndrome, Tabanca, Carnival Mentality, Demon Possession, Spiritual Travel and Playboy (Player or Macho) Personality. A tenth behaviour, Obeah, was excluded because 62 per cent of the respondents felt it was also widespread in other Caribbean territories.

# Description of Behaviours Under Study

## LIMING

'Liming' is a term commonly used in Trinidad for hanging out. Its origin is unclear with villagers' view that it originated from sailors afflicted with vitamin C deficiency sitting in the sun on the limestone covered areas. Another view is that it is a description of inhabitants sitting under the shaded citrus fruit trees, socializing with alcoholic beverages, sometimes gambling, idling their time away.

## CARNIVAL MENTALITY

Trinidadians have been dubbed as having a carnival mentality. This is a preoccupation with leisure, music, dance and a slack and laid-back attitude to work. It is seen as a behavioural pattern that has emanated from the carnival celebrations. Carnival has its origins in the emancipation of slavery and is annually celebrated with two days of street dancing, revelry, debauchery and 'freeing up'. This behaviour is considered to be pervasive throughout the year.

## PLAYER OR PLAYBOY PERSONALITY

The courtship cycle is generally absent among the male gender in Trinidad and Tobago. The origin of the playboy has been fashioned by many factors, such as, emancipation from servitude, the American presence during World War II and later the influences of the electronic media and of the country's oil wealth. The player is described as a well-dressed, slick, seemingly rich charmer with a fancy car, and who has many women with whom he is sexually but not emotionally involved. Such a person gains the admiration of the younger generation.

## TABANCA

'Tabanca' is a form of 'love sickness', derived from the French expression meaning 'to be thrown onto a bank'. It is described as 'a state of depression' accompanied by withdrawal symptoms (inability to eat, sleep, or think) that occurs when one has been rejected by a loved one or experiences unrequited love. It is the loss of a love object.

## OBSESSIONAL LATENESS

The people of Trinidad and Tobago show little concern for being on time. They walk at a leisurely pace, stop to greet others with little regard for punctuality or lateness.

Being fashionably late culturally confers respectability to the person, underlining his importance or heavy work schedule.

## SMARTMAN SYNDROME

Trinidadians are regionally referred to as 'Trickidadians', having a history of being dishonestly smart using techniques of lying, deceit, trickery and fraud. These individuals are well known con-artists or hagglers who are constantly attempting to make a fast dollar by defrauding someone else.

## DEMON POSSESSION

Steeped in superstitious and religio-magical occurrences, the people of Trinidad and Tobago believe in the existence of 'jinns', demons and powers that can possess them. These spirits can take over or possess the body of a person and control their behaviour. Many mental disorders are interpreted as demon possession.

## SPIRITUAL TRAVEL

Spiritual travel is practised by members of the Spiritual Baptist religion. Through a process of sensory deprivation in the mourning ground ceremony, a person's spirit can travel out of the body to far-off lands, meeting people of all walks of life from whom prescriptions can be obtained for healing. It's a method of transcendence that unifies one with God.

## MIDDLE-AGE INDIAN WOMAN SYNDROME

A common finding among Indo-Trinidadian women in their fourth and fifth decades is the occurrence of somatic complaints of headaches, body aches and pains, cardiac and gastrointestinal symptoms. There is no physical disease on investigation with causation being attributed to social and psychological disorders. They are viewed as Somatoform disorders that are more common in Indo-Caribbean women.

# Analysis of Cultural Behaviours

## SAMPLE AND INSTRUMENTS – MEASURING CULTURAL BEHAVIOURS

Through quota sampling, a new sample of respondents (N=536) was administered a questionnaire that gathered self-reported data on Trinidad culture (the nine behaviours identified). The sample population was similar to the population distribution of Trinidad and Tobago with respect to employment, religion, ethnicity, gender and social class (Central Statistical Office, 1992). The questionnaire collected data on the following:

- *Demographic Information*

  Data were gathered along the variables of age, sex, ethnicity (Afro-Trinidadians, Indo-Trinidadians, Mixed and Other), nationality and social class (low, middle and upper). Ethnicity or an individual's ethnic group was determined on the basis of the following criteria: (1) having at least three out of four grandparents belonging to the same ethnic group or if criteria (1) was not met, they were then categorized as Mixed. Mixed ethnicity refers to individuals who are the resulting offspring of a union between two different ethnic groups and who usually have distinctive physical traits that mark him or her from both parent ethnic groups, but who may also possess some characteristics of manner, thought and speech, which are derived from both lines of ancestry. The ethnicity category of Other includes those individuals who cannot be placed in the ethnic categories of Afro-Trinidadians, Indo-Trinidadians or Mixed. They also belong to ethnic groups that comprise a small percentage of the total population of Trinidad, e.g. Chinese, Syrian and Caucasian (Lewis, 1973). Social class was derived using both occupation and income brackets (Meltzer, Gill & Petticrew, 1995).

- *Awareness of behaviour*

  This variable was dichotomous and respondents were asked if they had ever heard of each of the nine behaviours. The response set was either "yes" or "no".

- *A description of the behaviour*

  If respondents were aware of a particular behaviour, they were asked to give a brief description of the behaviour, state whether it was an entity or not, and if it was associated with any particular symptoms. The descriptions of the behaviours were then coded into several categories by two raters. It must be noted that the coding of the descriptions were done twice to ensure that there would be inter-rater reliability.

- *Perception of the behaviour as being part of Trinidad culture*

  The response set was again either "yes" or "no". Respondents were asked for each of the nine behaviours whether they perceived it to be part of the culture of Trinidad and Tobago.

Data were entered and analyzed by the use of SPSS (Statistical Package for the Social Sciences, Version 8.0). The statistical test chosen for awareness of behaviour and perception of the behaviour as being part of Trinidad culture was Chi-Square tests as data were collected along a nominal level. In order to distinguish behaviours that were strongly perceived as being part of Trinidad culture, percentiles that were within the upper quarter (75% cutoff point) were utilized (Kurtz, 1999). Additional correlation analyses were also performed. The level of significance was set at a $p < 0.05$ level.

## RESULTS

From the questionnaire survey of 536 participants, the nine behaviours (Obsessional Lateness, Smartman Syndrome, Liming, Middle-age Indian Woman Syndrome, Tabanca, Carnival Mentality, Demon Possession, Spiritual Travel and Playboy Personality) were analysed in the following categories:

a) Demographic data of sampled population

b) Awareness of the behaviour

c) Description of the behaviour

d) Perception of the behaviour as part of culture

## a) Demographic Data of Sampled Population

The majority of the sample (98%) was Trinidadian with 2% non-Trinidadian. Indo-Trinidadians accounted for 39% of the sample, Afro-Trinidadians 35%, Mixed 24% and Other 2%. Ages of the respondents ranged from 14-56 with the mean age being 35. Sixty per cent (60%) were in the 14-25 age group, 18% in the 26-35 age group, 12% in the 36-45 age group and 10% in the over 45 age group. With respect to social class, 52% were from the middle class, 27% from the lower class and 21% from the upper class.

## b) Awareness of Behaviour

Overall, 99% of the sample were aware or familiar with the behaviour of Liming, 97% each for Carnival Mentality and Playboy Personality, Tabanca 95%, Obsessive Lateness 92%, Smartman Syndrome 80%, Demon Possession 73%, Spiritual Travel 66%, and Middle-age Indian Woman Syndrome 11%. A significantly greater percentage of Afro-Trinidadians were familiar with the behaviour of Obsessional Lateness than Indo-Trinidadians, Mixed Persons and Others ($X^2 = 8.404$, df = 3, p < 0.05). Indo-Trinidadians were also significantly more familiar with smartman syndrome than Afro-Trinidadians, Mixed and Other individuals ($X^2 = 11.590$, df = 3, p < 0.01).

Significant differences existed for the awareness of carnival mentality and smartman syndrome between social classes. Middle class individuals (55%) were more aware of the behaviour of carnival mentality than lower class (24%) and upper class (22%); and also were more aware of demon possession (53%) than lower class (25%) and upper class individuals (21%). These differences were significant where $X^2 = 13.337$, df = 2, p < 0.001 and $X^2 = 7.150$, df = 2, p < 0.05, respectively.

The 14-25 age group was more aware of the terms 'smartman syndrome' and 'carnival mentality' than other age groups, where $X^2 = 15.049$, df = 3, p < 0.01 and $X^2 = 12.721$, d.f. = 3, p < 0.001. No other significant differences were found between this variable and other demographic data.

In addition, awareness was not a determinant of cultural behaviour, but was strongly correlated with the perception that the behaviour was part of culture (r = 0.894, p<0.001) and there was an inverse relationship between the behaviour as part of culture and the number of the descriptive levels constituting that behaviour (r = -0.677, p<0.05)

## c) Description of Behaviour

The following descriptions of different behaviours are summative characteristics based on answers given by respondents who were familiar
with the culture.

*Liming* was described as a scheduled or non-scheduled event where a
group of people (friends, family, acquaintances etc.) takes time to "hang
out". The concept transcends ethnicity, class and religious barriers. It is
an activity geared towards relaxation, stress relief through the means of
talking, eating and drinking or just "doing nothing". As clearly put by
one respondent, liming is a major cultural activity, whether from 'river
lime', 'after-work lime' or 'duck lime'; and can also be seen as working in
sync with our "poor work ethic" and "carnival mentality" (*see* Table 1,
Appendix 2).

*Carnival Mentality* was seen as having two dimensions: during carnival season and outside of carnival period. During the carnival season,
carnival mentality has been viewed as a "time to free up", "time to break
away and get on bad" or take part in every carnival activity or event, and
indulging in alcohol, immoral, vulgar, and promiscuous activities without thinking of the consequences. Outside of the carnival season, carnival
mentality refers to the "non-stop party mentality" that is practised
throughout the year; where every event or occasion is treated as a excuse
"to lime or party". Some respondents have regarded carnival mentality
as "extreme liming" or "continuous fun in the sun". Carnival mentality
was also seen as having filtered into the workplace where individuals
have a very casual, 'laid-back' or 'don't-give-a-damn' attitude towards
work. Carnival mentality was also referred to by a minority of respondents as mindlessness, "when you hear music nothing could stop you
from dancing", having too many parties in the calendar and events having attributes of carnival (*see* Table 2, Appendix 2).

*Playboy Personality* was described as Trinidadian men who have multiple girlfriends but seek only attention and sexual satisfaction from
them. They dress sharp, have lots of money and drive expensive cars.
They are sexually involved with all of their partners but are never emotionally involved. A player (one who has a playboy personality) was also
identified as one who thinks he is God's gift to women, a real charmer
and is said to tackle "anything in a skirt that pass". He is identified as a
'sweetman', that is, someone who knows all the right words to say

(lyrics) and how to wine and dine the women he is currently seeing. Less than 1% of respondents viewed playboy personality as a person who commits adultery, behaviour that is adopted from another culture or passed on by adults, when a guy says he is in love but he is lying (*see* Table 3, Appendix 2).

*Tabanca* is a form of 'love sickness'. It was described as 'a state of depression' accompanied by withdrawal symptoms (inability to eat or sleep) that occurs when one has been rejected by a loved one or experiences unrequited love. It is an adjustment disorder of losing a loved one. The term is also used to describe the feeling of being in love where one is constantly thinking, daydreaming and totally 'head over heels' with someone, the mental anguish of getting 'horn' and having girlfriend/boyfriend worries or 'a case of Love Jones'. Severe tabanca has been described as 'tabantruck' (*see* Table 4, Appendix 2).

The respondents have clearly defined *obsessional lateness* as having no regard for punctuality, and lateness as being a part of our nature. In short, it is functioning with 'Trini time'. It is arriving for any event or occasion at least 15-45 minutes after the scheduled time. According to respondents, "Any time is Trini time" shows exactly how casual individuals are in their behaviour; and it has often been said, "A Trini will be late for his own funeral". Arriving late was seen by some as being fashionably late and was due to being disorganized, waiting until the 11th hour to do something that leads to rushing and thus being late (*see* Table 5, Appendix 2),

Individuals who have the ability to outsmart anyone or "hoodwink anyone" usually by means of lying, trickery, deceit and dishonesty display the *Smartman Syndrome*. These individuals are con artists who seek to get things for little or no value. In local parlance, it refers to individuals who are trying to get "something for nothing" or "trying to pull a fast one." This behaviour is also used to describe people who always have an answer for everything, a "smart retort" or "a bandage for every cut". Few respondents described a smartman as being one who fools and uses many women for their own benefit (similar to player), being a bully, being quiet and not talking too much and acting very stupid, that is, "playing dead to catch corbeaux alive" (*see* Table 6, Appendix 2).

*Demon Possession* was mostly viewed as when a spirit or demon took over the body and the person was unaware of what is happening. It was also seen to be attributed to an individual acting in a strange and unexplainable manner not consistent with his/her normal behaviour pattern, or acting crazy. Some people referred to demon possession as similar to evil, obeah, witchcraft and bad things constantly happening to you. Few described demon possession as an anxiety attack, talking constantly, folklore and myths and as a manifestation of abnormal behaviour usually schizophrenia. Table 7 describes the characteristics associated with demon possession (*see* Table 7, Appendix 2).

*Spiritual Travel* was defined as the ability of a spirit to travel out of the body; more specifically, respondents identified the transcendental travel of the soul on the mourning ground as a practice of the Spiritual Baptist faith. It was also associated with other religious sects involved in the practices of "ketching power" and loud singing and clapping. Other views of spiritual travel were that it was an episode that occurs while praying and one that brings you closer to God; is Obeah/Voodoo or it is when you are given the word of God in order to practise religion properly. It occurs in a state close to death when the spirit gradually leaves the body and is a state when one can have visions or dreams. It was described as a mostly religious related activity (*see* Table 8, Appendix 2).

*Middle-age Indian Woman Syndrome* was neither clearly nor consistently defined within one category. It was referred to as Indian women who stay at home, are extremely obsessional about their family and who neglect their physical appearance. In addition, the syndrome was seen as being associated with behaviour directed to recapture a youthful past, being fat around the waist and complaining of pains in the joints, forever quarrelling with the children and husband and having extra marital affairs (*see* Table 9, Appendix 2).

### d) Perception of Behaviour as Part of Culture

The measurements of respondents' perception of behaviours seen as part of the culture of Trinidad and Tobago were as follows: Liming (96%), Carnival Mentality (93%) were perceived as being part of the culture of Trinidad and Tobago, followed by Playboy Personality (83%), Tabanca (82%), Obsessive Lateness (77%, Smartman Syndrome (65%), Demon Possession (55%), Spiritual Travel (46%) and Middle-age Indian Woman Syndrome (9%).

Significant differences existed between ethnic groups and their view of Demon Possession as a part of Trinidad culture. Indo-Trinidadians were more likely (50%) than Afro-Trinidadians (30%), Mixed (17%) and Other (3%) individuals to view Demon Possession as a part of Trinidad culture. This was significant where $X^2 = 16.369$, d.f. = 3, p < 0.001.

Middle-class individuals (52%) and lower-class individuals (32%) were more likely than upper-class individuals (16%) to view Demon Possession as being a part of Trinidad culture. This difference was near significance where $X^2 = 5.3481$, d.f. = 2, p = 0.06.

The 14-25 age group was more likely than other age groups to view Smartman Syndrome and Playboy Personality as a part of culture, this was significant where $X^2 = 10.014$, d.f. = 3, p < 0.01 and $X^2 = 8.449$, d.f. = 3, p < 0.05 respectively. No other significant differences were found between this variable and other demographic data.

## LINK BETWEEN AWARENESS AND PERCEPTION OF BEHAVIOUR AS PART OF CULTURE

A strong correlational relationship existed between awareness and the perception that the behaviour was a part of culture. This was significant where r = 0.894, p < 0.001. However, it was discovered that high awareness is not a necessity for a determinant of culture. This is evident especially for demon possession where 73% of respondents were aware of culture but only 55% perceived it as being a part of culture.

Another significant correlational relationship existed between the perception of the behaviour as a culture and the number of levels constituting a behaviour where r = –0.677, p < 0.05. Therefore, as the number of levels in describing a behaviour increases the less likely it is to be considered a part of the culture. However, this relationship did not pertain to demon possession and spiritual travel.

## Discussion

Nine behaviours, namely: Liming, Carnival Mentality, Player or Playboy Personality, Tabanca, Obsessional Lateness, Smartman Syndrome, Demon Possession, Spiritual Travel and The Middle-age Indian Woman Syndrome were identified as existent cultural behaviours. Attempting to validate whether a particular behaviour was part of the culture of Trinidad and Tobago was no easy task. Using a cut-off point of more than a 75 per cent respondent rate (Kurtz, 1999) resulted in the rejection of four behaviours, namely Smartman Syndrome, Demon Possession, Spiritual Travel and the Middle-age Indian Woman Syndrome which fell below the 75 percentile.

There were, however, a number of limitations. The use of an opportunity sample may have resulted in lower figures in awareness and perception of behaviour as part of culture due to the skewing of the age groupings to the younger working groups. This, in our opinion may have resulted in lower figures in awareness and perception of the behaviour as part of culture. The strong correlation between awareness and perception that behaviour was part of culture was not always robust. In the case of demon possession, 73% of respondents were aware of the culture, but only 55% perceived it as part of culture. This substantiates the view that awareness of a phenomenon is not sufficient to categorize it as a cultural behaviour. In addition, it was found that the greater the number of levels used in describing a culture, the less likely it was found to be part of the culture ($r = -0.677$, $p < 0.05$). However, it must be noted that the correlation coefficient be interpreted with caution, as correlation does not equal causation and there is the possibility of third variables that may have an impact on the investigated variables (Martin, 2000)

Another interesting finding was that while respondents viewed social and traditional practices as cultural behaviour, they were less likely to perceive religious related behaviour as part of culture. This may have resulted in the low response rates for Demon Possession and Spiritual Travel. The divide of religion and culture in Trinidad and Tobago is promulgated by the dichotomy of one culture (East Indian) with many religions and one religion (Christianity) with many cultures, often in competition with each other. The post-slavery emphasis of distancing religion from culture may have been an attempt to gain reputation and respectability for religious beliefs.

## LIMING – 'THE ART OF DOING NOTHING'

Almost all the respondents (99%) were aware of liming and 96% described it as a scheduled or non-scheduled episode where a group of people take time off to hang out, be idle, get together or do nothing. The concept of liming as a social institution and cultural state of mind in Trinidad was reviewed by Eriksen (1990). He described it as a unique Trinidadian pastime of 'the art of doing nothing' and noted that whereas idling and inactivity are frequently perceived unequivocally as shameful and immoral in most societies, liming in Trinidad is an activity that one would not hesitate to indulge in proudly. Despite its occurrence elsewhere, in Trinidad it is different; it is a social situation acknowledged as a form of the performing art linked to the key symbols of carnival, calypso and steelband. In our study, liming was a feature of all groups, regardless of age, ethnicity, religion or class that utilized cultural archetypal mechanisms for the relief of stress.

## CARNIVAL MENTALITY – 'A HAPPY GO LUCKY PEOPLE WITH A NON-STOP PARTY MENTALITY'

Carnival is the Republic's best known festival ushering the season of Lent. The carnival season extends from Christmas to Lent, but outside this period 'a carnival mentality of having attributes to carnival' was described (Table 2, Appendix 2). There is abandonment of the social structures of work, family life, education and law. One commentator, the Prime Minister of Singapore, a country well known for its industry, has argued that the behaviour depicted at carnival is pervasive throughout the year and has referred to the population of Trinidad as having a carnival mentality (Panday, 2000). In response, Liverpool (1990) has pointed out that "in speaking of Trinidadians as having a carnival mentality, they seek to degrade our people, for they seek to say that to possess such a mentality is to live for today, to play 'mas', to have a good time and then to beg on Ash Wednesday morning. In other words, it is to live aimlessly." The urgency of carnival to many is well portrayed in Lovelace's novel, _The Dragon Can't Dance_ in the characterization of Aldrick Prospect. He would get up at midday from sleep, not knowing where his next meal was coming from, 'his brain working in the same smooth, unhurried nonchalance with which he moved his feet, a slow cruising crawl which he quickened only at carnival" (Lovelace, 1979). Thus, the enthusiasm and energy devoted to carnival is not displayed in everyday life. Trinidadians, especially those of African descent, are often described as a 'happy-go-lucky people' with little commitment to hard work. According to Eriksen (1990) "a common assumption, not least common in the urban working class itself is that Black working-class Trinidadians don't invest themselves in respectable activities such as wage work and family life. Life is too sweet".

In our study the carnival mentality was described as having a "non-stop party mentality", a time to indulge in "bad or immoral activities" and having a "slack and laid back attitude to work" (Table 2, Appendix 2). The invariable negative connotation of carnival mentality in our sample goes against the possibility of subgroup bias or stereotypy. A significant number, 97% of our respondents were aware of the carnival mentality behaviour and 92% identified it as being part of the islands' culture. A significant finding was that the middle social class was more aware of the carnival mentality (p < 0.001). A possible explanation is that members of this group are employed with the Civil Service and will be aware of the established work ethic. A common word of affirmation by mechanics after tuning up cars is "boss, your car idling like a civil servant".

## THE MACHOMAN OR PLAYER PERSONALITY – 'GOD'S GIFT TO WOMEN'

It has been argued that this phenomenon is more Caribbean than Trinidadian. It is unique to the region since it is argued that the Caribbean man or the 'Carib-being man' is polygamous in nature but jealously guards fidelity in his woman. The courtship cycle from introduction to intimate relationship with women is foreshortened in the Caribbean, with an emphasis on sexual conquest rather than a meaningful relationship.

The Trinidadian male, and by extension the Caribbean man, attains social ascendancy and status if he is perceived as 'macho'. Such behaviours of male individuals with multiple partners as "sexually involved but not emotionally involved" and "God's gift to woman" (Table 8, Appendix 2) have been met with exaltation and reinforcement in many national songs such as the Mighty Sparrow's calypso, "The Village Ram" (Roehler, 1975). The playboy personality or 'player' – the term commonly used by teenagers – is a 'woman charmer or sweetman', who is by nature polygamous, but will jealously guard fidelity in his partners. For him, there are no restrictions in making a 'play' on any woman. Contingencies of marital or social status, the feelings of others or moral issues are non-consequential. Within society there are social sanctions that undermine values of honesty, integrity and morality. The young age group of 14–25 years was more convinced that the playboy personality was a part of the culture of Trinidad and Tobago, and more common among Afro-Trinidadians.

## TABANCA – 'LOVE SICKNESS; LOSS OF A LOVE OBJECT'

Eighty-two per cent of the respondents felt that tabanca was part of the Trinidad culture. In Trinidad and Tobago, tabanca, or the loss of a loved one with ruminations of the lost object, has been described as an indigenous conceptualization of depression (Littlewood, 1985). Local researchers have argued that this love-struck behaviour is the feeling one gets when rejected by a partner or love object and is circumscribed in the pathos of culturally-determined confrontational humor known as 'picong' (Maharajh & Hutchinson, 1999). This process allows the individual to work through his feelings of loss and rejection in a cognitive behavioural context of minimization, levity, and social support. Although contemporarily considered to be a 'culture bound syndrome' this behaviour has been locally described as an adjustment disorder. It is culturally recognizable, particularly when the loss is known to one's peers. The individual may experience a temporary decrease in worth, humour, and esteem by way of the satirical and jocular treatment from his or her peers. This in itself is cathartic and leads to resolution. Trinidadians have popularized four stages of love sickness, namely: tabanca – feeling down after the departure of a lover; 'fufooloo' – behaving in a foolish or doltish manner; 'kairkathay' – so dazed, spinning like a top; and 'tirangebanji'– when one gives up and is psychotic or suicidal.

## OBSESSIONAL LATENESS – 'ANYTIME IS TRINIDAD TIME'

In Trinidad and Tobago, there is a pervasive cultural attitude of disrespect or unconcern for time. It is customary for individuals, even in high office, to arrive late for all events without any regard for protocol or punctuality. There is no feeling of shame, since such lateness is culturally perceived as a commitment to duty and dedication to hard work that prevented them from being on time. In addition, this behaviour is reinforced since their late appearance is often announced with adequate excuses of 'circumstances beyond their control' and being late due to the latecomers' 'busy schedule and commitment to hard work'. Due to the looseness of time, "just to show your face" is considered sufficient. Ninety-nine per cent of the sampled population correctly described this behaviour.

Obsessional lateness, or the inability to be on time, is inherent in our population and is well tolerated. In this behaviour, appointments are made and never met, and lateness is culturally accepted. Trinidadian sportsmen in the UK have been disciplined and heavily fined for lateness. In the recent World Trade Center disaster, the *Trinidad Guardian* newspaper carried the following story: "Many Trinidadians and Tobagonians are thanking God, and some because of their place of birth they were either late for work, still making their way to work or took a day off on Tuesday when two hijacked planes hit New York's World Trade Centre, killing an unknown number of people" (Wanser, 2001).

## Summary and Conclusion

It is noteworthy that the cultural behaviours – liming, carnival mentality, playboy personality, tabanca and obsessional lateness – are closely related. These behaviours have as their themes negative characteristics of doing nothing, sexual liaison with its sequaelae, and a lack of respect for time. The last two can be interpreted as subsets of the carnival mentality, all interrelated to the basic instincts of primary process thinking.

From our analysis, Smartman Syndrome, Demon Possession, Spiritual Travel and Middle-age Indian Woman Syndrome were rejected by the respondents as being part of the culture of Trinidad and Tobago. The summative characteristics, for the most part, were multidimensional with many levels of description. The Trinidadian 'smartman' is not unique in his ability to contrive, connive, scheme and outdo other people when compared with other countries. Guyanese and Barbadians are similarly perceived as schemers and 'smartmen' in the Caribbean region. Indo-Trinidadians were more familiar with the Smartman Syndrome. A possible explanation is their heavier involvement in business.

Demonical Possession and Spiritual Travel were not considered to be culture-based behaviours. This may be due to the perception that they are established religious practices ordained by the Christian and Baptist churches respectively. Indo-Trinidadians, however, were more likely to view demon possession as part of the Trinidadian culture while the majority of Afro-Christians attributed it to their religious beliefs. A cross-sectional study indicated that 71% of the total sample believed in the existence of demons and 65% thought that demons could possess people (Maharajh & Parasaram, 1997). It is, however, difficult to separate religion from culture since all religious groups have incorporated religio-magical thinking and exorcism as part of their theological practices and are engaged in faith-healing and the casting out of demons.

Many religious groups in Trinidad and Tobago believe in the concept of spiritual or astral travel. This is an out-of-body experience, induced by sensory deprivation whereby the soul of the pilgrim (mourner) leaves the body and travels to distant lands, meeting new people and becoming exposed to experiences that serve to strengthen one's faith and allow his/her ascendancy within the hierarchy of the church. This practice is not well known locally and commonly performed by followers of the Baptist religion in the mourning ground ceremony. It is not unique to Trinidad (Griffith, 1984). The Middle-age Indian Woman Syndrome is a somatoform disorder of mostly female Indo-Trinidadians who present for treatment with multiple somatic complaints at clinics and hospitals. This was rejected by the respondents, as it was not clearly or consistently defined within one particular dimension. This, in itself, gave statistical credibility to the respondents' responses by incorporating an entity known in the medical circles and testing it within the general population.

The question must be asked as to whether these phenomena are unique to Trinidad and Tobago. The obvious response will be no. However, on more detailed analysis, it will be evident that these are culturally determined behaviours that are specific to a mixed cultural heritage in a geographical region that has a uniqueness of its own. Similar syndromes may be present in other Caribbean countries but their presentations will be coloured by historical, social, economic, political and cultural antecedents with a difference in emphasis. The phenomena may be the same, but the presentations will vary.

Trinidad and Tobago is a socially stratified society with a large middle-class population. The latter being more educated tends to identify and popularize local customs giving them social sanctions. The working class is rarely involved in self-analysis of their behaviour, being too busy making ends meet. The younger age groups are invested in behaviours in which their peer groups are involved, such as liming, playing and tabanca. Ethnicity is not a major determinant of behaviour in the younger age groups, especially in urban areas. Among the over-forty population, there is a tendency for ethnic sub-grouping with particular emphasis, for example alcohol use among Indo-Trinidadians, with increased Tabanca and polygamy among Afro-Trinidadians who are more invested in carnival and liming.

In conclusion, using a 75% response rate, respondents were aware of six of the nine identified behaviours and perceived five of them to be part of the Trinidadian culture. Smartman Syndrome and The Middle-age Indian Woman Syndrome were rejected as cultural phenomena, both with respect to awareness and perception. The religious nature of the people of Trinidad and Tobago and their tolerance and respect for each other strengthened by elements of cultural fusion are plausible explanations for respondents exclusion of religious-related activities as culture based. This would have resulted in the exclusion of Spiritual Travel and Demon Possession. Carnival Mentality, Liming, Obsessional Lateness, Tabanca and the Player Personality were accepted as cultural behaviours in Trinidad and Tobago. The validity of these findings are supported by the triangulation of the results with previous reports and descriptions. In addition, inter-rater reliability (95%) demonstrated no differences in dimensions of behaviours of the people of Trinidad and Tobago.

Cultures are dynamic rather than static and, while the wheel of culture can go around for centuries without notable disturbance (Toner, 2001), cultures can change when the value system of a society changes. Nevertheless, the relics of a culture can still remain even when the culture changes. According to Jones (2001), many cultures see their future in terms of preserving the past. It is important, therefore, that documentation be made of the cultural behaviours of immigrants from both the sending and receiving countries in order to understand their emotional, behavioural, and thinking processes. For many, the old culture remains fixed at the time of migration, despite changes in the country of origin.

## GLOSSARY

**Trinidad** – term used in this study to mean the islands of Trinidad and Tobago

**River lime** – activity of liming that takes place near or on the bank of a river

**After-work lime** – liming that takes place after working hours, usually on Fridays, at the end of the working week

**Duck lime** – liming that involves the cooking and eating of a duck

**Time to free up; Time to get on bad** – chorus from calypsoes urging the population to relax. Sometimes refers to indulgence in alcohol, vulgar and immoral activities without even thinking of the consequences of one's actions

**Anything in a skirt that pass** – refers to an attraction to all female individuals regardless of age, ethnic group or marital status

**Macho** – refers to an individual, usually a male who is domineering, assertive and polygamous. Taken from the advertisement, "Rum is macho".

**Sweetman** – someone who is considered to be very charming and doesn't hesitate to spend money entertaining a woman

**Horn** – refers to the act when the your partner is unfaithful to you in the relationship – infidelity

**Tabantruck** – symptoms of tabanca so severe they cannot figuratively, fit in a car but needs a truck ("taban-truck" as opposed to "taban-car")

**Trini time** – is the term coined by Trinidadians to refer to their own inherent nature of being late to any event

**Just to show your face** – the term used to describe when someone only makes an appearance at an event or occasion.

**Picong** – communication pattern of mild but humorous confrontation with persons

**Something for nothing; Trying to pull a fast one** – refers to when an individual tries to outsmart someone or tries to negotiate an offer where he is the only one gaining

**Bandage for every cut** – having an answer for every question or problem

**Obeah** – refers to an African tradition of sorcery

**Mourning ground** – refers to the place where a follower of the Spiritual Baptist faith goes in order to perform Spiritual travel

**Ketching power** – refers to acting in a state similar as if one were possessed by a spirit or demon (shaking and trembling of body, eyes rolling etc.)

**Playing dead to catch corbeaux alive** – corbeaux are vultures that feed on dead carcasses. 'The smartman' will pretend to be stupid to gain an advantage.

# Appendix 1

**Semi-structured Interview for Identifying Cultural Behaviour Patterns of Trinidad and Tobago**

*Introduction*: We are conducting a survey on people's behaviour in Trinidad and Tobago and we are requesting your participation in answering a few questions.

*Demograhpics*
1. Age _____
2. Sex:            Male [1]        Female [2]
3. Ethnic Group:   African [1]     Indian [2]    Mixed [3]    Other [4]
4. Marital Status: Single [1]      Common-Law [2]    Married [3]
                   Separated [4]   Divorced [5]
5. Education Level: Primary [1]    Secondary [2]   Tertiary [3]
6. Occupation & Monthly Income _____
7. Social Class    Lower [1]       Middle [2]      Upper [3]

*Culture*
8. What do you understand by the word behaviour?
9. Does behaviour include culture – lifestyle, food, music etc. of people?
10. If yes, to question 9, what are the cultural practices (handed down behaviour) that you are aware of in this country?
11. Are there any other social patterns i.e. how people generally behave that are unique to our people?
12. If hitherto not mentioned, do you consider religious or spiritual beliefs or practices as part of behaviour or culture?
    If yes, can you describe them?
    If no, how would you interpret these religious practices?
13. Are your descriptions only found in:
    (a) Trinidad and Tobago
    (b) Other regions
    (c) Don't know.
    ***Thank You.***

# Appendix 2

*Table 1: Characteristics of Liming*

| Characteristics | % |
|---|---|
| 1. Major cultural activity/Scheduled or Non-scheduled episode where a group of people take time off to "hang out"/be idle/get together/do nothing | 96 |
| 2. Activity geared towards stress relief | 3 |
| 3. Mentality of liming causes laid back attitude/ poor work ethic/carnival mentality | 0.5 |
| 4. Turn any place into a liming spot | 0.5 |

*Table 2: Characteristics of Carnival Mentality*

| Characteristics | % |
|---|---|
| 1. Non-stop party mentality/ continuous fun in the sun "extreme liming" | 51.4 |
| 2. Take part in every carnival activity or event/time to break away and get on bad, immoral vulgar activities/ time to free up | 21.0 |
| 3. Attitude to work very laid back, slack/don't give a damn | 19.0 |
| 4. Mindlessness, not thinking of consequences/ indulging in alcohol, promiscuity | 3.0 |
| 5. Time to free up | 3.2 |
| 6. When you hear soca, nothing could stop you from dancing | 0.9 |
| 7. Having attributes of carnival e.g. cricket or football match | 0.9 |
| 8. Too much parties in calendar | 0.5 |

_Table 3: Characteristics of Playboy Personality_

| Characteristics | % |
|---|---|
| 1. Trini men with multiple girlfriends who just crave attention, sexual interests/sexually involved but not emotionally involved | 74.5 |
| 2. One who thinks he is God's gift to women and plays the hearts of many women/charmer/sweetman/player/ have to have "anything in a skirt that pass" | 23.5 |
| 3. Commits adultery or cheats on partner | 0.8 |
| 4. Player attitude passed on by adults | 0.4 |
| 5. Adopted from a different culture | 0.4 |
| 6. Guy says he is in love but he is lying | 0.4 |

_Table 4: Characteristics of Tabanca_

| Characteristics | % |
|---|---|
| 1. Love sickness; person who gets dumped goes through a state of depression and withdrawal symptoms: can't eat, sleep/ adjustment disorder of losing a loved one/ if symptoms severe known as 'tabantruck' | 71.2 |
| 2. Being in love, fall head over heels with someone, daydreaming etc. | 17.9 |
| 3. Mental anguish of getting 'horn' | 6.1 |
| 4. Girlfriend/boyfriend worries/ 'Love Jones' | 3.1 |
| 5. Don't eat, don't sleep | 1.3 |
| 6. When a male and female think they should be together | 0.4 |

*Table 5: Characteristics of Obsessional Lateness*

| Characteristics | % |
|---|---|
| 1. Reaching late for all events, may even reach late for own funeral/No regard for punctuality/Fashionably late, "just to show your face"/Operating on "Trini time" | 99 |
| 2. Watching too much T.V. at night | 1 |

*Table 6: Characteristics of Smartman Syndrome*

| Characteristics | % |
|---|---|
| 1. The ability to outsmart or "hoodwink" somebody, usually through dishonest means/conmen/trying to get "something for nothing" or "trying to pull a fast one" | 65 |
| 2. Always a smart retort/"bandage for every cut" | 19 |
| 3. People who act smart | 5 |
| 4. Getting things for little or no value | 4 |
| 5. Player who uses many women/fooling them | 3 |
| 6. Bully | 2 |
| 7. Quiet, not talking much | 1 |
| 8. Playing very stupid – "playing dead to catch corbeaux alive" | 1 |

_Table 7: Characteristics of Demon Possession_

| Characteristics | % |
| --- | --- |
| 1. When spirits/demon take over body and person unaware of what is happening | 55.5 |
| 2. Acting crazy/acting similar to if a demon possessed a person/strange unexplainable behaviour | 29.4 |
| 3. Obeah/evil/witchcraft | 11.3 |
| 4. Folklore and myths as part of culture | 1.7 |
| 5. Manifestation of abnormal behaviour, usually schizophrenia | 0.8 |
| 6. Anxiety attack | 0.8 |
| 7. Talks constantly/overly energetic and frisky | 0.4 |

_Table 8: Characteristics of Spiritual Travel_

| Characteristics | % |
| --- | --- |
| 1. The ability to travel out of the body/ transcendental travel on mourning ground/practice of Spiritual Baptists. | 65.0 |
| 2. Religious sect involved in practices like that/"ketching power" and loud clapping and singing | 17.2 |
| 3. Going through an episode that brings you closer to God/ holy trans evoked while praying | 8.0 |
| 4. Obeah/Voodoo | 4.3 |
| 5. After baptism, given information to practice religion/ behaviour when speaking the word of God | 3.1 |
| 6. Stage close to death and spirit gradually leaving body | 0.6 |
| 7. Visions, dreams, or dazed while in that state | 1.8 |

*Table 9: Characteristics of Middle Age Indian Woman Syndrome*

| Characteristics | % |
| --- | --- |
| 1. Extremely obsessive about family, stays at home and neglects physical appearance | 30 |
| 2. Types of behaviour associated with youthful past | 23 |
| 3. Behaving like an Indian woman at middle age | 10 |
| 4. Fat around the waist and complaining of joints | 10 |
| 5. Individual attracted to middle-age Indian women | 10 |
| 6. Looking old and tired but they are young | 7 |
| 7. Forever quarrelling with children and husband | 3.3 |
| 8. Extra marital affairs between 30-40 | 3.3 |
| 9. Menopause | 3.3 |

## REFERENCES

American Psychiatric Association (2000). *Diagnostic and statistical manual of mental disorders IV,TR.* Washington DC: American Psychiatric Association.

Burton-Bradley, B. G. (1968). The Amok Syndrome in Papua and New Guinea. *Medical Journal of Australia,* 1: 252-256.

Burton-Bradley, B.G. (1975). *Stone age crisis: A psychiatric appraisal.* Nashville: Vanderbilt University Press.

Bhugra, D., Hilwig, M., Hossein, B. et al. (1996). Incidence rate and one year follow up of first contact schizophrenia in Trinidad. *British Journal of Psychiatry,* 169: 587-592.

Central Statistical Office (1992). *Statistical Pocket Digest, Republic of Trinidad and Tobago.* Port of Spain, Trinidad: Office of the Prime Minister.

Dein, S. (1997). Mental health in a multiethnic society. *British Medical Journal,* 106: 473-477

Durkheim, E. (1951). *Suicide: A study in sociology.* (trans. Spaulding, J.A. and Simpson, G.), Glencoe, III: Free Press.

Eriksen, T. H. (1990). Liming in Trinidad: The art of doing nothing. *Folk,* Vol. 32.

Griffith, E. E. H., & Mahy, G. E. (1984). Psychological benefits of Spiritual Baptist "Mourning". *American Journal of Psychiatry,* 141: 769-73.

Jilek, W. G. (1986). Epidemics of "genital shrinking" (koro). _Curare. (Heidelberg)_ 9: 269-282.

———. (2000). Culturally related syndromes. In M. G. Gelder, J. J. Lopez-Ibor, & N. Andreasen (Eds.), _New Oxford Textbook of Psychiatry. Vol. 1._ Oxford: Oxford University Press, 1061-1066.

Jilek, W. G., & Jilek-Aall, L. (1977). A koro epidemic in Thailand. _Transcultural Psychiatric Research Review,_ 14: 57-59.

———. (2000). Kulturspezifische psychische storungen. In H. Hemlchen, F. Henn, H. Lauter, & N. Sartorius (Eds.), _Psychiatrie der Gegenwart. Vol. 3: Psychiatrie spezieller Lebenssituationen._ Berlin-Heidelberg: Springer.

Jones, D. (2001). Learning culture. Presented at 2001 AERC Conference Proceedings.

Kiev, A. (1972). _Transcultural psychiatry._ New York: The Free Press.

Kimura, B. (1995). _Zwischen Mensch and Mensch: Strakuren japanischer Subjaktivitat._ Darmstadt: Wissenschaftliche Buchgesellschaft.

Kirmayer, L. J. (1991). The place of culture in psychiatric nosology: taijin kyofusho and DSM-III-R. _Journal of Nervous and Mental Disease,_ 179: 19-28.

Kraeplin, E. (1909). _Psychiatrie. 8te Auflage,_ Leipzig: Barth.

Kurtz, N. (1999). _Statistical analysis for the social sciences._ Massachusetts: Allyn and Bacon.

Lee, S. H., Shin, Y. C., & Oh, K. S. (1994). A clinical study of social phobia for 10 years. _Journal of the Korean Neuropsychiatric Association,_ 33: 305-312.

Lewis, L. F. E. (1973). _Admission of schizophrenic patients at St Anns Hospital._ Port of Spain, Trinidad: Archives St. Anns Hospital.

Littlewood, R. (1985). An indigenous conceptualization of reactive depression in Trinidad. _Psychological Medicine,_ 15: 275-281.

Liverpool, H. (1990). _Culture and education. Carnival in Trinidad and Tobago – Implications for education in secondary schools._ London: Karia Press.

Lovelace, E. (1979). _The dragon can't dance._ London: Andre Deutsxh.

Maharajh, H. D., & Hutchinson, G. (1999). Tabanca in Trinidad and Tobago – myth, mirth or mood disorder. _Caribbean Medical Journal,_ 61, 1: 21-24.

Maharajh, H. D., & Parasram, R. (1997). Mental illness – Demons or Dopamine. _West Indian Medical Journal, Suppl._ 46: 17.

Maharajh, H. D., Clarke, T. D., & Hutchinson, G. (1989). Transcultural psychiatry. (Corres.) _Psychiatric Bulletin,_ 10: 574-575.

Martin, D. (2000). _Doing psychology experiments. 5th Edition._ Belmont, CA: Wadsworth, Thompson Learning.

Meltzer, H., Gill, B., & Petticrew, M. (1995). _The prevalence of psychiatric morbidity among adults aged 16-64 living in private households in Great Britain._ OPCS Surveys of Psychiatric Morbidity in Great Britain Report No. 1. London: HMSO.

Murphy, H. B. M. (1973). History and the striking evolution of syndromes: The striking case of Latah and Amok. In M. Hammer, K. Salzinger, & S. Sutton (Eds.), *Psychopathology – Contributions from the Biological, Behavioural and Social Sciences*. New York: Wiley, pp. 33-35.

Panday, B. (2000). *Speeches made by the political leader – The expansion on the LNG operations*. Trinidad and Tobago:The United National Congress.

Paris, J. (1992). Dhat: The semen loss anxiety syndrome. *Transcultural Psychiatry Research Review*, 29: 109-118.

Pfeiffer, W. M. (1994). *Transkulturelle Psychiatrie, 2nd rev. edn*. Stuttgart, New York: Thieme.

Prince, R. (1960). The "Brain-Fag" syndrome in Nigerian students. *Journal of Mental Science*, 106: 559-570.

Prince, R. (1985). The concept of culture-bound syndromes: Anorexia nervosa and Brain Fag. *Social Science and Medicine*, 21:197-203.

Rohlehr, G. (1975). Sparrow as poet. In M. Anthony & A. Carr (Eds.), *David Frost introduces Trinidad & Tobago*. London: André Deutsch.

Simons, R. (1996). *Boo! Culture, experience and the startle reflex*. Oxford, New York: Oxford University Press.

Toner, B. (2001). An Ethic for the Third Millennium. Working Notes. Dublin, Ireland: Jesuit Centre for Faith and Justice.

Tseng, W-S., Mo, K. M., Hsu, J., Li, L. S., Ou, L-W., Chen, G-Q., & Jiang, D-W. (1988). A sociocultural study of Koro epidemics in Guangdong, China. *American Journal of Psychiatry*, 145: 1538-1543.

Van Wulfften Palthe, P.M. (1991). Amok. *Nederlandsch Tijschrifl voor Geneeskunde*, 77: 983-991.

Voss, G. (1915). Die Aetiologie der Psychosen. In G. Aschaffenburg, (Ed.), *Handbuch der Psychiatrie*. Leipzig: Deuticke.

Wanser, D. (2001). "Mad Scramble for Safety". *Trinidad Guardian*, September 14: 15.

Westermeyer, J. (1972). A comparison of Amok and other homicide in Laos. *American Journal of Psychiatry*, 129: 703-709.

Westermeyer, J. (1973). On the epidemicity of Amok violence. *Archives of General Psychiatry*, 28: 873-876.

Winzeler, R. L. (1995). *Latah in Southeast Asia: The ethnography and history of a culture bound syndrome*. New York: Cambridge University Press.

Yap, P. M. (1965). Koro – A culture-bound depersonalization syndrome. *British Journal of Psychiatry*, 3: 43-50.

# PART II

## APPLICATIONS AND INTERACTIONS OF PSYCHOLOGY IN EVERYDAY LIFE

*Edited by*

Brigitte K. Matthies

# 7 Developmental Psychology in Caribbean Infants and Pre-schoolers

*Maureen Samms-Vaughan*

## Introduction

Developmental psychology is the scientific study of the changes experienced by an individual as he or she progresses through the human life cycle, from conception to old age and death. This chapter, which is confined to infants and pre-schoolers, begins by describing the domains and stages of development through which all children progress. There is as yet no available information to suggest that Caribbean children's sequence and stages of development or the underlying developmental theories are any different from children from other regions of the world. Theories of development are not covered in detail in this chapter and readers are directed to general texts on child development for this information (e.g. Berk, 2006; Santrock, 2007).

As development is recognized as a combination of nature (genes) and nurture (environment), the unique culture and way of life of Caribbean people can be expected to exert its influence on our young children. This chapter, therefore, describes the environment in which young Caribbean children grow and develop, from the earliest stages, and highlights what we know of how this environment impacts our young children's development.

## Domains of Development

Development is typically considered in three main domains, described below.

*Physical development* includes changes in body size (height, weight) and body proportions, brain development (brain growth and maturation), development of the motor system, pubertal changes and physical health.

*Language and cognitive development* includes advancing skills in a variety of areas such as perception; information processing; reasoning and intellect; memory and attention; language and communication.

*Social and emotional development* includes growth in the ability to understand and respond to ones' own feelings and the feelings of others, interpersonal skills and friendships and moral reasoning.

A fourth domain, sensory development, encompassing hearing and vision, is often added. Speech and language development is sometimes included within the domain of sensory development, with cognitive development as a separate domain.

Despite the domain classification, it is recognized that human development does not take place in a compartmentalized way but is a comprehensive, integrated, holistic process with all aspects of development taking place simultaneously in all domains, albeit at different rates. Additionally, the developmental processes in each domain impact on and are impacted on by the processes in other domains.

## Stages of Development

In addition to domains, the development process is divided into a number of stages across the life cycle: the prenatal period; infancy, the toddler years and the pre-school years; middle childhood; adolescence; young adulthood; middle age; old age and death. This chapter confines itself to the developmental psychology of Caribbean infants and pre-schoolers, and, therefore, considers only the stages prior to middle childhood as indicated below.

- Prenatal Period     Conception to birth
- Infancy     Birth to the first year of life

- Toddler Years        One to two years

- Pre-School Years     Three to five years

It is important to note that the period from birth to six years was previously known as the early childhood period. However, the current internationally accepted definition of the early childhood period is the period from birth to eight years (Puckett & Black, 2004). This broader definition of the early childhood period, not only encompasses infancy, the toddler years and the pre-school period, but also includes the early primary years, typically the first and second grades of Caribbean primary schools.

# The Pre-Natal Period

## PHASES OF DEVELOPMENT

The prenatal period has three phases: the germinal phase from conception to two weeks, the embryonic phase from two weeks to two months and the foetal phase from two months to birth. In practical terms, however, parents are more familiar with the trimesters of birth, in which the nine-month pregnancy period is divided into three month segments.

### Genetic Beginnings: Genes and Chromosomes

The human being is made up of trillions of cells. Each cell contains a nucleus, within which are rod-like structures known as chromosomes which contain genetic information. The number of chromosomes is fixed for each species and is 46 in humans. Chromosomes occur in matching pairs, one of each pair provided by the mother and the other by the father. In humans, there are twenty-two pairs called autosomes. Autosome pairs are similar in size, shape and the nature of the genetic information being carried. The 23rd pair, the human sex chromosomes, is different from each other, and carry only 23 chromosomes each. The XX sex chromosome identifies the female of the specie and the XY the male.

Chromosomes are made up of the chemical, deoxyribonucleic acid (DNA), a complex double helix molecule that looks like a twisted ladder. The ladder is made up of four chemical bases Adenine (A), Thymine (T), Guanine (G) and Cytosine (C). The chemicals pair up in specific ways across the rungs of the ladder, A pairs with T and C pairs with G. However, bases may occur with any sequence along the sides of the ladder. Segments of chromosomes are known as genes and these are considered to be the basic units of heredity. Genes may have from 2,000 to 2,000,000 base pairs. Genes transmit their information by coding for the making of a wide variety of proteins in the cytoplasm of the cell. Proteins, in turn, code for the production of enzymes which influence cell growth, development and function (Roca, Serrano, & Tenllado, 1995).

### The Germinal Phase

Conception marks the commencement of the development of a human being and the commencement of the germinal phase. Conception occurs when a single-celled organism, the zygote, is formed from the union of the gametes or sex cells, a sperm from the male and an egg from the female, during the process known as fertilization. Gametes are formed through a cell division process known as meiosis, which results in 23 chromosomes, half the number normally present in body cells, in each gamete. Fusion of the two gametes results in a cell with 46 chromosomes.

A few days after fertilization, the zygote undergoes rapid cell division to form a multi-celled mass called a blastocyst, while travelling along the mother's fallopian tube to the uterus. On about the seventh day, the blastocyst implants itself in the wall of the uterus. Approximately 80% of blastocysts are rejected at this time. Successful implantation is followed by formation of the placenta, a temporary structure which allows nutrients and oxygen to reach the foetus from the mother's blood and also allows waste matter to be passed from the developing human being into the mother's blood stream for excretion. The placenta is connected to the embryo by the umbilical cord. Occasionally, the zygote splits into two identical cells, producing monozygotic (identical) twins. Twins can also be formed when two ova are fertilized by two different sperm, producing dizygotic (fraternal) twins.

### The Embryonic Phase

During the embryonic phase, the cells become specialized and vital organs and systems begin to be formed. The developing organism is now known as an embryo. By the end of this phase, the embryo has taken on human form, though it is only two to three centimetres long. The embryonic phase is particularly important as any interference with the developmental processes at this time can have multiple and devastating effects. As a result, it is during this period that most miscarriages and structural birth defects occur.

## The Foetal Phase

In the foetal phase, there is growth and maturation of the newly formed organ systems. In the third month, the brain and the nervous and muscular systems are so developed that movement of limbs occurs. The foetus also begins breathing movements, moving fluid in and out of the lung, a necessary part of lung development. By the end of the third month, the genitalia can be identified. By the end of the second trimester, almost all the brain cells, called neurons, are in place. The development of the brain and its sensory organs is advanced enough at this stage to be associated with responsive behaviours in the foetus. For example, the foetus will shield itself from light as will a baby born at this stage. During the third trimester, between 22 and 26 weeks gestation, the foetus reaches viability, the stage at which it is likely to survive if born. Death rates are still quite high at this gestation period, particularly because the supporting brain structures are not well developed and brain haemorrhage sometimes occurs, the lungs are not mature enough to breathe on their own and mechanical ventilation is often necessary. In addition, the immune system is immature, resulting in susceptibility to infection. During the third trimester as organ development continues, the foetus becomes covered with a cheesy substance called vernix, and with tiny hairs called lanugo. Together, these protect the foetal skin from chafing due to prolonged contact with the amniotic fluid.

In the third trimester, there is rapid physical growth, with some five pounds of weight added. A layer of fat develops under the skin to provide insulation. Antibodies are passed from the mother to the foetus to offer protection from infection as the newborn infant still has an immature immune system. The cerebral cortex develops rapidly and this is associated with a change in foetal behaviour. Neuronal organization results in cycles of movement, sleep/wake activity and heart rate activity (DiPietro et al., 1996). The foetus assumes the head down position in this trimester in preparation for the birth process.

## PATTERNS OF INHERITANCE

The genetic composition of an organism is called the genotype. This sets limits within which variations can occur and is the reason individuals of the same species are recognisably similar.

The genotype is largely inherited from parent organisms, but occasionally, spontaneous changes in genotype, known as mutations, can occur. The observable characteristics of each individual are determined by the interaction between the genotype and the environment, and are called the phenotype. Changes in phenotype are known as modifications, and are not inherited. An example would be differences in a person's body size (e.g. height) or shape based on the content of one's diet.

Genes, the basic units of heredity, are inherited in four main ways: dominant/recessive inheritance, co-dominance, sex-linked inheritance, and polygenic inheritance. Each pair of genes, one from the mother and one from the father, coding for the same characteristic, is called an allele.

### Dominant/Recessive Inheritance

This occurs in conditions that are only influenced by one pair of genes and is best explained using an example. Extra digits, particularly fingers, are among the most common congenital problems identified at birth in Caribbean children. Indeed, some Caribbean fathers use extra digits as proof of paternity. The gene for extra digits is dominant; the gene for five digits is recessive. Depending on the contributions from each parent, a child can have alleles consisting of two dominant genes, two recessive genes or a combination of a dominant and a recessive gene. When both genes are similar, whether dominant or recessive, the child is said to be homozygous and will manifest the genes present. When the inherited genes are different (that is, one is recessive and one is dominant), the child is heterozygous. In the heterozygous state, the dominant gene is manifested. A child born with extra digits can, therefore, be homozygous for the dominant gene or heterozygous. Are our Caribbean fathers correct? Not quite! The father who has an extra digit may be homozygous or heterozygous. If he is heterozygous, though possessing a dominant gene, he may have passed on the recessive gene to his child. If the mother also passes on a normal recessive gene, their child will actually have five digits.

Many physical features such as dimples, hair colour and pigment, are due to dominant alleles, while most life-threatening conditions are inherited through homozygous recessive inheritance, thereby making them much rarer conditions. Since heterozygous persons can pass on the recessive trait to their child, they are called carriers.

## Codominance

Codominance occurs when both genes exert an influence on the condition. In some situations, for example blood groups, both genes have equal influence. This allows for persons to have not only blood groups A (genotype AO), B (genotype BO), or O (genotype OO) but also blood group AB.

## Sex-linked Inheritance

This is determined by genes located on the sex chromosomes, mainly on the X chromosome. As females have two X chromosomes, they can be homozygous or heterozygous. Males, with only one X chromosome are hemizygous for any gene on the X chromosome. X-linked disorders can be dominant or recessive.

In X-linked recessive inheritance, males are typically affected, and females are either normal or have mild manifestations. Affected males pass the abnormal gene on to all their daughters (who become carriers) but their sons will not be affected, as they pass on a Y chromosome to their sons.

Females play an important role in this type of inheritance, as the sons of females who carry an abnormal X gene have a 50% chance of getting the abnormal gene and daughters have a 50% chance of becoming a carrier of the abnormal gene. Common examples include haemophilia and colour blindness.

In X-linked dominant inheritance, conditions are twice as common in females as they have two X chromosomes. Offspring of affected females have a 50% chance of inheriting the condition, regardless of gender. All daughters of affected males will inherit the condition, but no sons will.

X-linked dominant disorders are rare; some are lethal in males and in homozygous females, resulting in an increased incidence of spontaneous abortion and miscarriages in women so affected. A common example is Vitamin D resistant rickets.

**Polygenic or Multifactorial Inheritance**

The inheritance of many common characteristics and some disorders may be the result of multiple genes, each with differing effects. Some characteristics and disorders may also be influenced by the environment. When the combination of predisposing genes from both parents and environmental factors exceed the threshold, the characteristic or disorder is expressed. Common examples include skin colour, diabetes or autism.

# Developmental Disorders of the Pre-natal Period

## FERTILITY

The fertility rate (i.e. the average number of children born to a woman over her lifetime) of Caribbean countries and territories ranges from 1.5 – 4.4,with only three countries (Barbados, Trinidad and Tobago and Antigua and Barbuda) reporting rates lower than replacement levels i.e. less than 2.0. (cited in Regional Report on the Achievement of the Millennium Development Goals in the Caribbean Community, UNDP, 2004). Fertility is important to adults in the Caribbean; children are valued and desired and a home is considered 'empty' in their absence (Barrow, 2002). Indeed, women who are childless are often teased. Contraception is not popular within the region, and an unwed mother is seen as having provided 'proof of fertility' before marriage. The infertility rate for Jamaican couples is 10-15%, with the majority being due to male infertility of unknown cause (personal communication, Fertility Management Unit, UWI, Jamaica). When women are infertile, the cause is usually medical in origin from polycystic ovarian syndrome, endometriosis, or the effects of sexually transmitted diseases.

The value placed on children has led to the development of Assisted Reproductive Technology in three Caribbean nations, Barbados, Jamaica and Trinidad and Tobago. Jamaica had 75 technologically assisted births up to early 2007 and Trinidad and Tobago had over 150 such births. Adoption of children, defined as the legal act of permanently placing a child with a parent or parents other than the birth parent, is also an option for infertile couples. In developed countries, the number of children available for adoption has fallen due to low fertility rates, legalisation of abortion and increased acceptance of the single-parent family. The majority of adoptions in these nations are now international adoptions.

There is little information available on adoption in the Caribbean region. In Jamaica, the majority of adoptions are family adoptions, from known relatives (personal communication, Child Development Agency). However, much fostering of children occurs without legalized status, utilising the extended family.

## CHROMOSOMAL AND GENETIC DISORDERS

Chromosomal and genetic disorders may affect either the autosomes or the sex chromosomes.

### Chromosomal Disorders

The most common chromosomal disorders are abnormalities of number or structure. Numerical abnormalities are due to unequal division (non-disjunction) of cells and result in one set of autosomes having an additional chromosome (trisomies) or only a single chromosome (monosomy). Structural abnormalities are due to breaks and random connections to other chromosomes, resulting in deletions of parts of some chromosomes; translocation of parts of one chromosome to another, or inversion, where there is a double break in the chromosome and the detached section re-attaches in an inverse manner. Another type of chromosomal abnormality is mosaicism, describing the presence of two or more different chromosome constitutions in different cells in the same individual. For example, some cells may have 47 chromosomes and others 46.

In general, autosomal abnormalities are more severe than sex chromosome and numerical abnormalities, where whole chromosomes are affected. They are also more severe than structural abnormalities, where only a part of a chromosome is affected. Chromosomal abnormalities typically result in dysmorphic features (unusual facial and other features), malformations of organs and mental impairment.

The commonest chromosomal abnormality is Down syndrome. In Down syndrome, chromosome 21 is affected, either by the presence of an additional chromosome (Trisomy 21), or as a structural abnormality (translocation or mosaicism). Down syndrome occurs in one in every 600 births, with a greater incidence among children of mothers over the age of 35 years. Children have facial features including a small and flattened head (bracycephaly), small posteriorly rotated ears, extra skin folds by the eyes (epicanthic folds), and a flattened nasal bridge. The most significant features of the condition are the presence of congenital heart disease, affecting up to half of the children, and mild to moderate mental impairment in the majority of cases. A few children with this condition have severe mental impairment (Rondal & Perera, 2006).

## Genetic Disorders

The commonest genetic disorder in the Caribbean, affecting a single gene, is sickle cell disease. The abnormal gene affects the blood protein haemoglobin; and normal adult haemoglobin (HbA, genotype AA) is replaced by the abnormal sickle Haemoglobin (HbS). Under conditions of oxygen deprivation, HbS units stick together and result in a change in shape of the red blood cells, from their normal round and flat shape to that of the shape of a sickle. Blood vessels become clogged by the sickled cells, resulting in severe pain, due to a lack of oxygen to tissues.

The sickle cell gene is present in 7% of the population in Barbados, 10% of the population in Jamaica and many Caribbean countries, and 13-14% in St. Lucia and Dominica (Sickle Cell Trust Publication, Sickle Cell Disease in the Caribbean). The gene is inherited in an autosomal recessive manner, resulting in homozygous and heterozygous (HbAS or sickle cell trait) forms. Sickle cell disease occurs when the sickle gene is present with another abnormal haemoglobin, e.g. Hb SS disease (homozygous sickle cell disease), HbSC disease or HbS-beta thallasemia disease.

In the heterozygous condition (sickle cell trait), some symptoms, though considerably milder, are expressed under extreme physiological conditions such as mountain climbing, where oxygen level is reduced as a result of high altitude.

The diagnosis is typically made in the first few years of life, but there are increasing efforts being made in the Caribbean towards antenatal diagnosis and newborn screening. Children with the most severe forms of sickle cell disease suffer medical complications of anaemia, jaundice, painful episodes (crises), acute chest syndrome (pain and infection), serious infections and a shut-down of the bone marrow (aplastic crisis). The affected children are often shorter than their peers (Thomas, Singhal, Hemmings-Kelly & Serjeant, 2000), suffer the mental health problems associated with a chronic illness, and may have mild intellectual impairment. Intellectual impairment in older children, ages 15-17 years, with the disorder is not associated with parental educational levels nor with school attendance, but is strongly associated with height, suggesting that early nutritional impairment may be a factor (Knight, Singhal, Thomas, & Serjeant, 1995). Family members are also affected, with psychological distress among younger siblings of affected children reported (Foster-Williams, Hambleton, Hilton, & Serjeant, 2000). Survival beyond the age of 30 years is common in the Caribbean and many persons live beyond 50 to 60 years.

## MATERNAL HEALTH AND WELL BEING

Maternal health and well being are intricately linked to the health and well being of young Caribbean children. In the majority of Caribbean countries, more than 90% of women attend antenatal facilities at least four times ,and more than 95% of births are attended by skilled health personnel (WHO, 2005). The lowest rates in the region occur in Haiti, with 42% of women attending antenatal facilities and 24% having births attended by skilled personnel.

### Maternal Illness

Maternal illnesses during pregnancy, which are common in the Caribbean population and which impact on the growth and development of the foetus, include hypertension, diabetes and sickle cell disease. Growth and maturity effects of these conditions commonly include prematurity, low birth weight and growth retardation (Winn & Hobbins, 2000). Uncontrolled maternal diabetes may result in a large infant leading to a difficult delivery, with the potential for physical injury, including brain injury (Winn & Hobbins, 2000). Though not an illness, another factor impacting on foetal growth and development is young maternal age. The Caribbean region reports a rate of 63 births per 1,000 women aged 15-19 years, with the Dominican Republic (89/1,000) and Jamaica (74/1,000) having the highest rates of the six countries documented (UNFPA, 2006). Young maternal age in Jamaican mothers has been associated with lower birth weight infants (Thame, Wilks, Matadial, & Forrester, 1999) and the consequent developmental problems can be anticipated.

**Maternal Lifestyle**

Caribbean women are generally well nourished and primary under-nutrition causing growth and developmental disorders is uncommon. There is little information on the use of drugs in pregnancy in Caribbean women and their impact on foetal growth and development. During the 1986 island-wide Jamaican Perinatal Mortality and Morbidity Study, the prevalence of drug use in mothers was as follows: cigarette smoking (7%), marijuana smoking (2.1%), and alcohol consumption (16.4%) (Samms-Vaughan, 1993). Despite its low prevalence, tobacco smoking was a significant independent risk factor for low birth weight and growth retardation, but not preterm birth on multivariate analysis (Samms-Vaughan, 1993). In this study, alcohol consumption and marijuana use did not affect foetal growth and development.

Anecdotal reports of the prevalence of foetal alcoholic syndrome in Caribbean countries, such as the Bahamas and Belize, suggest that alcohol use among pregnant mothers may be higher in some Caribbean countries. Foetal alcoholic syndrome is a direct result of the impact of alcohol on the developing foetus, primarily affecting growth, facial development and central nervous system development (Soby, 2006). Affected children are of small size, have small heads with narrow eye openings (palpebral fissures) and a smooth area between the nose and upper lip (smooth philtrum). Neuro-developmental effects include developmental delay and mental retardation, learning disorders, poor memory, poor coordination, hyperactivity, impulsivity, sleeping and feeding disorders. Less severely affected children may have only cognitive and behaviour disorders affecting memory, reasoning, impulsivity and attention, known as Alcohol-related Neuro-developmental Disorder (ARND). In the most severe cases, still birth or foetal death occurs (Soby, 2006).

**Maternal Death**

As is the case elsewhere, maternal death impacts significantly on the young Caribbean child. The maternal mortality ratio, the number of maternal deaths per 100,000 population, is often an inaccurate statistic in countries with small populations, partly because maternal death is a relatively rare occurrence, but also because of inadequate registration and reporting of cause of death. Methods to estimate the maternal mortality ratio have been developed and used in the Caribbean. The majority of countries have maternal mortality ratios of between 100 and 200 per 100,000. Haiti has a maternal mortality ratio of just below 700. Comparatively speaking, maternal mortality is the most elevated of all health statistics in the region, and the one that has been most resistant to reduction (UNDP, 2004).

The common causes of maternal death in the region are the hypertensive disorders of pregnancy and bleeding after delivery (postpartum haemorrhage). Bleeding after delivery is most common in women who have had a large number of pregnancies, and many of whom choose to have their deliveries at home. Since the late 1990s, some countries with continuous maternal mortality surveillance, such as Jamaica, have reported increasing maternal deaths associated with the HIV/AIDS epidemic (UNDP, 2004). The rate of HIV/AIDS among adults 15-49 years in the region is 1.2%, with wide variation from a low of 1.2% in Jamaica to a high of 5.6% in Haiti (UNAIDS, 2004). The region has the second highest HIV/AIDS rates in the world, behind sub-Saharan Africa, and so the epidemic is having a significant impact on the lives of young children in the Caribbean region. Haiti is estimated to have some 280,000 AIDS orphans and Jamaica, Guyana and Trinidad some 5,100, 4,200 and 3,600, respectively (UNAIDS, 2004). Regional efforts to reduce the impact and transmission of HIV/AIDS from mother to child include voluntary screening in pregnancy and the provision of free anti-retroviral drugs in pregnancy and follow-up of mothers, spouses and children together with treatment as necessary.

## Brain Development in the Early Years

The rapid brain growth in the first few years of life is testament to the tremendous brain development that occurs during this period. At birth, the brain has some 100 billion nerve cells (neurons) that are connected by approximately 50 trillion very thin, web-like connections. The connections present at birth are determined by the genes inherited from parents, which code for the basic functions of life, such as breathing and maintaining the heart and circulatory system. Within the first few months of life, the number of connections increases by more than 20 times to over 1,000 trillion. After the increase, some connections slowly die away. Scientists have determined that the existing genes are unable to account for the rapid increase in connections and that a baby's experiences with the environment play a large role in determining how connections are made. Based on the 'use it or lose it' principle, those connections that are frequently used are strengthened and those that are not stimulated die away (McClelland & Siegler, 2001).

Additionally, there are 'critical periods' for development, during which the brain must receive appropriate stimulation for specific aspects of development. For vision and emotional control, the main critical period is the first two years of life, with waning of this period occurring gradually from two years and ending completely by five years. If the brain is not exposed to visual stimuli during this period, the child will never have perfect (20:20) vision. Similarly, if a child is not exposed to appropriate emotional responses, their socio-emotional development will be impaired. For example, children who grew up in orphanages, where they were unable to develop appropriate emotional bonds, continue to have challenges with attachment, despite being adopted from as early as three years. Language development has its critical period from 18 months to four years, with waning complete by seven years. For understanding of symbols – the basics of reading and mathematics – the critical period is from 18 months to three years, with a waning period up to five years. The early childhood period is, therefore, recognized as an important period of life, setting the stage for all aspects of a child's future development.

Brain development is commonly monitored using its external expressions of developmental milestones. Some important milestones are shown in the Appendix to this chapter. Ethnic and/or cultural differences in attainment of milestones have been reported. For example, advanced motor development has been identified in children of African origin and specifically in Caribbean children since the 1970s (Grantham-McGregor & Back, 1971). The persistence of advanced motor development over time has been shown by a more recent study, in which the mean age of walking independently for Jamaican children is 10 months, and some 90% of children walk by one year (Samms-Vaughan, 2005). When a child shows a marked delay in meeting common developmental milestones, concerns of possible mental retardation, learning disorders, motor skills or communication disorders or more pervasive developmental disorders (e.g. autism) might be raised (American Psychiatric Association, 2000).

# The Infant, Toddler and Pre-school Years: Physical Growth and Development

Healthy children generally follow a pathway of increasing physical size (growth) and complexity of function (development). Monitoring of children's growth and development typically occur at well child visits, that occur in association with immunization and anticipatory guidance on child health and development. Immunization schedules and growth monitoring typically occur more frequently in the first 18 months of life, but at least annual well child visits are recommended for all children past 2 years.

## PHYSICAL GROWTH

Physicians commonly monitor children's physical growth using three parameters (weight, height and head size) and plot these on standardized growth charts. The shape of the growth charts will show that growth is not equal in these parameters. Head growth is more rapid than weight gain or height in the first two years of life.

The average birth weight of a healthy newborn in western societies has been reported as 3.5 kg (7 lbs.). The mean birth weight of Caribbean babies may be somewhat lower, as the mean birth weight of Jamaican babies during the Jamaican Perinatal Mortality and Morbidity Survey (1986) was 3.1 kg (Report of the Perinatal Mortality and Morbidity Survey, 1989). This is consistent with lower mean birth weights for the African American population in the USA (e.g. Kleinman & Kessel, 1987). The average child doubles his or her birth weight by four months and triples it in a year. Weight gain slows considerably in the second year of life. The average one-year-old weighs 10 kg and the average two-year-old weighs 12.5 kg. Another easy to remember growth fact is that a seven-year-old typically weighs 72 (49) lbs.

The average length of a newborn baby is 50 cm. In one year, length increases by 50% (25 cm.) to 75 cm. and in three years, another 25 cm. is added to give a length of 75 cm. At two years, a child is approximately half his or her adult height. The average head circumference of a newborn baby is 35 cm. A child achieves two-thirds of his or her brain size by two and a half to three years. Head growth then occurs slowly but steadily until 18 years, when adult head size is achieved.

## PHYSICAL DEVELOPMENT

Physical development follows basic principles. First, it is cephalo-caudal in nature, i.e., development occurs first at the head then progresses downwards to the feet. This is why babies first lift their heads, then roll over, then crawl and finally walk. Second, physical development first occurs proximally and then moves distally. Babies first make whole body movements to reach at objects, then attempt to reach out using the whole upper limb, then use the whole hand and finally develop a fine pincer grasp using the thumb and index finger. Third, after tasks are accomplished, further development results in increased speed and efficiency. For example, a three-year-old will run stiffly, a four- to five-year-old will run more smoothly and a five- to six-year-old will run with greater speed.

# The Infant, Toddler And Pre-School Years: Cognitive And Language Development

## COGNITIVE DEVELOPMENT

Cognitive development describes the changes that occur in children's mental skills and abilities throughout their lives. Piaget is credited with initiating the study of cognitive development in children (Piaget, 1929). He posited that children play an important role in their own development by being active explorers of their environment. The term 'schemes' was used to describe the mental structures created to represent, organize and interpret our experiences. According to Piaget, children modify their intellectual schemes by innate intellectual processes of organization and adaptation. Adaptation is comprised of assimilation, in which children interpret new experiences in terms of their existing models, and accommodation, in which existing structures are modified to account for new experiences. He described four invariant and universal stages of development: the sensori-motor stage (birth to two years); the pre-operational stage (two to seven years); the concrete operational stage (seven to 11 years); and the formal operational stage (11 years and over). The ages covered by this chapter are limited to Piaget's first two stages.

In the sensori-motor stage, children change from responding to their environment by reflex actions, to being capable of mental representation, as displayed by object permanence (recognition that an object is still present when hidden from view); deferred imitation (the ability to copy behaviours when the model is no longer present); and pretend play. In the pre-operational stage, mental representation advances further to include more advanced pretend play, of a socio-dramatic type, where children are able to combine pretend play with that of their peers. Children are also able to understand the use of symbols, such as drawings and photographs, to represent real world situations. Piaget felt that at this stage, children were too egocentric to undertake the more logical and organized thought processes required in the concrete operational stage.

Piaget's theories had a major influence on early childhood education. Children were encouraged to discover through activities and exploration; individual differences in accomplishing developmental tasks were acknowledged and children's learning experiences were designed to build on existing abilities. Although Piaget's theories and stages of development have been challenged fully or partially, there is as yet no universally accepted theory of cognitive development.

Vygotsky also advanced a theory of how children develop. This theory emphasizes the importance of socio-cultural influences on children's development, influences largely neglected by Piaget, and explains the wide cultural variation in cognitive skills. Vygotsky proposed that children learn culture, values and problem-solving strategies by their interactions with more skilled associates, both adults and peers. While acknowledging the role of symbol systems in cognitive development, he also felt that language was the most important symbol. Vygotsky's theory also impacted on the classroom environment. Teachers guide children's learning through a rich menu of learning experiences, using assisted discovery. Peer collaboration is also encouraged through classmates of varying abilities working with each other (Vygotsky, 1962).

A more recent set of theories, the information processing approach, views the mind as a complex system which manipulates symbols much like a computer. One such, Case's neo-Piagetian theory, posits that cognitive development occurs as a result of gains in working-memory capacity. Brain development occurs when practice results in automaticity of procedures and releases working memory. This allows a combination of old schemes and development of new ones (*see* Demetriou, Shayer, & Efklides, 1994).

## LANGUAGE DEVELOPMENT

There are four components of language: phonology, the use of phonemes, the basic units of sound singly or in combination; semantics, understanding of the meaning attributed to sounds; syntax, knowing the rules specifying how words combine to form phrases, sentences, and pragmatics, using language to communicate effectively. There are three main theories of language development. Learning theorists propose that children learn language by imitating another's speech; proponents of the nativist theory believe that humans have innate linguistic processing ability, a language acquisition device (LAD), which functions most efficiently in childhood; and interactionists believe that children are biologically designed to acquire language through interaction with their environment (Pence & Justice, 2007). Similar to cognitive development theories, no single theory fully explains what is known about language development.

Infants are born prepared to learn language; they are sensitive to a wider range of phonemes than older children and adults, including phonemes from all languages. It is well known that it is easier for children to learn a new language than an adult. Within the first few days of birth, infants show a preference for the sounds of their native language, attending less to phonemes that are not within their own language. The first vocal milestones are cooing and using vowel sounds by two months, and babbling, simple repetitive combinations of consonants and vowels by four to six months. Babbling is accompanied by a rhythmical pattern, but by 10 months, this pattern is typical of the child's native language. Though producing a limited number of sounds, babies learn to be effective communicators using joint attention. Joint attention is the process of sharing one's experience of observing an object or event, by following gaze or pointing gestures. During this process, two communicators attend to the same object or event. Joint attention is believed to be important to early language development and is impaired in autistic spectrum disorders. At the end of the first year, with the development of fine motor skills, infants combine these behaviours with communication skills and use preverbal gestures which are protodeclarative and protoimperative in nature. In protodeclarative gestures, infants touch, hold or point to an object while making eye contact with others to ensure their attention. In protoimperative gestures, infants get another person to initiate an activity by gesturing and using sounds.

Gradually, over time, words are formed and pronunciation improves. The size of a child's vocabulary increases rapidly in the pre-school years (_see_ Appendix), with receptive language (comprehension) preceding expressive language. Girls' acquisition of vocabulary is faster than boys in the early years; and children from lower social class homes have smaller vocabularies due to limited verbal stimulation (Pence & Justice, 2007). Between 18 and 24 months, toddlers begin to use two and three word sentences, known as telegraphic speech, because they omit the least important words (e.g. "Mummy come"). As children make longer sentences, they begin to express grammatical morphemes, such as 's' for plurals and 'ed' for past tense. At the late pre-school period, the beginning of pragmatics emerges. Further language expansion and refinement take place during later childhood.

In many Caribbean countries, the majority of the population uses a local creole or patois as the primary communication form, while the official language is a standard one, such as English or French. The ability to master the verbal rules of both the official language and the creole and to move comfortably between both is known as 'code switching." Code switching occurs frequently within the Caribbean, but many persons also experience difficulty in code switching. For example, while persons may be able to read and understand English, they may be unable to speak and write it (Muysken, 2005).

Learning in the official language is typical in pre-schools and primary schools throughout the world, including the Caribbean. Research, however, shows that children who learn in their mother tongue for the first six to eight years of life, including the early primary years, perform better than their peers who were taught in the official language (EFA Global Monitoring Report, 2007).

## The Infant Toddler and Pre-school Years: Socio-Emotional Development

Theories of emotional development have long existed. Erikson's psychosocial theory, with its stages of trust versus mistrust (birth to one year), autonomy versus shame and doubt (one to three years), and initiative versus guilt (three to six years) occurring in the infant and pre-school years, was developed in the 1950s and Bandura's social learning theory was developed in 1977. Important aspects of socio-emotional development are discussed further in the sections below (*see* Dowling, 2005).

## THE DEVELOPMENT OF EMOTIONS

Human beings are capable of expressing only few undifferentiated emotions at birth; babies are attracted to pleasant stimuli, withdraw from unpleasant stimuli and cry when distressed. With the further development of the nervous system, basic emotions, i.e. emotions that can be inferred from facial expressions, become better differentiated and the baby can be seen to express interest, happiness, disgust, distress and contentment. Happiness and distress, exhibited by a social smile and crying, respectively, are the most commonly expressed emotions. As the central nervous system develops further, the remaining basic or primary emotions of anger, fear, sadness and surprise are able to be expressed, usually in the second half of the first year of life (Dowling, 2005).

More complex, secondary or self-conscious emotions, such as embarrassment, pride, envy, guilt and shame, do not emerge until the second or third year of life, when cognitive development allows self-recognition and self-evaluation. This is assisted by the instruction and guidance provided by adults, particularly in the home and school setting. After the second year of life, language development allows young children to express their emotions verbally. Their emotional expressions continue to be impacted by adult instruction throughout childhood.

The commonly monitored early socioemotional milestones are the emergence of the social smile by 12 weeks, laughter by three to four months and separation anxiety by six to eight months. Other socioemotional milestones are reported in the Appendix.

## UNDERSTANDING OTHER'S EMOTIONS

Between eight and ten months, babies are able to interpret facial expressions. Subsequently, infants seek out the emotions of adults, particularly to provide guidance in unfamiliar social situations. This is termed social referencing. Infants first begin to appreciate that persons may have different emotional reactions in the second year of life, but the process of fully understanding and interpreting the emotions of others is a slow one that continues throughout childhood.

## EMOTIONAL SELF-REGULATION

The rudiments of emotional regulation begin in the first few weeks of life when parents and guardians respond more readily and positively to emotions of happiness, than to upset. This subtle form of behaviour modification encourages babies to suppress negative emotions and promote more positive ones. By the end of the first year of life, infants begin to regulate their own emotions. They use their motor skills, crawling and walking, to avoid unpleasant emotions. The earlier development of motor skills in Caribbean infants would suggest that they would accomplish physical avoidance earlier than infants from other cultures. The potential impact of this on emotional regulation is unknown.

After age two, when language develops, children are able to verbalize their emotions and use more directed physical activity, such as covering their eyes to unpleasant visual stimuli. Parents who intervene too readily in infant's distress signals, delay the development of self-regulation (Dowling, 2005). Similar to the ability to understand other's emotions, emotional self-regulation is a slow process that continues well into childhood.

## TEMPERAMENT

Temperament has been defined as the ability of a person to respond emotionally to environmental changes in predictable ways. Three main types of temperament were identified in the New York Longitudinal Study (Thomas & Chess, 1977): the easy child (40%), who is positive in mood, predictable and adapts easily to new experiences; the difficult child (10%) who does not have regular routines and frequently reacts negatively and intensely to new experiences; and the slow-to-warm-up child who is inactive and moody and shows low-key responses to environmental changes, with slow adaptation. The remaining 35% of children do not fit into any of these types, demonstrating the existence of unique temperamental patterns. There has been much recent interest in the temperament of infants, as it has been associated with long-term cognitive and social outcomes, particularly when assessed after the second year of life when responses are more predictable (Caspi, Elder, & Bem, 1988; Caspi & Silva, 1995). Temperament is believed to be determined by a combination of heritable factors, cultural support and environmental influences.

However, temperament has also been shown to be modulated by responsive parenting practices.

In the Profiles Project, just under a quarter of Jamaican children (24.3%) were reported to be of difficult temperament in at least one of three areas; 15.7% of parents retrospectively reported their children to be irritable and to have cried excessively as infants, 9.7% reported feeding difficulties and 7.1% reported sleeping difficulties (Samms-Vaughan, 2005). Some 6% of children had difficulties in two areas and 1% in all three areas. Univariate analysis identified associations between temperament in infancy and development at six years. Irritability was associated with internalizing and externalizing behaviours observed by parents, particularly aggression. Sleeping difficulties were associated with aggression observed by parents and with withdrawn behaviour, social problems and attention problems observed by teachers. No associations with feeding difficulties were found (Samms-Vaughan, 2005).

## ATTACHMENT

Attachment is defined as the strong emotional and affectionate ties that we feel for special persons in our lives. Infants first have an asocial phase that lasts from birth to six weeks, when any form of stimulus produces a response. A phase of indiscriminate attachment lasting for approximately 6 months follows, when they respond to adult faces more than to inanimate objects. Between 7 and 9 months of age, they form specific attachments, typically to their primary caregiver. The security associated with a specific attachment allows them to leave their secure base to explore their environment. The next stage is the formation of multiple attachments to a number of persons.

## SELF-CONCEPT AND CONCEPT OF OTHERS

Infants are believed to be born without self-concept, but quickly learn to distinguish themselves from their environment by the age of six months. By two years of age, toddlers proudly identify themselves as being within age bands and gender categories. Up to about five years, children define themselves and others primarily by physical features, possessions or capabilities. At this time, they also learn to evaluate themselves and develop a general feeling of self-worth. Differentiation of self-worth into academic, social, athletic and other categories does not usually occur until age eight. Between the ages of three and four years, however, another significant development takes place. It is during this period that children learn about the existence of people's beliefs and how these may influence behaviour. They learn as well to differentiate between the self they display publicly and the self they know privately. These represent the beginnings of 'theory of mind' (_see_ Saxe & Baron-Cohen, 2007). Concepts of self continue to develop further in childhood, progressing to identity formation in adolescence. The development of a sense of self is contributed to by advancing cognitive development, social interaction with family and peers and a culture that supports self-concept development.

## SELF-CONTROL

Self-control in the young child is first manifest as compliance with adult guidance in the second year of life. The nature of compliance is determined by the parental response to the child's increasing independence. Where parenting is responsive, the child's compliance is based on internalization of the parental rules; where parenting is authoritarian, as has been described in Caribbean societies, compliance is based on parental power and there is failure of internalization of parental rules. Compliance is, therefore, short-lived. By the third year of life, children begin to learn to delay gratification. The ability to delay gratification increases with age, as children learn strategies to reduce the stresses associated with delayed gratification. Children who become competent at delaying gratification typically become highly successful adolescents and adults (Goleman, 2006).

# Caribbean Influences On Child Development

## CARIBBEAN FAMILY STRUCTURE

In the Caribbean, like all other cultures, the family has a major influence on children's development. The family has responsibility for social, emotional and economic support of children and also for their socialization, a process in which the family's beliefs and morals are passed onto the offspring. Though the family is not the only institution that takes responsibility for children's development, support and socialization, it has particular importance in the lives of infants and pre-schoolers, most of whom spend their first few years of life in the family environment.

There is tremendous diversity in Caribbean family structure, varying both across and within countries, and by ethnicity. For example, the structure and functioning of the Afro-Caribbean and Indo-Caribbean family are somewhat different. This makes the typical Caribbean family difficult to define. Within these recognized limitations, some generalizations are attempted. Unlike Western and other societies where the nuclear family, consisting of a wife/mother, a husband/father and dependent children pre-dominates, the Caribbean family has been more diverse. Caribbean conjugal unions are classified as legally married; common-law (cohabitation without being legally married); the visiting relationship (conjugal relationships where partners live in other households, often with a parent or older family member); and the casual relationship, which is self-explanatory.

Using two Jamaican population samples, the changes in conjugal relationships between biological parents and, therefore, the family structure that children must adjust to over time are shown in Figure 1 (Samms-Vaughan, 2006). Few children are born into a married union, and much of the change in parental relationships occurs in the first six years of the child's life, the infant and pre-school period. The greatest increase in marriages and the greatest decline in visiting relationships occur during this period. Roberts and Sinclair (1978), in their Jamaican study, reported that visiting unions were more likely to be converted to marriages than common-law unions.

Some 44% of six-year-old Jamaican children live within a nuclear family, with 36% living with the biological mother, 5% living with the biological father and 15% living with neither biological parent (Samms-Vaughan, 2005). If the Jamaican situation is similar to that in most Caribbean countries, then most Caribbean children (80%) live with and are parented by their biological mothers in the early years of life. In contrast, fewer Caribbean children (40%) live with their biological fathers. Young Caribbean children, therefore, live in a largely matrifocal environment, with women providing the nurturing, socialization and stability for children. The recognition of the matrifocal society was highlighted by the title of Edith Clarke's seminal work, *My Mother who Fathered Me* (Clarke, 1957). That this has changed little over time is supported by work in the 1980s, which reported that approximately a half of fathers lived with their families (Grant, Leo-Rhynie, & Alexander, 1983; Grantham-McGregor, Landman, & Desai, 1983).

*Figure 1: Changes in Relationships between biological parents by child's age*

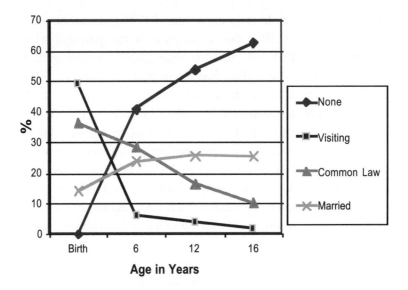

It is important to note that as many as three-quarters of Caribbean fathers continue their parenting role, despite a non-residential relationship (Samms-Vaughan, 2005). This concept has been termed 'parenting from a distance' (Samms-Vaughan, 2005). The Caribbean father, as in other societies, was previously thought to play largely an economic role. As early as 1993, there was scientific documentation showing that Caribbean men played important roles in rearing their young children. Some 67% reported playing with their children, 60% having discussions with them ("reasoning with them"), 44% staying with them, 42% helping with homework and 31% assisting with toileting and dressing ('tidying') (Brown, Anderson, & Chevannes, 1993). A more recent report from Jamaica supports this earlier finding, in which men, particularly those under 40 years of age, report an increasing role in nurturing their children (Ricketts & Anderson, 2005). Paternal involvement with children improves with increasing socio-economic status and education (Wilson & Kposowa, 1994). Ethnic differences are also apparent as Indo-Guyanese fathers show greater involvement than Afro-Guyanese, where there is a stronger maternal influence (Wilson & Kposowa, 1994)

The Profiles Project found that when the biological mother is absent from the home of the young child it is most frequently because of external migration (28.2%), perceptions of parental inadequacy by a relative and removal of the child from the mother (17.9%), abandonment (15.4%), financial reasons (12.9%), the dissolution of the parental relationship (7.7%) and death (2.6%) (Samms-Vaughan, 2005). The biological father is most frequently absent if there has never been a cohabiting relationship between parents (26.1%), the dissolution of the parental relationship (25.0%), external migration (20.5%), abandonment (9.1%), financial reasons (8.0%) and death (4.5%). In the absence of the biological mother, the maternal grandmother or a female relative undertakes the maternal role towards young children. When the biological father is absent, the paternal role is undertaken by a variety of persons: mother's partner, stepfather, grandfather or a male relative (Samms-Vaughan, 2005).

Child shifting, defined as fostering of a child, involving the re-allocation of dependent or minor children to a household not including a natural parent (Gordon, 1987), is a reality for many Caribbean children. Parental migration accounts for child shifting in large measure, but children being 'wanted' by a relative, particularly the grandmother, and many other incidental situations, also occur. Sociologists explain the child shifting phenomenon as a responsive strategy to economic circumstances, where the child is relocated to a more economically capable household (Gordon, 1987). Whatever the reason, there are often households that will accept the responsibility of caring for children. The extended family, therefore, plays an important role in the socio-emotional development of Caribbean children. Child shifting is less frequent among the young, on whom this chapter is focused.

## CARIBBEAN FAMILY STRUCTURE AND CHILDREN'S DEVELOPMENT

Kinship studies in African-American families in the USA suggest that, given appropriate parenting support, children in extended families can have positive academic and behaviour outcomes (Zimmerman, Salem, & Maton, 1995). Others have suggested that with the mix of nuclear, patrifocal, matrifocal and quasi-matrifocal families being the norm, Caribbean children might be expected to have fewer adverse consequences. Though there are a number of studies on Caribbean family structure and functioning, there are few on the impact on children's development, particularly their socio-emotional development in the early years. In Jamaica, six-year-olds who had been exposed to child shifting, as measured by multiple father figures had more withdrawn behaviour than their peers. Similarly, young children living with a biological father and surrogate mother were more withdrawn than those living in other family structures (Samms-Vaughan, 2005). This suggests that the Caribbean family structure does have an impact on children's emotional development and demands further and more detailed study, particularly for younger children.

## CARIBBEAN CHILD REARING PRACTICES

### Socialization

Most research on children's social experiences has been undertaken among low income families which form the majority of Caribbean populations. These families are often comprised of single parent, female headed households where females have had primary or incomplete secondary education. Even in situations where the father is present, the rearing of children is considered the role of the mother, and/or other maternal figures (Clarke, 1957), though, as indicated earlier, more and more fathers are reporting their involvement in childrearing experiences. Older siblings also play an important role in caring for and supervising younger children.

Children are highly valued and are welcome expressions of both manhood and womanhood (Barrow, 1996). In these early years, children are indulged and receive much attention and affection; they are frequently carried from place to place by their mothers and are doted on by the mother's friends and relatives. They are usually very well dressed for outings, and in recent times, this has come to include jewellery, including chains and earrings for both boys and girls, as well as flamboyant hair styles. A well-dressed, well-nourished child is perceived socially as evidence of good parenting, and in some cases, is indicative of the father's interest in and financial support for the child.

In these pre-school years, children live an unstructured life, with no specific mealtimes, bedtimes or other structured family activities. In homes with large families or in situations where children's homes are located with others in a yard, there is rich opportunity for young children to play with peers. Much of this play takes place outside (in yards), as homes are small and crowded, and contain valuables that may be destroyed by children. In these situations, children are also in the company of adults, but little time is spent engaging children in conversation or participating in developmentally stimulating activities (Jarrett, 1976; Grantham-McGregor, Landman, & Desai, 1983). Most communication is directed at children, rather than conversing with them in a reciprocal manner. Some mothers respond to questions asked, but much of the conversation initiated by parents and other adults is in response to children's misbehaviour and occurs in a verbally aggressive manner – sometimes accompanied by corporal punishment. Few children (26.3%) receive positive communication, such as praise (Leo-Rhynie, 1997). The authors in the 1983 study attribute much of the lack of stimulation to poverty and urbanization, with its correlates of limited parental education and the like. Though there are these negative consequences, it is also this type of family life that offers children exposure to the varied and rich social experiences that occur in their environments.

The limited attention to developmental stimulation has been objectively documented. In a sample of over 600 Barbadian parents, respondents were more strongly supportive of parenting practices of physical or emotional nurturance, than of practices that support a child's natural reasoning and curiosity, using a modified Block Child Rearing Practices Report (Payne & Furnham, 1992). The approach to children's curiosity was social class dependent. Anecdotal reports and perceptions of Caribbean children in middle and upper class environments also suggest that their lives are more structured and that more time is spent engaging them in conversation and in developmentally appropriate activities. There are also concerns, however, that in some of these environments, raising of the young child is the responsibility of the domestic helper in the home, as some working or socially active women spend little time at home with their children.

Studies on family function in Jamaica among parents of six-year-olds, using the Family Adaptability and Cohesion Environment Scale, FACES II (Olson, Portner, & Bell, 1982), indicate that Jamaican and North American families, on whom the instrument was normed, had similar means and standard deviations for measures of adaptability and cohesion (Samms-Vaughan, 2005). Some 56.2% of families were considered balanced or moderately balanced, 32.7% mid-range, and only 11.4% extreme.

## Discipline

Caribbean families utilize an authoritarian parenting style. Obedience of children is valued, and harsh methods of discipline are used to ensure it. The use of harsh discipline has been related by some to the influence of slavery and is believed by others to be supported by the Bible. Regardless of the underlying reasons for such discipline, a badly behaved child is seen as evidence of inadequate and ineffective parenting (Arnold, 1982). Among older school-aged children in Barbados, more than 90% of primary school children reported being flogged or caned at school, and more than 80% received the same type of punishment at home (Anderson & Payne, 1994). Similarly, in Jamaica, 85% of 11-12-year-olds report being beaten at home and 75% at school (Samms-Vaughan, 2007). Arnold also reported that even parents of higher educational levels seemed unaware of alternative forms of punishment.

Caribbean parents expect children to interpret beatings as an act of love, but the children have reported feelings of rejection directly associated with the punishments received, despite also reporting that beatings were an appropriate form of punishment (Rohner, Kea,n & Cournoyer, 1991). Though early reports on discipline of young children supported frequent corporal punishment use (Landman, Grantham-McGregor, & Desai, 1983), more recent research has suggested that alternative methods to corporal punishment are being used by Caribbean parents, with scolding (spoken to firmly) used with approximately two-thirds of six-year-olds, and a form of time-out (confining to room) used with a half (Samms-Vaughan, Williams & Brown, 2005). Corporal punishment use was still relatively common by slapping (31.3%) or hitting with an implement (14.6%), as were inappropriate verbal methods such as shouting (63.6%) and threatening (22.7%).

## Play and Leisure Activities

Young children are allowed to play freely with each other, but homes of children from the lower socio-economic groups have little store-bought material, such as books and blocks, to stimulate children's development (Grant, Leo-Rhynie & Alexander, 1983; Samms-Vaughan, 2005). The limited supervision of children's play afforded by parents, either results in purchased play items being easily destroyed by children or, alternatively, being put away from children to prevent destruction. Children often play with materials found in their environment, such as cans, plastic bottles etc., sometimes engaging in elaborate pretend play or making toys. The impact of this play on their creative development has not been studied.

Activities among older children (six-year-olds) were investigated during the Profiles Project. The most common children's leisure activity was watching television (Samms-Vaughan, 2005). Children watch television approximately 14 hours per week, with five of these hours on the weekend. One-fifth of the children watch more than 20 hours of television. Children of all social classes and both genders spend the same amount of time watching television. At six years of age, boys already show a preference for action and adventure programmes; all other types of programmes were watched equally by both genders. Half of the children are involved in some organized activity; activities are also gender associated. Boys are more likely to be involved in sports and girls in hobbies. A large proportion of six-year-olds (75%) also look at books other than school books, with girls and children of higher social class groups reading more, but the frequency of reading over a week is low. As with the free play of younger children, there was little parental involvement in children's activities, regardless of the nature of the activities.

## Attendance at Faith-Based Organizations

Churches, mosques or synagogues, are common features of Caribbean life. Reports from Jamaica, where the main religion is Christianity, indicate that over 80% of young children attend church weekly and most have visited a church within the last six months (Samms-Vaughan, 2005). Older Jamaican children, similar to children in other countries who attend church, have fewer behaviour problems and perform better at school (Samms-Vaughan, 2000).

## Exposure to Violence

Caribbean residents have become more concerned in recent times about the high prevalence of community violence in their countries. High levels of societal violence result in high levels of exposure of children to violence. Older Jamaican children have reported high rates of exposure to violence (Samms-Vaughan, Jackson, & Ashley, 2005). Young Caribbean children also report high levels of exposure to violence. While few six-year-olds report personal experiences of violence and over 90% report feeling safe at school and at home, 70% report having seen someone beaten up, a half report hearing gun shots, and more than a third report having seen someone stabbed. Caribbean children also witness violence within their homes. Just under a third of Jamaican six-year-olds watch adults shout at or hit each other, while one-tenth listen to adults threaten to shoot or stab each other ((Samms-Vaughan, Jackson, & Ashley, 2005).

### Caribbean Child Rearing Practices and Child Development

Child rearing practices in the Caribbean have largely been studied using a deficit model. The impact of the rich social environment that some young children grow in on their development has not been adequately studied. The lack of cognitive stimulation and responsive care-giving have been identified as significant factors impairing the development of young children in developing countries (Walker et al., 2007). Research in many countries consistently shows the importance of early literacy experiences, such as reading books to children and the number of books in the home, on language development, reading outcomes and school success (EFA Global Monitoring Report, 2007). Research in the Caribbean also demonstrates that the absence of stimulating material in young Caribbean children's home environments and limited parental participation in child activities is associated with impaired cognitive development (Samms-Vaughan, 2005).

Participation in structured activities is associated with improved cognitive and academic functioning in older Caribbean children, but excessive television viewing (more than 20 hours per week) is associated with poor school performance and internalizing problems of withdrawn behaviour, anxiety and social problems (Samms-Vaughan, 2000). The type of programme watched is also important. Watching action shows, talk shows and soap operas is associated with externalizing behaviour patterns, including delinquent and aggressive behaviours. Excessive television viewing by younger children is associated with delinquent behaviour in the school setting only.

Corporal punishment has been shown to be ineffective in changing behaviour in the long-term and to have negative consequences of aggressive and violent behaviour in childhood, as well as aggression, anti-social, delinquent and criminal behaviour in adolescence and adulthood (Gershoff, 2002). Its impact on older Caribbean children has also been mentioned above. Among Jamaican six-year-olds, the use of corporal punishment was associated with behaviour problems reported by parents, but not by teachers (Samms-Vaughan, 2005). This is in keeping with other reported findings, but the absence of a correlation with reports of behaviour problems by teachers also suggests the possibility that high levels of parental stress may lead to a perception of behaviour problems in children in the home setting.

Exposure to violence by older Jamaican children has been linked with externalizing behaviours of delinquency and aggression; and exposure to domestic violence has been linked with behaviour problems and depressive symptoms (Samms-Vaughan & Jackson, 2002). Similar findings have been documented elsewhere in the Caribbean (Perks & Jameson, 1999). No associations were found between exposure to violence and development or behaviour in six-year-old Jamaican children, but this may have been due to the small sample size.

## CARIBBEAN EARLY CHILDHOOD LEARNING ENVIRONMENTS

The learning environments of young children include both the home and pre-school. The home learning environment and its impact on children's development was described earlier. Among world regions, Latin America and the Caribbean have shown the greatest increase in pre-primary gross enrolment ratios (EFA Global Monitoring Report, 2007).

Two main types of early childhood education programmes exist in the Caribbean, those providing nursery or day-care services for the birth to two-year-old cohort and those providing pre-school services from three years to school entry. Nursery or day care programmes typically provide custodial services for a full day. Services are offered year-round in some countries and aligned to school terms in others. Participation rates for pre-school services vary widely among countries, from 5% to 53% (Charles & Williams, 2006).

Pre-school services are aligned to school terms. Participation rates are higher in this group, ranging from 55 to 95%. Using the Early Childhood Environment Rating Scale, early childhood environments across the Caribbean region lacked adequate space, material, furniture and programme structure. In particular, they lacked books and other literary material (Samms-Vaughan, 2005; cited in Charles & Williams, 2006). A relative strength in two-thirds of the learning environments in Caribbean countries was the quality of staff-child interaction. It has been postulated that the combination of teacher-directed learning strategies and the lack of educational material, of necessity promote staff-child interaction (cited in Charles & Williams, 2006). Teacher education was generally low in the region.

A third type of early childhood education programme, the home visiting programme, is present in five countries. Using the Roving Caregiver Model developed in Jamaica, services are provided particularly to children birth to two years in deprived communities, by trained caregivers. Caregivers make regular visits to homes, provide stimulation activities for children and encourage mothers to continue the activities in the home (Charles & Williams, 2006).

Home visiting programmes result in improved developmental scores for children and some have also changed parental practice (Powell, Baker-Henningham, Walker et al., 2004; Powell, 2006). Research on home visiting in the region has been limited to populations where children have multiple risk factors for poor development, including poverty, low maternal education and childhood under-nutrition.

## CARIBBEAN EARLY CHILDHOOD LEARNING ENVIRONMENTS AND CHILD DEVELOPMENT

The IEA (International Association for the Evaluation of Educational Achievement) pre-primary project which investigated children's learning experiences at age four and children's development at age seven in seventeen countries found that higher language scores were associated with unstructured, but child-centred activities in the early childhood environment, rather than with teacher-directed literary activities. The frequency of child interaction and adult participation in children's activities, together with the teacher's educational level, were also important factors in language development (Bracey, Montie, Xiang, & Schweinhart, 2007). While Caribbean learning environments have strengths in teacher interactions, there are challenges in the existence of many programmes, particularly with teacher-directed activities and teachers' educational level. Universities and teachers' colleges provide degree level training in early childhood education. Some countries have developed competency based standards for vocational training in early childhood development, but others continue to lag behind.

# Appendix 1

## Developmental Milestones

| | Gross Motor | Fine Motor | Expressive Speech | Receptive Speech | Socio-emotional | Cognitive |
|---|---|---|---|---|---|---|
| 6 months | Sits unsupported | Reaches out, grasps and transfers objects from hand to hand | Babbles freely to persons; Imitates sounds | Upset by 'no' | Anticipates social activities, e.g. stretches arms to be lifted | Shows interest in toys; Takes toys from table |
| 1 year | Stands independently | Uses neat pincer grasp sto pick up objects; Points; Builds a tower of 2 cubes | Says "mama" and "dada" specifically plus one other word; Uses mainly jargon | Gives objects on request | Waves "bye"; Gives affection. | Searches for hidden toy; Investigates toys, e.g. pulls lids off boxes |
| 2 years | Jumps with both feet on solid surface. Walks upstairs with both feet on each step, before advancing | Builds a tower of 6-7 cubes; Scribbles on paper | Calls food items by name; Says short phrases of 2-3 words; Vocabulary of 300 words | Points to common objects on request; Points to 3 or 4 main body parts on request | Verbalizes toilet needs; Helps to dress and undress | Can complete shape sorting tasks with 2 to 3 shapes |
| 3 years | Rides tricycle; Walks upstairs in an adult manner, using alternate feet | Copies circle and cross shapes; Can make a cut on paper with scissors | Uses verbs and simple adjectives of colour and size; Says phrases of 4 words; Vocabulary of 900 words | Can report first and last name on request; Can identify gender | Actively assists with dressing | Can compare size; Can complete shape sorting tasks of 6 shapes; |

## Developmental Milestones (contd.)

| | Gross Motor | Fine Motor | Expressive Speech | Receptive Speech | Socio-emotional | Cognitive |
|---|---|---|---|---|---|---|
| 3 years (contd.) | | | | | | Can recall a sequence of 2 to 3 digits or objects |
| 4 years | Runs and turns without stopping; Hops on one leg | Does buttons; Draws a 'stick' man | Uses personal pronouns; Says 5-word sentences; Vocabulary of 1500 words | Can report age; Can answer simple comprehension questions | Puts on shoes and socks | Can identify five to six colours; Can compare length and height; Can count to 5 |
| 5 years | Catches a ball; Runs to kick a ball; Walks downstairs in an adult manner | Draws a stick man; Draws more complex shapes: square, ladder | Says 6-word sentences | Can report street address on request; Can explain likes and dislikes on request | Can dress and undress self | Completes shape sorting with multiple angular shapes; Can make patterns; Can count to 15; Can compare speed |
| 6 years | Runs fast; Can throw a ball a short distance in the air and catch it | Draws a person with at least 8 body parts; Can write name | Says 7-word sentences | Can answer more complex comprehension questions | Can name a 'best' friend | Can remember sequence of five digits or objects |

## REFERENCES

American Psychiatric Association (2000). *Diagnostic and Statistical Manual of Mental Disorders, Fourth Edition, Text Revision (DSM-IV-TR)*. Washington, DC: American Psychiatric Association.

Anderson, S., & Payne, M. A. (1994). Corporal punishment in elementary education: views of Barbadian schoolchildren. *Child Abuse and Neglect*, 18, 377-386.

Arnold, E. (1982). The use of corporal punishment in child rearing in the West Indies. *Child Abuse and Neglect*, 6(2), 141-145.

Barrow, C. (1996). Child socialisation, relocation and abandonment. In *Family in the Caribbean*. Ian Randle Publishers, Kingston, Jamaica.

———. (2002). The overall context for children. Paper presented at CARICOM Council for Human and Social Development (COHSOD) Meeting, Guyana.

Berk, L. E. (2006). *Development through the lifespan, Fourth sdition*. Needham Heights, MA: Allyn and Bacon.

Bracey, G., Montie, J., Xiang, Z., & Schweinhart, L. J. (2007). *The IEA preprimary study: Findings and policy implications*. Ypsilanti, MI: High/Scope Educational Research Foundation. Available at: http://www.iea.nl/fileadmin/user_upload/docs/IEA_PPP_Findings_and_Policy_Implications.pdf

Brown J., Anderson, P., & Chevannes, B. (1993). *Report on the contribution of Caribbean men to the family: A Jamaican pilot study*. Kingston, Jamaica: The Caribbean Child Development Centre, School of Continuing Studies, UWI.

Caspi, A., Elder, G. H. Jr., & Bem, D. J. (1988). Moving away from the world: Life course patterns of shy children. *Developmental Psychology*, 24 (6), 824-831.

Caspi, A., & Silva, P.A. (1995). Temperamental qualities at age three predict personality traits in young adulthood: Longitudinal evidence from a birth cohort. *Child Development*, 66 (2), 486-498.

Charles, L. D., & Williams, S. (2006). Early childhood care and education in the Caribbean (CARICOM States). Background paper for the Education for All Global Monitoring Report 2007. UNESCO. Available at: http://unesdoc.unesco.org/images/0014/001474/147446e.pdf

Clarke, E. (1957; 1999). *My mother who fathered me: A study of the family in three selected communities in Jamaica. Revised edition*. Kingston, Jamaica: The Press, University of the West Indies.

Demetriou, A., Shayer, M., & Efklides, A. (1994). *Neo-Piagetian theories of cognitive development: Implications and applications for education*. New York, NY: Routledge.

Department of Child Health, University of the West Indies, Jamaica (1989). *Report of the Perinatal Mortality and Morbidity Survey*. Kingston, Jamaica: Author.

DiPietro, J. A., Hodgson, D. M., Costigan, K. A., Hilton, S. C., & Johnson T. R. B. (1996). Fetal neurobehavioral development. *Child Development*, 67 (5), 2553-67.

Dowling, M. (2005). *Young children's personal, social and emotional development, Second edition*. London: Paul Chapman Educational Publishing.

EFA Global Monitoring Report (2007). *Strong foundations: Early childhood care and education*. Paris: UNESCO.

Foster-Williams, K., Hambleton, I. R., Hilton, C., & Serjeant, G. R. (2000). Psychological distress among younger siblings of patients with homozygous sickle cell disease in the Jamaican cohort study. *West Indian Medical Journal, 49* (1), 52-54.

Gershoff, E. T. (2002). Corporal punishment by parents and associated child behaviors and experiences: A meta-analytic and theoretical review. *Psychological Bulletin, 128*, 539-579.

Goleman, D. (2006). *Emotional intelligence: Why it can matter more than IQ, 10th anniversary edition*. New York: Bantam Books.

Gordon, S. (1987). 'I go to Tanties': The economic significance of child shifting in Antigua, West Indies. *Journal of Comparative and Family Studies, 18* (3), 427-443.

Grant, D. R. B., Leo-Rhynie, E., & Alexander, G. (1983). *Children of the lesser world in the English-speaking Caribbean, Vol. 5: Household Structures and Settings*. Kingston: UWI, PECE.

Grantham-McGregor, S. M., & Back, E. H. (1971). Gross motor development in Jamaican infants. *Developmental Medicine and Child Neurology, 13* (1), 79-87.

Grantham-McGregor, S., Landmann, J., & Desai, P. (1983). Child rearing in poor urban Jamaica. *Child Care, Health and Development, 9*, 57-71.

Jarrett, J. (1976). A Survey of the experiential background of a sample of lower class pre-school Jamaican children. B.Ed. I. Study (unpublished). Faculty of Education, UWI, Mona.

Kleinman, J., & Kessel, S. (1987). Racial differences in low birth weight: Trends and risk factors. *New England Journal of Medicine, 317*, 749–53.

Knight, S., Singhal, A., Thomas, P., & Serjeant, G. R. (1995). Factors associated with lowered intelligence in homozygous sickle cell disease. *Archives of Diseases in Childhood, 73*, 316-320.

Landman, J., Grantham-McGregor, S., & Desai, P. (1983). Child-rearing practices in Kingston, Jamaica. *Caribbean Quarterly, 29*, 40-52.

Leo-Rhynie, E. (1997). Class, race and gender issues in child rearing in the Caribbean. In J. L. Roopnarine & J. Brown (Eds.), *Caribbean families: Diversity among ethnic groups*. Norwood, NJ: Ablex.

McClelland, J. L., & Siegler, R. (2001). *Mechanisms of Cognitive Development: Behavioral and Neural Perspectives (Carneqie Mellon Symposia on Cognition)*. Mahwah, NJ: Lawrence Erlbaum.

Muysken, P. (2005). *Bilingual speech: A typology of code-mixing*. Cambridge, UK: Cambridge University Press.

Olson, D. H., Portner, J., & Bell, R. (1982). Family adaptability and cohesion evaluation scales. In D. H. Olson, H. I. McCubbin, H. L. Bames, A. Larsen, M. J. Muxen & M. Wilson (Eds.), *Family inventories: Inventories used in a national survey of families across the family life cycle* (pp. 5-24). St. Paul: Family Social Science, University of Minnesota.

Payne, M., & Furnham, A. (1992). Parental self reports of child-rearing practices in the Caribbean. *Journal of Black Psychology*, 18 (2), 19-36.

Pence, K. L., & Justice, L. M. (2007). *Language development: From theory to practice*. Englewood Cliffs, NJ: Prentice Hall.

Perks, S. M., & Jameson, M. (1999). The effects of witnessing domestic violence on behavioral problems and depressive symptomology. A community sample of pupils from St Lucia. *West Indian Medical Journal*, 48 (4), 208-211.

Piaget, J. (1929). *The child's conception of the world*. New York, NY: Harcourt Brace.

Powell, C. (2004). *An evaluation of the roving caregivers programme of the Rural Family Support Organisation, May Pen, Clarendon, Jamaica*. New York, NY: UNICEF. Available at: http://www.unicef.org/infobycountry/jamaica_36354.html

Powell, C., Baker-Henningham, H., Walker, S., Gernay, J., & Grantham-McGregor, S. (2004). Feasibility of integrating early stimulation into primary care for under-nourished Jamaican children: cluster randomised control trial. *British Medical Journal*, 329 (7457), 89.

Puckett, M. B., & Black, J. K. (2004). *The young child. Development from prebirth to age eight. Fourth edition*. Upper Saddle River, NJ: Prentice Hall.

Ricketts, H., & Anderson, P. (2005). Parenting in Jamaica. A study conducted on behalf of the Planning Institute of Jamaica.

Roberts, G., & Sinclair, S. (1978). *Women in Jamaica: Patterns of reproduction and family*. Millwood, New York: KTO Press.

Roca, N. B., Serrano, M., & Tenllado, A. M. (1995). *Cells, genes and chromosomes (Invisible World)*. New York, NY: Chelsea House Publications.

Rohner, R. P., Kean, K. J., & Cournoyer, D. E. (1991). Effects of corporal punishment, perceived caretaker warmth, and cultural beliefs on the psychological adjustment of children in St. Kitts, West Indies. *Journal of Marriage and the Family*, 53, 681-693.

Rondal, J. A., & Perera, J. (2006). *Down Syndrome: Neurobehavioural specificity*. New York: Wiley.

Samms-Vaughan, M. (2000). *Cognition, educational attainment and behaviour in a cohort of Jamaican children: A comprehensive look at the development and behaviour of Jamaica's eleven year olds*. Kingston, Jamaica: Planning Institute of Jamaica Publication.

———. (2005). *Profiles: The Jamaican pre-School child. The status of early childhood development in Jamaica*. Kingston, Jamaica: Planning Institute of Jamaica Publication.

———. (2006). *Children caught in the crossfire. Grace, Kennedy Foundation Lecture, 2006*. Kingston, Jamaica: Grace, Kennedy Foundation Publication.

Samms-Vaughan, M. E., & Jackson, M. (2002). Improving behaviour in Jamaican children: A model for intervention based on epidemiological analysis. Report prepared for the Inter-American Development Bank.

Samms-Vaughan, M. E., Jackson, M. A., & Ashley, D. C. (2005). Urban Jamaican children's exposure to community violence. *West Indian Medical Journal*, 54 (1), 14-21.

Samms-Vaughan, M. E., Jackson, M., Ashley, D., & Lambert, M. (2007) (In press). Jamaican children's experience of corporal punishment at home and school. *Child Abuse and Neglect*. (In press).

Samms-Vaughan, M. E., Williams, S., & Brown, J. (2005). Disciplinary practices among parents of six year olds in Jamaica. *Journal of the Children's Issues Coalition*, 1, 58-70.

Santrock, J. W. (2007). *Child development, Eleventh edition.* New York: McGraw-Hill.

Saxe, R., & Baron-Cohen, S. (2007). *Theory of mind: A special issue of social neuroscience.* London: Psychology Press.

Sickle Cell Trust Publication (Leaflet). *Sickle cell disease in the Caribbean: Some questions and answers.*

Soby, J. M. (2006). *Prenatal exposure to drugs/alcohol: Characteristics and educational implications of fetal alcohol syndrome and cocaine/polydrug effects.* Springfield, IL: Charles C. Thomas Publisher.

Thame, M., Wilks, R., Matadial, L., & Forrester, T. (1999). A comparative study of pregnancy outcome in teenage girls and mature women. *West Indian Medical Journal*, 48 (2), 69-72.

Thomas, A., & Chess, S. (1977). *Temperament and development.* New York: Brunner/Mazel.

Thomas, P. W., Singhal, A., Hemmings-Kelly, M., & Serjeant, G. R. (2000). Height and weight reference curves for homozygous sickle cell disease. *Archives of Diseases in Childhood*, 82 (3), 204-208.

UNAIDS (2004). *Report on the global AIDS epidemic 2004.* Geneva: The United Nations Joint Programme on HIV/AIDS. Available at: http://www.unaids.org/bangkok2004/GAR2004_html/GAR2004_00_en.htm

UNDP (2004). *Regional report on the achievement of the Millennium Development Goals in the Caribbean Community.* New York: United Nations Development Program. Available at: www.undp.org/latinamerica/docs/RegionalMGDCaribbean.pdf

UNFPA (2006). *State of the world's population 2006. A passage to Hope: Women and international migration.* New York, NY, United Nations Population Fund. Available at: http://www.unfpa.org/publications/detail.cfm?ID=311&filterListType=

Vygotsky, L. S. (1962). *Thought and language.* Cambridge, MA: MIT Press.

Walker, S. P., Wachs, T. D., Meeks-Gardner, J., Lozoff, B., Wasserman, B., Pollitt, E., & Carter, J. A. (2007). Child development: Risk factors for adverse outcome in developing countries. *Lancet*, 369 (9556), 145-157.

WHO (2005). *The World Health Report 2005 – Make every mother and child count.* Geneva, Switzerland: World Health Organization. Available at: http://www.who.int/whr/2005/en/index.html

Wilson, L. C., & Kpososwa, A. J. (1994). Paternal involvement with children: Evidence from Guyana. _International Journal of Sociology of the Family_, 24 (1), 23-44.

Winn, H. N., & Hobbins, J. C. (2000). _Clinical maternal-foetal medicine_. London: Taylor and Francis.

Zimmerman, M. A., Salem, D. A., & Maton, K. I. (1995). Family structure and psychosocial correlates among urban African American adolescent males. _Child Development_, 66, 1598-1613.

# 8 Developmental Psychology in Caribbean School-aged Children, Ages 13-17

*Stacey N. Brodie-Walker*

Adolescence is defined as a period of time from the dependence of child-hood to the independence of adulthood. It begins with puberty and lasts through the teen years (Gerow & Bordens, 2000). Erikson (cited in Siegel & Senna, 1995) posits that adolescence is developmentally the most chal-lenging period of the life span. The challenges faced by adolescents are unique to this stage of development.

## Physical Development and Challenges

Puberty, which marks the beginning of adolescence is accompanied by two biological changes and represents the first major challenge. During puberty adolescents experience what is known as a **growth spurt**; that is, there is a sudden increase in both height and weight (Gerow & Bordens, 2000). This growth spurt occurs in girls at an earlier age than it does in boys. Girls begin their growth spurt as early as age 9 or 10, while boys experience it between ages 12 and 17. One of the most noticeable areas of growth in boys is that of the larynx and vocal cords. Squeaking and crack-ing of the voice occurs with the change of pitch. Boys develop facial and chest hair, the neck and shoulders expand and hips narrow. With girls their breasts begin to develop, hips broaden and become more rounded, and the shoulders narrow (Gerow & Bordens, 2000).

The other biological change of puberty is **sexual maturation**, which occurs when one becomes physically capable of sexual reproduction

(Gerow & Bordens, 2000). In males this begins with the appearance of live sperm in the semen. Boys seldom know when this has begun because "one would need a laboratory test to determine the appearance of sperms in the semen" (Gerow & Bordens, 2000), and other than this, there are no other consistent physical signs of the change; however, some boys may experience penile erections and nocturnal emissions of seminal fluid. In females, the change is noticeable and is marked by the first menstrual period called the **menarche**. Girls also have continued breast development and widening of their hips. Both sexes develop pubic hair (Gerow & Bordens, 2000).

Adjusting to these physical changes is challenging within itself, but with both sexes there are early and late bloomers which reinforce the already challenging period. For some girls being an early bloomer is an advantage as they are taller, stronger and more athletic than other girls (and many boys). Early blooming girls are more likely to be sexually active earlier and to marry earlier than their peers of the same age (Malim & Birch, 1998). On the other hand, being an early bloomer may be disadvantageous and may impact one's self-image. For example, if the early blooming girl is the only girl in her class who has put on weight because of the increased widening of the hips, and to show marked breast development, she may feel "different" at a time when she is trying to identify and align with her peers. Early blooming girls may also receive unwanted sexual advances from older men (Peterson, 1987), a common phenomenon in the Caribbean and elsewhere.

The advantages for early maturing boys are that they will have more dating and sexual experiences in comparison to their peers of the same age, which will raise their status and popularity. They will have better body image, higher self-esteem, be more athletic – excelling in competitive sports (Malim & Birch, 1998). However, cognitive, social and emotional development does not occur at the same time as physical development and early blooming boys who may become sexually active may not make rational and appropriate choices (*see* section on Sexuality).

Late bloomers for both boys and girls impact negatively. Late-maturing boys may have a sense of inadequacy and poor self-esteem; likewise late-maturing girls may experience self-image problems; research (Clausen, 1975) shows that these effects are not long-lasting in girls, but can persist to adulthood in boys.

## Emotional Development and Challenges

Adolescence can be a time of turmoil, joy, confusion, depression and overall mood swings. It has been said that adolescents have more swings in moods when compared to older individuals (Hall, 1904). These mood swings are caused by the biological changes that occur during adolescence and are often the source of misunderstanding, and at times misdiagnosing of adolescents. This is understandable as the mood swings resemble symptoms associated with disorders such as Major Depressive, Bipolar and Schizoaffective Disorder. Studies (Lewinsohn, Hops, Roberts, Seeley, & Andrews, 1993) have reported that incidents of affective disorders among adolescents are high and comparable to adult levels.

Depression, one of the most prevalent psychiatric disorders diagnosed in adolescence, is associated with many psychosocial factors such as substance abuse, low self-esteem or negative body image, lack of social support from friends and family, and most often, negative relationships with parents that include angry discussions over common parent-adolescent issues (i.e. choice of friends or clothes) (Hibbs & Jensen, 2001). Another issue related to the presentation of depression during adolescence is the fact that comorbidity of depression with other psychiatric disorders is higher in adolescents than in adults (Rohde, Lewinsohn, & Seeley, 1991). The disorders that were most often cormorbid with adolescent depression were eating, anxiety, disruptive and substance use disorders. Furthermore, boys are more likely to be disruptive when depressed, while girls are more likely to develop eating disorders (Connelly, Johnston, Brown, Mackay & Blackstock, 1993).

Caribbean females are less likely to express dissatisfaction about their bodies and embrace a plumper physique (Hodes, Jones, & Davies, 1996), however, eating disorders are becoming increasingly more prevalent within the Caribbean. As is seen globally, the presentation of eating disorders in the Caribbean is comorbid with other psychiatric disorders and usually occur as a response to internal and external stressors. In other words, the adolescent who is presenting with depression may be facing various psychosocial challenges that are later identified as the causative factors. One such case comes to mind as an example:

> A 16-year-old female, Paula, presented to me with a diagnosis of bulimia nervosa, purging type. Paula had clear symptoms such as eating at discrete periods of time; feeling that she could not stop eating or that she did

not have control over what or how much she ate; evaluating self, based on body shape and weight; displaying compensatory behaviours in order to prevent weight gain; and engaging in self-induced vomiting (American Psychiatric Association, 2000). After several sessions, Paula was also diagnosed as having major depression and was placed on anti-depressants. Paula revealed that because she was overwhelmingly "sad" about her life, specifically, her relationship with her parents, who were no longer together and "hated" each other, she started controlling the part of her life that she could – herself. After gaining insight about the psychosocial factors that were impacting her mood (major depression) and behaviour (bulimia nervosa, purging type), Paula was able to stabilize her mood and control her behaviours. Interestingly, I also treated Paula's 17-year-old brother, Paul, who presented for substance abuse, but showed signs of depression. Paul later reported that he started using illicit substances because of the stressors associated with his home environment.

This case substantiates the research (Rohde et al., 1991) that reports on the high prevalence rates of depression and other psychiatric disorders, and draws attention to the fact that understanding adolescent depression means understanding the interrelationships among biological, psychological and social factors (Cicchetti & Toth, 1998).

## Social Development and Challenges

Erik Erikson (1902-1994) proposed a stage theory of human development stating that all human beings pass through eight stages. In each stage there is a crisis/conflict that has to be resolved in order to successfully move to the next stage. According to Erikson (cited in Baron, 2001), we naturally go through the resolution of each conflict and resolution is determined by our relationships with significant others and our social environment. The fifth stage, which occurs from approximately age 12 to 18, is relevant for adolescence and is characterized by the crisis of identity vs. role confusion.

During this period, the adolescent is trying to formulate his or her identity by attempting to answer the question, "Who am I?" In doing so, the adolescent displays fickle and inconsistent behaviours in an effort to acquire the best fit. This is reflected in the constant changes in styles, i.e., lifestyle, hairstyle or dress style. Resolution of the conflict of this stage occurs when the adolescent receives support from others and is encouraged to seek answers on his or her own. If adolescents experiment with various styles they will eventually find one that is appropriate. It is during this time of experimentation that adolescents may become involved with gangs, drugs and sex.

## GANGS

Further attempts are made to answer the question "Who am I" through the formulation of friendships and the distancing from parents. The distancing from parents and the seeming rejection of parental authority and rules are part of normal adolescence (Shaw, 1966). By formulating friendships, adolescents reduce confusion about self, aligning themselves and identifying with an individual or group that can provide them with a sense of belonging. In doing so, adolescents may become involved with a gang, a religious (e.g. Rastafarian) or sports group (Gerow & Bordens, 2000).

Most adolescents, in their striving for other identifications, are able to make this transition without major problems. They seek relationships with people who are similar to them in gender and interest in order to satisfy not only their need to belong, but also their need to have frequent, positive on-going relationships.

The challenge, on the other hand, is the adolescent who attempts to achieve this sense of identity through gang membership or other antisocial associations/behaviours. Such an adolescent may choose to become involved with a gang because the gang provides him or her with opportunities for success and ego gratification (Siegel & Senna, 1995); that is, adolescents who have found little acceptance in healthy groups (i.e. religious or sports groups) may find acceptance and gratification with delinquent groups (Shaw, 1966).

Many factors have been highlighted as being contributory to adolescents becoming involved in delinquent gangs/activities, such as the need to identify. Other factors that are relevant to the Caribbean are discussed below.

*Lack of education,* and its ultimate link with *lack of employment,* are the first two factors examined. According to strain theory (Merton, 1957), delinquency (involvement with antisocial gangs/behaviours) results when individuals are unable to achieve their goals through legitimate channels. Individuals will then turn to illegitimate means to achieve their goals or they will strike out in anger. Merton (1957) goes on to say that we live in a society that promotes "the good life." Jamaican adolescents are constantly bombarded with music videos and other television programmes telling them that flashy cars, flashy jewellery and flashy women/men represent "the good life." Success and happiness are often measured in terms of whether or not one has these material things, which Merton calls "culturally prescribed goals."

Society tells us that we should attain these goals and society also directs us towards the way by which we should attain them. There are set rules, or "socially sanctioned means." We are told that it is socially correct to go to school, get a job and save money to buy material things, but it is wrong to steal (Merton, 1957). However, the problem is that the social structure in Jamaica blocks certain members from attaining these goals in acceptable ways. An estimated 6.8 per cent (11,342) of 12–16 year olds are not enroled in school; these are predominantly males from various inner-city communities. Some of the major reasons cited for this included financial difficulties (23 per cent), lack of interest in school (20 per cent) and pregnancy (12.6 per cent) (UNICEF 2005). Commonly seen on the streets of Jamaica are street children, the majority of whom are male and not in school, begging and involved in delinquent behaviours. If the educational means of achieving "the good life" is blocked, then the ability to attain a decent job is also blocked. Employment becomes out of reach and those who are able to find work (window washing and hustling), will only get enough money for the essentials, such as food, leaving little or no money for "the good things in life." Unemployment rates in Jamaica are high and lack of education, resulting in a lack of qualified workers, is a major factor in this situation. According to the 2004 Economic and Social Survey of Jamaica (UNICEF, 2005), the unemployment rate stood at 11.7 per cent in 2004 with 30.6 per cent of youth (14–24yrs) being represented. Sensing that their legitimate means for attaining their goals are blocked, they then turn to illegitimate means, that is, delinquent activities (Merton, 1938).

Second, adolescents who are exposed to delinquent behaviours/ gangs within their communities will be more apt to align with these antisocial groups. Social learning theory (Bandura, 1977, 1986) states that a person's learning and social experiences determine their behaviour. More specifically, the theory purports that children learn their behaviours by observing "social models." Social models are persons with whom we have consistent contact, persons to whom we are exposed (parents, peers and community). This theory goes on to say that persons are more likely to model behaviours if they witness their model being rewarded for their behaviour – **vicarious reinforcement**. Vicarious reinforcement increases the chances that the observer will imitate the model.

The learning history of youths in Jamaica is one in which the rewards of crime and violence are obvious. For example, most inner-city communities are lead by "Dons" who regulate the daily functions of the residents within these communities through both legitimate and illegitimate means. These "Dons" have acquired power, wealth, prestige and have achieved the prescribed "good things in life", mainly through criminal behaviours such as drug trafficking and murder (personal communication, K.A.D. Morgan & S.N.A. Brodie-Walker, 2006). Youths who live in these communities often perceive these Dons as role models and aspire to be like them. They then form gangs, most of which are fighting gangs (Cloward & Ohlin, 1947), which enable their members to gain approval of persons like them – identification – by showing their bravery and strength through fighting and displaying other criminal behaviours.

As was indicated earlier, not all youths join antisocial gangs in striving to identify and belong. "Some adolescents remain loyal to the values and rules of conventional society. Furthermore, some adolescents are temperamentally incapable of following criminal or conventional rules and in their strivings to find self may instead retreat by taking drugs and alcohol" (Cloward & Ohlin, 1947, p. 140).

## DRUGS

Many adolescents experiment with drugs; many use drugs on a regular basis and many abuse drugs. Drug use among adolescents in the USA rose during the 70s, dropped slowly during the 80s, and increased in the 90s and 00s (Gerow & Bordens, 2000). Research (Gans & Blyth, 1990) shows that American adolescents smoke (79 per cent) and drink alcohol (65 per cent), with the drug of choice being marijuana. Marijuana use among American adolescents has doubled since 1992, with an estimated 1.3 million adolescents using marijuana on a monthly basis (Gerow & Bordens, 2000).

Similar trends exist among Jamaican adolescents with marijuana representing 80 per cent of the illicit drug use. Douglas (2000) conducted a survey of 7,996 secondary school adolescents from grades 9, 11 and 13 to investigate the patterns of substance use in 1987 and 1997. The results indicated that marijuana was the drug of choice, with males being more likely to smoke five times per week in comparison to females, with an average of 7.7 per cent of students then smoking.

Another study (De La Haye & Harris, 2004) looked at 103 adolescents between the ages of 10 and 18 years, who received treatment in the Detoxification Unit of the University Hospital of West Indies. All participants were diagnosed with marijuana abuse, with the majority of them abusing marijuana only (54.5 per cent), followed by a combination of marijuana and alcohol (20.4 per cent). Interestingly, most of the adolescents (68.9 per cent) reported that they were introduced to substance use by a friend, indicating that peer pressure and the need to identify and belong are primary factors in adolescents' drug use.

Although drug use by adolescents is of great concern, there is evidence that we need not get hysterical about infrequent or experimental drug use among this group. A study by Shedler and Block (1990) looking at *abstainers, few time users (experimenters)* and *frequent users* (abusers) found that frequent users were maladjusted, alienated, deficient in impulse control, and distressed. The *abstainers* were overly anxious, emotionally constricted and lacked social skills. The *experimenters* were adjusted and psychologically "healthier" than either of the two groups. The explanation for these results lies in the belief that if the adolescent 'tests the waters' in relation to drug use he or she, having experimented, will be better able to refuse this lifestyle, while maintaining peer relations – thus remaining well adjusted. However, what is of greater concern are the adolescents who abuse drugs. Although the above-mentioned research states that experimenting with drugs may enhance the adolescents' sense of self/identity, we need to be clear about the fact that the majority of drug abusers were at one time experimenters.

## SEXUALITY

Adolescence is marked by an increase in sex hormones. Sex hormones give rise to sex drives which lead to sexual behaviours. Incidence of premarital sex has risen in the last two decades with adolescents experimenting with sex at an earlier age. By the age of 16, 71 per cent of Jamaican adolescents have had sex at least once. The Adolescent Condom Survey of 2001 conducted by Hope Enterprises reports that the age of sexual initiation for girls is 15 and for boys 13 (*Jamaica Observer*, April 19, 2004). Increased sexual activity among adolescents has led to an increase in teenage pregnancy. Jamaica's adolescent pregnancy rate has been among the highest in the Caribbean. Forty per cent of Jamaican women have been pregnant at least once before the age of 20 and more than 80 per cent of adolescent pregnancies are unplanned (Eggleston, Jackson, & Hardee, 1999).

Early sexual activity has also led to an increase in sexually transmitted infections (STIs) among adolescents. The Jamaica AIDS Report (Ministry of Health, 2002), states that close to one out of every 60 AIDS cases between 1982 and the end of 2001 were among those aged 10 to 19 years. During 2001, there were 69 new cases in the 15 to 24 age group, representing 7.4 per cent of the total. In addition, adolescent females, aged 10 to 14 and 15 to 19 years, had two and three times the risk of HIV infection, respectively, than boys of the same age group, "a result of social factors, whereby young girls are having sexual relations with HIV-infected older men" (Brown, 2003). (As was noted earlier, early maturing girls are attracting and having sex with older men.) The Adolescent Condom Survey 2001 (Brown, 2003), shows that 41 per cent of sexually active boys aged 15 to 19 years are at higher risk of contracting STIs, because they had had more than one partner in the previous year and did not consistently use condoms. The survey also found that while some 86 per cent of adolescents knew about HIV/AIDS, only 11 per cent of young men aged 15 to 19 years perceived themselves to be at personal risk.

One reason for this is because adolescents who are now physically mature are expected to show higher levels of cognitive development/ maturity. Physical maturity usually progresses faster than cognitive development and even though the adolescent is now capable of logical thinking because they have entered Piaget's (Baron, 2001) final stage of cognitive development – **formal operations** – most don't demonstrate such thinking in their everyday life. Research also shows that only about 40 per cent of the adolescents tested for formal operational thinking were able to solve the problems (Stankovich, 1993). When adolescents did demonstrate logical thinking, it was in association with problems in which they had direct experiences (Rogoff & Chavajay, 1995). Many adolescents reported that they did not plan to have sex – "It just happened", or that they did not plan to become pregnant. Many are ignorant about the consequences of their sexual behaviours, and some believe that they cannot become pregnant the first time they have intercourse.

In a survey of Jamaican students aged 11 to 14, less than 6 per cent of girls and 11 per cent of boys correctly identified the point during the menstrual cycle when a girl is most likely to become pregnant. Only one-third of girls and half of boys knew that pregnancy was possible at first sexual intercourse; and about 21 per cent of girls and 26 per cent of boys believed that oral contraceptives could protect against STIs (Jackson, 1998 cited in Ward, 2001). To make matters worse, "myths long thought to have been replaced by facts" are rendering Jamaican adolescents helpless in taking precautionary measures before engaging in sex (*Jamaica Observer*, April 27, 2004). In one study three out of seven girls reported that they believed drinking Pepsi-Cola after having sex or engaging in the activity in the sea would prevent pregnancy (Oritheneer & Isaacs, 2000 cited in *Jamaica Observer*, April 27, 2004). Further to this, 27 per cent of girls and 44 per cent of boys believed that sex with a virgin would cure STIs (Jackson, 1998 cited in Ward, 2001).

Another factor that places adolescents at risk is that many of them have negative attitudes about discussing and/or using contraceptives. As was reported in the *Jamaica Observer* (2005), Michael a 17-year-old, infected with HIV, confessed that not having a condom was not the problem, it was that the condoms were not being used; "Wi (including his friends at school) have di rubbers dem, but wi naa use dem." This young man later explained that even though he had heard about sexually transmitted diseases, his attitude was that such things could never happen to him. In a Case Study of the Women's Centre of Jamaica Foundation, 1997 (Ward, 2001), adolescent mothers reported that it was the fear of contraceptive side-effects that prevented them from using contraception. The young women stated that they heard that oral contraceptives could cause infertility, infections, brain damage and memory loss. Other reasons for not using contraceptives include fear of violence or rejection from their partners, (Boyd, 2000 & Senderowitz, 1998); as well as positively equating pregnancy and having a baby to womanhood.

## Relationship with Parents: A Challenge of Wills

Another area that represents a challenge is the transitional relationship between this group and their parents. The challenges of trying to formulate one's identity are intensified by the arising conflict between the adolescent and their parents. With adolescents distancing themselves from parents and moving towards their peers, they begin to give up the values and beliefs of their parents in favour of their own. They begin to ask questions, disagree and argue against the established rules. They become more independent, talking less to their parents, choosing rather to share intimate details of their lives with friends. Parents don't understand this change in behaviour and make the mistake of responding to their children by using the same techniques/discipline styles that were once effective.

One thing that has an impact on the relationship between adolescents and their parent is parenting styles. Baumrind (1991) describes four broad parenting styles and states that some have more beneficial effects than others. The first – the **authoritarian** style – is marked by parents responding in restrictive, rigid and rejecting manners. Parents set rules and children are expected to obey them without questioning. Children reared under these conditions, instead of being compliant, are later seen as insecure, apprehensive, socially withdrawn, low in both self-reliance and self-control. They may develop manipulative behaviours that passively express their aggression (i.e. depression) or explode into delinquency (McWhirter et al., 1998).

Next, the **authoritative**, is the parenting style in which parents respond with warmth; they adopt an inductive and non-punitive style of discipline (talking and explaining); and there is consistency in child rearing. Children exposed to this style are later seen as socially assertive, competent, responsible and having high self-esteem.

**Neglectful** or detached parents respond to their children in a nonchalant manner. These parents lack involvement and do not supervise their children; individual members function separately and autonomously with little family interdependence (McWhirter et al., 1998). In such families, one common characteristic is parental inconsistency towards rules and the behaviour of the children. Inconsistency may take various forms: (1) certain behaviours are permitted at one time but not at another; (2)

what the child is told to do is inconsistent with what the child sees other family members doing; and (3) one parent may enforce a rule, while the other parent allows for the breaking of the rule (McWhirter et al., 1998). Children are later seen as irresponsible – even about matters that effect their physical health and well being.

The fourth type, according to Baumriind (1991), are **indulgent** parents who respond with submission. They don't have rules and give into the demands of their children. This style is associated with children who later become involved in drug and alcohol use, antisocial groups/behaviours and are indisciplined at home and in school.

Within families in Jamaica and other parts of the Caribbean corporal punishment (authoritarian) is the dominant form of discipline. Physical assault (i.e. spanking, beating, pinching, tying of hands and shaking) is the most widely used method at 46.6 per cent; second, psychological methods (itself another form of authoritarian style) are used, including stern looks, spiting, scolding, shouting, threatening to hit (24.4 per cent); and last, non-violent methods (authoritative style) such as talking, explaining, time-out and removal of privileges were used by 28 per cent of parents (UNICEF, 2005). With the authoritarian style of parenting, parents set rules and expect the children to respond to the established rules without questioning: "Do wah me seh!" "Who yu a talk back to, yu nuh 'ave nuh manners?" As the adolescents try to assert their freedom, they start to question decisions being made for them by their parents. They start to re-think their ideals, values and norms and set new rules to govern their attitudes and behaviour. To reduce the conflict between adolescents and their parents, parents are encouraged to adjust their style of parenting to encompass the changes of their children. In other words, parents should move from an authoritarian to an authoritative style. In doing so, they should maintain their role of authority and continue to set rules. However, they should respect their children's right to make decisions by including them in the development of the rules. Additionally, the rules should be adaptive to the on-going physical, social and emotional developmental needs of the adolescent. For example, a child who at the age of 10 was not allowed to stay up past 8 p.m. and was not allowed to go out independently of parents should be allowed to do so at the age of 16, or thereabout.

## FAMILY CONFIGURATION

The relationship between adolescents and their parents is not only affected by parenting style, but by the family's configuration. More than half of marriages end in divorce, leaving a large proportion of children and adolescents living in one-parent, blended, or dysfunctional family homes (Baron, 2001). Adolescents in *one-parent homes*, typically single-mother households, are at an increased risk of depression, anxiety, impaired cognitive and school performance. They also experience difficulty in forming meaningful relationships, and thus show increased involvement in anti-social/delinquent groups. Children reared in *blended (step) families* are more likely to have problems with aggression, dropping out of school, and drug abuse when compared to children from nuclear families. *Dysfunctional families* are more harmful than nourishing, often neglecting or even mistreating their children (Baron, 2001). Studies (e.g. Stice & Barrera, 1995) show that in dysfunctional families where children and adolescents are exposed to addictive parents, parents with psychological problems and/or abusive parents, the children have an increased risk of problems such as drug abuse and externalizing behaviours (stealing, overt aggression). Where the abuse is specifically sexual in nature, this leads to depression, withdrawal, running away, substance abuse and promiscuity.

By the end of 2002, 45.5 per cent of Jamaican households were female-headed, "a trend which persisted for much of the 1990s" (UNICEF, 2005). Female-headed households were more common in urban areas (50.8 %), than other towns (45.6%) or rural areas (40.1%). Although single-headed households appear to be the consistent trend in Jamaica, children being reared in dysfunctional homes is also prevalent, specifically, homes in which children and adolescents are sexually abused. Children and adolescents were victims of 70 per cent of the sexual crimes reported to the police in 2004, with 959 having been sexually abused; 517 raped; 409 carnally abused (statutory rape); and 33 having been victims of incest. The Jamaican Injury Surveillance System (UNICEF, 2005) reported that 86 per cent of sexual assault cases reported in 2002 and 2003 were committed by a relative, friend or acquaintance, with strangers committing 11.67 per cent of these offences. What is even more distressing is that violence committed against children and adolescents occurred most frequently in their homes.

# A Generation at Risk

Now, more than ever, adolescents in the USA and in many other countries are dangerously at risk. Statistics reveal that adolescents living in the USA are 15 times more likely to die from homicide than their peers in other developed countries (Baron & Richardson, 1994). There has been an increase in armed assaults in high school, in incidents of sexually transmitted disease among adolescents between 1960 and 1997, and in children being reared in fatherless homes (Baron, 2001).

Jamaican youth are also at risk as they are exposed to the country's endemic problems of drugs, violence, stress, unemployment, motor vehicle accidents and an increase in sexually transmitted diseases (*Jamaica Observer*, April 19, 2004). Along with the developmental challenges of adolescence, the Jamaican child is expected to be more susceptible to psychiatric disorders, drug abuse, low self-esteem, becoming teenage parents, depression, suicide, crime, and delinquency. However, all is not lost. A study conducted by the Ministry of Health in 1998 revealed that Jamaica's youth are resilient. The report states that 78 per cent of adolescents are motivated to achieve and 88 per cent think it is important to stand up for what they believe in (*Jamaica Observer*, April 19, 2004). Nevertheless, many of our adolescents are externalizing their stress through delinquency and crime. This, as was mentioned earlier, is done as a form of identity formulation; that is, these adolescents have defined themselves among others like themselves with varying issues or problems and have found a way to establish themselves – thereby uncovering a pathway to resilience in their setting. Ungar (2005) has noted that this is sometimes one way in which children and adolescents create an identity for themselves from the resources they have available. In other words, when these resources are scarce, as is the case in Jamaica, children and youth turn to problem behaviours to find a powerful way to assert a preferred identity as a survivor. Cross (1991) also underscores this point, highlighting the general resilience of Africans across the Diaspora, suggesting, in opposition to much of the literature, that individuals of African descent maintain a strong sense of identity and that it is this that has brought them through their struggles.

Other accepted views about adolescents also appear to be incorrect. For example, it is a widely held belief that most adolescents are depressed, unhappy and lack self-esteem. Diener and Diener (1996) report that most adolescents report feeling happy and self-confident (having high self-esteem), as against being unhappy and distressed. Self-esteem is a widely used concept and is considered the evaluative component of the self-concept, which includes cognitive and behavioural aspects, as well as affective ones (MacArthur & MacArthur, 1997). Because self-esteem is based on life experiences, it is generally considered a stable characteristic of adults (www.bsos.umd.edu), however, it is a concept which clearly develops throughout adolescence. Self-esteem is closely connected to the notion of identity and it is the adolescent's self-esteem that is fundamental in determining identity and behaviour. Many assumptions have been made about adolescents' self-esteem, such as low self-esteem being linked to depression, suicidal ideation and delinquent/criminal behaviour (Messier & Ward, 1993). A study conducted on adolescents residing in a Place of Safety in Jamaica contradicts these assumptions (Morgan & Brodie-Walker, 2006). Adolescents who were assessed to be depressed and who displayed internalizing and/or externalizing behaviours all scored average to very high on the measure of self-esteem. Although studies (Bachman, 1974; Schwartz & Tangri, 1965; Reckless, Simon & Murray, 1956) have identified a link between self-esteem and externalizing and internalizing behaviours in adolescents, other studies (Jang & Thornberry cited in Grabmeier, 1998) have found healthy self-esteem among adolescents who exhibited behaviour problems. These authors theorized that it was the social support of delinquent friends, replacing social support of family, that boosted their self-esteem. Other researchers (Messier & Ward, 1993) presumed that striving for favourable impressions among a peer group with behaviour problems, partially motivates the inclination for delinquent acts. It was also presumed that committing delinquent acts may increase the self-confidence of the youth exhibiting behavioural problems, as self-confidence scores among such youth were higher than for their non-delinquent peers.

Even more surprising are studies that report findings contrary to long held views of adolescents and their parents being in constant conflict. One such study (Bachman, 1987) states that most adolescents report that they enjoy relatively good relations with their parents and that they agreed with them on basic values and future plans, as well as many other matters. This is of great importance as it is this family relationship that is instrumental in helping the adolescent to successfully make the transition through the challenges of this stage. According to reality therapy (McWhirter et al., 1998), the best environment in which to affect change when dealing with delinquency or antisocial behaviours, depression and other psychiatric disorders, teenage pregnancy and unsafe sexual practices exhibited by adolescents, is the family environment. The necessary characteristics of an effective family relationship include: parents being positively involved with their children, (i.e. monitoring their children's activities); consistently enforced rules with strict but fair supervision; and healthy communication that encourages and supports the expression of independent thought, and allows for give-and-take communication between parents and children. Children who have a good relationship with even one caregiver demonstrate great resilience and are more likely to make safe and rational decisions in their quest for identity (McWhirter et al., 1998). Thus, what is significant is not the configuration of the family but the relationship between the parent and the adolescent, even one parent, as is prominent in single-parent households in Jamaica.

Helping parents to be involved in their children's educational process is a great place to start in fostering a better parent-child relationship. Parents will become more invested in the lives of their children – monitoring their children activities, friends and their overall futures (McWhirter et al., 1998). Mobilizing parents to become more involved with their children's education can be a difficult task, especially in poor Caribbean families. Surveys of low income Black parents show that these parents have high aspirations for their children, but may not have the tools, the means, nor the abilities to follow through; that is, they don't know what to do to help their children achieve (Poussaint, 1990). Parents who don't have a secondary school education shun away from helping their children in school because they believe that this would reveal their own deficiencies (Poussaint, 1990). Therefore, educators and administrators need to be sensitive to the needs and deficiencies of parents and express interest in parental involvement by ensuring that there are outreach programmes in which parents can become involved. If parents are unwilling to come to the schools, educators, administrators, counselors and social workers have an obligation to go to the parents.

Parental involvement is the ultimate goal because parents who are uninvolved with their children are less attached to them and tend to produce youngsters who form inadequate or dysfunctional relationships outside the home (McWhirter et al., 1998). As was stated earlier, parental consistency (authoritative) with rules enforced in a strict, but fair manner is the discipline style that impacts positively on a child's social and emotional development. Parents who occupy this position are positively involved with their children and use reward, praise, and encouragement to engage them. They have open and healthy communication with their children, allowing for the expression of independent thought without emotional turmoil. If adolescents are emotionally attached and feel that they can communicate openly with their parents, they are less likely to become involved in early sexual activity, crime, delinquency and drugs. When they face stress, they will have their family relationships as another outlet to deal with these feelings and, therefore, avoid involvement in negative behaviours. Emotionally attached and healthy families also produce children who are responsible, conscientious, self-confident, and who have their self-esteem intact (McWhirter et al., 1998).

## Summary

In summary, adolescence is defined as the most developmentally challenging period of the life-span. Some of the developmental challenges experienced by adolescents include, but are not limited to, issues of a physical, emotional, social and parental (relationship with parents) nature. During the matriculation through these challenges what is common is the adolescents' striving for identity. This striving for identity is displayed by the adolescent experimenting as a way of finding the "best fit" for him or herself. Experimentation may take the form of gang involvement, drug use and/or early sexual activity. The relationship with parents is also a source of challenge for the adolescent. Although at one time thought to be an area of constant conflict, research (Bachman, 1987) assures us that the gap between adolescents and their parents is not as large as we may believe and, in general, adolescents do get along with their parents. This was highlighted as an area of great importance, as it is the relationship between adolescents and their parents that is deemed the most important variable in militating the challenges and deterring internalizing (i.e. depression and other affective disorders) and externalizing (gang and early sexual involvement) behaviours. It is my strong belief that it is the family that is ultimately responsible for ensuring the educational achievement of the adolescent; encouraging employment aspirations of the adolescent; providing physically and financially for the adolescent; being a source of stress management and, overall, emotional control for the adolescent; fostering high self-esteem and positive self-regard in the adolescent; and, protecting the adolescent against the impact of exposure to deviant persons/groups.

## REFERENCES

American Psychiatric Association. (2000). *Diagnostic and Statistical Manual of Mental Disorders.* (4th ed.). Washington, D.C.

Bachman, J. G. (1974). *Young men in high school and beyond: A summary of findings of the youth in transition project, 1966-1974.* Ann Arbor: Survey Research Center, University of Michigan.

———. (1987). An eye on the future. *Psychology Today,* February, pp. 6-7.

Bandura, A. (1977). *Social learning theory.* Englewood Cliffs, NJ: Prentice-Hall.

———. (1986). *Social foundations of thought and action: A social cognitive theory.* Englewood Cliffs, NJ: Prentice-Hall.

Baron, R.A. (2001). *Psychology* (5th ed.). Boston: Allyn and Bacon.

Baron, R. A., & Richardson, D. (1994). Human aggression. In R. A. Baron (Ed.), *Psychology* (5th ed.). Boston: Allyn and Bacon.

Baumrind, D. (1991). The influence of parenting style on adolescent competence and substance abuse. *Journal of Early Adolescence,* 11, 56-95.

Boyd, A. (2000). *The world's youth.* Washington, DC: Population Reference Bureau.

Brown, S. F. (2003). *Small successes, big ideas: Jamaica's adolescent reproductive health focus.* Retrieved April 24, 2006, from www.prb.org.

Cicchetti, D., & Toth, S. L. (1998). The development of depression in children and adolescents. *American Psychologist,* 53, 2, 221-241.

Clausen, J. A. (1975). The social meaning of differential physical and sexual maturation. In S. E. Dragastin and G. H. Edler (Eds.), *Adolescence in the life cycle.* New York: Halsted.

Cloward, R., & Ohlin L. (1947). Delinquency and opportunity. In L. J. Siegel and J. J. Senna (Eds.), *Juvenile Delinquency* (3rd ed.). New York: West Publishing Company.

Connelly, B., Johnston, D., Brown, I. D., Mackay, S., & Blackstock, E. G. (1993). The prevalence of depression in a high school population. *Adolescence,* 28 (109), 149-158.

Cross, W E. (1991). *Shades of Black: Diversity in African-American identity.* Philadelphia: Temple University Press.

De La Haye, W., & Harris, J. (2004). Early age of onset of substance abuse in clients treated in an adolescent substance abuse clinic in a general hospital in Jamaica. *West Indian Medical Journal,* November, 2005.

Diener, E., & Diener, C. (1996). Most people are happy. *Psychology Science, 7,* 181-185.

Douglas, K. (2000). *Patterns of substance use and substance abuse among post primary students in Jamaica.* Kingston, Jamaica: Planning Institute of Jamaica.

Eggleston, E., Jackson, J, & Hardee, K. (June 1999). Sexual attitudes and behaviour among young adolescents in Jamaica. *Family Planning Perspective, 25,* 2.

Gans, J. E., & Blyth, D. A. (1990). American adolescents; How healthy are they?. In J. Gerow and K. Bordens (Eds.), *Psychology: An introduction* (6th ed.). Carrollton, Tx: Alliance Press.

Gerow, J., & Bordens, K. (2000). *Psychology: An Introduction* (6th ed.). Carrollton, Tx: Alliance Press.

Grabmeier, J. (1998, November). *Low self-esteem does not cause delinquency, study finds.* Retrieved March 7, 2006, from http://www.eurekalert.org

Hall, G. S. (1904). *Adolescence.* Englewood Cliffs, NJ: Prentice-Hall.

Hibbs, E. D., & Jensen, P. S. (2001). *Psychosocial treatments for child and adolescent disorders: Empirically based strategies for clinical practice.* Washington D.C.: American Psychological Association.

Hodes, M., Jones, C., & Davies, H. (1996). Cross-cultural differences in maternal evaluation of children's body shapes. *International Journal of Eating Disorders,* 19 (3), 257-263.

Jamaica Observer. (2004, April 19). Early sex and your child. Retrieved April 24, 2006, from http://www.jamaicaobserver.com

———. (2004, April 27). Myths causing high teenage pregnancy in Mandeville?. Retrieved April 24, 2006, from http://www.jamaicaobserver.com

———. (2005, March 8). Safer sex message, why is it so difficult to heed particularly among young men?

Retrieved April 24, 2006, from http://www.jamaicaobserver. com

Lewinsohn, P. M., Hops, H., Roberts, R. E., Seeley, J. R., & Andrews, J. (1993). Adolescent psychopathology: Prevalence and incidence of depression and other DSM-III-R disorders in high school students. *Journal of Abnormal Psychology,* 102, 133-144.

MacArthur, J. D., & MacArthur, C. T. (2000). *Self-esteem.* Research Network on Socioeconomic Status and Health.

Malim, T., & Birch, A. (1998). *Introductory Psychology.* New York: Palgrave.

McWhirter, J. J., McWhirter, B. T., McWhirter, A.M., & McWhirter, E.H. (1998). *At-risk youth: A comprehensive response* (2nd ed.). New York: Brooks/Cole Publishing Company.

Merton, R. K. (1938). Social structure and anomie. *American Sociological Review,* 3, 712-719.

————. (1957). *Social theory and social structure.* New York: Free Press.

Messier, L. P., & Ward, T. J. (1993). Self-esteem among juvenile delinquents. In G. McEachron-Hirsch (Ed.), *Student self-esteem: Integrating the self* (pp.345-378). Lancaster, PA: Technomic.

Ministry of Health (2002). *Jamaica's Aids Report 2001.* Retrieved April 24, 2006, from www.prb.org.

Morgan, K.A., & Brodie-Walker, S. N. (2006). Impact of environment and behaviour on self-esteem in Jamaican adolescent girls. Unpublished.

Peterson, A. C. (1987, September). Those gangly years. *Psychology Today,* pp. 28-34.

Poussaint, A. (1990). Mobilizing the parents. Paper presented at the conference on the Role of parents in mobilizing for excellence, Washington, DC.

Reckless, W. C., Simon, D., & Murray, E. B. (1956). Self-concept as an insulator against delinquency. *American Sociological Review,* 21, 744-746.

Rogoff, B., & Chavajay, P. (1995). What's becoming of research on the cultural basis of cognitive development? *American Psychologist,* 50, 859-877.

Rohde, P., Lewinsohn, P. M., & Seeley, J. R. (1991). Comorbidity with unipolar depression II: Comorbidity with other mental disorders in adolescents and adults. *Journal of Abnormal Psychology,* 100, 214-222.

Schwartz, M., & Tangri, S. S. (1965). A note on self-concept as an insulator against delinquency. *American Sociological Review,* 30, 922-926.

Senderowitz, J. (1998). *Reproductive health programs for young adults: Health facility programs.* Washington, DC: FOCUS on Young Adults.

Shaw, C.R. (1966). *The psychiatric disorders of childhood.* New York: Meredith Publishing Company.

Shedler, J., & Block, J. (1990). Adolescent drug use and psychological health: A longitudinal study. *American Psychologist,* 45, 612-630.

Siegel, L.J., & Senna, J. J. (1995). *Juvenile delinquency.* (3rd ed.). New York: West Publishing Company.

Stankovich, K.E. (1993). The development of rationality and critical thinking. *Merrill-Palmer Quarterly,* 39, 47-103.

Stice, E., & Barrera, M., Jr. (1995). A longitudinal examination of the reciprocal relationship between perceived parenting and adolescents' substance use and externalizing behaviors. In R. A. Baron (Ed.), *Psychology* (5th ed.). Boston: Allyn and Bacon.

Ungar, M. (2005). *Delinquent or simply resilient? How "problem" behaviour can be a child's hidden path of resilience.* Retrieved March 31, 2006, from http://www.voicesforchildren.ca/report-August2005-1.htm

UNICEF. (2005). *Situational analysis of Jamaican children.* Retrieved January 10, 2006 from http://www.unicef.org/jamaica

Ward, M. (2001). *The reproductive and sexual health of Jamaican youth.* Retrieved April 24, 2006, from www.advocatesforyouth.org

# 9 Measuring and Predicting Severe Psychopathology in Caribbean Adults

*Michael C. Lambert, Clement T. M. Lambert, Frederick W. Hickling, & Kena Douglas*

The direct and indirect economic costs of behavioural and emotional problems are comparable to those of cancer and cardiovascular diseases. The indirect economic and human costs are even more substantial (American Psychological Society, 1996; U.S. Department of Health and Human Services, 1999). Effective intervention to minimize and eradicate such human suffering is, therefore, important. Screening and clinical assessment procedures with rigorous scientific bases are critical for the identification of at-risk individuals, constructive intervention planning, measurement of treatment effectiveness, and for facilitating research on causative and ameliorative factors for such dysfunctions. In contrast to the medical sciences, which can often employ biological markers in researching and treating pathology in most individuals, the absence of such markers for most forms of psychopathology makes the availability of psychometrically sound assessment procedures critical.

Ethnic and cultural diversity worldwide provides a challenge for the development of psychometrically sound measures. If such measures are designed for the assessment of specific socio-ethnic groups, they should not be used on other groups, as such use might lead to inaccurate measurement information. Despite this knowledge, many professionals con-

224

tinue to use measures to assess individuals although these measures were not designed for them. The concern generated by this practice is relevant to Caribbean nations, including Jamaica, where considerable work has been conducted, using measures designed to assess children in North America and Europe or adapting such measures for Jamaican children (*see* Lambert, Essau, Schmitt & Samms-Vaughan, 2007 for review). Little work has, however, been done on adapting existing measures or developing screening and clinical assessment procedures for the rest of the Caribbean, and especially for adults residing in the Caribbean Basin.

These concerns are similar to those described by McLoyd and Steinberg (1998) in the preface to their edited volume on Minority Adolescents. That is, they likened the dearth of research on persons of colour to the weather, in that everyone complains about it, but no-one ever does anything to ameliorate it. McLoyd and Steinberg (1998) further noted that despite the acute need for research on persons of colour worldwide, and in this case Caribbean adults who are the focus of this study, the literature base on this group is surprisingly thin. Equally problematic, is that most existing research uses Whites from North America and Europe as the gold standard in studies focused on Caribbean people or in comparative studies focused on individuals of European and Caribbean heritage. Moreover, much of this research focuses disproportionately or entirely on problematic behaviour (Lambert, Hickling, Lambert Douglas, & Samms-Vaughan, 2005; Lambert, Lambert, & Douglas, 2005). A shift from comparing individuals from the Caribbean with predominantly White inhabitants from Europe and North America to country and region-specific research is, therefore, critical in addressing these problems (McLoyd & Randolph, 1986). This shift would require the study of Caribbean people on their own terms. It would also require the development of new measures with appropriate psychometric properties for clinical assessment and research involving such individuals (Phinney & Landin, 1998). This perspective has been echoed by others concerned about the use of measures developed for Whites in other continents to assess persons of Caribbean heritage, the majority of whom are persons of colour (*see* Lambert, Essau, Schmitt, & Samms-Vaughan, in press). This practice, they believe, makes it difficult to determine whether findings regarding group differences or similarities reflect the true trends identified in such research, or whether they are artifacts of measurement (i.e., measurement error) (Knight & Hill, 1998). Furthermore, since effective clinical practice is often guided by accurate research, inaccurate research findings due to measurement error can have profound effects on research-guided clinical practice, including ineffective intervention (*see* Haynes, Nelson, & Blaine, 1999).

This chapter describes the steps taken to meet some of the challenges many researchers have presented regarding culturally appropriate measurement of behavioural and emotional functioning in Caribbean adults, especially those in Jamaica. Furthermore, it documents how we used information derived from the measurement procedure developed to identify factors which contribute to severe psychopathology. It is hoped that by describing a new measure with appropriate content and cultural validity, designed to measure the behavioural and emotional strengths and difficulties that Caribbean adults present, we are no longer just "talking about" the challenges of working with individuals of Caribbean heritage, but that we have begun "doing" something about them. A brief review of the literature relevant to our task and a description of the goals of the study follow, which highlight the underlying principles that guided the tasks.

Many researchers who study persons of colour focus primarily on deviant behaviour in high risk contexts (Gibbs, 1998; McLoyd & Ceballo, 1998). When such investigators find differences among these individuals with high risk factors and their European or North American peers, they typically interpret these differences using a deficit model, which labels individuals of colour as deviant (Garcia Coll & Garcia, 1995). This practice ignores the contribution of complex personal and ecological factors to such individuals' behaviour. For example, the adjustment of persons who are of Caribbean heritage is influenced by socio-demographic factors including gender, ethnicity, the socioeconomic realities of living in developing nations, and the interaction of such factors with their environmental contexts (Holmbeck & Shapera, 1999; McLoyd, 1995). Many researchers also ignore the behavioural and emotional strengths (e.g., spirituality and value of education) that people of colour and their families have developed (Boyd-Franklin, 1991; Resnicow, Ross-Gaddy, & Vaughan, 1995). Many of these strengths are not only rooted in a rich cultural heritage in Africa and other world regions, but were also developed to address the challenges that societies, based on colonialist ideals, often present (Coll et al., 1998; Staples, 1999). Research efforts, therefore, not only ignore the risk factors that impinge on persons of Caribbean heritage and other individuals of colour, but also the protective factors that mediate and moderate their functioning (Culbertson, 1999; Kazdin, 1999). An accurate yet economical assessment of such strengths and difficulties, therefore, represents a critical concern for researchers interested in such constructs, as well as for clinicians and other interventionists who often scaffold their intervention upon such strengths.

In addressing these concerns, we acknowledge that diversity exists within the Caribbean community, but that there are specific cultural characteristics (e.g., ethnic heritage) that almost universally influence the functioning of persons in Caribbean nations. For example, although evident in other groups, like those of the African Diaspora, most Caribbean families stress more collectivism than families of European heritage, which more often emphasize autonomy and self-reliance (Boyd-Franklin, 2003; Brice-Barker, 1996). Good relationships with biological relatives, peers, and elders are, therefore, important characteristics for many persons who are of Caribbean heritage. We do not argue that empirically derived psychological constructs (i.e., dimensions) of strengths and difficulties identified in Europeans are necessarily absent in persons residing in the Caribbean Basin. Nevertheless, we posit that the absence of appropriate content in most established measures for persons from the Caribbean makes it difficult to confidently assess these dimensions in such persons. The present chapter, therefore, describes an effort that focuses on positive functioning and the behavioural and emotional difficulties Caribbean adults possess. Thus, we focus on the development of the Caribbean Symptom Checklist-Self Report measure, an assessment procedure designed with considerable input from the Jamaican community, with the goal of assessing behavioural and emotional strengths and difficulties Caribbean adults present.

In addition to describing the procedures used to develop this measure (*see* Development of Measure under Method), the present study was designed to identify factors that might predict severe psychological disorders. For example, it has been repeatedly demonstrated that lower socioeconomic standing is associated with various forms of psychopathology (e.g., Dohrenwend et al., 1992). Moreover, the burgeoning literature base on risk factors for the development of psychopathology has linked physical and emotional trauma to poor psychological outcomes. Much of this work has focused on Post-traumatic Stress Disorder or other less severe disorders (e.g., Ruggiero, McLeer, & Dixon, 2000; Katerndhal, Burge, & Kellogg, 2005). Most existing studies have placed little emphasis on whether behavioural and emotional strengths might buffer the effects of physical and emotional trauma on psychopathology. In addition, most studies addressing risk factors (e.g., Ruggiero et al., 2005) such as low educational levels, resulting especially from poor intellectual development (see Mattisohanni et al., 2005) and protective factors (e.g., behavioural and emotional strengths) associated with outcomes in adults, have achieved their goals via traditional methodological designs, including general linear models methodology, such as analysis of variance and multiple regression (Greenberg et al.,1999). These studies have furthered our understanding of the outcomes for individuals who are victims of physical and emotional trauma, but like most research, the methodology used has limitations. Among drawbacks inherent in such methodology is the limited number of risk and protective factors one may examine in a given analysis, and the failure to simultaneously account for critical issues such as measurement error in addressing mediation – an issue that is important to most social scientists (Hoyle & Smith, 1994). Finally, it is also important to underscore that studies on risk factors have not focused on individuals in developing countries such as those in the Caribbean. It is, therefore, inappropriate to generalize and apply the findings from these studies to citizens in developing countries and the Caribbean.

To address these shortcomings, the present study was designed to use causal (also known as structural equation) models to determine the direct effects of factors such as educational level and occupational status on severe psychopathology in Caribbean adults. These factors have been established as appropriate predictors of psychological functioning. Some of the benefits of structural equation modeling (SEM) are that besides accounting for measurement error, it combines factor analytical and regression capabilities. Moreover, SEM allows the researcher to first determine whether the data fit a hypothesized model, and whether hypothesized pathways from one variable to the next are significant. Furthermore, SEM can also determine whether such pathways are mediated (i.e., in this case buffered or exacerbated) by other factors. Finally,

SEM models are capable of determining whether hypothesized pathways are identical for different groups such as males versus females, or persons in the general population versus those who are referred for clinical intervention.

Toward this end we tested the hypothesized model shown in Figure 1 (Appendix 2). Based on studies conducted on other groups that used more general linear modeling procedures (e.g., Ruggiero, et al., 2000) this model hypothesizes a direct relationship between occupational status and severe psychopathology. The same assumption is evident for educational level and strengths. Nevertheless, these pathways are hypothesized to be mediated by indirect effects through other latent variables. For example, it is hypothesized that the effect of one's educational level is mediated by an indirect path through occupational status and that some of the variance (i.e., effects) between educational level and severe psychopathology is shared though an indirect relationship through occupational status. A similar trend is predicted between occupational status and severe psychopathology, where some of this variance is shared through an indirect path through physical and emotional trauma. The model also posits that some of the variance from occupational status and also that from educational level is mediated through social and emotional strengths.

With the hypothesized model in mind, the present study was designed to achieve the following five objectives:

1. describe the development of a set of measures of behavioural and emotional strengths and difficulties presented by Caribbean adults that are called the Caribbean Symptom Checklist (CSC);

2. establish appropriate factor model(s) for the strength items in the CSC;

3. identify factor model(s) for the items reflecting problems in the CSC;

4. demonstrate how data derived from the measure might be used in causal models to identify which factors might contribute to severe forms of psychopathology in adults within the Caribbean; and

5. determine whether the model was identical across males versus females and referred versus nonreferred adults.

# Method

## SAMPLE DESCRIPTIONS

The sample consisted of 695 adults aged 18 to 89 years (Mean age = 29.7, SD = 12.94), who reported on their own functioning. Socioeconomic Status (SES) was derived from the respondent's occupation and was coded according to the Smith (1984) five-step scale where 1 = the lowest and 5 = the highest (Mean SES = 2.00, SD = 1.08). We recognize that the Smith system does not include income level, which might be especially critical in providing accurate SES information for Jamaicans. We excluded questions that would provide such information and those related to wealth, because respondents in our pilot study viewed such questions as invasive or offensive. Moreover, since many Jamaicans receive unearned income (e.g., monetary contributions from relatives living overseas) and often do not consider this part of their income, information on total income might have been inaccurate.

## DATA COLLECTION PROCEDURES

All participants in the study were drawn from Jamaica. Of this sample, 456 were nonreferred and were randomly sampled from parishes within the three counties of the country – parishes such as Kingston, Portland, St Ann, St Andrew, St Catherine, and St James. It is important to note that many of the persons sampled from these parishes were from other regions of the island and were only temporarily residing in the parish where the data were collected. Thus, the sample included individuals from virtually all parishes in the island, and was stratified to reflect individuals from various socioeconomic levels nationwide. The remaining 239 participants were individuals who were referred for treatment in various clinical services (e.g., casualty, day hospital, in-patient services) at the University Hospital of the West Indies. Of the total sample, 236 were males and 459 were females. For most factor analyses (*see* exploratory factor analyses below), data were either combined or analyzed simultaneously. Combining groups afforded greater variance in item scores (i.e., more than conducting separate analyses for each individual group), which is critical for accurate measurement parameter estimation (Embretson & Reise, 2000).

Upon recruiting the participants, we obtained their informed consent prior to their participation in the study. For nonreferred participants, data collection occurred immediately or within a week thereafter. Referred participants completed the CSC at the time of intake. To minimize discomfort for individuals with reading difficulties, interviewers presented the measures to all participants, noting that some persons preferred to complete the measure independently, while others preferred the interviewer to read it aloud to them. The interviewer asked the respondents to make their preferences known. Interviewers were always available for consultation if the respondents desired it. Virtually all nonreferred participants completed their forms by self-administration, whereas most referred participants completed the form by interviews. Respondents received no monetary or other material incentives for participation in the study.

## Measure
### DEVELOPMENT OF THE MEASURE

The CSC is a set of two forms, the first designed to assess behavioural and emotional strengths and the second, the problems adults in the Caribbean present. We relied on the expertise of adults within the rural and urban communities of Jamaica to generate culturally relevant items for the measures. Therefore, the first author trained five graduate and undergraduate research assistants to conduct focus groups in areas of the country that were reflective of its rural, suburban, and urban areas. Our choice of focus group methodology included our desire to consult with the group for whom the measures were designed, especially in the initial phase of measurement development (Vogt, King, & King, 2004). We were interested in obtaining the 'voice' of the participants, as well as constructing the measures with idioms reflective of the language used, thereby increasing the likelihood of the measures having adequate content and cultural validity for people within the Caribbean (Vogt et al., 2004). A trained leader and an assistant conducted each focus group, which included five to ten participants. It is also important to note that while the focus groups were primarily concerned with the behavioural and emotional strengths that Jamaican adults exhibit, the participants were also asked to describe abnormal psychological functioning in persons they have encountered. Furthermore, the participants were asked to describe their reactions and attitudes, as well as other person's behaviour and attitudes toward individuals who exhibited signs of psychological problems.

## Composition of Focus Groups and Findings

The six focus groups included a total of 34 adults. Participants stated that strengths Jamaican adults exhibit include spirituality, cooperation, respect for others, a sense of humor, and the ability to perform appropriately at work – qualities that are deemed important to families of the African Diaspora and other families of colour. Several problem items emerged from the focus group, which were not evident in widely used measures, such as being boisterous, acting like police officers or other persons in authority, brandishing a machete, giving away clothing or other belongings, throwing stones at people, and using indecent language. It is also important to note that we conducted focus group sessions to the point of saturation of themes, so that subsequent sessions yielded no new information (Kline, 2005; Vogt et al., 2004).

## Clinic Record Study

During the period 1995 to 1996, the presenting problems of 600 Jamaican adults, 18 years and older, were sampled from in-patient and out-patient clinic records throughout the island of Jamaica. The samples were drawn from large hospitals such as Cornwall Regional, Kingston Public, Spanish Town, and the University Hospital of the West Indies. Records were also sampled from other hospitals throughout the island, such as Port Antonio, Morant Bay, and Mandeville, and from hospitals in other parishes such as St. Ann and Westmoreland. All presenting problems reported at intake and recorded by the interviewing clinician, including psychiatrists, mental health officers, general medical practitioners, and other clinicians were copied verbatim by the first author of the study.

The clinic record survey revealed a significant number of items reflective of symptomatology in the Caribbean, which were not included in existing measures developed in North America or Europe. Although Table 1 (Appendix 1) is a factor analysis table (see Results), many of the items from the clinic record survey are included in this table. Nevertheless, we highlighted some of these items, among which were: rolling sensation in the head; head feeling heavy; the sensation of being touched in one's sleep; walking naked in public; believing someone obeahed or put spirits on one; and preaching excessively.

## The Caribbean Symptom Checklist

The CSC consists of a self-report measure and a third party measure designed to assess the emotional and behavioural strengths and problems in adults who are 18 and older. The measures have open-ended questions that collect demographic data such as gender, age, educational level, and type of occupation. Other open-ended questions that might be relevant for clinical assessment – such as a history of learning difficulties, sexual abuse/rape, victimization by violence, witnessing violence, serious physical illness/hospitalizations, chronic illnesses, history of mental health care, legal problems, and homelessness – are also included.

As mentioned earlier, each CSC form contains separate sets of items. One set is designed to measure emotional and behavioural strengths and the other set is designed to measure emotional and behavioural problems. As discussed in the preceding paragraph, the family of measures includes a self-report tool (CSC-S), on which adults report on their own functioning. It also includes a third-party report (CSC-T) measure, on which a family member, friend, or other person acquainted with the person's functioning might provide ratings. The third party measure was developed to allow others to report on an individual's functioning, as some individuals' symptomatology makes it difficult for them to report accurately on their own functioning. It is worth noting that the CSC forms were designed with considerable input from the Caribbean community. All 31 items for the section of the measure that assesses strengths were derived from the focus groups. The 147 items that measure problematic functioning were derived primarily from the clinic record survey and to a lesser extent, from the focus group study.

Besides the input from focus groups in Jamaica, we also asked six behavioural scientists from other Caribbean nations, such as Trinidad and Tobago, Barbados, and Guyana, to review the items and to determine whether they were reflective of functioning in their countries. These professionals concluded that the items were not only appropriate for the measurement of behavioural and emotional functioning in adults residing in their own countries, but that they were also worded in such a manner that their fellow citizens could understand. In addition, the measure has been successfully used to examine functioning in a three-nation study of Barbados, Jamaica, and Trinidad and Tobago (unpublished data). To further ensure the cultural and content validity of the measures, we also asked 30 adults in Jamaica, who did not participate in the focus groups, to complete the forms and to provide us with feedback on their difficulties with them. As an additional safeguard of content and cultural validity, we assembled another 30 adults who had not previously participated in the study in any way, to rate the items of psychological strengths and difficulties, as well as instructions written on the different forms, in relation to their clarity, and to their relevance for the Caribbean. More than 90 per cent of the respondents indicated that the instructions and item content were very clear and relevant for persons residing in countries within the Caribbean Basin. Respondents suggested slight modifications for some items but did not recommend the exclusion of any item from the measure.

### Scoring Format for the CSC

The CSC measures are designed to be administered by paper and pencil format and computerized adaptive testing. In this study, however, the data were collected in paper and pencil format, where respondents rated items of psychological strengths and difficulties as 0 = not true (as far as they knew), 1 = somewhat or sometimes true, and 2 = very true or often true.

## DATA ANALYSIS

### Overview

We conducted data analyses in three waves. In the first wave, we subjected the items on the CSC to exploratory factor analyses (EFA). Thus, we implemented separate principal axis factor analyses for items on strengths and difficulties, using SPSS 14.0 to identify factors from answers that respondents gave. In the second wave, we used the factors, as well as other predictors from the CSC to develop a causal model to determine what factors might contribute to severe psychological problems in the adults' surveyed. To achieve this, we used AMOS-6, a structural equation modeling (SEM) application that allows the testing of multiple contributors to severe psychopathology and also the identification factors which might potentially buffer the effect of these contributors. It is important to note that a preliminary test was used prior to conducting the SEM procedures, where AMOS-6 was also used to conduct confirmatory factor analyses on all factors used in the model. That is, to determine whether the factor models chosen were psychometrically appropriate.

## Exploratory Factor Analyses

EFA defines the internal structures of psychometric measures (Nunnally & Bernstein, 1994) and condenses multiple variables (i.e., items) into coherent subsets (i.e., factors) that are relatively different from one another. Thus, the variables in each subset are highly correlated with one another but are relatively independent from other subsets of items (Tabachnick & Fidell, 2001). While there are different criteria for the selection of factors to be retained and rotated, the Kaiser-Guttman rule of selecting as many factors as the number of eigenvalues greater than one and the examination of a scree plot (Cattell, 1966), are most often used to guide factor retention and rotation. Such criteria, however, produce inconsistent conclusions regarding factor structure (Hakstian, Rogers, & Cattell, 1982). Therefore, in making retention and rotation decisions, we included findings of a recent study (Fabrigar, Wegener, MacCallum, & Strahan, 1999), which suggested that the scree test was a more reliable indicator of the number of factors to retain and rotate. This study further underscored that like most psychological constructs, factors representing them are usually correlated. Oblique rotations that allow correlations across factors are, therefore, most appropriate. Nevertheless, we conducted both orthogonal (the assumption that factors are uncorrelated) and oblique rotations. Thereafter, we examined several factor solutions and made our final decision on the basis of theoretical meaningfulness.

## Confirmatory Factor Analyses

Subsumed under the rubric of structural equation modeling, confirmatory factor analysis (CFA) represents a procedure where hypotheses regarding the relationship between latent variables and indicators are tested. This occurs where a series of regression equations are solved simultaneously and thus generate estimated covariance matrices (Marshall, Orlando, Foy, & Belzberg, 2002). The $X^2$ statistic is used to assess model fit, but it is known to be sensitive to large sample sizes (Schumacker & Lomax, 1996) such as those used in the present study and can result in the commission of Type I error where a good fitting model is inappropriately rejected. Using other 'goodness-of-fit indices', such as the Comparative

Fit Index (CFI), the Tucker Lewis Index (TLI), and the Root Mean Square of Approximation (RMSEA), the hypothesized covariance matrix can be compared with the observed covariance matrix from a specific sample to determine whether the hypothesized matrix is appropriately represented in the data (Kline, 2005). CFI and TLI over .90 are indicative of good data-to-model fit, while those above .80 are indicative of a moderate fit. RMSEA values under .05 are indicative of good data-to-model fit, whereas estimates below .08 represent an acceptable fit. All CFA models were tested using the maximum likelihood (ML) analyses in AMOS 5.0 (Arbuckle, 2003). For all latent variables (i.e., constructs derived from measures used) such as strengths, academic achievement, type of occupation, and behaviour and emotional problems in the model shown in Figure 1 (Appendix 2), a confirmatory factor analysis was run to assess the degree to which multiple indicators reflected single latent constructs (Newcomb, 1994).

CFAs can also be used to test measurement invariance, a critical assumption in multi-group analyses. Measurement invariance assumes that when different groups of individuals (e.g., males and females, referred and nonreferred) are compared according to the measurement of a given construct (e.g., depression), their scores vary only according to the level of the construct they possess, and not because their responses vary as a result of the group to which they belong. If different groups of individuals are compared using measures that are not invariant, the findings from such comparisons could, therefore, be reflective of measurement artifacts and as such might lack psychometric soundness. In testing for measurement invariance, a model where the paths from the latent variables to the indicators are constrained across two or more groups is nested in (i.e., compared with) a model where such paths are constrained. Although the $X^2$ statistic is not appropriate for testing model fit it is especially useful in testing whether nested models differ from one another. Therefore, the $X^2$ and its degrees of freedom (DF) from the constrained model are respectively subtracted from those emerging from the unconstrained model. The difference in $X^2$ (i.e. $\Delta X^2$ or $X^2$ difference test) values and the difference between the degrees of freedom is then examined for significance where nonsignificant $X^2$ indicates that invariance exists across the groups to be compared.

## Structural Equation Modeling

Structural Equation Modeling (SEM) is documented to have numerous advantages over more traditional analyses. This is so because a single analysis can accommodate multiple potentially dependent predictors and outcomes. It therefore allows the researcher to simultaneously estimate a measurement model, make specifications regarding measured variables and the latent construct they theoretically measure and specify the structural relationships between latent constructs (DeShon, 1998; Hoyle, 1994). Like the CFA described earlier, using specific statistical programmes, the SEM technique provides fit indices that are used to assess whether a hypothesized model fits the researcher's data (DeShon, 1998). After testing for invariance in all latent variables, a subtractive approach, which includes paths (hypothesized or not) in the model and the subsequent removal of non-significant paths was chosen to capture the 'true model' (MacCallum, 1986). Thus, after trimming non-significant paths, the SEM analysis is repeated. As outlined under the Confirmatory Factor Analysis subheading above, the $\Delta X^2$ emerging from nested trimmed and untrimmed models is then examined for significance where non-significant $\Delta X^2$ indicates that trimming the non-significant path resulted in no loss of information from the model. Similar procedures were applied when the paths between latent variables in structural equation models were constrained to determine whether they predicted identical outcomes across two groups. Finally, it is important to note that the same indices (i.e., TLI, CFI, and RMSEA) used to test for fit in CFA models are also used to test for overall model fit in SEM models.

The theoretical model in Figure 1 (Appendix 2) was used to test model to data fit. The Educational Level variable was coded on a five-point scale where 1 = did not complete primary school; 2 = completed primary school; 3 = completed all-age school/commercial school/vocational school/H.E.A.R.T.; 4 = completed high/secondary school; and 5 = completed college or university. Occupational status was derived from the Smith code outlined in the sample descriptions section above. Physical and emotional trauma consisted of two latent variables: 'Physical Stress' and events that might cause 'Emotional Trauma'. The Physical Stress indicator was created by totaling the following three dichotomous variables, where study participants responded to questions as yes or no where no = 0 and 1 = yes: experienced serious non-violent physical injury; experienced severe illnesses/hospitalizations; and experienced chronic illnesses. Similarly, the Emotional Trauma variable consisted of responses to each of the following two dichotomously scored items: experienced sexual abuse or rape; has been a victim of other types of violence; and has witnessed (without being a victim) serious violence inflicted on others. The indicators for severe psychopathology (i.e., the Prodromal Psychosis, Active Psychosis and Bipolar syndromes) variables were derived from outcomes of the factor analyses described below in the heading, Results. Likewise, social and emotional strengths were derived from the results of the factor analyses (*see* Results).

## Results

### STRENGTHS FACTOR SOLUTION

The scree plot revealed that a single factor might be the best factor solution for the strength items. Although we retained and rotated other factor solutions, they had several cross-loaded items (indicating shared variance across factors) and some factors that were not theoretically meaningful. Thus, for this study the factor loadings from a solution with a single factor that we labeled Social and Emotional strengths are presented in Table 1 (Appendix 1).

### BEHAVIOURAL AND EMOTIONAL PROBLEMS FACTOR SOLUTION

The scree plot suggested the retention and rotation of three factors. Nevertheless, we retained and rotated factor solutions with as many as 10 factors and as few as two. Theoretical meaningfulness suggested the retention of five factors labeled Active Psychosis, Prodromal Psychosis, Somatization, Depression, and Bipolar disorders. All factors except Depression and Somatization were used in the SEM model, as they are more reflective of severe psychopathology (*see* Table 2, Appendix 1).

### CONFIRMATORY FACTOR ANALYSES

To ensure that all latent variables and their indicators were used in the SEM analyses, a series of CFAs were conducted to address model fit as well as to determine whether measurement invariance (i.e., that the constructs are measured across the groups in psychometrically identical fashion) emerged when the models were compared across groups. The model tested is shown in Figure 2 (Appendix 2). The results shown in Table 2 (Appendix 1) show that the $X^2$ for all but one model was not significant and that all fit indices revealed good model to data fit for all models tested. Furthermore, they also show that all $\Delta X^2$ values were not significant and that the assumption of measurement invariance across the groups studied is not violated.

## STRUCTURAL EQUATION MODELING

Figure 1 (Appendix 2) shows the theoretical SEM model tested; Figure 2 (Appendix 2) shows the theoretical CFA model; and Figure 3 (Appendix 2) shows the SEM model with non-significant paths removed. Table 2 (Appendix 1) shows that trimming the original model tested resulted in no deterioration of model fit. Prior to interpreting this trimmed model, we tested for invariance of the paths in the model across males and females and also across referred and nonreferred adults. The results show that each of the more complex two-group models did not produce a significant decrement in $X^2$ and that the single-group model provided significantly better model-to-data fit. Although some paths were significant for one of the groups tested but not the other, Table 2 (Appendix 1) also revealed that the paths in these models did not significantly differ even when they were constrained. The results of the trimmed two group models are presented in Table 3 (Appendix 1) and in Figures 4-7 (Appendix 2). Because the findings described above revealed the presence of invariance across all groups tested, only the single-group model is interpreted.

### Direct Pathways

As expected, the direct path from Educational Level to occupational status is positive and significant. The direct paths from occupational status to physical and emotional trauma, as well as to severe psychopathology is in the direction expected where higher education, together with occupational status significantly decreases the risk of physical and emotional trauma and severe psychopathology. The pathway between occupation and social and emotional strengths is negative, and the same trend is evident for the pathway from physical and emotional trauma to severe psychopathology. The path from social and emotional strengths to severe psychopathology is in the direction expected, where a higher strength level is significantly related to decreased levels of severe psychopathology.

### Indirect Paths and Mediated Effects

Because all indirect paths are part of mediated relationships between two variables, indirect paths are only presented as part of mediated paths. The direct path between occupational status and severe psychopathology is mediated by a positive indirect path through physical and emotional trauma. Some of the variance from occupational status to severe psychopathology is mediated by a positive indirect pathway through social and emotional strengths. The direct path between educational level shows that a higher educational level is associated with a decrement in the risk of severe psychopathology. However, the direct effect of education is mediated by a significant negative indirect pathway through occupational status, as well as a negative indirect pathway through physical and emotional trauma.

## Discussion

The present study described efforts toward developing a set of culturally relevant measures of behavioural and emotional strengths and problems for Caribbean persons aged 18 and over. Thus, it has demonstrated that culturally relevant measures which have both content and cultural validity are possible if qualitative methodology such as focus groups are used to capture and include the voice of the people (Kline, 2005; Vogt et al., 2004). By combining this procedure with the clinic record search (another qualitative procedure), and sampling data to the point of saturation of themes, it is possible to derive items that might be useful in the assessment of adults from the Caribbean. The power of this methodology is evident in the items loading on each factor in Table 2 (Appendix 1), where items such as taking clothes off in public, throwing stones at people, and running away from people are items that load under the Active Psychosis syndrome. Most Caribbean clinicians are aware that that such behaviour might be indicative of a psychotic process, but the items would not be found on measures developed in North America or Europe. The same statement might be made for brandishing a machete, acting like the police, and feeling like something is rolling in one's head – items loading under the Prodromal Psychosis Syndrome; feeling like head is expanding and gazing into space – items loading on Depression; and voicing religious beliefs too forcefully and excessive preaching – items loading under Bipolar syndrome. These findings suggest that measures from North America and Europe which do not include these culture specific items risk missing important symptomatology that persons from the Caribbean present and might, therefore, provide inaccurate information on these individuals' functioning (Lambert et al., 2003).

Turning to the model tested, the absence of a significant direct path between Educational Level and Strengths is noteworthy, especially when interpreted within the context of the significant indirect negative path through occupational status, as well as the significant direct path indicating a negative relationship between occupational status and social and emotional strengths. These findings suggest that individuals' educational levels only influence their strengths indirectly, and only through the occupational level in which one is classified. These findings might also underscore that persons of Caribbean heritage with limited means might have to develop significantly more social and emotional strengths in order to survive in their society, than those with more resources.

The direct paths between educational level and occupational status indicating a negative relationship between these variables and severe psychopathology are in the expected direction. That is, our own research on children and youth in the Caribbean together with the work of others, has indicated that variables such as educational and occupational levels that are often used to proxy SES are negatively associated with psychopathology within the Caribbean region and in other international settings (Dohrenwend, 1990; Dohrenwend et al., 1992; Lambert, Rowan, & Lyubansky, 2002; Lambert, Russ, Samms-Vaughan, Achenbach, & François-Bellas, 2001). This finding is further potentiated by the indirect pathway from educational level through occupational status to severe psychopathology. Thus, while higher educational level is an important factor in decreasing the risk for severe psychological disturbance, it can have an even more profound effect on this concern if individuals are employed.

The direct negative effect of occupational level on physical and emotional trauma is also worthy of note. This finding suggests that individuals in higher occupational levels are significantly less likely to be at risk for such trauma. The direct negative effect of physical and emotional trauma on severe psychopathology is counterintuitive. Viewed in the context of the indirect positive pathway of occupational status through physical and emotional trauma, this finding shows that although individuals of higher occupational levels and even some with higher educational levels are less likely to experience severe physical and emotional trauma or severe forms of psychopathology, those who are subjected to this trauma might be more at risk of severe psychopathology than those who are not. By contrast, some individuals with high educational levels, and who are also subjected to severe physical and emotional trauma might be less likely to develop severe psychopathology.

While some of the findings described above are difficult to interpret they might be explained by the mechanisms hypothesized in the diathesis stress model (Wicks-Nelson & Israel, 2003). That model posits that although some individuals might have high educational levels and high status jobs, if they are subjected to undue stress the interaction of this stress with their diathesis might make them more vulnerable to severe psychopathology. In addition, while some who are educated are at significantly lower risk of severe psychopathology, some who suffer severe trauma might also be at reduced risk. If education is used as a proxy for intellectual capabilities, it might also be inferred that some individuals with high levels of cognitive functioning might be capable of using this capability to inoculate themselves from the effects of severe stress, or be capable of using this capability to address the concerns emerging from such stressors.

Finally, the indirect positive pathways from occupational status through strengths, as well as that from educational level through occupational status and strengths which mediate the negative association between educational level, as well as occupational status, on severe psychopathology through strengths, are also puzzling. While these findings might be artifactual they might suggest that individuals who are highly educated and also hold higher status occupation and also rely extensively on strengths, place themselves at risk for severe psychopathology. As discussed previously, individuals with more resources might rely less on their social and emotional strengths because it is less necessary for their survival than those with limited means. It is possible that some individuals who are highly educated and have higher occupational status might have the diathesis for psychological vulnerability and that some of the effects of stress associated with acquiring higher education and maintaining their functioning in high status jobs, might place them at risk of psychopathology. These individuals might, therefore, have to cultivate and also maintain high strength levels to function. It is, however, difficult to appropriately tease out these findings without further research with samples that are large enough to permit the examination of these pathways across groups of individuals with low, moderate and high educational levels, together with occupational status.

Turning to the shortcomings of this study, it is important to note that while the sample size is adequate for the measurement-related section, and also adequate for the models tested, larger samples would allow testing of the models across more distinctly defined groups. For example, while the study has focused on invariance across referred and non-referred adults as well as males and females, it was not large enough to permit testing of the models across groups of nonreferred males versus females and referred males versus females. Furthermore, as mentioned in the preceding paragraph, it is also impossible to test the model across other groups such as individuals from low, moderate, and high occupational and educational levels. It is also important to note that events reflecting severe psychological and physical trauma have low population base rates and that problems emerging from such low base rates are magnified in small to moderately sized samples. To provide sufficient variance for the analyses, multiple questions reflecting trauma had to be combined in order to create the indicators in the model. Thus, it was impossible to include each item as an indicator of the trauma latent variable in the model. Finally, although the data used in this study were collected across multiple Caribbean nations, the analyses presented here were conducted only on samples from Jamaica. Hence the findings should be generalized across other Caribbean countries with caution.

Shifting focus to recommendations, the first set of recommendations focus on research-related recommendations. It is important that larger samples are obtained to test more complex models, to include items with low base rates as indicators in models, as well as to test different models across groups of individuals in less grossly defined segments. It is also important to examine the factor structure of the measures across more Caribbean nations and to test the SEM models across these countries.

The second set of recommendations suggests that although inferences drawn from the present study must be interpreted within the context of its limitations, it might have some important policy implications. Although further research is necessary to more clearly address causality, the association between educational level, as well as occupational status, on psychological adjustment could suggest that increasing the educational levels and also the occupational status of persons in the country might reduce the risks of severe psychopathology. While the investment in education and training of the nation's people might be costly, the treatment of severe psychological problems might be equally costly. Furthermore, the costs of such problems to families and communities can be tremendous. Furthermore, individuals with severe forms of psychopathology do not usually produce the income necessary to generate governmental tax revenues; and because most individuals with such problems generally lack resources, the cost of their treatment often further depletes governmental resources.

To conclude, it is important to note that despite its shortcomings, a thorough search of the literature and relevant records reveals that this is the first study which has used cutting-edge methodology to develop culturally appropriate measures of strengths and psychological problems for Caribbean people. This extensive sample, whose responses to the measures are being used to establish its psychometric properties, will provide an empirically rigorously designed and calibrated measure for clinical assessment, research, programme evaluation and other forms of professionally appropriate use. Item response theory (IRT) analyses, for example, will estimate the parameters of each item in the measure and will allow for accurate estimation of emotional and behavioural strengths in the Caribbean. IRT procedures will also permit relatively easy development of short forms that screen different types of psychopathology in persons residing in the Caribbean Basin. Additionally, these procedures will also provide the means of more in-depth testing for individuals who need it. The present study, therefore, represents the first method we know of that continues to use arguably more psychometrically rigorous statistical models to evaluate some of the psychometric properties of a measure designed to assess Caribbean citizens' functioning. This measure will also be used to predict multiple factors that contribute to severe psychopathology and those which potentate or buffer the effects of such factors. Finally, the study suggests that increasing education, facilitating increments in SES and reducing physical and emotional trauma might contribute to a reduction in severe psychological problems and increase resources available to families, communities, and societies.

# Appendix 1 – Tables

*Table 1:* *Factor Loadings for the Caribbean Symptom Checklist Self-Report*

| Item descriptions | Social and Emotional Strengths |
|---|---|
| 1. Able to read social cues | .42 |
| 2. Accept consequences for your actions | .43 |
| 3. Appropriate social skills/get along with others | .43 |
| 4. Behaviour usually consistent across situations | .32 |
| 5. Creative | .46 |
| 6. Communicate well | .48 |
| 7. Feel loved | .46 |
| 8. Feel safe when in safe surroundings | .41 |
| 9. Focused when working | .47 |
| 10. Have a variety of interests | .47 |
| 11. Friendly | .42 |
| 12. Have positive attitude, hopeful/ good outlook on the future | .63 |
| 13. Have a variety of friends | .40 |
| 14. Have confidence/good self-esteem | .52 |
| 15. Have good physical health | .43 |
| 16. Have good problem solving skills | .56 |
| 17. Have healthy competitiveness | .53 |
| 18. Interested in your history and culture | .44 |
| 19. Involved in exercise and fitness | .32 |
| 20. Involved in the arts | .36 |
| 21. Loving, appropriately affectionate | .53 |
| 22. Make appropriate choices | .53 |
| 23. Mediate or solves conflicts with others | .54 |

| Item descriptions | Social and Emotional Strengths |
|---|---|
| 24. Motivated, hard working | .54 |
| 25. Practise good hygiene | .45 |
| 26. Responsible | .53 |
| 27. Set appropriate goals | .57 |
| 28. Socially active with friends | .48 |
| 29. Take leadership role when appropriate | .55 |
| 30. Tolerate/accept differences in others | .48 |
| 31. Work well with others | .59 |

_Table 2: Factor Loadings for the Caribbean Symptom Checklist Self-Report for Behavioural and Emotional Problems_

| Item descriptions | Psychosis | Prodromal | Depression | Somatic | Bipolar |
|---|---|---|---|---|---|
| 1. Abusing alcohol/ drinking too much | | .525 | | | |
| 2. Acting like others (e.g., act like police) | | .533 | | | |
| 6. Afraid to be alone | | | | | .370 |
| 7. Afraid of germs or getting diseases | | | | | .400 |
| 9. Angry/upset | | | .312 | | |
| 10. Anxious/nervous/ shakiness inside | | | | | .325 |
| 11. Attacking family members/assaulting others | | .591 | | | |
| 12. Attempting suicide or attempting to harm yourself | | .533 | | | |
| 13. Bad dreams/ nightmares | | | .336 | | |
| 14. Behaviour don't fit this person moods | | | | | .382 |

*Table 2 (contd.):  Factor Loadings for the Caribbean Symptom Checklist Self-Report for Behavioural and Emotional Problems*

| Item descriptions | Psychosis | Prodromal | Depression | Somatic | Bipolar |
|---|---|---|---|---|---|
| 15. Believe others are evil | .442 | | | | |
| 16. Believe you have superior powers | .481 | | | | |
| 17. Believe people put spirits on you | .440 | | | | |
| 19. Boisterous/loud/ raucous | .612 | | | | |
| 20. Burning, throwing away or destroying belongs | .491 | | | | |
| 21. Can't complete tasks | .491 | | | | |
| 22. Carrying or brandishing knife/ machete | .550 | | | | |
| 24. Collecting and hoarding things | .440 | | | | |
| 26. Constantly active/ restless | | | .333 | | |
| 27. Constantly checking things | | | | | .356 |
| 30. Crying easily | | | | | .310 |
| 32. Destroying others' things/destructive | .638 | | | | |
| 33. Dizziness/giddiness/ weakness/light- headedness | | | | .323 | |
| 34. Disruptive/annoying and provoking others | .550 | | | | |
| 36. Don't speak | | | | | .303 |
| 37. Drinking ganja tea | .600 | | | | |
| 39. Elated, extremely happy, cheerful or energetic | | | | | .483 |

_Table 2 (contd.):  Factor Loadings for the Caribbean Symptom Checklist Self-Report for Behavioural and Emotional Problems_

| Item descriptions | Psychosis | Prodromal | Depression | Somatic | Bipolar |
|---|---|---|---|---|---|
| 40. Excessively singing to yourself | | | | | .462 |
| 42. Fainting, unconsciousness | | .459 | | | |
| 43. Fast and pressured speech | | .531 | | | |
| 44. Feeling like you are overpowered by demons | | .628 | | | |
| 45. Feeling like you are out of control | | .483 | | | |
| 46. Feeling someone is touching you in your sleep | | .523 | | | |
| 47. Feeling like something is rolling in your head | | .481 | | | |
| 49. Feeling dead inside | | | .348 | | |
| 50. Feeling that something bad is going to happen | | | .533 | | |
| 51.feeling others do not understand you | | | .727 | | |
| 52. Feeling like your body is not yours | | | | .356 | |
| 53. Feeling guilty or responsible for things | | | .541 | | |
| 54. Feeling helpless | | | .425 | | |
| 55. Feeling like your head is expanding | | | .327 | | |
| 56. Feeling lonely | | | .575 | | |
| 57. Feeling that you are being watched | | | .557 | | |
| 58. Fixed gaze into space | | | .503 | | |

*Table 2 (contd.):* Factor Loadings for the Caribbean Symptom Checklist Self-Report for Behavioural and Emotional Problems

| Item descriptions | Psychosis | Prodromal | Depression | Somatic | Bipolar |
|---|---|---|---|---|---|
| 59. Frightened | | | .346 | | |
| 60. Giving away your belongings | | | | | .343 |
| 61. Gossiping/broadcasting | .343 | | | | |
| 63. Hate or cannot stand noise | | | | | .367 |
| 64. Having little or no interest in things | | | .315 | | |
| 65. Having urges to beat, injure or harm someone | | .350 | | | |
| 69. Hearing voices or sounds that others do not hear | | | | .482 | |
| 71. Heavy feelings in arms or legs | | | | .624 | |
| 72. Hot or cold spells/ flashes | | | | .476 | |
| 73. Jumping from task to task | | | | .385 | |
| 74. Jumping out of sleep | | | | .578 | |
| 75. Laughing inappropriately to yourself | | | | .393 | |
| 77. Making strange noises | .379 | | | | |
| 78. Moody/fast changes in moods | | | .388 | | |
| 79. Nausea, bad feelings or upset stomach | | | | .404 | |
| 81. Not sure who you or others are | .490 | | | | |
| 83. Numbness or tingling in parts of body | | | | .678 | |

*Table 2 (contd.): Factor Loadings for the Caribbean Symptom Checklist Self-Report for Behavioural and Emotional Problems*

| Item descriptions | Psychosis | Prodromal | Depression | Somatic | Bipolar |
|---|---|---|---|---|---|
| 86. Others think your religious beliefs are too strong | | | | .479 | |
| 87. Pain in head or neck | | | | .658 | |
| 88. Pain in lower neck | | | | .533 | |
| 89. Pain in heart or chest | | | | .444 | |
| 90. Parts of face or other muscle move uncontrollably | | | | .681 | |
| 91. People believe you dress strangely or unusually | | | | .483 | |
| 95. Poor attention to hygiene or cleanliness | | .345 | | | |
| 96. Preaching excessively | | | .424 | | |
| 97. Problems at work or school | | | | .315 | |
| 98. Problems falling asleep | | | .391 | | |
| 100. Racing thoughts | | | .423 | | |
| 101. Responding to voices nobody else hears | .576 | | | | |
| 102. Repeating certain acts over and over | .375 | | | | |
| 103. Restless or disturbed asleep | | | .376 | | |
| 104. Ringing sound in ears | .444 | | | | |
| 105. Seeing things that nobody else sees | .590 | | | | |
| 106. Seizure or fit | .693 | | | | |

*Table 2 (contd.): Factor Loadings for the Caribbean Symptom Checklist Self-Report for Behavioural and Emotional Problems*

| Item descriptions | Psychosis | Prodromal | Depression | Somatic | Bipolar |
|---|---|---|---|---|---|
| 108. Setting fires | .817 | | | | |
| 110. Smoking ganja | .644 | | | | |
| 112. Speaking very slowly | .599 | | | | |
| 113. Speaking foolishness /incoherent speech | .482 | | | | |
| 114. Strange feeling in head and body parts | .650 | | | | |
| 115. Strange behaviour | .587 | | | | |
| 116. Stubborn behaviour | | | .457 | | |
| 117. Taking off clothes in public | .740 | | | | |
| 118. Taking other people's things/stealing | .694 | | | | |
| 119. Talking to yourself a lot | | | .466 | | |
| 122. Thinking about killing yourself | | .316 | | | |
| 123. Thoughts being taken out of your mind | | | .317 | | |
| 124. Threatening others | .537 | | | | |
| 125. Throwing stones or other objects | .617 | | | | |
| 126. Throwing stones or other objects at people | .739 | | | | |
| 127. Trembling or shaking all over | .456 | | | | |
| 128. Trouble falling asleep | | | .774 | | |

_Table 2 (contd.):_ _Factor Loadings for the Caribbean Symptom Checklist Self-Report for_
_Behavioural and Emotional Problems_

| Item descriptions | Psychosis | Prodromal | Depression | Somatic | Bipolar |
|---|---|---|---|---|---|
| 129. Trouble concentrating | | | .535 | | |
| 130. Trouble getting or catching your breath | .378 | | | | |
| 131. Trouble remember-ing things/forgetting | | | .581 | | |
| 132. Tunnel vision | .423 | | | | |
| 133. Unhappy, depressed, sad, or low in spirit | | | .748 | | |
| 134. Using cocaine or other drugs | .465 | | | | |
| 135. Violent, aggressive behaviour | .593 | | | | |
| 136. Vomiting | .679 | | | | |
| 138. Walking up and down aimlessly | .372 | | | | |
| 139. Weakness | | | .425 | | |
| 140. Withdrawn | | | .569 | | |
| 141. Head feels heavy | | | | .429 | |
| 142. Worrying a lot | | | .684 | | |
| 143. Perspiring more than usual | | | .351 | | |
| 145. Feeling nervous | | | .560 | | |
| 146. Runs away from home and relatives | | .421 | | | |

*Table 3: Fit Indices for Confirmatory Factor Analytical and Structural Equation Models*

| Model Tested | $X^2$ | DF | TLI | CFI | RMSEA | $\Delta X^2$ | DF | p |
|---|---|---|---|---|---|---|---|---|
| *Invariance tests for Factors Used in Two Group Structural Equation Modeling* | | | | | | | | |
| Males vs. females unconstrained | 15.72 | 8 | .99 | .99 | .04 | | | |
| Males vs. females constrained | 20.41 | 11 | .99 | .97 | .04 | 4.69 | 3 | ns |
| Referred vs. nonreferred unconstrained | 14.84 | 8 | .99 | .99 | .04 | | | |
| Referred vs. nonreferred constrained | 19.57 | 11 | .99 | .99 | .04 | 4.73 | 3 | ns |

| Model Tested | $X^2$ | DF | TLI | CFI | RMSEA | $\Delta X^2$ | DF | p |
|---|---|---|---|---|---|---|---|---|
| *Structural Equation Models* | | | | | | | | |
| Total sample untrimmed | 16.27 | 13 | .99 | .99 | .02 | | | |
| Total sample trimmed | 18.76 | 15 | .99 | .99 | .02 | 2.49 | 2 | ns |
| Males vs. females untrimmed | 39.37 | 26 | .98 | .99 | .03 | | | |
| Males vs. females trimmed | 52.76 | 34 | .98 | .99 | .03 | 13.39 | 8 | ns |
| Males vs. females trimmed constrained | 64.99 | 40 | .98 | .98 | .02 | 12.23 | 6 | ns |
| Referred vs. nonreferred untrimmed | 33.56 | 26 | .99 | .99 | .02 | | | |
| Referred vs. nonreferred trimmed | 42.41 | 32 | .99 | .99 | .02 | 8.85 | 6 | ns |
| Referred vs. nonreferred trimmed const. | 50.67 | 39 | .99 | .99 | .02 | 8.26 | 7 | ns |

**Note:** For all CFA tests $X^2$ values are significant at $p < .05$ emerged only for the male/female unconstrained model.

For SEM models significant $X^2$ emerged for only the males vs. females trimmed and for the males vs. females trimmed and constrained models. DF = degrees of freedom; TLI = Tucker-Lewis index; CFI = Comparative Fit Index; RMSEA = Root Mean Square Error of Approximation; $\Delta X^2$ = test of invariance calculated from $X^2$ constrained – $X^2$ unconstrained, with the degree of freedom for this index = DF constrained – DF unconstrained; ns = nonsignificant;

Total Sample vs. Referred/nonreferred $\Delta X^2$ (13) = 19.25, p > .05;

Total Sample vs. Male/Female $\Delta X^2$ (13) = 23.1, p < .05.

# Appendix 2 – Figures

_Figure 1: Theoretical Model for Structural Equation Analyses_

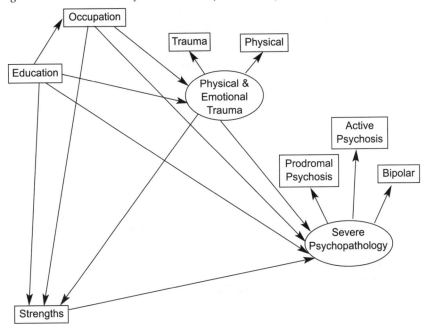

_Figure 2: Theoretical Confirmatory Factor Analysis Model_

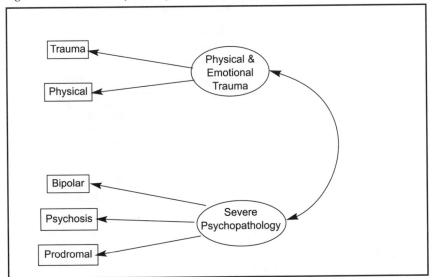

*Figure 3: Trimmed Model for Total Sample*

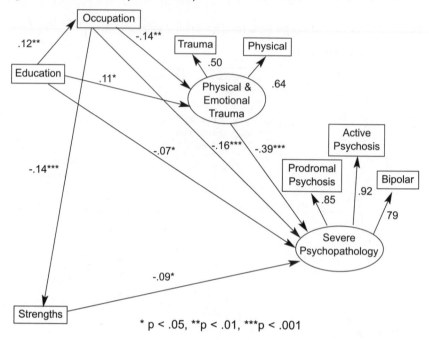

\* p < .05, \*\*p < .01, \*\*\*p < .001

*Figure 4: Model for Females*

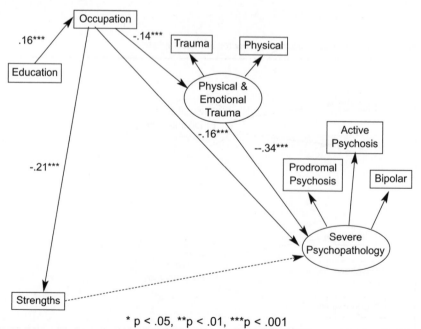

\* p < .05, \*\*p < .01, \*\*\*p < .001

*Figure 5: Model for Males*

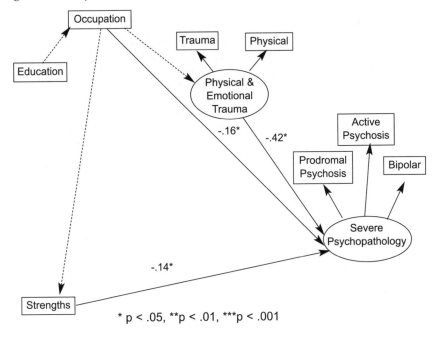

* p < .05, **p < .01, ***p < .001

*Figure 6: Model for Nonreferred Adults*

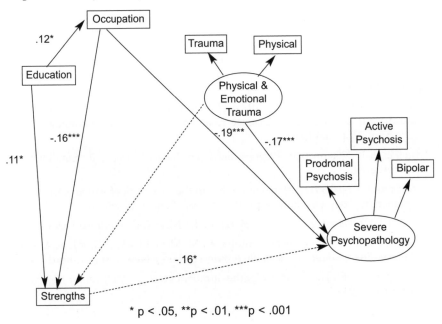

* p < .05, **p < .01, ***p < .001

*Figure 7: Model for Referred Adults*

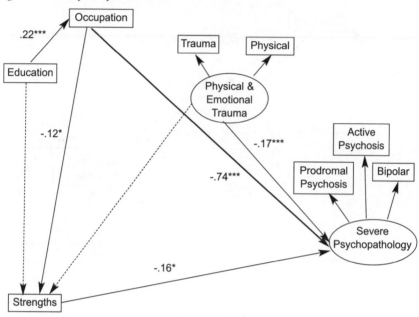

\* p < .05, \*\*p < .01, \*\*\*p < .001

## REFERENCES

American Psychological Society. (1996). Human Capital Initiative: Reducing mental disorders: A behavioral science research plan for psychopathology. *APS Observer*, 3 (Special Issue).

Arbuckle, J. L. (2003). *Amos Program and Users Guide*. Chicago, IL: Smallwaters Corporation.

Boyd-Franklin, N. (1991). Recurrent themes in the treatment of African-American women in group psychotherapy. *Women and Therapy*, 11, 25-40.

―――. (2003). *Black families in therapy* (2nd ed.). New York: Guilford Press.

Brice-Barker, J. (1996). Jamaican Families. In M. McGoldrick, J. Giordano & J. K. Pearce (Eds.), *Ethnicity and family therapy* (2nd ed.). New York: Guilford Press.

Cattell, R. B. (1966). The scree test for the number of factors. *Multivariate Behavioral Research*, 1, 245-276.

Coll, C. G., Lamberty, G., Jenkins, R., McAdoo, H. P., Crnic, K., Wasik, B. H., & Garcia, H. V. (1998). An integrative model for the study of developmental competencies in minority children. *Child-Development*, 67, 1891-1914.

Culbertson, J. L. (1999). Research methods with children. In P. C. Kendall, J. N. Butcher, & G. N. Holmbeck (Eds.), *Research Methods in Clinical Psychology* (pp. 619-633). New York: John Wiley & Sons.

DeShon, R. P. (1998). A cautionary note on measurement error corrections in structural equation models. *Psychological Methods*, 3, 412-423.

Dohrenwend, B. P. (1990). Socioeconomic status (SES) and psychiatric disorders: Are the issues still compelling? *Social Psychiatry and Psychiatric Epidemiology*, 25, 41-47.

Dohrenwend, B. P., Levav, I., Schrout, P. E., Schwartz, S., Naveh, G., Skodol, A. E., et al. (1992). Socioeconomic status and psychiatric disorders: The causation-selection issue. *Science*, 225, 946-952.

Fabrigar, L. R., Wegener, D. T., MacCallum, R. C., & Strahan, E. J. (1999). Evaluating the use of exploratory factor analysis in psychological research. *Psychological Methods*, 4 (3), 272-299.

Embretson, S. E., & Reise, S. P. (2000). *Item Response theory for psychologists*. Mahwah, NJ: Lawrence Erlbaum.

Garcia Coll, C. G., & Garcia, H. A. (1995). Theory and research with children of color: Implications for social policy. Paper presented at the Biennial meeting of the Society for Research in Child Development, Indianapolis.

Gibbs, G. T. (1998). High-risk behaviors in African American Youth: Conceptual and methodological issues in research. In V. C. McLoyd & L. Steinberg (Eds.), *Studying minority adolescents: Conceptual, methodological, and theoretical issues* (pp. 55-85). Mahwah, NJ: Lawrence Erlbaum.

Greenberg, M. T., Lengua, L. J., Coie, J. D., Pinderhughes, E. E., Bierman, K., Dodge, K. A., et al. (1999). Predicting developmental outcomes at school entry using a multiple-risk model: Four American communities. *Developmental Psychology*, 35 (2), 403-417.

Hakstian, A. R., Rogers, W. T., & Cattell, R. B. (1982). The behavior of number-of-factors rules with simulated data. *Multivariate Behavioral Research*, 17 (2), 193-219.

Haynes, S. N., Nelson, M. A., & Blaine, D. D. (1999). Psychometric issues in assessment research. In P. C. Kendall, J. N. Butcher & G. N. Holmbeck (Eds.), *Research methods in clinical psychology* (pp. 125-154). New York: John Wiley and Sons.

Holmbeck, G. N., & Shapera, W. E. (1999). Research Methods with adolescents. In P. C. Kendall, J. N. Butcher & G. N. Holmbeck (Eds.), *Research methods in clinical psychology* (pp. 634-661). New York: John Wiley and Sons.

Hoyle, R. H. (1994). Introduction to the special section: Structural equation modeling in clinical research. *Journal of Consulting and Clinical Psychology*, 62(3), 427-428.

Hoyle, R. H., & Smith, G. T. (1994). Formulating clinical research hypotheses as structural equation models: A conceptual overview. *Journal of Consulting and Clinical Psychology*, 62(3), 429-440.

Katerndahl, D., Burge, S., & Kellogg, N. (2005). Predictors of development of adult psychopathology in female victims of childhood sexual abuse. *Journal of Nervous and Mental Disease*, 193, 258-264.

Kazdin, A. E. (1999). Overview of research design issues in clinical psychology. In P. C. Kendall, J. N. Butcher & G. N. Holmbeck (Eds.), *Research methods in clinical psychology* (2nd ed., pp. 3-30). New York: John Wiley & Sons.

Kline, J. J. B. (2005). *Psychological testing: A practical approach to design and evaluation*. Thousand Oaks: Sage.

Knight, G. P., & Hill, N. (1998). Measurement equivalence in research involving minority adolescents. In V. C. McLoyd & L. Steinberg (Eds.), *Studying minority adolescents: Conceptual, methodological, and theoretical issues* (pp. 183-210). Mahwah, NJ: Lawrence Erlbaum.

Lambert, M. C., Essau, C. A., Schmitt, N., & Samms-Vaughan, M. E. (2007). Dimensionality and psychometric invariance of the Youth Self-report Form of the Child Behavior Checklist in cross-national settings. *Assessment*, 231-245.

Lambert, M. C., Lambert C. T. M., Douglas (August 2005). Attitudes of nonreferred Jamaican adults toward mental Health Problems in their Fellow Citizens. Paper presented at the Conference of Caribbean Psychiatric Association, Kingston, Jamaica, W. I.

Lambert, M. C., Hickling, F., Lambert C. T. M., Douglas, K., & Samms-Vaughan, M. (August 2005). Contributors to Thought Disorders in Caribbean Adults: A Focus on Jamaica Paper presented at the Conference of Caribbean Psychiatric Association, Kingston, Jamaica, W. I.

Lambert, M. C., Rowan, G. T., & Lyubansky, M. (2002). Behavior and emotional problems of clinic-referred African American children and adolescents: Parent reports for ages 4-18. *Journal of Child and Family Studies*, 271-585.

Lambert, M. C., Russ, C. M., Samms-Vaughan, M. E., Achenbach, T. M., & Francois-Bellas, V. (2001). Comparisons of behavioral and emotional problems among referred and nonreferred children of the African Diaspora: Parent and teacher reports for African American and Jamaican children. *Caribbean Journal of Psychology*, 2, 50-68.

Lambert, M. C., Schmitt, N., Samms-Vaughan, M. E., An, J. S., Fairclough, M., & Nutter, C. A. (2003). Is it prudent to administer all items for each Child Behavior Checklist cross-informant syndrome? Evaluating the psychometric properties of Youth Self-Report dimensions with confirmatory factor analysis and item response theory. *Psychological Assessment*, 15 (4), 550-568.

MacCallum, R. (1986). Specification searches in covariance structure modeling. *Psychological Bulletin*, 100 (1), 107-120.

Marshall, G. N., Orlando, M., Foy, D. W., & Belzberg, H. (2002). Development and validation of a modified version of the Peritraumatic Dissociative Questionnaire. *Psychological Assessment*, 14, 123-124.

McLoyd, V. C. (1995). Poverty, parenting, and policy: Meeting the support needs of poor parents. In H. E. Fitzgerald, B. Lester & B. S. Zuckerman (Eds.), *Children of poverty: Research, health, and policy issues. Reference books on family issues, Vol. 23 and Garland reference library of social science, Vol. 968.* (pp. 269-303): New York: Garland Publishing, Inc.

McLoyd, V. C., & Ceballo, R. (1998). Conceptualizing and assessing economic context: Issues of race and child development. In V. C. McLoyd & L. Steinberg (Eds.), *Studying minority adolescents: Conceptual, methodological, and theoretical issues.* Mahwah, NJ: Lawrence Erlbaum Associates.

McLoyd, V. C., & Randolph, S. M. (1986). Secular trends in the study of Afro-American children: A review of Child Development, 1936-1980. *Monographs of the Society for Research in Child Development,* 50 (4-5), 78-92.

McLoyd, V. C., & Steinberg, L. (1998). Preface to "Studying Minority Adolescents: Conceptual, methodological, and theoretical issues". In V. C. McLoyd & L. Steinberg (Eds.), *Studying minority adolescents: Conceptual, methodological, and theoretical issues.* Mahwah, NJ: Lawrence Erlbaum Associates.

Mattisohanni, E. L., Moilanen, K., Issohanni, I., Kemppainen, H., Koponen, H., Miettunen, J., et al. (2005). Predictors of schizophrenia. *British Journal of Psychiatry,* 187 (suppl, 48), s4-s7.

Newcomb, M. D. (1994). Drug use and intimate relationships among women and men: Separating specific from general effects in prospective data using structural equation models. *Journal of Consulting and Clinical Psychology,* 62 (3), 463-476.

Nunnally, J. C., & Bernstein, I. H. (1994). *Psychometric theory* (3rd ed.). New York: McGraw-Hill Humanities.

Phinney, J. S., & Landin, J. (1998). Research paradigms for studying ethnic minority families within and across groups. In V. C. McLoyd & L. Steinberg (Eds.), *Studying minority adolescents: Conceptual, methodological, and theoretical issues.* (pp. 89-109). Mahwah, NJ: Lawrence Erlbaum Associates.

Resnicow, K., Ross-Gaddy, D., & Vaughan, R. D. (1995). Structure of problem and positive behaviors in African American youths. *Journal of Consulting and Clinical Psychology,* 63, 594-603.

Ruggiero, K. J., McLeer, S., & Dixon, J. F (2000). Sexual abuse characteristics associates with survivor psychopathology, *Child Abuse and Neglect,* 24, 651-964.

Schumacker, R. E., & Lomax, R. G. (1996). *A beginner's guide to structural equation modeling.* Mahwah, NJ: Lawrence Erlbaum.

Smith, A. G. (1984). *Culture, race and class in the Commonwealth Caribbean.* Mona, Jamaica, WI: University of the West Indies, Department of Extramural Studies.

Staples, R. (1999). *The Black family: Essays and studies* (6th ed.). Albany, NY: Wadsworth.

Tabachnick, B. G., & Fidell, L. S. (2001). *Using multivariate statistics* (4th ed.). Needham Heights, MA: Allyn & Bacon.

U.S. Department of Health and Human Services (1999). *Mental health: A report of the Surgeon General.* Rockville, MD: Department of Health and Human Services, Substance Abuse and Mental Health Services Administration, Center for Mental Health Services, National Institutes of Health, National Institute of Mental Health.

Vogt, D. S., King, D. W., & King, L. A. (2004). Focus groups in psychological assessment: Enhancing content validity by consulting members of the target population. *Psychological Assessment,* 16, 231-243.

Wicks-Nelson, R., & Israel, A. C. (2003). *Behavior disorders of childhood* (5th ed.). Upper Saddle River: Prentice Hall.

# 10 Redefining Personality Disorder in Jamaica

## Frederick W. Hickling, Jacqueline Martin, & Allison Harrisingh-Dewar

Blacks and whites are proportionately bad as well as proportionately good, living under the conditions and environments of our imperfect civilization. All beauty, virtue and goodness are the exclusive attributes of no one race.

*Marcus Garvey (1967).*

There is special interest today in an understanding and clarification of the contradictions surrounding the human personality, the concept of personality disorder, and the dynamic inter-relationship of these to the ever-changing and complex human societies in which we live (Francis & Widiger, 1986; Hirschfield 1986). Information on personality disorders currently available is restricted in volume when compared to a number of other disorders such as schizophrenia and depression (Lenzenweger, et al., 1997). The types of personality disorders have also changed throughout the years, and these modifications have thus far been placed in each successive version of the *Diagnostic Statistical Manual of Mental Disorders* of the American Psychiatric Association. Over the past three decades, the World Health Organization Mental Health Program has been placing great emphasis on developing reliable and cross-culturally applicable diagnostic criteria and relevant instruments for the assessment of mental disorders (Pilgrim & Mann, 1990).

Personality traits are enduring patterns of perceiving, relating to, and thinking about the environment and oneself. When personality traits are

263

inflexible, maladaptive and cause either significant impairment in social or occupational functioning, or subjective distress, they constitute a personality disorder (DSM III-R, American Psychiatric Association, 1980). By 1994 the American Psychiatric Association had refined this definition as "an enduring pattern of inner experience and behavior that deviates markedly from the expectations of the individual's culture, is pervasive and inflexible, has an onset in adolescence or early adulthood, is stable over time, and leads to distress or impairment" (DSM- IV, 1994). Personality disorders have been placed on Axis II in the third and fourth edition of the *Diagnostic Statistical Manual of Mental Disorders* (DSM-III-R, DSM-IV-TR, American Psychiatric Association, 1980, 2000).

Personality disorders usually become visible within the early adult years. Over time, difficulties experienced become woven into the individual's persona and, as such, inner conflicts and problems relating to others become increasingly strengthened. Individuals with a personality disorder exhibit specific cardinal personality traits to an unusual and inappropriate extreme. Once an individual's personality traits become maladaptive and inflexible, thereby resulting in significant functional impairment or distress, a personality disorder is considered. Many mental health professionals use the DSM-IV-TR criteria for diagnosing personality disorders and for categorizing individuals into specific clusters and subgroups of personality disorder. Individuals who suffer from a personality disorder, or any mental illness, will have difficulty adjusting to societal demands, and are likely to experience prejudice and discrimination due to the stigma attached to having a mental illness.

Liebert & Spiegler (1997), in  paraphrasing Hans Jürgen Eysenck, a psychologist most remembered for his work in human personality and intelligence, define personality as " the more or less stable and enduring organization of a person's character, temperament, intellect, and physique, which determines his unique adjustment to his environment ". Hence, it appears fair to say that an individual with a disordered personality may, therefore, have difficulty in adjusting to the acceptable norms of his environment and, as is stated in the DSM IV-TR definition of personality disorder, will display maladaptive behaviours resulting in social and occupational malfunction. The social malfunction of individuals or groups in a society will ultimately leave that society itself disordered, unhealthy and prone to despair. Thus the diagnosis and treatment of mental disorders, and in particular, personality disorders, have become of paramount importance for the creation of a safe well-ordered and progressive society. Epidemiological studies indicate that personality disorders are common, with a lifetime prevalence of 15 per cent of adults in the USA. One in seven adults in that population has a personality disorder and may have more than one (Zimmerman et al., 2005).

An important characteristic of the longitudinal course of personality disorder is the frequent co-occurrence with other illnesses, both psychiatric and non-psychiatric, as well as social and occupational dysfunction. For example, there is an association between borderline personality disorder and depression, histrionic personality disorder and somatization (Tryer et al., 2006). Chakroun et al. (2004) documented the causal association between personality disorder and substance abuse. Houston et al. (2001) showed that personality disorder was present in 29.6 per cent, and accentuated personality traits were present on psychological autopsy of 55.6 per cent of young people who committed suicide. Antisocial personality disorder is a strong predictor of criminal recidivism, particularly violent recidivism and, as such, 50–70 per cent of the prison population in Canada has antisocial personality disorder (Hucker, 2005). Similarly, Singleton (1998) showed that 78 per cent of all males remanded, 64 per cent of all males sentenced and 50 per cent of all females sentenced in a random sample of all prisoners in Wales and England had antisocial personality disorder.

Personality disorder as a cause of crime and violence is often underestimated in patients of African Caribbean origin. While persons of Afro Caribbean origin were admitted to forensic facilities three times more often than their White counterparts in Britain, their diagnoses were mainly psychotic illnesses, compared to a diagnosis of a personality disorder in Whites (Maden et al., 1999). This discrepancy in findings implies that studies of the pathways by which African Caribbean and other minorities reach a forensic facility are needed, as a personality disorder that is potentially treatable may be the cause of the antisocial behaviour for which they are serving time in the forensic facilities. The tailoring of assessment and diagnostic tools to take into account ethno-cultural differences is often recommended but also often ignored. The major benefit of the creation of these tools would be to decrease the percentage of undiagnosed personality disorders in the population and institute early intervention and treatment in this potentially lethal "hidden" population. Given that personality disorder has its roots in childhood and adolescence, the case for early diagnosis and intervention is further strengthened by the findings of a study by Aggrey Burke (1980) where two per cent of a group of delinquent West Indian boys in an approved school were found to meet the criteria for personality disorder. There is a paucity of published material on psychiatric conditions, other than schizophrenia, in the Caribbean. This may be due to the fact that the currently available validated instruments (1990) for the diagnosis of personality disorder tend to be tedious, time-consuming and perceived as racially and culturally biased towards the developed countries.

Fanon (1965) was one of the first psychiatrists to challenge the established concepts of behaviour and personality originating in a eurocentric and capitalistic socio-economic system, and to demand a re-evaluation of the behaviour of oppressed people, based on their own historical and sociocultural realities. The concept of psychopathy becomes of even greater interest to Blacks and other minority groups once it is recognized that the definitions of psychopathy are dictated by a worldview that is predominantly eurocentric (Nobles et al., 1997). Although the DSM-IV cautions therapists to consider an individual's ethnic, cultural and social background in applying a personality disorder diagnosis, Alarcon (1996), as cited in Iwamasa, Larrabee, and Merritt (2000), determined that less than two-thirds of the recommendations made by the DSM-IV Group on Culture and Diagnosis were included in the final version of the DSM-IV. It should also be noted that the DSM-IV does not provide clinicians with guidelines or recommendations on how to make a diagnostic judgment when assessing patients from varying cultures.

Personality disorders continue to receive limited attention from cross-cultural psychiatry. This is likely a result of the huge methodological problems involved, and the value judgements about what is "abnormal" in relation to cultural values and norms (Mumford, 1995). Considerable responsibility is, therefore, placed on the clinician to make a determination of whether the diagnosis is applicable to the individual – given the cultural context in which he or she lives. This is very problematic when a clinician has little knowledge or experience in the various cultural aspects of a patient's life.

# Personality Disorders in Jamaica

The Jamaican population consists of a combination of individuals from African, Chinese, Indian and European descent. Here, religion is an essential part of everyday life and as a result, morals and values may differ from those in the North America and Europe. Experiences and lessons from the past have contributed to the recognition that self-confidence and self-reliance bring about full freedom, and this has resulted in a vibrant cultural richness. The Jamaican heritage to which many peoples have contributed has evolved into what has become known as the "Jamaican Personality" (The National Library of Jamaica and the Urban Development Corporation, 1984). In the Jamaican society, pervasive levels of stress and coping difficulties have led to the surfacing of a number of disordered personality traits. Jamaicans experience racial, class, sexual, political and religious conflicts in their lives, which have originated from the historical experience of European imposed slavery. Slaves in Jamaica had no rights and, as such, any thoughts or concerns they had often went unheard. Jamaican slaves experienced dislocation from their African homeland, the horrors of the Trans-Atlantic middle passage, and the genocidal enforcement of their labour on the British-owned plantations (Patterson, 1967; Sherlock and Bennett, 1998). They were forcibly separated from their families, their women raped and beaten by plantation owners and the men tortured and belittled by their masters (Hall, 1989). Emotions had to be internalized for fear of punishment, thereby immortalizing these experiences and this way of life, which have become ingrained in the contemporary Jamaican psyche. Today, many members of Jamaican society have difficulty taking personal responsibility for their actions, preferring to put blame on something or someone else, or denying that they are even aware of what took place. Some Jamaican people turn a blind eye to illegal and immoral actions in order to avoid punishment, just as their ancestors were forced to do during slavery. Maladaptive personality traits have been passed down from generation to generation into present-day society, which in many ways parallels the conditions that existed during slavery; and these traits, consequently, have become the foundations of contemporary personality disorders. Jamaican sociologist Carl Stone (1992) opined that the problems in Jamaica were rooted in serious personality disorders, with violent crime being the tip of the iceberg of violent behaviour in the country. He suggested that hypersensitivity about status – the 'dis' syndrome[1] was rife in the island, and that aggression was a standard tool for asserting personhood. Most Jamaicans saw authority as social oppression, and colonization and the plantation system were the parents of the tarnished authority system. He concluded that no new authority systems had been established in independent Jamaica to replace colonialism.

The psychiatric study of personality disorder in Jamaica emerged in the 1970s following exchange programmes of young psychiatrists between the Department of Psychiatry at the University of the West Indies, Mona, and the Department of Psychiatry of the University of Edinburgh. Professor of Psychiatry and Psychotherapist, Henry Walton, was a pioneer in the study of personality disorder, and focused the attention of his students on a classification of personality disorder based on a nosology of insight (Walton et al., 1970). The principal author of the present chapter, on his return to Jamaica in the early 1970s, began to apply this perspective to the study of personality disorder in Jamaica, having been exposed to, and influenced by Walton's perspectives of personality disorder, while a psychiatric resident at the University of Edinburgh.

Work with a number of patients who came seeking assistance led to a study of personality disorder in the Jamaican people who were being seen in the author's private practice at that time. The purpose of the study was to investigate the behaviour of a group of predominantly Black Jamaican men and women and their socio-cultural realities, and to analyze the findings in relation to the demographic, clinical, and diagnostic characteristics of this group of patients. A critical component of this study was the application of a dialectical framework (Cornforth, 1952) to the phenomenological, behavioural and sociological characteristics presented by these patients. Thirty-four men and women seen between 1974 and 1980 provided the raw data for the study. These people all came voluntarily to the psychiatrist to seek assistance in the resolution of thoughts, feelings and actions which they were experiencing in their lives, and which they perceived as a problem to their existence. All remained in individual psychotherapy for a minimum of six months, involving one-hour weekly sessions with the therapist. The written reports of these sessions and their case histories were analyzed in respect of each patient, and their phenomenological and sociocultural factors were disaggregated, collated on a spreadsheet, tabulated and statistically analyzed. In each case, the diagnosis of personality disorder was based on the subjective phenomenon perceived by the patient and the objective phenomenon reported by the external observers, including the therapist (Walton et al., 1970).

Of the sample, the majority – 20 (59 %) – was female. The average age of the sample was 31.0 years, the youngest being 19 and the oldest 51 years old. The vast majority – 29 (85%) – was of African origin, four (12%) were Caucasian and one (3%) was Indian. Of the 29 of African origin, 13 were mixed African-European origin, two of African-Chinese origin and 14 (48%) were of totally African descent. Twenty-one (61%) belonged to social class I, II and III, using the UK General Register Office's classification of social class by occupation. All had lived in Jamaica continuously for five years or more prior to consultation. Thirty (88%) were born and raised in Jamaica, two from other Caribbean islands and one from the USA.

Of the 34 patients referred to the psychiatrist, 12 (33%) were referred from general practitioners, 13 (38%) were self-referred and nine (27%) were referred by a relative or another interested person. Slightly less than half of the sample had been referred for the reported or observed psychological problems of nervousness, tension and depression. The most common complaints were of subjective psychological phenomena (personal problems) such as depression and anxiety. These were the major symptoms in over 45 per cent of the sample. Interpersonal behavioural problems were next in the rank sequence. These included marital, domestic and sexual conflicts, but this was much less of importance to the patients as the main identifiable problem, and did not account for more than 23 per cent (N = 8) of the complaints of the sample. For a still smaller segment of the sample, (5, 14%), the major complaint was of a social behaviour problem, e.g. police arrest or suicidal attempts. More than half of the sample (18 patients) had received previous psychiatric treatment and of those 18 patients, nine (27%) had a previous psychiatric admission. A further ten patients had received treatment for a psychosomatic or physical illness. Suicide attempts were rare (five patients, accounting for 14%) and were four times more common in females than males.

The pattern of drug use revealed the next major – male as compared to female – difference of this analysis. Alcohol and cannabis were used three times more commonly by males than females, whereas females used anxiolytics and antidepressants five times more commonly than males. Both groups used cigarettes with equal frequency. Use of hard narcotics was found in only three patients (9%)

Most males (21, 63%) reported few and infrequent sexual encounters, a suspiciousness of, hostility to, and insecurity with men and women. More than half of the sample reported florid heterosexual and homosexual fantasies and 'uptight' sexual attitudes. A very high percentage (17, 85%) of the females reported marked hostility and aggressive behaviour towards men and recounted incidents of sexual manipulative and emasculatory practices in their behaviour with men. Over 75 per cent (N = 15) of the women reported feelings of sexual frigidity with associated florid heterosexual fantasies. A half of the sample reported homosexual fantasies and up to 70 per cent (N = 24) of the total sample reported few actual sexual contacts and a lack of sexual desire. 'Uptight' sexual attitudes, absence of orgasm and a lack of enjoyment of sex with mates were reported in 12 of the 20 women. Twelve women (60%) of the sample reported a paradoxical craving for a dominant aggressive man.

Taken together as a group, the most significant emerging psychosexual trend was a marked hostility, suspiciousness and fear of men  by both male and females of this sample, which was less marked in intensity compared to the hostility displayed towards women. Frigidity and quantitative lack of sex are the other major trends, along with sexual manipulatory behaviour. Twenty-nine per cent (4) of the males and 20 per cent (5) of the females were overt, practising homosexuals and 80 per cent of the sample reported florid homosexual and heterosexual fantasies. Thirty per cent (10) of the sample was married at the time of assessment, 24 per cent (8) separated or divorced, and 21 per cent having visiting relationships with a regular mate. Twenty (60%) reported power struggles in the relationships with their mates, while 15 (44%) persons reported poor sexual relationships with their mates.

Sixteen (47%) of those examined were the progeny of a broken home, with their parents either separated or divorced, while 14 (41%) reported an absent father-figure during childhood. Twenty-four persons (71%) reported memories of a power struggle between their parents, and seven reported memories of severe parental floggings and abuse during childhood. Twenty-two (65%) patients expressed hostility towards their mother and father. They reported that their mothers were controlling and manipulative and described their fathers as being authoritarian and aggressive.

During the course of the therapy the patients' behaviour was observed and recorded. Major conflicts surfaced and were ventilated, and psychological phenomena and mechanisms commonly employed and presented by the patients were identified. Over 80 per cent of the patients reported racial, class, sexual and political/religious conflicts in their lives and their thinking. Analysis of the phenomenology of the cohort revealed a very high percentage of manipulative (87%), controlling (81%), sadistic (69%) and seductive, flirtatious (66%) behaviour. Psychological symptoms of anxiety (78%), depressed mood (66%), and paranoia (66%) were also exhibited by a high proportion of the cohort. Pathological defensive mechanisms were exhibited by over 80 per cent, and dependency was a marked feature in 72 per cent of the sample. Seventy per cent of the males showed features of introversion, where 75 per cent of the females showed features of extroversion and histrionic behaviour.

Twenty-one patients (63%) showed features of a bona fide psychiatric illness on first assessment, that masked the characterological features of the personality disorder. The diagnosis of depression was made in 24 per cent, anxiety state in 18 per cent, and schizoaffective illness in 14 per cent of the cases. Two patients had features of an amphetamine psychosis, and two others were diagnosed as having alcoholism. Thirteen patients, all female, were seen as having DSM III-R diagnoses of hysterical personality disorders, and 13 (11 males and 2 females) were assessed as having paranoid personality disorder. Five patients were classified as psychopaths, and three showed an obsessional personality disorder.

This initial study in 1978 pointed to a clinical triad (Figure 1) in this cohort of patients diagnosed with a personality disorder of **dependency, psychosexual problems and anxiety,** and **power management problems** manifested as interpersonal conflict. The problems of dependency presented as psychological/emotional dependency on family members, loved ones, or social contacts; physiological dependency on legal drugs like cigarettes and alcohol, illegal drugs like cannabis and cocaine, or propriety drugs such as benzodiazepines and/or antidepressants. The problems in managing power in their relationships ranged from recurrent conflicts, quarrels and fights with spouses, family members, work colleagues and social conflicts; power struggles at home, in the workplace or organizations to which they belonged; and conflicts with/within organizations, authority, social and legal structures; and poor impulse control. The psychosexual problems represented the third leg of the triad: inadequate or poor sex, sexual dysfunction, homosexual activity, and inability to sustain emotional relationships. These features were widespread among this group.

*Figure 1: The clinical triad of personality disorder*

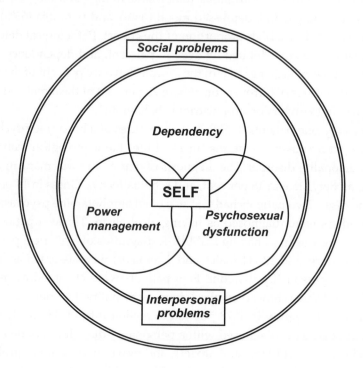

This clinical triad appears to be a vehicle through which the psychic contradictions and antagonisms were manifested as abnormal thoughts, feelings and actions. These factors can be seen as the different faces of intrapsychic aggression, which finds expression directed against the self (personal psychological problems), against other individuals (interpersonal behavioural problems), or against society (sociological problems).

These people who sought psychiatric assistance for their problems reflected a personal need to change self, which in terms of this analysis must be seen as a non-conscious need to change the oppressive social system in which they lived. This is reflected in the fact that eight (24%) of the initial cohort had been involved in significant political activity with recognized local political organizations and four (12%) were active in the local Rastafarian movement (_see_ Barrett, 1977; Chevannes, 1995). The hostility and aggression which found its main outlet against self, against others and against society in a disorganized and unconscious manner as discussed earlier, also recognized and found tangible expression against the oppressive system through active political work. This has also been closely associated in this sample with an attempt to deal with the racial conflicts which also disturbed them. More than half of the initial cohort under study were of mixed African/European racial background and these, along with the White persons under study, exhibited severe racial identity crisis in a political period which was demanding a release from European cultural repression, and the establishment of recognizable African cultural organizations and expression of self.

The psychosexual anxieties displayed by the patients revealed another major area of maladaptive behaviour in their lives. Unable to truly express their feelings of love, and tied up by artificial roles and expected patterns of behaviour, aggression found another outlet – this time man against woman in the sexual arena. Grossly repressed sexually by a Victorian Judeo-Christian system of morals, they continued to act out their unconscious feelings of rage and hostility, meant for the oppressors, on their mates. They had learnt this from their parents, their own educational environment, and their social involvement with Judeo-Christianity. The results of this study also tend to support the thesis of the Black macho defence, resulting from inadequate male psychosexual identification, due to absent or authoritarian male parenting, and overprotective, domineering and manipulative female parenting. The resultant hostility and aggression has, therefore, been directed at convenient targets – self, mate and the society itself. The Black women, while craving their Black man's aggressivity, at the same time hated him for it. They (male and female) both explored the homosexual role and felt guilty. They smoked, drank, partied, attempted suicide, and popped pills – all in an effort to try to deal with this uncomfortable nagging psychic hostility which they could not explain. Ultimately they had tried to change themselves and their society with limited success.

For these 34 Jamaicans who came for treatment, the role of the therapist in this situation was to facilitate insight into their individual psychopathology and the inevitable dialectical interrelatedness of their present position within the sociopolitical system. It was also to encourage behavioural change within the sociopolitical system to reduce morbidity and to actualize their future adaptive position in society.

Perhaps the most important finding of this study was the generalized hostility and conflict of all the patients towards men and women – the hostility being greater towards the opposite sex for both samples of males and females. Investigation and analysis revealed that this hostility originated from two unconscious psychopathologic sources: (i) psychosexual anxiety and (ii) authority rebellion. The conscious feelings of hostility, rage and anxiety were modified by the patients' overactive defence mechanisms of repression, denial, sublimation and reaction formation, similar to those described by Anna Freud (1934) and others. These psychopathological conditions, in turn, gave rise to (a) the abnormal feelings of anxiety, depression and inadequacy (subjective factors), and (b) maladaptive interpersonal and social behaviour (objective factors) on which the diagnosis of personality disorders was made.

All the patients showed evidence of an abnormal acculturation growth and development process in their lives. The major vehicle for this maladaptive acculturation process was the abnormal family dynamics, with broken homes, matriarchal mothers and authoritarian and/or absent fathers being the major predetermining factors. These and other factors formed the source of the deep-seated racial, religious, class and gender conflicts, which were the precursors of the psychosexual anxiety and authority rebellion that characterized the psychic unconscious world of these patients.

All the variables fall into one of the three areas of study – those present in the mind of the patients; those present in the conscious life of the patients, and those relating to the sociocultural environment of the patients. All variables represented in this schema arose from the investigation and analysis of the patients of this study.

# Etiologic Insights

An attempt has been made to extend the etiological enquiry further by the use of a dialectic analysis of the findings. Jaspers (1959), in clarifying basic patterns of meaning in psychic connections, indicates "psychic life and its contents are polarized into opposites (dialectics). It is through opposites that everything is once more reconnected ...dialectical transformation is a universal and basic form of thought" (pp. 340-343). He describes the process as a reversal through time without consciousness taking part. It starts with an initial event or construct (the thesis), proceeding to a battle of opposites (antithesis) and ending with a resolution or final choice (synthesis) of a new event or construct. For the purpose of this analysis, the internal conflicts and behaviour of the patients in the sample have been divided into their dialectic components; these are then viewed in conjunction with the wider social dialectics also expressed by these patients, in addition to the individual clinical findings identified by this study.

An important aspect of the initial study on personality disorder carried out in Jamaica in the 1970s was the attempt to tease out the behavioural and social dialect vectors, and to interpret these within the context of the Jamaican society. Table 1 represents behavioural dialectical opposites experienced and exhibited by these patients in the course of their lives and expressed in their life histories.

*Table 1: Experienced behavioural dialectic vectors by the 34 patients.*

| Vector | # | % | Opposing Related Vector | # | % |
|---|---|---|---|---|---|
| Experience of racial prejudice | 27 | 79 | Miscegenation (Mixed racial ontogeny) | 17 | 50 |
| Experience of violent behaviour | 15 | 44 | Substance abuse | 27 | 79 |
| Experience of migration | 12 | 35 | Family fragmentation | 16 | 47 |
| Experience of cultural/ religious repression | 13 | 38 | Anti-authority rebellious behaviour | 15 | 44 |

The behavioural dialect vectors experienced by these patients in their therapeutic sessions were often related to deep-seated emotional conflicts that were teased out during therapy. Four major emotional conflicts were identified. These were racial, class, gender and political conflicts, and they were often linked to opposing emotions that the patient was experiencing. The dialect expressions of these conflicts are illustrated in Table 2.

*Table 2: Relationship between dialectic emotional vectors and internal conflicts*

| Conflict | | | Dialectic Emotional Vectors | | | | | |
|---|---|---|---|---|---|---|---|---|
| | # | % | | # | % | | # | % |
| Racial conflicts | 22 | 65 | Hostility to Blacks | 15 | 44 | Hostility to Whites | 12 | 35 |
| Class conflicts | 27 | 79 | Shame of origin in poverty | 22 | 65 | Guilt of origin in wealth | 12 | 35 |
| Gender conflicts | 22 | 65 | Hostility to males | 24 | 70 | Hostility to females | 18 | 53 |
| Political conflicts | 27 | 79 | Anger against state authorities (oppressor) | 15 | 54 | Frustration with inability to change social conditions (oppressed) | 12 | 35 |

In an attempt to link the dialectic interplay (causation) between the individual and the society, Figure 2 was developed to show the relationship, at least at a two-dimensional level, of the social factors which influence individual behaviour and vice versa. The resultant vector produced from this complex interplay of dialectic vectors can be seen as a resultant force, helping to shape the nature of the society as a whole. The importance of this dialectic understanding of the person and the society in which he or she lives lies in the therapeutic strategies designed to relieve the problem. Until there is conscious negation of the dialectic vectors which lay at the root of the personal pathology, the problems will continue unabated and, in fact, will be personally and socially self-perpetuating. The role of psychotherapy in the treatment of the personality disorder lies, therefore, in the identification of the dialectic vectors and the establishment of psychological manoeuvres to negate these vectors, thereby producing sustained change in individual behaviour. This must affect in the long term, the social pathologic conditions as the vicious cycle of psychopathological self-perpetuation is broken.

_Figure 2:  Etiological relationship between social and psychological phenomena_

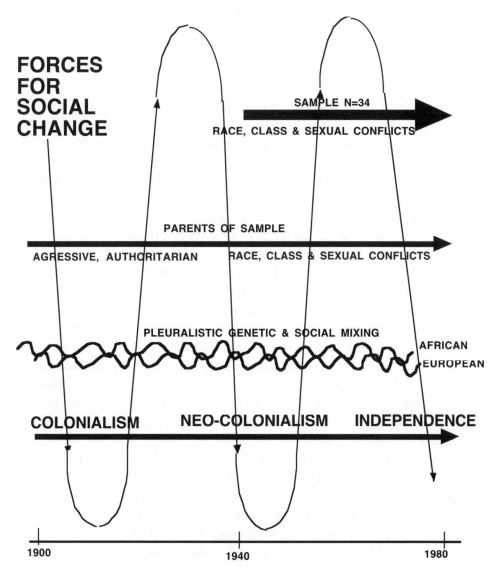

As mentioned earlier, nearly 60 per cent of the patients were from social class I and nearly 25 per cent from social class II, with a mean age of 36 years. They were predominantly White or of mixed race (27% were White, 45%, brown), and 28 per cent Black. There were twice as many female as males. However, the fact that 20 per cent of these patients belonged to social classes III, IV and V indicates that the poor and the middle-classes of this society are not exempt from this psychopathology. In short, all classes of this society show features of this essentially upper-class psychopathology. All of these patients have presented with the clinical triad identified in the initial study, and psychotherapeutic analysis revealed religious, class, racial and sexual conflicts at a deep-seated psychological level. They nearly all showed features of manipulative, controlling behaviour, and ego-defensiveness. Paranoia and introversion were the predominant clinical features in the males, while histrionic behaviour and extroversion were the main clinical findings in the females.

Since 1975, the principal author has worked psychotherapeutically with over 300 patients in Jamaica diagnosed with personality disorders, and has devised psychotherapeutic programmes to assist in their transformation and change. The patients described were all treated using Psychohistoriographic Brief Psychotherapy (see Hickling, 2007).

In summary, it is apparent that the various stressors which were predominant a century ago continue to influence Jamaican culture, and this has forced many Jamaicans to behave, think, and feel in certain ways which are maladaptive and which eventually force them to seek psychiatric or psychological assistance. A number of antagonisms emerge within the individual, males and females alike, and result in dependency issues, psychosexual anxiety, and various interpersonal conflicts that were also present during slavery, as a result of ill treatment or abuse from plantation "masters", and which seem to have become embedded in the Jamaican consciousness.

These unresolved conflicts can be linked to the various facets of aggression apparent in Jamaican society, aggression directed against self (personal psychological problems), against other individuals (interpersonal behaviour problems), or against society (sociopathic problems). This aggression has led to marital discord, relational problems between parent and child, and rivalry between siblings. Seeking assistance for such problems can be seen as reflecting a personal need to change self and an unconscious need to change the oppressive social system which continues to control Jamaicans, thereby maintaining maladaptive behaviour and thinking passed down from their Jamaican ancestry since slavery.

Maladaptive personality traits also continue to exist in Jamaica due to an abnormal acculturation growth and development process in the individuals' personal life. This process results from abnormal family dynamics with broken homes, matriarchal mothers and authoritarian and/or absent fathers being the major predetermining factors. Inadequate male psychosexual identification, due to the absent or authoritarian father and an overprotective, domineering or manipulative mother has created hostility, aggression and resentment for some offspring, which becomes directed towards self or other members of society. Those who do not "lash out" at self or others become inhibited, frail and dependent, unable to face the reality of what Jamaican society has to offer. These factors, and the various defence mechanisms being used to cope with them, create and maintain maladaptive thoughts and behaviour leading to the development of personality disorders and personality disorder traits in the Jamaican population. However, many Jamaicans' suffering from personality disorders are unaware of their maladaptive behaviour or are unwilling to take responsibility for their actions and, therefore, do not seek treatment. This may result in fewer diagnoses of personality disorders being made and the necessary treatment plans not being implemented. It also means that little research is available on these disorders in the Jamaican population and, as such, clinicians do not have all the resources and information needed to diagnose personality disorders in Jamaica and provide the best possible treatment plan.

## Limitations of the IPDE and DSM-IV Classification

Problems have been identified by some researchers such as Koerner et al. (1996) with the use of the _Diagnostic and Statistical Manual of Mental Disorders_ in detecting personality disorders. The manual states that "it is only when personality traits are inflexible and maladaptive and cause either significant functional impairment or subjective distress that they constitute Personality Disorders" (American Psychiatric Association,

2000). However, it is not clear when a clinically significant level of inflexibility, maladaptivity, impairment or distress occurs. Further, in determining if the criterion for the diagnosis of a personality disorder is met, the point at which personality traits have become maladaptive needs to be identified and this will vary with different interviewers or clinicians. What is considered to be maladaptive and adaptive of a personality trait, may also vary across situations. Widiger and Costa (1994) suggest that any particular personality trait can have adaptive as well as maladaptive consequences, and the maladaptivity of a trait needs to be assessed within the social and occupational context in which the person is operating, to determine if impairment in functioning has occurred. At present, not much work has been done on determining the severity of personality disturbance and the means by which it can be properly measured.

The International Personality Disorder Examination is an outgrowth of the Personality Disorder Examination (PDE) that was modified for international use and compatibility with the *International Classification of Diseases, Tenth Revision* (ICD-10) and the DSM-III-R classification systems (Loranger et al., 1994). This instrument has been developed as a standardized interview for personality disorders and is intended for use by clinicians experienced in the assessment of personality disorders (Janca et al., 1994). The International Personality Disorder Examination was designed for use in clinical research around the world. In 1985, representatives of the international psychiatric community discussed the format of the interview, the wording of items, as well as the development of the scoring manual for the instrument. A field trial was then done in 14 participating centres in 11 countries. This included North America, Europe, Africa and Asia (*International Personality Disorder Examination Manual,* 1999). The ICD 10 definition of personality allows for the possibility of criteria developed to describe personality in different countries (Presley & Walton, 1973).

In Jamaica at present, there are limited testing materials available to determine the existence of a personality disorder in accordance with Axis II of DSM-IV. Comprehensive clinical assessments comprising interviews, a range of intellectual tests and self-reports on various aspects of the individual's persona, have been used in the past to determine if a personality disorder is, in fact, present and to distinguish what type of personality disorder exists. These assessments can be time consuming, inconvenient and frustrating for patients who will need to complete a series of tests. There has also been some difficulty experienced in the past with the accurate assessment of personality disorders in Jamaica. No _specific_ instrument is being used at present in mental health facilities to give a _complete_ assessment of personality disorders; and such disorders can be very difficult to diagnose at times and, as such, misdiagnosis is possible. The test used most commonly in Jamaica for detecting the presence of a personality disorder, is the Minnesota Multiphasic Personality Inventory (MMPI). However, no diagnosis can be given solely on the basis of this instrument. This test is very time consuming – consisting of 567 items, and can be administered only by a properly trained psychometrist, psychologist or psychological assistant. Psychiatrists are, therefore, limited as they would not have been trained to use this test and so can administer it, but not interpret it.

Given the need for testing materials which are both culturally relevant and accurate in their diagnosis of personality disorders, and which can be used by psychologists and psychiatrists alike, a validation of the International Personality Disorder Examination (IPDE) among the Jamaican population was made (Harrisingh, 2004). Findings from Harrisingh's study suggested that the IPDE was valid, based on the considerable agreement on the prevalence of definite personality disorder diagnoses after examination by both the psychologist/psychiatrist and the IPDE, and the fact that the consensual clinical diagnosis was set as the validity standard. The estimated prevalence of personality disorders in this Jamaican sample (16.66 %) is what might have been expected, based on information that is currently available in the literature, and as the testing instrument appears to be culturally relevant in the Jamaican population.

Several limitations were noted, however, in reference to diagnoses given or assessments conducted by a psychologist/psychiatrist based on test results (Harrisingh, 2004). The question was raised as to whether some personality disorders and traits may be misrepresented by clinicians as a result of varying meanings given to words in the Jamaican culture. There was also concern that some personality disorders such as Borderline may be over diagnosed, while others might remain under diagnosed because of co-existing Axis I mental disorders, or the failure to consider the possibility of more than one Axis II personality disorder.

There are ten specific personality disorders listed in the DSM-IV-TR. These personality disorders are divided into three clusters.

- Cluster A – These individuals often appear odd or eccentric: Paranoid personality disorder, Schizoid personality disorder, Schizotypal personality disorder; a pattern of acute discomfort in relationships, cognitive or perceptual distortions, and eccentricities of behaviour.

- Cluster B – These individuals often appear dramatic, emotional or erratic: Antisocial personality disorder, Borderline personality disorder, Histrionic personality disorder, Narcissistic personality disorder.

- Cluster C – These individuals often appear anxious or fearful: Avoidant personality disorder, Dependent personality disorder, Obsessive-compulsive personality disorder.

The present chapter advances the view that the separation of personality disorders into categories (histrionic, paranoid, obsessive etc.) is clinically and therapeutically irrelevant, and does not advance our epistemological understanding of the condition.

## Creating the Jamaica Personality Disorder Index

Recently, great emphasis has been placed by the World Health Organization on the development of valid and reliable instruments which are both cross-culturally relevant and applicable to aid in the diagnosis, and subsequent treatment of mental disorders. Whereas the use of structured interviews seems to have significantly improved interrater reliability for the diagnosis of Axis II disorders, minimum data is available on evidence of validity for Axis II diagnostic interviews and structured clinical ratings. Of the limited information available, it has been determined that the validity of a semi-structured interview assessment depends substantially on the training, care, and dependability of the interviewers (Zimmerman, 1994). In the last three decades there has been, resurgence in interest in personality and its relationship to psychopathology. This resurfacing has led to the development of a variety of instruments to draw inferences about personality. Psychologists rely on structured interviews, self-report questionnaires, clinical ratings, direct observation, impressions of others, detailed personal histories, and life records for the identification of personality disorders (Liebert & Spiegler, 1997). Some problems have been experienced with the poor reliability of some of these new instruments, particularly in the form of very limited agreement among diagnosticians (Mellsop et al., 1982, as cited in Pilkonis, Heape, Ruddy, & Serrao, 1991).

The area of personality disorders continues to be a somewhat 'grey' one as there is still inadequate information on its origin and development, oftentimes leading to both under diagnosis and misdiagnosis of the condition. This revelation formed the basis of a collective decision to create a short personality disorder questionnaire specifically for Jamaican people. This questionnaire shows the presence or absence of a personality disorder, based on the clinical triad described, but it will not attempt to describe the type of personality disorder. The questionnaire, while testing the _clinical triad_, was also mandated to take into account the social and cultural norms of the Jamaican people. It was also mandated that, on completion, the questionnaire should take a much shorter time to administer, compared to the full version of the IPDE which, depending on the patient, can take several hours to administer. This questionnaire will establish a diagnosis of personality disorder and will identify patients who are possible candidates for psychotherapy. It is in this sense that it will differ from the brief screening section of the IPDE, as this questionnaire does not attempt to further sub-classify the diagnosis of personality disorder. The questionnaire would then be validated against the existing gold standard personality disorder assessment instrument – the IPDE – which had been validated in the Jamaican population by Harrisingh (2004).

The cultural bias of existing questionnaires poses a distinct problem as it relates to accurate diagnosis of the disorder. This is so because both the ICD-10 and the DSM-IV place emphasis on the cultural abnormality of a behaviour as an integral part of the requirement for making the diagnosis of a personality disorder. In addition, there is much research where the findings emphasize the need for ethno-cultural differences to be highlighted in the diagnosis of mental illness, especially where the first language is not English (Saddock and Saddock, 2003; Iwamasa, 2000). Therefore, the value which the development of a brief questionnaire that will detect both the presence and severity (Walton et al., 1970) of a personality disorder will bring, is clear. The questionnaire, in addition to being socially and culturally relevant, should also be religiously appropriate and linguistically acceptable. This will ensure accuracy as the essence and intended meaning of a question can be lost in the translation from one language or dialect to another. In Jamaica, there has been no large-scale population-based study to estimate the prevalence of personality disorders or their impact on criminality, even though the number of violent crimes in the island continues to increase.

The instrument designed to assess personality disorders in Jamaica was meticulously created, analyzed and reformatted by the research team which comprised mental health professionals including consultant psychiatrists, resident psychiatrists, a senior registered mental health nurse and post-graduate psychology students, as well as research assistants. Once the name "Jamaican Personality Disorder Index" (JPDI) was chosen by consensus, the discussions about the development of the survey instrument commenced. The three issues of power management, psychosexual dysfunction and dependency were discussed in detail, so as to make a checklist of the phenomenology of each issue – thus ensuring that the questions related to each area found on the survey instrument captured the essence of that aspect of the disorder and were relevant. Owing to the identifiable limitations of the DSM classification, the perceptions of Walton et al. (1972), based on the patient's level of insight into the disorder, were used to guide the creation of this instrument. Three groups were then formed, each having the responsibility to create at least ten questions for issues relating to the three components of personality disorder, according to the clinical triad: **dependency, psychosexual dysfunction and power management**. After a series of weekly meetings of the team – resulting in seven drafts of the JPDI being fine-tuned, reworded and reformatted – a 30-question survey instrument to elicit the required information on personality disorder was created, ready for pre-testing.

The second pre-test primarily highlighted difficulty with semantics; however, a decision was taken that once there was an issue of clarity or misunderstanding of a question, then that question should be discarded. As a result, a new questionnaire, increasing the number of questions to 39, was agreed on as the final product, and pending approval from the ethics committee, the JPDI is now ready for validation. The format of the final questionnaire was a landscape layout with 39 closed-ended questions to be read to the person being assessed by the examiner and the answer recorded. It takes approximately 15–20 minutes to administer the questionnaire. Concurrent validation of the newly developed instrument will be tested, as the IPDE will be administered to the subject by the same person immediately following the administration of the JPDI. All members of the team are required to administer both the JPDI and the IPDE at the same time to a total of 12 psychiatric patients on Ward 21, the psychiatric admission ward of the University Hospital of the West Indies. The same person is to administer both tests to the same subject so as to minimize interviewer bias. The JPDI is to be administered first, as it is the instrument that needs the validation. Once the JPDI has been validated, the prevalence studies of both the patients on Ward 21 and the Jamaican population will begin.

This study currently being conducted addresses how Jamaican clinicians actually assess and diagnose personality disorders. It is anticipated that a more structured and reliable way of detecting personality disorders in Jamaica will replace the MMPI as the primary method of assessment in this country.

## NOTE

1. 'Dis' is the shortened version of the word 'disrespect'. Thus the 'dis syndrome' is the pattern of aggressive and assertive behaviour that results from an individual who perceives that he/she has been 'dissed' or disrespected. Often there are elements of paranoid misunderstanding in the perception of being 'dissed.'

## REFERENCES

American Psychiatric Association. (1980). *Diagnostic and Statistical Manual of Mental Disorders DSM III-R*. Washington, D.C.: Author.

————. (1994). *Diagnostic and statistical manual of mental disorders DSM-IV*. Washington, D.C.: Author.

————. (2000). *Diagnostic and statistical manual of mental disorders DSM-IV-TR*. Washington, D.C.: Author.

Barrett, L. (1977). *The Rastafarians*. Kingston, Jamaica: Heinemann/Sangster's.

Burke A.W. (1980). A cross cultural study of delinquency among West Indian Boys. *Internal Journal of Social Psychology* 26 (1), 81-8.

Burke, V. W. (1992). Associates of lifestyle and personality characteristics. *B.P & Journal Clinical Epid* 45 (10),1061-70.

Chakroun, N., Doron, J., & Swendsen, J. (2004). Substance use, affective problems and personality traits, tests of two association models. *Journal Encephale*, 30 (6), 549-59

Chevannes, B. (1995). *Rastafari: Roots and ideology*. New York: Syracuse University Press

Cornforth, M. (1952). *Dialectical materialism – Materialism and the dialectical method*. London: Lawrence and Wishart.

Coid, J., Nadji, K., Gault, S., et al. (2000). Ethnic differences in admission to secure forensic facilities. *British Medical Journal*, December 177, 241-247.

Coid, J., Yang, M., Tyrer, P., Roberts, A., & Ullrich, S. (2006). Prevalence and correlates of personality disorder in Great Britain. *British Journal of Psychiatry*, 188, 423-431.

Fanon, F. (1965). *The wretched of the earth*. New York: Grove Press.

Frances, A. J., & Widiger, T. (1986). The classification of personality disorders: An overview of problems and solutions. *American Psychiatric Association Annual Review*. 5, 240.

Freud, A. (1934). *The ego and mechanisms of defence*. London: Hogarth.

Garvey, A. J. (1967). *Philosophy and opinions of Marcus Garvey, or Africa for the Africans*. New Jersey: Frank Cass. p. 134.

General Register Office. (1966). *Classification of occupations*. London: H.M.S.O.

Hall, D. (1989). *In miserable slavery: Thomas Thistlewood in Jamaica, 1750-86*. London: Warwick University Caribbean Studies Series.

Harrisingh, A. (2004). Validation of the IPDE in the Jamaican Population. M.Sc. thesis (Clinical Psychology), University of the West Indies.

Hickling, F. W. (2007). *Psychohistoriography: A post-colonial model of psychoanalysis and psychotherapy*. Kingston, CARIMENSA University of the West Indies.

Hirschfield, R. M. (1986). Personality disorders. *American Psychiatric Association Annual Review*, 5, 233.

Hucker, S. J. (2005). The Canadian contribution to violence risk assessment history and implication for current psychiatric practice. *Canada Journal of Psychiatry*, 50 (1) 3-11

Iwamasa, G.Y., Larrabee, A.L., & Merritt, R.D. (2000). Are personality disorder criteria ethnically biased? A card-sort analysis. *Cultural Diversity and Ethnic Minority Psychology*, 6 (3), 284-296.

Janca, A., Ustun, T. B., & Sartorius, N. (1994). New versions of World Health Organization instruments for the assessment of mental disorders. *Acta Psychiatrica Scandinavica*, 90, 73-83.

Koerner, K., Kohlenberg, R. J., & Parker, C. R. (1996). Diagnosis of personality disorder: A radical behavioral perspective. *Journal of Consulting and Clinical Psychology*, 64 (6), 1169-1176.

Liebert, R. M., & Spiegler, M. D. (1997). _Personality strategies and issues_ (8th ed.). California: Brooks/Cole Publishing Company.

Lenzenweger, M. F., Loranger, A. W., Korfine, L., & Neff, C. (1997). Detecting personality disorders in a nonclinical population. _Archives of General Psychiatry_, 54, 345-351.

Loranger, A. W. (1999). _IPDE: International personality disorder examination DSM-IV and ICD-10 Interviews_. Psychological Assessment Resources, Inc.

Loranger, A. W., Sartorius, N., Andreoli, A., Berger, P., Buchheim, P., Coid, B., et al. (1994). The International Personality Disorder Examination. _Archives of General Psychiatry_, 51, 215-224).

Loranger, A. W., Susman, V. L., Oldham, J. M., et al (1987). The personality disorder examination: A preliminary report. _Journal of Personality Disorders_, I, 103.

Jaspers, K. (1959). _General psychopathology_. Translated by J. Hoenig and M. W. Hamilton. Manchester: Manchester University Press.

Maden, A., Friendship, C., McClinhock, T., & Rutter, S. (1999). Outcome of admission to a medium secure psychiatric unit. 2. Role of ethnic origin. _British Journal of Psychiatry_, 175, 317-321.

Mellsop, et al., (1982.) as cited in Pilkonis, P. A., Heape, C. L., Ruddy, J., & Serrao, P. (1991). Validity in the diagnosis of personality disorders: The use of the LEAD standard. _Psychological Assessment_, 3 (1), 46-54.

Mumford, D. B. (1995). Cultural issues in assessment and treatment. _Current Opinion in Psychiatry_, 8, 134-137.

National Library of Jamaica and the Urban Development Corporation, (1984). _Freedom to be: The abolition of slavery in Jamaica and its aftermath_. Kingston: Auhor.

Nobles, W. W., Goddard, L. L, W. E.; & George, P. Y. (1987) _African-American families: Issues, insights and directions_. Oakland California: Black Family Institute Publications.

Patterson, O. (1967). _The sociology of slavery. An analysis of the origins, development and structure of Negro slave society in Jamaica_. London: Grenada Publishing Ltd.

Pilgrim, J., & Mann, A. (2003, 1990). _Standardized assessment of personality_. Cambridge: Cambridge University Press.

Presley, A. J., & Walton, H. J., (1973). Use of a category system in the diagnosis of personality disorder. _British Journal of Psychiatry_, March 122, 568-68.

Sarason, I. G., & Sarason, B. R. (1999). _Abnormal psychology: The problem of maladaptive behavior_ (9th ed.). New Jersey: Prentice Hall.

Saddock, B. J., & Saddock V. A., (2003). _Kaplan and Saddock's synopsis of psychiatry: Behavioral sciences_, (9th Ed) Clinical psychology p. 821. Philadelphia: Lippincott, Williams & Wilkins.

Sherlock, P., & Bennett, H. (1998). _The story of the Jamaican people_. Kingston: Ian Randle Publishers; Princeton: Marcus Wiener Publishers.

Singleton, N., Meltzer, H., & Gatward, R. (1998). *Psychiatric morbidity among prisoners in England and Wales.* London: Stationery Office.

Stone, C. (1992). "The anatomy of aggression." *The Daily Gleaner,* Wednesday October 21, 1992.

Tryer, P., Coombs, N., Ibrahimi, F., Mathilakath, A., Bajaj, P., Ranger, M., Rao, B., & Din ,R. (2007). Critical developments in the assessment of personality disorder. *British Journal of Psychiatry,,* 190, s51-s59

Walton, H. J., Foulds, G. A., Littman, S. K., & Presley, A. S. (1970). Abnormal personality. *British Journal of Psychiatry,* 116, 497.

Widiger, T. A., & Costa, P. T. (1994). Personality and personality disorders. *Journal of Abnormal Psychology,* 103 (1), 78-91.

Zimmerman, M. (1994). Diagnosing personality disorders. *Archives of General Psychiatry,* 51, 225-245.

Zimmerman, M., Rothschild, L., & Chelminski, I. (2005). The prevalence of DSM-IV personality disorders in psychiatric outpatients. *American Journal of Psychiatry,* 162, 1911-1918, October 2005.

# 11 Psychology and HIV/AIDS in the Caribbean

## An Introduction and Overview

*Peter D. Weller & Katija Khan*

## Introduction: Psychology and the AIDS Pandemic

The Acquired Immune Deficiency Syndrome (AIDS) pandemic, a world-wide behavioural challenge, has engaged the field of psychology as part of an interdisciplinary response to the threat. The use of behavioural indicators is now recognized as an important part of monitoring the course of the HIV/AIDS epidemic. A number of psychological disciplines contribute to the collection of this data and thus increase our understanding of, and response to, this pandemic. The clinical and counselling psychologist; the industrial and organizational psychologist; the social psychologist; as well as the developmental, school, physiological and child psychologists, amongst others, must all be part of a collaborative effort in the development of interventions to address prevention and care.

Health psychology is one field of applied psychology that seeks to use psychological theory and knowledge to promote personal and public health. Campbell (2003, p. 2) notes that health psychologists ". . . have produced a steady stream of scholarly studies, linking sexual behaviour to properties of the individual such as cognitive processes, instincts, attitudes, sense of personal vulnerability, or perceived social norms". This type of information is valuable, as it can facilitate the prediction of future directions of the epidemic, thus facilitating prevention interventions, and it can be related to the psychosocial needs and planning of care of persons living with HIV / AIDS (PLWHA).

In the Caribbean, where we are only now developing competencies in the sub-disciplines of psychology listed above, it is imperative that we ensure that this interdisciplinary and collaborative effort is informed by culturally relevant, but not limited, research and shared 'best practices'. However, it is important to consider the recommendation made by Campbell (2003) who, paraphrasing Peter Piot, has noted that it is not just about best practices but (perhaps more importantly) about new practices. She reminds us that epidemics, by definition events outside of the 'ordinary', require new interventions because existing understandings and systems have been unable to prevent the spread.

It is not possible in this chapter to address all the ways in which psychological theories can and should be applied as we in the Caribbean respond to the AIDS pandemic, but it is anticipated that the material covered will serve as an introduction to the field and lead to an increased awareness, thirst for knowledge, and the innovation necessary for an effective response.

# The AIDS Pandemic

In its third decade, HIV / AIDS continues to pose a serious threat to public health and is one of the greatest challenges to the attainment of the Millennium Development Goals, developed by the United Nations and adopted as a blueprint by countries around the world. Many are only now beginning to appreciate the extent to which this pandemic can destroy communities and families as well as the people who are living with HIV / AIDS, and while efforts for prevention continue with partial success, finding a cure continues to be a challenge.

## ACQUIRED IMMUNE DEFICIENCY SYNDROME (AIDS)

Acquired Immune Deficiency Syndrome, or AIDS, was first identified in the USA in 1979 and came to the attention of the medical community in 1981. Gallo et al. (1983; 1984) established the retrovirus Human Immunodeficiency Virus (HIV) as the cause of AIDS. However, while the presence of HIV antibodies is indicative of infection with HIV, it is not diagnostic of AIDS. A case definition of AIDS was established in 1982 by the Center for Disease Control (CDC) in the USA. The diagnosis necessitated the presence of certain opportunistic infections and/or malignancies predictive of cellular immune deficiency (Harris, Segreti & Kessler, 1989).

## HUMAN IMMUNODEFICIENCY VIRUS (HIV)

The Human Immunodeficiency Virus (HIV) is a member of the family of RNA (ribonucleic acid) viruses which are characterized by the presence of RNA-dependent DNA (deoxyribonucleic acid) polymerase or reverse transcriptase. These are enzymes which enable RNA viruses to produce a DNA copy of the genome, which is then incorporated into the host genome. The HIV virus itself is not responsible for the signs and symptoms of AIDS, but rather weakens the immune system and damages the cellular structure of organs leaving them susceptible to opportunistic infections (*see* below) which cause severe impairment and illness – AIDS.

Infection with HIV includes a progressive loss of CD4+ T cells. It is the loss of these critical lymphocytes, which serve as regulators and effectors of the immune system, that is thought to underlie the immunodeficiency characteristic of AIDS (Fauci, 1995). HIV also infects monocytes, which serve as a cellular reservoir for, and allows further dissemination of, the virus into other organs of the body including the brain.

Different clinical classification and staging schemes for persons with various stages of HIV infection have been developed. Most utilize a combination of CD4 lymphocyte counts and symptoms. Classification schemes are useful in guiding the clinical and therapeutic management of the patient. The Centre for HIV/AIDS Research, Educations and Services (CHARES) clinic at the University Hospital of the West Indies (UHWI), Jamaica, uses the two-part classification scheme below to guide the treatment of the patient (D. Thompson, personal communication, 2005):

*Category A:* Asymptomatic HIV infection –CD4 count >200
cells/mm^3 ,

*Category B:* Symptomatic HIV Infection- CD4 count < 200
cells/mm^3 or the presence of an AIDS defining condition.

Once a person has been classified as Category B, they remain a Category B whether or not their CD4 count improves. Patients classified as symptomatic are recommended to start a regime of HIV medication.

## Transmission of HIV

Transmission of HIV may occur by exposure to infected body fluids. These include blood, semen, vaginal fluids and breast milk. HIV is most commonly spread by unprotected sex with an infected partner. Today, the risk of becoming infected with HIV through blood transfusions is very small due to screening procedures as well as heat treatment. HIV may also be spread among intravenous (i.v.) drug users who share needles or syringes contaminated with small quantities of infected blood. Women can transmit HIV to their babies during pregnancy or birth. This is referred to as mother-to-child transmission (MTCT). HIV also can be spread to babies through the breast milk of mothers infected with the virus. However, the risk of MTCT can be significantly reduced by treating the mother during pregnancy and by delivering the baby through caesarean section.

While HIV has been found in the saliva of infected persons, there is no evidence that HIV is spread through saliva by kissing. However, the lining of the mouth can be infected by HIV and as such, HIV can be transmitted via oral intercourse. Thus far, there is no evidence that HIV is spread through sweat, tears, urine, faeces or through casual contact such as sharing of kitchen utensils, towels, bedding, telephones, swimming pools and toilet seats. HIV is not spread by biting insects such as mosquitoes or bedbugs.

## HIV-related Opportunistic Infections

Opportunistic infections generally do not pose a great threat to healthy persons but can be quite severe and harmful in persons with AIDS, since their immune system is considerably weakened and cannot fight off the threat posed by certain fungi, bacteria, parasites, viruses and other microbes. Some of the most common opportunistic infections include: bacterial diseases such as tuberculosis, bacterial pneumonia and septicaemia (blood poisoning); protozoal diseases such as pneumocystis carinii pneumonia (PCP); toxoplasmosis and leishmaniasis; fungal diseases such as candidiasis, cryptococcosis and penicilliosis; viral diseases such as those caused by cytomegalovirus, herpes simplex and herpes zoster virus; and HIV-associated malignancies such as Kaposi's sarcoma, lymphoma and squamous cell carcinoma (UNAIDS, 1998). Symptoms of

HIV-related opportunistic infections may include:

- Coughing and shortness of breath
- Seizures and lack of coordination
- Difficult or painful swallowing
- Mental symptoms such as confusion and forgetfulness
- Severe and persistent diarrhea
- Fever
- Vision loss
- Nausea, abdominal cramps, and vomiting
- Weight loss and extreme fatigue
- Severe headaches
- Coma

Children with AIDS may get the same opportunistic infections as infected adults, but could also have severe forms of common childhood bacterial infections, such as conjunctivitis (pink eye), ear infections, and tonsillitis (National Institute of Allergy and Infectious Diseases, 2007).

## HIV/AIDS: Epidemiology

An estimated 39.5 million persons are living with HIV/AIDS around the world (UNAIDS, 2006). Worldwide, approximately 16,000 new infections occur daily with 90% of these new infections occurring in developing countries and most commonly in young adults aged 15 to 25. The prevalence rate in the Caribbean is 2.3% and growing, second only to sub-Saharan Africa. UNAIDS (2006) estimates that 27,000 adults and children in the Caribbean were infected during 2006 and that about 19,000 residents of the Caribbean died of AIDS in that period. Approximately 330,000 persons are living with AIDS with women accounting for 51% (_see_ Table 1 for country specific figures). The countries most affected are The Bahamas and Haiti with prevalence rates exceeding 3%, and Trinidad and Tobago, with 2.6%. The least affected country is Cuba with prevalence rates of less than 0.1 %. The relative success in Cuba has been attributed to a vigorous national response which includes universal access to antiretroviral (ARV) treatment for PLWHA as well as the successful prevention of mother-to-child transmission (Camara et al., 2003).

*Table 1: Estimated number of people living with HIV in Caribbean countries*

| Country | Number of Adults (>15 yrs) | Prevalence (%) Adults (15–49) Rate |
|---|---|---|
| Caribbean | 330,000 | 1.5 |
| Bahamas | 6,800 | 3.3 |
| Barbados | 2,700 | 1.5 |
| Cuba | 4,800 | 0.1 |
| Dominican Republic | 66,000 | 1.1 |
| Haiti | 190,000 | 3.8 |
| Jamaica | 25,000 | 1.5 |
| Trinidad and Tobago | 27,000 | 2.6 |

*Source: UNAIDS 2006 Report*

## HIV Transmission in the Caribbean

Unprotected heterosexual intercourse is the main mode of HIV transmission in the Caribbean (UNAIDS, 2006). For example, in Jamaica, 60% of all reported AIDS cases are due to heterosexual transmission with mother-to-child transmission accounting for an additional 7%. Caribbean women (particularly young women) are proving especially vulnerable. Physiological susceptibility, and the relatively common practice of younger women establishing relationships with older men (who, by virtue of their age and experience, are more likely to have acquired HIV) are thought to account for this finding (UNAIDS, 2006). A significant minority of cases (12%) of reported HIV infections in the Caribbean is attributable to unprotected sex between men. Homophobia and strong sociocultural taboos that stigmatize same sex relations mean that the actual proportion could be somewhat larger (Inciardi, Syvertsen & Surratt, 2005). The age group 15-19 years has the highest sero-prevalence rate (2.5%) followed by the 25-29 and 30-34 age groups (2%) and (1%) respectively.

Walker et al. (2004) found that of 25 HIV positive adolescents attending a clinic in Jamaica, consensual sexual intercourse was the main mode of transmission for 56%, and vertical transmission (mother–to–child) accounted for a further 16%. Across the Caribbean, at least 3,000 children are born each year to mothers infected by HIV, and it can be predicted that 10,000 children will be infected over the next few years if HIV-positive mothers do not get antiretroviral (ART) treatment. Weller, Hambleton, Bain, Christie and Bain (2005) discuss the psychosocial implications of the impact of ART, noting that approximately 25-35% of HIV positive pregnant women could pass HIV to their newborns without this treatment.

The increased availability of treatment including the new antiretrovirals has significantly changed the 'face of AIDS' in the Caribbean. No longer is AIDS automatically perceived as a 'death sentence'. In many Caribbean countries, the life expectancy for persons with AIDS exceeds 60 years (UNAIDS, 2004). In this regard, quality of life and the standard of everyday functioning of the seropositive person becomes of paramount importance.

## HIV/AIDS – Introducing the Behavioural Context

Campbell (2003) warns that, internationally, psychologists may have hindered the change process by focusing attention on the individual-level phenomena and away from the societal changes which are prerequisites for sustained behaviour change.

This section of the chapter will introduce the reader to current practices in the field of HIV/AIDS prevention and care, with a particular focus on some of the psychosocial/ behavioural dimensions of these interventions, and some of their theoretical underpinnings. Unfortunately due to space limitations, not all of the issues that contribute to the challenge of the HIV/AIDS epidemic can be covered here. Particular areas for consideration are highlighted that we hope will be addressed in more detail in future publications of this nature. Hence, a few of the psychosocial issues are presented, besides the economic and political dynamics which are beyond our remit, and which contextualize the challenges which are facing us as we craft a response to HIV/AIDS in the Caribbean.

The first issue, a contemporary Caribbean challenge and currently a major focus of concern, relates to stigma and discrimination. Stigma refers to a visible characteristic which is used to shame, condemn, or ostracize. Describing the stigmatization of HIV/AIDS in the USA, Kalichman, Rompa and Cage (2000) quote from Herek's (1990) list of six stigmatization dimensions:

> ... although concealable early in its course, later stages of HIV infection and AIDS are rarely hidden from others; HIV infection interferes with social relationships; the disease physically disables and disfigures and is therefore aesthetically repellent; its origin is often, although not always, blamed on behaviours and choices; the course of HIV infection is degenerative and not alterable; and, HIV is a high-peril condition in that poses risks to others. Thus, HIV infection falls on the negative end of all dimensions.

The implications of this stigmatization process run the gamut of consequences from stress-related effects on disease progression, through fear of accessing services, to the effects of discrimination, for example denial of human rights and loss of employment opportunities.

The prejudice and the discrimination currently associated with HIV/AIDS have proven to be a major challenge in our fight against the pandemic, as it significantly decreases the availability of social support for the affected person. Social relationships are known to have a powerful influence on health (Herek & Glunt, 1988). The following definition of social support highlights the negative impact that stigma and discrimination are having on all persons who are affected by the HIV/AIDS epidemic. Social support refers to aid and assistance exchanged through social relationships and interpersonal interactions and can be categorized into the following four broad types of supportive behaviours or acts (House, 1981):

- Emotional support – empathy, love, trust, caring

- Instrumental support – tangible aid and services

- Informational support – advice, information, suggestions

- Appraisal support – information that is useful for self-evaluation

Sir George Alleyne (2005, p.5), speaking about the Caribbean response to the HIV/AIDS pandemic, reminds us that "the nature and depth of stigma and discrimination bear the colour of their cultural environment and we cannot easily translate findings from other cultures to this environment." Caribbean psychologists and behavioural scientists must therefore play a greater role in collecting reliable data and valid information regarding the Caribbean nature of HIV/AIDS stigmatization and discrimination. This information must inform the policies and programmes created to address the Caribbean experience if we are to stem the pandemic that is occurring here.

Psychologists must also learn to use a gendered perspective as we examine the issues contributing to the pandemic. Appropriate use of the tools of gender analysis helps us to understand how men and women attach meanings to elements of sexual and social behaviour. Research from the Caribbean indicates significant differences in the dynamics of HIV/AIDS infections among men and women (UNIFEM, 2004). Inequities in power and access to services, inability to negotiate safer behaviours, and role expectation are just some of the factors we know contribute to these differences. We know that these gender norms and expectations influence women and men and their sexual behaviours and that these, in turn, influence the extent to which men and women are vulnerable to HIV/AIDS (UNAIDS, 2004) There are, therefore, implications for prevention as well as for treatment and care, for example in terms of adherence to treatment protocols.

A related issue and one which has, both in the Caribbean and worldwide, influenced the social response to the pandemic, relates to sexuality and, specifically, sexual orientation. In the Caribbean, HIV is primarily spread by sexual activity and Ramsammy (2005, p 14) notes that for "religious reasoning or mis-reasoning, people have concluded that having HIV is a result of moral fault, such as promiscuous or deviant sex, and deserves punishment." The psychological implications of the Caribbean attitudes and beliefs about sexuality and the even broader area of gender and the impact on HIV/AIDS prevention and care are a significant area of research which we have only just begun to explore.

Camara et al. (2003) also note that although several English-speaking Caribbean countries have modified legislation criminalizing certain sexual acts in recent years, stigma continues to be strongly influenced by the Bible-based religious beliefs of many Caribbean Christians (the majority religion of the region), who perceive certain sexual behaviours and lifestyles as morally repugnant and deserving of punishment. It is clear, therefore, that the role of religion, spirituality and the formal structures such as the church, another broad issue we highlight, must also be examined from a psychosocial perspective. Religious organizations are among the most influential stakeholders in the region (Alleyne, 2005) and are also very involved in the delivery of services including education and care. Continued collaboration with umbrella groups such as the Caribbean Council of Churches, as well as other non-Christian faith-based groups, must also be informed by the data gathered by Caribbean psychologists, as all players including, for example, pastoral counsellors must be kept up to date on best and new practices. This admittedly brief snapshot of the sociocultural context of the Caribbean AIDS epidemic serves to remind us not only of the challenges we face but, we think, reinforces the urgent need for collaboration among behavioural scientists.

## HIV/AIDS – Behavioural Interventions

The complexity of the health behaviours associated with HIV/AIDS (e.g. risk assessment, condom negotiation, testing and adherence to medication) has led to a variety of interventions (*see* below). It is clear that the design of behaviour change interventions should be guided by a theoretical model and that psychologists interested in and working in this field should be at least familiar with some of these formal theories and models. These theories and models are important, not only for the design and implementation of effective interventions for prevention and care from a public health perspective, but also for the development of the professionals and practitioners in the field who may need to change their own behaviour.

Across the Caribbean region there are thousands of people who, each day, find themselves cast in the role of psychologist or behavioural scientist as they provide healthcare services, including those needed by people affected by HIV/AIDS. That is, many healthcare workers must function in roles requiring the application of psychological theories and techniques, frequently without the theoretical background, the training or sometimes even the awareness of the extent or complexity of the tasks they are being asked to perform. Uninformed attempts at counselling for behaviour change sometimes end up being not only ineffective but frustrating for both the providers and the recipients. For example, there are many AIDS service providers in the Caribbean who subscribe to the belief system that 'God' or 'Nature' have predetermined (wo)man's behaviour and "that's just how (wo)men are" (Weller et al., 2005). Clearly an individual who subscribes to this belief system may be less likely to buy into behaviour change programmes and so may be less effective as communicators of change messages. The professional or other provider seeking to apply principles of psychology to the prevention of HIV / AIDS therefore requires a personal awareness of his or her own mindset and philosophy of what can and will lead to behaviour change.

These mindsets exist along with other internalized psychological principles. Some individuals focus on early experiences which are seen as the 'cause' of the behaviour and feel that people need to examine their pasts and gain insights in order to change (psychodynamic/psychoanalytic approach), others believe that if you have strong enough 'motivating' factors (the carrot – e.g. money, or the stick – e.g. prosecution) you can achieve change (behavioural approach). Carried to one extreme this latter perspective supports the belief that punishment is the strongest deterrent and you can "beat it out of him/her". At the other end of the spectrum there are some who feel that it is immoral to 'manipulate' people by playing on their feelings and fears. Some feel that you need only 'reason' with people, and that given the knowledge a 'reasonable' person will change behaviour (cognitive behavioural). The pedagogical approach of teaching and preaching as a mode of influencing others is deeply ingrained in our Caribbean culture and, while it has a role to play, we know that knowledge alone does not often lead to the changes we desire. There are also those who see peer pressure as an important mode of influence and so place an emphasis on reinforcement of normative behaviours and use, for example, influential spokespersons to carry messages (social learning theory).

A contemporary appreciation of the complexity of human behaviour has led to an understanding that behaviour change interventions need to address cultural 'mindsets' in order to be effective. In the same way that we target those who are potentially at risk for HIV/AIDS due to their risky sexual or drug-seeking behaviour, we must also target the 'mindsets' of policy and programme managers. These individuals are products of the same sociocultural processes and will have their own values and issues which may influence the ways in which they respond to the HIV epidemic. For example, in a number of Caribbean territories programmes such as the Champions for Change, have been initiated to work with civic leaders, the political directorate and especially the members of Parliament to facilitate their involvement in the national response (Hackett, 2005).

## Psychology and Models for the Prevention of HIV/AIDS

Interventions based on the application of psychological principles to the prevention of HIV/AIDS in the Caribbean have run the gamut of the aforementioned perspectives. The authors believe that much of the research conducted on behaviour change and most of the interventions intended to change behaviour implemented in the Caribbean region have been based on a relatively narrow range of theoretical models promoted by various international development agencies partnering with regional health agencies. In fact, in a proposal to study adolescents' sexual behaviour in Jamaica, Jemmot et al. (2005), noted that it was difficult to identify a uniquely Caribbean theoretical model to provide the foundation for their proposed research. Camara et al. (2003) commenting on the early use of Information, Education and Counseling (IEC) material in the Caribbean, remind us that frequently material designed for certain target groups identified in North America and Europe have been used inappropriately for general Caribbean audiences. They note that in Trinidad and Tobago, for example, early AIDS prevention messages may have been interpreted as saying that women were not at risk.

In their meta-analysis testing major assumptions of behaviour change, Albarracin et al. (2005) provide a helpful overview of theories used in HIV-prevention interventions. They found that the most effective interventions were those that contained attitudinal arguments, educational information, behavioural skills arguments, and behavioural skills training, whereas the least effective ones were those that attempted to induce a fear of HIV. The impact of different interventions and strategies are also contingent on factors such as gender, age, ethnicity, risk group and past condom use (Albarracin et al., 2005).

Motivational and cognitive health antecedents of health behaviour are two important concepts which are advocated in the *theory of reasoned action* (Fishbein and Ajzen, 1975) and *theory of planned behaviour* (Ajzen and Madden, 1986). These models state that protective behaviours are contingent on the perceived desirability of the behaviour (i.e., positive attitudes and expectancies about the behaviour) and the normative pressure to engage in the behaviour (i.e., social norms). The theory of planned behaviour also considers perceptions that the behaviour is easy and up to the individual (i.e., perceived behavioural control). In *social–cognitive theory* (Bandura,1986; 1989; 1994) which is based on Bandura's earlier work on social learning theory (1977), the emphasis is placed on two areas of expectancy: outcome efficacy – believing it can work, and self efficacy – believing you can do it. Social cognitive theories have been the basis for most theoretical approaches to behaviour change intervention in the Caribbean. Furthermore, social- cognitive theory (Bandura, 1989) and the *information-motivation-behavioural skills model* (Fisher & Fisher, 1992) both assume that people are more likely to perform a behaviour once they acquire relevant knowledge and behavioural skills.

Other models have focused on the perceived threat of the health problem and the conflicting predictions. The *health belief model* (Rosenstock, 1974) and the *protection motivation theory* (Floyd, Prentice-Dunn, & Rogers, 2000; Rogers, 1975), suggest that people are motivated to initiate healthy behaviours when they believe they are susceptible to a disease and fear its severity. However, Rothman and Salovey (1997) have found that threatening (loss framed) persuasive measures are only effective when the target behaviour consists of avoiding a risk factor and can actually be detrimental when promoting a proactive measure (cited in Albarracin et al., 2005). Based on this information, we have learned in the Caribbean that the early "AIDS kills" messages may not have been as effective as intended and that gain-framed messages, e.g. touting the benefits of condom use, may be more effective.

Fisher and Fisher's (1992) information-motivation-behavioural skills model posits that information, motivation, and behavioural skills predict actual behaviours. They advocate that prevention messages will not be successful unless they manage to increase behavioural skills. Thus a persuasive campaign promoting condom use would not only mention the advantages but also describe how success depends on preparatory actions such as carrying condoms around all the time, or discussing use with potential partners. Albarracin et al. (2005) note that strategies such as having individuals role-play condom application or negotiation facilitates the acquisition of behavioural skills and are likely to increase perceptions of control, which are critical elements in the theory of planned behaviour and social-cognitive theory.

The *transtheoretical model (TTM)* (Prochaska, DiClemente, & Norcross, 1992) is an integrative model of behaviour change which states that individuals pass through five stages of change when modifying a behaviour: precontemplation, contemplation, preparation, action, and maintenance. During precontemplation, the individual does not recognize the behaviour as a problem. In the contemplation stage, the individual begins to recognize the behaviour as problematic but is not yet ready to take action. In the preparation stage, there is a firm intention to change and some attempt is made to change. In the action stage, the new behaviour is being consistently performed and after six months the individual enters the maintenance stage, in which he/she works to prevent relapse and endeavours to integrate the changes made during the previous phases into his/her life. The TTM recognizes that persons at different stages of readiness may be receptive to different types of interventions and that rather than treating behaviour as an "all or nothing" phenomenon, it should be viewed as a sequence of steps with interventions tailored to each step (Center for Disease Control and Prevention, 1999).

In investigating condom use among adolescent males in Jamaica, certain effective strategies were identified. The 1997 Jamaica Reproductive Health Survey and other data indicated that 60% of sexually experienced young men ages 15 to 24 and 40% of sexually experienced male adolescents ages 10 to 14 reported using condoms for their last or most recent sexual intercourse. Four types of interventions were found to have contributed to increased condom use among adolescent males in Jamaica and led to the following recommendations (Pathfinder International, 2002):

1. *Perceived Peer Acceptance.* Interventions that promote peer endorsement, peer promotion, and condom skills training by peer facilitators will significantly increase condom use because adolescent males are far more likely to accept and use condoms if they believe that their peers are using condoms.

2. *Communication Campaigns.* Effective communication campaigns should (a) address issues of sexually transmitted infections

(STI's) and pregnancy prevention; (b) promote messages that desensitize condom inhibitions, popularize condom usage, and establish social acceptance (using a condom is the "cool" thing to do); and (c) create a healthy, positive image of condoms and condom users.

3. _Youth-Friendly Access and Wide Availability._ Youth-friendly access includes: (a) establishing a variety and large number of outlets, with emphasis on nontraditional retail points that are more anonymous and have convenient opening hours; (b) sensitizing "providers" to be more accommodating and encouraging to adolescents who wish to use and purchase condoms; and (c) creating a non-threatening environment for access to condoms.

4. _Skills Training._ Training in correct condom usage should include instructional leaflets, "older" youth as demonstrators or instructors, and a relaxed and open group environment.

# Behaviour Change Communication (BCC) Model

In the Caribbean, most behaviour change interventions are designed and implemented based on an integration of several of these models and theories. Behaviour change practitioners have drawn upon what is called the _Behaviour change communication (BCC)_ model to design effective interventions. BCC refers to "an interactive process with communities (as integrated with an overall program) to develop tailored messages and approaches using a variety of communication channels to develop positive behaviours; promote and sustain individual, community and societal behaviour change; and maintain appropriate behaviours" (Family Health International, 2002, p. 3).

Family Health International (2002) identified BCC as an integral component of any HIV/AIDS prevention programme and identified its role as helping to: increase knowledge; stimulate community dialogue; promote essential attitude change; reduce stigma and discrimination; create a demand for information and services; advocate; promote service for prevention, care and support; and promote skills and sense of self-efficacy. As mentioned above, BCC uses a combination of theories and practical steps that are based on field realities, rather than relying on any single theory or model. BCC practitioners believe that when changing behaviour there are a series of steps through which the individual, group or institution moves, from a lack of awareness to sustained behaviour change. These steps are taken at different rates and not always consistently – that is, sometimes they move forward, sometimes backward and some steps may even be skipped. Practitioners of behaviour change must therefore understand the enabling factors and use the available channels of communication.

The steps involved in creating a BCC strategy (AIDSCAP, 1997; 2003) are as follows:

1. State programme goals

2. Involve stakeholders

3. Identify target population

4. Conduct formative BCC assessments

5. Segment target populations

6. Define behaviour change objectives

7. Design BCC strategy monitoring and evaluation plan

8. Develop communication products

9. Pre-test

10. Implement and monitor

11. Evaluate

12. Analyze feedback and revision (return to 7 if necessary)

In a number of Caribbean countries, ongoing community-based programmes are attempting to influence the behaviour of specific target groups. In Trinidad, the Men-Touring programme of the YMCA; UWI-HARP (University of the West Indies HIV AIDS Response Programme) on the campuses of the University of the West Indies; in Grenada and across the region, the Red Cross youth programmes – all are using behaviour change campaigns specifically designed to address the knowledge, values and attitudes of their target groups.

Needless to say, behaviour change communication continues to be a complex endeavour. Even as we in the region develop and apply our own constructs and theories, we must continue to monitor the process as we fine-tune these messages so as to have the desired impact on our target audiences.

A cautionary note should be made at this point: targeted interventions may carry corollary messages causing collateral damage. As a case in point, as we de-stigmatize HIV/AIDS and promote ARV benefits – "Positive Living" – we may also sending the message that there is less to be concerned about contracting HIV/AIDS. For example, young men are reporting that some no longer feel that AIDS is a big deal. After all, for many young men, especially in urban low income communities, there are far greater risks to their health and life to be faced on a daily basis (Weller et al., 2007). These observations emphasize the importance of monitoring, evaluation and revised targeting as critical components, if these behaviour change communication programmes are to remain effective.

# HIV/AIDS: Psychological Counselling Interventions

Kelly and Freeman (2005) point to evidence that both medical and non-medical interventions, such as psychotropic medications and counselling, have been demonstrated to significantly improve the health and well-being of people living with infectious health conditions. A variety of interventions, utilizing various counselling techniques, have been developed and are perceived as international best practices. A number of these interventions have been applied in the Caribbean and are described in the following sections.

## VOLUNTARY COUNSELLING AND TESTING: PRE- AND POST-TEST COUNSELLING

The acronym "VCT" (voluntary counselling and testing) is used internationally to refer to HIV testing and counselling. VCT programmes have been implemented in the Caribbean and are a service used to help people examine their risk for HIV infection, identify the ways in which they can avoid infection, facilitate accessing the blood test to find out if they are infected, and manage the results of the test. These programmes are seen as an important gateway to prevention, treatment and support services for people affected by HIV/AIDS.

The standard components of the VCT process may be described under the headings below.

### Pre-test Counselling
- Introduction and orientation to VCT

- Assessment of risk
- Exploration of options for reducing risk
- HIV testing information

### Post-test Counselling – Negative

- Provide HIV negative result
- Develop risk reduction plan
- Identify support for risk reduction
- Discuss disclosure and partner referral

### Post-test Counselling – Positive

- Provide HIV+ test result
- Provide result and ensure understanding
- Explore emotional reaction and support
- Identify sources of support and provide referrals
- Refer to appropriate providers e.g. medical, social, pastoral
- Discuss disclosure and partner referral
- Identify partners to be informed
- Help prepare for disclosure to significant others
- Address remaining risk reduction issues

A comprehensive Voluntary Counselling and Testing (VCT) programme has been initiated in a number of Caribbean territories and standardized manuals and training programmes have been used to improve the quality of VCT provided (JHPIEGO, 2002). Notably, voluntary counselling and testing offered in antenatal clinics and by other health providers is often the best opportunity to initiate and manage behaviour change communication in support of those interventions intended to reduce MTCT.

One of the principal components of the protocols designed for conducting pre-test counselling sessions is the assessment of risk and the exploration of options for reducing risk. In addition, a major component of post-test counselling sessions is the exploration and recommendation of psychosocial support, as well as negotiation of disclosure issues. The training manual for VCT emphasizes the appropriate use of selected questions which match the client's life situation (JHPIEGO, 2002).

Counsellors are also encouraged to "develop a picture of the client's life" e.g., related to life experiences, risk behaviour and coping/support. Revised guidelines for HIV Counselling, Testing and Referral (CTR), developed by the CDC, emphasize the importance of including in-depth, personalized risk assessment. It must be noted that the terminology used by the CDC puts equal emphasis on counselling, testing and referral. Referral has not been emphasized in the current terminology of VCT used in the Caribbean, perhaps to the detriment of the patient who may not receive appropriate referrals for comprehensive care, and to the detriment of the regional response which has not harnessed nor developed the skills of all pertinent stakeholders in the care network.

Given the limited amount of time available during most VCT sessions, counsellors must be efficient in the topics they explore as they try to help their clients come to terms with their situations and make healthy choices with regard to their future. VCT counsellors should be able to:

- Describe how people get infected with HIV
- Describe how people can avoid getting infected with HIV
- Describe how HIV becomes AIDS
- Describe safer sex behaviours
- Describe local Counselling and Testing Services
- Describe the options for HIV testing and the possible HIV test results
- List the benefits of counselling and testing
- Describe healthy living

## PROVIDER INITIATED COUNSELING AND TESTING (PITC)

There have been a number of changes in the way VCT is approached worldwide with a greater emphasis on facilitating rapid testing, diagnosis and treatment. In fact the CDC in the USA has recommended that the HIV test should be a routine part of healthcare and has set aside previous requirements for pre-test counselling and a separate written informed consent in the USA (Centers for Disease Control, 2001). In the Caribbean,

CAREC/PAHO recently provided new guidelines for developing Caribbean VCT programmes that are intended to increase provider- initiated approaches (primarily by doctor and nurses). PITC is intended to encourage more people to do the HIV test in order to know their status, but also to give them the choice to 'opt out' of testing. In this context, standard VCT pre-test counselling is modified to simply ensure informed consent and to provide minimal education and counselling.

The authors are concerned that, from a psychological perspective, one of the most serious implications of this new Caribbean protocol is the potential effect of decreasing pre-test counselling requirements. Though not as drastic as the CDC recommendations, the implication is that less communication about HIV, especially from respected sources such as medical professionals, will be provided. This means that there will be fewer opportunities to educate people about HIV and to facilitate decreased risk behaviour. This will be particularly true for persons whose test was negative, allowing an important opportunity to promote prevention to pass. Unfortunately, post-test counselling is unlikely to pick up the slack unless effective systems are put in place to ensure referral to psychosocial providers who are able to counsel effectively.

Providers initiating this testing will need more effective psychosocial profiling skills, given the limited time allocated to this process. There needs to be a greater emphasis on the potential benefits of psychosocial profiling – identifying psychological and social characteristics as a means of appropriately assessing needs for care and referral. This should include an assessment of the individual's:

- knowledge of disease
- attitude towards the illness
- literacy level including health literacy
- emotional status/stress level
- level of cognitive functioning
- pre-morbid and present coping style
- social support network
- spiritual/religious orientation

There must of course be an accessible network of referral support services to meet the needs of these individuals (Patterson & Francis, 2006).

One of the present authors (Weller), along with colleagues at The University of the West Indies (Mona) Health Centre, is currently developing a model to address the concerns articulated here. The concept being developed is the creation of a model which integrates the role of the medical provider as facilitator of testing with a degree of screening or profiling allowing appropriate referral to other services. It is anticipated that the initial provider, whether a physician or nurse, will access certain information which will allow the referral resource, a psychosocial provider, to follow-up and target necessary behaviour change issues.

## Psychology and the Treatment and Care of PLWHA

Psychological distress associated with HIV infection can compound adjustment difficulties and increase barriers to accessing care and support services, especially in a society fraught with stigma and discrimination. However, we know very little about the incidence and implications of these psychological variables as they affect health behaviour and coping strategies among people living with HIV/AIDS (PLWHA) in the Caribbean.

Social psychological theories provide an understanding and explanation of how the thoughts, feelings and behaviours of an individual can be influenced by the actual, imagined or implied presence of other people. Psychosocial factors are frequently identified as critical variables in the effective treatment of HIV/AIDS. Psychosocial factors include the psychological variables which operate on an intrapersonal level e.g. emotional state; self variables e.g. self esteem; cognitive factors; e.g. belief systems; problem solving styles, etc., all of which influence knowledge, attitudes and practices.

Studies have shown the impact of psychosocial variables on different aspects of HIV infection. Adherence to one's medical regime was found to be negatively affected by lack of social support; belief about health/wellness; concurrent alcohol or illicit drug use; negative provider; and patient's beliefs, including cultural beliefs about health issues (All et al., 2004). In one study, persons with a low HIV viral load were found to have a more internal locus of control than those with higher loads, suggesting a relationship between perceived self-efficacy and response to the virus (All et al., 2004). Another study (Grassi et al., 1998) found that patients who were adjusting well to their HIV-positive status tended to have a higher level of fighting spirit and lower degree of hopelessness than those patients who were not adjusting well to their HIV-positive status. Also a coping style that included an inability to face and confront HIV infection was associated with symptoms of psychological stress, repression of anger, external locus of control, and low social support in the latter group.

Safren, Radomsky, Otto, and Saloman (2002) investigated the impact of certain cognitive and behavioural variables on psychological well-being (assessed by measures of depression, self-esteem and quality of life), in HIV infected persons. They found that while stressful life events explained some of the variance in psychological well-being, these effects were negated when the factors of social support, coping styles and punishment beliefs (for example, "I have HIV because I am being punished for things I have done") were included in the analysis. Thus, social psychological factors must be considered inasmuch as we seek to understand and influence the social behaviour – interactions and social thoughts which may mediate the targeted behaviour patterns.

## Challenges of Living with HIV/AIDS

Infection with HIV and the progress of the illness through the stages of AIDS bring a sequence of challenges. Reactions to the diagnosis invariably include shock and fear, no matter how much pre-test counselling has been provided. Issues of death and dying, impact on families, stigma and discrimination, loss of dreams all may weigh heavily on the individual. Facing a life with HIV often means loss of social support at a time when it is so crucial, and this may lead to an increased vulnerability to stress; mental disorders may be a result of this inability to cope. On the other hand, there are those who are able to cope and provide support to their peers in dealing with this process.

Challenges for PLWHA come in all the dimensions that constitute wellness – physical, intellectual, environmental, emotional, social and spiritual. Here we will focus on the last three mentioned. The emotional challenges faced by PLWHA have been well documented (e.g. Sweetland, Lazarus, Freeman, & Saloner, 2005) and vary from individual to individual in terms of severity, sequence, and situation. These challenges are often likely to influence willingness to commence treatment in a number of ways. Coping with the stress of living with HIV may be more difficult for some than for others, depending on their personality and pre-morbid coping skills.

Depression and a sense of hopelessness can prevent an individual from even bothering to take the medication or, worse, perhaps motivate them to abuse the medication as a suicidal gesture. On the one hand, the medication may be seen as giving hope, but on the other, it is a constant reminder of the life-threatening condition. Initial assessment and ongoing monitoring of the emotional well-being of the patient, are important parts of an adherence intervention.

Spiritual challenges are frequently underestimated as providers do not usually initiate discussions of this issue. However, whether or not patients attend church, they are products of a culture which puts great emphasis on spirituality. These beliefs can, on the one hand, serve a protective and supportive role in coping with HIV/AIDS, but on the other hand, they can raise many uncomfortable feelings of guilt, rejection, shame and anger at the unfairness of life.

## MENTAL DISORDERS AND PSYCHOLOGICAL EFFECTS OF HIV/AIDS

Mental disorders have been found to be more common in PLWHA than in non-infected people (Kelly & Freeman, 2005). Patients being treated for HIV infection have been found to have much higher prevalence rates for substance abuse and psychiatric disorders than members of the general population. Prevalence rates vary widely (50% to 83%). Psychiatric disorders may be due to co-morbidity with other existing conditions, e.g. substance abuse, neuropathology of the illness itself, other opportunistic infections or as a result of anti-retroviral treatment. Prevalence rates for depression are as high as 40% (Angelino & Treisman, 2001), while psychotic disorders (schizophrenia, schizophreniform and brief psychotic disorder) range from 0.2% to 15.5% (Sewell, 1996). Other disorders found in HIV populations include dysthymia, generalized anxiety disorder and panic attacks (Bing et al., 2001).

It can therefore be seen that there are many stressors associated with HIV infection and even more with the advent of antiretroviral (ART) treatment. Kelly and Freeman (2005) summarize some of the mental health correlates seen in PLWHA:

- Cognitive impairment, dementia, and psychosis as a result viral infection of the brain

- Depression and anxiety due to the impact of the infection on the person's life

- Alcohol and drug abuse

- Psychiatric side effects of ARVs (notably efavirenz), e.g. depression

- Social difficulties faced as a result of stigma and discrimination.

## NEUROPSYCHOLOGY AND HIV/AIDS

It is well known that PLWHA have relatively high rates of delirium, dementia and psychiatric disorders. A variety of factors contribute to this, including pre-existing mental illnesses, the effects of HIV on the neurological system, opportunistic infections, and malignancies sometimes seen in stages 3 and 4 of the clinical progression. Other contributing factors are the medications, such as anti-retrovirals, which can cause neurological side effects (Bartlett & Gallant, 2003; Bartlett, 2005).

HIV-positive persons are at significant risk for cognitive impairment which increases with each successive stage of HIV disease. Ziefert, Leary and Boccellari (1995) suggest that between 55 and 65 per cent of persons living with HIV/AIDS will experience cognitive difficulties. The first abilities to be affected include: information processing speed, psychomotor skills, learning efficiency, and the retrieval of stored information. More recent data echo similar rates with estimates that over 60 per cent of persons living with HIV/AIDS will develop cognitive difficulties during their illness and that the progression of cognitive decline secondary to HIV infection parallels the progression of systemic HIV disease (Canadian Psychiatric Association, 2004).Thus cognitive deficits are least common in persons with asymptomatic HIV infection and most common in patients with an AIDS defining condition.  While some neuropsychological impairment may occur early in infection, it most often develops when patients are symptomatic or are diagnosed with AIDS.

Impairments may stabilize or become worse as the disease progresses. They also impact different aspects of the patient's life, e.g. interpersonal relationships, work performance, medication compliance, and the ability to live independently (Canadian Psychiatric Association, 2004). The degree to which the person is affected can vary.

One of the most significant and prevalent brain disorders affecting persons with AIDS is HIV Associated Dementia (Ziefert et al., 1995). HIV Associated Dementia can exert its toll on the cognitive, motor and behavioural functioning of the affected individual. In more severe cases, cognitive impairment includes forgetfulness, decreased concentration and attention, mental slowing (e.g. new learning, sequencing and problem solving), difficulty reading and slowed executive functioning (Reitan and Wolfson, 1993; Canadian Psychiatric Association, 2004).

Behavioural or physical changes include fatigue, loss of motivation, malaise, headaches, increasing social isolation, apathy and diminished emotional responsiveness. Loss of sex drive may also be present (Reitan & Wolfson, 1993; Canadian Psychiatric Association, 2004; Navia et al., 1986). Mania may develop in some patients and is thought to be a primary manifestation of HIV-associated dementia. Patients with HIV-associated dementia may also suffer from depressed mood, and a challenge lies in differentiating the two. While both may coexist, the presence of apathy, amotivation, lethargy and indifference, along with the presence of cognitive deficits, as well as the absence of reports of a sense of sadness are more suggestive of HIV dementia than a major depressive disorder (Canadian Psychiatric Association, 2004; Greenwood, 1991). Motor symptoms include psychomotor slowing, clumsiness, tremor, weakness of the legs, poor balance, unsteady gait, hyperreflexia, deficits in motor speed and control and deterioration of handwriting (Reitan & Wolfson, 1993; Canadian Psychiatric Association, 2004; Navia et al., 1986).

HIV-associated dementia usually progresses slowly and presents initially with mild cognitive changes including loss of memory, an inability to concentrate, mild confusion and mental slowness (Barnes, 1986; Herman, 1986; Navia et al., 1986; Perry & Jacobsen, 1986). Persons with mild symptoms may often remain stable and appear within normal limits on a mental status examination. As the disease progresses, persons with AIDS may become increasingly confused and require assistance to function. They may also fail to realize how ill they are. Greenwood (1991) suggests that this is a crucial point in the development of the illness and not only may the person be unable to care for themselves, but persons who previously practised safe sex may forget to do so as their dementia advances. They thus place themselves and their partners at risk for infection and re-infection with HIV. Another important area of concern is medication management. Studies have suggested that HIV-positive persons with impairments in memory, executive functioning and psychomotor functioning may show difficulty with medication management and adherence to medication regimes (Albert, Weber, Todak et al., 1999; Hinkin, Castellon, Durvasula et al., 2002).

While progressive cognitive impairment in HIV infection significantly influences the medical and social prognosis of afflicted patients (Oechsner, Moller & Zaudig, 1993), there are also implications for vocational prognosis in determining real-life occupational functioning and competence (UNAIDS, 1998). Those patients who are most immuno-compromised and systemically unwell are at great risk of rapid progression. Thus the progression of HIV dementia appears related to the patient's overall health and immune function (Canadian Psychiatric Association, 2004). Other factors associated with increased risk and rapid progression include a high viral load, low CD4 counts (e.g. below 200), depression, executive dysfunction, presence of MCMD, prominent psychomotor slowing, injecting drug use and non injecting cocaine use (Childs, 1999; Bouwman, 1998; Maschke, 2000; Stern, 2001).

Cournos, Wainberg and Horwath (2005) note that the patient thought to be suffering from HIV dementia should be assessed for the following: cognitive problems, motor problems, behavioural problems and decrements in functioning. Brief screening instruments such as the Mini Mental Status Exam, Mental Alternation Test and HIV Dementia scale may be used, but these are not very sensitive and may not detect subtle and early signs of cognitive impairment. Neuropsychological assessment should include an assessment of premorbid functioning, including measures of age, educational level, substance use history, current medications and results from medical examinations. Psychologists can support these clinical assessments by using standardized tests, some of which are described by Spreen and Strauss (1998) and include the Hopkins HIV screen, non-dominant hand grooved pegboard test, WAIS-R (Wechsler Adult Intelligence Scale- revised), Boston Naming Test, COWA

(Controlled Oral Word Association Test), Trail Making Test, MMPI-2 (Minnesota Multiphasic Personality Inventory) and the Wechsler Memory Scale.

Those who are involved with providing care for PLWHA should be aware that accurate and early detection of cognitive impairment has implications not only for the clinicians' ability to manage the disease but also for the patient's ability to perform social and occupational tasks effectively.

## Psychological Correlates of Medication

Psychologists and other providers of psychosocial services must be familiar with the treatment regimes of PLWHA. ARVs and other medications can play a pivotal role in the lives of these individuals and can have a great impact on the person's mental health. While some studies link psychological distress to physical health (Rabkin et al., 2000), others have highlighted the negative psychological side effects of HIV medication. One study by the United Kingdom Coalition of Persons Living With HIV/AIDS (2000) which sought to discover the existence of psychological side effects of HIV medication asked PLWHA whether they had noticed psychological or mood changes since starting therapy. Changes were reported by 79% of persons. The following specific effects were reported: depression 67%, irritability 46%, mania 10%, anxiety 58%, hallucinations 12%, vivid dreams 35%, suicidal thoughts/actions 30% and other 6%. Premorbid psychological well-being, the stage of HIV infection, and emotional reaction to the diagnosis may all have contributed to the psychological responses noted.

However, many patients attributed their psychological difficulties to their treatment medication and this has implications for compliance and adherence to treatment regimens. Additionally, more than half stated that they had not been warned of possible psychological side-effects. In this study, 80% of patients also started using antidepressant and sleeping medication since starting anti-HIV therapy, and although antidepressants are most efficacious when combined with psychotherapy, only 55% of persons reported receiving psychotherapy. Thus the impact of treatment on mental health and the collaboration between doctor and psychologist must be explored and encouraged.

## ADHERENCE AND THE PSYCHOLOGICAL IMPACT OF ARV TREATMENT

A particular challenge faced by PLWHA, and their providers relates to the decision to start HAART/ARV therapy. Sustaining and adhering to treatment, as well as the complexity of some regimes, can be very difficult and demanding and may add to existing stressors. Patients may struggle to manage factors such as increased demands on food intake, numerous dosing times, shifts in schedules and activities to maintain regimens, coping with side-effects, economic costs of treatment, psychological distress due to survivor guilt, and potential employment-related impairment. "Will I be able to fit my medication regime around shift hours? Will working harm my health?" (Kalichman et al., 2000; UK, Coalition of People Living with HIV and AIDS, 2003).

It is imperative that we act in a proactive manner to identify those factors which might have a negative influence on adherence, and thus pose a threat to the health of the individual and the wider community. It is also very important that we identify the factors which will support adherence. These factors are significant, not only in terms of how they influence the 'health seeking' behaviour of the PLWHA, but also in terms of the 'health providing' behaviours of medical and other service providers.

Weller et al. (2005) found that spiritual beliefs, concerns re confidentiality, and attitudes towards generic medications could be important factors in facilitating adherence. The specific effect of these factors may vary between individuals. For example, it was found that some women with strong Christian beliefs did not put their faith in the medication and so might be less compliant, while other Christian women felt that they should comply, as this indicated their faith that God would work through the medications (Weller et al., 2005). The researchers recommended that, as they engaged in psychosocial profiling of patients, providers should be more concerned about assessing these concerns.

The challenge, then, for psychologists and others responding to the AIDS epidemic, is to develop a network of care providers who are sensitized to the needs and dynamics surrounding ARV treatment and who perceive the needs of PLWHIV through a "wellness" lens, which acknowledges the importance of providing a state of physical, mental, and social well-being.

As mentioned before, one of the challenges which may be a part of

ARV treatment programmes is the complexity of treatment schedules, as this may be a problem for some people. One method of instructing patients, the provision of printed material, may not be as useful as anticipated because of the varying levels of literacy among the population. Interventions to increase adherence frequently rely on the use of calendars, meal schedules, charts, etc. also assume a certain level of cognitive competence and literacy.

Concern has also been expressed that, as noted before (Weller et al., 2006; 2007), (1) as the medications become cheaper and more easily obtained, their perceived value may diminish and may influence adherence to regimen; and (2) as the stigma of HIV is reduced and as it becomes seen in the same light as other chronic diseases, it is possible that the fear factor may decrease and, along with it, the preventive and protective behaviours.

## PSYCHOTROPIC MEDICATION

Psychologists who are involved in the treatment and care of PLWHA should be aware of the implications of treatment with psychotropic medications. The well-being of the PLWHA, their compliance with interventions in general, and adherence to medication in particular may be significantly enhanced by proper management of their mental health, with appropriate use of psychotropic medication.

Psychosocial providers must be familiar with issues such as symptoms and treatment of specific disorders, side-effects, dosages, interactions between psychotropic drugs and antiretroviral medications, use of multiple psychotropic medications, and the specific needs of HIV Clinical stages 3 and 4 patients, who may be on complex medication regimens.

The three main categories of ARVs – nucleoside reverse transcriptase inhibitor (NRTI), non-nucleoside reverse transcriptase inhibitor (NNRTI), and protease inhibitors (PI) – have specific interactions with certain antipsychotics, antidepressants, mood stabilizers and anxiolytics. The levels and efficacy of the ARVs may be affected and dosages may need to be modified. In some cases there may be the danger of toxicity (Bartlett, 2005). In the Caribbean where PLWHA may seek medical services from a number of providers, there can be serious consequences if the patients are not educated to the potential danger of drug interactions. Sharing of medications may also exacerbate this danger.

# Living with HIV/AIDS: Types of Psychosocial Support

Catalan et al. (2005) emphasize the importance of treating the mental disorders of PLWHA (*see* below) and they also believe that the provision of psychosocial support is equally important. They note that the positive consequences extend beyond the well-being of the individuals and affect the society in terms of the economy, and quality of public health.

As has been noted, HIV disease progression is likely to be slowed down by improving mental health. From the period of time when the individual is making the decision to take the HIV test to the period of time when the individual is living with HIV/AIDS, psychological support, both formal and informal, can make all the difference in the well-being the patient experiences. Psychological support encompasses a wide variety of interventions provided both by professionals and non-professionals trained in medicine, as well as by other providers in the wider realm of healthcare, including psychosocial (social workers, counsellors, human resource professionals) and pastoral (clergy) providers.

This support is also provided by families, friends, and peers living with HIV/AIDS. It is therefore critical to include in this discussion the needs of the people who are caregivers as they too are affected and may suffer considerable emotional pain and dysfunction. They must learn to deal with their own emotional struggles, burn-out and need for self-care. Interventions to facilitate psychological support therefore extend beyond the provision of services to PLWHA, to those whose lives have also been affected by the diagnosis.

## SUPPORTIVE COUNSELLING TO MEET THE NEEDS OF PEOPLE LIVING WITH HIV/AIDS

The purpose of supportive counselling is to help people who are living with HIV and others affected by HIV, such as families and friends, to cope with the emotional stressors associated with this life experience. Key elements are encouragement and hope, and in simple terms, a shoulder to lean on. In the Caribbean context of limited resources, stigma and discrimination, it is often very important to have someone you can trust, confide in and who can help you to 'live positively'. Helping the individuals to develop problem-solving skills includes assessing their needs and competencies as well as facilitating access to other service providers by making appropriate referrals. Obviously, time must be taken to get to know the individual, to establish rapport and to understand what the experience of living with HIV/AIDS means to that individual. Provision of this type of support may take place in both individual and group interventions.

Female participants in a study of HIV-positive mothers found that the opportunity to discuss their issues in a safe group of peers was of considerable benefit. These participants requested additional opportunities for this group support (Weller et al., 2005). Support groups, such as those provided by the Centre for HIV/AIDS Research Education and Service (CHARES) and KPAIDS at the University of the West Indies, and by Caribbean Network of Seropositives (CRN+) groups in the region, may be expected to become more available and acceptable as stigma and discrimination decrease. More providers need to be trained in conducting peer support groups for individuals affected by HIV/AIDS. It is important to emphasize that PLWHA may need special interventions to help them deal with their own issues before attempting to facilitate groups such as these. In any case, before individuals are ready to discuss their concerns in a group setting they may need help in dealing with disclosure issues.

## COUNSELLING FOR DISCLOSURE

Though there may be a desire for emotional and social support, many people are too afraid of the negative emotional reactions of others to share their HIV status. Stigma and discrimination continue to be inhibiting factors for many PLWHA. The decision to disclose one's HIV status is, for many, a complex process and thus counselling can be very helpful as the individual assesses the many relevant factors. It is important to realize that disclosure is really a process and not an event. It takes time, so the individual must be encouraged when possible to think it through and plan ahead. Potential benefits and also the potential negative consequences must be considered.

Some key points to consider include the fact that the decision to disclose must be made by the clients themselves as it can have significant implications for the subsequent quality of their lives. The counsellor's own perceptions should not be the basis for the decision, but can have a significantly influential effect. The counsellor must, therefore, be very careful that his or her judgements re public health impact, fears for the safety of the individual, and other personal beliefs do not unduly influence the client's decision.

Lazarus and Saloner (2005) suggest that the counsellor should among other things:

a. help the individual explore the implications of disclosure on relationships with family, friends and co-workers, for example

b. help the person develop a plan on how he/she is going to disclose, to whom, and in what sequence

c. explore things they can do to prepare people to receive this news

d. role play the disclosure and prepare for a variety of responses

e. provide support for the consequences.

Clearly, the role of the counsellor is important and emphasizes not only the need for key psychological competencies and counselling skills for those providing care, but also the need for ongoing access to these services. Psychosocial support groups, such as those run by the CRN+ throughout the region, and Jamaica AIDS Support in Jamaica, provide an important resource for people living with HIV/AIDS, in that they are able to provide psychosocial support in a group-setting to their peers.

Other aspects of counselling for which interventions are often required include relationship counselling; crisis counselling; and grief, survivor guilt and bereavement counselling. These require specific techniques which must be learned by providers if interventions are to be effective (Catalan et al., 2005).

## HIV/AIDS and Children and Adolescents

While many of the issues addressed in previous sections apply to Caribbean children and adolescents, the needs of these young people whose lives are affected by HIV/AIDS often provide a unique challenge (Dicks, 2001). As noted previously, mother–to-child prevention programmes in the Caribbean have improved the chances of survival of children of HIV-positive mothers (Christie, 2004). The prevention of infection among these children is only one of the benefits of these interventions. In addition, these programmes facilitate the identification of the needs of, and the provision of services to, HIV-positive children.

Pierre, Ramsay and Loudon (2005) remind us that children are particularly vulnerable, not only because they are so dependent on others, but also because they are not yet emotionally mature and thus are less capable of coping with the psychosocial challenges. Children affected by HIV/AIDS require coordinated interventions involving a range of professionals. Pierre et al. (2005) also note the growing phenomenon of AIDS orphans in the Caribbean and the need for psychosocial programmes to meet their needs. Another significant phenomenon relates to the increasing number of Caribbean teenagers living with HIV, some of whom have been HIV-positive all their lives (Dunkley-Thompson, Figueroa & Christie, 2006). These young people are now, or may soon be, sexually active and face unique challenges as they try to make healthy decisions regarding intimate relationships.

CHARES (the Centre for HIV/AIDS Research Education and Service), based at UWI, Mona provides treatment and social/ emotional support for children and teenagers living with HIV. Similar centres exist elsewhere in the Caribbean region. CHARES has also served as a practicum site for psychology students and others in the field of psychosocial services. In Trinidad, services are provided for HIV/AIDS orphans and for children and teens living with HIV/AIDS by agencies such as the Cyril Ross Nursery, which runs a home and an outpatient clinic. In addition, support groups are run by a number of NGOs (UNGASS, 2006).

The number of HIV infected children and adolescents may be expected to continue to increase, due partly to the increase in mother-to-child transmission, and partly to the early age of sexual activity. Rodriguez et al. (2004) note that as the highest AIDS seroprevalence may be found among those in their twenties, it is likely that they were infected during their teenage years.

As has been noted previously, young people are particularly vulnerable to messages from the media and to the influence of peers and adults. This increases the chance of risky behaviour among them although it also provides the opportunities for intervention. One of the goals of the 2002 Joint United Nations Programme on HIV/AIDS (UNAIDS) was to provide reproductive health services, including contraceptives, counselling, and treatment of sexually transmitted infections (STI's) to adolescents. Unfortunately, in the Caribbean, access to services, especially for prevention, are often limited due to sociocultural beliefs about sexuality, and beliefs about the options which should be made available to the youth, e.g. sex education and condom promotion.

Caribbean psychologists, especially those working in the educational and school systems, have a very important role to play in the development of age- and stage-appropriate interventions, and the institutionalization of these interventions. The psychologist's role as an advocate for these and other vulnerable groups cannot be overstated.

## Creating the Psychosocial Network

Kelly and Freeman (2005) note the frequency with which mental health problems among PLWHA can go unnoticed and untreated. This may be true for psychosocial needs in general. Both clinical and non-clinical healthcare workers, including those involved in primary care, frequently need help to identify these problems and also must learn how to provide appropriate support and referrals to other service providers when necessary. Weller et al. (2005) make a series of recommendations for the development of psychosocial services in the Caribbean/ CARICOM region, which include revisiting the psychosocial role of the healthcare provider to meet the needs of PLWHA. They recommend that this provider must be not only a provider of medication/clinical services, but also a sensor assessing needs, a gatekeeper providing direction to other service providers, a supporter during the process, and a sentinel identifying trends and patterns. Implications for training of providers include a greater focus on a teamwork approach for building networks, psychosocial assessment/ profiling, creation of an effective referral network, use of appropriate levels of literacy material, public education, and continuing/in-service education (Kelly and Bain, 2003).

We must continue to modify curricula in relevant professional schools, e.g. medical, nursing, pharmacy, psychology, counselling, and social work. One such initiative by UWIHARP (the UWI HIV/AIDS Response Programme) included a series of interventions to enable faculty to integrate material in their courses to address contemporary issues related to AIDS (Bain, 2004; SIRHASC Project Report, 2006).

Healthcare Providers need to improve their:
- communication skills

- ability to assess psychosocial needs
- counselling skills
- patient education skills
- knowledge of appropriate referral resources
- ability to make effective referrals

Other competencies to be promoted among non-medical psychosocial providers e.g. social workers, pastoral and other counsellors, etc include:
- knowledge of ART regimes/protocols
- relationship/communication skills
- ability to assess psychosocial needs
- sensitization to unique psychosocial needs of PLWHA
- patient education
- knowledge of behaviour change theories
- HIV counselling skills
- knowledge of appropriate referral processes and sources
- access to supervision/skills

All providers should be competent to make effective psychosocial referrals and should be able to:
- identify providers of psychosocial services
- be familiar with how agencies operate
- be familiar with specific people at agencies – know names
- be aware of public perception of provider
- be prepared to promote use of service or address barriers

Development of a network to provide these services requires expansion and modification of existing programmes. The creation of a more effective network will be helped by the development of adjuncts to VCT/PICT programmes, including training additional psychosocial providers in adherence, disclosure, grief/bereavement and relationship counselling issues, promotion of these services to PLWHIV, supervision of counsellors and other psychosocial providers by trained professionals, and improved referral mechanisms to VCT/adjuncts and by VCT.

Given the rapidly growing access to, and utilization of, telephone technology in the Caribbean, telephone counselling programmes should be expanded to include more training for counsellors to provide guidance in psychosocial, and especially adherence, issues; access to appropriate information re treatment protocols so that counsellors are able to answer frequently asked questions; and the promotion of these services to PLWHIV and those affected.

The excellent work of Caribbean organizations for PLWHA (CRN+, JN+ etc) must be supported and the providers must be integrated into the region's health response. There is a benefit to educating these individuals and organizations with regard to psychosocial issues; helping PLWHA to deal with their own issues regarding HIV and medication before they try to help others; facilitating development of communication/counselling skills in support of psychosocial issues especially adherence, and promoting referrals to appropriate agencies.

An initiative by CARICOM to develop a code of practice to be used by psychosocial professionals bodes well for ethical and effective provision of services to those affected by HIV/AIDS (Patterson and Francis, 2006). It is anticipated that the professional collaboration facilitated by this and other current processes will enhance the abilities of all psychosocial providers in the region to develop increased competencies, share culturally relevant experiences and scale up their roles as advocates for the needs of people affected by HIV/AIDS.

## Conclusion

As we in the Caribbean continue to struggle together to respond to the HIV/AIDS pandemic it is clear that the challenges we face must be met with unity and a shared vision that is translated into integrated and strategic policies and programmes. Some of the behavioural implications of this pandemic have been reviewed in this chapter and we feel that they indicate not only the complexity of the problem but the need for input of the behavioural scientists, and in this case particularly that of the psychologists, at all levels of intervention. As we continue to collect data from our surveillance systems and from the multitude of formal and informal research projects, it is imperative that the behavioural issues are included as we seek to identify patterns and trends. As we increase our use of targeted interventions based on the data we collect we must be careful that, in our design of behaviour change communication campaigns, we monitor the corollary messages we send and minimize the 'collateral damage' we may cause. We must include more robust qualitative research and we must, in our quantitative efforts, ensure that we are not just 'counting events/behaviours' but are including questions to help us understand the motivations, facilitators and barriers to behaviour change.

Psychologists and other behavioural scientists must avoid the tendency to focus on the 'other' and appreciate the reality that those affected by HIV/AIDS include 'us' – the 'we' who are involved in the response. We must continue to look at ourselves to see how our own issues as individuals and professionals should be examined to ensure that we are facilitators and not barriers in the Caribbean's response to the AIDS pandemic. The cultural diversity of the Caribbean must be harnessed as a strength, yet can act as a barrier if we do not acknowledge the differences, sometimes subtle but significant, that exist among us. One aspect – too often under-examined and unappreciated – relates to the impact that the provision of psychosocial and other services may have on the providers themselves. Emotional and other effects of burn-out can be a normal part of the caring process and psychosocial providers should be equipped with the skills to help themselves and others so affected.

The Caribbean psychologist's role must not be narrowly defined in terms of individual-level processes (e.g. counselling and therapy) but must embrace all levels of analysis (e.g. social and communications issues). As policy makers and programmers become aware of the value of the contribution of psychologists and other psychosocial providers, it is hoped that more of these professionals will be included in the decision-making process at all levels and that the Caribbean will benefit as it should from their input.

## REFERENCES

AIDSCAP (1997). *Family Health International, AIDS control and prevention project, August 21, 1991 to December 31, 1997. Final report, Volume 1.* Retrieved March 20, 2008 from http://www.fhi.org/en/HIVAIDS/pub/Archive/aidscapreports/aidscapfinalvol1/FHI_AIDSCAP_Fnl_Rprt_Vol1_Tech_BCC.htm

—— (2003). *How to create an effective communication project.* Retrieved January 29, 2008, from http://www.fhi.org/en/HIVAIDS/pub/guide/BCC%20Handbooks/effectivecommunication.htm.

Ajzen, I., & Madden, T. (1986). Prediction of goal-directed behavior: Attitudes, intentions, and perceived behavioral control. *Journal of Experimental Social Psychology, 22,* 453–474.

Albarracín, D., Gillette, J. C., Earl, A. N., Glasman, L. R., Durantini, M. R., and Ho, M. H. (2005). A test of major assumptions about behavior change: A comprehensive look at the effects of passive and active HIV-prevention interventions since the beginning of the epidemic. *Psychological Bulletin,* 131 (6), 856-897.

Albert, S. M., Weber, C., Todak, G., Polanco, C., Clouse, R., McElhiney, M. et al. (1999). An observed performance test of medication management ability in HIV: Relation to neuropsychological status and adherence outcomes. *AIDS and Behavior,* 3, 121-128.

All, A., Nishakawa, H., Vinson, N., & Huycke, M. (2004). Psychosocial variables that relate to blood HIV virus load levels. *The Internet Journal of Advanced Nursing Practice,* 6(2). Retrieved February 8, 2008, from http://www.ispub.com/ostia/index.php?xmlFilePath=journals/ijanp/vol6n2/hiv.xml

Alleyne, G. (2005). HIV/AIDS Stigma and discrimination: Challenges in the Caribbean. In V. Hackett, (Ed.), *Champions for change: Reducing HIV/AIDS stigma and discrimination in the Caribbean.* CARICOM/PANCAP.

Angelino, A. F., & Treisman, G. J. (2001). Management of psychiatric disorders in patients infected with HIV. *Clinical Infectious Disorders,* 33, 847–56.

Bain, B. (2004). The UWI HIV/AIDS Response Programme. *Caribbean Quarterly,* 50 (1).

Bandura, A. (1986). *Social foundations of thought and action: A social cognitive theory.* Englewood Cliffs, NJ: Prentice Hall.

————. (1989). Human agency in social cognitive theory. *American Psychologist,* 44, 1175-1184.

————. (1994). Social cognitive theory of mass communication. In J. Bryant & D. Zillmann (Eds.), *Media effects: Advances in theory and research* (pp. 61-90). Hillsdale, NJ: Lawrence Erlbaum.

Barnes, D. (1986). AIDS related brain damage explained. *Science,* 232, 1091-1093.

Bartlett, J. G. (2005). *Adult HIV/AIDS treatment.* Baltimore: Johns Hopkins University Press.

Bartlett, J. G., & Gallant, J. E. (2003). *Medical management of HIV infection.* Baltimore: Johns Hopkins University Press.

Bing, E. G., Burnam, M. A., Longshore, D., Fleishman, J. A., Sherbourne, C. D., London, A. S. et al. (2001). Psychiatric disorders and drug use among human immunodeficiency virus–infected adults in the United States. *Archives General Psychiatry,* 58, 721-728.

Bouwman, F. H., Skolasky, R., Hes, D., Selnes, O. A., Glass, J. D., Nance-Sproson, T. E. et al. (1998). Variable progression of HIV-associated dementia. _Neurology_, 50, 1814–1820.

Camara, B., Lee, R., Gatwood, J., Wagner, H., Cazal-Gamelsy, R., & Boisson, E. (2003). The Caribbean HIV/AIDS epidemic epidemiological status – Success stories: A summary. _CAREC Surveillance Report Supplement_, 23 (1).

Campbell, C. (2003). _Letting them die: Why HIV/AIDS interventions fail (African Issues)_. Cape Town: Double Storey.

Canadian Psychiatric Association (2004). _HIV and psychiatry: A training and resource manual_. Retrieved February 10, 2005, from http://www.cpa-apc.org/Publications/HIV/HIV.asp

Catalan, J., Collins, P., Mash, B., & Freeman, M. (2005). _Psychotherapeutic interventions in anti-retroviral (ARV) therapy: For second level care_. World Health Organization: WHO Press.

Centers for Disease Control and Prevention (1999). _STD surveillance 1999, special focus profiles: STDs in adolescents and young adults_. Retrieved January 29, 2008, from http://www.cdc.gov/nchstp/dstd/Stats_Trends/1999Surveillance/99PDF/99Section8.pdf

———. (2001). _Revised guidelines for HIV counseling, testing and referrals_.

Childs, E. A., Lyles, R. H., Selnes, O. A., Chen, B., Miller, E. N., Cohen, B. A. et al. (1999). Plasma viral load and CD4 lymphocytes predict HIV-associated dementia and sensory neuropathy. _Neurology_, 52 (3), 607–613.

Christie, C.D.C. (2004). A paediatric and perinatal HIV/AIDS initiative in Kingston Jamaica. _West Indian Medical Journal_, 53, 283 -29.

Cournos, F., Wainburg, M., & Horwath, E. (2005). _Psychiatric care in anti-retroviral (ARV) therapy: Second level care_. Johannesburg: World Health Organization.

Dicks, B.A. (2001). _Journal of HIV/AIDS Prevention and Education for Adolescents and Children_, 4 (2/3).

Dunkley-Thompson, J., Figueroa, J. P., & Christie, C. D. C. (2006). The missed population of perinatally HIV-infected adolescent slow progressors in Jamaica. _West Indian Medical Journal_, 55, 1-7.

Family Health International. (2002). _Behaviour change communication (BCC) for HIV/AIDS: A strategic framework_. Arlington, Virginia: Family Health International.

Fauci, A. S. (1995). Studies in subjects with long-term nonprogressive human immunodeficiency virus infection. _New England Journal of Medicine_, 332, 209-216.

Fishbein, M., & Ajzen, I. (1975). _Belief, attitude, intention, and behavior: An introduction to theory and research_. Reading, Mass.: Addison-Wesley.

Fisher, J. D., & Fisher, W. A. (1992). Changing AIDS risk behavior. _Psychological Bulletin_, 111, 455-474.

Floyd, D. L., Prentice-Dunn, S., & Rogers, R. W. (2000). A meta-analysis of research on protection motivation theory. *Journal of Applied Social Psychology,* 30, 407-429.

Gallo, R. C., Sarin, P. S., Gelmann, E. P., Robert-Guroff, M., Richardson, E. et al. (1983). Isolation of human T-cell leukemia virus in Acquired Immune Deficiency Syndrome. *Science,* 220 (4599), 865-867.

Gallo, R. C., Salahuddin, S. Z., Popovic, M., Shearer, G. M., Kaplan, M., Haynes, B. F. et al. (1984). Frequent detection and isolation of cytopathic retroviruses (HTLV-III) from patients with AIDS and at risk for AIDS. *Science,* 224 (4648), 500-503.

Grassi, L., Righi, R, Sighinolfi, L, Makoui, S., & Ghinelli, F. (1998). Coping styles and psychosocial-related variables in HIV-infected patients. *Psychosomatics: Journal of Consultation Liaison Psychiatry,* 39 (4), 350-359.

Greenwood, D. (1991). Neuropsychological aspects of AIDS dementia complex: What clinicians need to know. *Professional Psychology: Research and Practice,* 22 (5), 407-409.

Hackett, V. (ed.) (2005). *Champions for change: Reducing HIV/AIDS stigma and discrimination in the Caribbean.* CARICOM/PANCAP.

Harris, A. A., Segreti, J., & Kessler, H. A. (1989). The neurology of AIDS. In P. J. Vinken, G. W. Bruyn, H. L. Klawans, & R. R. McKendall (Eds.), *Handbook of Clinical Neurology* (Series Volume 56, Revised Series #12). Elsevier.

Herek, G. (1990). Illness, stigma, and AIDS. In G. M. Herek, S. M. Levy, S. Maddi, S. Taylor, & D. Wertlieb (Eds.), *Psychological aspects of chronic illness: Chronic conditions, fatal diseases, and clinical care,* pp. 107-150. Washington, DC: American Psychological Association.

Herek, G. M., & Glunt, E. K. (1988). An epidemic of stigma: Public reactions to AIDS. *American Psychologist,* 43 (11), 886-891.

Herman, P. (1986). Neurologic effects of HTLV-III infection in adults. An overview. *The Mount Siniai Journal of Medicine,* 63, 616-621.

Hinkin, C. H., Castellon, S. A., Durvasula, R. S. et al. (2002). Medication adherence among HIV+ adults: Effects of cognitive dysfunction and regimen complexity. *Neurology,* 59, 1944-1950.

House, J. S. (1981). *Work, stress and social support.* Reading, MA: Addison-Wesley.

Inciardi, J. A., Syvertsen, J. L., & Surratt, H. L. (2005). HIV/AIDS in the Caribbean Basin. *AIDS Care,* 17 (Suppl.1), S9-S25.

Jemmott, L., Bain, B., Hewitt, H., Hutchinson, M.K., Jemmot, J., Kahwa, E. et al. (2005). Reducing HIV risk behaviour among Jamaican adolescent males. Department of Health and Human Services Grant Application.

JHPIEGO (2002). *Voluntary counseling and testing – Caribbean specific. Reference Manual.* Baltimore: Johns Hopkins University Press.

Kalichman, S. C., Rompa, D., & Cage, M. (2000). Distinguishing between overlapping somatic symptoms of depression and HIV disease in people living with HIV-AIDS. *Journal of Nervous and Mental Disease,* 188 (10), 662-670.

Kaplan, R. M., Sallis, J. F., & Patterson, T. L. (1993). *Health and human behaviour.* New York: McGraw-Hill.

Kelly, M., & Bain, B. (2003). *Education and HIV/AIDS in the Caribbean.* Paris: International Institute for Educational Planning.

Kelly, K., & Freeman, M. (2005). *Organization and systems support for mental health interventions in anti-retroviral therapy programmes.* World Health Organization: WHO Press.

Lazarus, R., & Saloner, K. (2005). *Basic counseling guidelines for anti-retroviral (ARV) therapy programmes.* World Health Organization: WHO Press.

Maschke, M., Kastrup, O., Esser, S., Ross, B., Hengge, U., & Hufnagel, A. (2000). Incidence and prevalence of neurological disorders associated with HIV since the introduction of highly active antiretroviral therapy (HAART). *Journal of Neurology, Neurosurgery and Psychiatry, 69*(3), 376-380.

National Institute of Allergy and Infectious Diseases (2007). *HIV infection and AIDS: An overview.* Retrieved January 29, 2008, from http://www.niaid.nih.gov/factsheets/hivinf.htm.

Navia, B. A., Jordan, B. D., & Price, R. W. (1986). The AIDS dementia complex: 1. Clinical features. *Annals of Neurology, 19,* 517-524.

Oechsner, M., Moller, A., & Zaudig, M. (1993). Cognitive impairment, dementia and psychosocial functioning in Human Immunodeficiency Virus infection. A prospective study based on DSM-III-R and ICD-10. *Acta Psychiatric Scandinavia, 87* (1), 7-13.

Pan-Caribbean Partnership on HIV/AIDS (2002). *The Caribbean regional strategic framework for HIV/AIDS.* Georgetown, Guyana: PANCAP.

Pathfinder International FOCUS on Young Adults Project (2002). *Family Health International.* Retrieved February 8, 2008 from http://www.fhi.org/en/Youth/YouthNet/FAQs/FAQsbehaviorchangecommunication.htm

Patterson, D., & Francis, C. (2006). Workshop to develop a regional model code of practice for counselors, social workers, and psychologists. In *National HIV/AIDS responses in the Caribbean.* Workshop Report. CARICOM.

Perry, S., & Jacobsen, P. (1986). Neuropsychiatric manifestations of AIDS-spectrum disorders. *Hospital and Community Psychiatry, 37,* 135-142.

Pierre, R., Ramsey, D. H., & Loudon, M. (2005). HIV/AIDS and affected Jamaican children: A vulnerable generation. *Caribbean Childhoods, 2,* 82-99.

Prochaska, J. O., DiClemente, C. C., & Norcross, J. C. (1992). In search of how people change: Applications to addictive behaviors. *American Psychologist, 47,* 1102-1114.

Rabkin, J. G., Ferrando, S. J., Lin, S., Sewell, M., & McElhiney, M. (2000). Psychological effects of HAART: A 2-year study. *Psychosomatic Medicine, 62,* 413-422.

Ramsammy, L. (2005). Equality and human rights in HIV/AIDS stigma and discrimination. In V. Hackett, (Ed.), *Champions for change: Reducing HIV/AIDS stigma and discrimination in the Caribbean,* CARICOM/PANCAP.

Reitan, R. M., & Wolfson, D. (1993). *The Halstead-Reitan Neuropsychological Test Battery: Theory and clinical interpretation,* (2nd Ed.). Tucson, Ariz.: Neuropsychology Press.

Rodriguez, B., Steel-Duncan, J.C., Pierre, R., Evans-Gilbert, T., Hambleton, I., Palmer, P., Figueroa, J. P., & Christie, C. D. C. (2004). Socio-demographic characteristics of HIV-exposed and HIV–infected Jamaican children. *West Indian Medical Journal,* 53, 303-307.

Rogers, R. W. (1975). A protection motivation theory of fear appeals and attitude change. *Journal of Psychology,* 91, 93-114.

Rosenstock, I. M. (1974). Historical origins of the health belief model. *Health Education Monographs,* 2, 328–335.

Rothman, A. J., & Salovey, P. (1997). Shaping perceptions to motivate healthy behavior. *Psychological Bulletin,* 121, 3-19.

Safren, S. A., Radomsky, A., Otto, M. W., & Saloman, E. (2002). Predictors of psychological well-being in a diverse sample of HIV-positive patients receiving highly active antiretroviral therapy. *Psychosomatics,* 43, 478–485.

Sewell, D. (1996). Schizophrenia and HIV. *Schizophrenia Bulletin,* 22, 465-73.

SIRHASC Project Report. (2006). UWIHARP/CARICOM.

Spreen, O., & Strauss, E. (1998). *A compendium of neuropsychological tests: Administration, norms, and commentary* (2nd Ed.). NY: Oxford University Press.

Stern, Y., McDermott, M., Albert, S., Palumbo, D., Selnes, O., McArthur, J. et al. (2001). Factors associated with incident Human Immunodeficiency Virus–Dementia. *Archives of Neurology,* 58 (3), 473-479.

Sweetland, A., Lazarus, R., Freeman, M., & Saloner, K. (2005). *Psychosocial support programmes in anti-retroviral (ARV) therapy programmes.* World Health Organization: WHO Press.

Thompson, D. (2005). Personal communication.

United Kingdom Coalition of Persons Living with HIV/AIDS. (2000). *Psychological impact project.* Retrieved January 29, 2008, from http://www.ukcoalition.org/Psychology/psychology.html.

UNAIDS. (1998). HIV- related opportunistic diseases: UNAIDS Technical Update. Geneva: UNAIDS.

———. (2004). *AIDS epidemic update 2004.* Geneva: UNAIDS.

———. (2006). *AIDS epidemic update 2006.* Geneva: UNAIDS.

UNGASS. (2006). *HIV/AIDS Country Report: Trinidad and Tobago.* Retrieved January 29, 2008, from http://data.unaids.org/pub/Report/2006/2006_country_progress_report_trinidad_tobago_en.pdf.

UNIFEM, (2004). *Inter-agency roundtable on the gender assessment of HIV/AIDS programming in the Caribbean.* Retrieved January 29, 2008, from www.unifemcar.org/documents/Inter-Agency%20Meeting%20Report.pdf.

Walker, E., Mayes, B., Ramsey, H., Hewitt, H., Bain, B., & Christie, C. D. C. (2004).

Socio-demographic and clinical characteristics of Jamaican adolescents with HIV/AIDS. _West Indian Medical Journal_, 53, 332-338.

Weller, P. D. (2007). Study of perceptions, attitudes and beliefs regarding masculinity, gender, gender equity and HIV/AIDS among men in St Lucia and Grenada. _CariMAN Technical Report_ (Jan – March). CARICOM.

Weller, P. D., Hambleton, I., Bain, S., Christie, C., & Bain, B. (2005). _Psychosocial determinants of health behaviour: Pre- and Post-natal women in Jamaica._ Project Report for SIRHASC Project Coordinating Unit, UWI HARP. CARICOM.

Weller, P. D., Prendergast, P., & Hyatt, S. (2006). Study of perceptions, attitudes and beliefs regarding masculinity, gender, gender equity and HIV/AIDS among men in Jamaica. _MAN Initiative Technical Report._ CARICOM.

Ziefert, P., Leary, M., & Boccellari, A. (1995). _AIDS and the impact of cognitive impairment._ Retrieved January 29, 2008, from http://www.ucsf-ahp.org/HTML2/services_providers_publications_excerpt8.html.

# 12 Neuropsychological Assessment in the Caribbean

*Tony Ward*

## Summary

This chapter outlines the use of the Wechsler Adult Intelligence Scale as a neuropsychological assessment battery in Jamaica and tentative norms are provided. Some data on the validity of the measure, in particular the factor analysis and correlation with another set of cognitive measures, are also provided. A similar presentation is given for the Wechsler Memory Scale, as it is suggested that the Wechsler Memory Scale forms a useful adjunct to the Wechsler Adult Intelligence Scale. The chapter also addresses the utility of reaction-time-based tests of cognitive function as described in a study on Lupus Erythematosus. Finally, limitations of screening instruments such as the Mini-Mental State Examination within the Jamaican context are discussed.

## Introduction

Neuropsychology is the application of psychological knowledge to the understanding and remediation of neurological conditions, such as head injury, stroke, Alzheimer's disease, etc. (*see* Halligan, Kischka & Marshall, 2003, for a thorough recent overview). Recently, the approach has also been extended to include applications to non-neurological medical conditions, such as high blood pressure and diabetes. These are now known to produce neurological complications (_see_ Tarter, Butters & Beers, 2nd edition, 2001, for one of the few comprehensive reviews of this area).

The main area of psychological theorizing which is brought to bear in neuropsychology is our understanding of cognitive processes. Theories developed in the psychology laboratory to explain normal human performance have been found to have high utility in explaining the impairments and performances of patients with neurological difficulties. Furthermore, such theories are useful in explaining to patients the difficulties they are now experiencing. It should not be underestimated how important it is to patients to be able to make sense of the mental challenges they are facing. Finally, such insights can be useful in guiding clinicians as to how they may be able to help patients overcome their difficulties. Whilst the outlook for patients with severe conditions may not be optimistic in terms of full recovery of function, the extent to which they can compensate for their difficulties can be remarkable.

A good illustration of the above points can be drawn from Evans (2003). In this chapter, Evans suggests that patients with various conditions can experience loss of memory. It has proven useful to conceive such difficulties in terms of short- and long-term memory. Short-term memory refers to retaining information on a moment- by-moment basis. It is the ability we use, for example, to follow a conversation. Long-term memory, on the other hand, is the recollection of an event or fact some time after we have ceased attending to it. Remembering what we had for breakfast this morning would be one example, or what we did last year in August, another. Different brain regions have been implicated in these different types of memory. The ways we might help a patient to cope with losses of each could be very different. For example, short-term memory deficits can be remediated through structuring the everyday environment, with tasks broken down into simple steps and lots of cues provided. The act of brushing one's teeth, for instance can be broken down into smaller steps such as finding the brush and toothpaste, placing paste on the brush, wetting the brush, moving the brush over the teeth, spitting out excess paste, etc. In contrast, patients with long-term memory deficits may be trained to keep detailed diaries organized so that the patient can easily refer back to the information within them.

The range of cognitive functions which neuropsychologists typically assess cover the whole gamut of human abilities. They include perception, memory, problem solving, attention, language and movement. Each of these can be further subdivided into specialist functions, for example, within language we can assess reading, writing, speech production and oral comprehension. Goldstein and McNeil (2004) present a thorough account of these various domains and the types of tests used to assess them.

By the time a clinician has narrowed down a patient's difficulties into very specialist domains, such as written word comprehension, the types of tests being used to assess the deficit are likely to be highly specialist in nature. Prior to that stage, however, the clinician is likely to employ a more wide-ranging battery of tests, capable of screening patients over a variety of functions. The most commonly used of such batteries is the Wechsler Adult Intelligence Scale (1997). There is insufficient scope in this chapter to give a comprehensive account of the ways in which the WAIS can be used in neuropsychological assessment. The reader is, therefore, directed to comprehensive texts on neuropsychological assessment, such as Groth-Marnat (2000). Only a brief description will be offered here.

## The Wechsler Adult Intelligence Scale III

### DESCRIPTION

As it currently stands, the Wechsler Adult Intelligence Scale, Version III, consists of the following sub-tests divided into two main areas: Verbal and Performance Abilities.

### VERBAL SUBTESTS

As the name implies, these tests frequently involve complex linguistic skills. However, another property they tend to have in common is testing of learned and stored concepts and knowledge. As such, they might be seen tapping into crystallised ability.

### Information

This subtest focuses on retrieval of factual knowledge from long-term memory, and may be influenced by the extent of school-based learning.

## Vocabulary

This is a test of the patients' word knowledge, in which they have to define a set of words which become increasingly more complex. Performance on this test is frequently used as an index of general ability. Since crystallized ability is thought to be relatively resistant to change, this is often taken as an estimate of pre-morbid ability.

## Similarities

This is a test of abstract reasoning in which the patient has to say in what way two concepts are similar. It falls within the verbal items, reflecting the necessary linguistic skill. In practice it is often found to be sensitive to fluid reasoning problems, in particular frontal lobe damage.

## Arithmetic

As its name suggests, this scale involves a variety of numerical manipulations. Given the variety of complex mathematical problems, the scale taps into a number of cognitive skills, including: computation, concentration, short-term memory, and numerical reasoning. It may be questioned why this is considered a verbal subtest. It should be noted that although arithmetic is not obviously a verbal subtest, it loads on the verbal factor, in factor analytic studies, as was the case with this Jamaican sample. In cognitive terms, good mental arithmetic skills may be predicated on working memory processes – either phonological or visuo-spatial scratchpad in Baddeley's working memory model (_see_ McCloskey, 1991).

## Digit Span

The digit span task requires the patient to repeat back sequences of digits, which gradually increase in length. This is generally seen as giving a classic measure of short-term verbal working memory capacity. In a second phase, the patient has to repeat the sequences in reverse order, which increases the working memory load (in other words, the digits have to be retained mentally while the patient works backwards through them in turn, to give them in reverse order). A comparison of the latter with the former may give an indication of reduced attentional capacity or working memory manipulation, possibly implicated in frontal lesions.

## Letter-number Sequencing

This is a recent addition to the WAIS, which requires the patient to manipulate random sequences of letters and digits, first, reporting the digits back, followed by the letters, in ascending and alphabetical orders, respectively. It is likely to involve working memory, concentration and sequencing.

## PERFORMANCE SUBTESTS

The performance items are generally abstract, novel problems requiring immediate solutions. These items could be considered as more akin to fluid reasoning, as opposed to crystallized ability. It should be noted that many of the tests are timed, and therefore, decreasing performance with age is very evident. (There is a debate within the literature that decreasing cognitive performance with age might be due either to quality of processing or to speed of processing – though these two might be closely related concepts – *see* Ward, 2004).

### Picture Completion

Here, the patient looks at a sequence of pictures, in each case, identifying what important thing is missing from the picture. The solution is sometimes quite subtle. Some of the items involve cultural bias, and in our experience, it is unlikely that many Jamaicans will be able to determine the final item unless they have travelled abroad, as the item requires familiarity with snow and its properties.

### Digit-Symbol Coding

In this task the patient copies symbols from a key into a numbered grid. It has generally been seen as a classic test of attention and concentration, but it undoubtedly also involves dexterity and some degree of memory (better candidates will gradually learn the number-symbol correspondence as the test progresses).

A new amendment to this test assesses transcribing speed, which allows the examiner to better interpret the patient's performance on the digit symbol encoding task. If a patient has a low transcribing score, then his or her performance on the digit symbol task is less likely to be due to attention and concentration difficulties, and more likely to be due to dyspraxia (i.e. a motor inability which makes manipulation of the pencil across the page difficult).

## Block Design

This is one of the clinicians favourites, and widely seen as one of the most useful subtests in the battery. The patient uses a set of coloured cubes to recreate bi-coloured designs, within strict time limits. This subtest requires good perception and visualization, planning and co-ordination. Block design is generally seen as a test sensitive to frontal lobe lesions.

## Matrix Reasoning

Another new addition to the battery, this subtest is very similar to the Ravens Progressive Matrices, where patients have to decide which of several design fragments complete an overall pattern. The task involves fluid reasoning, but there is no imposed time limit (though in practice patients are likely to impose their own deadlines). This is another useful addition, which might serve as a good estimator of current fluid reasoning skills, though the full utility remains to be determined by researchers. Some of the items, however, seem to be more reliant on complex perception rather than fluid reasoning. As such, it is probably not a pure measure. Nevertheless, these perceptual items could be useful indicators of visual disturbance.

## Picture Arrangement

In this test the patient has to arrange a sequence of pictures to tell a logical story. Some of the later items involve ascribing complex human reasoning and motivation, which might be useful, for example, for identifying theory of mind deficits, concrete thinking, or poor perception of social skills.

## Symbol Search

This is another new task, which gives a measure of scanning, perception and attention or concentration. The testee has to scan a long a set of symbols as quickly as possible and indicate which ones correspond to a target.

## Object Assembly

Object assembly is generally an easy subtask, which is often neglected by clinicians. It requires the patient to assemble a set of parts to make up a larger object. It also requires good perceptual and organization skills.

# Jamaican Norms for the Wechsler Adult Intelligence Scale III

Between 2001 and 2003, the University of the West Indies (UWI) sponsored a research project to collect normative data for the Wescher Adult Intelligence Scale. A full description of this study and the data can be found elsewhere (Ward et al, in press). What will be presented here is, therefore, a summary.

### RATIONALE FOR COLLECTING NEW JAMAICAN NORMS

The widespread adoption and use of the WAIS tests in the USA undoubtedly reflected the early availability of extensive and good quality normative data for the American population. The tests soon came to be used elsewhere, and not surprisingly, given the effort required in norming such tests, it was hoped that they could be used with little adaptation, even relying on the original American norms. This may seem a plausible strategy for English-speaking cultures which share aspects of American culture. However, certain test items have been shown to be problematic even in Canada (Pugh & Boer, 1989; Violato, 1986), and Canadian normative data shows differences from the American sample (Hildebrand & Saklofshi, 1996). Studies on earlier versions of the WAIS in the UK suggested that there were differences from the American sample (Wilson et al, 1987), though recent work on the WAIS-III suggests that the data from the two populations are currently very similar (Crawford & Allen, 1995). Recent work in Australia has also highlighted differences with the American data (Shores & Carstairs, 2000).

Given the above findings, it seemed to this author that the utility of the existing North American norms should at least be evaluated, and this could be done through assessing a small representative sample of the Jamaican population. If it emerged then that the Jamaican data was somewhat different from the American, then this would provide the initial basis for the inclusion of a new set of Jamaican norms.

**OUTLINE OF THE PROJECT**

One hundred and fifty participants from the Kingston metropolitan area were assessed using the Wechsler Adult Intelligence Scales. The participants were selected to include a representative sample, using the factors of age, sex, and occupation.

To validate the WAIS in the Jamaican context, patients were also assessed on a battery of computerized cognitive tests, so that the two sets of measures could be compared. These latter tests might be useful in their own right, particularly for assessing subtle cognitive deficits, and norms are presented for these. Their use will be briefly illustrated with reference to a study in Jamaica of deficits in patients with Lupus. Lupus is an auto-immune disorder which causes widespread physiological changes and can involve the central nervous system.

# Modifications of the WAIS-III for Use in Jamaica

The research team decided, after careful consideration, to try to use the WAIS as much as possible in an unmodified format. It was recognized that some items would be very difficult for most Jamaicans, e.g. the final item of the picture completion task, but it was felt that the new norms would take this into account. However, it was also felt that in some cases earlier items were inappropriate, and would jar the sensibilities of Jamaican patients, therefore, they were altered. The two such changes were as follows:

a) On test 9 – information – it was felt that few Jamaicans would be able to name an American Civil War president. Instead, they were asked to give the year of the emancipation of slaves in the British West Indies (1838).

b) On test 11 – comprehension – the proverbs in items 17 and 18 were felt to be inappropriate to a Jamaican audience. Item 17 was substituted with "Make hay while the sun shines" and item 18 was substituted with "Silent rivers run deep".

Table 1* gives the descriptive statistics for the Jamaican sample used to construct these norms.

---

*   See Appendix for tables, showing Jamaican norms for the Wechsler Adult Intelligence Scales.

Tables 2–3 present the scaled scores for the various Wechsler subtests for three age groups. The age groups are 18-44, 45-64 and 65+. Table 4 gives overall IQ scores based on the total scaled scores. We suggest that clinicians substitute these tables for the ones given in the WAIS manuals. Table 1 gives details of the sample sizes so that clinicians can judge the amount of data on which the norms are based.

For any subtest a scaled score of 10 is average, with each scaled score point representing one-third of a standard deviation. Therefore, a scaled score of 13 is one standard deviation above the average (IQ115), while 16 is 2 standard deviations above (IQ130). Similarly, a score of 7 is one standard deviation below the mean (IQ 85) and 4 is two standard deviations below (IQ 70). On this basis, IQ can be estimated based upon the verbal subtest score.

This is a small sample, so caution should be urged in using these norms. Of particular note, they were drawn from the Kingston area, and so may not be fully representative of the island as a whole. However, it is the author's opinion that these norms are infinitely more appropriate than either the British or American ones. The Jamaican norms allow for conditions prevailing in the country, and Jamaican cultural differences. The norms which exist for the UK and USA are based on very different circumstances. In our opinion use of foreign norms will, therefore, do an injustice to Jamaican patients, with the likelihood of grossly over estimating the frequency and severity of deficits.  FOR WAIS-II

## VALIDITY OF THE WECHSLER ADULT INTELLIGENCE SCALE IN JAMAICA

We established the validity of the WAIS scales for Jamaican use in two ways. First of all, we looked at the factor analysis, as a measure of construct validity. Second, we looked at the relationship of the WAIS to a battery of computerized cognitive assessments based upon reaction time.

The factor analysis which resulted from the Jamaican data demonstrates the classical two-factor structure which has so often been found in previous studies over many years. The factor structure can be seen in table 6 (*see* Appendix).

It is very clear from table 6 that factor 1 consists of all those tests which make up the verbal subscale, while factor 2 consists of all the performance items. Thus, the traditional way of viewing the WAIS, as being made up of verbal and performance subscales, is consistent with the patterns of performance observed in Jamaica.

### Computerized Cognitive Tests

The sample of participants who provided the normative data for the WAIS were also assessed on a battery of computerized reaction time measures, which collectively were known as the University of the West Indies Cognitive Assessment Battery (UWICAS). This battery of tests was developed for neuropsychological screening, and in particular, for use in medical neuropsychological research, for example, where patients have subtle deficits as a consequence of conditions such as diabetes and hypertension. The battery of tests may be accessed through the Psychiatry unit at the UWI. The measures are based upon average reaction time in milliseconds and number of correct responses, where appropriate. Stimuli were displayed on a computer screen, and responses were made, using the left and right mouse keys. Test administration was performed with Superlab experimental software. The tests included:

**Simple reaction time** The average time in milliseconds in which participants are able to respond to a simple stimuli which appears on the computer screen.

**Choice reaction time** The average time to respond to a stimuli where there are two choices.

**Vigilance** A sequence of stimuli is presented, with one stimuli per minute being designated as a target. Thus the participant has to monitor the task carefully and be ready to make a fast, but rare, response.

**Working memory** The participant is given 3 digits to remember and then has to monitor a random sequence of digits, responding whenever one of the 3 targets appears.

**Visual working memory** The participant has to remember a complex abstract grid based design, and then verify whether a subsequent pattern matches the original.

**Picture memory** Twenty random pictures are shown to the participant. After a delay, they have to pick out the original 20 pictures from 20 distracters. Some of the distracters are very similar to the originals, thus requiring a fine degree of discrimination, and reducing the participants' ability to rely solely on verbal coding strategies.

**Word memory** Twenty words are presented to the participants. After a delay, they have to identify the original 20 words from 20 distracter items. The new items are matched for word length and semantic content.

This battery of tests may well prove useful for assessing cognitive function in Jamaica, for example, in conditions such as diabetes, hypertension and others. For this reason, norms based on the original 150 normative project sample are presented here (*see* table 7, Appendix). This is the first time these norms have been presented, and they are given for two age groups, 18-44 and 45+. The reason for choosing to cut the sample at 45 is that it is in the mid-forties that decline on cognitive tests first becomes evident. Extreme scores in the older age group due to advanced age were excluded as outliers.

## Use of the UWICAS in Jamaica

A small study by O'Brien (2003) evaluated the utility of the UWICAS tests in a Jamaican sample of patients with Lupus Erythmatosus. O'Brien found that the Lupus patients had significantly slower scores on most of the UWICAS assessments administered, with the exception of memory accuracy. Thus, the patients were much slower to make cognitive responses on a variety of tasks. This indicated an overall deficit in attention, concentration, and/or speed of processing. The results of the study are given in table 8 (*see* Appendix).

This research indicates the utility of computerized assessments of cognitive function for the evaluation of subtle deficits in medical neuropsychological contexts within Jamaica.

### RELATIONSHIP OF THE UWICAS MEASURES TO THE WAIS

When factor analysed, the UWICAS tests yielded a three-factor solution. These were conceptualized as attention, memory and response accuracy.

As previously described, the factor analysis of the WAIS produced a two-factor solution, along classical lines. The two factors reflect verbal and performance subscales.

To determine the relationship between the UWICAS and WAIS in a succinct manner, the factor scores from the two sets of tests were correlated. None of the correlations with the verbal test factor were significant, but all three correlations with the WAIS performance factor were. The correlation between WAIS performance and UWICOG attention was −0.42, while for the UWICOG memory it was −0.46 and for the UWICOG response accuracy it was 0.21. The significance in each case was <0.05, n =104. It can therefore be seen that in the Jamaican sample, performance on the WAIS performance factor correlates moderately well with current performance on a set of abstract laboratory style cognitive tests. As might be expected, past achievement and knowledge acquisition as indexed through the verbal factor, does not correlate with current cognitive performance. (It should be noted that the sample included a significant number of older individuals in the top end of the age distribution, whose speed and dexterity could be expected to have suffered somewhat.)

# Norms for the Wechsler Memory Scales

When Wechsler constructed the WAIS in the 1930s from a candidate set of tests, he found that he was left with a number of unused items, several of which related to aspects of memory functioning. These were pooled together to form the Wechsler Memory Scales, which like the WAIS, have subsequently been revised a number of times.

### DESCRIPTION

The Wechsler Intelligence Scale consists of the following tests:

**Logical memory**  In this task the patient has to remember a short story which consists of 21 ideas.

**Verbal paired associates**  Here the patient has to learn a number of word pairs, which are repeated several times, the first word being presented as a cue.

**Faces**  A set of faces is presented, which then have to be recognized from a set of distracters.

**Family pictures**  A set of pictures are shown, which depict several family members performing activities in various locations. Patients are prompted to provide various pieces of information about the pictures they have seen.

All of the above tests are re-administered after a delay, giving a set of delayed memory measures.

**Letter-number sequencing**  This is administered as per the new WAIS test described above.

**Spatial span**  A set of blocks is presented and tapped in a particular order. The patient has to repeat the order of presentation.

**Word lists**  This is a classic list-learning paradigm. Twelve words are presented over four trials, followed by a distracter list and finally, a request for the original words.

**Mental control**  Here a number of mental control items are administered, for example, saying the alphabet as fast as possible, forwards and backwards.

These various tests can be combined in various ways to give composite scores, for example, for verbal memory or working memory.

Of all the domains assessed in depth by neuropsychologists, probably one of the most important is memory, and for many years the Wechsler Memory Scales (WMS) have been one of the important batteries available for doing this. The advent of co-norming for the WMS alongside the WAIS is seen as an important step forward, since it is now possible and valid to compare patients' performance across the two sets of measures. Thus, a patient with a poor memory in the context of a generally good WAIS performance can be seen as having specific memory deficits, as opposed to being generally poor on cognitive tests, as might be indicated by a poor overall WAIS score.

It was, therefore, felt to be important, particularly as the WMS was being taught as part of the UWI's Clinical Psychology programme, to include this facility alongside the new Jamaican WAIS norms. Thus Jamaican clinicians should be able to tentatively interpret memory scores in the light of current and estimated prior functioning according to WAIS scores.

While some studies suggest that the US norms for the WMS can be useful in other countries (e.g. Bosnes, 1999; Bosnes & Ellertsen, 2000 [for Norway]), there are indications that re-norming is advisable (Ivison, 1977; Shores & Carstairs, 2000 [both in relation to Australia], Demsky, Mittenberg, Quintar, Kattell, & Golden, 1998 [in relation to US Spanish translations]).

WMS norms, collected on the same sample used for the WAIS norms above are, therefore, presented in tables 9–11 (_see_ Appendix).

Factor analysis of the Wechsler Memory Scales Jamaican data yielded a single overall factor, conceived as a memory factor. Correlation of the memory factor with the WAIS verbal factor was 0.42, and with the performance factor was 0.80. Thus, it can be seen that the memory performance on the WMS relates to ability on the WAIS, but is much more strongly related to current performance on the performance scale items. That is, it is much more strongly implicated in current problem solving and processing, but is also clearly and significantly related to past achievement.

## USE OF THE MINI-MENTAL STATE EXAMINATION IN JAMAICA

Whenever new assessment instruments or scales are used within a cultural context for which they were not originally intended, careful consideration should be given to their usefulness and appropriateness in the new context. These comments are based upon our experiences in assessing patients as part of a memory clinic run at the University Hospital of the West Indies.

The mini-mental state examination (MMSE) was originally published in the 1970s (Folstein et al, 1975), and has for many years been the screening instrument of choice used for diagnosing possible dementia. Copies and instructions can be readily obtained on the internet (_see_, for example, the UK Alzheimer's society webpage).

The MMSE is a convenient and easy-to-use measure. However, there are a number of reasons to exercise caution within the Jamaican context. First of all, there is no evidence that the usual cut-off score of 21 is appropriate to the Jamaican elderly population. As Crum et al (1993) point out, the median score changes as a function of age and education. It is unlikely that the dynamic interplay of these two factors within the Jamaican context is going to be equivalent to that found in the West. For example, many elderly Jamaicans may have had inadequate education, stemming from former colonial times when the educational infrastructure was underdeveloped. As a consequence, the rate of functional illiteracy may be relatively high in the current older age groups. This would lead to misleading scores on several of the MMSE items, such as the serial sevens and spelling 'WORLD' backwards. There is no evidence that the elderly segment of the Jamaican population will relate well to the phrase 'No ifs ands or buts', with which they may not be familiar.

Finally, there is a cultural and geographical issue with asking persons what season it is, in a country where they do not exist in the same sense as in the northern climes. In practice, we found patients using northern-style seasons (winter, spring, etc), as well as more appropriate local ones (namely rainy and dry). Our solution was to credit any response which was logical – given the time of year (although one could no doubt debate at length the actual limits of the wet seasons).

To overcome the inadequacy of the MMSE and to provide a quick and reliable measure of overall memory functioning, we used the word-list learning task from the WMS, norms for which were given earlier in this chapter. This takes about 15 minutes to administer, and is very acceptable to elderly Jamaicans. The words are reasonable to the Jamaican ear, with none causing undue difficulty. This is quite a sensitive test, with the same trial of 12 words being presented four times. A score below 14 is fairly clear evidence of a significant memory deficit, which may be an indicator of dementia. Even quite severely demented patients will manage to score a few points, which makes the measure useful for monitoring the impact of the new acetylcholinesterase inhibitors, such as Aricept.

To summarise, there may well be times when it is tempting to use Westernized screening instruments in the Jamaican context. As this example shows, this needs to be done with considerable caution, and ideally, with work done to adapt and re-norm the measure for the local population. We began this work for the mini-mental state examination, but to date, have not collected sufficient data.

## Further Perspectives – Use of Neuropsychological Assessment in Schools

While neuropsychological assessment as a tool has been traditionally used by neuropsychologists and clinical psychologist in hospital settings, more recently, its scope has transcended this arena. Merz (1990) has noted that educators have begun to recognize the value of neuropsychological assessment and that many school psychologists are being trained to use it as a regular part of assessing children with special needs.

Hale and Fiorello (2004) indicate that a student's classroom presentation, for example, slow and sloppy work, can well be caused by a neuropsychological disorder. Similarly, Shawitz (2003), as well as Feifer and Phillip (2000; 2002), acknowledge that deficits in spoken and written language and skilled reading, as in dyslexia, often have their genesis in the integrity of the related neural pathways. Such presentations, it is being implied, suggest the need for neuropsychological assessment.

Historically in the Caribbean, neuropsychological assessment has not been brought to bear upon the process of schooling. With modern technological advances such as magnetic resonance imagining (MRI) and functional magnetic imaging (fMRI), hitherto unexplored frontiers of the brain are now within the reach of the clinician and clinician-educator.

For these reasons, neuropsychological assessment must become centrally located in the educational process in the Caribbean, in an effort to transcend traditional models of teaching and learning. Perhaps the way forward is actually already being charted by approaches to neuropsychological assessment being adopted at the University of the West Indies Hospital, as part of the Clinical Psychology Programme. In this respect, the Jamaicanizing/Caribbeanizing of the Wechsler Adult Intelligence Scale III and the Wechsler Memory Scale for the purpose of neuropsychological assessment, as outlined in this chapter, is particularly instructive.

# Appendix

*Table 1: Descriptive statistics for the three age groups used to construct normative tables.*

| Ageband | Mean age (sd) | Years of education (sd) | Male:female ratio | n |
|---------|---------------|-------------------------|-------------------|-----|
| 18-44   | 27.9 (8.5)    | 12.0 (2)                | 17:39             | 56  |
| 45-64   | 54.3 (5.2)    | 12.1 (3)                | 21:36             | 57  |
| 65+     | 76.0 (7.3)    | 10.7 (3)                | 19:19             | 38  |

Table 2: *Scaled Score Equivalent of Raw Scores. Wechsler Adult Intelligence Scale. Ages 18-44.*

| Scaled Score | VERBAL | | | | | | | Scaled score | PERFORMANCE | | | | | | Scaled score |
| --- | --- | --- | --- | --- | --- | --- | --- | --- | --- | --- | --- | --- | --- | --- | --- |
| | Spot the word | Vocabulary | Similarities | Arithmetic | Digit span | Information | Compre-hension | | Picture completion | Digit symbol | Block design | Matrix reasoning | Picture arrange-ment | Symbol search | |
| 19 | 51-53 | - | - | 22 | - | 28 | - | 19 | - | 120-133 | 67-68 | - | - | 60 | 19 |
| 18 | 48-50 | 66 | - | 21 | 26 | 26-27 | - | 18 | - | 114-119 | 63-66 | - | - | 57-59 | 18 |
| 17 | 46-47 | 61-65 | - | 20 | 25 | 24-25 | - | 17 | - | 107-113 | 58-62 | - | - | 53-56 | 17 |
| 16 | 44-45 | 58-61 | 31-33 | 18-19 | 23-24 | 23 | 33 | 16 | - | 101-106 | 53-57 | 26 | 22 | 49-52 | 16 |
| 15 | 42-43 | 53-57 | 29-30 | 17 | 22 | 21-22 | 30-32 | 15 | 24-25 | 94-100 | 48-52 | 24-25 | 20-21 | 45-48 | 15 |
| 14 | 40-41 | 49-52 | 26-28 | 16 | 21 | 19-20 | 28-29 | 14 | 22-23 | 87-93 | 44-47 | 22-23 | 19 | 42-44 | 14 |
| 13 | 38-39 | 45-48 | 24-25 | 15 | 20 | 17-18 | 25-27 | 13 | 20-21 | 81-86 | 39-43 | 20-21 | 17-18 | 38-41 | 13 |
| 12 | 36-37 | 41-44 | 21-23 | 13-14 | 18-19 | 16 | 23-24 | 12 | 19 | 74-80 | 34-38 | 18-19 | 15-16 | 34-37 | 12 |
| 11 | 34-35 | 37-40 | 19-20 | 12 | 17 | 14-15 | 20-22 | 11 | 17-18 | 68-73 | 30-33 | 16-17 | 13-14 | 30-33 | 11 |
| 10 | 32-33 | 33-36 | 17-18 | 11 | 16 | 12-13 | 18-19 | 10 | 15-16 | 61-67 | 25-29 | 14-15 | 12 | 27-29 | 10 |
| 9 | 29-31 | 28-32 | 14-16 | 10 | 14-15 | 10-11 | 15-17 | 9 | 13-14 | 55-60 | 20-24 | 12-13 | 10-11 | 23-26 | 9 |
| 8 | 27-28 | 24-27 | 12-13 | 9 | 13 | 8-9 | 13-14 | 8 | 12 | 48-54 | 15-19 | 10-11 | 8-9 | 19-22 | 8 |
| 7 | 25-26 | 20-23 | 9-11 | 7-8 | 12 | 7 | 10-12 | 7 | 10-11 | 42-47 | 11-14 | 8-9 | 6-7 | 15-18 | 7 |
| 6 | 23-24 | 16-19 | 7-8 | 6 | 10-11 | 5-6 | 8-9 | 6 | 8-9 | 35-41 | 6-10 | 5-7 | 4-5 | 11-14 | 6 |
| 5 | 21-22 | 12-15 | 5-6 | 5 | 9 | 3-4 | 5-7 | 5 | 6-7 | 28-34 | 1-5 | 3-4 | 3 | 8-10 | 5 |
| 4 | 19-20 | 7-11 | 3-4 | 4 | 8 | 2 | 3-4 | 4 | 5 | 22-27 | 0 | 2 | 1-2 | 4-7 | 4 |
| 3 | 17-18 | 3-6 | 1-2 | 3 | 7 | 1 | 1-2 | 3 | 3-4 | 15-21 | - | 1 | 0 | 1-3 | 3 |
| 2 | 15-16 | 1-2 | 0 | 2 | 5-6 | 0 | 0 | 2 | 1-2 | 8-14 | - | 0 | - | 0 | 2 |
| 1 | <15 | 0 | - | 0-1 | 0-4 | - | - | 1 | 0 | <8 | - | - | - | - | 1 |

Table 3: Scaled Score Equivalent of Raw Scores. Wechsler Adult Intelligence Scale. Ages 45-64.

| Scaled Score | Spot the word | Vocabulary | Similarities | Arithmetic | Digit span | Information | Comprehension | Scaled score | Picture completion | Digit symbol | Block design | Matrix reasoning | Picture arrangement | Symbol search | Scaled score |
|---|---|---|---|---|---|---|---|---|---|---|---|---|---|---|---|
| | | VERBAL | | | | | | | | PERFORMANCE | | | | | |
| 19 | - | - | - | - | - | - | - | 19 | - | 104-133 | 54-68 | 26 | - | 49-60 | 19 |
| 18 | 59-60 | - | - | - | 30 | - | - | 18 | - | 96-103 | 52-54 | 24-25 | 22 | 45-48 | 18 |
| 17 | 56-58 | - | - | 21-22 | 28-29 | 28 | - | 17 | - | 89-95 | 48-51 | 22-23 | 20-21 | 41-44 | 17 |
| 16 | 52-55 | 66 | - | 20 | 26-27 | 26-27 | - | 16 | 24-25 | 82-88 | 44-47 | 20-21 | 18-19 | 38-40 | 16 |
| 15 | 49-51 | 60-65 | 32-33 | 18-19 | 24-25 | 24-25 | 32-33 | 15 | 22-23 | 75-81 | 40-43 | 19 | 16-17 | 35-37 | 15 |
| 14 | 46-48 | 55-59 | 28-31 | 17 | 22-23 | 22-23 | 28-31 | 14 | 20-21 | 67-74 | 36-39 | 17-18 | 14-15 | 31-34 | 14 |
| 13 | 43-45 | 50-54 | 25-27 | 15-16 | 20-21 | 20-21 | 26-27 | 13 | 18-19 | 60-66 | 33-35 | 15-16 | 13 | 28-30 | 13 |
| 12 | 40-42 | 45-49 | 22-24 | 14 | 19 | 18-19 | 23-25 | 12 | 16-17 | 53-59 | 28-31 | 13-14 | 11-12 | 25-27 | 12 |
| 11 | 37-39 | 40-44 | 19-21 | 12-13 | 17-18 | 15-17 | 20-22 | 11 | 14-15 | 45-52 | 24-27 | 11-12 | 9-10 | 21-24 | 11 |
| 10 | 34-36 | 35-39 | 15-18 | 11 | 15-16 | 13-14 | 17-19 | 10 | 12-13 | 38-44 | 21-23 | 9-10 | 7-8 | 18-20 | 10 |
| 9 | 31-33 | 30-34 | 12-14 | 9-10 | 13-14 | 11-12 | 14-16 | 9 | 10-11 | 31-37 | 17-20 | 8 | 5-6 | 15-17 | 9 |
| 8 | 28-30 | 24-29 | 9-11 | 8 | 11-12 | 9-10 | 11-13 | 8 | 8-9 | 24-30 | 13-16 | 6-7 | 3-4 | 11-14 | 8 |
| 7 | 25-27 | 19-23 | 6-8 | 6-7 | 9-10 | 7-8 | 8-10 | 7 | 6-7 | 16-23 | 9-12 | 4-5 | 1-2 | 8-10 | 7 |
| 6 | 23-24 | 14-18 | 3-5 | 5 | 7-8 | 5-6 | 6-7 | 6 | 4-5 | 9-15 | 5-8 | 2-3 | 0 | 5-7 | 6 |
| 5 | 20-22 | 9-13 | 1-2 | 3-4 | 5-6 | 3-4 | 3-5 | 5 | 2-3 | 2-8 | 2-4 | 1 | - | 2-4 | 5 |
| 4 | 17-19 | 4-8 | 0 | 2 | 3-4 | 1-2 | 1-2 | 4 | 1 | 1 | 1 | 0 | - | 1 | 4 |
| 3 | 14-16 | 1-3 | - | 1 | 1-2 | 0 | 0 | 3 | 0 | 0 | 0 | - | - | 0 | 3 |
| 2 | 11-13 | 0 | - | 0 | 0 | - | - | 2 | - | - | - | - | - | - | 2 |
| 1 | 0-10 | - | - | - | - | - | - | 1 | - | - | - | - | - | - | 1 |

Table 4:  Scaled Score Equivalent of Raw Scores. Wechsler Adult Intelligence Scale. Ages 65+.

| Scaled Score | VERBAL | | | | | | | Scaled score | PERFORMANCE | | | | | | Scaled score |
|---|---|---|---|---|---|---|---|---|---|---|---|---|---|---|---|
| | Spot the word | Vocabulary | Similarities | Arithmetic | Digit span | Information | Compre-hension | | Picture completion | Digit symbol | Block design | Matrix reasoning | Picture arrange-ment | Symbol search | |
| 19 | 54+ | 66 | - | 19+ | 25+ | 26+ | - | 19 | 22-25 | 63+ | 44+ | 14+ | 15+ | 35+ | 19 |
| 18 | 52-53 | 62-65 | 33 | 18 | 24 | 24-25 | - | 18 | 21 | 59-62 | 41-43 | 13 | 14 | 33-34 | 18 |
| 17 | 50-51 | 58-61 | 30-32 | 17 | 22-23 | 22-23 | 31-33 | 17 | 19-20 | 54-58 | 37-40 | 12 | 12-13 | 30-32 | 17 |
| 16 | 47-49 | 54-57 | 28-29 | 16 | 21 | 21-22 | 29-30 | 16 | 17-18 | 49-53 | 34-36 | 11 | 11 | 27-29 | 16 |
| 15 | 45-46 | 50-53 | 25-27 | 15 | 20 | 19-20 | 26-28 | 15 | 16 | 45-48 | 30-33 | 10 | 10 | 25-26 | 15 |
| 14 | 43-44 | 45-49 | 22-24 | 14 | 18-19 | 17-18 | 23-25 | 14 | 14-15 | 40-44 | 27-29 | 9 | 9 | 22-24 | 14 |
| 13 | 40-42 | 41-44 | 19-21 | 12-13 | 17 | 16 | 21-22 | 13 | 12-13 | 35-39 | 24-26 | 8 | 8 | 19-21 | 13 |
| 12 | 38-39 | 37-40 | 17-18 | 11 | 16 | 14-15 | 18-20 | 12 | 11 | 30-34 | 20-23 | 7 | 6-7 | 17-18 | 12 |
| 11 | 36-37 | 33-36 | 14-16 | 10 | 14-15 | 12-13 | 15-17 | 11 | 9-10 | 26-29 | 17-19 | - | 5 | 14-16 | 11 |
| 10 | 33-35 | 28-32 | 11-13 | 9 | 13 | 11 | 13-14 | 10 | 7-8 | 21-25 | 13-16 | 6 | 4 | 11-13 | 10 |
| 9 | 31-32 | 24-27 | 8-10 | 7-8 | 12 | 9-10 | 10-12 | 9 | 6 | 16-20 | 10-12 | 5 | 3 | 8-10 | 9 |
| 8 | 29-30 | 20-23 | 6-7 | 6 | 10-11 | 7-8 | 7-9 | 8 | 4-5 | 12-15 | 6-9 | 4 | 2 | 6-7 | 8 |
| 7 | 26-28 | 14-19 | 3-5 | 5 | 9 | 6 | 4-6 | 7 | 2-3 | 7-11 | 3-5 | 3 | 1 | 3-5 | 7 |
| 6 | 24-25 | 11-13 | 1-2 | 4 | 8 | 4-5 | 2-3 | 6 | 1 | 2-6 | 1-2 | 2 | 0 | 1-2 | 6 |
| 5 | 22-23 | 7-10 | 0 | 3 | 6-7 | 2-3 | 1 | 5 | 0 | 1 | 0 | 1 | - | 0 | 5 |
| 4 | 19-21 | 3-6 | - | 2 | 5 | 1 | 0 | 4 | - | 0 | - | 0 | - | - | 4 |
| 3 | 17-18 | 1-2 | - | 1 | 4 | 0 | - | 3 | - | - | - | - | - | - | 3 |
| 2 | 15-16 | 0 | - | 0 | 2-3 | - | - | 2 | - | - | - | - | - | - | 2 |
| 1 | 0-14 | - | - | - | 0-1 | - | - | 1 | - | - | - | - | - | - | 1 |

Table 5: _IQ equivalents of sums of scaled scores._

**VERBAL**

| sum of ss | IQ | sum of ss | IQ | sum of ss | IQ |
|---|---|---|---|---|---|
| 6 | 48 | 46 | 86 | 86 | 125 |
| 7 | 49 | 47 | 87 | 87 | 126 |
| 8 | 50 | 48 | 88 | 88 | 127 |
| 9 | 51 | 49 | 89 | 89 | 128 |
| 10 | 52 | 50 | 90 | 90 | 129 |
| 11 | 53 | 51 | 91 | 91 | 130 |
| 12 | 54 | 52 | 92 | 92 | 131 |
| 13 | 55 | 53 | 93 | 93 | 132 |
| 14 | 55 | 54 | 94 | 94 | 133 |
| 15 | 56 | 55 | 95 | 95 | 134 |
| 16 | 57 | 56 | 96 | 96 | 135 |
| 17 | 58 | 57 | 97 | 97 | 136 |
| 18 | 59 | 58 | 98 | 98 | 137 |
| 19 | 60 | 59 | 99 | 99 | 138 |
| 20 | 61 | 60 | 100 | 100 | 139 |
| 21 | 62 | 61 | 101 | 101 | 140 |
| 22 | 63 | 62 | 102 | 102 | 141 |
| 23 | 64 | 63 | 103 | 103 | 142 |
| 24 | 65 | 64 | 104 | 104 | 143 |
| 25 | 66 | 65 | 105 | 105 | 144 |
| 26 | 67 | 66 | 106 | 106 | 145 |
| 27 | 68 | 67 | 107 | 107 | 145 |
| 28 | 69 | 68 | 108 | 108 | 146 |

**PERFORMANCE**

| sum of ss | IQ | sum of ss | IQ | sum of ss | IQ |
|---|---|---|---|---|---|
| 5 | 46 | 45 | 94 | 85 | 142 |
| 6 | 48 | 46 | 95 | 86 | 143 |
| 7 | 49 | 47 | 96 | 87 | 144 |
| 8 | 50 | 48 | 98 | 88 | 145 |
| 9 | 51 | 49 | 99 | 89 | 146 |
| 10 | 52 | 50 | 100 | 90 | 148 |
| 11 | 54 | 51 | 101 | 91 | 149 |
| 12 | 55 | 52 | 102 | 92 | 150 |
| 13 | 56 | 53 | 104 | 93 | 151 |
| 14 | 57 | 54 | 105 | 94 | 152 |
| 15 | 58 | 55 | 106 | 95 | 154 |
| 16 | 60 | 56 | 107 | | |
| 17 | 61 | 57 | 108 | | |
| 18 | 62 | 58 | 110 | | |
| 19 | 63 | 59 | 111 | | |
| 20 | 64 | 60 | 112 | | |
| 21 | 65 | 61 | 113 | | |
| 22 | 67 | 62 | 114 | | |
| 23 | 68 | 63 | 115 | | |
| 24 | 69 | 64 | 117 | | |
| 25 | 70 | 65 | 118 | | |
| 26 | 71 | 66 | 119 | | |
| 27 | 73 | 67 | 120 | | |

**FULL SCALE**

| sum of ss | IQ | sum of ss | IQ | sum of ss | IQ | sum of ss | IQ | sum of ss | IQ |
|---|---|---|---|---|---|---|---|---|---|
| 11 | 45 | 51 | 67 | 91 | 89 | 131 | 112 | 171 | 134 |
| 12 | 45 | 52 | 68 | 92 | 90 | 132 | 112 | 172 | 135 |
| 13 | 46 | 53 | 68 | 93 | 91 | 133 | 113 | 173 | 135 |
| 14 | 46 | 54 | 69 | 94 | 91 | 134 | 113 | 174 | 136 |
| 15 | 47 | 55 | 69 | 95 | 92 | 135 | 114 | 175 | 136 |
| 16 | 48 | 56 | 70 | 96 | 92 | 136 | 114 | 176 | 137 |
| 17 | 48 | 57 | 70 | 97 | 93 | 137 | 115 | 177 | 137 |
| 18 | 49 | 58 | 71 | 98 | 93 | 138 | 116 | 178 | 138 |
| 19 | 49 | 59 | 72 | 99 | 94 | 139 | 116 | 179 | 138 |
| 20 | 50 | 60 | 72 | 100 | 94 | 140 | 117 | 180 | 139 |
| 21 | 50 | 61 | 73 | 101 | 95 | 141 | 117 | 181 | 140 |
| 22 | 51 | 62 | 73 | 102 | 96 | 142 | 118 | 182 | 140 |
| 23 | 51 | 63 | 74 | 103 | 96 | 143 | 118 | 183 | 141 |
| 24 | 52 | 64 | 74 | 104 | 97 | 144 | 119 | 184 | 141 |
| 25 | 53 | 65 | 75 | 105 | 97 | 145 | 120 | 185 | 142 |
| 26 | 53 | 66 | 75 | 106 | 98 | 146 | 120 | 186 | 142 |
| 27 | 54 | 67 | 76 | 107 | 98 | 147 | 121 | 187 | 143 |
| 28 | 54 | 68 | 77 | 108 | 99 | 148 | 121 | 188 | 143 |
| 29 | 55 | 69 | 77 | 109 | 99 | 149 | 122 | 189 | 144 |
| 30 | 55 | 70 | 78 | 110 | 100 | 150 | 122 | 190 | 145 |
| 31 | 56 | 71 | 78 | 111 | 101 | 151 | 123 | 191 | 145 |
| 32 | 57 | 72 | 79 | 112 | 101 | 152 | 123 | 192 | 146 |
| 33 | 57 | 73 | 79 | 113 | 102 | 153 | 124 | 193 | 146 |

*Table 5 (contd): IQ equivalents of sums of scaled scores.*

### VERBAL

| sum of ss | IQ | sum of ss | IQ | sum of ss | IQ |
|---|---|---|---|---|---|
| 29 | 70 | 69 | 109 | 109 | 147 |
| 30 | 71 | 70 | 110 | 110 | 148 |
| 31 | 72 | 71 | 111 | 111 | 149 |
| 32 | 73 | 72 | 112 | 112 | 150 |
| 33 | 74 | 73 | 113 | 113 | 151 |
| 34 | 75 | 74 | 114 | 114 | 152 |
| 35 | 76 | 75 | 115 | | |
| 36 | 77 | 76 | 115 | | |
| 37 | 78 | 77 | 116 | | |
| 38 | 79 | 78 | 117 | | |
| 39 | 80 | 79 | 118 | | |
| 40 | 81 | 80 | 119 | | |
| 41 | 82 | 81 | 120 | | |
| 42 | 83 | 82 | 121 | | |
| 43 | 84 | 83 | 122 | | |
| 44 | 85 | 84 | 123 | | |
| 45 | 85 | 85 | 124 | | |

### PERFORMANCE

| sum of ss | IQ | sum of ss | IQ | sum of ss | IQ |
|---|---|---|---|---|---|
| 28 | 74 | 68 | 121 | | |
| 29 | 75 | 69 | 123 | | |
| 30 | 76 | 70 | 124 | | |
| 31 | 77 | 71 | 125 | | |
| 32 | 79 | 72 | 126 | | |
| 33 | 80 | 73 | 127 | | |
| 34 | 81 | 74 | 129 | | |
| 35 | 82 | 75 | 130 | | |
| 36 | 83 | 76 | 131 | | |
| 37 | 85 | 77 | 132 | | |
| 38 | 86 | 78 | 133 | | |
| 39 | 87 | 79 | 135 | | |
| 40 | 88 | 80 | 136 | | |
| 41 | 89 | 81 | 137 | | |
| 42 | 90 | 82 | 138 | | |
| 43 | 92 | 83 | 139 | | |
| 44 | 93 | 84 | 140 | | |

### FULL SCALE

| sum of ss | IQ | sum of ss | IQ | sum of ss | IQ | sum of ss | IQ | sum of ss | IQ |
|---|---|---|---|---|---|---|---|---|---|
| 34 | 58 | 74 | 80 | 114 | 102 | 154 | 125 | 194 | 147 |
| 35 | 58 | 75 | 80 | 115 | 103 | 155 | 125 | 195 | 147 |
| 36 | 59 | 76 | 81 | 116 | 103 | 156 | 126 | 196 | 148 |
| 37 | 59 | 77 | 82 | 117 | 104 | 157 | 126 | 197 | 149 |
| 38 | 60 | 78 | 82 | 118 | 104 | 158 | 127 | 198 | 149 |
| 39 | 60 | 79 | 83 | 119 | 105 | 159 | 127 | 199 | 150 |
| 40 | 61 | 80 | 83 | 120 | 106 | 160 | 128 | 200 | 150 |
| 41 | 62 | 81 | 84 | 121 | 106 | 161 | 128 | 201 | 151 |
| 42 | 62 | 82 | 84 | 122 | 107 | 162 | 129 | 202 | 151 |
| 43 | 63 | 83 | 85 | 123 | 107 | 163 | 130 | 203 | 152 |
| 44 | 63 | 84 | 86 | 124 | 108 | 164 | 130 | 204 | 152 |
| 45 | 64 | 85 | 86 | 125 | 108 | 165 | 131 | 205 | 153 |
| 46 | 64 | 86 | 87 | 126 | 109 | 166 | 131 | 206 | 154 |
| 47 | 65 | 87 | 87 | 127 | 109 | 167 | 132 | 207 | 154 |
| 48 | 65 | 88 | 88 | 128 | 110 | 168 | 132 | 208 | 155 |
| 49 | 66 | 89 | 88 | 129 | 111 | 169 | 133 | 209 | 155 |
| 50 | 67 | 90 | 89 | 130 | 111 | 170 | 133 | | |

*Table 6: Factor analysis of the WAIS-III.*

| Test | Verbal | Performance |
|------|--------|-------------|
| Picture Completion | 0.46 | **0.76** |
| Vocabulary | **0.89** | 0.30 |
| Digit Symbol-Coding | 0.25 | **0.85** |
| Similarities | **0.78** | 0.44 |
| Block Design | 0.49 | **0.70** |
| Arithmetic | **0.71** | 0.44 |
| Matrix Reasoning | 0.40 | **0.82** |
| Digit Span | **0.68** | 0.38 |
| Information | **0.87** | 0.28 |
| Picture Arrangement | 0.34 | **0.81** |
| Comprehension | **0.80** | 0.39 |

*Table 7: Normative data for the University of the West Indies Cognitive Assessment System. (5% cut-off scores are given, which may be used as an indication of poor performance.)*

| Measure | Age 18-45 (n=50) | | | Age > 45 (n=53) | | |
|---------|-------|-----|-----|-------|-----|-----|
| | *Score* | *SD* | *5%* | *Score* | *SD* | *5%* |
| Simple Reaction Time | 297 | 63 | 401 | 416 | 170 | 696 |
| Choice Reaction Time | 483 | 90 | 631 | 607 | 194 | 927 |
| Choice RT Accuracy | 95 | 4.5 | 87 | 96 | 7.3 | 84 |
| Vigilance | 463 | 76 | 588 | 526 | 90 | 674 |
| Vigilance Accuracy | 97 | 7.6 | 84 | 92 | 11.9 | 72 |
| Numeric WM | 837 | 280 | 1299 | 957 | 332 | 1504 |
| Numeric WM Accuracy | 93 | 17 | 65 | 92 | 12 | 72 |
| Visual WM | 998 | 288 | 1473 | 1222 | 538 | 2109 |
| Visual WM Accuracy | 90 | 15 | 65 | 82 | 23 | 44 |
| Picture Memory | 1028 | 235 | 1415 | 1238 | 334 | 1789 |
| Picture Memory Acc. | 87 | 11 | 69 | 82 | 13 | 60 |
| Word Memory | 967 | 241 | 1364 | 1210 | 397 | 1865 |
| Word Memory Acc | 79 | 14 | 56 | 73 | 13 | 51 |

*Note: Reaction times are in milliseconds, accuracy is % correct responses.*

*Table 8: Systemic Lupus Erythematosus (SLE) compared to matched controls on various UWICOG measures in Jamaica.*

| Factor | SLE (N=31) in seconds Mean | Control (N=31) in seconds Mean (SD) | p value |
|---|---|---|---|
| Simple Reaction Time | 324.16 (64.00) | 239.12 (31.26) | .000 |
| Choice Reaction Time | 518.90 (105.76) | 424.00 (45.26) | .000 |
| Choice Reaction Time Correct | 31.41 (0.886) | 30.77 (1.36) | .031 |
| Vigilance | 478.90 (70.20) | 449.19 (43.39) | .050 |
| Vigilance Correct | 15.35 (1.112) | 14.96 (1.168) | .187 |
| Words | 1123.45 (275.65) | 796.93 (123.41) | .000 |
| Words Correct | 31.12 (5.39) | 30.74 (3.71) | .743 |
| Pictures | 1127.32 (255.12) | 805.12 (172.62) | .000 |
| Pictures Correct | 35.83 (3.55) | 34.00 (4.83) | .093 |

Table 9: Scaled Score Equivalent of Raw Scores. Wechsler Memory Scale. Ages 18-44.

| Scaled score | IMMEDIATE MEMORY | | | | GENERAL (DELAYED) MEMORY | | | | | WORKING MEMORY | | SUPP. TESTS | | |
|---|---|---|---|---|---|---|---|---|---|---|---|---|---|---|
| | Auditory | | Visual | | Auditory | | | Visual | | Auditory | Visual | Word Lists | | Control |
| | LM1 recall TS | VPA recall TS | Faces1 recog TS | Fam Pic recall 1 TS | LM 2 recall 1 TS | VPA 2 recall 1 TS | Aud rec del TS | Faces 2 recog TS | Fam Pic 2 TS | Let Num seq TS | Spatial span TS | Word list TS | Word list sh del TS | Mental control TS |
| 19 | 75 | - | - | - | 49-50 | - | - | - | - | 19-20 | 26-32 | - | - | 40 |
| 18 | 71-74 | - | - | - | 46-48 | - | - | - | - | 18 | 25 | - | - | 38-39 |
| 17 | 67-70 | - | - | - | 43-45 | - | 52-54 | 48 | - | 17 | 23-24 | 47-48 | - | 36-37 |
| 16 | 63-66 | - | - | - | 40-42 | - | 48-51 | 48-47 | - | 16 | 22 | 45-46 | - | 34-35 |
| 15 | 59-62 | 32 | 47-48 | 64 | 37-39 | - | 45-47 | 44-45 | 63-64 | 15 | 21 | 43-44 | 12 | 32-33 |
| 14 | 55-58 | 29-31 | 45-46 | 60-63 | 34-36 | - | 42-44 | 42-43 | 59-62 | 13-14 | 19-20 | 41-42 | 11 | 30-31 |
| 13 | 51-54 | 26-28 | 42-44 | 56-59 | 31-33 | 8 | 38-41 | 41 | 55-58 | 12 | 18 | 39-40 | - | 28-29 |
| 12 | 47-50 | 23-25 | 40-41 | 52-55 | 28-30 | 7 | 35-37 | 39-40 | 50-54 | 11 | 16-17 | 37-38 | 10 | 26-27 |
| 11 | 43-46 | 20-22 | 38-39 | 48-51 | 26-27 | 6 | 31-34 | 37-38 | 46-49 | 10 | 15 | 35-36 | 9 | 24-25 |
| 10 | 39-42 | 17-19 | 35-37 | 44-47 | 23-25 | 5 | 28-30 | 35-36 | 42-45 | 9 | 14 | 33-34 | 8 | 22-23 |
| 9 | 35-38 | 13-16 | 33-34 | 40-43 | 20-22 | 4 | 24-27 | 33-34 | 38-41 | 8 | 13 | 31-32 | 7 | 20-21 |
| 8 | 31-34 | 10-12 | 30-32 | 36-39 | 17-19 | - | 21-23 | 32 | 33-37 | 7 | 11-12 | 29-30 | 6 | 18-19 |
| 7 | 27-30 | 7-9 | 28-29 | 32-35 | 14-16 | 3 | 17-20 | 30-31 | 29-32 | 6 | 10 | 26-28 | 5 | 16-17 |
| 6 | 23-26 | 4-6 | 26-27 | 28-31 | 11-13 | 2 | 14-16 | 28-29 | 25-28 | 5 | 8-9 | 24-25 | 4 | 14-15 |
| 5 | 19-22 | 1-3 | 23-25 | 24-27 | 8-10 | 1 | 11-13 | 26-27 | 21-24 | 4 | 7 | 22-23 | - | 12-13 |
| 4 | 15-18 | 0 | 21-22 | 20-23 | 5-7 | 0 | 7-10 | 24-25 | 16-20 | 3 | 6 | 20-21 | 2-3 | 10-11 |
| 3 | 11-14 | - | 19-20 | 16-19 | 2-4 | - | 4-6 | 23 | 12-15 | 2 | 4-5 | 18-19 | - | 8-9 |
| 2 | 7-10 | - | 16-18 | 12-15 | 1 | - | 1-3 | 21-22 | 8-11 | 1 | 3 | 16-17 | 1 | 6-7 |
| 1 | 0-6 | - | 0-15 | 1-11 | 0 | - | 0 | 0-20 | 0-7 | 0 | 0-2 | -0-15 | 0 | 0-5 |

Table 10: *Scaled Score Equivalent of Raw Scores. Wechsler Memory Scale. Ages 45-64.*

| Scaled score | IMMEDIATE MEMORY | | | | GENERAL (DELAYED) MEMORY | | | | | WORKING MEMORY | | SUPP. TESTS | | |
| --- | --- | --- | --- | --- | --- | --- | --- | --- | --- | --- | --- | --- | --- | --- |
| | Auditory | | Visual | | Auditory | | | Visual | | Auditory | Visual | Word Lists | | Control |
| | LM1 recall TS | VPA recall TS | Faces1 recog TS | Fam Pic recall 1 TS | LM 2 recall 1 TS | VPA 2 recall 1 TS | Aud rec del TS | Faces 2 recog TS | Fam Pic 2 TS | Let Num seq TS | Spatial span TS | Word list TS | Word list sh del TS | Mental control TS |
| 19 | 65-75 | - | - | - | 44-50 | - | 51-54 | 48 | 63-34 | 20-21 | 25-32 | 47-48 | - | 37-40 |
| 18 | 61-64 | 30-32 | 47-48 | 61-64 | 40-43 | - | 47-50 | 46-47 | 59-62 | 19 | 24 | 45-46 | - | 35-36 |
| 17 | 57-60 | 27-29 | 45-46 | 57-60 | 37-39 | - | 44-46 | 44-45 | 55-58 | 18 | 22-23 | 43-44 | 12 | 33-34 |
| 16 | 54-56 | 25-26 | 43-44 | 53-56 | 34-36 | - | 40-43 | 42-43 | 50-54 | 17 | 21 | 41-42 | 11 | 31-32 |
| 15 | 50-53 | 22-24 | 41-42 | 49-52 | 31-33 | 8 | 37-39 | 41 | 46-49 | 15-16 | 19-20 | 39-40 | 10 | 29-30 |
| 14 | 46-49 | 20-21 | 39-40 | 45-48 | 28-30 | 7 | 33-36 | 39-40 | 42-45 | 14 | 18 | 36-37 | 9 | 27-28 |
| 13 | 42-45 | 17-19 | 37-38 | 41-44 | 25-27 | 6 | 30-32 | 37-38 | 38-41 | 12-13 | 16-17 | 34-35 | - | 25-26 |
| 12 | 38-41 | 14-16 | 35-36 | 36-40 | 22-24 | 5 | 26-29 | 35-36 | 34-37 | 11 | 15 | 32-33 | 8 | 23-24 |
| 11 | 34-37 | 12-13 | 34 | 32-35 | 19-21 | 4 | 23-25 | 33-34 | 30-33 | 10 | 13-14 | 30-31 | 7 | 21-22 |
| 10 | 31-33 | 9-11 | 32-33 | 28-31 | 17-18 | 3 | 19-22 | 31-32 | 26-29 | 8-9 | 12 | 27-29 | 6 | 19-20 |
| 9 | 27-30 | 7-8 | 30-31 | 24-27 | 14-16 | 2 | 16-18 | 29-30 | 22-25 | 7 | 10-11 | 25-26 | 5 | 17-18 |
| 8 | 23-26 | 4-6 | 28-29 | 20-23 | 11-13 | 1 | 12-15 | 28 | 18-21 | 5-6 | 9 | 23-24 | 4 | 15-16 |
| 7 | 19-22 | 1-3 | 26-27 | 16-19 | 8-10 | - | 9-11 | 26-27 | 14-17 | 4 | 7-8 | 21-22 | 3 | 13-14 |
| 6 | 15-18 | - | 24-25 | 11-15 | 5-7 | - | 5-8 | 24-25 | 10-13 | 3 | 6 | 18-20 | 2 | 11-12 |
| 5 | 11-14 | - | 22-23 | 7-10 | 2-4 | - | 2-4 | 22-23 | 6-9 | 1-2 | 4-5 | 16-17 | 1 | 9-10 |
| 4 | 8-10 | - | 20-21 | 3-6 | 1 | - | 1 | 20-21 | 4-5 | 0 | 3 | 14-15 | 0 | 7-8 |
| 3 | 4-7 | - | 18-19 | 1-2 | 0 | - | 0 | 18-19 | 1-3 | - | 1-2 | 12-13 | - | 5-6 |
| 2 | 1-3 | - | 16-17 | 0 | - | - | - | 16-17 | 0 | - | 0 | 10-11 | - | 3-4 |
| 1 | 0 | - | 0-15 | - | - | - | - | 0-15 | - | - | - | 0-9 | - | 0-2 |

Table 11: _Scaled Score Equivalent of Raw Scores. Wechsler Memory Scale. Ages 65+._

| Scaled score | IMMEDIATE MEMORY | | | | GENERAL (DELAYED) MEMORY | | | | | WORKING MEMORY | | SUPP. TESTS | | |
| --- | --- | --- | --- | --- | --- | --- | --- | --- | --- | --- | --- | --- | --- | --- |
| | Auditory | | Visual | | Auditory | | | Visual | | Auditory | Visual | Word Lists | | Control |
| | LM1 recall TS | VPA recall TS | Faces1 recog TS | Fam Pic recall 1 TS | LM 2 recall 1 TS | VPA 2 recall 1 TS | Aud rec del TS | Faces 2 recog TS | Fam Pic 2 TS | Let Num seq TS | Spatial span TS | Word list TS | Word list sh del TS | Mental control TS |
| 19 | 59-75 | 24-32 | 44-48 | 50-64 | 36-50 | 7-8 | 39-54 | 48 | 52-64 | 17-21 | 23-32 | 42-48 | 11-12 | 33-40 |
| 18 | 55-58 | 22-23 | 43 | 46-49 | 33-35 | 6 | 36-38 | 46-47 | 48-51 | 16 | 22 | 39-41 | 10 | 31-32 |
| 17 | 51-54 | 20-21 | 41-42 | 42-45 | 30-32 | 5 | 33-35 | 44-45 | 44-47 | 15 | 20-21 | 37-38 | - | 29-30 |
| 16 | 47-50 | 18-19 | 39-40 | 39-41 | 27-29 | - | 30-32 | 42-43 | 40-43 | 13-14 | 18-19 | 35-36 | 9 | 27-28 |
| 15 | 43-46 | 16-17 | 38 | 35-38 | 25-26 | 4 | 27-29 | 41 | 36-39 | 12 | 17 | 32-34 | 8 | 25-26 |
| 14 | 28-42 | 14-15 | 36-37 | 31-34 | 22-24 | - | 24-26 | 39-40 | 32-35 | 11 | 15-16 | 30-31 | 7 | 23-24 |
| 13 | 34-37 | 12-13 | 34-35 | 27-30 | 19-21 | 3 | 21-23 | 37-38 | 29-31 | 9-10 | 14 | 28-29 | 6 | 21-22 |
| 12 | 30-33 | 10-11 | 33 | 24-26 | 16-18 | - | 18-20 | 35-36 | 25-28 | 8 | 12-13 | 25-27 | - | 19-20 |
| 11 | 26-29 | 8-9 | 31-32 | 20-23 | 14-15 | 2 | 15-17 | 33-34 | 21-24 | 7 | 11 | 23-24 | 5 | 17-18 |
| 10 | 22-25 | 5-7 | 29-30 | 16-19 | 11-13 | 1 | 12-14 | 31-32 | 17-20 | 6 | 9-10 | 21-22 | 4 | 16 |
| 9 | 18-21 | 3-4 | 28 | 12-15 | 8-10 | - | 9-11 | 29-30 | 13-16 | 4-5 | 7-8 | 18-20 | 3 | 14-15 |
| 8 | 13-17 | 2 | 26-27 | 9-11 | 5-7 | 0 | 6-8 | 28 | 9-12 | 3 | 6 | 16-17 | 2 | 12-13 |
| 7 | 9-12 | 1 | 24-25 | 5-8 | 3-4 | - | 3-5 | 26-27 | 5-8 | 2 | 4-5 | 14-15 | - | 10-11 |
| 6 | 5-8 | 0 | 23 | 1-4 | 1-2 | - | 1-2 | 24-25 | 2-4 | 1 | 3 | 11-13 | 1 | 8-9 |
| 5 | 1-4 | - | 21-22 | 0 | 0 | - | 0 | 22-23 | 1 | 0 | 1-2 | 9-10 | - | 6-7 |
| 4 | 0 | - | 19-20 | - | - | - | - | 20-21 | 0 | - | 0 | 7-8 | 0 | 4-5 |
| 3 | - | - | 18 | - | - | - | - | 18-19 | - | - | - | 4-6 | - | 2-3 |
| 2 | - | - | 16-17 | - | - | - | - | 16-17 | - | - | - | 2-3 | - | 1 |
| 1 | - | - | 0-15 | - | - | - | - | 0-15 | - | - | - | 0-1 | - | 0 |

## REFERENCES

Alzheimer's Disease Society. Accessed 2/2/07 at http://www.alzheimers. org.uk/Working_with_people_with_dementia/Primary_care/ Dementia_diagnosis_and_management_in_primary_care/mmse.html

Bosnes, O. (1999). Wechsler Memory Scale og Wechsler Memory Scale-Revisited: En sammenligning med et klinisk utvalg i Norge. /Wechsler Memory Scale (WMS) and Wechsler Memory Scale-Revisited (WMS-R): Comparison in a clinical sample in Norway. *Tidsskrift for Norsk Psykologforening*, 36, 853-857.

Bosnes, O., & Ellertsen, B. (2000). Wechsler Memory Scale – Revised (WMS – R) anvendt pa barn i Norge./The Wechsler Memory Scale – Revised (WMS – R) used with children in Norway. *Tidsskrift for Norsk Psykologforening*, 37, 717-723.

Crawford, J. R., & Allan, K. M. (1995). The WAIS – R (UK): Basic psychometric properties in an adult UK sample. *British Journal of Clinical Psychology*, 34, 237-250.

Crum R. M., Anthony J. C., Bassett S. S., & Folstein M. F. (1993). Population-based norms for the mini-mental state examination by age and educational level, *Journal of the American Medical Association*, 18: 2386-2391.

Demsky, Y. I., Mittenberg, W., Quintar, B., Katell, A. D., & Golden, C. J. (1998). Bias in the use of standard American norms with Spanish translations of the Wechsler Memory Scale – Revised. *Assessment*, 5, 115-121.

Evans, J., (2003). Assessment of memory. In L.H. Goldstein & J. McNeil (Eds.), *Clinical neuropsychology: A practical guide to assessment and management for clinicians*. New York: Wiley.

Feifer, S. G., & Phillip, A. D. (2000). *The neuropsychology of reading disorders: Diagnosis and intervention workbook*. Middletown, MD: School Neuropsychology Press, LLC.

Feifer, S. G., & Phillip, A. D. (2002). *The neuropsychology of written language disorder: Diagnosis and intervention*. Middletown, MD: School Neuropsychology Press, LLC.

Folstein M. F., Folstein, S. E., & McHugh P. R. (1975). Mini-mental state: A practical method for grading the state of patients for the clinician. *Journal of Psychiatric Research*, 12: 189-198.

Goldstein, L. H., & McNeil, J. E. (2004). *Clinical neuropsychology – A practical guide to assessment and management for clinicians*. Chichester, UK: Wiley.

Groth-Marnat, G. (2000). *Neuropsychological assessment in clinical practice: A guide to test interpretation and integration*. New York, Chichester, Brisbane, Singapore, Toronto: Wiley.

Hale, J., & Fiorello, C. (2004). *School neuropsychology: A practitioner's handbook*. New York: Guilford Publications, Inc.

Halligan, P. W., Kischka, U., & Marshall, J. C. (2003). *Handbook of clinical neuropsychology*. Oxford and New York: Oxford University Press.

Hildebrand, D., & Saklofske, D. H. (1996). The Wechsler Adult Intelligence Scale-

Third Edition: A Canadian standardization study. _Canadian Journal of School Psychology_, 12, 74-76.

Ivison, D. J. (1977). The Wechsler Memory Scale: Preliminary findings toward an Australian standardisation. _Australian Psychologist_, 12, 303-312.

McCloskey, M. (1991). Cognitive mechanisms in numerical processing: Evidence from acquired dyscalculia. In S. Dehaene, (Ed.), _Numerical cognition_. Cambridge and Oxford: Blackwell.

Merz, W. (1990). Neuropsychological assessment in schools. _ERIC Digest_.

O'Brien, A. (2003). Cognitive function in Lupus Erythematosus in Jamaica. Unpublished MSc thesis, University of the West Indies, Mona, Jamaica.

Pugh, G. M., & Boer, D. P. (1989). An examination of culturally appropriate items for the WAIS--R Information subtest with Canadian subjects. _Journal of Psychoeducational Assessment_, 7, 131-140.

Shaywitz, S. (2003). _Overcoming dyslexia_. New York: Vintage Books, Random House Inc.

Shores, E., Arthur, C., & Jane R. (2000). The Macquarie University Neuropsychological Normative Study (MUNNS): Australian norms for the WAIS-R and WMS-R. _Australian Psychologist_, 35, 41-59.

Tarter, R. E., Butters, M., & Beers, S. R. (2001). _Medical neuropsychology_, 2nd edition. New York, Dorderecht, London and Moscow: Kluwer Academic/Plenum Publishers.

Violato, C. (1986). Canadian versions of the information subtests of the Wechsler tests of intelligence. _Canadian Psychology_, 27, 69-74.

Ward, T. (2004). _Attention, a neuropsychological approach_. Hove and New York: Psychology Press.

Ward, T., Bender, N., Harrisingh, A., & Wilson, L. (In press). Jamaican normative data for the Wechsler Adult Intelligence Scale – third edition and the Wechsler Memory Scale – third edition. Caribbean Journal of Psychology.

Wechsler, D. (1997). _The Wechsler Adult Intelligence Scale – Third Edition_. San Antonio, Texas: The Psychological Corporation.

———. (1997). _The Wechsler Memory Scale – Third Edition_. San Antonio, Texas: The Psychological Corporation.

Wilson, A., McCullough, J. A., & Morris, R. C. (1987). WAIS scores for a non-clinical British sample. _British Journal of Clinical Psychology_, 26, 57-58.

## Acknowledgement

The author would like to acknowledge the contribution of Dr. Dennis Edwards, for his material on neuropsychological assessment in schools.

# 13 The Evolution of Sexual Behaviour in the Caribbean

## A Psychological Perspective

*Tamika Haynes-Robinson*

## Introduction

The exploration of human sexuality is rife with challenges. First and foremost is the fact that sexuality, as evolutionists have already found, does not follow a straight line. It grows, is stunted, masquerades as something else, combines and shifts as it evolves. The Caribbean is neither one persona, nor one evolution, however, with regard to sexuality there are common threads throughout the region that overlap and contribute to the evolution of sexuality. These threads will be discussed in turn, with close attention to the context of the Caribbean territory being described.

The wide variety of the uses of the word 'sexuality' in psychological literature necessitates a precise definition and use of the term in this context. The use of 'sexuality' in this chapter refers to "the array of sexual behaviours, roles and sexual identities demonstrated by different cultural populations across the Caribbean."

The evolution of sexuality in the Caribbean will be explored from a psychohistoriographic perspective, charting the historical evolution of the Caribbean and the development of sexual expression through this construction. It explores the development and psychological impact of polygamy, empowerment of the female sexuality, "rent-a-dread", incest and prostitution. The chapter concludes with the modern expression of sexualities from culturally "conventional" expressions of sex, to dance-hall and carnival.

## Historical Expressions of Sexuality in the Caribbean

### AMERINDIAN EXPERIENCE

The word 'Taíno' is an Arawak word for "friendly people." It refers to the Taíno Indians, a subgroup of the Arawakan Indians (a group of the original inhabitants of north-eastern South America). The Tainos inhabited the Greater Antilles (comprising Cuba, Jamaica, Hispaniola [Haiti and the Dominican Republic], and Puerto Rico) in the Caribbean Sea prior to the Spanish invasion in 1492.

Historically, these tribes (commonly referred to as the tribe of either Arawak or Carib) existed from the Palaeolithic era (Palaeo-Indians reached the New World at least 20,000 years ago; possibly much earlier). The Taíno migrated to the Caribbean islands from Guyana and Venezuela. Initially they settled in Trinidad. However, some of the sub-tribes eventually made their way north and west into the entire Antilles by 1000 BC.

Most of the history of the Taíno is seen through the eyes of the colonizers; however, there are primary sources of their history found in Taíno oral history, artefacts and interpretation of inscriptions. Numbering up to 5 million (according to historical estimates), the Taíno Indians lived in theocratic kingdoms and had hierarchically arranged chiefs or _caciques_.

The Taino were of average stature with bronze-coloured complexions, dark, flowing, coarse hair, and large and slightly oblique dark eyes. Men generally went naked or wore a breech cloth, called _nagua_, single women walked around naked and married women wore an apron over their genitals, made of cotton or palm fibres, the length of which was a sign of rank. Both sexes painted themselves on special occasions; they wore ear-rings, nose rings, and necklaces, which were sometimes made of gold (Las Casas cited in Wilson, 1990).

## SOCIETY, SEXUAL CULTURE AND RITES OF SUCCESSION IN THE TAÍNO

### Gender Roles

Both men and women in the elite were seen and treated as equals in this matrilineal and avunculocal society. Matrilineal refers to the practice of assigning kinship categories through female lines of decent. Avunculocal refers to the practice of men moving to live with their uncles in the village of their lineage (avunculocal residence).

Research on Taíno gender constructions demonstrates that gender roles among the Taíno were generally fluid and often demonstrated evidence of females at the highest "level" of cacique, even though this was a predominantly male position. Certainly, both genders participated in most activities, ranging from political leadership and fighting as warriors to food and craft production (Las Casas cited in Wilson, 1990).

Although the roles and duties appeared equal, Columbus himself noted that "it appears [to me] that the women work more than the men." As such, the expression of sex roles and sexuality among the Taíno reflected similar freedoms.

### Polygamy and Family among the Taíno

The Taíno practised polygamy, most notably among the upper echelons of their society, the caciques (most notably Cacique Behecchio) had thirty wives. Both men and women had the ability to have more than one spouse. More specifically, sexual intercourse was not restricted to the marriage partner. However, as with other ancient cultures, polygamy was tied to resources. Access to woven goods, craft and food usually accentuated one's ability to provide for one's family and attain higher social status among the Taíno. Usually marriages fulfilled both political and social ends by joining competing tribes of any one or group of islands (Wilson, 1990).

Unique to the Taíno is succession based on matrilineage. The succession of offspring to the highest position of cacique, was determined by matrilineal ties, in that the male child of the cacique's sister was next in line. If she had no male child then the cacique's own biological son would be the heir apparent. However in cases where there was no male present to ascend, it was not uncommon for a female to be cacique.

## Sexual Expression of the Taíno

The Taíno people's mode of dress represented their connection to the earth as well as the openness of their relationship to each other. Some of the first Columbian invaders recounted shock and amazement on encountering the Amerindians.

Accounts by Las Casas (in Martyr, 1970) explicitly describe the beauty of the Taíno women of the Xaraguán tribe in Hispaniola:

> As for the young girls, they covered no part of their bodies, but wore their hair loose upon their shoulders and a narrow ribbon tied around the forehead. Their face, breasts, hands, and the entire body was quite naked, and of a somewhat brunette tint.

> All were beautiful, so that one might think he beheld those splendid naiads or nymphs of the fountains, so much celebrated by the ancients.

The Amerindians were not without rules for engagement as they had specific guidelines for welcoming the visitors. According to further reports from Columbus's log, the Taíno considered lending their wives to visitors whom they considered important as a sign of hospitality (Carey, 1997, p. 32). This custom was not comprehended by the invaders, who mistook these women as prostitutes. Their misunderstanding would later cost them their lives.

Also astonishing to the colonizers was the free sexual expression reflected in Taíno art and religion (Arrom, 1989). Expressions of sexual behaviour among the Taíno were recorded by Columbus's doctor, Diego Alvarez Chanca, in his 1495 notes (Kempadoo, 2004). Chanca describes the native peoples as normalizing the rape of men by men over time in their society. This, he opines, served to cultivate "transsexuals, transvestites, eunuchs, "berdaches," and other third-gendered groupings" (cited in Kempadoo, 2004). He summarizes that the Taíno were "largely sodomites". However, according to Kempadoo (2004), this reference was born out of a misunderstanding of the Taíno fluid gender roles as well as a desire to de-masculinize the Taíno men.

Of further interest is Columbus's account of Matinino, an island inhabited exclusively by women in the Eastern Caribbean. According to his report the women of this Taíno tribe made annual warrior treks to other islands demanding sexual intercourse with men in order to become pregnant to secure the future existence of their own tribe.

From these accounts it is suggested that gender equality and a certain amount of freedom in sexual relationships was part of the psychosexual makeup of the Taíno people. Specifically, sexual behaviour in the Taíno was no different from other ancient matrilineal societies in which the focus of its sexuality lay in communal sex and polygamy (Kempadoo and Doezma, 1999).

## Colonizer Influence on Sexuality: From the Spanish to the British

### THE RISE AND FALL OF SPANISH INFLUENCE IN THE CARIBBEAN

Besides inflicting mass murder, starvation, rape and near annihilation of the indigenous people in the Caribbean, colonization enacted significant cultural change, including infringements on physical as well as social and psychological space (LaFont, 2001).

In terms of culture, the Spaniards, in most of their acquired territory, settled into a mode of relatively amicable living with the Amerindians by the mid 16th century. In some cases intermarrying occurred, while in other cases Taíno, in revolt, migrated to other islands or to their own territory's hinterland. Taíno women were subjected to the mores and values of the conquerors and no longer held their egalitarian positions alongside their men. Over time, the social and sexual cultures of the Taíno were systematically destroyed or assimilated and transformed by the conquistadors.

In terms of sexual transformation, in one hundred years, the remaining Taíno became "chattel", the women were property of the Spanish conquistadors and polygamy was outlawed except where it befitted the Spanish. A new sexuality began to emerge. By the 1600s there emerged further historical accounts of homosexuality and bisexuality in the Caribbean colonies. Sexuality scholars Antonio De Moya and Rafael Garcia (2000, p. 152) note:

> Historical records from the sixteenth century onwards suggest that bisexual and homosexual behaviour involving adolescent/adult partners was probably relatively common in the Spanish colony of Santo Domingo. Because of homophobia, most of these transgressive relations had to be clandestine, relatively impersonal and publicly denied .... It is not clear when adult men in the colony started paying poorer adolescent males for

sex, but it is likely that up until 1844, when slavery was abolished, some masters used to have sexual relations with enslaved adolescent males.

## BRITISH INFLUENCE ON SEXUALITY

The British invasions, beginning in the 16th century, signalled the end of the overarching Spanish influence on Amerindian culture. Formal slavery was reintroduced to the Caribbean and the trans-Atlantic trade burgeoned, with numerous shipments of human cargo. With this change came cultural change, which in turn brought changes in sexual expression. These were not fluid nor equal changes but changes based on skin colour and occupation: elite versus slave. These sexual changes were based on opportunity, economy, new religious-based mores, and the quest to 'civilize' the desires of the slave.

## SLAVERY AND SEXUALITY

It appears from historical records that slavery not only destroyed the native customs of the captive labour but also gave birth to a new social and sexual order. This order was by all accounts based on psychology and economics, and involved the introduction of a complex new relationship between the owned and the owners. Commonly not thought of as human beings, but as possessions, the slaves were not allowed to express their own cultural forms of sexuality, but were automatically included in the sexual fantasies and behaviours of their owners.

As chattel, the slaves were first inducted into slavery through humiliation – both physical and mental. Direct evidence of this behaviour is clearly documented in Thomas Thistlewood's diaries (Douglas, 1999). Thistlewood's diaries contained 10,000 pages of daily details of his interactions with the slaves he managed, and then owned, on plantations in Jamaica during 1750-1786. In his journals, Thistlewood clinically reports sexual "rites of passage" such as the act of forced sex for slave women. Often it was a females slave's initiation into slavery after her capture. She was made to know her role was simply to work and provide a vessel for bearing offspring into slavery.

Burnard (2004) describes the common and condoned practice of sexual encounters between slave and slave master; the fruit of these liaisons were the many children born into slavery of White masters and Black slave women. According to James Walvin, author of _Black Ivory: A History_ *of British Slavery,* (1994) "A female slave could ...also be used as a...breed-er...and provider of sexual services for the slave-owner and his coterie".

Thomas Thistlewood's daily firsthand accounts of slavery and slave-owning provide a remarkable window into relationships between the slave master and slave. His diary tells a tale of regular sexual intercourse with many of his female slaves. The descriptions of these encounters were recorded with no more emotion than brushing teeth or using the bathroom. Thistlewood's recount of his days is filled with records of his aggressive and opportunistic sexual acts with slaves. He had forced or unforced sex with slaves anywhere he pleased with great abandon (Douglas, 1999).

Ironically, the relatively sparse contact with other White people allowed Thistlewood freedom in interacting with his slaves. For great stretches of time his only human interaction was with the slaves from whom he learnt and documented the sexual effect of cane juice as a lubri-cant on the slave women and the male slave practice of using hog lard to make their penises larger. He also surmised that African women must "be very sensual" from the female slaves' recount of their sexual experiences and the practice of shaving their genitals.

In part, this "relationship" between master and female slave was spurred on by the relatively few White women in the colonies (except in Barbados). With so few women to men in the planter class, many of the White men sought the sexual company of slave women. In fact, there was a variety of relationships existing between the owners and the owned, from the purely sexual (with or without violence) to long-term monoga-mous relationships akin to 'marriage' (Walvin, 1994). Make no mistake, slave women were not seen as equals and did not hold the same value as Black male slaves. As a result, the slave women often resorted to either prostitution or becoming 'mistresses' of their slave masters in an attempt to raise their social status. Having children for her White master also increased the status of the female slave and as such, her wanting to advance her position would ensure she had the offspring of the White master. Psychologically, the effect of this social order was demonstrated in female slaves actively competing for any mode of ascension. They were unhappy with their status and thus sought to change it through independent acquisition of money or through liaisons with their White masters (LaFont, 2001).

Prostitution was a common occupation of slave women and the ports in many of the West Indian islands provided ample support for this trade (Douglas, 1999; Kempadoo, 1991). Thistlewood himself describes being seduced by female slaves upon his arrival in Antigua. His first encounters formed his concept of African women as sexually licentious (Burnard, 2004).

Freedom of sexual expression was clearly seen in the West Indies among White male slave owners or overseers. However, the Black male's sexual role was only for breeding with the females, and their families were often split up by auction or sale to other landowners (Walvin, 1994).

The European perception of the Black male slave was rife with sexual connotation and denotation. Literature at the time of slavery documents the nature of Black men and women as lascivious, of being well-endowed by nature and sexually voracious in comparison to their White counterparts (Walvin, 1994). However, these attitudes seemed to be more a means of repression and propaganda serving to further dehumanize the slaves. Indeed, there is contrary evidence suggesting the sexual expression of the White slave owners to be more "rapacious" than those they owned (*see* Thistlewood diaries and Lady Nugent diaries). Lady Nugent, wife of the then Governor of Jamaica, Lord Nugent, reports (April 8, 1802):

> white men of all descriptions, married or single, live in a state of licentiousness with their female slaves; and until a great reformation takes place on their part, neither religion, decency nor morality, can be established among the negroes...The overseers, too, are in general needy adventurers, without either principle, religion, or morality. Of course, their example must be the worst possible to these poor creatures. (p. 104).

The end of slavery in 1834 brought with it the end of this overt power over sexuality. Domination took place in more subtle forms. The nineteenth century saw the continued influence of the former slave masters ideas of sexual expression and, the continued use of sex as a means of accentuating status among the former slave women. This period was also witness to the final destruction of the Black working class family. The former slaves, now bereft of land and finances, worked in much the same way as they had under slavery, only at minimal wages from their former masters. The only improvement was that they could now work for themselves (Walvin, 1994).

Sexually, the former slaves were still viewed as lascivious and wanton by the Europeans who intended to study this licentious behaviour. Many such studies focused on expressions of Black sexual relations, commonly defined as "mating." Kamala Kempadoo (1994) states:

> Concerns about "immoral" and "loose" sexual practices, "promiscuity," "unstable" or "irregular" conjugal relations, and "illegitimacy" of children often propelled early-twentieth-century studies into "the Negro" condition.

By the twentieth century the psychology of Caribbean sexuality seemed to be available only through the precepts of European sociologists and anthropologists. Their thoughts on the matter of Black sexuality were, of course, tinted by their continuing notion of Blacks as animals. Franz Fanon (1963) reflects this concept by noting that, "when the settler seeks to describe the native fully in exact terms, he...refers to the bestiary". The use of "bestiary" figuratively and literally placed the Black person in the animal class, separate from humans. Fanon opines that this attitude permeated any elitist description of Black sexuality in the Caribbean. That being the case, the psychology of the settlers and the natives in the Caribbean depicted a struggle to reconcile the African and European influences on sexual expression and sexuality.

## Polygamy in the Caribbean of the Twentieth Century

Ostensibly the European "nuclear" family was presented as the ideal. However, what became the sociological norm for the post-slavery era in the Caribbean was an informally polygamous society. Many Caribbean men have a formal wife and family as well as an 'outside' family. This is clearly documented and discussed in studies by R. T. Smith (1956) and M. G. Smith (1962), investigating family types in the Caribbean. These authors found this polygamous state as an "indigenous" or "sui generis" expression and assigned full responsibility for this experience to slavery and its effects. The combination of African cultural aspects with British cultural norms in a newly discovered land had provided fertile ground for a new sexual identity and expression, complete with its own rules of engagement. Indeed, slavery in the Caribbean produced a sexual evolution quite unlike anywhere else in the world at that time and since.

Shepherd, in 1999, pointed out that during and after slavery a disconnect was apparent between the sexes, " so little are the sexes attached to each other... that it is common for the men to have several wives at a time besides transient mistresses; ... and the women to leave their husbands for others, and to submit to the embraces of white men for money and clothes" (quoted in Shepherd 1999, p. 58 in Barriteau, 2003.)

The evolution of sex and sexuality in the Caribbean was a movement from pre-Columbian equality and fluidity to the post-slavery use of sex and sexuality to gain power and hold status, as well as to influence the prevailing sexual culture. The twentieth century hegemony of the White male therefore formed the features of the sexual culture of this era: hegemonic masculinity. This masculinity was articulated through the avenues of "socio-political leadership; economic dominance; heterosexuality; headship of nuclear family; chivalric defence of property, empire and family" (Reddock, 2004, p. 107). Physical prowess was the penultimate expression of the hegemony and was in fact the truest expression of the "naturalness of male power" (Reddock, 2004, p. 107).

The historical perspective presented above illustrates the theme of necessity being the mother of invention, as the society existing during and after slavery did not change much in reality. The same gender dynamics and sexual politics existed as was deemed implicitly necessary by the persons involved. The post-slavery societies were still relatively small communities with a variety of ethnicities and cultures thrust together for better or worse. The intimacy of these peculiar societies fashioned a crucible of sexual relationships, sexual dynamics and politics peculiar to the slavery and post-slavery culture. The resulting sexual culture was born out of necessity, and the lack of change in the economic and psychological climate made for fertile ground for the burgeoning of multiple partners, prostitution, and disconnected families.

## Contemporary Expressions of Sexuality

British slavery is said to be the origin of the concept of women being validated through bearing children and men validated as truly "male" by their ability to impregnate (MacCormak and Draper, 1987). According to Royes, contemporary ideas of sexuality in Jamaica are the same in 1999 as they were in 1899. Her position may have merit as the Twentieth century saw little change in the male hegemony and validity of the female through childbirth. Heterosexuality was still the popular demonstration; however homosexuality continued to develop, and a re-emergence of diverse family and sexual structures was evident.

By the 1970s 'visiting unions', common-law unions and 'outside relationships' were depicted as the cultural norm, having gained the status of being formally defined and accepted as typical of Caribbean sexuality and family (Babbie, 1990). Women were still not sexually equal to men, and double standards of behaviour were clearly defined. Women who were open with their sexual desires and needs were viewed as "wanton" and "loose", while men were encouraged to develop and advertise their sexual prowess with as many women as they could (Bowla, 2004). Homosexuality remained an illegal and hence underground expression.

## Homosexuality: Perceptions and Realities

Positions on homosexuality and its origins in Caribbean cultures point to the advent and effects of colonization. Some Caribbean scholars posit homosexuality throughout ancient cultures to be the result of bourgeoisie society (Smith, 1956; Smith, 1962). However, the reality is that homosexuality existed long before the advent of a bourgeoisie society and long before colonization, even though the term "homosexuality" did not exist until 1868 (Fone, 2000). To be sure, documented cultural norms included the expression of masculinity through sexual relations with both women and adolescent boys throughout ancient, pre-reformation and Victorian Europe (Trumbach, 1994).

Conservative views on homosexuality in the Caribbean however strongly indicate the history of polarized tension between the African slaves and their White owners (LaFont, 2001). In her essay on "very straight sex" Lafont contends that the intolerance of homosexuality originated in the pious nature of the missionaries sent to indoctrinate the chattel. The slave, in existence and in deed, personified sin, especially when they had several sexual partners or when they engaged in same sex intercourse. The thin line between church and state in the 1700s no doubt reflected the sentiment prostrated in the anti-buggery act of 1533.

LaFont continues the discussion by linking the formation of the cultural expressions of sexuality with the past. In her essay (2001) she discusses the impact of slavery, the slave culture itself, Christianity and the importance of respectability on the evolution of contemporary Caribbean expression of sexuality. The view of oral, anal and same sex intercourse as "nastiness" originates from slavery; as the slaves, freedmen and ex-slaves needed to find some ground on which they could think of themselves as "head and shoulders" above the White elite. With the well documented sexual forays of the plantocracy in full view, the slaves could gain moral ground, though no social or economic ground, in their stance on sexuality. They achieved this through the establishment of respectability. In the eyes of the transposed African people, their sexuality and sexual mores were distinct from those of their White masters (LaFont, 2001).

The abolition of slavery further propelled respectability, as the ex-slaves were now able to freely construct and express their sexual mores. It became more common for single unions between Black people to exist, and virginity became a prized possession (Nugent, 1839). Adultery was condemned, however pre-marital sex was expected but not without careful consideration of the first sexual experience. In effect, the ex-slaves chose to become more pious in some respects than their former masters, in rejection of all that was slavery. Social mobility was only achieved through respectability, and in turn, one of the ways to earn respectability was to be sexually irreprehensible (Wilson, 1973).

For a hundred years, five British territories in the Caribbean maintained British laws that made homosexual intercourse illegal, with punishment varying from island to island. During the twentieth century the laws were rarely enforced, although the Cayman Islands turned away a cruise liner chartered by 1000 gay men in 1999.

In Jamaica, the act specifically outlawing homosexual sex is referred to as the buggery law (The Buggery Act, sec 76 of the Offences Against the Person Act, 1553).

> The Offences Against the Persons Act prohibits 'acts of gross indecency' – generally interpreted as referring to any kind of physical intimacy – between men, in public or in private. The offence of buggery is specified in section 76, and is defined as anal intercourse between a man and a woman, or between two men. However, most prosecution under the Act in fact involves consenting adult men suspected of indulging in anal sex. (IGLHRC, 2000 in LaFont, 2001).

The Act prohibits homosexual activity in public or private places and, if caught, perpetrators can be punished with prison time and fines.

Layman's law in Jamaica grants unofficial permission to impart violent "justice" on perpetrators caught before the police arrive. It is this public behaviour and condemnation that has given rise to international outcry and condemnation of lawless violence and prejudice against homosexual persons in many Caribbean territories.

The British government has taken the view that the anti-buggery laws violated international human rights agreements that it had signed. For some years it tried without success to persuade Caribbean politicians to repeal the laws in island legislatures. However, in January 2001 the British Privy Council, which acts as the highest court for the remaining British West Indian territories, made an order that decriminalized homosexual acts between consenting adults in private. The order applied to five Caribbean territories: Anguilla, the Cayman Islands, the British Virgin Islands, Montserrat, and the Turks and Caicos.

> Britain has scrapped anti-gay laws in its five Caribbean territories, acting after legislatures of the socially conservative and deeply religious islands refused to do so themselves... London's move angered religious leaders, who say homosexuality is immoral and goes against the grain of their culture and religions. 'This is totally unacceptable to the minds of the Christian community here,' Nicholas Sykes, chief pastor of the Church of England in the Cayman Islands, said Friday. (*The Guardian*, 6th January, 2001, p. 7).

Some Caribbean islands have chosen to delineate and uphold their own laws against homosexuality. Jamaica is one of these islands and is renowned for its low tolerance level of homosexuality. According to the World Policy Institute (2003):

> In the Caribbean, Jamaica is by far the most dangerous place for sexual minorities, with frequent and often fatal attacks against gay men fostered by a popular culture that idolizes reggae and dancehall singers whose lyrics call for burning and killing gay men. Draconian laws against sexual activity between members of the same sex continue to be in force not only in Jamaica, but in most of the English-speaking Caribbean.

According to sociologist Robert Carr, director of the non-governmental organization, Jamaica AIDS Support, gay men in Jamaica face significant threats of violence. An article in a daily newspaper in Jamaica in April 24, 2000 documents an attack on several gay men:

> Among the victims was a man cornered in a Baptist Church hall ... in Kingston about 3:30 on Saturday afternoon and shot dead as he begged for

his life. Sources say his killers jeered him before pumping several bullets into his body. The man ... was accused of being a homosexual. (_The Daily Gleaner_, 2000).

A report from Amnesty International (2005) states, the gay and lesbian community in Jamaica faces extreme prejudice. Sexual acts in private between consenting male adults remain criminalized and punishable by imprisonment and hard labor."

Thomas Glave, a Professor of English at the State University of New York, who was raised in Kingston, reports that when gays are arrested under Jamaican sodomy laws, their names and addresses are published in the local press and it is common for neighbours to attack them. Glave has cited cases of Jamaican gays being attacked with bottles of acid.

In 2002, a Jamaican gay man, David, was granted asylum in Britain because of repeated violent attacks he suffered at the hands of gay bashers in his country. His throat was slashed once, but he survived; another time his arm was broken (Stern, 2003).

These stories are more or less replicated in the other English-speaking Caribbean territories. In St. Lucia, the legal and informal hostility towards homosexuality also exists. Homosexual citizens of this island live a closeted double life, reinforced by their fear of being discovered at work. They have no bars to go to, and it is totally impossible for them to form an association or to meet openly. Gay life in St. Lucia revolves around private parties and several networks of gay men who maintain contact with each other (Stern, 2003).

According to the laws of St. Lucia, buggery, or anal sex, between consenting adults, whether homosexual or heterosexual, is punishable by 25 years in prison. An adult who has anal sex with a minor could get a life sentence. This has a huge effect on gay men. While the government does not go around arresting people who are suspected of being gay, a climate of fear and intolerance is the rule (Stern, 2003).

The legal opposition to homosexuality continues to be reflected in the operation of CARICOM, which has as one of its responsibilities the coordination of healthcare programmes in the non-Hispanic Caribbean region. CARICOM (1997) published its "model legislation for sexual offences." This model, however, continues to endorse the criminalization of same-sex acts between adults, specifying a penalty of up to five years in prison.

In 1998, the island state of Dominica enacted anti-gay laws which are apparently based on the model CARICOM legislation, providing a five-year prison sentence for the 'gross indecency' of any homosexual act. Furthermore, anal sex, even between consenting adults, is punished by ten years in prison.

Religion plays a major role in forming the strong opinions held by the people in the territories across the Caribbean. Although there is a distinct formal separation of church and state among most Caribbean territories, religion continues to have strong legal and social clout. The Caribbean territories are home to a variety of religions each with its own levels of influence. These religions include Christianity, Santeria, Rastafarianism, and Vodun. Among the religions the interwoven belief about homosexuality is that it is against the moral and universal laws set by the various gods that govern these doctrines.

## WINDS OF CHANGE

Of note, a curious phenomenon has begun to occur in Jamaica with regard to homosexuality. In the past five to ten years there have been a greater number of openly homosexual persons voicing their concerns about violations of their human and economic rights as citizens. Once a completely underground group, those involved began to fight for their rights. Jamaica's Federation of Lesbians, All-Sexuals and Gays (JFLAG) proved to be a strident advocate for the rights of homosexuals in Jamaica and continues to press for a repeal of the Anti-buggery Act – which is itself over 200 years old, and moreover, does not apply to female homosexuality.

In Guyana, Parliament approved a constitutional amendment in 2000 that would have prohibited discrimination on the basis of sexual orientation. The law was vetoed on religious grounds by Guyana's President. According to the Guyana Human Rights Association, the Chairperson of the Guyana Council of Churches, Bishop Juan Edghill, said that the new legislation would, "open the door to homosexuality, bestiality, child abuse and every form of sexual perversion being enshrined in the highest law of this land." The constitutional amendment is about to be reconsidered by the Guyanese Parliament, but opposition to it has apparently grown since 2000.

In Belize – another CARICOM country linked more to the region by language, culture and history, than by geography – there is apparently less overt violence against gays, but the gay community still remains completely underground.

In Barbados, homosexuality exists and is treated with more tolerance and is even incorporated into aspects of revelry and 'playing mas' during Crop Over festival. It is not uncommon to see 'bands' of homosexual men. In Trinidad and Tobago, homosexuality has seen a more fluid transition into regular society; there are gay and lesbian clubs, parties and sections in carnival. The group has its own identity and has its own colours and symbols that are openly displayed.

## HOMOSEXUAL IDENTITY

Troiden (1989) posits that the homosexual identity is a cognitive construct; a representation of the self, of "who I am" rather than "what I do." It is developed in direct relation to the social norm of sexuality, and therefore is bound to be outside of the social and individual identity. Sexual proclivity is no longer an act but an entire category of person (Dank, 1971; Troiden, 1989; Plummer, 1980).

The phases of homosexual identity are described in many different ways by authors; however, the main theories discuss similar elements. Ponse (1978) explains that the homosexual identity is formed through five distinct phases. First is a subjective sense of difference from heterosexuals, emotionally as well as sexually. Second is a sense of understanding of these homosexual feelings and third is an acceptance of these feelings and what they mean in the context of their micro and macro environment. The fourth element is seeking "sameness", in an attempt to identify one must find something with which to identify. As such, seeking other homosexuals and the formation of an unofficial and mostly underground group occurs. It is of note, however, that Ponse's theory was constructed based on lesbian identity alone.

Cass formed the most widely held theory of the development of the homosexual identity. He posits six clear stages of identity formation in homosexuals: identity confusion, identity comparison, identity tolerance, identity acceptance, pride and finally identity synthesis (Cass, 1985).

Identity studies of homosexuality in Jamaica assert that the phases of identity development occur at a slower rate than in developed societies because of the extreme oppression of its existence and the strong heterocentric nature of the people on the island (Blackwood, 2000). When applied to Jamaica, homosexual identity followed a similar path as outlined by Cass, with Blackwood positing that homosexuals in Jamaica are in the latter stages of identity formation: acceptance, pride, and synthesis (Blackwood, 2000).

# The New Millennium and Sexual Overdrive

Centuries of sexual repression coming from the heterosexual majority has impacted on sexual expressions outside of the heterosexual norm. Eduardo Campana in the *Ecumenical Review* (October 2004) discusses the impact of sexual repression on the peoples of the Caribbean. In his article he contends that false morality and repression have had disastrous effects on humankind. He expounds on the rapid spread of HIV/AIDS through the Caribbean and the resulting devastation, as well as the massive psychological damage, often involving things that go beyond the law, like sexual abuse, and its physical and psychological consequences; and the hyper-sexualizing role of eroticized society.

The concept is simple cause and effect. The psychological impact of sexual repression is the explosion of demonstrative sexuality. This is no more visible than in dance and music in the Caribbean.

## CARIBBEAN KARMA SUTRA

Dance and music is in essence the vena cava of the Caribbean. It is a vehicle for sexual expression as well as a crucible of African retention. Dance and music communicate the pulse of sexuality and female empowerment, as well as the economy and politics in the Caribbean. Nowhere is the sexual role of music and dance more evident in the Caribbean than in carnival and the evolution of reggae and dancehall culture.

### Carnival

The festival of Carnival or bacchanal is a direct derivative of slavery. After reaping the sugar cane (crop over) a festival was held by the slaves in celebration of the end of their hard work. It was during these festivities that the African traditions mingled with the colonial traditions to form the dance and music of the period.

Feathers were frequently used by Africans in their motherland on masks and headdresses as a symbol of their ability as humans to rise above problems, pains, heartbreaks, illness — to travel to another world to be reborn and to grow spiritually.

Trinidad and Tobago's Carnival is rife with sexual denotations, and very few connotations. Calypso music, the forerunner of *soca*, had more connotative sexual suggestions than contemporary soca. The music of carnival is filled with metaphors such as needing "injections" to cure illnesses and Trinidadian cannibals "eating" White women, out of hunger and curiosity. Soca today leaves out speculation and directly refers to "horn" meaning infidelity, who will get it, and who will not get it, and why. Penis size and ability to have sex for extended periods of time are also referred to in songs as signs of prowess and the dances are usually demonstrative of the sexual act they intend to depict.

From the calypso lyrics of the Mighty Sparrow (Slinger Francisco) to soca in the lyrics of Destra and other performers, sexual expression abounds. In the lyrics of soca one can find both male and female expression of sexual liberation in making sexual partners know their sexual tastes, likes and dislikes. Sparrow, is the best known calypsonian in the Caribbean, winning, among other accolades, soca monarch in Trinidad and Tobago eight times. He is most notably known for his sexually suggestive lyrics connoting themes from the sexuality of Hispanic and Indian women, prostitution, infidelity and the prowess of Caribbean men.

Destra Garcia is famous in the Caribbean not only for her lyrics but also for her liberated sense of fashion and her passionate performances. Her songs speak to the unspoken rule of "don't ask, don't tell" during carnival. This rule applies to Trinidad carnival and requires freedom of sexual expression without reproach, despite any relationship one might be involved in before or after carnival.

The carnival groups or 'bands' on parade during a week of festivities are mostly 'pretty mas'. This consists of highly decorated costumes which reveal most of the body of the person wearing the costume. This scene of "pretty mas" has changed in the last quarter century, where carnival, as described by Peter Minshall, internationally famous costume designer and carnival winner, used to be about the presenting moving human works of art. The costumes then spoke of political or historical topics and often involved more thought. Minshall disparages today's version of "Trini" carnival, as mere revelry without substance, demonstrative of greed and power (Callaloo Company; Minshall, 1990).

Carnival transformed, nonetheless, is still reflective of the sexual discourse which continues long after carnival is over. The playing of 'mas' is more liberal than contemporary society, however, the bacchanal does speak to the desire for sexual freedom, love relationships, adultery and, of course, high energy lyrics designed specifically for dancing.

## Sexuality and Dancehall

Dancehall embodies culture, music, fashion and style in Jamaica. Its history lies in the roots of the neo-liberalist ideologies and materialism which developed in Jamaica in the late 1970s and early 1980s. Psychologically, it represents the pulse of Jamaican popular opinion and expression. New ideologies, political stances, dances and language constantly evolve from Dancehall. Dancehall culture is highly sexual and relies on the erotic and liberal expression of sexuality in capturing the attention of its audience. Most performers gained and held their place in the dancehall through sexually explicit dress and lyrics. Lady Saw (Marion Hall) is one female performer whose lyrics are frank expressions of female sexuality and liberation, despite public outcry and possible detriment to her career. Jamaica's double standard between men and women's expectations of sexual behaviour is thoroughly tested and found wanting in her lyrics. She speaks to her sexual dislikes and likes, her prowess, taunting men and empowering women.

Other performers speak of the distinct sexual difference between men and women of lighter skin colour and different classes. Buju Banton and his song, "Brownin", glorify the sexual talents of brown-skinned women over her black-skinned counterpart, extolling the virtues long sought by many Jamaican men. In contrast, Beenie Man's "Ghetto Gyal" reports on the sexual satisfaction to be found only in sex with a girl from the ghetto. According to a sociological analyst, Donna Hope (2002) reports:

> One obtains a ghetto slam from a 'trang' (strong) black woman from the lower or working class or from the inner city – a black, lower working class phenomenon. This woman is perceived as possessing the physical attributes that make her suitable for engagement in overtly physical dis-

plays of sexual activity - large breasts, large posterior, big frame, together with the social positioning that makes her more accessible for use and/or abuse by men. The oftentimes lighter-skinned, more feminine upper/middle class counterpart is perceived as too 'ladylike' and pure for engagement in any overtly physical displays of sexual prowess on the one hand and less accessible on the other.

The lyrics in Dancehall music often describe the popular notions, held by both males and females of 'rough' or aggressive sex being better than more traditional intercourse, and that longer and larger penises denote better sexual prowess.

Carolyn Cooper, an advocate for the formalizing of patois (the indigenous language spoken in Jamaica) and a pioneer in the study and recording of gender politics and relationships in Jamaica, explains that dancehall lyrics, though labelled "misogynistic" and violent, offer empowerment of the female through worship and liberation. According to the often controversial Cooper, dance-hall culture affords Jamaican women a chance to try on roles that may not be available to them ordinarily. This is a view that extends outside Jamaica and into the Caribbean among social scientists.

In a paper presented by Donna Hope at the Second Conference on Caribbean Culture (January 2002), at the University of the West Indies, entitled 'Love Pu-nany Bad: Negotiating Misogynistic Masculinity in Dancehall Culture', she discusses the nature of power expressed through sexuality and procreation in the Caribbean. She begins by recounting societal rules and mores from slavery that may still exist today, manned by Eurocentric racial and classist rules.

> In the Caribbean context of slavery, white men were placed at the helm. Notions of sex and sexuality were effectively created and perpetuated... Black people, men and women, were stereotyped as sexual animals, driven by insatiable sexual desires and in need of constant supervision. (Hope, 2002).

Contemporary Jamaican society, in Hope's description, continues to psychologically and physically bind itself to valuing European traits above African in terms of descent, appearance and sexuality. Power is reflected by various means depending on the class in society one occupies. In the same presentation, Hope points out that sexual power represents the only perceived power among poor people in the Jamaican society.

Research in the dancehall shows that the concept of a 'wukka man' (worker man) who have "nuff gyal inna bungle" (many girls in a bundle) is one that is actively subscribed to by men and women who find themselves precariously placed on the edge of the race/class/gender nexus. As the socio-economic tensions deepen, these groupings find themselves with increasingly diminished access to the traditional and emerging symbols of social mobility and power in Jamaica, including socio-economic background, education and a white-collar career, among others. For the women, meaningful monogamous relationships are traded for polygamous liaisons with 'powerful' men.

In essence, Hope describes the creation of sexual symbols of power in demanding the 'demeaning' of the female through sex in order to extinguish her potential power over men.

## Anal and Oral Sex in The Caribbean

The areas of anal and oral sexuality are expressed in rather unique variations in the Caribbean. Particularly vocal against the inclusion of oral or anal sex in sexual intercourse are the people of Jamaica. Intolerance of anal sex stems from the anti-sodomy laws, and oral sex is viewed as abhorrent and 'nasty'.

Carolyn Cooper acknowledges this sentiment by giving evidence of the negative portrayal of oral sex in the lyrics of many popular dancehall DJ's. Eating of 'fur burger' is seen as repulsive and repugnant. Persons who are deemed to have committed such acts often feel compelled to publicly deny such allegations. Such is the case of Coco Tea, a popular Jamaican DJ who was rumoured to have had oral sex with his wife. He was compelled to make a public statement denying such acts (White, 2001).

LaFont (2001) in her article on "very straight sex" looks at the evolution of intolerance in Jamaican sexual expression. In her discussion she expounded on the revulsion many Jamaican men feel towards men and women who engage in fellatio:

Heterosexual anti-sodomy is also blatant and is illustrated in the following examples. Men who date tourist women are ostracized for potentially engaging in oral sex (a sex act Western women are said to demand). A musician I know threw an American groupie out of his hotel room in the middle of night after she tried to fellate him. He complained that if she was willing to do that to him, she had surely done it to other men. How could he kiss lips that had been on a penis?

She also noted that in her interviews, engaging in oral sex was denied vehemently en masse.

Considering the notorious anti-homosexual laws in the Caribbean, it is not surprising therefore that engaging in anal sex is also not tolerated. Admitting to anal sex is almost as condemning as admitting to homosexuality. As such, the subject is not usually broached in public and rarely is it broached in private (Kempadoo, 1991; LaFont, 2001). There is an obvious split between private behaviour and public display, as shame and fear of ridicule and stigmatization control the outward demonstration of sexuality in many Caribbean territories.

LaFont's discussion on the abhorrence of anal sex in Jamaican society deems:

> Current discourse on anti-sodomism invariably emanates from religious sources and popular culture. Anti-sodomism is championed as evidence of Jamaica's moral superiority over Western liberal sexual morés. Tolerance of sodomy is seen not only morally reprehensible but also as un-Jamaican -- tarnishing the national image. Anti-sodomism, on the other hand, is regarded as a virtue that Jamaicans willingly share.

Age seems to be a defining factor in the expressions of sexual behaviour in Jamaica. According to a recent quantitative survey of knowledge, attitudes and practices of sexual behaviour among Jamaican adolescents, there is evidence of a shift in perspective. In a prospective survey of 800 adolescents from a representative cross-section of Jamaican high schools, it was discovered that frank discussions of oral and anal sex do occur among adolescent peer groups (Halcon et al., 2003). Whether or not they would admit to such discussions outside their own peer group was not identified. These discussions appear to take place among trusted friends, while in public anal sex is not discussed and is even condemned, representing the cultural double standard. Again the influence of religion, law and myth abound in forming, reflecting and compounding popular constructs of anal and oral sex in Jamaica. This reticence to discuss or admit to engaging in anal sex also exists to a lesser extent in the other Caribbean territories.

## 'Swinging' in the Caribbean

Do we 'swing'? The practice of couples, married or dating, engaging in wife/husband/partner swapping in a singular or group setting, is one that has been around from the advent of the couple. This practice is not considered 'normal' nor accepted in the Caribbean, and as such has been relegated to the underground of sexual practice. As one swinger told the author of this chapter, "if you don't know about the swingers club in Kingston, then you clearly are not their type", suggesting both the secretive nature and the exclusivity of these 'clubs'. Information on swingers clubs in the Caribbean is sparse at best, and the topic is hardly scrutinized or analysed in research. Bowla (2003) found that there was a significant difference in the sexual practices of men and women attending the University of the West Indies in that more men than women admitted to engaging in multiple sex/orgies. The attitudes and sexual practices of younger persons also seem more sexually permissive than in older generations. Literature searches of other psychological and sociological articles from the Caribbean find brief mention of multiple sex partners, but once again the secretive nature of this kind of activity makes a frank examination of the topic difficult. At best, one must rely on anecdotal information from informal conversations. The topic does remain a possible area of research.

On the Internet, vacations for swingers in upscale 'all-inclusive' resorts throughout the Caribbean are easily available. Some of the better known and more liberal hostels across the Caribbean advertise schedules with names such as 'Latin swing week'. Reviews posted by swingers highlight the best hotels with the widest array of offerings across the diaspora.

## The Establishment of the Oldest Profession in the Caribbean

As mentioned earlier, the oldest profession in the world has been evident in the Caribbean since the Columbian era. Beginning with the Taíno, prostitution – by force and eventually by economy – worked its way into the society, but remained largely underground. By the advent of slavery prostitution became a way of life for many female slaves (Kempadoo and Doezema 1999; LaFont, 2001). The widespread belief in the voracious libido of female slaves naturally influenced the flourishing of prostitution among slaves. It was not long before one's skin colour graded the 'quality' of the sex worker. In Cuba, the _jineteras_ were often mulatto slaves, as White women were for marrying, Black women were for work and mulattoes were valued for sex (Kempadoo and Doezema, 1999). According to Kempadoo (1994) for the White elite males in the plantocracy, the insatiable, wantonly sexual Black slave naturally opened the door for sexual opportunity and, hence, exploitation. Enabling this opportunity was the fact that the White males' families were often well over five hundred miles away.

The absence of the slave owner's family led to the incorporation of sexual activity into the daily life of the slave owner (as was the case with Thomas Thistlewood, mentioned earlier in this article) or to outright prostitution of the female slaves by the plantation owners (Brathwaite, 1971), as evidenced by an editorial in the local newspaper:

> It is quite common for an attorney to keep a favourite black or mulatta girl on every estate, which the managers are obliged to pamper and indulge like goddesses. (_Royal Gazette_ 1814:17, reprinted in Brathwaite, 1971).

For the female slave, prostitution had the indirect benefit of relative empowerment, a benefit which was psychological and economic if not social. Indeed, many female slaves aspired to prostitution for the economic, social (possibly even marriage) and emotional benefit. They used their looks, skin colour, and wiles to achieve the status of favoured prostitute. Offspring of slave and White owners often received the privilege of being housed, clothed, educated and fed alongside the plantation owners' White children (Higman, 1976). Historical literature also indicates the formation of White female and Black male slave relationships, some also leading to marriage. At this time, however, this was seen as an aberration (Brathwaite, 1971).

Prostitution in the Caribbean has continued much along this path through slavery's abolition in 1834, the labour struggles of the nineteenth and early twentieth centuries, political and economical upheaval in the 1960s, 1970s and 1980s and up until today. The sex trade has become more prolific over time, as well as more formalized. This is due, in no small part, to the onset of tourism and immigration, and tied inextricably to the economic environment. Kempadoo (1994; 1996) records the establishment and effect of the International Congress of Whores, and the

National Mujeres Unidad among others, in developing and enforcing the rights of sex workers. Notably these formalized bodies exist in the Latin American Caribbean countries of Cuba, and the Dominican Republic.

## SEX TOURISM IN THE CARIBBEAN

Another variation of sexuality occurs as sexual tourism. Sexual tourism is the informal industry whereby foreigners travel to destinations known for a wide variety of sexual offerings. Though prostitution is often involved, for many the sex occurs as an informal part of the vacation. Sexual tourism includes prostitution, gigolos, sex shows, and all aspects of the sex trade. Sex tourism, as it is now popularly called, is directly related to the occurrence of tourism generated purely by sex. As in the Netherlands, the popularization of sexual destinations garners money for the agencies involved, whether formal or informal.

Certain countries worldwide are known for their sexual offerings as tourist attractions, apart from sightseeing, monuments, sand or sea. Thailand and Cuba are but a few of the places known for their thriving sex tourism, with some countries having a more formalized sex trade than others.

In the Caribbean, Cuba and the up-and-coming Jamaica are known for their sex tourism trade. A recent furore in the Caribbean occurred surrounding the formalizing of sex workers in the English-speaking Caribbean prior to the Cricket World Cup (*Gleaner*, Nov 2006). Although no one denies the existence of the sex industry, the importance of formalizing it in the Caribbean has been downplayed. Indeed, the very mention among government officials of the idea of formalizing sex workers for such a prestigious event as the World Cup seemed preposterous. The proponents of formalizing the sex trade for this event posited that it was the negative impact of the stigma attached to prostitution which allowed for this means of sexual expression to be swept under the carpet.

In Jamaica, due to the underground nature of sex tourism, records of the number or ratio of female to male sex workers vary, if they exist at all. The organization Jamaica AIDS Support estimates up to 2,000 workers in the sex tourism and prostitution trade (Steve Harvey in an interview held on August 16, 2005), with approximately 150 employed in 'Go Go' (strip) clubs in Kingston alone. Other studies have placed that figure at 900 (The Panos Institute Caribbean, Downer, 2006).

Clearly, sex is a robust industry in Jamaica with segmented markets comprising escort services, bars, clubs, cruise ships, streetwalkers, brothels and massage parlours. In a study entitled "Realities of Commercial Sex Work in Jamaica" by Patricia Watson (December 1, 2002, p.19), it was reported that some prostitutes earn between JA$500 (minimum) and JA$10,000 (maximum) per sexual act, plus tips (U$20-$50).

With regard to male sex workers, Kempadoo (2001) asserts that, unlike other nations around the world, Jamaica stands out as one of the few countries where male sex workers outnumber female sex workers. It is posited that the male sex trade in Jamaica is fuelled by the flourishing needs of the heterosexual and homosexual male population rather than heterosexual females (Wignall, 2004). The homosexual reacts to being pushed underground by seeking sex in underground places, such as the side streets of Kingston and Montego Bay or at 'liberated' house parties. Homosexuality being underground tends to attract both homosexual and heterosexual liaisons that are outside of the norm or outside of a marriage. In an article in the _Jamaica Observer_, a male sex worker revealed the rationale behind heterosexual males having sex with male homosexual prostitutes:

> [Ques.] Who is their biggest clientele – homosexuals or bisexuals? [Ans.] "Most of the men are married with children who say that it (sex) is better with us than with their wives," says Joyce [a male homosexual sex worker] ... "The man that I'm with says that I am tighter than his wife, who has three children for him," chimes in Tamara Goodas [street name]. (_Observer_, January 31, 2005).

However, according to the 2004 'Knowledge, Attitude, Practice and Behaviour Survey', commissioned by the Ministry of Health in 2000, males in the age group 15–24 years accounted for two per cent of the sex worker population. This increased to six per cent in 2004. The increase in males aged 25–49 was even more significant, moving from a low of 1.2 per cent in 2000 to 15 per cent of the sex worker population. Those advocating for children's rights have become alarmed at the occurrence of younger male sex workers, especially the large numbers engaged in homosexual prostitution.

Patricia Watson's article in the _Gleaner_ (April 21, 2002) describes the following scene:

> Within Kingston and St. Andrew 's fancy houses and hotels, and outside

along those daytime busy streets, twilight hides a sombre reality: scores of boys below the age of 19 years, frolicking with men two or three times their age in exchange for money.

The young men described in these articles often are pursued by older men and give in as their initiation to homosexuality. The money and the sexual preference become the hook for the continuation of their sex trade.

This is not to say that the rise of the male sex worker is not in part due to the emerging sexuality of Jamaican women. This rise has coincided with a rise in patronage by middle to upper-class women who, according to reports, have financial independence but lack sexual happiness (The Panos Institute, Downer, 2006). This proliferation also parallels the boom in the adult entertainment industry in Jamaica. It is also interesting to note that the majority of male sex workers, according to Jamaica AIDS Support, are from the middle to upper classes. This in itself warrants study.

Male sex work in the Caribbean traditionally is more underground than that of females, presumably due to a more stringent stigma attached to the behaviour. There is one type of male sex work that does not seem to attract the same stigma. That is the male 'rent-a-dread'.

## The "Rent-a-Dread" Phenomenon

According to a Reuters report (2003):

The beach boy, or "rent-a-dread" phenomenon sees fair-skinned North American and European women seeking exotic, dark-skinned Jamaican men wearing dreadlock hairstyles for sex. Ian Edwards, a Washington-based spokesman for the Organization of American States, said at a recent conference on sustainable tourism held in Jamaica.

"There 's a mystique that apparently comes attached with the dreadlocks. I 've seen it here and I 've seen it in Barbados and it is not rare," Edwards said.

Some say the expression of "rent-a-dread" originated out of the Jamaican concert Reggae Sunsplash. Reggae Sunsplash began in the 1970s as an annual stage show lasting seven days in Montego Bay, Jamaica. It became an internationally famous concert and a must-see event. With tourists flocking to the island during the staging of this concert an opportunity for many dreadlocked Jamaican men arose. It became commonplace for White female tourists to be seen with Black dreadlocked men for the duration of, and sometimes following, the concert. During the period it was clear that the men profited substantially from the affections of these women and often remained 'kept' long after the concert ended and after the female patrons had returned home. Sometimes these liaisons ended with migration of the man, marriage, and children with the White female in her foreign country. Other times it ended with the White woman leaving her home to live in Jamaica with her "rent-a-dread." Whether the trade occurred first with dreadlocked or shaven men remains a moot point.

## ADULT ENTERTAINMENT

According to the Ministry of Health (2000):

> The (adult entertainment business) is recognized as a growing industry and like any other business, there is competition. Freaky Nights are a feature in almost all the nightclubs, pushing at the barriers and boundaries. It is a marketplace where people buy sex and the service.

Live sex is the new frontier in sexual entertainment in Jamaica. Any "go-go" club worth its salt will have a headlining sex act night as part of its package (The Panos Institute Caribbean, Downer, 2006). Providing lucrative careers for men and women alike, this new addition embodies the piqued curiosity and broadening sexual taste of the Caribbean people.

The rise in male sex workers and the advent of public sex acts in go-go clubs can be said to be a reflection of rebellion in sexual expression against the status quo. It could also be the changing of the guard in terms of sexual norms. A psychological struggle currently ensues between the mores of Christianity and European-based sexuality and the underground sexual swell of creativity, freedom and, some would say, empowerment (Cooper, 2004). This argument is often hotly discussed in the media. Amidst cries of 'nastiness', there are retorts of "keeping it real". The argument may be said to be won by the rising popularity of the Freaky Fridays or Wednesdays at exotic dance clubs islandwide and the booming Internet pornography industry in Jamaica.

## Summary and Conclusion

In summary, Caribbean sexuality and its expression are firmly rooted in its past and are connected and subject to the economic, political and ideological winds of change. This makes our sexuality, in one respect, very similar to many 'westernized' countries. However, the stark economic and social realities of the Diaspora force a unique embodiment of sexuality. So as not to group Caribbean sexuality into one melting pot, it is strongly recommended that further detailed exploration of the different expressions and roots of expression of Caribbean sexuality from a psychological perspective be carried out.

Our sexuality represents our individuality as members of the Caribbean, in itself a rare and exceptional diverse grouping of human beings. If necessity is the mother of invention, sexual necessity has definitely given birth to the expression of multiple sexualities throughout the Caribbean.

## REFERENCES

Allen, S. M. (1982). Adolescent pregnancy among 11-15 year old girls in the parish of Manchester. Ph.D. Diss., University of the West Indies.

American Journeys Collection. (2003). Letter from Columbus to Luis de Santangel. Document no. AJ-063. Retrieved June 12, 2007 from http://www.americanjourneys.org.

Amnesty International Report. (2005). Retrieved June 1st 2006 from www.web.amnesty.org/report2005/index.

Arrom, J. J. (1989). (Ed.), An account of the antiquities of the Indians, and: The discoverie of the large, rich, and bewtiful empyre of Guiana (review) Ethnohistory 48 (3), Summer, 547-550.

Babbie, E. (1990). Survey research methods (2nd Edition). California: Wadsworth Publishing Co.

Barriteau, E. (2003). Confronting power, theorizing gender: Interdisciplinary perspectives in the Caribbean. Kingston, Jamaica: University Press of the West Indies.

Beals, C. (1961). Sex life in Latin America. In A. Ellis & A. Abarbanel (Eds.), The encyclopaedia of sexual behaviour, Vol. 2. London: W. Heinemann, pp. 599-613.

Blake, J. (1961). Family structure in Jamaica. New York: Glencoe.

Blum, R. W., Halcón, L., Beuhring, T., Pate, E., Campell-Forrester, S., & Venema, A. (2003). Adolescent health in the Caribbean: Risk and protective factors. American Journal of Public Health, 93 (3), 456-460.

Bowla, K. (2003). Frequency, gender and attitude correlates of sexual practices among UWI, Mona students. MSc. Thesis. University of the West Indies.

Bozon, M. (2003). At what age do women and men have their first sexual intercourse? World comparisons and recent trends. _Population & Sociétés_, 391, 1-4. Available at: http://www.ined.fr/en/resources_documentation/publications/pop_soc/bdd/publication/542/.

Brathwaite, E. K. (1971). _The development of creole culture in Jamaica 1770–1820._ Oxford: Clarendon.

Brody, E. (1981). _Sex, contraception and motherhood in Jamaica._ Cambridge: Harvard University Press.

The Buggery Act, Sec 76 of the Offences against the Person Act, (1553).

Burg, B. R. (1995). _Sodomy and the pirate tradition: English sea rovers in the seventeenth-century Caribbean._ New York and London: New York University Press.

Burnard, T. G. (2004). _Mastery, tyranny, and desire: Thomas Thistlewood and his slaves in the Anglo-Jamaican world._ Chapel Hill: University of North Carolina Press.

Campana, E. (2004). Sexuality, CLIA, and the Church: Experiences in Latin America and the Caribbean. _The Ecumenical Review_, 56 (4), 461-469.

Carey, B. (1997). _The Maroon story: The authentic and original history of the Maroons in the history of Jamaica, 1490-1880._ Gordon Town, Jamaica: Agouti Press.

Carrim, R. L. (2000). Attitudes toward sexuality and spiritual well-being among Nazarene pastors in the English-Speaking Caribbean. Diss., Faculty of Asbury Theological Seminary.

Cass, V. C. (1985). Homosexual identity: A concept in need of definition. In J. P. De Cecco and M.G. Shively (Eds.), _Origins of sexuality and homosexuality._ New York: Hawthorne Press, p.p. 105-126.

Chevannes, B. (1992). _Sexual practices and behaviour in Jamaica: A review of the literature._ Washington, D.C.: AIDSCOM Academic for Educational Development.

Clarke, E. (1957). _My mother who fathered me: A study of the families in three selected communities of Jamaica._ London: George Allen & Unwin Ltd.

Cohen, Y. A. (1955). Character formation and social structure in a Jamaican community, _Psychiatry_ 18 (3), 275-96.

Cooper, C. (2004). _Sound clash: Jamaican dancehall culture at large._ New York: Palgrave.

_The Daily Gleaner_, April 24, 2000.

Dank, B. M. (1971). Coming out in the gay world. _Psychiatry._ 34(2),180-97.

De Moya E. A., & Garcia, R. (1999). Three decades of male sex work in Santo Domingo. In P. Addleton (Ed.), _Men who sell sex – international perspectives on male prostitution and AIDS._ London: UCL Press.

Downer, A.(2006). _Diamond and the sweetie shop._ Kingston, Jamaica: The Panos Institute of the Caribbean.

Eggleston, E., Jackson, J., & Hardee, K. (1999). Sexual attitudes and behavior among young adolescents in Jamaica. _International Family Planning Perspectives_, 25 (2), 78-84, 91. Available at: http://www.guttmacher.org/pubs/journals/2507899.html

Eggleston, E., Leitch, J., & Jackson, J. (2000). Consistency of self-reports of sexual activity among young adolescents in Jamaica. *International Family Planning Perspectives* 26(2), 79-83. Available at: http://www.guttmacher.org/pubs/journals/2607900.html

Fone, B. (2000). *Homophobia: A history*. New York: Metropolitan Books.

Hafner-Burton, E. M., & Tsutsui, K. (2005). *Human rights in a globalizing world: The paradox of empty promises*. AJS: University of Chicago Press

Fanon, F. (1963). *The wretched of the earth*. New York: Grove Press.

Foucault, M. (1980).*The history of sexuality: The use of pleasure (Vintage) Vol. 2*. New York: Random House Inc.

Francoeur, R. T. (1990). Current religious doctrines of sexual and erotic development in childhood. In M. E. Perry (Ed.), *Handbook of Sexology, Vol. VII: Childhood and Adolescent Sexology*. Amsterdam: Elsevier, pp 80-112.

Green, H. B. (1960). Comparison of nurturance and independence training in Jamaica and Puerto Rico, with consideration of the resulting personality structure and transplanted social patterns. *Journal of Social Psychology*, 51, 27-63.

Greenfeld, S. M. (1966). *English rustics in black skin*. New Haven: College and University Press.

*The Guardian*. January 6, 2001, page 7.

Halcon, L., Blum, R. W., Beuhring, T., Pate, E., Campbell-Forrester, S., & Venema, A. (2003) Adolescent health in the Caribbean: A regional portrait. *American Journal of Public Health*, 93 (11),1851-1857.

Hall, D. (1998). *In miserable slavery: Thomas Thistlewood in Jamaica 1750-1786*. Kingston Jamaica: University of the West Indies Press.

Hendriques, F. (1953). *Family and colour in Jamaica*. London: Eyre and Spottiswoode.

Higman, B. W. (1976). *Slave population and economy in Jamaica, 1807-1834*. Cambridge, New York: Cambridge University Press.

Hope, D. (2002, January 27). Origins of Black bedroom conflict. In Love punany bad: Negotiating misogynistic masculinity in dancehall culture. *The Sunday Gleaner*, p.p. E3.

Jackson, J., Leitch, J., & Lee, A. (1998). *The Jamaica adolescent study. Final Report*. Women 's Studies Project, Family Health International Research. Triangle Park, NC, USA.

Kempadoo, K. (1994). Exotic colonies: Caribbean women in the Dutch sex trade. Ph.D. Diss., University of Colorado.

————. (1998). *The sex trade in the Caribbean*. Boulder, CO: Project Steering Committee.

————. (1999). *Sun, sex, and gold: Tourism and sex work in the Caribbean*. Lanham, MD: Rowman and Littlefield Publishers.

————. (2001). Freelancers, temporary wives, and beach-boys: researching sex work in the Caribbean. *Feminist Review*, 67, 39-62.

———. (2004). *Sexing the Caribbean: Gender, race and sexual labor.* New York, NY: Routledge.

Kempadoo, K., & Doezema, J. (Eds.) (1999). *Global sex workers: Rights, resistance and redefinition.* New York, NY: Routledge.

LaFont, S. (2001). Very straight sex: The development of sexual mores in Jamaica. *Journal of Colonialism and Colonial History,* 2 (3). Available at: http://muse.jhu.edu/journals/journal_of_colonialism_and_colonial_history/v002/2.3lafont.html.

Lim, A. M. (2005). A night with male prostitutes. *Jamaica Observer,* January 31, 2005.

MacCormack, C. P., & Draper, A. (1987). Social and cognitive aspects of female sexuality in Jamaica. In P. Caplan (Ed.), *The cultural construction of sexuality.* London and New York: Tavistock Publications Ltd, p.p.143-65.

Martyr d'Anghiera, P. (1970). Las Casas: "muchos señores y nobleza, que se ayuntaron de toda la provincia con el rey Behecchio y la reina" – *Historia,* I:441. Cited in Wilson, S.M. (1990). *Hispaniola: Caribbean chiefdoms in the age of Columbus.* Tuscaloosa, AL: University of Alabama Press.

Ministry of Health (2004). *Annual Report.* Kingston, Jamaica.

Minshall, P. (1990). Essay on 'The Mas'. Callaloo Company. Retrieved June 1 2006 from http://www. Callaloo.co.tt

Morris, L. 1988. Young adults in Latin America and the Caribbean: Their sexual experience and contraceptive use. *International Family Planning Perspectives,* 14 (4),153-8.

Mukerjee, D. (1982). A study of the characteristics and community leadership role of family planning acceptors attending the community health centre [etc.]. Diss., University of the West Indies.

Murphy, V. J. (1982). Factors associated with adolescent pregnancy in St. Vincent and the Grenadines. Diss., University of the West Indies.

Nugent, M. Lady & Wright, P. (1966). *Lady Nugent's journal of her residence in Jamaica from 1801 to 1805.* Kingston, Jamaica: Institute of Jamaica.

Olenick, I. (1999). Among young Jamaicans, sex and childbearing often begin during adolescence. *International Family Planning Perspectives,* 25 (4), 206-7.

Ponse, B. (1978). *Identities in the lesbian world: The social construction of self.* Westport, CT: Greenwood Press.

Reddock R. (Ed). (2004). *Interrogating Caribbean masculinities: Theoretical and empirical analyses.* Kingston, Jamaica: University Press of the West Indies.

Roberts, G. W., & Sinclair, S. A. (1978). *Women in Jamaica.* Millwood, NY: KTO Press.

Rubenstein, H. (1987). *Coping with poverty.* Boulder, CO: Westview Press.

Sanford, M. (1975). To be treated as a child of the home. In T. Williams (Ed.), *Socialization and communication in primary groups.* The Hague and Paris: Mouton, p.p. 159-81.

Sharpe, J., & Pinto, S. (2006). The sweetest taboo: Studies of Caribbean sexualities; A review essay. *Journal of Women in Culture and Society*, 32, 247-274.

Shepherd, V. A. (1999). *Women in Caribbean history: The British-colonised territories*. Princeton, NJ: Markus Weiner Publishers.

Smith, M. G. (1962). West Indian family structure. *American Ethnological Society*. Seattle: University of Washington Press.

Smith R. T. (1956). *The Negro family in British Guiana*. London: Routledge and Paul, New York: Humanities Press. In association with Institute of Social and Economic Research, University College of the West Indies, Jamaica.

Stern, R . (2003). *Homosexuality in the Caribbean*. Retrieved January 20th 2007 from http://www.thegully.com/essays/gaymundo/030731_caribbean_AIDS_hate.html.

Thompson, T. (1982). Views of 13-15 year olds in high and secondary school in Hanover concerning their parents/guardians as sex educators. Diss., University of the West Indies.

Troiden, R. R. (1989). The formation of homosexual identities. *Journal of Homosexuality*, 17(1/2), 43-74.

Trumbach, R. (1994). London's sapphists: From three sexes to four genders in the making of modern culture. In G. Herdt (Ed.), *Third sex, third gender: Beyond sexual dimorphism in culture and history*. New York, NY: Zone Books, p.p. 111-136.

Waite, N. A. (1993). *Caribbean sexuality: A pastoral counsellor looks at family patterns and the influences of culture on Caribbean people*. Winston-Salem, NC: Moravian Church in America.

Walvin, J. (1994). *Black ivory: A history of British slavery*. Washington, DC: Howard University Press.

Warren, C. W., Powell, D., Morris, L., Jackson, J., & Hamilton, P. (1988). Fertility and family planning among young adults in Jamaica. *International Family Planning Perspectives*, 14 (4), 137-41.

Williams, L. (2000). Homophobia and gay rights activism in Jamaica". *Small Axe* Vol. 7 (March): 106 -11.

Wilson, S. M. (1990). *Hispaniola: Caribbean chiefdoms in the age of Columbus*. Tuscaloosa, AL: University of Alabama Press.

Wilson, P. J. (1969). Reputation and respectability: A suggestion for Caribbean ethnology. *Man*, N. S., 4 (1), 70-84.

———. (1973). *Crab antics: The social anthropology of English-speaking Negro societies of the Caribbean*. New Haven: Yale University Press.

World Policy Institute (2003). Working papers. New York, NY: Columbia University Press.

# 14 Issues of Violence in the Caribbean

*Brigitte K. Matthies, Julie Meeks-Gardner,
Avril Daley, & Claudette Crawford-Brown*

## Introduction

Violence has been a significant aspect of Caribbean life for a very long
time, and is perhaps the single most discussed issue in many Anglophone
Caribbean societies today (Bogues, 2006). Despite advances in economic,
political and social development within the region, crime and violence
continue to increase in our society. Rates of interpersonal violence are
extremely high in some countries, and seem to be on the increase even in
islands with traditionally low levels of violence (Krug et al., 2002;
UNODC & WB, 2007). Caribbean society seems very tolerant and even
accommodating of violence, and the subject has become the concern of
diverse disciplines, including criminology, psychology, psychiatry, social
work, sociology, child development, public health, and law and justice.
This is because violence occurs at a variety of levels, and different disciplines usually take responsibility for studying and/or controlling it at
their respective levels (Kaplan et al., 1993). Personal violence, or suicide,
is the province of mental health workers because depression is closely
linked with this risky behaviour. Interpersonal violence is often studied
by social psychologists and sociologists; the control of interpersonal violence is left to the criminal justice system; while war and group conflict
are the domain of political science and governments (Kaplan et al., 1993).

## Legacy of Violence in the Caribbean

The countries of the Caribbean share similarities in their cultural and historical backgrounds, including the destruction of their native populations following the arrival of the Europeans in the late 15th century, the use of African slaves to work the sugarcane plantations, and the subsequent use of Asians as indentured labourers. The legacy of slavery and of the brutal plantation life are seen as a major contributor to the continued violence experienced in the Caribbean. Slavery was a form of domination in which the slave's body was not only property but turned into an object. Hickling (1994) has written extensively about the historical origins of aggressive attitudes and behaviour among Caribbean people as being adaptive to the extermination of the indigenous peoples and to the brutal conditions of slavery and the post-emancipation period, and has suggested a historiographic psychoanalytic perspective on the development of violence in the region. In that article, Hickling presents an analytic framework of the causes of this violence, using a historical-biological model, based on his psychiatric and psychoanalytic experience with Jamaican people, together with the historical, sociological, anthropological and political research findings of Caribbean scholars. He concludes that the Jamaican people, who have survived in the New World with heightened attributes of adaptive aggression, have serious problems with authority, poor impulse control and difficulty handling power – all originating from the 500-year history of violence and migration born of European slavery and colonialism. This history has spawned a social environment of marked unequal distribution of wealth, poor educational and economic opportunities, and a political system based on patronage and clientelism. Hickling argues that violence, originally manifested as rebellion against political, economic and racial exploitation, was turned inward as tribalism and self-destruction, following the development of Universal Adult Suffrage under the Westminster system of parliamentary democracy in the decade of the 1940s. This resulted in a psychological environment which has been dubbed 'the graveyard of champions', where crime, migration and entrepreneurial aggression seem to be the surest avenues for social advancement.

## POLITICAL TRIBALISM

Independence from British rule did not end the culture of violence, and in several Caribbean countries it has extended into violence-related to political rivalry. This is very apparent in Jamaica where the two major political parties have had a turbulent relationship that has deteriorated into what can best be called 'war' at times (_see_ Harriot, 2004). Stone (1987) described the relationship between many of the politically powerful, their supporters, and party workers as one of 'patron-client'. For many years the 'client' partners were obedient to their 'patron' partners, who in turn provided scarce resources, jobs, cash or kind. However, more recently, there has been a breakdown of these relationships, with the patrons unable or unwilling to provide in kind, resulting in a gap which drug dealers have been only too willing to fill. This has resulted in relatively autonomous gangs which carve out territory and create their own rules, and has spawned a new source of violence. Caribbean countries have a history of armed conflict (e.g. Suriname, Grenada), riots (e.g. Jamaica), assassinations, military coups or insurrection (e.g. Guyana), and human rights crises (e.g. Haiti) in which there are reports of escalating violence, including government-sponsored killing in poor neighbourhoods, arbitrary arrests, detention and shortages of food and medicine.

Bogues (2006) gives an interesting account of the development of the culture of political violence and gang activity in Jamaica. After the abolition of slavery, the oppression of colonial rule extended into a vigorous effort to turn the ex-slave into a wage labourer and a 'Christian Black'– an effort which was rejected by Black Nationalism, as part of its practices and narratives. This movement has now been virtually silenced by the emergence of 'modern' political movements. Bogues writes that after political and constitutional independence in 1962, a hegemonic ideology about 'Jamaicaness' developed, and rebellion emerged in the form of Rastafarianism and the figure of the 'Rude Bwoy' (Bogues, 2006). The Rude Bwoy was "that person, native totally disenchanted with the ruling system, who generally descended from the 'African' in the lower class and who was now armed with ratchets and other cutting instruments and increasingly guns and explosives" (White, 1967). Violence was an integral part of the Rude Bwoy's repertoire of rebellion, and was actually a strategic instrument of self-fashioning (Bogues, 2006). Violence was often seen as a means of creating and safeguarding zones of Black mas-culinity that were at odds with the hegemonic conceptions of the Jamaican nation state. There was a different set of normative terms for self-conception – in particular, a profound notion of respect. There was no real cultural guerilla warfare, but an identification with Bob Marley (the Rastafarian singer), Marcus Garvey (the Jamaican Black nationalist) and Malcolm X (the US civil rights leader) and an effort to challenge the norms of citizenship and its values.

Over time, however, Rude Bwoys developed into gang formations and became attached to the Jamaican two-party political system. This was accomplished at two levels: first, the Bwoys became a protective force within their respective communities, and then central figures for the distribution of various forms of public works, embracing the patronage system of the two parties. The Bwoys were transformed from postcolo-nial rebellious figures into political enforcers; and the Jamaican two-party system inscribed a friend or foe difference onto localized geographical spaces. This was reinforced through notions of belonging, and enacted through political dramaturgy – songs, colour, party conferences, dances, popular music and the appropriation of the religious symbols of Rastafari and other Afro-Jamaican religious practices. The split between friend and foe was often unequivocal and a matter of life and death (Bogues, 2006).

Bogues believes that it is not just that political parties have recently lost complete control over communities, but that a different logic may now be at work, one that seeks to break the absolute domination of the two-party system. The Rude Bwoy now emerges as another figure – the area leader, also called a 'don'. The 'base' of the leader is often organized around some economic venture (e.g. small shop), with leaders function-ing through a set of community codes enforced by male individuals, and once war breaks out between communities it is often to the death. Young men in these communities expect death as an affirmation that they have lived, and the ritual of burial is marked not only by the fashion show, but also by graveyard gun salutes.

There are now two types of area leaders in many communities: one deeply connected to the two-party system, the other semi-independent and of more concern. The latter is a reflection of a new form of politics in which organized communities operate outside the constitutional and judicial norms of the nation state. However, in this case it is no longer a prelude to a revolution, as the radical self-fashioning, based on black suffering, has collapsed. The collapse is reflected in the fact that the area leader is rapidly losing his dominance and is being replaced by the 'shotta don', so named for his reliance on the gunshot. This is partly a result of area leaders' inability to obtain and maintain peace, as well as deficits in economic development. Shottas do not buy into either of the two central ideological forces of radical Afro-Jamaica, whether Rastafari or Black Nationalism. These shottas have challenged many area leaders, and are themselves becoming dons and predators. Bogues (2006) believes it is the sign of a crisis – with no allegiance to any logic of black suffering for them. There is only one way out – accumulate enough capital through extortion, government contracts or the haulage business, then use these resources to influence the formal two-party system. Rule is enforced through death, a norm to be deployed. Rule is about the absolute power in death. Violence, too, must now be especially brutal, and rape has become a regular feature of violent attacks. He asserts that Jamaican society must come to grips with this new form of power.

Not surprisingly, most Jamaican inner-city residents believe that the increase in violence since the late 70s and early 80s is due mainly to political tribalism, which has extended into the violence in our communities today (Levy & Chevannes, 1996). Levy's research consisted of a Participatory Urban Appraisal in 1995 on violence and poverty within five urban communities. The study also found that inner-city residents believe that their problems stem from a combination of crime, violence and unemployment. Violence appears to harshly penetrate and rule every layer and corner of the personal and community life of Jamaican inner-city residents (Levy & Chevannes, 1996). Similar results have been found in other islands (e.g. McCree, 1998).

## RACE RELATIONSHIPS

Historically, the planter classes imposed divisions between the ethnic East Indian and African labourers to control the labour force more effectively. Today, in countries where East Indian descendants are dominant (e.g. Guyana and Trinidad), there are seemingly incurable racial problems, with leading political parties depending on one race or the other for support (Howe, 1998). Every issue is apparently tainted by race. However, the problem is more complex than a simple struggle for dominance, as issues of access to wealth and power are implicated by shade and ethnic origin as well. Despite these countries' similarities in history, demographics and politics, significantly different manifestations of ethnic violence have evolved. Intense competition between post-independence political parties led to violence and arson between Afro- and Indo-Guyanese communities during the early 1960s (*see* Parris, 1988). In Trinidad this did not happen. Since the 1990s, both countries have shifted from primarily Afro-majority governments to ones ruled primarily by Indo-based political parties. This has resulted in ethnic violence in Guyana, but not in Trinidad. In countries such as these with populations of barely a million, racial violence can devastate an economy (Howe, 1998).

## Violence in the Caribbean Today

Advertisements beckoning tourists to the Caribbean region present an image of joy and luxury and a perception of a 'laid-back', 'no-problem' way of life, but violence is on the rise all across the English-speaking Caribbean (UNOCP & WB, 2007). The homicide rate is as high in tiny, seemingly idyllic places such as the British Virgin Islands and St Kitts as it is in busy Trinidad – although there it is only about 40 per cent of the incidence in Jamaica (*Economist*, 2004). By 1998, violence was the leading cause of death among people in the 15- to 44-year-old age group in Latin American and the Caribbean, and it was the fourth most important cause of death for the population as a whole (Krug et al., 2002).

Most of the available literature refers to the situation of Jamaica, which not only has the largest population of the English-speaking Caribbean countries, but also has by far the highest levels of violence by many criteria. In 2002, there were over 14, 000 offences against the person in Jamaica (Planning Institute of Jamaica [PIOJ], 2003). A United Nations Development Programme (UNDP) report revealed that Jamaica's homicide rate was four times higher than the world's average rate (UNDP, 1999). The report also noted a very close link between the murder rate and the rate of other violent crimes such as robbery and rape. After 1,600 persons were murdered in 2005 (55 per 100,000), Jamaica claimed the number one homicide rate in the world (Caribbean News Net, 2005; Jamaica Constabulary Force, 2006). Another country of concern is

Trinidad which showed a large increase in its homicide rate (moving from seven to 30 per 100,000) between 1999 and 2005 (UNOCP & WB, 2007). According to a 2007 Joint Report of the United Nations Office on Drugs and Crime and the Latin America and Caribbean region of the World Bank, the Caribbean region now has the highest homicide rate in the world (30 per 100,000), greater than South/West Africa (29 per 100,000) and South America (26 per 100,000), with many Caribbean countries showing rates for assault and rape that are higher than world averages (UNOCP & WB, 2007).

## VIOLENCE AMONG YOUTH

The fact that violence is on the rise among youths throughout the Caribbean is also a matter of much concern (Ohene et al., 2005; UNICEF, 2007). Youths both contribute to, and are victims of, violence within the home and community. Forty-seven per cent of Guyanese children knew someone who had been killed (UNICEF, 2000), 60 per cent of 9- to 17-year-old Jamaican children indicated that a family member had been a victim of violence, and 37 per cent had a family member who had been killed (Meeks Gardner et al., 2003). Soyibo and Lee (2000) found that in a sample of Jamaican youths, 78.5 per cent had witnessed violence in their communities, 60.8 per cent in their schools and 44.7 per cent in their homes. In addition, 29 per cent of these young people reported that they had injured someone else. Similarly, a recent PAHO/WHO survey of 15,695 adolescents aged 10-18 years in nine CARICOM countries (Antigua, The Bahamas, Barbados, British Virgin Islands, Dominica, Grenada, Guyana, Jamaica and St. Lucia) found that 20 per cent of the males surveyed had carried weapons to school in the previous 30 days. Ten per cent of the boys and five per cent of the girls reported that they had been knocked unconscious in a fight, with similar numbers reporting that they had been stabbed or shot. Forty per cent of youths reported thinking about hurting or killing someone else "sometimes" or "most of the time." Finally, 17 per cent of this group felt they would not live to the age of 25 (Halcón et al., 2003). In Jamaica, the major crimes against youths in the 15- to 24-year-old group are robbery, rape, shooting and murder (PIOJ, 2003). Moreover, youths are being arrested, jailed and murdered at twice the rate of the general population (MOEYC, 2002).

## Factors Contributing to Violence in the Caribbean

The global literature on violence provides no single explanation for its causes, which vary from one society to the next, and from one community to the next. In small societies like most of those in the Caribbean, the causes of violence tend to differ, based on community factors, socio-economic factors and class differences.

### SOCIAL FACTORS

#### Migration

Caribbean people have embraced emigration as a way to expand opportunities ever since the abolition of slavery. They emigrate in order to take advantage of available work (e.g. to assist with the construction of the Panama Canal), to seek a better life (e.g. the extensive emigration to Great Britain post-World War II), to escape unfavourable social situations (e.g. the extremely high violence and fear of socialism in Jamaica in the late 1970s or the major ongoing volcanic eruption in Montserrat during the 1990s) and to take advantage of new fortune (e.g. intra-regional migration to oil-rich Trinidad since the 1970s) (UNICEF, 2007). In many cases, only one member of the family migrates, resulting in a complex situation for the children left behind who are often raised by relatives or neighbours. Though remittances and gifts (often clothing, shoes and other items sent periodically in 'barrels') may result in some material benefits for the child, the loss of the primary caregiver is an undoubtedly traumatic event that can cause psychological damage, manifested through deviant 'acting out' or withdrawn depressive behaviours. In a study comparing delinquent and non-delinquent adolescent boys in Jamaica, Crawford-Brown (1993) found that maternal absence was significantly more common in the delinquent group, and that the biggest cause of maternal absence was migration. Pottinger (2005) reported that having a negative reaction to their parents' migration was directly related to inner-city children's poor school performance (especially in mathematics), reduced feelings of popularity among their peers, and psychological difficulties, including depressive symptoms and suicidal ideation. Many children in her study had not been prepared for the migration, had no-one to talk to about it, and reported somatic complaints, and feelings of anger and loneliness. It is argued that these children may wait in vain for the return of their parent and become angry when this does not happen. Furthermore, when the caregiving system that was put in place breaks down, these children may be left unprotected and unsupervised. This leaves the children vulnerable to harmful consequences such as physical, emotional and sexual abuse; child prostitution; and adolescent drug use (Crawford-Brown & Rattray, 2001; Morrison, 1993; Leo-Rhynie, 1993). Of course, migration is not the only cause of separation and loss for children, for example, absent fathers are common in the Caribbean, and these findings are not unique to this group.

## Education

The quality of education provided to Caribbean children varies immensely. Excellent facilities and teachers are available in some countries, especially within certain private schools. For others, the facilities are completely inadequate, and teachers are few and often have not had adequate training. This is particularly true for the youngest children in the poorer countries (UNICEF, 2007). Poor quality education leads to reduced potential for employment or opportunities for self-improvement through further education. Youth who drop out of school or leave without an adequate education are more likely see their options as few, and to be drawn into a life of crime and violence (Smith, 2000; Brodie-Walker & Morgan, 2007). It is important to highlight the fact that Caribbean teachers lack training or access to options for dealing with students with behavioural problems. When students present with disruptive behaviour in the classroom, they are often sent outside, which simply reinforces the negative behaviour. The efforts from the educational system to meet the specialized needs of these students are severely limited. This situation creates an atmosphere where those most at risk move further away from the formal learning environment. Only a few schools have their own initiatives for dealing with inappropriate behaviour among students, for instance, having consultations with parents, while leaving suspension and expulsion as a last resort (UNICEF, 2007).

## Economic Issues

The struggling state of the economies of many Caribbean countries is also implicated in the levels of violence. For example, in Jamaica the period since the late 1970s has been described as one of 'economic pressure driving the violence' (Austin & Richards, 1989; Levy & Chevannes, 1996; Moser & Holland, 1997). Others have argued that the problem is not poverty per se as there are many poor countries without this problem. Instead, it is suggested that the obvious inequality and close proximity of both high-income earners and the very poor that are to blame (Headly, 1994; Robotham, 1984).

### Marginalization of Males

Another social phenomenon which may be influencing the levels of violence regionally is the so-called 'marginalization' of males and the rise of women in academia and business. As mentioned before, the abolition of slavery created confrontation with other aspects of colonial rule – the vigorous application of Christianity and a push to wage labourer status, which was rejected by young males, but more willingly embraced by females who put their efforts into education and creative ways of earning a living (e.g. 'higglering' – the term for informal vending in Jamaica). It has been suggested that shifting gender roles have affected the traditional patterns of authority within the homes, with the result of increased domestic violence attributed to men's 're-asserting authority' (Chevannes, 2001; Miller, 1997).

### Foreign Penetration

Foreign penetration into the Caribbean way of life through the media and through tourism, disrupts traditional mechanisms of social control. Tourism is a constant reminder of the disparities of wealth and a motivation for crime. Tourists are often the targets of burglaries and opportunistic crime carrying minimal risk for the perpetrator, as the victims will soon leave the country (King, 1997).

### Policy, Justice and Police Issues

In many Caribbean countries the police are seen as contributing to, rather than preventing, crime in the communities, and are criticized for having an apathetic approach to crime fighting, poor detective and crime scene investigatory skills, slow response time, and for being corrupt or involved in the drug trade themselves. Stories of so-called police abuse abound (e.g. Mars, 2004). There is, therefore, a prevalent mistrust of law enforcement agencies in many communities. There are also issues related to the legal system, such as the subjectivity of judgments and sentencing (Gayfoor, 1989), slowness of the system, and the very small likelihood of conviction. Intimidation of witnesses, lawyers, and judges is common. Furthermore, there is the absence of laws to fight some crimes (e.g. Menon, 1983; Parsad, 1992).

## Drugs

For several decades the Caribbean has been used as a trans-shipment point for illegal narcotic drugs. There is widespread acknowledgement that the increase in drug-trafficking in the Caribbean region has brought associated violent crimes (De Albuquerque & McElroy, 1999; O'Connor, 1992; UNODC & WB, 2007). Most of the drugs flow from production areas in South and Central America to the ready markets of North America and Western Europe – joining the already established conduits for transmitting ganja (marijuana) from Jamaica and other islands, where it had been grown and exported to North America and England. The drug trade is said to be conducted through both cash transactions and through exchanges for weapons. As a result, dealers have extensive disposable income which is used not only for personal aggrandizement, but also for community benefits which serve to cement community loyalty to the dealers. The exchange of weapons for drugs allows the dealers to become well armed, arms which they use to defend their 'turf' or respective areas of control, and to commit acts of intimidation and murder, which further cement their control. The secondary trade in weapons further contributes to the resulting violence (UNICEF, 2007). The link between addiction and violent crimes, and results of a rehabilitation programme in the Bahamas are described in Allen (1990).

## Deportees

Changes in US immigration policy have provided Caribbean governments with a deluge of Caribbean criminals, since the 1990s, deported after completing their sentences (Griffin, 2002). Upon their return to their countries, deportees use their big city skills to run gangs, or live quietly as consultants, using overseas contacts to facilitate the exporting of cocaine or instructing eager students in credit card fraud (_Economist_, 2004). Deportation is not likely to stop. It is also too easy for hardened criminals to stay in the Caribbean and fight extradition. Smart traffickers with expensive lawyers face understaffed state prosecutors and inadequate judicial systems and argue they cannot get a fair trial in the USA (Economist, 2004; UNOCP & WB, 2007). Others have argued, however, that deportees are not responsible for increased crime rates since the great majority was deported for only minor infractions (*see* Headly, 2006).

# Development of Violent Behaviour in Caribbean Individuals

## INDIVIDUAL FACTORS

The historical, economic and broader social contributors to the development of violence in the Caribbean have been discussed earlier in this chapter. The following section focuses on violence at the level of the individual (for background, *please see* Headley, 1994; Harriot, Brathwaite, & Wortley, 2004; UNICEF, 2007).

There has been extensive investigation into the development of aggression and violent behaviour, primarily from industrialized countries including the USA, Canada and those of Western Europe (e.g. Cairns & Cairns, 1984; Nagin & Tremblay, 2001; Olweus, 1979; Paternoster & Brame, 1997; Patterson, Reid, & Eddy, 2002; Tremblay, 2006), though numerous questions still remain (Tremblay, 2006). One issue is the definition of 'aggression' (we will use it here to refer to physical aggressiveness), and another is the lack of data describing the development of aggression from infancy. There are only few cross-cultural studies. However, it is acknowledged that aggressive behaviour in childhood may be a predictor of later violence (Loeber & Hale, 1997; Hill, Howell, Hawkins & Battin-Pearson, 1999) so efforts to contain and reduce violence must, in part, focus on developmental stages. There is also general agreement that aggression and violence are products of a complex interplay of biological, psychological and social factors. Genetic and other biological factors are most likely to be similar across cultures, but social factors, including their effect on psychological well-being, may be less robust. Some research has described factors associated with aggression in Caribbean youth, and there are studies describing many of the factors which have been associated with aggression and violence both in the Caribbean and elsewhere (Meeks Gardner, Powell & Grantham-McGregor, 2007; UNICEF, 2007; UNOCP & WB, 2007).

Identifying associated factors is helpful in order to identify those at highest risk so as to target interventions, and to also design interventions which might reduce the risk factors. A number of studies have examined risk factors associated with childhood aggression and juvenile delinquency. The data from the PAHO/WHO Caribbean nine-country study mentioned earlier showed that the major risk factors for youth involvement in violence were physical and sexual abuse, skipping school, and rage (Blum & Ireland, 2004). In a case-control study of aggressive and prosocial 10-13 year old boys in Kingston, Jamaica (Meeks Gardner, Powell, & Grantham-McGregor, 2000; 2007) the aggressive boys came from poorer homes with more marijuana use, less parental affection or supervision, and more family discord. They were less exposed to religious instruction, their parents had lower occupational levels and were more likely to be in common-law unions than married. They were more exposed to neighbourhood violence and were punished more often at home and at school. Statistical analyses to determine the independent risk factors for aggression showed that exposure to neighbourhood violence, physical punishment at home, and family discord were associated with increased risk. Parents being married, practising religion as a family, and having less tattered school uniforms were associated with reduced risk. Another Jamaican study found that conduct disorder in adolescence was associated with absent mothers, the presence of a negative role model and multiple changes of primary caregivers (Crawford-Brown, 1997). The link between a number of these risk factors in the international literature (as reviewed by Hawkins et al, 1998), and the studies describing the situation in the Caribbean, including findings from these studies are summarized below.

## Biological and Psychological Factors

A number of biological factors have been shown to be related to aggressive and violent behaviour. These include anatomical and physiologic differences in the brain (Strueber, Lueck, & Roth, 2006), complications of pregnancy and delivery, and a low resting heart rate (Hawkins et el., 1998). Although no Caribbean studies of these specific associations were found, biological associations are likely to be robust across cultures.

Psychological factors related to aggression include hyperactivity, attention deficit, impulsivity and risk-taking. The Jamaican case-control study did not formally measure these, but a rating suggestive of hyper-activity differentiated between aggressive and prosocial boys (Meeks Gardner et al., 2000; 2007). Another study of Jamaican college students found that those with ADHD (attention deficit-hyperactivity disorder) reported more physical aggression, anger and hostility (Minor, Lipps, Shetty et al., 2004) consistent with findings elsewhere.

**Family Factors**

There is agreement that family-related variables are important determinants of aggressive behaviour (Hawkins et al., 1998), although the exact relationships – whether direct or indirect, additive or interactive, and the impact of these variables within larger social contexts – are less clear. Family-related factors identified through extensive review of the literature include parental criminality (not reported from the Caribbean), child abuse and neglect, parent-child relationships, family conflict, and early separation from parents. The Crawford-Brown study (1993) confirms the importance of neglect as a risk factor for conduct disorder (which includes aggression), while the Jamaican case-control study, mentioned above, identifies a range of family factors which were associated with aggression. These included sub-optimal parent-child relationships as shown by little affection and supervision by parents, and what were likely markers for parental attention (school uniform quality, praying, and going to church as a family). In addition, family conflict was a strong predictor of boys' aggression (Meeks-Gardner et al., 2000; 2007).

Crawford-Brown (1993) looked at family factors, peer group factors and biological factors associated with conduct disordered behaviour in 70 Jamaican males aged 12-17 years, and found that family factors were the most important factors associated with such behaviour. These family factors included absence of the mother (because of death or migration) and/or little contact with father. The degree of contact with conduct-disordered peers was also related to Conduct Disorder. Similarly, an earlier study of Jamaican children with emotional and behavioural problems found that 73 per cent of the children studied were not living with parents (Crawford-Brown, 1986).

Corporal punishment (physical punishments including beatings and being made to stand in uncomfortable positions) at home are a special case in the Caribbean where there is widespread support for this form of discipline (see below). This has been identified as probably the greatest source of child abuse in the Caribbean, and was strongly related to aggressive behaviour in the Jamaican case-control study. (It should be noted that this was a cross-sectional study, so it is not possible to assign causation.)

## School Factors

According to the international literature, school factors related to the development of aggression include academic failure, truancy and drop-out, and multiple transitions. The nine-country PAHO/WHO Caribbean study confirmed truancy as a risk factor here (Blum & Ireland, 2004). The Jamaican case-control study also showed poorer school achievement among the more aggressive boys in all areas tested: math, spelling and reading. A follow-up of the same sample of boys six years later confirmed that the aggressive boys were twice as likely to have dropped out of school (Meeks-Gardner et al., 2007).

The school environment itself has also been shown to influence aggressive behaviour, and there is evidence that modifications of the school environment can reduce aggressive behaviour (e.g. Poole, Ushkow, Nader et al., 1991). Schools where teachers praise children, act as good role models, and with smaller class sizes have beneficial effects, while those with frequent disciplinary interventions, including corporal punishment, are associated with worse behaviour in children. A study of 30 primary-level schools including principals, teachers and students, and classroom and playground observations, found that the level of community violence around the school and children's exposure to violence, as well as the use of corporal punishment, less homework and fewer rewards, were related to greater aggression (Meeks Gardner, et al., 2000).

## Peer-related Factors

The major peer-related influences on violent behaviour have been the presence of delinquent siblings and peers, and participation in gang activities. Recent investigations into child and youth participation in gang activities in Jamaica suggest that this is also the case there, but these connections have not been thoroughly investigated in the Caribbean (see below).

### Community and Neighbourhood Factors

Poverty, community 'disorganization', including levels of crime and exposure to violence, drug selling, gang activity, and poor housing describe the most important community and neighbourhood factors that have been related to aggressive and violent behaviour. The level of exposure to violence is especially high in Jamaica (Samms-Vaughan et al., 2005; Meeks Gardner, Powell, Thomas & Millard, 2003). Exposure includes having seen victims of homicide, knowing someone who has been murdered, and having family members murdered. This was an independent predictor of aggression in the Jamaican case-control study. In a study by Brodie-Walker and Morgan (2007) assessing six psychosocial factors that impact on juvenile delinquency (family relationships, exposure to violence, employment, education, self-esteem and frustration), only exposure to violence was found to differentiate delinquents from non-delinquents. The association between aggression on the one hand, and gang and drug selling activities on the other, has not been reported from the Caribbean.

Another form of exposure to violence is through the media (discussed later), especially violent television, music and video games (e.g. Ostrov, Gentile & Crick, 2006). The wide penetration of American cable television to much of the Caribbean has made this particularly worrying. An analysis of television viewing among the boys in the Jamaican case-control study found that those boys exposed to television violence were three times as likely to belong to the aggressive group (Campbell, 2006).

# Types of Violence

The World Health Organization (WHO) has defined violence as: "The intentional use of physical force or power, threatened or actual, against oneself, another person or against a group or community that either results in or has a high likelihood of resulting in injury, death, psychological harm, mal-development or deprivation" (Dahlberg & Krug, 2002, p. 5). Similarly, according to the American Psychological Association (2000) violence refers to "immediate or chronic situations that result in injury to the psychological, social, or physical well-being of individuals or groups" (APA, 1993, p. 1). Violence occurs between people who are related (domestic violence), as well as between people who do not know each other well or not at all (community violence).

## COMMUNITY VIOLENCE

Community violence includes intentional or volitional acts of crime or violence that occur between humans (Raia, 1999). It is also violence that occurs between individuals who are unrelated, and who may or may not know each other, generally taking place outside the home (Dahlberg & Krug, 2002). However, community violence may spill over into the home when unrelated persons attack someone within their own home. Community violence includes frequent and continual exposure to bullying; physical fights; the use of guns, knives, and drugs; youth violence; random violence; and rape or sexual assault by strangers, occurring in public, or in institutions, including schools (Buka et al., 2001; Mercy, Butchart, Farrington & Cerdá, 2002; Osofsky, 1995). A Ministry of Health study conducted in Jamaica by Dr. Elizabeth Ward (2001) found that 57 per cent of the sample of 1,419 persons treated at the Kingston Public Hospital had experienced personal injuries through violence in their communities, that it, in the street or public areas.

Meeks Gardner, Powell, Thomas and Millard (2003), conducted a study to examine the perception and experience of violence among 1,710 Jamaican adolescents in 11 randomly selected secondary schools. The mean age of the group was 13.2 years. They found that 84 per cent of the sample carried a weapon to school, 89 per cent were worried about violence at school, 50 per cent had witnessed violence in their neighbourhood, and 34 per cent had been victims of violence. Students over 13 years of age were more likely to know more victims of violence than students under 13. Boys reported higher neighbourhood and school violence, and worried more about violence than girls did. The factor of lower income range also placed children at risk for aggression. In another study of a sample of 1,416 grade five Jamaican school children, Meeks Gardener, Powell and Graham-McGregor (2000) found that approximately 45 per cent of the students had seen fights involving an implement or had seen someone carrying a weapon to school. More than half of the participants had been involved in a fight during the term. The students also reported that they had heard (75%) or seen (50%) someone involved in violence within their communities. The study concluded that community violence and corporal punishment are related to aggressive behaviours, while rewards for school work were linked to lower aggression levels.

## Homicide

The most fear-inducing aspect of community violence is homicide. Homicide is the leading cause of death in the Caribbean today, and is particularly high among males. As mentioned earlier, homicide rates in the Caribbean are nearly three times as high as the world average – 30 per 100,000 compared to 10.7 per 100,000 (UNOCP & WB, 2007; WB, 2003). These high homicide rates reflect the high prevalence of crime and violence at the community level.

In the USA only about 4 per cent of all homicides are considered justifiable on the basis of self-defence or police action, so the vast majority are murder. In 40 per cent of cases, the murderer is a friend or acquaintance of the victim and in 15 per cent of cases, the murderer is a family member. Thirteen per cent of murders are committed by strangers, but in one in three cases the murderer has an unknown relationship to the victim (Rosenberg & Mercy, 1992). The tendency for murderer and victim to know each other suggests that many murders reflect a breakdown in nonviolent conflict resolution. In fact, in the USA, verbal disagreements are the most common circumstances leading to a homicide with almost 40 per cent of all murders starting that way. Approximately 20 per cent of homicides are committed during the commission of a felony, such as a robbery or drug-related offence. Brawls, gangs and prison killings account for another 20 per cent, while the circumstances of the remainder are unknown (Rosenberg & Mercy, 1992). Research to determine any similarities in the Caribbean is recommended.

## Violence against Children

The issue of child-related violence is also of major concern. According to the WHO 2002 World Report on Violence and Health, globally, an average of 565 children, adolescents and young adults between the ages of 10 and 29 years died as a result of interpersonal/community violence each day in 2000, (Dahlberg & Krug, 2002). According to the UNICEF (2007) regional assessment of violence against children, Caribbean children are frequently victims of severe violence. In Jamaica, the most extreme example, that is, the murder and shooting of children, increased in 2004, resulting in 119 children (under the age of 18 years) being killed, representing 8 per cent of all murders. Of these murders, 86 per cent involved boys. In the same year, 430 children were shot and injured, according to police reports.

The involvement of young people in crime and violence in the Caribbean region is also a serious problem. In Jamaica, 25 per cent of those arrested for major crimes – including armed robbery, assault, rape and murder – were male youths aged 13-19 (World Bank, 2003). According to the PAHO/WHO Caribbean nine-country study, 40.1 per cent of teenagers reported that they were sufficiently angry some or most of the time that they "could kill someone." Respondents who reported rage were much more likely than their peers to report involvement in violence, particularly if male (Halcón et al., 2003). Youths view violence as a useful tool for survival and social mobility, given their lack of faith in the efficacy of justice, law, and order. Marginalized youths are often recruited into crime by others in their community. Boys who drop out of school are easy targets for the criminal elements in their community, and involvement in a life of crime can provide them with the recognition and power that they have been deprived of at home and at school. De Albuquerque and McElroy (1999) describe "the emergence of a violent subculture of marginalized, unemployed youth" as one of the primary reasons for the serious crime wave affecting the Caribbean region.

Studies also report high rates of physical, sexual and emotional abuse (see below) and as children get older this abuse is more likely to take place in the community and at school rather than at home. Certain groups of children are at greater risk of continued victimization out in the community and these include children who have dropped out of school or who do not attend school regularly, street children and working children. In addition, children who attend school are not immune to being victims of abuse in a community setting. For example, in Jamaica, school children have reported experiencing physical, sexual and emotional abuse when using public transportation (UNICEF, 2007).

School violence also appears to be on the increase. The incidence of homicides, wounding, sexual and physical assault in schools has risen sharply over the last decade, commanding the attention of most Caribbean governments and their citizens (UNICEF, 2007). However, reporting of school-based violence is neither consistent nor standardized. In Jamaican schools, violence is manifested in the lower grades by aggressive behaviours such as kicking, hitting, spitting and name-calling and in the upper grades by bullying, extortion, physical fighting, use of weapons and gang activity (Flannery & Singer, 1999; Mercy et al., 2002). As mentioned above, a disturbing number of Caribbean school children have witnessed a physically violent act at some point in their lives, with a notable proportion occurring at school. As a result, many students no longer feel safe in their schools and some drop out, or attend irregularly. Children can also suffer emotional and psychological abuse at the hands of teachers and school administrators. Teachers are known to use corporal punishment, and are not immune to the use of verbal and psychological abuse, e.g. the use of harsh words, and even humiliation and intimidation (Samms-Vaughn et al., 2007). This can lead to the development of low self-esteem and self-efficacy and other behavioural problems, such as truancy.

One major concern is that the response to youth crime in the Caribbean is often punitive rather than rehabilitative. Holding youth trials in adult criminal courts, detaining children in adult correctional centres, and the long time period between arrest and sentencing, are some of the reported problems in the current systems (UNICEF, 2007). Holding children in adult jails often leads to their witnessing of more violence, and becoming the victims of physical, emotional and sexual abuse.

**Factors involved in Youth Violence**

The Jamaican Ministry of Health report mentioned above looked at victims of violent injury (Ward, 2001). The report suggested that there were specific characteristics associated with perpetrators, and found that males were more likely than females to present with violence-related injuries, and that those males in the age group 20-29 were the largest group of victims, while males in the age group 10-19 were the second largest group of victims. Other data from this Jamaican study suggested that when the circumstances of the injury were investigated, the majority of the injuries (75%) were due to involvement in a fight or argument. The majority of violent injuries (51%) occurred as a result of sharp objects, and the majority of violent incidents (57%) occurred in streets or public areas. The researcher also came to the conclusion that significant factors related to youth violence included academic underachievement, exposure to or interest in violence, as well as exposure to drugs, alcohol or suicidal thoughts. Factors mitigating against youth violence included church involvement and a warm and nurturing family environment.

## DOMESTIC VIOLENCE

The family is supposed to be a source of love, affection and security, but for many it is an environment of terror and barbarity (Rawlins, 2000). Domestic violence has been defined as "any act committed within the family by one of its members which seriously impairs the life, body, psychological well being or liberty of another family member" (Antony & Miller, 1986). Domestic violence would include an ongoing experience of physical, psychological, and/or sexual abuse in the home that is used to establish power and control over another person (Stiles, 2002). Domestic violence might take the form of serious verbal abuse, or psychological terrorization of the targeted individual. It might include kicking, pushing, shoving and choking (Seemungal, 1994). This abuse may also include clubbing, stabbing or shooting (WHO, 1998). The resulting burden on the heath and social service systems is enormous (Mansingh & Ramphal, 1993; McDonald, Duncan, Mitchell & Fletcher, 1999).

In 1998, Kingston's Woman's Crisis Centre, a non-profit organization that provides counselling for women who are victims of violent crimes, reported that domestic violence and domestic crisis were the most prevalent type of assaults they encountered in their treatment programme (UNDP, 1999). In Jamaica, nearly 30 per cent of homicides in 2002 were linked to domestic violence (PIOJ, 2003). Other studies have reported that 50 per cent of men reported having hit their partner and 30 per cent of adolescents worry about the fighting and violence they see in the home (Brown et al., 1993). In the British Virgin Islands and Barbados, 30 per cent of women reported having been physically abused (UNICEF, 2001).

Incidents of domestic violence, including physical assault, sexual assault, incest and child abuse, reported to the police have increased in the Caribbean over the past several years. Incidents of domestic violence in Anguilla increased from 37 in 1987 to 317 in 1993; in The Bahamas from 150 to 436, in Jamaica from 50 to 392 and in St Kitts/Nevis from 26 to 32. Between 1991 and 1993 there were 1,670 cases of domestic violence in Trinidad and Tobago, 156 in the Virgin Islands, 50 in Montserrat, and 18 in the Turks and Caicos. Child abuse cases increased from five to 15 in St Kitts/Nevis and in Dominica from 5 in 1995 to 252 in 1993 (Mondesire & Dunn, 1998). The trend continues (UNOCP & WB, 2007).

Rawlings (2000) studied 200 persons in two communities in Trinidad to determine attitudes toward, and experiences of, domestic violence via a questionnaire. Based on the participant's responses, 27 per cent had lived in homes where there was domestic abuse in their childhood, with 16 per cent reporting incidents occurring in adulthood. Of those injured enough to go to hospital, 40 per cent did not discuss the true nature of their injuries. For both physical and psychological abuse reported in childhood, 61 per cent said fathers were responsible, 32 per cent other males, and 7 per cent cited their mother. Eight per cent said it was they themselves who had been the victim (hitting, chopping, sexual abuse). In the adult cases, most victims were female and the main perpetrators were husbands, with many reporting substance abuse before the attack. Only 35% per cent reported the violence they had seen or experienced to the police, and in the majority of the cases the officer did nothing. The respondents believed that drugs, finances, and lack of communication were the reasons for the violence, but the great majority (95%) felt that domestic violence was never justified.

Historically, Caribbean countries have addressed domestic violence by utilizing existing assault and battery laws. With increasing levels of violence, some countries have passed domestic violence legislation in an attempt to make it easier to apply for protection orders and for the criminal justice system to prosecute offenders. Another reason for the legislation is to send the message that domestic violence is unacceptable to society and offenders will be punished (Joseph et al., 1998). Most of the English-speaking countries have passed domestic violence Acts, but notable exceptions include Montserrat, Antigua and Barbuda, and St. Kitts and Nevis. In the Acts that have been passed, both parties are covered, as well as a number of family members, including parents and children. All the Acts prohibit physical violence, some include persistent verbal abuse (e.g. Barbados), and some include willful destruction and seizure of property, as well as stalking (Joseph et al., 1998). Few contain prohibitions against sexual violence, in particular marital rape, which is usually covered by rape and sexual assault laws. The overall response to women is still negative, however, with few arrests made. The police view domestic violence as a personal problem, and the legal system is often hostile, indifferent, time-consuming, expensive and humiliating (Rodriquez, 1990; Luciano, Esim & Duvvury, 2005). Additionally, police may fail to arrest violators of protection orders.

Domestic violence is usually divided into three categories based on the victim of the abuse: child abuse, spouse (or partner) abuse and elder abuse.

### Spousal or Partner Abuse

Statistics show that women all over the world are being abused and killed by their intimate partners (United Nations, 1995; 1996). According to the WHO, 16-52 per cent of women suffer physical violence from their male partners (WHO, 1997). Domestic violence affects the lives of women regardless of race, ethnicity, class, educational status or geographic location. It is becoming widely recognized as a serious public health problem with grave implications for a woman's physical and psychological well-being (Ellsberg, Caldera, Herrera et al., 1999). There is no country in which this problem is absent (United Nations, 1995). In most countries, 17-50 per cent of women are assaulted at least once in their lives by an intimate partner (Ellsberg et al., 1999; United Nations, 1995). The WHO (1998) has observed that in most communities women appear to be at greatest risk from intimate male partners or from men they know.

Intimate violence against women is also quite common in the Caribbean. For example, in Jamaica, in one month alone there were 409 acts of violence committed against women, most by men with whom they were intimately involved. In 1994, 17 per cent of Jamaican women between the ages of 15 and 55 experienced physical violence perpetrated by a male (Haniff, 1995). A 1999 Trinidad study showed that 9 per cent of ante-natal women had experienced abuse in their most recent pregnancy (Patel, Lee Pow, Kawal et al., 1999). In the Caribbean, as is the case elsewhere, there is significant under-reporting, so that official figures are unlikely to represent the true magnitude of the problem. For example, in Dominica, only 14 per cent of women who admitted being victims of domestic violence had reported it to the police (Le Franc, 2002).

Though women do use force against men during arguments (Moore, 1996; Sukhu, 2000), battering is almost always done by men to women. Half the men who batter reportedly do so at least three times per year.

Women are more likely to be battered when they have higher education-al or occupational status than their partners or when the man is unem-ployed or consistently underemployed (Kaplan et al., 1993). In addition, men who beat their partners are also more likely to beat their children. A similar connection has also been made between wife abuse and physical or emotional abuse of children (Campbell, 1995). When women are abused other members of the family, including unborn children, are also at risk (Perks & Jameson, 1999). Spousal abuse rarely corrects itself and active prevention and treatment programmes are needed to reduce this form of violence.

The WHO (1998) report notes that as well as causing physical damage, gender-based violence can lead to psychological distress and trauma, with the resulting distress often lasting a lifetime. Abused women often turn to alcohol. Women who have been abused are often debilitated by anxiety about the next attack and may suffer post-traumatic stress disor-der (PTSD) (Koss, 1990). Abused women have increased rates of depres-sion, some turn to substance abuse (e.g. Andrews & Brown, 1988), while others see suicide as the only way out (Plichta, 1992). The medical pro-fession is starting to recognize the seriousness of violence against women. It brings with it the risk of unwanted pregnancy, STDs, and other serious health problems. The physical result of domestic violence also includes miscarriage, fractured skulls, chronic ailments, and even death (WHO, 1998).

Finally, children are often witnesses of domestic violence between their caregivers and this leads to a variety of outcomes. Some children identify with their mother and become depressed or fearful. Others wish to protect their mother and this leads to them staying by her side and being reluctant to play, go to school, stay over with a friend, or sleep. In some cases, they may try to intervene in order to prevent the violence and may themselves get injured. Some children identify with the aggressor and start to criticize or abuse their mother themselves, or verbally and physically abuse a young sibling (UNICEF, 2007). In the Caribbean, many children emerge out of violent experiences ready to respond with vio-lence (Bailey, Le Franc & Branche, 1999).

In 1991 Trinidad enacted one of the region's strongest laws to protect women from abuse. However, this law still requires a witness, and a man cannot be convicted of raping his wife unless they were legally separated at the time. Such laws have been criticized as simply ad hoc responses to the problem (Bissessar, 2000).

## Explaining Spousal Abuse

Spousal abuse is a multifaceted phenomenon which is related to: cultural norms that condone and hide violence against women; a lack of social and economic resources; the man's and the woman's personality characteristics; and role models during childhood (Della-Guistina, 2000). When women are the victims of attack, the perpetrator may be motivated directly by the desire to demonstrate his masculinity, to enforce his (male) power, and to control the woman (Rawlins, 2000). The general belief is that men should show control over women, so friends and family members will rarely intervene or interfere when a woman is abused publicly (Danns & Parsad, 1989). Cultural influences perpetuate the violence, including the belief that the victim provokes the attacks. Furthermore, anthropologists argue that domestic violence is rooted in the patriarchal family system, which rose alongside family property (Della-Guistina, 2000), and is socially determined. Prior to the development of patriarchy, strong communities were the norm and incidents of violence, including domestic violence, were minimal. When domestic violence did occur, community members intervened to stop any escalation. Women enjoyed equal, sometimes elevated status in these primitive communities. As communal living gave way, gender-based divisions in labour developed within the family, resulting in the intensification of gender equality, including domestic violence against women, and community members became less inclined to intervene. Later, during feudalism and early capitalism, a woman's status as chattel justified domestic violence against her (Della-Guistina, 2000).

Three models are often used to explain spousal abuse (Stark & Flitcraft, 1992). The _interpersonal violence model_ states that violence occurs when adults lack the skills to respond appropriately to stress and conflict. Lack of interpersonal skills, psychological problems, and specific personality profiles are believed to lead to domestic violence. Cognitive behavioural therapy for victims and skills-training programmes for batterers have been shown to be effective. The _family violence model_ emphasizes the effect of norms for using violence to resolve conflict, with violence seen as even more likely when a family member experienced violence in childhood. The clustering of spouse and child abuse in the same family supports the concept that this is a 'family' problem (Kaplan et al., 1993). However, most spousal abusers were not subjected to violence when they were children. This model does not lead to specific intervention strategies. The *gender-politics model* views family violence as one of the many examples of male domination in our society. When men perceive that their access to money, status or sex is threatened by a woman's actions, then violence is one type of response. This model is supported by evidence that arguments about women's traditional responsibilities at home are the most common topics of conflict that lead to abuse. This model leads to recommendations for punishment of male offenders, funding for women's shelters, and support for women's economic independence. However, the effectiveness of such approaches has not been documented (Kaplan et al., 1993).

## Child Abuse and Neglect

Violent behaviour in the family also includes the physical, sexual, and emotional or psychological abuse of children. Child abuse is an ancient and global problem. Reports from many cultures throughout history tell of infanticide, mutilations, abandonment and other forms of child abuse and neglect (Krug et al., 2002). Child abuse is thought to be deeply rooted in cultural and social practices, and its causes, as well as consequences, need to be examined in specific contexts in order to be understood and effectively tackled. In the USA, as recently as several decades ago, child abuse was rarely talked about and abusive parents were thought to be mentally ill. This attitude changed dramatically in the 60s and 70s when the approach shifted to helping parents become more effective caregivers (Kaplan et al., 1993). As a result, child abuse came to be seen within the context of other family disturbances. The definition of child abuse has shifted from a focus on physical injury to include child neglect, emotional injury, sexual maltreatment, and deprivation of medical care (Newberger, 1992). Child abuse and neglect are defined differently across cultures, as expectations regarding acceptable parental practices vary. For some experts, abuse or neglect must be the result of the actions or inactions of parents, while for others, child abuse includes violence against children in institutions such as schools. Here we will use the following WHO definitions (Krug et al., 2002):

- *Physical abuse*: acts that cause actual physical harm or have the potential for harm

- *Sexual abuse*: acts where a caregiver uses a child for sexual gratification

- *Emotional abuse*: acts that have an adverse effect on the emotional health and development of a child, including denigration, ridicule, threats and intimidation, discrimination, rejection, withholding affection, and other non-physical forms of hostile treatment

- *Child neglect*: the failure of a caregiver to provide for the development of a child (where the caregiver is in a position to do so) in one or more of the following areas: health, education, emotional development, nutrition, shelter and safe living conditions.

Physical abuse includes acts such as hitting, slapping, choking, or the forced ingestion of an unwanted substance. Sexual abuse is unwanted sexual intimacy forced on another person, including acts such as oral, anal, or vaginal stimulation or penetration, forced nudity or exposure to sexually explicit material or activity, or any other unwanted sexual activity (Volpe, 1996). Psychological abuse is the use of derogatory statements or threats of further abuse such as being killed. This may involve isolation, economic threats, and emotional abuse – the overt or covert direction of hostility to a child by repeatedly threatening, withholding affection, and belittling the child's capabilities, qualities and desires.

The available data on the extent of child abuse and neglect indicate that these problems are endemic and widespread in the Caribbean. Surveys of adults' and children's experiences generally reveal higher prevalence figures of child abuse, neglect and violence than official reports, suggesting that there is a high degree of under-reporting (Eldemire, 1986). Some of the suggested reasons for under-reporting are: the fear of reprisal; shame and the view that abuse is a private matter; the family's economic dependence on the perpetrator; the child's fear of the perpetrator; a lack of awareness of what constitutes abuse and neglect by parents and other adults including professionals (e.g. police, teachers, health workers); a lack of awareness of the consequences; the social and cultural sanctioning of child abuse; and a lack of or inefficient reporting procedures (UNICEF, 2007). "Violence within the home is hidden since culturally it may be seen as normal. Also because of allegiance to the home, children are compelled to remain silent about instances of abuse. Abused children are torn emotionally...loving and hating the abuser in the home..." (UNICEF 2007, p.16; Original Source: The Report on the Adolescent Forum/Caribbean Regional Consultation, for the UN Study on Violence Against Children, UNICEF, March 2005).

In the joint PAHO/WHO survey of 15,695 adolescents in nine CARI-COM countries, many of the young people surveyed reported a history of abuse in their lives (Halcón, 2003). Sixteen percent stated they had been physically abused, mostly by an adult in their home, and 10 per cent stated that they worried about being physically abused. Ten per cent reported sexual abuse, most frequently by adults outside of the home or other teens, but many reported abuse by adults in the home and by siblings. A small proportion (5%) reported a history of both physical and sexual abuse, and about 15 per cent reported a history of one or the other. A nearly equal rate of sexual abuse in boys and girls was found with many forced into first intercourse by age 11. This finding is unusual, as studies elsewhere typically report much lower rates of sexual abuse in males (e.g. Finkelhor, Hotaling & Lewis, 1990).

Reports from Jamaica and Guyana show that child abuse and neglect occur across all socio-economic groups and family structures (Cabral & Speek-Warney, 2004; UNICEF, 2000). Children from homes of low socio-economic status, children from inner-city areas and those who have a parent with mental health problems or drug/alcohol problems, appear to be the most vulnerable. In addition, those with disabilities (Payne, 1989; UNICEF 2000), orphans and children with absentee parents, younger children (birth to 12 years), and children from minority groups (e.g. Carib children from St. Vincent and the Grenadines and Dominica (Joseph, 2002), Amerindian children in Guyana (Danns, 2002) and Maroon children in Suriname (Terborg, 2002) have been reported to experience higher levels of abuse and neglect than children from the general population.

The type of abuse with the highest reported incidence differs by country. In Jamaica and Dominica, sexual abuse has the highest incidence, whereas in Grenada abandonment and neglect, and in Belize and Barbados, neglect had the highest reported incidence (UNICEF, 2007). In Dominica, risk factors for child abuse and neglect were identified as: the child not living with both parents; the loss of one or both parents (for example, through family separation or migration); not sharing social activities with parents; parental mental health problems and drug and alcohol abuse (Benjamin, Mahy, Harvey & Benjamin, 2001).

One recent development in the area of child abuse is the fact that in countries such as Jamaica and Trinidad and Tobago, there are a growing number of children who are involved in commercial sexual activities, especially in tourist areas. In these settings, the children are not only sexually exploited, but are often exposed to other forms of verbal and physical abuse, as well as sexually transmitted infections (UNICEF 2007).

In many developed countries there are laws requiring professionals (e.g. psychologists, doctors and social workers) and paraprofessionals (e.g. persons developing film, day care workers) to report suspected child abuse. This is not the case in most of the Caribbean. At the present time, only Jamaica has laws relating to the mandatory reporting of child abuse and neglect. Instituting such laws needs to be carefully considered by other countries in the region and the necessary resources need to be made available to ensure that children can be provided with appropriate and effective services to prevent further abuse and to mitigate against the serious consequences of child abuse. Another serious concern relating to sexual abuse against boys is that in some countries (e.g., Belize, Grenada and Guyana), sexual abuse is not recognized under the law if the victim is male (UNICEF, 2007).

## CHILD ABUSE – PHYSICAL

There are few data on the prevalence of physical abuse across the Caribbean. Rates of physical abuse, as reported by children themselves, do not differ significantly by gender (Cabral & Speek-Warnery, 2004; Payne, 1989), and parents generally support the use of corporal punishment for their sons and daughters. However, there is some anecdotal evidence that boys are more likely to be victims of more severe forms of physical abuse, and this is supported by data on hospital cases in Jamaica which reported treating more boys than girls for injuries due to physical abuse (National Child Month Committee Report, 1997). Reports from Guyana, Jamaica and Barbados indicate that the main perpetrators of physical abuse in the home are caregivers (Cabral & Speek-Warnery, 2004), particularly mothers (Rock, 2002). Physical abuse perpetrated by children, e.g. older siblings, is in the minority. Injuries to children seen by health professionals may be described as accidental.

Caribbean children may also experience physical violence in the home from a very young age as part of the process of being disciplined (Meeks Gardner et al., 2000; Smith & Mosby, 2003), and this can be especially brutal. Arnold (1982) examined the use of corporal punishment as a form of discipline in the West Indies. She concluded that an excessive amount of discipline may be the result of the legacy of slavery, which handed down physical punishment as a form of discipline. An alternative explanation that has been forwarded is the Freudian concept of displacement – shifting or redirecting anger or hostility from a threatening object to a less threatening one (Freud, 1965). It is often purported that harsh, stressful social and economic conditions create anger, frustration and hostility in low income parents – but this cannot explain the fact that extreme disciplinary practices are pervasive at all levels of society (Leo-Rhynie, 1997).

Corporal punishment is internationally considered to be child abuse (Global Initiative to End All Corporal Punishment, 2005), but there is widespread support for the use of corporal punishment by parents in the Caribbean (Krug et al., 2002; UNICEF, 1992), although severe forms of punishment leading to injury are generally not condoned (Payne, 1989, Samms-Vaughan et al., 2007). Similarly, surveys of children's views report that the majority of children themselves believe that physical punishment is a valid and necessary form of discipline (Cabral & Speek-Warnery, 2004).

The widespread support for and use of corporal punishment has been described as a result of the complex interplay of cultural and social norms, including the belief that children are born 'bad' or 'wicked' and need correcting; the belief that physical punishment is a necessary part of character development; the lack of awareness of non-violent disciplinary approaches; the importance placed on children being obedient and respectful to adults; the Biblical admonishment to 'spare the rod and spoil the child'; and the repeated assertion by adults that they were not harmed by, and even benefited from, the physical punishment they received as children (UNICEF, 2007). Physical punishment is meted out for many reasons including: disobedience, disrespect to parents or elders, stealing, lying, answering back, indecent language, fighting, poor school work, deliberate defiance, laziness and neglect of chores, disregarding the rules of the home or the community, playing in the house, crying too much, and not eating the meal provided. (Barrow, 1996; Payne, 1989). Gopaul-McNicol interviewed 50 child care workers in seven Caribbean countries. Participants were instructed to report on acceptable and unacceptable disciplinary practices in their culture. Few regional differences were noted in the responses of the various Caribbean islanders. Physical discipline was used as a means of 'training' as well as punishing (e.g. child was slapped for touching a valued object), and its use was seen as evidence of caring enough to take the time to train their children properly (Gopaul-McNicol, 1999).

While these harsh childrearing practices may not be seen as physical abuse by the people of the Caribbean, research suggests that its use is linked to deficits in psychosocial adjustment of children (Smith & Mosby, 2003). Harsh punishment is also linked to later violent behaviour in adolescents and adults (Dahlberg & Krug, 2002; Meeks Gardner et al., 2000; Smith & Mosby, 2003). More recent studies, conducted in a variety of settings and societies, have indicated that physical punishment, used even in moderation, has an adverse effect on psychosocial adjustment and behaviour. Exposure to physical punishment predicts impaired cognitive processes (low IQ and academic failure), socioemotional dysfunction, low empathy, hostile aggressive and oppositional tendencies, severe depression, conduct disorders in childhood and criminality in adulthood (Cicchetti & Toth, 1998; Evans & Davies, 1997; Frias-Armenta, 2002; Swinford, DeMaris, Cernkovich et al., 2000). Physical punishment inhibits children's development of internal controls, conformity to rules, and concern for the welfare of others. It also creates in children the propensity to misunderstand how power is appropriated and wielded, and teaches them to become beaters themselves (Smith & Mosby, 2003; Swinford et al., 2000).

In Jamaica, parenting style has been shown to negatively affect children's and adolescent's psychosocial outcomes, leading to serious concerns (_see_ Crawford-Brown, 1999; Leo-Rhynie, 1997). In this country, like many other Caribbean countries, discipline is often inconsistent and developmentally inappropriate, and includes public humiliation of adolescents. Jamaican schools validate the use of the severe punishment children receive at home, and reinforce a punitive, power-assertive, authoritarian approach to relationships and conflict resolution (Evans & Davis, 1997). Parents lack the know-how to establish trusting and cordial relationships with their children (Smith & Mosby, 2003). There is poor communication between parent and child, including an unwillingness to have extended conversations or to reason with children.

In one study, only Haiti, of the six countries (St. Lucia, Grenada, Guyana, Haiti, Belize, and Dominica) which submitted completed government questionnaires, had laws prohibiting the use of corporal punishment at home. However, the law in Haiti is not enforced and perpetrators are not prosecuted. Eliminating violence in Caribbean schools becomes particularly problematic when the issue of corporal punishment arises. Not only is the use of it written into law in many Caribbean nations, but it is also so engrained in Caribbean culture that in Trinidad and Tobago there have been calls from parents, teachers and even students for the Parliament to reinstate the recently-abolished corporal punishment in schools (Trinidad Guardian, 2006).

It is important to note that there is disagreement about the effects of physical punishment on children. While some researchers have noted a direct relationship between physical punishment and psychological maladjustment (Frias-Armenta, 2002; Swinford et al., 2000) as noted above, others have contended that the outcomes are culture-dependent (e.g. Barrow, 1996). Others posit a mediating role of the child's perception of the punishment as rejection by the caretaker (e.g. Rohner et al., 1991). One of the greatest challenges is identifying where along the continuum appropriate discipline becomes child abuse. Cultural differences substantially add to the existing complexity of defining maltreatment, neglect or abuse (Giovannoni & Becerra, 1979; Gopaul-McNicol 1999). However, it is important to note than when a culture views corporal punishment as an acceptable form of discipline then 'physical abuse' is more likely to occur (Gopaul-McNicol, 1999).

Several studies in the USA indicate that physical abuse is more common in poor homes, when the mother is young, and when the child is unwanted (Kaplan et al., 1993). Past approaches to child abuse focused on punishment of abusers, but a human service model is now more common. It is often unclear whether a child should be removed from the home after abuse has been detected. Important strengths of the family may not be readily apparent, and group and foster homes are often not ideal nurturing environments. On the other hand, the risk of leaving a child with an abusive family may be great. Child protective service workers are typically so overburdened that they do not have the time to do thorough assessments before deciding whether to remove the child or not. Interventions need to both protect the child and develop support for the family, so that the child can be safely returned to an improved family environment. Approaches involving a multidisciplinary team in the hospital, coordination with social service agencies, and systematic follow-up produce shorter hospitalizations, lower cost of treatment and lower re-injury rates (Newberger et al., 1973). The most promising method of preventing child abuse is by providing child care aides on a regular basis to high-risk families. These may be trained volunteers who visit weekly and provide various forms of assistance. They can answer questions about child care, demonstrate how to take care of the baby, provide transportation and simply be companions. Studies in the USA have shown a reduction of maltreatment rates by 75 per cent when child care aides are provided (Olds, Henderson, Chamberlin et al., 1986).

## CHILD ABUSE – SEXUAL

In the Caribbean, there are discrepancies in the legal terminologies used to describe sexual abuse among children. For example, in Jamaica where children younger than 16 years of age are involved, the term 'carnal abuse' is used, whereas in the case of children 16 to 18, the term 'rape' is used. This has serious implications, particularly as 'carnal abuse' is often treated as a lesser crime than 'rape'. The younger children are therefore offered less protection under the law than older children and adults (UNICEF, 2007).

In the USA, sexual abuse is equally likely in both rich and poor homes (Kaplan et al., 1993). The vast majority of sexual abuse victims are female, and the peak ages of risk are six to seven years and 10 to 12 years. Sexual abuse is more likely when there is discord among parents, when a parent is absent, and when parents are cold and punitive (Christoffel, 1990). Similarly in the Caribbean, in the overwhelming majority of reported cases of sexual abuse, the victims are girls. Although there is a general belief in the Caribbean community that girls in single parent households are most at risk and that the perpetrator is most often the stepfather or mother's boyfriend, the statistics do not always support this view. For example, Le Franc (2002) reported on a study by Wyatt which found that sexual abuse was most common in two-parent households. Overall, the data are conflicting; with some reports of non-relatives being the main perpetrators of sexual abuse, while others report that the most common perpetrators are the child's father or a relative of the father. The settings in which the abuse take place are not generally differentiated and it may be that the father or relative of the father is the most common perpetrator in the home, and a non-relative outside of the home. It is generally agreed that the perpetrators of sexual abuse are usually male and known to the victim.

A number of cultural and social beliefs continue to reinforce sexual abuse of children. Allowing young children to run around naked is often the norm. In Jamaica, some men believe that they have the right to a sexual liaison with a girl who is under their care and protection (Williams, 2002). The use of violence to gain sexual favours is also reportedly common among male adolescents of the Maroon people in Suriname (Terborg, 2002). Some girls believe that sexual harassment is 'normal' and is usually instigated by a women's choice of clothing and behaviour (Cabral & Speek-Warnery, 2004). The influence of alcohol abuse on the practice of incest is discussed by Mahy (1990).

Although there are few reported cases of boys being the victims of sexual abuse, this may be due to the fact that sexual abuse of boys is less likely to be reported than sexual abuse of girls. As mentioned above, in the PAHO/WHO study of school-going youth, there was only a marginal difference (9.1% versus 10.5%) in the percentage of boys and girls admitting to having been victims of sexual abuse (Halcón et al, 2003). In another study, sexual abuse of boys was reportedly most common at younger ages (age five to nine) than that of girls (Terborg, 2002). The former study also reported that of the third of adolescents who had had intercourse, almost half reported that their first sexual intercourse was forced. More than 50 per cent of sexually active boys and about 25 per cent of females stated that the age of first intercourse was 10 years of age or younger, and almost 67 per cent had intercourse before the age of 13 (Halcón et al., 2003). Early sexual intercourse (ESI) (at 10 to 12 years of age) was associated with rage, physical and sexual abuse (Blum et al., 2003), alcohol use, gang involvement, weapon-related violence, running away, and skipping school for both genders (Ohene et al., 2005). It is clear that ESI is not a normative behaviour among Caribbean youth – given the correlation between violence involvement and ESI, and this is a source of concern.

Anecdotal reports suggest that one of the consequences of sexual abuse is that the children (and sometimes the mother) are forced to leave the home or community where they live and experience severe disruption of their lives. In contrast, the perpetrator often remains unpunished and without any rehabilitative services, leaving a strong likelihood that he or she will sexually abuse another young child in the future. A review from Trinidad also suggests that in the long term there may be manifestations of violent behaviour in some sexually abused children (Oates, 1990).

As mentioned earlier, the failure to report sexual abuse is most likely due to the acceptance of the relationship by other household members, due to financial dependence on the perpetrator. Prosecution of offenders is also difficult. For example, in Guyana, children need to be able to give credible evidence and the defence lawyers are often so intimidating that the child becomes upset and confused, and the evidence is declared not credible (UNICEF, 2007). Educational programmes to prevent child abuse have become common in recent years, particularly in North America, most of them teaching children how to recognize and protect themselves from sexual abuse (e.g. Wurtele, 1990). Caribbean versions of these programmes need to be implemented as soon as possible.

## CHILD ABUSE – PSYCHOLOGICAL

There is much less information on the prevalence of psychological abuse in the Caribbean than on physical and sexual abuse. However, verbal aggression and threatening children with physical punishment and/or abuse are common. In Belize, as many as 80 per cent of the school-aged children taking part in a study reported being unloved by their mother while they were growing up (Rosberg, 2005) In Jamaica, 97 per cent of the 11 to 12-year-olds interviewed reported verbal aggression from an adult at home (Samms-Vaughan et al., 2007). Parents appear to be the most common perpetrators of psychological/emotional abuse in the home, especially mothers (UNICEF, 1999-2000; Cabral & Speek-Warnery, 2004) and there are some reports of boys being more vulnerable to psychological abuse than girls (GoPaul-McNicol, 1999). In most studies, emotional abuse consisted of a lack of public display of affection, verbal abuse and a lack of tactile communication. Many authors have concluded that Caribbean families do not show affection to their children, at least not in traditional ways – but rather by sacrificing their own needs, educating the children despite few resources, and calling them by nicknames.

## CHILD NEGLECT

Very little attention is given to child neglect in the Caribbean literature, despite this having the highest prevalence rate among forms of abuse or neglect in countries such as Belize, Barbados, and Grenada (UNICEF, 2007). The most common perpetrators of neglect appear to be parents (National Child Month Committee, 1997), especially mothers (Rock, 2002) and, as with psychological and/or emotional abuse, there are some reports of boys being more vulnerable to neglect than girls.

### Consequences of Child Abuse and Neglect

The international literature describes extensive negative sequelae to child abuse, including both short-term and long-term psychological damage. Psychiatric symptoms may include depression, anxiety, substance abuse, aggression or cognitive impairments, sleep disorders, and post-traumatic stress disorder. Manifestations may be sub-clinical, and later become overt. Physical abuse can lead to injury of every organ system, depending on the form of abuse. Common examples include scalding, burns, poisoning, cuts, bruises on the skin and internal organs, brain damage and malnutrition. Psychological outcomes include aggression, language disorders, decreased intellectual functioning, phobias, nightmares, changes in eating and sleeping patterns, abdominal pain and headaches. Psychological symptoms appear to be more severe when force is used in sexual acts (Newberger, 1992). Additionally, it has been argued that females who have been sexually abused as young girls may be especially damaged, and some are never able to make a full recovery (Browne & Finkelhor, 1998). Physical health may also be impaired. Child abuse has been associated with major forms of adult illnesses (including ischaemic heart disease, cancer, chronic lung disease, irritable bowel syndrome and fibromyalgia). Apparently, early child abuse may lead to the adoption of behavioural risk factors such as smoking, alcohol or drug abuse, poor diet and lack of exercise.

There is some evidence from the Caribbean that child abuse and neglect is associated with not attending/ dropping out of school, being put into institutional care, living on the street and child labour (Cabral &

Speek-Warnery, 2004) and involvement in violence in adolescence (Meeks Gardner, Powell & Grantham-McGregor, 2000). Furthermore, in the PAHO/WHO study, 9 per cent of young people who did not indicate sexual abuse had attempted suicide, whereas 23 per cent who had experienced sexual abuse reported having done so. There are similar findings for physical abuse (Blum et al., 2003) and both physical and sexual abuse were associated with depression and rage. Longitudinal studies would be useful to confirm the associations between child abuse and neglect and adult functioning in the Caribbean.

Financial costs at the level of the individual or society also result from child abuse, for example, treatment costs for the resulting psychiatric and physical problems; the costs of investigating, apprehending and prosecuting perpetrators; as well as costs to the employment sector resulting from absenteeism and low productivity (Krug et al., 2002).

**Prevention of Child Abuse and Neglect**

Although prevention of child abuse is widely considered to be vitally important, most efforts are aimed at mitigating the effects on victims, rather than on primary prevention. Programmes may be aimed at family support, such as parent training or home visiting; at health services – including screening by health care professionals; approaches at the legal or national policy level, such as mandatory reporting, child protection services, and the implementation of various policies; community-based or in-school education programmes; or at the level of international agreements and treaties, such as the Convention on the Rights of the Child, which has been ratified by all Caribbean countries (e.g. Bishop, 1990). Therapeutic approaches for child victims of abuse, for children who have witnessed violence or for adults abused as children are also important. These need to be appropriate for the victim, with age, developmental level and other factors taken into consideration. Except for a single report of case studies with positive treatment findings from young victims of child abuse (Hamel-Smith, 1990), there were no other reports of interventions put in place to reduce the widespread problems of physical and sexual abuse.

**Elder Abuse**

This is a relatively new topic on the public agenda. In the Caribbean, as elsewhere, more and more people are living longer lives, and the mal-treatment of the elderly has become a more important issue. Elder abuse typically arises as a result of a decline in physical or cognitive function-ing, or both, which makes many elderly persons dependent on others to meet some of their basic needs. Elder abuse can occur in a variety of ways: physical violence, psychological or emotional abuse, misuse or theft of the elder's property or finances. Finally, intentional failure of a designated caregiver to meet the needs of an elder is also considered mal-treatment (Kaplan et al., 1993). Elder abuse is a serious problem, and many elders have few resources with which to defend themselves. Elder abuse has been related to caregiver stress and also to the possibility that the caregiver may be dependent on the elder (e.g. financially or for a place to live), and unhappy with his or her own powerlessness. Public recognition of elder abuse is limited in the Caribbean, and few studies mention elder abuse or abuse of persons with handicaps (e.g. Creque, 1995). As such, both lay people and health professionals need to increase their awareness of this problem. Finally, the facilities in the region that provide care for the elderly are often woefully inadequate.

## Special Topics

### VIOLENCE AGAINST HOMOSEXUALS

The Caribbean is known for its high level of homophobia, and anti-gay violence is a common occurrence, for example, Jamaica's best known gay rights activist, Brian Williamson, was found brutally murdered in 2004 (Advocate, 2004). He had helped to found the Jamaica Forum for Lesbians, All-Sexuals and Gays (J-Flag) in 1998 in a failed attempt to pres-sure the government to overturn Jamaica's 140-year-old sodomy law, which cites 'buggery' (anal sex) as a punishable offence. The group cur-rently provides counselling to gays. In spite of the strong anti-gay senti-ment, the people of the Caribbean show rates of homosexuality compa-rable to those in more developed countries. In the PAHO/WHO study, approximately equal percentages of males (9.8%) and females (9.5%) reported a history of same gender sexual experience and attraction. Reasons for the deep negative reaction to homosexuality in the region include a lack of education regarding the causes of homosexuality and of HIV/AIDS, strong religious and cultural influences, and spreading of anti-gay views through gay bashing in popular music. So inciting of hatred are the lyrics, that Caribbean musicians have been refused permission to play at several events abroad (e.g. Beenie Man, Sizzla and Buju Banton in the UK). The level of ignorance and fear is so high that great lengths are taken to reduce the exposure of Caribbean people to homosexuality. Recently, the island of Tobago considered refusing to allow Elton John, an openly gay singer and musician, to play at a jazz festival as religious ministers there were afraid that his presence may tempt young people to pursue his lifestyle and he might "turn the youth gay". Finally, many islands refuse to allow gay cruise ships access to their ports. The fact that the same anti-gay sentiment is not expressed for lesbians, who are much less likely to become victims of violence, and who do not receive the same negative treatment in popular music, suggests that Caribbean society may have a strong underlying fear of emasculation.

## SUICIDE

In general, suicide rates in the Caribbean are low. In the USA, suicide rates are 19.8 per 100,000 for males and 4.4 per 100,000 for females. In Jamaica, by comparison, the rates are 0.5 per 100,000 for males and 0.2 per 100,000 for females. Suicide appears to be of increasing concern in some islands of the Caribbean, however, with a 319 per cent increase in the male suicide rate in Trinidad and Tobago between 1978 and 1992 (up to 20.76 per 100,000) (Hutchinson & Simeon, 1997). Fred Hickling, a Professor of Psychiatry at UWI, Mona, has argued that the low suicide rate in the Caribbean may be the result of a general tendency among persons in the region to express their anger outwardly (in the form of violence towards others) rather than inwardly (resulting in suicide).

According to the PAHO/WHO study, one in nine (about 12%) of Caribbean youth had attempted suicide, and many reported that they had a friend or relative who had tried to kill him or herself. Among the risk factors associated with ever having attempted suicide was a history of a friend's or family member's suicide (the strongest predictor), followed by rage, then a history of physical abuse, sexual abuse, or both. Girls were consistently more likely to have attempted suicide but not significantly so. Conversely, parental connectedness was strongly protective against suicide attempts in all age groups. No other factors were found to be protective (Blum et al., 2003).

## CHILD AND YOUTH INVOLVEMENT IN GANG VIOLENCE

In trying to understand youth gang involvement in the Caribbean, it is important to be clear about the meaning of the term 'gang' which continues to be difficult to define. There is little written about youth gangs in the Caribbean. However, there is a great deal known about the criminal gangs, especially out of Jamaica where the 'posses' and 'yardies' became infamous for their involvement in the drug trade in North America and Britain in the 1980s (Behrns & Dang, 2006). These were (and continue to be) highly organized, extremely violent groups with transnational connections, dealing in drugs and arms, and also in legitimate businesses, in many cases. The confusion arises because most gang members fall in the age group of 'youth' (approximately 15 to 24 years, for the purpose of this discussion). The leaders, or 'dons', however, tend to be older, experienced male adults. These gangs often lack the typical characteristics of youth gangs described elsewhere. For example, members of Jamaican gangs are not more likely to use drugs or alcohol, there is very little female membership in gangs, and there is little use of identifying signs, symbols, clothing etc. However, data from Trinidad and Tobago suggest that youth gangs there may be more similar to North American/Western European gangs. Typically, youth gangs form when peers join together (for friendship, protection, a sense of belonging), and together commit illegal acts which may be violent, including assault, theft, robbery and murder. There has been disagreement as to the relative weight of individual, family, cultural and other factors in understanding gang participation and violence (Hagedorn, 1998). Recent work being undertaken in the Caribbean among groups ranging from young school children, through to organized crime groups will address these issues in the Caribbean context. According to the PAHO/WHO study, 13 per cent of females and 22 per cent of Caribbean males have at some time ever belonged in a gang, up from 10 per cent in 1998 (McCree, 1998), however, the inclusion of membership in benign 'gangs' is possible. In 2004 Jamaican police counted 85 criminal gangs, up from 35 in 1994 (*Economist*, 2004).

In a study of gangs in the Trinidad community of Laventille, Cain (1995) found that 84 per cent of participants had no knowledge of gangs in the community. A greater proportion of youth (aged 15-24 years) were aware of gang activity, with many knowing of more than four gangs. Slightly more young females were aware of gang activity, but this does not mean they were in a gang, as traditionally, crime and gang membership tend to be male-dominated (Cain, 1995). Indirect involvement includes offering alibis, refuge from the law or helping to manage, protect or consume the loot. Gang members may be serving their material needs or those of their children. The Laventville gangs were variously involved in four major activities: robbery-muggings, drug trafficking, assault and the making of guns. When participants in the study were asked to state who wielded the most power, 33 per cent cited drug lords and criminals, 26 per cent cited the opposition political party, and 22 per cent cited politicians generally.

In the USA, community-gang relations may be of three main types: (1) antagonistic/hostile/non supportive; (2) apathetic (community ignores gang); and (3) mutual cooperation/supportive. The groups may provide mutual benefits for each other and on this basis, develop a working relationship or social contract (Jankowski, 1991). Benefits for the community include the provision of protection from intruders/criminal elements and unscrupulous businessmen. Gangs may actually regulate or determine who may or may not live and work in the community. In turn, the community benefits the gang by (a) offering protection or a place of refuge from the police, (b) providing information on possible police action and their rival gangs, and (c) serving as a source of recruitment for new gang members. Gangs also receive the support or sympathy of many community members because they identify with the community member's struggles to resist their poor socioeconomic position. Failure of either party to live up to the 'contract' can result in the termination of the relationship, which will be more detrimental to the gang, as it seriously weakens its ability to work effectively (McCree, 1998). In light of their social function, eradication or controlling of gangs is extremely difficult, if not impossible. The solution will likely depend on ameliorating the social conditions out of which gangs have developed. Some have argued that gangs may even be reducing criminal activity – given the benefactor's role they play. In fact, in Jamaica there is evidence of the existence of a 'protection racket' similar to that of early to mid 20th century Mafia in the USA.

In 2004, big drug gangs were successfully 'cracked' in Jamaica, The Bahamas and Guyana (_Economist_, 2004). The Bahamas, where five gangs have been broken since 2001, is one of the few Caribbean countries where the murder rate has fallen. Many counties have anti-gang initiatives vetted by inter-agency teams with on-board lawyers and international support such as Operation Kingfish in Jamaica (*Economist*, 2004). Charging gang leaders with crimes will hopefully follow but the picture may not be so simple. The increase in the homicide rate in Jamaica in 2005, for example, has been blamed on successful action against known gang leaders which, thus resulting in turf wars, as rising leaders battled for a piece of the pie.

## VIOLENCE IN MUSIC AND MEDIA AND VIDEOGAMES

Persons are also exposed to violence in music, books, videogames, and through media. The influence of the media in increasing violence is widely discussed in the literature from developed countries (e.g. Villani, 2001). A leading behavioural-psychological theory for this effect is the General Affective Aggression Model, which proposes that repeated exposure to violence on television and videogames causes changes in aggressive beliefs, aggressive perceptual schemas, aggressive expectations, aggressive behaviour scripts and desensitization that interacts with the individuals personality and the situation to cause aggressive behaviour (*see* Anderson & Bushman, 2001).

A Jamaican study found a very high level of exposure to violence in print, TV and on the radio and the authors expressed the belief that the violence is portrayed as 'normal' and 'acceptable' (Women's Media Watch, 2000). Some of the violence was perpetrated by local celebrities and this is likely to encourage the involvement of youth in crime. Perpetrators were portrayed as being rewarded for violence almost twice as often as they were punished, and an alternative to violence was seldom portrayed. Another Jamaican survey suggested that media workers concur with the public that violence is depicted too frequently in the media (Robinson, 2003).

In the USA, studies have shown that media violence exposure is related to poorer executive functioning based on neuropsychological evaluation, and that this relationship may be stronger for adolescents who have a history of aggressive-disruptive behaviour (Kronenberger, Mathews, Dunn et al., 2005). Furthermore, frontal lobe activation was reduced in aggressive subjects, compared to control subjects as measured by fMRI, and this finding was associated with differences in media violence exposure (Mathews, Kronenberger, Wang et al., 2005).

More and more persons in the Caribbean have access to video game systems, and play games with the potential to influence violent and other socially undesirable behaviour. In the USA, arcades are frequented by children during school breaks and after school, particularly young males aged seven and up. This is also true in the Caribbean. There are several major consequences to this: first, increased exposure of youths generally, and male youths in particular, to violence, and on a more continuous basis (McCree, 1998). Second, from a very early age those who play these games are being socialized into viewing violence as (1) a main means of resolving conflict and differences, and (2) as entertainment; and third, the new games inadvertently serve to add to the all-pervasive culture of violence which already exists in the society. Studies show that exposure to violent videogames increases physiological arousal and aggression-related thoughts and feelings (Andersen & Bushman, 2001). A recent US study of brain activity in teens aged 13 to 17 years after playing violent video games for 30 minutes revealed increased activity in a part of the brain that governs emotional arousal. The same teens showed decreased activity in the parts of the brain involved in focus, inhibition and concentration (Springen, 2006). Playing violent videogames is also related to a decrease in pro-social behaviour (Anderson & Bushman, 2001).

In Jamaica, there are reports of the influence of the 'sound system' dance, that is. community gatherings, where loud dancehall music is played and which have a notorious reputation for promoting violence through song lyrics and through the culture which promotes respect for ruthlessness (e.g. Stolzoff, 2000). According to Pereira (1994), dancehall music shows a marked preference for themes of violence and sex. The focus on the former is of more recent vintage and reflects the increasing stress of urban ghettoization. Violence stems from the daily experience of class oppression and police brutality, supported by images in the media showing little value for human life. Dancehall is primarily a form of entertainment, and is most heavily supported by ghetto and urban working-class communities, for whom violence is an everyday reality. Males tend to respond in a positive way to the themes of violence, and women react positively to the sex themes. The lyrics also show a link between sex and violence, though complicit. "The female may be a special type of opponent, and the weapon distinctive, but the language is violence and the objective annihilation" (Pereira, 1994, p. 211). Songs are also degrading to women, but a reflection of reality – the female is expected to provide the male his needed sense of power. In addition, males can have multiple partners, creating jealousy and a convenient deflection of responsibility to female-on-female violence. Male-on-female violence is less acceptable. According to Pereira, previously 'conscious' lyrics (i.e. those with important social commentary) have deteriorated into lyrics revealing a subversive disregard for all values. Popular lyrics cover: murder for pleasure; target dominant state figures (law-agents, bank, church), and figures associated with traditional values (woman, pastor, granny); and show destruction of the social symbol of the family (stealing from mother and brother). Even if 'fiction' these lyrics become harder to separate from recent reality. The divide between lyrical play and reality has at times become too blurred, with the gun murder of a number of DJ's (popular performers) over time. Although some songs have come out against violence, it appears that life is imitating art and not vice versa (Pereira, 1994).

Others suggest that many of the cultural principles that guide thought and behaviour in dancehall are already held by the larger Jamaican populace, and it is reality that is reflected in the music. More recently, women have been portrayed more positively, and more recent lyrics are simply about dancing, with some even have religious themes (Cooper, 2004). Stewart (2002) has argued that interventions aimed at tackling the violence in Jamaica should cease working from the premise that dancehall is a strong contributor to the problem.

## EXPOSURE TO VIOLENCE

Exposure to violence includes watching or hearing about violent events; direct involvement, such as trying to intervene to stop a violent act; being the direct recipient of violence; or experiencing the aftermath of the violence, that is, seeing the physical signs (Fantuzzo & Mohr, 1989; Maxwell, 1994; Runyan et al. 2002). This would include continual exposure to the use of knives, guns and drugs, knowing a victim, being a victim, or seeing an unfamiliar person being victimized in random violence in their home or community environment, and which causes the individual to feel threatened.

In particular, children experiencing violence, either as victims or witnesses, are of major concern worldwide (Berman, Silverman, & Kurtines, 2000; Dahlberg & Krug, 2002; Fantuzzo & Mohr, 1999; Hurt, Malmud, Brodsky, & Glannetta, 2001; Tolan, Guerra, & Kendall, 1995; Vermeiren, Ruchkin, Leckman, et al., 2002; Ward, Flisher, Zissis, et al., 2001). The matter of children being exposed to violence within the home and in the wider community is of great concern to parents, medical personnel, sociologists, psychologists and to many other groups. In fact, the exposure to the epidemic of violence is described as a public health problem (Dahlberg & Krug, 2002; Margolin & Gordis, 2000, 2004; Meeks Gardner et al., 2003; Meeks Gardner et al., 2000; Osofsky, 1999; Rosenthal, 2000; Thompson, 2002) as it drains a country's health care resources.

The statistics reported in this chapter indicate that Caribbean children are exposed to very high levels of violence in their communities, and they are definitely feeling the impact. One-third of school-going adolescents in a Caribbean 12-country study was concerned about violence in their community and wished to move elsewhere (PAHO/WHO, 2000; World Bank, 2003). In Jamaica, for example, only 28 per cent of children surveyed thought their home neighbourhood was very safe and 33 per cent were afraid of someone in their community or yard (UNICEF, 2001), while in Belize, 40 per cent of children felt unsafe on the streets (Rosberg, 2005).

A single, brief, traumatic experience can alter an individual's entire outlook on life and how he or she makes sense of the world (Bloom, 1999; Giller, 1999). Exposure to family and community violence is linked to involvement in violent or aggressive behaviours (Margolin & Gordis, 2004). Albert Bandura's Social Learning Theory may be used to explain this phenomenon. Social learning theorists believe that human behaviour is partially explained through the process of imitation and observational learning (Kaplan et al., 1993). Bandura's social learning theory argues that aggression is learnt in two basic ways: (1) from observing aggressive models, and (2) from receiving and/or expecting a reward following aggression. Social learning theorists believe that the value of observation or modelling serves as an introduction to aggression and violence (Brennan, 1998). The theory further offers an explanation for how children and adults operate cognitively on their social experiences, and how these cognitions then influence behaviour and development (Brown, 1998). Therefore, children learn from the aggressive models in their environments (Kaplan, 2000). Victimization further compounds their ability to regulate their emotions and this allows for aggressive acting out (Margolin & Gordis, 2004).

There is evidence suggesting that exposure to community violence is among the strongest predictors of aggression among youth (Halliday-Boykins & Graham, 2001). Young people feel unsafe; they feel that there is no way to escape the violence in their surroundings and so they, in turn, begin to display aggressive behaviour (Kuther, 1999). Girls tend to display more distress symptoms than boys, but boys tend to report more high-risk behaviours, such as fighting and carrying weapons, than girls (Berman et al., 2000; Runyan et al., 2002). Exposure to violence in the home also has a strong association with aggressive behaviour among children (Halliday-Boykins & Graham, 2001; Kolko, 1992; NCPS, 2003; Runyan et al., 2002). Experience of physical abuse and childhood victimization teach aggressive behaviour and the acceptance of aggression and violent behaviour as the norm (Margolin & Gordis, 2000; 2004; Stiles, 2002).

**Psychological Impact of Exposure to Violence**

While some studies have examined the prevalence of exposure to violence in Jamaican communities (Chevannes, 2004; Fernald & Meeks Gardner, 2003; Meeks Gardner, et al., 2003; Soyibo & Lee, 2000), there are few epidemiological studies done in Jamaica that have examined the relationship between exposure to violence and psychological traumas, symptomatologies or disorders (Knowles, 1999; Meeks Gardener et al., 2000; Daley, 2008).

An individual's reaction to exposure to violence is complex and multifaceted (Berman, et al., 2000) such that traumatic experiences vary in their potential to traumatize. There are many factors that may account for this phenomenon. Psychological trauma theory purports that a person's conceptualization of traumatization is a consequence of the interaction between the crisis event, the individual's unique crisis experience, and personal resiliency and vulnerability (Giller, 1999). An individual may label an experience as being traumatic, based on both the subjective and the objective view of the situation. Traumatization is, therefore, not simply a consequence of what happened; it is also a consequence of how survivors experience the crisis (individual crisis experience variables), coupled with the personal characteristics of the survivors (personal resiliency and vulnerability variables). That is, trauma is defined by the experience of the survivor, and two individuals may undergo the same traumatic experience, for example, being held up at gun-point and robbed, and one may be traumatized, while the other person is unaffected (Giller, 1999). An event is classified as a psychological trauma when "the individual's ability to integrate his or her emotional experience is overwhelmed or the individual experiences a threat to life, bodily integrity or sanity" (Giller, 1999, p.3). So, individuals will classify an event or situation as traumatic when it is overwhelming and they perceive that their life or sanity is threatened, and they feel unable to cope with the event or situation (Volpe, 1996). Other factors such as age, gender, personal characteristics, level of exposure, and level of family support can influence the impact of the individual's exposure to violence (Osofsky, 1999; Runyan et al., 2002).

For the most part, exposure to violence is a stressful experience that requires psychological adaptation and may give rise to psychological sequelae such as anger, anxiety, depression, post-traumatic stress, and dissociation (Breman et al., 2000; Jaycox et al., 2002, Kolko, 1992; Rosenthal, 2000; Rosenthal & Wilson, 2003; Song, Singer & Anglin, 1998). Victims of violence feel unsafe and their view of the world is affected. Life appears meaningless and the future uncertain (Margolin & Gordis, 2000). Children and adolescents are affected, not only physically but also psychologically, by exposure to violence (Fantuzzo & Mohr, 1989; Margolin & Gordis, 2000; Maxwell, 1994; Osofsky, 1999; Samms-Vaughan, 2000).

Internationally, research has linked adolescent exposure to community violence with a series of mental health problems, including internalizing symptoms such as anxiety, depression, withdrawal, (Hurt, et al., 2001; Kolko, 1992; Martinez & Richters, 1993; Mazza & Reynolds, 1999; Osofsky, 1995, 1999; Rosenthal, 2000; Stiles, 2002; Ward et al., 2001); psychosomatic complaints (Stiles, 2002); externalizing behaviour, such as conduct problems, physical aggression and antisocial behaviours (Brown & Kolko, 1999; Fantuzzo & Mohr, 1999; Halliday-Boykins & Graham, 2001; Kolko, 1992; Nygren, Nelson, & Klein, 2004; Vermeiren et al., 2002); oppositional defiant disorder (Nygren et al., 2004); low self-esteem (Hurt et al., 2001; Kolko, 1992; Vermeiren et al., 2002; ), symptoms associated with post-traumatic stress disorder (Berman et al., 2000; JIS, 2003; Mazza & Reynolds, 1999; Osofsky, 1999); approval of aggression (Mazza &

Reynolds, 1999); suicidal ideation (Mazza & Reynolds, 1999; Vermeiren et al., 2002) and withdrawal (Osofsky, 1995; 1999). Kuther (1999) found that post-traumatic stress symptomatology is a correlate of co-victimization in low-income urban children and adolescents. Exposure to community violence is also associated with lowered levels of cognitive, academic, and social functioning (Fantuzzo & Mohr, 1999; Hurt et al., 2001; Kuther, 1999; Margolin & Gordis, 2000; Samms-Vaughn, 2000; Stiles, 2002); interpersonal problems (Maxwell, 1996; Stiles 2002), and substance abuse (Stiles, 2002).

The age at which a child was exposed to violence has an impact on the behaviour of that child. Osofsky (1999) reported that there is a link between exposure to violence and negative behaviours in children across all age ranges. Osofsky (1999) went on to explain that pre-school and school-age children living in violent homes and/or communities display symptoms similar to adult post-traumatic stress. Child victims of violence, who have been exposed to multiple forms of abuse, may display more traumatic symptoms than a child victim of a single type of abuse (Osofsky, 1995). Direct victimization has more of an impact than indirect victimization (Kuther, 1999). Some chronically traumatized adolescents and young adults often appear to be deadened to feelings and pain, and show restricted emotional development over time (Osofsky, 1999).

The effect of traumatic stressors on children and adolescents appears to be modified by the young people's vulnerability to trauma, as youngsters who are exposed to more traumas, who lack family support and who have other emotional problems appear to have more severe symptoms. Levy (2000) reported that children who reside in single-parent homes are often at risk for the development of disorders. As mentioned earlier, parents who are unavailable emotionally may be unable to help their children to cope with trauma (Osofsky, 1998). However, Levy and Wall (2000) and Osofsky (1998) reported that one of the most important protective factors that enables a child to cope with exposure to violence is a strong relationship with a caring competent, positive adult, usually a parent. Osofsky (1998) further reported that children who received greater support from families showed less anxiety, even when living in violent neighbourhoods.

In one of the few studies conducted in the Caribbean, Daley (2008) looked at the relationship between exposure to violence and psychological symptoms, including anxiety, depression, post-traumatic stress and dissociation in 392 students aged 13-16 in four corporate area high schools in Jamaica. The results revealed that persons with a high level of exposure to violence had a greater likelihood of developing psychological symptoms that were diagnosable. The study also showed that males had a higher level of exposure and higher levels of depression. In addition, anger and acting out behaviours were associated with higher levels of exposure to violence.

There is no doubt that the Caribbean people are suffering psychologically as a result of the high levels of violence in the region. Action is required at all levels, including education, continued research, and the provision of psychological services for those directly affected.

## Recommendations for Research

There is a large discrepancy between the number of reports published from Trinidad, Barbados and Jamaica in particular, compared with other Caribbean countries. An effort should, therefore, be made to conduct and report studies from the under-represented countries. Many of the reports rely on subjective perceptions rather than detailed studies, using either quantitative or qualitative methodology. Such studies should be supported to allow for more empirical conclusions. The focus has largely been on describing violence, and not on presenting and testing possible solutions. In addition, certain types of violence that have been largely ignored, such as elder abuse, should be investigated. Intervention models should be widely explored and carefully evaluated in order to improve the high levels of violence described. The interventions should be tried at many levels including (i) law and policy; (ii) institutional reforms; (iii) the community; and (iv) at the individual level, especially for children. Where possible, interventions should employ a multi-sectoral approach.

## Violence Prevention

Many types of prevention efforts have been proposed, but few have been fully implemented in the Caribbean. There are only few published reports of interventions (Grantham-McGregor & Meeks Gardner, 2002; Samms-Vaughan & Jackson, 2002; Meeks Gardner et al., 2005; Sacco & Twemlow, 1997).

One on-going prevention programme that has shown some success in dealing with violent Caribbean youth was developed, implemented and studied by a senior Jamaican clinical social worker (Claudette Crawford-Brown), with the assistance of a clinical psychologist from UWI (Mona). The intervention consisted of a bi-monthly weekend community-based programme, which was combined with a weekly after-school programme in a primary and all-age school in urban Jamaica. The project was implemented over a 21-month period, with an initial cohort of 35 children, aged 11 to 16 years who were identified by their guidance counsellor and teachers as having emotional and behavioural problems.

The *community-based interventions* evaluated included an adolescent mentorship programme, and the range of *clinical interventions* examined included (i) psycho-educational intervention, (ii) group counselling, and (iii) play therapy, using art and story-telling, supplemented by puppetry and psychodrama. One of the primary tools for the intervention was a comprehensive package of culturally appropriate material for the assessment, counselling and training (ACT) of children and adolescents, in the areas of Anger Management and Behaviour Modification. This package was developed by a team of graduate social work students and academics in the Social Work Unit at the UWI (Mona), and implemented with the full cooperation of the administration and teaching staff of the school. A small group of staff members (the school guidance team) worked alongside the clinical team for the duration of the programme, to ensure sustainability.

The model chosen for the specialized intervention was a model of Community Care. The clinical interventions took place within the context of this community-based model, with the adolescents acting on a voluntary basis, as one tier of peer counsellors, working with the mentees once per week and on alternate weekends. Trained clinicians operated at a secondary level with the children in the after-school programme. In the weekend programme, there was a processing of information as the adolescents were helped to understand their mentee, and time was set aside for the training of the adolescents in academic topics such as the Psychology of Children and Adolescence. The adolescents were also exposed to yoga and martial arts as a way of paying them for their voluntary activities. The use of community adolescents as mentors is an adaptation of an intervention model known as the UNITAS model of violence prevention, developed by Edward Eismann. It has been used by him successfully to reduce violent incidents and to maintain low levels of community violence in a section of the borough of Bronx, New York for over thirty years (_see_ Eismann, 1982; 1996). This model was used and adapted with his permission. The model also includes a nurturing context for the intervention, which uses on-going positive reinforcement with large Behaviour Boards, the use of touch (hug therapy) and the provision of meals served to the children by the counsellors, who then sit and eat with the children as they would in a family.

The intervention team consisted of six persons – a team of three clinicians and two specially trained community-based care-givers, headed by a senior clinician. For one year prior to working on the after-school intervention programme, this team based at the UWI (Mona) Violence Prevention Family Clinic, had worked together with children and families who were victims and perpetrators of different forms of violence. The intervention team was supported by a number of community para-professionals, psychology and social work students and was constantly observed by members of the school's own guidance team, who also attended the sessions, interacting, having meals with the children at the end of each session, and engaging with the intervention team in de-briefing sessions.

Primary sources of data collected included self-report scales, used weekly with teachers and guidance counsellors, as well as a supplementary questionnaire which solicited information on household composition, parenting structure, function, as well as parenting practices. Broad-based assessment of the context of the children's feelings was done through weekly focus group discussions, and through the use of worksheets on Understanding Feelings, Understanding Anger, and Anger Management, all of which were specially developed for Caribbean children and adolescents. These worksheets were taken from the Assessment Counselling and Training Package for Caribbean Populations ACT NOW developed by the UWI Violence Prevention Programme.

The Reynolds Adolescent Screening Inventory was given to the children prior to the intervention to identify the major presenting problems they were experiencing. The presenting problems identified by the instruments included behavioural problems (e.g. lying, impulsivity, fighting) and emotional problems (e.g. suicidal ideation and low self-worth). The first six-week period of the programme was used as a pre-test or baseline, where the number of incidents for each type of problem found for each child, were documented.

Behavioural indicators documented for the duration of the programme were:

1) The number of *incidents of disrespectful behaviour* (e.g. walking out of class at will, and disregarding the teacher's instructions to return; not responding to an authority figure when called; verbal abuse to teachers or non-responsiveness; and a lack of remorse when engaged with an authority figure in discussion about misbehaviour). The intervention used to deal with these incidents of disrespectful behaviour included play therapy – specifically puppetry, using enactment and role play, and story-telling; and the ongoing behaviour modification system, using positive reinforcers for good behaviour. Children were rewarded weekly with stars on their Behaviour Board.

2) *Lying and/or lack of remorse* (e.g. children who lied consistently in relation to their own misbehaviour, or who had difficulty taking responsibility for their actions). Much of this behaviour involved bullying and assaulting other children.

3) *Hyperactivity/inattentiveness/impulsivity* (e.g. inability to complete tasks, interrupting class, and the inability to focus on a particular task in the classroom environment); and

4) *Aggression/anger management issues* (e.g. number of fights reported). Physical and verbal aggression were documented with the same weighting, based on the level of disruption created.

Graphical representations of the data obtained showed reductions in all behaviours over the course of the programme, though there were some children for whom the programme was less successful – particularly those with the most severe problems (e.g. those with Conduct Disorder). It is important to note that the improvements in the children's behaviour could not be attributed to any one specific intervention used, nor could it be determined whether gains would continue once the children left the programme. This was a particular concern for those with attention deficit type problems.

The study showed that with sustained and long-term, rather than short-term, intervention, using a training of trainers model, school-based professionals can be helped in reducing the incidence of behavioural problems that create some of the impetus for the violent incidents in the school system. From the weekly focus group discussions, the study also showed that the interaction of parents, school and community as contributory factors can inoculate the child against violence or exacerbate the problem of violence.

## General Recommendations

Violence prevention efforts typically fall into five general areas. The first is the _reform and strengthening of the legal, judicial and policing systems_ with emphasis on _reducing access to weapons_, and _controlling substance use and the drug trade_. There is a need for increased law enforcement in the region, including more police patrols and tougher penalties for perpetrators. Although this may have some effect on selected situations such as assaults on the streets, it is unlikely to affect the most common category of family and acquaintance homicides which are not committed by repeat offenders (Kaplan et al., 1993). More community policing is required, together with increased effectiveness in apprehending offenders and investigating crimes. There is a need to educate, train and discipline the police force. New laws should be created as necessary (e.g. laws relating to gangs). Domestic violence legislation must be enacted and enforced. Clear procedures for the reporting of child abuse, and wide dissemination of these procedures should be instituted and NGOs and civil society should also be allowed to file charges against perpetrators of violence.

Decreasing the availability of the most lethal and most frequently used weapons has been shown to reduce homicide rates elsewhere (Sloan, Kellerman, Reay et al., 1988). In most Caribbean countries guns are illegal, so there needs to be a focus on reducing the importation and smuggling of weapons, as well as the guns-for-drugs trade. There needs to be better policing to detect concealed weapons, particularly in the schools, using the search and seizure method. Some people have called for the legalization of drugs as a way of reducing violence. Whether this will gain currency remains to be seen, however, there is an urgent need for the regulation of the sale of drugs (especially ganja) to school children. Close monitoring and supervision by the community, as well as community education about the link between drug use and youth violence should also be encouraged.

The second recommendation supports the need for the *institution of strong anti-crime anti-violence campaigns*. Massive public education programmes with anti-violence themes – incorporating the use of billboards, TV, radio, psycho-drama, etc. targeting high-risk youth in particular – need to be developed. There should be a crackdown on all types of gangs (McCree, 1998). Reducing exposure to and glorification of violence in the media, film, video games, TV, and music videos should be addressed. Children's programmes should be monitored and regulated with regard to exposure to death and gore. In addition, business owners should be fined if they allow youngsters to play videogames in their establishments during school time.

The third approach to violence prevention is *education*. Parents need education on the detrimental effects of certain child-rearing practices on optimal child development. They need training in alternative methods of behaviour modification for their children. Parenting classes are almost nonexistent, and these are especially helpful for adolescent parents. The media can also be used to demonstrate good parenting. The public in general also needs education on the laws governing the treatment of children. Training in the detection, assessment and management of child abuse should be provided for all professionals dealing with children, including medical practitioners and health professionals, social workers, teachers, child care professionals and para-professionals and members of the police force.

Children also need to be educated in a comprehensive way about their rights – what constitutes abuse and neglect, and how to protect themselves from it. They need clear information on how to report incidents of abuse and neglect. This could be included as part of Family Life Education in the school curriculum. Child abuse hotlines should be established and made easily accessible to allow children to report abuse confidentially.

Many teachers are ignorant of alternative methods of guidance and discipline, and training in behaviour management needs to be a part of teacher training pedagogy. A core curriculum for managing violence in schools needs to be developed. The teaching of conflict resolution and mediation skills in schools at all levels within the curriculum or in specialized sessions is also needed. Additionally, the development of a cadre of peer counsellors, well trained in conflict resolution and mediation skills, and thus able to detect violence before it happens would be beneficial. Student assistance centres (SACs) could be used by peer counsellors to defuse potentially violent clashes in the absence of an adult. These centers should be equipped with resource material such as videos, brochures, and appropriate hand-outs, and should project a family-friendly environment. Educational policy should require specialized short-term and/or in-service training of guidance counsellors, to deal with problems such as anger management, behaviour modification, suicide prevention, and injury reduction programmes. Martial arts could also be taught in school as an alternative means of self defence. The development of a curriculum for managing trauma in communities for community workers, parents and NGOs is also recommended.

The fourth recommendation addresses the _provision of services_. There needs to be much greater emphasis on the detection and screening of children with emotional and behavioural problems at an early stage. Screening, followed up by appropriate interventions, should be done as early as pre-school, and at the latest, at the latency stage (age 8-12 years) before the behaviour has become intractable.

Counselling should be provided for victims and perpetrators of violence, in order to stop the cycle. Health-care workers should ask women directly about domestic violence in a supportive non-judgmental atmosphere, and victims should be told clearly that no one deserves to be raped or beaten. It should be established whether victims are in immediate danger, and action taken if necessary. Posters and leaflets should be available in relevant facilities. Victims should be encouraged to maintain contact with organizations that support such women and that manage shelters for battered women and their children (Rawlins, 2000). Adult and peer-based mentoring should be encouraged in schools, churches, and community organizations. This would include Big Brother and Big Sister models, Boys' Scouts, Boys' Brigade, and similar movements. It would also be beneficial to set up of a Rapid Response Team for schools, that would serve to provide a team of trained individuals to respond to violent crises in schools, such as incidents of stabbings, attempted suicide, murder, and the like. This team would comprise teachers and other experts, trained and hand-picked by the regional teachers' associations.

The responses to child abuse and neglect should be clear, comprehensive and operational, and should involve both medical and mental health care, as well as family interventions, (e.g. by social workers and psychologists), police investigations and legal services. Support for child victims should include specialized agencies and units, staff within the police force, social services, health and legal facilities. Children and their families need swift and easy access to appropriate treatment programmes. Increased childhood mental health services are required in the Caribbean region and the accessibility and acceptability of these programmes need to be improved. The perpetrators of violence need to be prosecuted and to undergo mandatory treatment.

In-class discussion of programmes on television and radio, involving the children themselves will help to reduce the shame associated with the experience of violence. Dialogue with youth about community violence will also provide opportunities for children to speak out about how violence affects them. Additionally, this will help perpetrators to take responsibility for violence they have committed, such as the raping of younger girls or bullying of younger children.

The fifth approach is to *change the structure of society*. Reducing poverty and the social disintegration and psychological stress that accompanies it may be required before significant decreases in violence will be seen (Blum et al., 2003). Family is central to the health of young people, in spite of differences in family structures. Young people who report connectedness to their parents, attendance at religious services, school connectedness and trying hard in school, are less likely to participate in, or be adversely affected by violence. Interventions that highlight strengthening the protective factors present in the lives of young people tend to be more effective than those focused only on risk reduction (Kirby, 2001). Risk is cumulative, as is protection. The greatest risk reduction is associated with school connectedness, stressing the importance of building protection and connectedness between teachers and students. Relationships between students should be fostered together with a mind-set that encourages them to see schools as safe havens, and to regard violence as anti-social. The establishment of codes of conduct rewarding positive behaviour at the classroom and school level, and Behaviour Halls of Fame would help to create an enabling environment for positive change.

Improving access and the quality of education for children and adolescents should be a focal point for policymakers. The actions required include increasing the number of spaces available and reducing class size; making financial assistance for school available; placing greater emphasis on life skills and basic job skills; banning corporal punishment and replacing it with non-violent methods of discipline; promoting attitude change; and teaching conflict resolution. The educational systems, particularly individual schools, should forge links with NGOs and community-based organizations to provide extracurricular activities for youth (e.g. character clubs, martial arts training) and to provide the youth with recreational and safe spaces in the community. The private sector should also be approached to assist with the provision of alternative education e.g. vocational training.

There is an urgent need to return their childhood to Caribbean children – create community play spaces for them; instill in the community a public sense of protection and responsibility for all children, and child safety (e.g. community crossing guards); engender communal responsibility for the rearing of young children and adolescents. Parents should be encouraged and given support to engage with their children and to build strong bonds with them, especially since 'connectedness' has proven to be a core protective factor for the reduction of risk behaviours, including violence. The cultural and social norms and beliefs that perpetuate violence against children need to be challenged. As mentioned earlier, a coordinated effort of government, non-government, and community organizations, together with the media – including the voices of children themselves, is required.

The active participation of young people in their own, their community's and their nation's development must be encouraged. Young people need to be allowed to voice their opinions on issues which affect them. This is a reality in St. Lucia which operates a National Youth Council with 162 youth organizations around the island. We need to inform and educate the youth on their rights and responsibilities, versus power and powerlessness. These ideas should be integrated into school curricula at all levels, and into community-based programmes with child friendly definitions and materials. We must tap into the strength of young people to help in reduction of violence in the schools. Finally we need to allow young people to contribute to developing the solutions. It is also important to explore the possibility of strengthening spiritual bases as a means of preventing violent behaviour and building resilience in our youth.

## REFERENCES

Bissessar, A. M. (2000). Policy transfer and implementation failure: A review of the policy of domestic violence in Trinidad and Tobago. _Caribbean Journal of Criminology and Social Psychology,_ 5 (1-2), 57-80.

Bloom, S. L. (1999). Trauma theory abbreviated. [Electronic Version]. _Community Works._ Retrieved April 25, 2006 from http://www.sanctuaryweb.com/Documents/Downloads/Trauma%20theory%20abbreviated.pdf

Blum, R. W., Halcón, L., Beuhring, T., Pate, E., Campbell-Forrester, S., & Venema, A. (2003). Adolescent health in the Caribbean: Risk and protective factors. _American Journal of Public Health,_ 93 (3), 456-460.

Blum R. W., & Ireland M. (2004). Reducing risk, increasing protective factors: Findings from the Caribbean youth health survey. _Journal of Adolescent Health,_ 35 (6), 493-500.

Bogues, A. (2006). Power, violence and the Jamaican "Shotta Don". Report: _Our Caribbean._ NACLA Report on the Americas, 21-26.

Brodie-Walker, S. N., & Morgan, K. A. D. (2007). Factors impacting delinquency in Jamaican and African-American adolescents. Unpublished Study.

Brennan, W. (1998). Aggression and violence: Examining the theories. _Nursing Standard,_ 12 (27), 36-38.

Brown, J., Anderson, P., & Chevannes, B. (1993). _Report on the contribution of Caribbean men to the family: A Jamaican pilot study. Mona._ Jamaica: The Caribbean Child Development Centre, School of Continuing Studies, UWI.

Brown, K. M. (1998). Social cognitive theory overview. Retrieved May 30, 2006 from http://hsc.usf.edu/~kmbrown/Social_Cognitive_Theory_Overview.htm

Brown, E. J., & Kolko, D. J. (1999). Child victims' attributions about being physically abused: An examination of factors associated with symptom severity. _Journal of Abnormal Child Psychiatry,_ 27 (4), 311-322.

Browne, A., & Finkelhor, D. (1986). Impact of child sexual abuse: A review of the research. _Psychological Bulletin,_ 99 (1), 66-77.

Buka, S. L., Stichick, T. L., Birdthistle, I., & Earls, F. J. (2001). Youth exposure to violence: Prevalence, risks and consequences. _American Journal of Orthopsychiatry,_ 71 (3), 298-310.

Cabral, C., & Speek-Warnery, V. (2004). _Voices of children: Experience with violence._ Ministry of Labour, Human Services and Social Security, Red Thread Women's Development Programme, UNICEF-Guyana, Georgetown, Guyana.

Cain, M. (1995). _Crime and punishment in Trinidad and Tobago: A collection of papers._ St. Augustine, Trinidad: Department of Behavioral Sciences UWI, St. Augustine.

Cairns, R. B., & Cairns, B. D. (1984). Predicting aggressive patterns in girls and boys: a developmental study. _Aggressive Behavior,_ 10 (3), 227-242.

Campbell, C. G. (2006). Media violence and aggression in Jamaican preadolescent boys. MPH thesis, Rollins School of Public Health, Emory University.

Campbell, J. C. (1995). Addressing battering during pregnancy: Reducing low birth weight and on-going abuse. *Seminars in Perinatology*, 19 (4), 301-306.

*Caribbean News Net* (2005). Jamaica's murder rate hits all time high. November 25, 2005, Kingston, Jamaica.

Chevannes, B. (2001). *Learning to be a man: Culture, socialization and gender identity in five Caribbean communities.* Kingston, Jamaica: University of the West Indies Press.

Chevannes, P. (2004). *Preliminary study on violence in Caribbean schools: A preliminary investigation on the situation of school violence in 6 CARICOM countries* (Dominica, Grenada, Jamaica, St. Lucia, St. Vincent and the Grenadines, Trinidad and Tobago) [Abstract]. Caribbean: Change from Within Project, UNESCO Caribbean.

Christoffel, K. K. (1990).Violent death and injury in US children and adolescents. *American Journal of Diseases of Children*, 144 (6), 697-706.

Cicchetti, G., & Toth, S. L. (1998). Perspectives on research and practice in developmental psychopathology. In W. Damon (Series Ed.), I. E. Siegel and K. A. Renninger (Vol. Eds.), *Handbook of child psychology: Vol. 4. Child psychology in practice* (5th Ed.), pp. 479-582, New York: Wiley.

Cooper, C. (2004). *Sound clash: Jamaican dancehall culture at large.* New York: Palgrave Macmillan.

Crawford-Brown, C. (1986). *Overcrowding in places of safety in the corporate area: A study of under six year olds: Vol. 1. The social work reality.* Kingston, Jamaica: Department of Sociology, University of the West Indies.

————. (1997). The impact of parent-child socialization on the development of conduct disorder in Jamaican male adolescents. In J. L. Roopnarine & J. Brown (Eds.), *Caribbean families: Diversity among ethnic groups. Advances in Applied Developmental Psychology 14.* Westport, CT: Ablex Publishing Corporation, pp. 205-222.

————. (1999). The impact of parenting on conduct disorder in Jamaican male adolescents. *Adolescence*, 34 (134), 417-436.

————. (2000). *Who will save our children? The plight of the Jamaican child in the 1990's.* Mona, Jamaica: University Press of the West Indies.

Crawford-Brown, C. P. J. (1993). A study of the factors associated with the development of conduct disorder in Jamaican male adolescents. *Dissertation Abstracts International, Section A: Humanities and Social Sciences*, 55 (2-A), pp. 375.

Crawford-Brown, C. P. J., & Rattray, J. M. (2001). Parent child relationships in Caribbean families. In N. Boyd Webb and D. Lum (Eds.), *Culturally diverse parent child and family relationships: A guide for social workers and other practitioners.* New York, NY: Columbia University Press, pp. 107-130.

Creque, M. (1995). *A study of the incidence of domestic violence in Trinidad and Tobago from 1991 to 1993.* Port of Spain: Trinidad and Tobago Coalition against Domestic Violence.

Dahlberg, L. L., & Krug, E. G. (2002). Violence: A global public health problem. In E. G. Krugs, L. L. Dahlberg, J. A. Mercy, A. B. Zwi, & R. Lozano (Eds.), _World report on violence and health_. Geneva: World Health Organization, pp. 1-22. Available: http://www.who.int/violence_injury_ prevention/violence/world_report/en/full_en.pdf

Daley, A. Z. (2008). Exposure to violence in Jamaican adolescents and its relationship to psychological trauma symptoms. Unpublished PhD Thesis. Department of Community Health and Psychiatry, University of the West Indies, Mona, Jamaica.

Danns, G. K. (2002). Amerindian children and human rights in Guyana. In C. Barrow (Ed.), _Children's rights: Caribbean realities_. Kingston, Jamaica: Ian Randle Publishers, pp. 243-282.

Danns, G. K., & Parsad, B. S. (1989). _Domestic violence in the Caribbean: A Guyana case study_. Women's Studies Unit, Georgetown, Guyana: University of Guyana Publishers.

De Albuquerque, K., & McElroy, J. L. (1999). A longitudinal study of serious crime in the Caribbean. _Caribbean Journal of Criminology and Social Psychology_, 4: 32-70.

Della-Guistina, J. (2000). Domestic violence against women – Community justice issue or individual crime?: Cross cultural implications. _Caribbean Journal of Criminology and Social Psychology_, 5 (1-2), 40-56.

The Economist (2004). "Bubba, Bobo, Zambo and Zeeks". Domestic and international issues fuel gang violence in the Caribbean. The _Economist_, 4 Nov 2004.

Eismann, E. P. (1982). _Unitas: Building healing communities for children: A developmental and training manual_. New York, NY: Fordham University Press, Hispanic Research Center.

————. (1996). _Unitas: Building healing communities for children_. New York, NY: Fordham University Press.

Eldemire, D. (1986). Sexual abuse of children in Kingston and St Andrew, Jamaica. _West Indian Medical Journal_, 35 (1), 38-43.

Ellsberg, M., Caldera, T., Herrera, A., Winkvist, A., & Kullgren, G. (1999). Domestic violence and emotional distress among Nicaraguan women: Results from a population based study. _American Psychologist_, 51 (4), 30-36.

Evans, H., & Davies, R. (1997). Overview issues in childhood socialization in the Caribbean. In J. L. Rooparine and J. Brown (Eds.), _Caribbean families: Diversity among ethnic groups_. Westport, CT: Ablex Publishing, pp. 1-24.

Fantuzzo, J. W., & Mohr, W. K (1999). Prevalence and effects of child exposure to domestic violence. _The future of children, Special Issue: Domestic Violence and Children_, 9 (3), 21-32.

Fernald, L. C., & Meeks Gardner, J. (2003). Jamaican children's reports of violence at school and home. _Social and Economic Studies_, 52, 121-140.

Finkelhor, D., Hotaling, G., & Lewis, I. A. (1990). Sexual abuse in a national survey of adult men and women: Prevalence, characteristics and risk factors. *Child Abuse and Neglect,* 14 (1), 19-28.

Flannery, D. J., & Singer, M. I. (1999) Exposure to violence and victimization at school. *Choices in Preventing Youth Violence* 4 [Online]. Available at http://iume.tc.columbia.edu/choices/briefs/choices04.html

Freud, A. (1965). *Normality and pathology in childhood: Assessments of development.* New York, NY: International Universities Press.

Frias-Armenta, M. (2002). Long-term effects of child punishment on Mexican women: A structural model. *Child Abuse and Neglect,* 26 (4), 371-386.

Gayfoor, G. (1989). Crime and punishment in the Caribbean: The conflict over sentencing. *Caribbean Affairs,* 2, 129-140.

Giovannoni, J. M., & Becerra, R. M. (Eds). (1979). *Defining child abuse.* New York, NY: Free Press.

Global Initiative to End All Corporal Punishment of Children (2005). Ending legalized violence against children. *Report for the Caribbean Regional Consultation – the UN Secretary General's Study on Violence against Children,* March 10-11, Trinidad.

Gopaul-McNicol, S. (1999). Ethnocultural perspectives on childrearing practices in the Caribbean. *International Social Work,* 42 (1), 79-86.

Grantham-McGregor, S., & Meeks Gardner, J. (2002). *Evaluation of the impact of the Peace and Love in Schools (PALS) Programme.* Mona, Jamaica: Tropical Metabolism Research Unit, UWI.

Griffin, C. E. (2002). Criminal deportation: The unintended impact of US anti-crime and anti-terrorism policy along its third border. *Caribbean Studies,* 30 (2), 39-76.

Griffin, T. M. (2004). *Haiti: Human rights investigation, November 11-21, 2004.* Miami, FL: Centre for the Study of Human Rights, University of Miami School of Law.

Giller, E. (1999). What is psychological trauma? *Sidran Institute, Traumatic Stress Education and Advocacy* [Online]. Available at http://www.sidran.org/whatistrauma.html. Retrieved on December 10, 2003.

Hagedorn, M. (1998). Discussion of gang definition. In M. Tonry and M. H. Moore (Eds.), *Youth Violence: Crime and Justice, Volume 24 (Crime and Justice: A Review of Research).* Chicago, IL; University of Chicago Press, pp. 366-368.

Halcón, L., Blum, R. W., Beuhring, T., Pate, E., Campbell-Forrester, S., & Venema, A. (2003). Adolescent health in the Caribbean: A regional portrait. *American Journal of Public Health,* 93 (11), 1851-1857.

Halliday-Boykins, C. A., & Graham, S. (2001) At both ends of the gun: Testing the relationship between community violence exposure and youth violent behavior. *Journal of Abnormal Child Psychology,* 29 (5), 383-402.

Hamel-Smith, A. (1990). Empowerment through education. Power and control from the perspective of the abused child. In UNICEF (Ed.), _Child Abuse: Breaking the Cycle_. Geneva: UNICEF, pp. 201-207.

Hannif, N. Z. (1995). Male violence against women and men in the Caribbean: The case of Jamaica. _Journal of Comparative Family Studies_, 20 (2), 361-369.

Harriott A., Brathwaite, F., & Wortley, S. (2004). _Crime and criminal justice in the Caribbean_. Kingston, Jamaica: Arawak Publications.

Headly, B. (2006). Giving critical context to the deportee phenomenon. _Social Justice_, 33 (1), 40-56.

Headley, B. D. (1994). _The Jamaican crime scene: A perspective_. Mandeville, Jamaica: Eureka Press Limited.

Hickling, F. W. (1994). Violence in Jamaica. _Caribbean Journal of Religious Studies_, 15, 3-13.

Hill, K. G., Howell, J. C., Hawkins, J. D., & Battin-Pearson, S. R. (1999) Childhood risk factors for adolescent gang membership: Results from the Seattle Social Development Project. _Journal of Research in Crime and Delinquency_, 36 (3), 300-322.

Hotton, T. (2003). Childhood aggression and exposure to violence in the home. Crime and Justice Research Paper Series, Catalogue No. 85-561-MIE2003002. Ottawa, Canada: Canadian Center for Justice Statistics, Statistics Canada [Online]. Available: http://ww4.ps-sp.gc.ca/en/library/publications/children/aggression/85-561-mie2003002.pdf

Howe, D. (1998). You will enjoy your Caribbean holiday as long as you ignore the endemic racial hatred. _New Statesman_, 127 (4396), 16.

Hurt, H., Malmud, E., Brodsky, N. L., & Giannetta, J. (2001). Psychological and academic correlates in child witnesses. _Archives of Pediatric and Adolescent Medicine_, 155 (12), 1351-1356.

Hutchinson, G. A., & Simeon, D. T. (1997). Suicide in Trinidad and Tobago: Association with measures of social distress. _International Journal of Social Psychiatry_, 43 (4), 269-275.

Jankowski, S. M. (1991). _Islands in the street: Gangs and American urban society_. Berkeley, CA: University of California Press.

Jaycox, L.H., Stein, B. D., Kataoka, S. H., Wong, M., Fink, A., Escudero, P., & Zaragoza, C. (2002). Violence exposure, posttraumatic stress disorder, and depressive symptoms among recent immigrant school children. _Journal of the American Academy of Child and Adolescent Psychiatry_, 41 (9), 1104-1110.

Joseph, F. (2002). Contravening the Convention on the Rights of the Child: Health care, education and quality of life among the Carib Indian children of Dominica and St Vincent. In C. Barrow (Ed.), _Children's Rights, Caribbean Realities_. Kingston, Jamaica: Ian Randle Publishers, pp. 257-268.

Joseph, J., Henriques, Z. W., & Ekeh, K. R. (1998). The legal response to domestic violence in the English-speaking Caribbean countries. _Caribbean Journal of Criminology and Social Psychology_, 3 (1-2), 174-187.

Kaplan, P. S. (2000). *A child's Odyssey: Child and adolescent development.* Belmont, CA: Wadsworth/Thomson Learning.

Kaplan, R. M., Sallis, J. F., & Patterson, T. L. (1993). *Health and human behavior.* New York, NY: McGraw-Hill, Inc.

King, J. W. (1997). Paradise lost? Crime in the Caribbean: A comparison of Barbados and Jamaica. *Caribbean Journal of Criminology and Social Psychology, 2* (1), 30-44.

Kirby, D. (2001). *Emerging answers: Research findings on programs to reduce sexual risk-taking and teen pregnancy.* Washington, D.C., National Campaign to Prevent Teen Pregnancy.

Knowles, L. M. (1999). The impact of physical abuse on the psychological and behavioural state of institutionalized children in the Bahamas and Jamaica. Unpublished Ph.D. Thesis, University of the West Indies, Mona, Jamaica.

Kolko, D. J. (1992). Characteristics of child victims of physical abuse: Research findings and clinical implications. *Journal of Interpersonal Violence, 7* (2), 244-276.

Koss, M. P. (1990). The women's mental health research agenda: Violence against women. *American Psychologist, 45* (3), 374-380.

Kronenberger, W. G., Mathews, V. P., Dunn, D. W., Wang, Y., Wood, E. A., Giauque, A. L., Larsen, J. J., Rembusch, M. E., Lowe, M. J., & Li, T. (2005). Media violence exposure and executive functioning in aggressive and control adolescents. *Journal of Clinical Psychology, 61* (6), 725-737.

Krug, E. G., Dahlberg, L. L. Mercy, J. A., Zwi, A. B., & Lozano, R. (Eds.). (2002). *World Report on Violence and Health.* Geneva, Switzerland: World Health Organization. Available: http://www.who.int/violence_injury_prevention/violence/world_report/en/full_en.pdf

Kuther, T. L., (1999). A developmental-contextual perspective on youth covictimization by community violence. *Adolescence, 34* (136), 699-714.

Le Franc, E. (2002). Child abuse in the Caribbean. Addressing the rights of the child. In C. Barrow (Ed.), *Children's rights, Caribbean realities.* Kingston, Jamaica: Ian Randle Publishers, pp. 285-305.

Leo-Rhynie, E. (1993). *The Jamaican family: Continuity and change* (Grace Kennedy Foundation lecture). Kingston Jamaica: Grace Kennedy Foundation.

————.(1997). Class, race and gender issues in child rearing in the Caribbean. In J. L. Roopnarine, and J. Brown (Eds.), *Caribbean families: Diversity among ethnic groups. Advances in Applied Developmental Psychology 14.* Westport, CT: Ablex Publishing Corporation, pp. 25-55.

Levy, H., & Chevannes, B. (1996). *They cry "respect"! Urban violence and poverty in Jamaica.* Mona, Jamaica: UWI Centre for Population, Community and Social Change, Department of Sociology and Social Work.

Levy, A. J., & Wall, J. C. (2000). Children who have witnessed community homicide: Incorporating risk and resilience in clinical work. *Families in Society, 81* (4), 402-411.

Loeber, R., & Hale, D. (1997). Key issues in the development of aggression and violence from childhood to early adulthood. _Annual Review of Psychology, 48,_ 371-410.

Luciano, D., Esim, S., & Duvvury, N. (2005). How to make the law work? Budgetary implications of domestic violence laws in Latin America, Central America and the Caribbean. _Journal of Women, Politics and Policy, 27_ (1-2), 123-133.

Mahy, G. (1990). _Incest and drug abuse. Breaking the cycle._ Port of Spain, Trinidad: Ministry of Social Development and Family Services, pp.154-158.

Mansingh, A., & Ramphal, P. (1993). The nature of interpersonal violence in Jamaica and its strain on the national health system. _West Indian Medical Journal, 42_ (2), 53-56.

Margolin, G., & Gordis, E. B. (2000). The effects of family and community violence on children. _Annual Review of Psychology, 51,_ 445-479.

————. (2004). Children's exposure to violence in the family and community. _American Psychological Society, 13_ (4), 152-155.

Mars, J. (2004). Police Abuse of force in Guyana: Applying lessons from the United States. In A. Harriott, F. Brathwaite & S. Wortley (Eds.), _Crime and justice in the Caribbean._ Kingston, Jamaica: Arawak Publications, pp. 206-224.

Martinez, P., & Richters, J. E. (1993). The NIMH community violence project: II. Children's distress symptoms associated with violence exposure. _Psychiatry: Interpersonal and Biological Processes, Special Issue: Children and Violence, 56_ (1), 22-35.

Mathews, V. P, Kronenberger, W. G., Wang, Y., Lurito, J. T., Lowe, M. J., & Dunn, D. W. (2005). Media violence exposure and frontal lobe activation measured by functional magnetic resonance imaging in aggressive and non aggressive adolescents. _Journal of Computer Assisted Tomography, 29_ (3), 287-292.

Maxwell, G. M. (1994). _Children and family violence: the unnoticed victim._ Minnesota Centre Against Violence and Abuse. [Online]. Available at http://mincava.umn.edu/documents/nzreport/nzreport.shtml

Mazza, J. J., & Reynolds, W. M. (1999). Exposure to violence in young inner-city adolescents: relationships with suicidal ideation, depression, and PTSD symptomatology. _Journal of Abnormal Child Psychology, 27_ (3), 203-213.

McCree, R.D. (1998). Violence: A preliminary look at gangs in Trinidad and Tobago. _Caribbean Journal of Criminology and Social Psychology, 1_ (1-2), 155-173.

McDonald, A., Duncan, N. D., Mitchell, D. I., & Fletcher, P. R. (1999). Trauma aetiology and cost in the accident and emergency unit of the university hospital of the West Indies. _West Indian Medical Journal, 48_ (3), 141-142.

Meeks Gardner, J. (1995). Documentation of interpersonal violence prevention programmes for children in Jamaica. Mona, Jamaica: Child Development Centre, unpublished work.

Meeks Gardner J., Powell C., & Grantham-McGregor, S. (2000). A case-control study of family and school determinants of aggression in Jamaican children. Working Paper No. 6. Kingston, Jamaica: Planning Institute of Jamaica.

Meeks Gardner, J., Powell, C. A., & Grantham-McGregor, S. M. (2007). Determinants of aggressive and prosocial behaviour among Jamaican school-boys. *West Indian Medical Journal*, 56 (1), 34-41.

Meeks Gardner, J., Powell, C. A., Thomas, J. A., & Millard, D. (2003). Perceptions and experiences of violence among secondary school students in urban Jamaica. *Pan American Journal of Public Health*, 14 (2), 97-103.

Menon, P. K. (1983). The law of rape and criminal law administration with special reference to the commonwealth Caribbean. *The International and Comparative Law Quarterly*, 32 (4), 832-870.

Mercy, J. A., Butchart, A., Farrington D., & Cerda, M. (2002). Youth Violence. In E. G. Krug, L. L. Dahlberg, J. A. Mercy, A. B. Zwi, & R. Lozano (Eds.), *World report on violence and health*, Geneva: World Health Organization, pp. 23-56.

Miller, E. L. (1997). *Marginalization of the Black male, 2nd Edition*. Kingston, Jamaica: University of the West Indies Press.

Ministry of Education, Youth and Culture (2002). *Youth in Jamaica Situation Assessment Report in Jamaica, 2001*. National Centre for Youth Development, Kingston, Jamaica: MOEYC.

Minor, S. W, Lipps, G., Shetty, G., Prescott, P., Burke, D., Holder, D., & Lamb, K. (2004). Attention-deficit/hyperactivity disorder and aggression in Jamaican students. *Caribbean Journal of Psychology*, 1 (1), 13-21.

Moore, S.A. (1996). The other victims. *Guyana Review*, 41-42.

Mondesire, A., & Dunn, L. D. (1997). *Toward equity in development: A report on the status of women*. Georgetown, Guyana: Caribbean Community (CARICOM) Secretariat.

Morrison, I. (1993). *Report of the task force on child abuse*. Kingston Jamaica: United Nations Children's Fund.

Moser, C., & Holland, J. (1997). Urban poverty and violence in Jamaica. In World Bank Latin American and Caribbean Studies. *Viewpoints*. Washington D.C.: World Bank.

Nagin, D. S., & Tremblay, R. E. (2001). Parental and early childhood predictors of persistent physical aggression in boys from kindergarten to high school. *Archives of General Psychiatry*, 58 (4), 389-394.

National Child Month Committee (1997). *Children and Violence Conference Report*. Kingston, Jamaica.

Newberger, E. H. (1992). Child abuse. In J. M. Last & R. B. Wallace (Eds.), *Public health and preventive medicine (13th Ed.)*. Norwalk, Conn.: Appleton and Lange, pp. 1046-1048.

Nygren, P., Nelson, H. D., & Klein, J. (2004). Screening children for family violence: Review of the evidence for the U.S. preventive services task force. *Annals of Family Medicine*, 2 (2), 161-169.

Oates, K. (1990). _Child sexual abuse and its aftermath. Child abuse: Breaking the cycle._ Port of Spain: Ministry of Social Development and Family Services, pp. 159-169.

O'Conner, F. (1992) Crime, violence and the criminal justice system, 10, Mona, Jamaica: Grassroots Development and the State of the Nation, Symposium in Honour of Carl Stone.

Ohene, S., Ireland, M., & Blum, R. W. (2005). The clustering of risk behaviors among Caribbean youth. _Maternal and Child Health Journal,_ 9 (1), 91-100.

Olds, D. L., Henderson, C. R., Chamberlin, R., & Tatelbaum, R. (1986). Preventing child abuse and neglect: A randomized trial of nurse home visitation. _Pediatrics,_ 78, 65-78.

Olweus, D. (1979). Stability of aggressive reaction patterns in males: A review. _Psychological Bulletin,_ 86 (4), 852-875.

Osofsky, J. D. (1995). The effects of exposure to violence on young children. _American Psychologist,_ 50 (9), 782-788.

————. (1999). The impact of violence on children. The future of children. Special Issue: Domestic Violence and Children, 9 (3), 33-49.

Ostrov, J. M., Gentile, D. A., & Crick, N. R. (2006). Media exposure, aggression and prosocial behaviour during early childhood: A longitudinal study. _Social Development,_ 15 (4), 612-627.

PAHO/WHO (2000). _A portrait of adolescent health in the Caribbean,_ 2000. Minneapolis: University of Minnesota, WHO Collaborating Centre on Adolescent Health, 2000.

Parsad, B. S. (1992). Conjugal violence and public policy: Evidence from Guyana. In M. Cain (Ed.), _New Directions,_ pp. 285-248.

Parris, M. (1988). _Violent crimes and ethnic diversity in Guyana._ UWI, St. Augustine, Trinidad: Research Contributions Series C, pp. 1-26.

Patel, S., Lee Pow, N., Kawal, R., Kahn, S., Mohess, D., & Sankar, S. (1999). Prevalence and factors associated with physical and emotional abuse against pregnant women in central Trinidad. Caribbean Health Research Council Conference, Barbados, April 1999.

Paternoster, R., & Brame, R. (1997). Multiple routes to delinquency? A test of developmental and general theories of crime. _Criminology,_ 35 (1), 49-84.

Patterson, G. R., Reid, J. B., & Eddy, J. M. (2002). A brief history of the Oregon model. In J. B. Reid, G. R. Patterson & J. Snyder, (Eds.), _Antisocial behavior in children and adolescents: A developmental analysis and model for intervention._ Washington, D.C.: American Psychological Association.

Payne, M. A. (1989). Use and abuse of corporal punishment: A Caribbean view. _Child Abuse and Neglect,_ 13 (3), 389-401.

Pereira, J. (1994). Gun talk and girls talk: The DJ clash. _Caribbean Studies,_ 27 (3-4), 208-223.

Perks, S. M., & Jameson, M. (1999). The effects of witnessing domestic violence on behavioral problems and depressive symptomology. A community sample of pupils from St Lucia. *West Indian Medical Journal*, 48 (4), 208-211.

Planning Institute of Jamaica (2003). *Economic and Social Survey. Jamaica 2002.* Statistical Institute of Jamaica Library. Kingston, Jamaica: PIOJ.

Plichta, S. (1992). The effects of woman abuse on health care utilization and health status: A literature review. *Women's Health Issues*, 2 (3), 154-163.

Poole, S. R., Ushkow, M. C., Nader, P. R., Bradford,B. J., Asbury, J. R., Worthington, D. C., Sanabria, K. E., & Carruth, T. (1991). The role of the pediatrician in abolishing corporal punishment in schools. *Pediatrics*, 88 (1), 162-167.

Pottinger, A. M. (2005). Children's experience of loss by parental migration in inner-city Jamaica. *American Journal of Orthopsychiatry*, 75 (4), 485-496.

Raia, J. A. (1999). Treatment of children and adolescents exposed to community violence. [Electronic Version]. National Center for Post-Traumatic Stress Disorder. *Clinical Quarterly*, 8 (4), 56-60.

Rawlins, J. M. (2000). Domestic violence in Trinidad: A family and public health problem. *Caribbean Journal of Criminology and Social Psychology*, 5 (1-2), 165-180.

Robinson, C. (2003). Coverage of crime and violence in the Jamaican media: Attitudinal survey of media workers, pp. 1-8, unpublished work.

Robotham, D. (1984). *"The notorious riot": The socio-economic and political base of Paul Bogle's revolt*. Kingston, Jamaica: Institute of Social and Economic Research, UWI, Mona

Rock, L. (2002). Child abuse in Barbados. In C. Barrow (Ed.), *Children's rights, Caribbean realities*. Kingston, Jamaica: Ian Randle Publishers, pp. 305-329.

Rodriquez, T. (1990). Violence and women. Washington, D.C.: *Conference proceedings on Inter-American Consultation on Women and Violence*, July 1990.

Rohner, R. P., Kean, K. J., & Cournoyer, D. E. (1991). Effects of corporal punishment, perceived caretaker warmth, and cultural beliefs on the psychological adjustment of children in St. Kitts, West Indies. *Journal of Marriage and the Family*, 53 (3), 681-693.

Rosberg, M. (2005). *Impact of crime and violence on children and adolescents.* Community Rehabilitation Department, Ministry of Human Development, UNICEF, Belize.

Rosenberg, M. L., & Mercy, J. A.(1992). Assaultive violence. In J. M. Last & R. B. Wallace (Eds.), *Public health and preventive medicine (13th Ed.)*. Norwalk, Connecticut: Appleton and Lange, pp. 1035-1039.

Rosenthal, B. S. (2000). Exposure to community violence in adolescence: Trauma symptoms. *Adolescence*, 35, 271-284.

Rosenthal B. S., & Wilson, W. C. (2003). Impact of exposure to community violence and psychological symptoms on college performance among students of color. *Adolescence*, 38 (150), 239-249.

Caribbean Regional Consultation (2005). *Report on the Adolescent Forum.* March 2005.

Runyan, D., Wattam, C., Ikeda, R., Hassan, F., & Ramiro L. (2002). Child abuse and neglect by parents and other caregivers. In E. G. Krug, L. L. Dahlberg, J. A. Mercy, A. B. Zwi, & R. Lozano (Eds.), *World report on violence and health.* Geneva: World Health Organization, pp. 57-86.

Sacco, F. C., & Twemlow, M. D. (1997). School violence reduction: A model Jamaican secondary school programme. *Community Mental Health Journal*, 33 (3), 229-234.

Samms-Vaughan M. E., & Jackson, M. (2002). *Improving behaviour in Jamaican children: A model for intervention based on epidemiological analysis.* Report prepared for the Inter-American Development Bank.

Samms-Vaughan, M. E., Jackson, M. A., & Ashley, D. E. (2005). Urban Jamaican children's exposure to community violence. *West Indian Medical Journal;* 54 (1), 14-21.

Samms-Vaughan, M. E., Jackson, M., Ashley, D., & Lambert, M. (2007) (In Press). Jamaican children's experience of corporal punishment at home and school. *Child Abuse and Neglect.*

Samms-Vaughn, M. (2000). *Cognition, educational attainment and behaviour in a cohort of Jamaican children: A comprehensive look at the development and behaviour of Jamaica's eleven year olds.* Working Paper Number 5. Kingston, Jamaica: Planning Institute of Jamaica.

Seemungal, F. (1994). Empowering "survivors" of domestic violence: Feminism as research for social response in Trinidad and Tobago. Report in fulfillment of the Certificate Course in Gender and Development Studies. Barbados, University of the West Indies, Cave Hill.

Singer, M. I., Anglin, T. M., Song L., & Lunghofer L. (1995). Adolescents' exposure to violence and associated symptoms of psychological trauma. *Journal of the American Medical Association,* 273 (6), 477-482.

Singer, M. I., Miller, D. B., Guo, S., Flannery, D. J., Frierson, T., & Slovak, K. (1999). Contributors to violent behavior among elementary and middle school children. *Pediatrics,* 104 (4), 878-884.

Sloan, J. H., Kellermann, A. L., Reay, D. T., Ferris, J. A., Koepsell, T., Rivara, F. P., Rice, C., Gray, L., & LoGerfo, J. (1988). Handgun regulations, crime, assaults and homicide. A tale of two cities. *New England Journal of Medicine,* 319 (19), 1256-1262.

Smith, B. J. (2000). Marginalized youth, delinquency, and education: The need for critical-interpretive research. *Urban Review,* 32 (3), 293-312.

Smith, D. E., & Mosby, G. (2003). Jamaican child-rearing practices: The role of corporal punishment. *Adolescence,* 38 (150), 369-381.

Song, L.Y., Singer, M. I., & Anglin, T. M. (1998) Violence exposure and emotional trauma as contribution to adolescents' violent behaviour. *Archives of Pediatric and Adolescent Medicine,*152 (6), 531-536.

Soyibo, K., & Lee, M. G. (2000). Domestic and school violence among high school students in Jamaica. *West Indian Medical Journal*, 49 (3), 232-236.

Springen, K. (2006). Teen brains changed by violent videogames. *Newsweek Health*, MSNBC.com, November 28, 2006.

Stark, E., & Flitcraft, A. H. (1992). Spouse abuse. In J. M. Last & R. B. Wallace (Eds.), *Public health and preventive medicine (13th Edition)*. Norwalk, Connecticut: Appleton and Lange, pp.1040-1043.

Stewart, K. (2002). "So wha, me nuh fe fi liv to?" Interpreting violence in Jamaica through the dancehall culture. *IDEAZ*, 1, 17-28.

Stiles, M. M. (2002) Witnessing domestic violence: The effect on children. *American Family Physician*, 66 (11), 2052-2066.

Stolzoff, N. C. (2000). *Wake the town and tell the people: Dancehall culture in Jamaica*. Durham, NC: Duke University Press.

Stone, C. (1987). *Class, race and political behavior in urban Jamaica: New challenges for public policy*. Kingston, Jamaica: University of the West Indies Press.

Strueber, D., Lueck, M., & Roth, G. (2006). The violent brain. *Scientific American Mind*, 17 (6), 20-27.

Sukhu, R. L. M. (2000). Domestic violence and power: A war of words and fists. *Caribbean Journal of Criminology and Social Psychology*, 5, 228-236.

Swinford, S. P., DeMaris, A., Cernkovich, S. A., & Giordano, P. G. (2000). Harsh physical discipline in childhood and violence in later romantic involvements: The mediating role of problem behaviors. *Journal of Marriage and the Family*, 62 (2), 508-519.

Terborg, J. (2002). Social change, socialization and sexual practice among Maroon children in Suriname. In C. Barrow (Ed.), *Children's rights, Caribbean realities*. Kingston, Jamaica: Ian Randle Publishers pp: 269-282.

Thompson, E. (2002). Children at risk: Television plus aggression equals aggressive children. *The Jamaican Gleaner*, August 28, 2002.

Tolan, P. H., Guerra, N. G., & Kendall, P. C. (1995). Introduction to special section: Prediction and prevention of antisocial behaviour in children and adolescents. *Journal of Consulting and Clinical Psychology*, 63(4).515-517.

Tremblay, R. E. (2006). Prevention of youth violence: Why not start at the beginning? *Journal of Abnormal Child Psychology*, 34 (4): 481-487.

*Trinidad Guardian*, The. (2006). Spare the rod and encourage the child. Editorial. March 13, 2006.

United Nations (1995). *Report on the world's women 1995: Trends and statistics*. New York, NY: UN.

———. (1996). *The Beijing Declaration and Platform for Action*. New York, NY: UN.

United Nation Development Programme (1999). *National Report on the situation of gender violence against women*. [Online]. Available: http://www.undp.org/rblac/gender/jamaicabigfile.pdf

UNICEF (1992). _UNICEF and intra-Caribbean technical cooperation in maternal and child health_, pp. 40-43. UNICEF.

———. (1999-2000). _Jamaican children and their families. A situation assessment and analysis._ Kingston, Jamaica: UNICEF.

———. (2000). _Jamaican children and their families. A situation assessment and analysis 1999-2000._ Kingston, Jamaica: UNICEF.

———. (2000). _Survey on the rights of the child in Guyana._ Bridgetown, Barbados: UNICEF Caribbean Area Office.

———. (2001). _Situational analysis of children and women in twelve countries of the Caribbean: Protection: Children 'at risk.'_ Barbados: UNICEF Eastern Caribbean.

———. (2005). _Violence against children in the Caribbean region. A desk review._ Kingston, Jamaica: UNICEF.

———. (2007). _Violence against children in the Caribbean region. Regional assessment. UN Secretary General's study on violence against children._ Panama: UNICEF.

UNODC and WB. (2007). _Crime, violence and development: Trends, costs, and policy options in the Caribbean. Report # 3720. A joint report by the United Nations Office on Drugs and Crime and the Latin America and the Caribbean Region of the World Bank._ March 2007. Washington, D.C.: World Bank.

Vermeiren, R., Ruchkin,V., Leckman, P. E., Deboutte, D., & Schwab-Stone, M. (2002). Exposure to violence and suicide risk in adolescents: A community study. _Journal of Abnormal Child Psychology, 30_(5), 529-537.

Villani, S. (2001). Impact of media on children and adolescents: A 10-year review of the research. _Journal of the American Academy of Child and Adolescent Psychiatry, 40_ (4), 392-401.

Volpe, J. S. (1996). Effects of domestic violence on children and adolescents: An overview. _The American Academy of Experts in Traumatic Stress, Inc._ [Online]. Available: http://www.aaets.org/article8.htm.

Ward, C. L., Flisher, A. J., Zissis, C., Muller. M., & Lombard, C. (2001). Exposure to violence and its relationship to psychopathology in adolescents. _Injury Prevention, 7_(4), 297-301.

Ward, E. (2001). _Injuries and exposure to violence among Jamaicans._ Kingston, Jamaica: Ministry of Health.

White, G. (1967). Rudie, oh Rudie. _Caribbean Quarterly,_ 13.

Williams, S (2002). The mighty influence of long custom and practice: Sexual exploitation of children for cash and goods in Jamaica. In C. Barrow (Ed.), _Children's rights, Caribbean realities._ Kingston, Jamaica: Ian Randle Publishers, pp: 330-349.

Women's Media Watch (2000). _A portrayal of violence in media to Jamaican youth: A content analysis._ Kingston, Jamaica.

World Bank (2003). _Caribbean youth development: Issues and policy directions._ Washington, D.C.: The World Bank. Available: http://wbln0018.worldbank.org.

World Health Organization (1997). *Violence against women – Health consequences.* Geneva: WHO.

———. (1998). *Gender and health.* Geneva: WHO.

Wurtele, S. K. (1990). Teaching personal safety skills to four-year-old children. A behavioral approach. *Behavior Therapy*, 21(1), 25-32.

# 15 Traditional Mental Health Practices in Jamaica

## On the Phenomenology of Red Eye, Bad-mind and Obeah

*Frederick W. Hickling & Caryl James*

Obeah and Myalism (Chevannes, 1995a) are African religious retentions practised in Jamaica and the Caribbean. They also represent forms of indigenous traditional medicine – used for protecting and restoring health – that existed in these societies before the arrival of modern Western medicine. These indigenous approaches to health and religion belong to the traditions of each country and have been handed down from generation to generation. In practice, the term 'traditional medicine' refers to acupuncture, traditional birth attendants, mental healers and herbal medicine (Hamilton, 2003), and it exists in Africa, Asia, China and the Caribbean (Bannerman, Burton & Wen-Chieh , 1983). In some parts of Africa traditional medicine is referred to as 'Obeye' and has taken on many names in the Caribbean islands such as Shango (in Trinidad), Santeria (in Cuba), Voodoo (in Haiti), Ju-Ju (in Bahamas) and Obeah in Jamaica (Giraldo, 2003).

Although traditional medicine has long since been an integral component in the maintenance of health in these countries, it has gone large-ly unrecognized for its contribution to the healthcare sector from a Western perspective. This method of treatment focuses on the spiritual and moral aspect of health. Therefore, illnesses that posit causation by witchcraft, sorcery, a broken taboo or spiritual imbalance, are dealt with by the traditional practitioner (Bhugra & Bhui, 2003). Despite the fact that these explanations for illness were strongly highlighted in traditional societies in the past, they became de-emphasized with the coming of the 19th century. This era "...introduced doubt where previously there has been belief and emphasized intellect and logic...", resulting in the new approach to health known as Western scientific medicine (Bannerman et al., 1983). The belief of Western medicine that its approach was the most effective approach to health, denigrated traditional medicine, and disregarded these practices as weird and outlandish, a product of ignorance and superstition, being unscientific and virtually unverifiable. The Western medicine approach to the diagnosis of ill health is thought to be more effective as it is viewed as "...rational and scientific..." (Hayes & Watrall, 2000 p.1). More recently, this perception has been challenged, and there has been a re-awakening of interest in the emotional, spiritual and the so-called 'irrational' aspects of health (Bhugra & Bhui, 2003). This shift has often been led by patients who insist on seeking the services of traditional practitioners in spite of the availability of highly developed Western medical systems, with free practitioner service and technologically advanced hospitals (Bannerman e. al., 1983). The efficacy and primacy of Western biomedicine is well established, and those brought up in the Western tradition are often at a loss to understand why rational thinking people should not choose Western medicine as their best option for health care. While it cannot be disputed that Western medicine has brought dramatic improvement in some physical health conditions, increasing numbers of patients today believe that the traditional practitioner has a better understanding of their 'total life style', diet, rest, human relations, sexuality and even the moral and spiritual factors – and this satisfies the patient's desire to be understood. Additionally, there is the belief that the healer can "...call on vital and even cosmic forces to reinforce his own skills and release the patient's own will to recover and add greatly to their confidence..." (Bannerman et al., 1983 p.4). The traditional, more holistic approach that includes mind-body-spirit and emotion in its formulation, is juxtaposed with the approach taken by Western medicine, which has tended to separate the mind from the body and largely ignored the importance of mental and spiritual health. Plato-Charmides (460 B.C.) wrote "...You ought not to attempt to cure the body without the soul... For this is the great error of our day in the treatment of the human body, that physicians separate the soul from the body..." (Hased, 1998 p. 3).

The degree of 'reductionism' and 'deconstructionism' in modern science has helped to negate the holistic understanding of the patient at the expense of an increasingly technological and pharmacological approach to health care. As such, Western medicine has broken down the human body into various systems, each having its own properties, functions and reactions to disease. This approach has resulted in the perception of the individual and his illness as being only physical. Based on this, many have argued that this approach has led Western practitioners to lose contact with basic human values of respect for the other person's beliefs and preferences which involved other spiritual and emotional aspects (Hased, 1998). To be more specific, it has also been argued that Western practitioners lack understanding when patients attribute their illnesses to anything other than that which is scientific. This lack of understanding, researchers reveal, is due largely to the fact that Western practitioners tend to have the misconception that the deeply held beliefs and values their patients have towards their illness can be changed through rational reasoning. Western practitioners may, therefore, think that if they show the patients how rational their approach is, as opposed to the patient's approach to his or her illness, then the patient will comply. The result can be catastrophic when Western practitioners refuse to acknowledge the patients' approach to health. Smith (1997) suggests that culture permeates all our social interactions, becomes ingrained in our beliefs and shapes our worldview. He argues that the 'dominant medicine', that is, Western medicine, instead of using Western culture as a reference point, forces many to view Western culture as "the truth", with the conclusion that other cultures must be wrong. Smith recognized that there are many cultures and many truths, and that no single culture has a controlling share of the truth. Harrah (2003) concludes, "We must remain knowledgeable about other theories and practices, because our patients are... it is our responsibility as physicians to be aware, non-judgmental, yet appropriately skeptical in order to provide the best care we can. This includes being unbiased when faced with a patient who wishes to pursue alternative treatment."

Mgobhozi et al. (2000) revealed that 70 per cent of the patients in

South Africa, whom they studied, consulted traditional healers as a first choice and that the Shangomas (traditional healer) sees as many as 20 patients per day. These traditional practitioners function as traditional birth attendants, herbalists and healers. WHO estimates that traditional birth attendants assist in up to 95 per cent of all rural births and 70 per cent of urban births in developing countries (Hamilton, 2003), and notes that not only is traditional medicine a potentially important resource for the delivery of health care in these countries, but also that medicinal plants used by these practitioners are of great importance to the health of individuals and communities.

## Traditional Medicine and Mental Illness

The belief systems of African society, like many Caribbean societies populated mainly with peoples derived from the African slave trade of the seventeenth and eighteenth centuries, consists of beliefs in god, divinities, spirits, ancestors and the practice of magic medicine (Chevannes 1995b). These phenomena are critical to the expression, interpretation, diagnosis, and treatment of behaviours that are seen by Western society as psychiatric disorders (Fabrega, 2003). Dein (1997) argues that in the West, emphasis is placed on psychological factors, life events, and the effects of stress as an explanation for mental illness. However, in many parts of the Third World, explanations for mental illness take into account spirit possession, witchcraft, the breaking of religious taboos, divine retribution and the capture of the soul by spirit. A prevalent belief among Jamaicans is that it is possible to influence the health or well-being of another person through the use of Obeah. The effect of this has been noted by Morrow (1983), who describes patients who, under the influence of Obeah become "inexplicably and inexorably sickened". Devisch (1993 p. 149) suggests that the traditional healer locates illness not in the individual but in his social relationships. For these people, healing is a physical, ritualistic method allowing the individual to "reconnect with others, his life world, the world of dreams with spirits and ancestral shades". Healing is not just about curing, but also about the protection and promotion of human physical, spiritual and material well-being. In distinguishing curing from healing, it should be noted that curing is an act of treating successfully a specific condition. In light of this, Western medicine deals with curing not healing. In contrast, the traditional practitioner deals with healing, which this refers to the whole person and is seen as an integrated system with both the spiritual and physical components (Stewart & Strathern, 1999).

## Christian and African Religious Syncretism

Chevannes (1995b) provides an account of the emergence of African religious retentions such as Myal, Revivalism, Obeah, Zion and Pukumina and their syncretic relationship with Christianity, the religious ideology of the European colonizer. There is no doubt, as he points out, that maintenance of slavery and colonialism was accomplished primarily by physical force and by the power of an enslaving ideology. Nowhere is this mental tug-of-war revealed as nakedly as in the manifestations of psychosis and madness in Jamaican people, where religiosity forms a major phenomenological buttress.

> A 32-year-old male, black, a rural farm laborer, married at age 27 and during the same year was converted to an evangelical Christian religion. Within two years of marriage he started acting strangely, displaying violent aggressive outbursts towards his wife. There were marked sexual problems in the marriage as conditions in the marriage became more strained. He became excessively religious and aggressive and was admitted to the Bellevue Mental Hospital. He claimed that nothing was wrong with him although he was displaying auditory hallucinations and paranoid delusions. He claimed that his wife was trying to work Obeah (death spiritualism) on him and that was the cause of his problems. His entire family came to the hospital and discharged him against medical advice, concurring with his belief that his wife was working Obeah on him in order to get him out of the way.

Poverty, conflicting religious syncretism, together with marital and sexual difficulty emerge as the major themes of this case study. This man's abnormal behaviour started with the stress of a poor marriage and coincided with his religious conversion to Christianity. Belief in Obeah, as a defence against his economic and emotional crisis, was a logical sequence in the cultural context; as the Christian belief system and Church failed to resolve the economic and psychosexual stressors. Jamaica, a land of predominantly African people, was totally immersed in the religious culture of European Christianity, and flight into the

Christian religion is a common and accepted way of coping with problems among Jamaicans. His problems, however, continued to intensify until the belief system of Christianity could no longer contain his psychic disturbance. His ultimate defence at the height of his illness was the African religious form of Obeah or necromancy – a belief in ancestral spirits that the British Anti-Obeah slave law of 1761 had ruthlessly but unsuccessfully tried to suppress. Not only did this further flight into a deeply culturally-bound religious belief system adequately cope with his aggressive paranoid state, but the concurrence by his family who discharged him from the mental hospital and Western therapy, effectively scapegoated his wife and absolved him of the economic and other responsibilities of the union. This represents an individual's attempt to deal with the problems of cultural and economic subjugation by the oppressive social system, through progressively retreating through the 'layers' of syncretic beliefs into madness.

The African healing religious retention is evident in Jamaica as Revivalism. Patients use both Western and Revival systems to satisfy their perceived healthcare needs. Individuals, therefore, use the Western system for physical symptoms (these are deemed to be natural) and the traditional system (Obeah) for dealing with the spiritual and the moral aspects of health and illness. Wirth (1995, cited in Weaver, 2003) suggests:

> Traditionally, spiritual healing practitioners believed illness manifested on the physical level is due to an imbalance in psychological or spiritual aspects of the individual. The role of the healer is to correct this imbalance by utilizing culturally accepted and proven methods of healing. (p. 249)

In an effort to protect themselves as well as their loved ones, Jamaicans who attribute their illness to Obeah resort to the Obeah man for help. Some Jamaicans believe that illness can result from a variety of spiritual activities which can be purposely positioned by practitioners of Obeah, and that these spiritual practitioners can also remove such illness. Obeah men and women can, therefore, be either purveyors of illness or healers of disease. Many Jamaicans incorporate concepts of Western medical sciences as well as African religious retention into their understanding of health and mental health problems. When Obeah is used for healing it is often called 'Myal'. The term 'Myal' is the description of a Pan-

African religion that may have Central African roots (Schuler, 1979), which posits a spiritual cause of disease and social disorder (Chevannes, 1995b). The doctor or Myal man, is resorted to, in order to neutralize the power of the Obeah man. The Myal man is often seen as the antipodal antidote to the Obeah man. Sometimes his remedies are of a very simple character, particularly if his object was to cure some local disease (Blyth, 1851 p. 174 quoted from Chevannes 1995b p. 7).

> The Myalman or Myalwoman, thus, operated like a practitioner treating a patient, one to one. Groups, led by Myalmen would gather at night, singing and dancing in circles and undergoing possession, and then would follow their leaders as they discovered and destroyed Obeahs, or released the shadows of those bewitched. The multiple concept of the soul is still found in Jamaica; the soul, which goes to hell or heaven; the spirit, which can journey during sleep; and the shadow, or inner self, of which the visible shadow is but a reflection. Through Obeah it is possible to hurt one by attacking one's shadow..." Chevannes 1995b, p. 7)

## The Role of Obeah in Treating Mental Illness in Jamaica

In an important study of the efficacy of Obeah in the treatment of psychiatric patients in Jamaica, James et al (2007) showed that traditional medicine has been and continues to be beneficial to patients' healthcare. The study by James and her colleagues evaluated mentally ill Jamaican patients' perspective of the diagnosis given to them by their Western practitioners as opposed to the Obeah man's diagnosis. The study also evaluated their perspectives of the after-effects of the treatment given from the Western practitioner as well as the Obeah man. Participants in this study were selected from the psychiatric ward (Ward 21) at the University Hospital of the West Indies and Bellevue Mental Hospital located in Kingston Jamaica. The sample comprised 51 participants, (55% female), most of whom (67%) were less than 35 years old, and 69 per cent of whom were employed. The majority (88.2%) was actively affiliated with an Afrocentric religion.

A Jamaican Healthcare Perception Questionnaire was developed at the University Hospital of the West Indies, after permission was received from the Massachusetts Department of Mental Health to employ some of the items from their Healthcare Preference Questionnaire that were modified for cultural applicability. The resulting 34-item questionnaire was designed to gather data on the perception that patients have about their selected treatment modality whether it be traditional medicine (including healers, herbalists, or Obeah men/women) or formal medicine (any form of Western medicine including psychiatry, medical doctor, hospital, or clinic). Of the sample, 30 (59%) incorporated traditional medicine in the treatment of their condition, while 21 (41%) of those sampled sought formal medicine as the first step in treating their healthcare problems. The choice of formal medicine as their first treatment option was influenced by the patients' belief that this was the most effective approach (53%) and by their family's influence (29%).

Although 36 (71%) of the sample indicated that their formal practitioner had given them a diagnosis, only 17 (55%) agreed with the formal Western diagnosis assigned. These diagnostic categories included schizophrenia, bipolar disorder and depression. Many who did not agree with the diagnosis given believed that their illness was due to the influence of spirits, individuals using Obeah against them, and fatigue. Of those participants who had also incorporated traditional medicine into their healthcare choice 77 per cent agreed with the diagnosis given by the traditional practitioner. Some of the diagnoses included 'someone working Obeah on them',' the influence of a 'duppy' [*duppy = ghost, the spirit of the dead, believed to be capable of returning to aid or more often to harm living beings, directly or indirectly* (Cassidy and Le Page, 1980)], or that they needed 'healing'. The small segment who disagreed (23%) with the diagnosis given by the traditional practitioner, felt that their illness was due to nerves, or fatigue.

The majority of the participants (94%) had received treatment from their formal practitioner. For the most part, formal practitioners gave their patients medication (82%) or medication and counselling (10%). Patients who had gone to a traditional practitioner received varied types of treatment, including something to drink (33%), baths and herbs (20%), spiritual healing (17%), and being rubbed with herbs (7%). Approximately half of the patients who were treated by the Western practitioner (51%) felt that their symptoms had not been addressed. When it came to the effectiveness of the treatment, both practitioners were given a positive rating. Seventy-four per cent of the patients felt that their condition improved as a result of the interventions of the Western practitioner and 73 per cent of those who had also accessed traditional medicine felt that their condition had improved as a result of the interventions of the traditional practitioner. The majority of the sample had faith in the formal healthcare system and believed that the formal practitioner and the traditional practitioner were to be trusted. Of the sample, 67 per cent concluded that it would be beneficial for traditional medicine to be incorporated in the healthcare system. Although both practitioners were credited for their actions in the improvement of their patients, often the traditional practitioner was given more credit. However, the results indicated that patients who had incorporated traditional medicine into their treatment were significantly less likely to think that the quality of service of Western medicine was good, and that incorporation of traditional medicine into their mode of treatment would be beneficial to the healthcare industry. Given the fact that Western medicine is given the sole right to practice in Jamaica, the patients' right to choose his or her preferred healthcare treatment becomes restricted on entering the healthcare system (Weaver, 2003). Despite the monopolistic pressures of Western medicine, Jamaicans resolutely seek alternative and traditional healing in Obeah. Although many practitioners of Western medicine in Jamaica might wish to deny the fact that many of their patients use Obeah, this study implies that many Jamaicans have never given up this mode of treatment. Much of the origin of the stigma towards traditional medicine is found in the history of slavery, where the European plantation owners forbade the practice of Obeah. Clearly the Anti-Obeah laws have not prevented patients from using Obeah, and its use has been a part of Jamaica's culture for over 400 years. The laws prohibiting the use of Obeah should be revisited and repealed.

## The Psychology of 'Red Eye' and 'Bad-mind'

A number of phenomenological terms exist in the Caribbean epistemology that escape meaning in the conventional European phenomenological descriptions, but recur repeatedly in Caribbean dialogue and cultural discourse. Included in these expressions are the terms 'red eye', 'bad-mind' and 'grudgeful'. These expressions are commonly encountered in Caribbean patients and play a profound role in patients' understandings of occurrences in their lives, and present particular challenges for the clinician in his or her attempt to comprehend and interpret the phenomenological expression of Caribbean people. These expressions are integrally bound to the worldview and belief systems of contemporary Caribbean people, and play an important role in the understanding of their behaviour.

Strict definitions of these expressions are elusive and often do not capture their full meaning. Moreover, the regularity and intensity with which these terms are used by Caribbean people belie the psychological clarity of their meaning and the critical importance of their causal and diagnostic relationship to every day life and in particular, to psychopathology. Cassidy and Le Page (1980) define 'red eye' as "…a greedy, miserly person…" and questions its allusion to a mongoose. But in common Jamaican parlance, 'red eye' describes much more than a greedy, miserly person; the term refers to persons who are jealous and envious, especially of a particular person's (usually the user of the term) achievement. Within the psychopathological context, the term has an even more profound meaning. In this context it takes on an assertion of an idea of reference, or even frank paranoia, often including elements of the religious belief system of Obeah.

> A 25-year-old man was admitted to hospital after a prolonged episode of status epilepticus (fits). Physical examination and a computerized axial tomography (CAT Scan) revealed a large left-sided frontal lobe tumor in his brain, complete with bilateral papilloedema (bilateral swelling of the optic disk visible from examination of the retina with an ophthalmoscope). He refused neurosurgery, giving the explanation that he had two girlfriends, and that when one girlfriend learned that he was going to marry the other, she was 'red-eye' and visited an Obeah-man who worked a 'science' that put a 'lick' on him that had caused his illness.

Note that he had not described her as *having* 'red eye', but that she *was* 'red eye'. 'Red eye' was not described as a noun, but as an adjective. The red eye was not a passive condition like a common cold, but an active condition; a descriptor for jealousy and anger which provoked her to mobilize the evil 'spirits' (science) of an Obeah man to provoke retributive damage (the 'lick'). If she could not have him, then certainly the other woman would not have him either, or at least the other woman would receive 'damaged goods'. Thus 'red eye' can simply mean 'jealous' and/or 'angry', as used in the sentence: "Go away, you are too red eye…" or can be used to describe the active intent of inflicting hurt and/or damage on another by the use of Obeah. Often, when the expression is used, there is an implication about the use of Obeah. However, the very act of confronting the person with the term, is a measure to counteract the potential for the other person to contemplate the use of Obeah. The concept of 'red eye' can be characterized as an emotion, but this chapter suggests that the concept also characterizes a behaviour that accompanies an emotion.

The word Obeah is described by Olive Senior (2003) as follows: "…to denote witchcraft, evil magic or sorcery by which supernatural power is invoked to achieve personal protection or the destruction of enemies…" Since Obeah was made illegal in 1761, and is still illegal today, and its use is shrouded in denial, fear and stigma, it is difficult to accurately assess its prevalence in today's society. What about the idea that talking about it may "spoil it"? 'Goat mouth' anyone?

> …Any Nega or other slave who shall pretend any supernatural power and be detected in making use of any blood, feathers, parrots beaks, dog's teeth, alligator's teeth, broken bottles, grave dirt, rum, eggshells or any other materials related to the practice of Obeah or witch craft in order to delude and impose on the minds of others shall upon conviction thereof before two magistrates and three freeholders suffer death or transportation. Anything in this act or any other act or any other law to the contrary not with standing… (Anti Obeah Law : January 1761)

There is no doubt, however, that Obeah occupies a pervasive position in the belief system of Caribbean people, and its practice is quite popular. It is used for personal protection in health, legal issues and matters of the heart. It is also commonly used to foil enemies. Many Jamaicans would routinely place powders and oils in their application forms for American visas and Green Cards. This has forced the American Embassy in Kingston to request that applicants submit their application forms in a clean and pristine condition, and refrain from placing said oils and powders with their applications. According to Senior, the word 'Obeah' has been used "loosely to describe any non-Christian beliefs, practices and rituals" in the Jamaican context, and can be used to do harm, or to achieve beneficial ends or 'healing'.

## The Exercise of Negative Power

It seems that one of the psychological legacies of European enslavement of African people is the exercise by the latter of negative power. In the harsh authoritarian culture of slavery, slaves would often resort to the use of covert activities embodied in the subservient posture of the slave in order to carry out sabotage and resistance, such as spitting in the slave masters food in its preparation. The exercise of negative power seems to have created a seeming intractable contradiction for the Jamaican society today, where authority seems almost irrelevant, and justice is fast becoming a farce. The syndromes of 'red eye' – unbridled greed and covetousness ('covitchousness' in the popular parlance), and 'bad-mind' – irrational wickedness and morbid jealousy, are major components of this phenomenon. The pervasiveness of this psychology is accompanied by an inverse pride, which seemingly applauds the most contrary exhibitions of this type of behaviour. It often hides behind the popular figure from African mythology, 'Anancy, the spider man', who is revered for his ability to 'con' or trick his way into a position of power and control. The more dangerous aspects of this phenomenon occur when lawful confrontation of criminal and illegal behaviour is deemed 'informing', and being gentle and generous is viewed as being soft ('soff' - in the popular parlance).

Many Jamaican people, to say nothing of visitors to the country, must marvel at the extremely common phenomenon, observed in Jamaican behaviour, where a Jamaican person or institution performs a seemingly irrational act out of entirely individualistic and selfish short-term interest. Low-income-housing residents, for example, have been known to deliberately block their own toilets in order to get the job contracts to clear the blocked sewer line, or steal the toilet bowls from the schools attended by their own children. Residents living beside a gully course continue to dump garbage into it, despite numerous warnings as to the consequences of a blocked gully, and in spite of having been flooded out of their homes when the blocked gully overflowed its banks after a heavy rain. After a frank and factual television programme on British Channel 4 TV on deplorable conditions at the Kingston Public Hospital, the former Minister of Health, the Honourable Peter Phillips, angrily ignored the critical realities exposed by the documentary and proceeded to attack the foreign press for failing to report the aspects of the hospital that did work (*The Daily Gleaner*, 28 January 1997, p. 1). The same Peter Phillips in an earlier essay on the Jamaican elite (1977), had sagely instructed: "...Transformation of Caribbean societies besotted with a lengthy past of colonialism and racisms must involve then, an attack on the psychological structures and patterns of relationships..." (p. 1), and concluded: "In any case, should the current elite, whatever their ideology, prove unequal to the task, the contradictions in the society which already seem to be producing vibrant counter-cultures and possible counter-elites will no doubt be sharpened and portend in time a new series of cataclysms, which, destructive though they may be, hold that 'better' which it is said, in popular parlance, 'must come'..." (p.13).

This no doubt, must be, in the popular parlance, an example of 'cock mout kill cock' (*what one says may come back to punish the speaker*). The present Jamaican society is replete with examples like these, of the intractable 'contradictions' that seem to plague our daily lives. A domestic helper, for example, on breaking a plate while washing it will proclaim" "The plate bruck" [*The plate broke*], not "I broke the plate". Few Jamaican people will take responsibility and full accountability for their actions. This also applies to many Jamaican institutions. In fact, one of the most debilitating realities of daily life in Jamaica is of individuals' and institutions' failure to critically analyze their behaviour, and to take full responsibility and accountability for their actions. The undoubted remnant of the dependency syndrome of the post-slave society described by Beckford (1972) must be one of the most agonizing conundrums facing Jamaica today. Few take responsibility; even fewer accept accountability. The politicians who designed the tribal 'garrison constituencies' and who win electoral power with a 101 per cent plebiscite (Kerr, 1997) refuse to acknowledge their role in the genesis of the lawless violent society which now seems to be beyond their control.

The term 'red eye' has become increasingly synonymous with a phenomenological or psychic state that describes a person's ability to experience jealousy born of a specific experience. This jealousy transforms itself into a rage which is sated only by revenge meted out by mobilization of a supernatural 'attack' on the object of the jealousy/revenge. Jamaican psychiatry is replete with case studies of this nature, where a psychological 'flight into religion' is often the major manifestation of the psychotic breakdown of the individual, and represents the ultimate psychological defence in situations of great stress, especially in the poorer classes. The phenomena of 'red eye' and 'bad-mind' are exceedingly common in contemporary Jamaican society and are found increasingly in the contemporary cultural forms of music, song and drama. Their use and occurrence crosses all classes.

## Bad-mind, Grudgeful and Obeah

The concept of 'bad-mind' or bad-mindedness' has been defined by Allsopp (2004) as "malice; spite; animosity; the harboring of active ill-will'. It is suggested that the derivation probably comes from African languages in which 'mind' is expressed by the same word for 'heart', 'chest', or 'inside-body' and supply the Yoruba derivation ni inu buruku meaning 'have a bad inside', or 'malevolent'. Allsopp also draws the fine distinction between 'bad-mind', and bad **mind** – a naturally malicious mind – but adds that the distinction might not be very great, although used differently in some instances, quoting: "He got a bad mind and is unreasonable, that is why he is sick, God is punishing him, she added" (*The Guyana Citizen*, 29 November 1976, p. 6)". On the other hand, Allsopp provides an example of the use of bad-mind as used conventionally in the Caribbean in a quotation from the *Trinidad Express*: "Dr Williams's closest friends should advise him that the politics of bad-mind will not do and that he should positively discourage any attempt to divide this nation." (*Trinidad Express*, 1 December 1979, p. 4). Allsopp defines the adjective bad-minded (spiteful; malevolent; envious; ungenerous) giving the following example of its use: "They don't lend us their wheelbarrow, so if we wanted to be bad-minded about it we needn't lend them our ladder" (Guyanese manuscript – Allsopp ( 2004) p. 67)". The noun 'bad-mindedness' is finally defined as 'spite; malevolence; malignant attitude' and a further example of its conventional usage is given: "The bad-mindedness and the roguishness are largely a product of the old-time manipulative Doctor Politics which simply cannot help but hold us in contempt, confident that we can be brambled over an over by these facile stratagems (*Tapia*, 21 December 1975, p. 6)

It is quite clear from the definitions provided, that 'bad-mind', 'bad-minded' and 'bad-mindedness' are phenomenological constructions of the Caribbean that connote a particular form of spite or malevolence that is not commonly found in conventional English parlance and would, therefore, never feature in the American Psychiatric Association's Diagnostic Statistical Manual or any other psychiatric nosological classificatory systems in conventional use. However, practitioners of mental health, without a clear understanding of this phenomenological construction, would be hard-pressed to understand the thinking and behaviour of most Caribbean people who use this construction in everyday life. These practitioners would often make diagnostic mistakes such as the misinterpretation for psychotic paranoia, based on their ignorance of this phenomenon when dealing with patients from the English-speaking Caribbean. The concept of 'bad-mind' is almost always linked in Caribbean phenomenology to 'red eye', that is described earlier in this chapter, and the concept of 'grudgeful', all of which are linked to the practice of Obeah. 'bad-mind' denotes an evil intent, 'red-eye' connotes jealousy/avarice, while 'grudgeful' embodies revenge.

Cassidy and Le Page (1980) define 'grudgeful' as an adjective meaning envious or jealous, and quote many folk songs of the region where the word 'grudgeful' is used as a phenomenological description of life events. For example, the folksong "Sammy plant piece a corn down a gully" says, "A no tief Sammy tief make dem kill him, But a grudgeful dem grudgeful make dem kill him." (Murray 1953), [_translation – They did not kill Sammy for being a thief, But because they were envious of him_].

The use of the adjective 'grudgeful' multiplies the potency of the phenomenon 'red eye' when used in conjunction with 'bad-mind', and both phenomena when used together are catapulted into the world and meaning of Obeah and 'higher science' (spiritualism) in the contemporary Caribbean. This phenomenological construction is further compounded when used in connection with 'red-eye' and is pervasive and common in conventional Caribbean usage. In this context 'the exercise of negative power' discussed earlier in the chapter becomes a compelling behaviour in day-to-day Caribbean activity that is magnified in patients with mental health problems, and often makes it difficult to distinguish from paranoia. These constructions are pervasive in the culture of Caribbean people, and are especially prevalent in the lyrics of the popular Caribbean singers and musicians. The following verse from Elephant Man's (given name, O'neal Bryan) popular Dancehall song "Bad Mind" is illustrative:

Bomb a drop, scobaay away,
Bomb a drop
Run for cover, save yuh mama
Yuh too bad mind (rept.3)
Alright then Christian dip (rept.4)
Shingle dips (rept.4) inna spirit (rept.2)
Praise the lord (rept.2)

*Chorus*
We bun bad mind for we hypocrites can't stay
Yuh too bad mind (rept.3)
So we draw our line and tell Satan scobaay
Yuh too bad mind (rept.3)
Kiss the cross and touch the sky
Christian dip, Revival dip, Christian dip, Revival dip
All bad mind things must stop
We a bun out bad mind

Elephant Man has at least two major Dancehall songs that feature the bad-mind theme. Some mental health professionals might interpret the lyrics as paranoid, as they refer to people saying bad things about him and spreading rumors about his life. However, this is a regular feature of Jamaican culture and is often reality-based. His lyrics invoke the Christian faith to drive away Satan (scobaay), but especially the Revival (African-based) religion to negate the bad-mind declaring 'All bad-mind things must stop we a bun out bad-mind'. In this context, 'bun' means 'burn', and signifies the symbolic usage of spiritual fire to vanquish the spiritually evil bad-mind. The repeated use of the word 'dip' is an allusion to the baptismal emersion in water for spiritual cleansing used in many Christian and Revival religious practices.

Dancehall icon, Beenie Man, also mirrors this aspect of the Jamaican culture in the lyrics of his hit feature "Bad Mind Is Active (My Perogative)". Although based on a song by African American Bobby Brown, Beenie Man transposes it into the Jamaican consciousness:

*Chorus 1: Everybody's talking all the crap about me*
Why they just don't let me live
Tell me why

(He's the girls dem sugar)
It's my decision and that's my peragative
They say I'm crazy and they even said I'm (beep)
While I'm living on the girls dem way
So move wid yuh nasty question
You try to destroy my life
Ooh, just llow a man
Mek him deejay him tune and try to survive

_Chorus 2: Bad mind is active (ah)_
Dem a watch nex people business
Bad mind is active (ah, ah, ah, ah)
And it's the way the they want to live
Bad mind is active (ah, ah)
Dem neva stop and think positive
Bad mind is active (ah, ah) but all pon dem mind is negative

In this, Beenie Man is asserting that people (_everybody_) are talking about him because he is so popular and loved by so many women. The lyrics indicate that his detractors call him crazy or homosexual (_beep_), and this is a reflection of their bad mind, which is an active phenomenon, and is used by these people to prey on and mind other people's business. Bennie Man suggests that this active bad mind is 'nasty' and is used in an attempt to destroy him, so he is demanding that these people leave him in peace and allow him practise his successful deejay skills, which he uses for his survival, and to live without their torment. The fact that the original lyrics are African American underscores the seminal relationship between the African Jamaican and African American cultures. Many African Americans are of Jamaican origin, and the current intercultural movement and linkages between these two societies are marked.

This bad mind is commonly linked with 'grudgefulness' in the popular culture, as is expressed in the lyrics of another Dancehall artiste Winston 'Niney' Holness – "Bad Mind Grudgeful":

Now, you say you are my friend
And you know I'll last to the end
Everywhere, every place I go

People ask if I don't know:
You're no good, bad mind grudgeful
You're no good, bad mind grudgeful

Say you trying to see me go down
But you know I'll forever wear a crown
What kind of friend you are
Trying to see me go down?
You're no good, bad mind grudgeful
You're no good, bad mind grudgeful

Say you trying to see me go down
You're no good, bad mind grudgeful
You're no good, bad mind grudgeful
You're no good, bad mind grudgeful.

The phenomenology of bad-mind occurs across the English-speaking Caribbean and is consistently linked to Obeah and demonic spiritualism. Calypsonian, The Mighty Sparrow (Hon. Dr. Slinger Francisco, D.Litt H.B.M., C.M.G., O.C.C.) born to a poor working-class family in Gran Roi, a small fishing village in Grenada, moved to Trinidad as an infant. At the age of 14, he formed a steel band to perform at Carnival, sparking his interest in Calypso. Teaching himself to play the guitar, Sparrow began to write his own songs and has become one of the Caribbean's most successful artists. In 1966 he wrote the Carnival award-winning Road March song, "Melda", which told the story of a woman who uses Obeah and necromancy to try to entrap him into marriage.

### "Obeah Wedding"
You making yourself a pappy show Melda
You making yourself a bloody clown
Up and down the country looking for Obeah
And you perspiration smell so strong
Girl, you only wasting time
Obeah wedding bells don't chime
And you can't trap me
With necromancy

The Calypsonian made it clear, however, that none of those primal African rituals were sufficient to ensnare him, and that her manipulation through Obeah was the foundation for conflict and disharmony:

Melda oh, you making wedding plans
Carrying me name to Obeah man
All you do, can't get through
I still ain't goin' marry to you

Look how many nights we hug up tight, tight, tight
All we ever know was love and peace
Now every minute is only fight, fight, fight
Till you using Obeah man for priest
You don't seem to understand
Obeah can't upset my plan
For Papa Niser
Is me Grandfather

It is sobering to realize from the last verse, however, that in spite of the Calypsonian's rational negation of the necromancy, the realization that the Obeah man who Melda visited to secure the entrapment was no other than the Calypsonian's grandfather, brings with it the thinly-veiled implication that through his bloodline, he has an even more powerful antidote to her Obeah!

## Conclusion

The mental health implications of Obeah in the Caribbean cannot be ignored, and mental health professionals within and outside the Caribbean who deal with Caribbean people must understand the phenomenological implications of 'red eye', 'bad mind' and 'grudgeful' in the daily lives of Caribbean people and the thin line between these phenomena and manifestations of mental illness in English-speaking people from the West Indies, despite their racial, ethnic or class backgrounds. The fact that the use and practice of Obeah is still extremely common throughout the Caribbean and in every area of the world where Caribbean people live, should alert mental health professionals who deal with these peoples to comprehend the power that these belief systems hold for West Indians. The fact that many Obeah men and women still practise their art and craft, must alert us to the fact that patients referred to psychiatrists and psychologists by these Obeah practitioners, recognize that, *ipso facto*, in the eyes of many Caribbean people, psychiatrists and psychologists are themselves seen as Obeah practitioners with additional skills, a wider armamentarium and even greater powers for healing.

## REFERENCES

Allsopp R. (Ed.) (2004). *Dictionary of Caribbean English usage.* Jamaica, Barbados, Trinidad & Tobago: University of the West Indies Press.

American Psychiatric Association (2000). *Diagnostic and Statistical Manual of Mental Disorders 4th Edition, Text Revision.* Washington, D.C: Author.

Bannerman, R. H., Burton, J., & Chen Wen-Chieh (1983). *Traditional medicine and health care coverage: A reader for health administrators and practitioners.* Geneva: WHO.

Beenie Man. Bad Mind Is Active (My Prerogative) http://www.lyricsfreak.com/b/beenie+man/bad+mind+is+active+my+perogative_20152710.html

Bhugra, D., & Bhui, K. (2003). Explanatory models in psychiatry. *British Journal of Psychiatry,* 183, 170-175.

Beckford, G. (1972). *Persistent poverty.* London: Oxford University Press.

Brown, B. (2005) http://www.lyricsfreak.com/f/frank+zappa/bobby+brown_20056812.html

Bryan, O. (Elephant Man) http://lyricstrue.net/bandsongtext/ELEPHANT_MAN/Bun_Bad_Mind.html

Cassidy, F. G., & Le Page, R. B. (1980). *Dictionary of Jamaican English (Second Edition).* Cambridge: Cambridge University Press.

Chevannes, B. (1995a). Introduction to native religions of Jamaica. In B. Chevannes (Ed.), *Rastafari and other Afro-Caribbean world views.* New Jersey: Rutgers University Press.

Chevannes, B. (Ed). (1995b) *Rastafari and other African-Caribbean worldviews.* London: Macmillan Press.

*Daily Gleaner.* 28th January 1997, p. 1. Kingston, Jamaica.

Dein, S. (1997). ABC of mental health: Mental health in a multiethnic society. *British Medical Journal,* 315, 473-476.

Devisch, R. (1993). *Weaving the threads of life: The Khita GYN-eco-logical healing cult among the Yaka.* Chicago: University of Chicago Press.

Fabrega, H. Jr. (2003). *Culture and history in psychiatric diagnosis and practice.* Pennsylvania: Department of Psychiatry, University of Pittsburgh.

Franscisco, S. (The Mighty Sparrow). Melda (Obeah Wedding). http://en.wikipedia.org/wiki/Mighty_Sparrow

Giraldo, A. (2003). Religion and resistance Obeah: The ultimate resistance. Resistancehttp://www.library.miami.edu/archives/slaves/Religion.religion.html

*Guyana Citizen.* 29 November 1976, p.6. Georgetown, Guyana.

Hamilton, L. L (2003). Recognition of Oriental Medicine and Traditional Chinese Medicine. The National Institute of Health (NIH). *Modern World Clinic* http://www.modernacupunctureclinic.com/mission.htm

Harrah, J. D. (2003). *A Western view of alternative medicine.* musom.marshall.edu/sharma/harrah-1.htm

Hased. C. (1998). Mind-body medicine in health promotion: Science, practice and philosophy. *Internet Journal of Health Promotion.* http://www.rhpeo.org/ ijhp-articles/1998/10/index.htm.

Hayes, M., & Watrall, E. (2000). *The Asclepion.* Indiana University Bloomington. http://www.iub.edu/~ancmed/intro.htm

Hewson, M. G. (1998). Traditional healers in South Africa. *Annals of Internal Medicine,* 128, 1029-1034.

Holness, W. 'Niney' Bad Mind Grudgeful. http://www.boldlyrics.com/lyrics/208824

James, C., Weaver, S., & Morgan, K. A. D. (2007). Psychiatric patient's evaluation of the efficacy of traditional medicine versus Western medicine (Submitted for publication).

Mgobhozi, Z. L. J., Mkhize, M., & Puckree, T. (2002). African traditional healers: What health care professionals need to know. *International Journal of Rehabilitation Research.* 25 (4), 247-51.

Morrow, R. C. (1983). On Obeah, Myalism and magical death in Jamaica. *West Indian Medical Journal.* 32 (4), 1-6.

Murray, T. (1953) *Folk songs of Jamaica.* London: Oxford.

Phillips, P. (1977) Jamaican elites: 1938 to present. Chapter 1. In C. Stone & A. Brown (Eds.), *Essays on power and change in Jamaica.* Kingston: Jamaica Publishing House.

Schuler, M. (1979). Myalism and the African religious tradition in Jamaica. In M. E. Crahan & F. Knight (Eds.), *Africa in the Caribbean: The legacies of a link* (pp. 65-79). Baltimore and London: Johns Hopkins University Press.

Senior, O. (2003). *Encyclopedia of Jamaican heritage.* Jamaica: Twin Guinep Publishers.

Smith, B. M. (1997). *Enhancing cultural proficiency in the management care environment.* Washington DC: United States Department of Health and Human Services.

Stewart P. J., & Strathern, A. (1999). *Curing and healing: Medical anthropology in global perspective.* North Carolina: Carolina Academic Press.

*Tapia.* 21 December 1975, p. 6. Port of Spain, Trinidad.

*Trinidad Express.* 1 December 1979, p. 4.Port of Spain, Trinidad.

Weaver, S. (2003). Health and illness in rural community. A study of traditional healthcare practices in the Parish of St. Thomas. Ph.D. Dissertation. University of the West Indies.

# PART III

## ROLES AND TOOLS OF THE CARIBBEAN PSYCHOLOGIST

*Edited by*

Frederick W. Hickling

# 16 The Roles and Responsibilities of Clinical Psychologists in the Caribbean

*Frederick W. Hickling, Ruth Doorbar, Jacqueline Benn, Elaine Gordon, Kai Morgan, & Brigitte K. Matthies*

## I. Frederick W. Hickling – The Psychiatrist's Perspective (Part 1)

It might seem paradoxical that a psychiatrist should anchor a chapter on the roles of clinical psychologists. It is precisely this paradox that speaks to the uniqueness of the process of the development of psychology in the Caribbean. Clinical psychology has been poorly understood in the Caribbean. Psychology is commonly confused with psychiatry, and even at the level of many professionals in medicine, the scope of psychiatry is not clearly defined; and the role of the clinical psychologist is virtually unknown. The retreating British colonizers, in their wisdom, left psychology out of the curriculum of the University of the West Indies at its inception in 1948. Psychiatry was only included in the Faculty of Medical Sciences in 1965, and has remained marginal in the Medical School in spite of the increasing acknowledgement that mental illness is one of the leading causes of morbidity worldwide. In the Caribbean, the scope of psychology and psychiatry is unclear and unrecognized. Additionally, because of the blinkered biological perspective of psychiatry taught at the University of the West Indies' Faculty of Medical Sciences (UWI FMS), the belief that psychopharmacology is the only therapeutic window available to clinicians has been the prevailing wisdom. The increasing role of psychology in health and mental health matters is only now being recognized in the Medical School. In trying to develop this chapter, I have attempted to weave together my experiences as a psychiatrist with those of a pioneering clinical psychologist in Jamaica, Dr. Ruth Doorbar. The opinions of a young Masters'-level clinical psychologist, trained in the newly established programme at UWI (Mona) are presented next. Experienced Jamaican clinical psychologist, Elaine Gordon, who is just completing the PhD Clinical Psychology programmme at UWI (Mona), then presents her experiences. This segment is followed by the opinions of Dr. Kai Morgan, who teaches in the Section of Psychiatry of UWI (Mona), and Dr. Brigitte Matthies, the clinical psychologist who co-authored and pioneered the MSc and PhD courses with me at UWI (Mona). The chapter ends with my attempt to combine these expressions into a coherent whole.

My initial experience as a psychiatric resident working with a clinical psychologist in Jamaica was 'underwhelming'. This person was a young White psychologist from the USA who had been assigned to the Psychiatry Unit on Ward 20 of the University Hospital of the West Indies. She spent much of her professional time performing psychological assessments and some time working with children in the fledgling Child Guidance Clinic, and made very little impact, it seemed to me, on the progress of our patients. I was given an inkling about my future relation-ship with psychologists, when a visiting psychiatrist from the University of Maryland, Professor Eugene Brody, questioned the necessity for stu-dents of psychopathology to spend 12 years in training, first as a medical practitioner, and then as a psychiatrist. I was surprised to learn from him that he had recommended to his daughter, once he realized that she was determined to become a psychopathologist, that she train as a clinical psychologist rather that studying medicine. My opinion of psychologists was broadened somewhat during the period I spent at the Royal Edinburgh Hospital in the UK in 1972 and 1973. What was particularly significant was my discovery of the psychologist's value in research, as well as in the philosophical understanding of psychopathology.

However, I was still unclear about the role of the clinical psychologist.

Insight was awaiting me when I returned to work in Jamaica as a consultant psychiatrist when I became involved in the pioneering work of establishing community psychiatry in Jamaica. During in that period, I spent one day each week working in the rural parishes of St. Mary and Portland setting up community mental health clinics in the hospitals of those parishes. I worked very closely with Headley Bertram, the Mental Health Officer for those parishes. Mental Health Officers were psychiatric nurses who were trained as community psychiatric nurse practitioners and case managers, and soon proved to be the backbone of the emerging Jamaican Community Mental Health Service. It was at the Port Maria Hospital that I met clinical psychologist, Ruth Doorbar, a White American practitioner who had retired from working as an upscale private clinical psychologist on Park Avenue in New York City, and had relocated to Jamaica. I was amazed at how easily she fitted into the Jamaican contemporary scene and how quickly she adapted her professional skills to the needs of the Jamaican people. I learned much about psychotherapy from her, and understood the practical reality that nearly 60 per cent of the psychiatrist's clinical role was in the practice of psychotherapy and psychology. My narrow perspective of the psychiatrist as a psychopharmacologist was about to be exploded. From her I learned new forensic psychopathology skills, and most importantly, having opened a private practice with her, I learned the intricacies of establishing a first-class upscale private psychopathology practice. Here I was learning three things: first, how much of the psychiatrist's work involved psychology; second, the range of the role of the clinical psychologist; and third, how easily the clinical psychologist can syncretize the role of the case manager within the mental health team, and as a psychotherapist. In addition, I learned that the roles of psychiatrists and psychologists were complementary. It became clear that they worked best together, and that they need not carry around the baggage of competitiveness and division that often seemed to beset psychiatrists and psychologists in North America and Europe.

## II. Ruth Doorbar – Reflections of a Pioneering Clinical Psychologist in Jamaica

Most mornings in Jamaica, with very few exceptions, are glorious, bright, sunshiny, and full of hope and encouragement. It was on just such a morning in July 1974 that I started out to report for my first job as a psychologist in Jamaica. The Ministry of Health had assigned me to a north coast hospital as a Consultant Psychologist. The north coast had been my choice as I was living there. I followed the winding road up the hill to the hospital. I later learned that many folks said that if you can make it up to the hospital, you really don't need to go there. Anyway, I proceeded, parked my vehicle, and went up the steep steps and into the wide front entrance.

I assumed that I should report to the Senior Medical Officer. So I went in search of his office. No nurse or secretary was in sight, so I knocked on his door. A deep, kindly voice said "Come in", and I complied. He was a middle-aged rather tired looking man, whose desk was piled with dockets and papers. He seemed a little startled to see me, so I introduced myself, adding that I was the new psychologist. "Yes," he said. "I heard your name. You are a psychiatrist." "No", I explained, "I am a psychologist." "Well, welcome . . . just what does a psychologist do?" I proceeded to explain about psychological tests and diagnoses, and then about psychotherapy. "So, you don't prescribe drugs?" I explained that psychologists do not prescribe medications, but see patients, who may otherwise be on medication, for counselling. He seemed pleased with "counselling", so I proceeded to explain that psychotherapy is more than counselling and involved methods of modifying thinking and changing behaviour. "Oh," he said. "Talk therapy". And he admitted he had heard of that, but had never met a practitioner.

He then phoned the Mental Health Officer (MHO) who soon came. A short, sturdy young man whose very presence spelled "helpful." That day began a 28-year relationship with one of the pillars of strength in the health system. He took me off to the out-patient clinic, and explained to me the process for handling new and repeat patients. He knew what a psychologist was – he had taken psychology in school, and had done some reading on his own. During the ensuing weeks, I began to see patients referred by the MHO, and we later discussed each day, our impressions of the patients' needs. Medication was prescribed by the doctor-on-duty, and psychotherapy on a once-in-two-weeks basis. Word seems to have spread quickly – by "Jamaican telegraph", so-called. Matrons from two nearby hospitals said they wanted me to visit their facilities and see referred patients. And finally, another hospital, in an adjacent parish, asked for my services. So, quickly, I was very spread out – travelling one day per week to all four hospitals, with an extra day to return to the hospital where I was first.

By then, I had acquired an apartment in Kingston, and I began spending weekends on the north coast, visiting those hospitals on Fridays, Mondays and Tuesdays, and adding yet a fifth hospital, in yet another parish, to my list – one near Kingston. Often I travelled to and from Kingston with a psychiatrist who was a consultant at the north coast hospitals. This was a most fortunate friendship for me, and we soon decided that we would open a private practice together in Kingston. We obtained a four-room suite atop the NCR building in Kingston – one office for him, one for me, a waiting room, and an extra room with a bed and a refrigerator. The psychiatrist was an absolutely brilliant and inspired man, and we shared great mutual respect and trust. The practice went very well for many months. Then the psychiatrist was offered the position of Senior Medical Officer at Bellevue Hospital. This meant that we separated, but only in terms of working space, and in 1978 I proceeded to Oxford Medical Centre where I continued to maintain an office. I continued to service the five hospitals as the Ministry of Health employee for a total of 28 years, while conducting my private practice on the side and on weekends.

## THE 36 DEATH ROW INMATES

And it came to pass in the mid-1970s, that a decision was taken to study condemned inmates and evaluate the St. Catherine District Prison. The Hon. Carl Rattray was then Minister of National Security and Justice (Justice and Security were combined in one ministry). A committee was appointed to head the study and two psychiatrists and one psychologist were selected to form the investigating team. The psychiatrists were Dr. Frederick Hickling and Dr. Frank Knight. I was the psychologist.

The selection of the psychologist was somewhat problematic. Having been chosen, I had three strikes against me. I was white, female, and a non-Jamaican. I was told that the only females allowed inside the prison (aside from in the visitors' area) were Catholic nuns, who conducted a literacy rehabilitation programme. I therefore believe that some influence by my co-workers had all to do with my being included in the study.

We went to the prison every day (including Saturdays and Sundays) for approximately three months. The psychiatrists conducted clinical interviews with each inmate individually, while I conducted psychological tests (intelligence and personality) and also did a clinical interview. The result was a two-volume work, the first of which dealt with analysis of and suggestions for solving problems found within the prison. The second volume consisted of individual case studies of each of the 36 men. When we first arrived at the prison, we were taken on a tour by the Superintendent – a very pleasant, cooperative man. After about an hour of our viewing the dilapidated walls and crumbling structure, the Superintendent asked me what I though about it. I commented that it resembled a 17th-century dungeon. He laughed and replied, "Sixteenth century." It soon became evident that the men were especially anxious to be examined by me. They drew lots to see who would go first. I soon realized that most of these men's problems had been with Black male figures – fathers, police, warders, etc. I became known as the 'White Angel from the north,' whom they perceived as someone who had come to help them out of their predicament. I corrected this misconception and told them I had come to give them some tests, and we got down to business.

In retrospect, the men seemed to fall into three categories. They all claimed innocence, of course, but judging from the type of sometimes seemingly unjust legal and police procedures, at least a third of the men may well have been innocent. (We had no access to police reports.) A second 'third' seemed to be cases for whom a plea of self-defence was applicable. In this group were cases where two men had gotten into a physical fight, and one succeeded in killing the other. The survivor was then charged with murder. The final 'third' were chiefly men who had attempted a robbery, for example, at a gas station, and wantonly killed an attendant or a security guard who happened to be in the way. The personality tests showed that this group of men scored very high as 'psychopathic' or 'sociopathic' personalities, and they were all quite obviously guilty of their crimes. In the area of intelligence, even more interesting results abounded. It turned out that a much higher percentage of these men had I.Q.s of 120 or over, in the superior range, higher than is the case of the general population. Prison populations the world over usually score an average IQ in the 80s and are classified as Dull Normal. Our condemned men are clearly not an average prison population.

From reports from the men, it seemed that the most painful punishment was the waiting – endless waiting for their appeals to be considered. At a somewhat later time, I was asked to examine two inmates: Pratt and Morgan. These men had protested the long wait for their appeals, and finally the Privy Council considered their case. The outcome of this legal decision was that it was illegal to hold a man awaiting the death sentence for more than five years. Thereafter, his sentence must be commuted to a life sentence. After this assignment was completed, the Department of Corrections in the Ministry of National Security and Justice, offered me a position as a Consultant. Thereafter, ensued ten years of steady work at the St. Catherine District Prison, examining men who were thought to be "unfit to plead" – many of whom were suffering from full-blown schizophrenia. Medication was suggested, and approved by the medical doctor, and the men had psychotherapeutic sessions to help them plan their futures, should they return to court. Most of these men were housed in one section of the prison, and while I felt that my work was helpful, it was woefully inadequate in relation to the magnitude of the task.

## III. Jacqueline Benn, MSc – A Young Practitioner's Perspective

The guiding principle of clinical psychologists in our Caribbean region has been provided by a perspective grounded in a North American and European philosophy, reflected in the view that clinical psychologists "...help people with psychological problems adjust to the demands of life...clinical psychologists evaluate problems through structured interviews and psychological tests. They help their clients resolve their problems and change maladaptive behavior through psychotherapy and behavior therapy..." (Rathus, 1997, p 5). This is understandable, since in the main, Caribbean clinical psychologists, have been educated in North American and European environments. If we accept the above-mentioned perspective, it follows that the psychologist fulfils the roles of therapist, educator, consultant, researcher, experimenter, diagnostician, treatment presciber and provider, as well as mentor. Along with these roles come responsibilities, which Caribbean clinical psychologists accept as an indispensable part of their practice. These include, but are not limited to the following: being competent, having a high level of integrity, being professionally and scientifically responsible, being respectful of others' rights and dignity, having concern for others' welfare, and having a high level of social responsibility which, when adhered to, ensures that he or she is practising in an ethical manner (Principles referenced: APA Code of Ethics, 2002).

Do we then as Caribbean clinical psychologists need to follow these principles and precepts and adopt these roles as our own, and should our behaviour be limited solely by these guidelines highlighted above? The answer, surprisingly, is 'yes and no'. Yes, it is incumbent upon us as clinical psychologists in the Caribbean to fulfill our roles and responsibilities ethically, having decided to enter the profession, remembering that our main duty is to our patients and society. However, it is because we are Caribbean psychologists that our roles and responsibilities may inherently have other facets and may also be coloured significantly by the environment in which we live. Different in what way, one may ask or wonder. As Caribbean psychologists, we should be aware of the potential impact of our historical background on our own and our peoples' psyche. Issues of colonialism and neo-colonialism, enslavement, ethnocentrism, color and race, together with emerging problems of globalization and economic position, all have an effect, subtle and overt, on our society and the people who live here. Colonialism has brought with it ethnocentrism and deep-rooted issues of race, colour and to some extent, class, which in recent times has been labelled as *crypto-racism* in one particular island. This has, in turn, affected and continues to affect how various racial groups relate to each other in all aspects of life. We must also remember that miscegenation is an incontrovertible factor which each side often tends to hide, deny or exaggerate, depending on which side of the divide he or she stands. This is merely one of the underlying factors which affect how people see themselves and others, and which fuel their behaviour. Thus, the Caribbean psychologist must have a full understanding of these unique patterns of existence and the psychological conflicts which they may engender. This is necessary so that when making a clinical assessment, a more thorough or deeper understanding is obtained of the individual as well as factors that affect him or her, which then should help to inform better decision-making.

Religion plays an integral role in the lives of Caribbean people and is often intertwined with how an individual perceives his illness and its outcome. Many patients and their relatives believe that religion, spirituality, and possession by some supernatural entity may influence the development and resolution of some mental illnesses, such as schizophrenia, or other types of psychotic illnesses. Hence, a Caribbean clinical psychologist who is attempting to treat an individual with such an illness, must be prepared to work, if necessary, with the family and/or a significant other, in a way that acknowledges and accepts such beliefs, while providing the best scientific and ethically sound treatment available. The vast majority of the instruments used by Caribbean psychologists to assess or test patients have been developed, normed and standardized on North American populations. While one may argue that an individual in North America is subject to, and displays the same emotions and behaviour as his Caribbean counterpart, the factors that influence and elicit some of these features may often be very different. The same must be said of tests used to assess aptitude and intelligence. Many items presented in these tools are unfamiliar to persons who do not live in northern societies and who have not been exposed to features of that landscape or information about those societies. Does this therefore mean that the Caribbean person is less intelligent or is in some way abnormal because he does not recognize or respond according to what is accepted as 'normal' in the instruments? This is hardly the case.

Thus, the psychologist who is assessing a Caribbean individual with tools that contain features which are more familiar to the North American patient, has to understand and be keenly aware of several factors. He must be aware, as a diagnostician, which results of testing may give erroneous conclusions, as these may have undesirable and longstanding effects on an individual's life when diagnoses are made. Being cognizant of the limitations of testing, while not dismissing the intent of testing, should be uppermost in the mind of the psychologist. This then should be an imperative that drives Caribbean psychologists to examine their roles as test developers. From a general perusal of the numerous tools available for testing, it is apparent that there are very few Caribbean test developers, as well as researchers based in the Caribbean. As a result, there is a dearth of assessment tools created for and normed on Caribbean populations. Therefore, tools that can have a wider reference, but which take fully into account the many factors which influence or impact upon the psychological, emotional and behavioural lives of our Caribbean patients, are sorely needed.

As consultants and advisors, we Caribbean clinical psychologists ought to take seriously our potential for influencing policy-makers and creating policies which are best suited to our unique environment. Our collective responsibility to the people of this region makes it necessary for us to become involved and advise our governments and policy-makers about factors which can impact negatively, as well as positively on our people. Among these issues that need to be addressed are some of the types of music and the accompanying lyrics which are heard daily on our airwaves, and which will affect the self and psyche of generations to come. On the other hand, being more aware of human behaviour and many of the things that can fuel thinking and behaviour, we can also provide assistance in areas of early childhood education, adolescent challenges and relationship issues from a Caribbean perspective. Of equal importance is the issue of the availability of alcohol and cigarettes to minors, health and environmental policies, as well as the effects of certain aspects of the work environment on employees, to name a few. Failure to make an input into controlling, preventing and solving these national and regional problems ensures that they continue unabated. What is more, they will come back to haunt us as practitioners when we treat those who have been so affected thereby underscoring our failure on the principle of social responsibility.

Finally, but of great importance, is the issue of the creation of a Caribbean code of ethics. This code of ethics would embody all of the precepts and principles of the international codes but it would go a step further, by incorporating aspects of life specific to our Caribbean society. This may include principles and standards that address our culture, our laws and the myriad roles which psychologists play in such closely-knit societies. It may be felt that the roles and responsibilities of clinical psychologists in the Caribbean, in many ways mirror those of their counterparts in North America and Europe. However, it is also apparent that there are several areas where differences exist in the scope of our roles and responsibilities. We, therefore, need to become more aware of these unique areas and having become aware, we need to incorporate these into our practice for the benefit of our patients, our Caribbean society and the furtherance of our profession as clinical psychologists in the region.

## IV. Elaine Gordon, MSc – A Practitioner's Perspective

Psychology as a phenomenon is not new to the Caribbean. It is woven into the rich tapestry of our cultural inheritance and its practice can be identified in many areas of our lives – from the village counsellor through religion, folk tales, superstition and obeah, to name a few. What is relatively new is psychology as a distinct professional discipline, practised by a body of trained individuals. This new group of practitioners was either trained in the USA or the UK, but localized training is gathering strength and numbers are set to soar. The emerging body of psychologists practising in the Caribbean, in my view, find themselves in an interesting and exciting era, in that they have the opportunity to define themselves in a way not open to psychologists of Caribbean origin, practising in Europe or the USA. Psychology as a discipline emerged as a science in Europe and the USA in the late 1880s. Psychologists were largely found in laboratories with some practice in analytic consultation rooms. However, a paradigm shift in the late 1940s saw the emergence of a scientist-practitioner model that merged clinical research and strategies for intervention.

The overwhelming majority of psychologists currently practising in the Caribbean were trained, and often gained their experience either in the USA or the UK and, therefore, bring with them the traditions of the discipline as articulated overseas. The challenge for these psychologists (myself included) is to apply our adaptive skills regardless of the area of work – teaching, training of psychologists, or clinical practice – to a Caribbean population, in order to promote mental health and well-being.

Filling the vacuum of professional psychologists in the Caribbean has inherent tensions as regards role definition. Apart from the laity referred to above, other professionals working in the general mental health arena – psychiatrists, mental health nurses, clinical social workers, counsellors, some paediatricians, etc. have, either by design or default, incorporated aspects of the psychologist's functions into their practice. This is not to say that there are no areas of overlap between the roles of psychologists and these professionals, but the psychologist's role is unique in its contribution to the understanding of human functioning. According to the theorists, roles consist of rules or norms that form a framework for behaviour, specifying factors such as goals, tasks and performance required in a given scenario. These specifications, in turn, give rise to role expectations from both the individual in the role and others on the outside. Role theory further helps us to understand the link between individual behaviour, social structures and their reciprocal interactions. Notwithstanding this, the role of a psychologist in the Caribbean cannot be totally open to negotiation between an individual and a given social structure, as this is not only against the convention within the profession, but a recipe for role confusion on all sides.

Over time, psychologists have formed professional associations, (e.g. the American Psychological Association (USA) and the British Psychological Society (UK), which act as regulatory bodies, not only within the profession but also at its boundaries. Thus, the role of the psychologist has a pattern of behaviour that is regular with sufficient predictability. This enables the individual to function effectively as expectations are clearly set out, which in turn, enable boundary definitions. In the Caribbean context, professional associations are either in their infancy or non-existent and this presents opportunities for confusion in terms of the patient population. Psychologists, professional colleagues and others seek to ascribe roles to psychologists that are conflicting and inconsistent with our training. It is, therefore, the prime responsibility of psychologists in the Caribbean to define and assert their role and to continue this assertion while the role is evolving. Otherwise, they face the possibility of being defined from outside the profession. Clearly this cannot be effectively accomplished on an individual basis, and it follows that the establishment of effective psychological associations in each territory with the aim of regionalization and developing links with specialist psychological associations such as the Association of Black Psychologists (ABPsi in the USA, ABP in the UK) is long overdue. Traditionally, psychologists working in a mental health setting, have been purely clinical psychologists. There has been a recent shift to acknowledge that colleagues working in other areas may not only have some of the skills of the clinical psychologists, but they also embrace the scientist-practitioner-model, (e.g. educational psychologists) and offer therapeutic interventions. However, what enables a psychologist to make the expected unique contribution by applying adaptive skills begins with training. Training as a scientist-practitioner prepares the psychologist for a wide range of professional functions. The aspiring psychologist is seeking a post-graduate place and it is, therefore, his or her responsibility to undertake the necessary research to ensure that the course chosen is not only approved by a body with oversight of the profession, but that it will also provide adaptive skills and learning experiences which will form a sound basis for further development. In the case of training courses outside the Caribbean, it is unlikely that there will be much emphasis on working with Caribbean people and it would, therefore, be the psychologist's responsibility to seek further experience to enable meaningful benefit for the Caribbean patient. For example, a psychologist may be very skilled in administration, scoring and writing reports on a battery of psychometric tests. There is no need to go into the vast amount of literature on psychometrics and Black people here, except to say that by itself, that skill is not sufficient. The psychologist would do well to keep in mind other issues such as standardization, item validity, and cultural norms (including language) and so on, in utilizing such assessment tools. After the initial training for clinical practice, it is vital that psychologists engage in continuing professional development activities. It is also important to keep abreast of new developments within the profession and to extend one's skills repertoire. This should be part of the professional commitment of both the psychologist and his or her employer. While Caribbean bodies charged with the oversight of the profession are still being formed, it is the responsibility of individual psychologists to lobby their employers for continuing professional development time and financial support. There are many existing models in countries where the profession is more firmly rooted, which may provide useful starting points. Once qualified and admitted to the profession, the psychologist has a responsibility to live up to the ethical code and protect the boundaries through role and function.

Psychologists working in clinical settings in the Caribbean have two distinct advantages, in that they have the opportunity to be at the forefront not only of role development, but also of defining their areas of service delivery. There has been a gradual shift from clinic to community settings overseas. This encompasses a shift from the individual to the ecological, where empowerment is key in the promotion of systemic change. As noted earlier, psychologists are relatively few in the Caribbean. This, coupled with the fact that some territories' mental health services are delivered on a community basis, has made it possible for policymakers to add psychological services without too much resistance. In providing community-based mental health services, the policymakers were no doubt persuaded by the argument that these services should be more readily available to all, and that effective interventions must take into account the system – family, culture, community, etc. – in which the problem arises. The psychologist working in the community, therefore, has to have clarity of role and be prepared to defend the professional boundary in order to avoid the trap of role confusion.

Caribbean psychological literature could be considered as being in its infancy and this is not surprising, given that we are few in numbers and practising psychologists have tended generally to place more emphasis on the practitioner aspect of the scientist-practitioner model, at the expense of the scientist element. The time has come, however, for each and every practising psychologist to take the need for research seriously and to set up their clinical practice in a way that enables them to gather data on a systematic basis. An example of this could be to track outcomes of interventions which may not necessarily assist the individual psychologist or community served, but through dissemination, may have an impact on a wider group of psychologists and patient population. There is readily available technology than can assist, so there is no excuse for the continued paucity of literature written by Caribbean psychologists about the mental health and other psychological issues relating to Caribbean people. While studies from abroad do have their place, we need to be in a position to compare our Caribbean empirical data and to be reliably guided by our own validated findings. An essential role, then, for the psychologist, is that of researcher and within this role, he or she is charged with the responsibility of generating empirically sound studies which can withstand the scrutiny of peers and professional journals across the world. Policymakers will need to acknowledge this role not only by providing professional development opportunities to obtain the requisite skills, but also in the allocation of time to carry out the activity. The role of the psychologist as researcher cannot be emphasized enough, as the future of a profession does not lie in the anecdotal and/or oral tradition, but in the establishment of a body of academically sound literature which will give accountability and, therefore, power to our practice.

Another essential role of a psychologist is that of providing assessments of individuals in the main areas of human functioning, for example, cognitive, academic achievement, type and severity of psychopathology, and neuropsychological dysfunction, to name a few. We are trained to select and administer standardized and validated tests in order to identify some possible answers to complex questions about the individual's level of functioning. Although these standardized tests may have included some "minorities" in the countries of standardization, (mainly the USA and the UK), the vast majority of the population sampled would have had European backgrounds. As such, the validity of these assessment instruments for a Caribbean population must always be in question and the psychologist must be sensitive to this. In the absence of more valid instruments, it must be borne in mind that the results may not be as reliable for our populations as for those where the tests were developed. The whole question of whether these standardized instruments are valid and reliable for Black populations has long been debated and there is a long history of campaigns against their use in the USA and the UK. There is no intention of rehearsing this matter here, as it is well documented. What some psychologists in the UK have reported is the successful diagnostic application of certain items from some psychometric instruments that, it is claimed, provides a more advantageous picture of the individual's functioning. This diagnostic application seems to provide a way through the controversy and could enable Caribbean psychologists to adapt their skills to the advantage of their patients or clinical interviews and this should be a powerful tool in any psychologist's skills repertoire. It is the responsibility of all psychologists to hone their interviewing skills on a continuing basis, as interviewing is the centerpiece of the assessment process. The psychologist has a duty to ensure that, as far as possible, the patient or client is put at ease. He or she may have come to the appointment with a variety of misconceptions, anxieties and/or questions, and the psychologist needs to be sensitive to these possibilities and develop the capacity for an appropriate response. The clinical interview is not a medium for a cozy chat but a time in which the psychologist is engaged in a number of activities including building an alliance with the patient, making assessments. During the interview, hypotheses are also being formed, developed and sometimes tested. Information from other sources (e.g., other professional colleagues, if involved) should be gathered as part of the process of assessment. In addition, the psychologist's knowledge as a community insider would be well grounded due to an increased understanding of the context within which the patient has to function, thereby creating a bridge to alliance formation, which will result in realistic strategies for intervention. In the development of interventions it is the responsibility of the psychologist to 'keep it real'. Indeed, we need to acquire the skills to deliver interventions adapted from the range available – manualized treatment, cognitive behaviour therapy, brief focused therapies, systemic work with families, and individual and group psychotherapy, to name a few. Contemporary professional literature could also be consulted as appropriate and psychologists should ensure that access to relevant journals and other material forms part of their conditions of service. This will enable the psychologist to better discharge the responsibility of developing meaningful interventions along with the patient, with clear targets, time-frames and success criteria. It is non-productive to develop a well-defined intervention for a patient who is either without the capacity or the interest to participate in any meaningful way. In such instances, there is a risk of increased frustration and feelings of failure on the part of the patient, who will most likely withdraw from the process.

The final two core areas of responsibility for the psychologist to be highlighted here generally fall under the umbrella of administration. Within the Caribbean, we need to develop a professional culture of giving and receiving supervision. Whether in groups or individually, supervision is to be experienced as a supportive process that enables the supervisee to reflect on practice, feel supported within a particular context or as part of the process of continuing professional development. Another rationale for supervision has to do with ethics. The vast majority of psychologists' interactions with patients tend to be as lone professionals, and supervision provides the opportunity for protecting both patient and psychologist, if a third party has oversight of the processes. It is the responsibility of every psychologist to secure the experience as a supervisee, as part of his or her conditions of service, regardless of years of experience or seniority. The supervisory process is also helpful in the maintenance of patient records. Supervision is a skill which requires thought and structure, and should be a positive experience to the benefit of the supervisee. It is the responsibility of every psychologist to acquire this skill, as "good and meaningful" supervision does not occur by accident. Psychologists need to support their work in the community through the dissemination of information to specific and/or general populations, as well as to professional colleagues. Psychologists therefore need to practise their teaching and training skills through regular seminars and workshops, journal presentations, and by providing reflective feedback, including evaluation of their work over a given period. In this paper, I have sought to identify some core roles and responsibilities (to the exclusion of others) for psychologists working in a Caribbean. The roles will not be radically different from elsewhere, but because there is the need for community focus, these roles will inevitably influence responsibilities and how they are discharged. Finally, it is urgent that psychological associations be formed and developed within the Caribbean to give psychologists professional authority – as responsibility without authority is courting disaster.

## V. Brigitte Matthies – An Academic Perspective

The discipline of psychology is relatively new to the English speaking Caribbean. It wasn't until 1995 that a Bachelor of Science degree in Psychology was instituted at the University of the West Indies (UWI), Mona Campus in Jamaica. In contrast, psychology has been taught in North America, South Africa, and Europe for well over 100 years (Hunt, 1993). Similar Bachelors programmes soon followed at the other UWI campuses in Trinidad and Barbados, as well as at other academic institutions in the region. Since the genesis of these early programmes was in the Departments of Sociology, the early curriculum emphasized the teaching of Social Psychology and Developmental Psychology. However, psychology is a broad discipline with many distinct divisions, including physiological psychology, sports psychology, health psychology and industrial/organizational psychology to name but a few (the reader is invited to consult the American Psychological Association (APA) website at http://www.apa.org/about/division.html for an in-depth description of these divisions). Psychology is currently one of the most popular degree programmes in universities throughout the world. At UWI Mona, Psychology is second only to Management Studies in terms of enrolment. From my perspective, psychologists are educators, and as such, their roles and responsibilities in the Caribbean are as described here.

## EDUCATING THE PUBLIC ABOUT PSYCHOLOGY AS A DISTINCT DISCIPLINE

Given the late introduction of Psychology to the region, the people of the Caribbean need to be educated about what it is as a discipline. They need to know that not all psychologists spend their time listening to people's problems, that psychology is a science, with most practitioners in academia having laboratories where scientific data is collected, that psychologists have expertise in a variety of areas related to behaviour. They need to know that the study of psychology requires higher education, and exactly how counselling and clinical psychologists differ from counsellors, social workers and psychiatrists. Employers need to be educated about what persons with a Bachelors degree in psychology can do. Increased opportunities for young people to be exposed to "the study of the mind and behaviour" (psychology) are necessary. At present, Caribbean high schools do not teach psychology until sixth form, and even then, classes are not available in all schools or in all islands. This can and should be changed.

## IMPLEMENTATION OF TRAINING PROGRAMMES OF SUFFICIENT SCOPE AND QUALITY

Because Psychology is such a popular discipline, psychology programmes are emerging all across the region. In many cases these programmes are designed and taught by persons who themselves are barely trained in the discipline. Furthermore, these new psychology programmes are offered by institutions that are not capable of competently teaching the research, nor of practising aspects of psychology. Many of these institutions bring in psychologists from abroad to teach classes but that raises the issue of cultural relevance. We need to guard against the ad hoc importation of teaching materials and ideas. We also need to guard against the churning out of mediocre psychology students. Where possible, Caribbean psychologists should lead and teach in these programmes. The quality and scope of the curriculum should be of paramount importance. In fact, all Caribbean psychologists should consider devoting part of their time to the teaching of their discipline in an academic setting.

## FOCUS ON RESEARCH AND GRANT WRITING

Psychology is both an art and a science. In the current climate of scarce resources, psychologists working in academic institutions are stretched thin between their teaching and administrative responsibilities. Research may seem to be a luxury. As a result, the research legacy of Caribbean psychologists is scant and this contributes to the belief of many people, that psychology is simply "common sense". Many people are not aware of the legacy of science that makes up the theories and practice of psychology. It is the science that sets psychology apart as a discipline, and it is the science that fascinates students. Academic psychologists should insist on laboratory space and start-up funds, consistent with what their colleagues abroad can access. Grant writing, research, conference presentations and publications should also be of primary focus. Regardless of whether they are in academia, in the public or private sectors, it is important to remember that dissemination of research findings is an ethical responsibility of all psychologists. Regional journals that publish psychology research, therefore, need to be developed and supported.

## INSTITUTION OF PROGRAMMES OF RESEARCH THAT INVOLVE STUDENTS

It is vital that psychologists not only conduct research, but also have students work with them on their projects. This is an important way to indoctrinate students into the worth and joy of research. It is also a medium for students to learn how to conduct research properly, and how to bring a project to completion (ethics reviews, research design, data collection, data analysis and interpretation, presentation and publication of findings). Wherever possible, psychology students should be exposed to research in a variety of areas, including animal research.

*Attitude*

## REDUCING THE STIGMA ASSOCIATED WITH MENTAL HEALTH

It is safe to say that the majority of Caribbean people are not 'psycholog-ically minded'. Because of economic pressures, most persons in the region focus on day-to-day issues – getting primary needs met – food, shelter, and sex. For many of our people, relationships are about the pro-vision of money, shelter and sexual satisfaction and not self-actualization. Feelings are not easily expressed, discussed nor understood. Giving and receiving affection is not a major focus of concern. There are numerous external attributions of problems, and little introspection. The idea of talking to a stranger – as a way of coming up with solutions to problems, to change one's behaviour or personality, to explore and deal with feel-ings and to help with life planning and decision-making – is not readily accepted by most. For most, only 'mad people' go to see a psychologist or psychiatrist. Even psychology students express hesitation in relation to visiting campus-counselling services to discuss their personal problems. As psychologists committed to the mental health of our people, we need to change all of this. It starts with us. We are the ones who must be brave enough to attack the stigma head-on by working on our own mental health, lobbying for the development of increased mental health facilities that provide culturally relevant services, and encouraging our students to do their part to educate their friends and families. If we can't meet the stigma head-on, we cannot expect others to do so. We also need to edu-cate the public about the ongoing nature of psychotherapy, which is in contrast to the medical model, deeply ingrained in our culture, of the expectation of one visit and a prescription.

*I like / I recommend this*

## COMMENTARY ON ISSUES OF IMPORTANCE TO THE COMMUNITY

The Caribbean has its share of problems, including obesity, the spread of HIV/AIDS, racism, substance abuse, violence and sexual dysfunction, to name but a few. Psychology has much to say about all of these maladap-tive behaviours, and Caribbean psychologists need to be part of the solu-tion. Additionally, the region shares a number of attitudes that are unhealthy. One example is the overwhelmingly negative reaction to peo-ple of a homosexual orientation. Psychologists know that anxiety and shame related to homosexual urges, coupled with the belief that there is no one to talk to, is a leading cause of suicide in adolescents. We need to address all of these issues. When the media portrays inaccuracies about human behaviour, or hurtful points of view, we need to respond and to educate. We cannot afford to stand idly by. We need to make our voices heard.

## GETTING INVOLVED IN INTERDISCIPLINARY PROGRAMMES THAT DON'T HAVE A PSYCHOLOGIST

There are many ongoing projects in the region with documented behavioural outcomes, but which do not have the involvement of a psychologist. Some examples include projects on sexual health and fertility, substance abuse, violence in schools, and community development. Psychologists need to become involved in these projects. They need to volunteer to be included on ethics boards, in sports organizations, schools, children's homes, old age homes, and churches. They also need to get involved in the legal system, and community service is a must.

## ETHICAL PRACTICE

Psychologists worldwide are governed by a code of ethics that provides guidelines for working with students, human and animal research and clinical practice, including psychotherapy and assessment (_see_ http://www.apa.org/ethics/). It is essential for Caribbean psychologists to commit themselves to these standards. This will help them to earn the respect that they deserve as professionals within the region. Among the other areas of particular importance to the Caribbean psychologist are sensitivity to diversity issues, commitment to pro bono work and community service, maintenance of patient and research participants' confidentiality, a commitment to publication, limiting practice to work within one's area of expertise, and prevention of dual relationships.

## SUPPORT OF LOCAL PSYCHOLOGICAL ASSOCIATIONS

Psychologists need to organize themselves. There is power in numbers. Psychologists need to form and get involved in local psychology associations. Such associations can take on the task of getting the discipline recognized. This will set the stage for: reimbursement from insurance companies for services rendered, the establishment of a registry of competent psychologists, devising a way to sanction those who are unprofessional, and creating a channel for expressing opinions to the government and to our people. Another important goal would be to liaise with other islands so that issues of relevance to the Caribbean can be addressed.

# VI. Kai Morgan – Psychology as a Profession

Dr. Ruth Doorbar founded the Jamaican Psychological Association in the 1970s. Other vanguards in the field in Jamaica have also worked assiduously for the promotion and recognition of Psychology, but in my estimation, the numbers were insufficient and the task was gargantuan. In 2001, a new name was registered and new faces began to emerge with the same vision. Dr Peter Weller, Dr Audrey Pottinger, Dr Brigitte Matthies, and Dr Tony Bastick were among the Executive Committee members at the time, who have made significant contributions to the growth of Psychology in Jamaica. As President of the Jamaican Psychological Society (2005–present), it is incumbent on me in a publication such as this, to advance the principles of our organization and to highlight our progress thus far in matters of great import to the profession. This segment of the chapter highlights the progress of the national body, and the roles that it has played and hopes to play in the future.

## THE PRACTICE OF PSYCHOLOGY IN JAMAICA

The Jamaican Psychological Society is cognizant of the critical need for the regulation of the practice of psychology in Jamaica, particularly in light of the growth of the field and its related disciplines, and the corresponding lack of cohesiveness and accountability. Two issues are paramount: protection of the public, who are often unaware of the role of a psychologist and the necessary training and qualifications that are essential for certification; and protection of psychologists as a mental health professionals, from individuals who, through malpractice (particularly lack of training), taint the dignity of the discipline. Since 2003, the Society has been giving priority to these issues, and has been strongly advocating for the final step to be taken. In February 2004, Professor Scott Minor (clinical psychologist), Dr. Peter Weller (clinical psychologist and then Immediate Past President of the Jamaican Psychological Society) and myself, Dr. Kai Morgan (clinical psychologist and then Vice President of the Jamaican Psychological Society), met to discuss what had been done thus far and the direction to be taken. Out of that meeting, a number of crucial issues were highlighted. First, there is the need for governmental recognition of psychologists as independent and capable professionals. Currently, in government agencies, the psychologist is under the 'supervision' of the psychiatrist, who is then liable for his or her actions from a medico-legal perspective. However, in the arena of private practice, there is absolutely no accountability and the public is open to the consequences of any malpractice by a psychologist. Second, there is need for a clear definition of the title, roles and functions of a psychologist. The public and other professional areas (e.g. forensic, organizational, medicine) are grossly unaware of or have misconceptions about these functions, roles and titles. Third, there is need for a two-tiered definition of those titles, roles and functions, for individuals at the Masters and the Doctoral levels. Fourth, given the general lack of information in this regard, it is necessary to have the formation of clear criteria which define the necessary qualifications of a psychologist (degree held, institution from which degree was obtained, requisite experience). There is also the need for a professional body to review these qualifications in order to sanction governmental and national registration. This procedure would have to include a grandfather clause for already established credible psychologists. Finally, there is need for a register of practising psychologists nation-wide, together with an on-going effort to educate the public about these issues.

In light of the foregoing, the decision was taken to draft a Psychology Practice Act, an Ethical Code of Conduct and a nation-wide register of practising psychologists. A committee was formed which included the following individuals: Kai Morgan (UWI), Peter Weller (UWI), Scott Minor (UWI), Garth Lipps (UWI), Barbara Matalon (UWI), Karla Lafayette (MICO CARE Centre), Barry Davidson (Family Life Ministries), Daniel Antwi (Institute for Theological Leadership Development), Grace Kelly (Northern Caribbean University) and Michele Alexander (student representative – UWI), representing varying specialty areas including clinical, counseling, applied, educational, marital and family psychology; as well as individuals from the Masters and Doctoral levels.

These documents were reviewed several times at monthly Licensure and Executive Committee meetings, posted on the JamPsych website, presented at Quarterly and Annual General Meetings of the Society and emailed to psychologists, and government officials for perusal and feedback, prior to the final documents being submitted to the Council for Professions Supplementary to Medicine for final approval.

The draft Jamaican Psychology Practice Act was approved by the Counsel Supplementary to Medicine and the Ministry of Health in June 2007 and offers registration under four specialty areas of psychology: clinical, counselling, school, and applied – at two levels, Masters (Associate Psychologist) and Doctoral (Psychologist). The proposal outlines that the individual must have received a psychology degree from an accredited institution of higher learning (which meets the approval of the Jamaica Psychology Board, members of whom are appointed by the Jamaican Psychological Society to give counsel to the governmental authorities). Applicants must pass a basic ethics examination and show that they have received the required hours of supervision in their training. They must also have the required clinical hours (1,000 over a five-year period for Masters, and 4,000 hours over a two-year period, including internship, for Doctoral) in order to practise independently.

The Jamaican Ethics Code of Conduct for Psychologists (2004) is primarily based on the American Psychological Association's Code of Ethics (2002) and includes: competency, a knowledge of dual roles and multiple relationships, issues of privacy and confidentiality, research competence, knowledge of psychotherapy and informed consent, and knowledge of sexual harassment and its assessment in human relations. (As of February 2007, the Executive Committee awaits a final response from the Council on how to proceed with the implementation of the proposed process.) It is important to note that this endeavour follows on initiatives made by the vanguards in earlier years. However, with the numerous psychology programmes being mounted and delivered in Jamaica today, the time is ripe, and hence the process has been facilitated more easily. Currently, our membership stands at 100, consisting largely of student members with few professionals. However, the Society is actively planning a drive for professional membership, and has only recently published a call to this group. A list of qualified professional members will then follow this call, in a bid for public education.

## FUTURE DIRECTION

Some of the areas in which the Society would like to be influential and lobby for its members and the public include

- *malpractice insurance coverage* for professionals which we believe will come with the proper registration at the governmental level;

- adequate *health insurance coverage* for patients – although there is some coverage currently offered by select insurance companies for 'counselling', there is more lobbying to be done in this area;

- *public education* – an ongoing endeavour which the Society hopes to continue through regular newspaper articles and fora about the field of psychology;

- *programme accreditation* – as the number of undergraduate and graduate programmes increase islandwide, the Society has an obligation to help the accrediting bodies (e.g. the University Council of Jamaica) in their attempts to ensure high quality programmes;

- *salary structure* – as psychologists begin to define themselves, they then begin to define their worth which is grossly understated in the current pay structure. Again, here the Society has a role to play in terms of defining such;

- *continuing education units* – JamPsych (as we affectionately refer to our organization) hopes to offer continuous opportunities for professional development and knowledge acquisition in the field of psychology and to keep a record of activities of its members in these areas to ensure that knowledge and practices are aligned and remain current.

We hope that in the upcoming years, these very critical issues will be addressed as psychology continues to be a force within society, the importance of which needs to be recognized.

## VII: Frederick W. Hickling – The Psychiatrist's Perspective (Part II)

The role of the clinical psychologist in the mental health team revolves around the provision of suitable psychometric testing, the enhancement of the psychotherapeutic processes and services applicable to the Caribbean, and the stimulation of research output. The establishment of professional training programmes in Clinical Psychology at the UWI revolved around these three basic principles; namely the teaching of psychometric testing, the development of psychotherapeutic services and the development of research. The narratives of the five clinical psychologists contributing to this chapter reflect this conclusion.

Few people recognize the advances that have taken place in the area of psychometric testing in psychology. There are literally thousands of psychometric assessment tools which have been developed to meet the needs of many areas of clinical medicine and other arenas. As such there is now an immediate need for the standardization of many of these tools for the Jamaican and Caribbean populations. To this end, the Section of Psychiatry, in collaboration with the Section of Psychology has recently undertaken collaborative research work with the Government of Jamaica to standardize basic clinical psychological instruments to be used in the Jamaican mental health services.

The provision of modern and culturally appropriate psychotherapy services is also a major priority for the Caribbean. While there has been a mushrooming of evidenced-based literature regarding the use of individual and group psychotherapies in a wide variety of clinical areas, Jamaica and the Caribbean have lagged behind in the area of research and publication in mental health. Clinical psychologists, by virtue of their specialized training in research methodology, statistics and epidemiology, play a vital role in the advancement of clinical research, and would play a major role in the Caribbean in this area of work.

In most countries with well developed psychology programmes, extreme rivalry and often enmity between psychologists and psychiatrists have ensued, usually resulting in significant loss to the end-user – the patient. The Caribbean can ill afford such a conundrum, and would be well advised not to make these mistakes, by learning from the experiences of other countries. In my experience, the principal reason for these difficulties arose from the administrative genesis of the psychology programmes. In most cases, particularly in the UK, psychology programmes were born in departments of Sociology and eventually evolved into stand-alone, autonomous departments. In other countries such as the USA, psychology programmes started as stand-alone, autonomous departments. In both countries these programmes evolved outside of clinical environments, but at the same time, were expected to function within them alongside other mental health providers, particularly medicine and psychiatry. This resulted in clinical competitiveness, enmity and isolation, with the mental health delivery team often operating in confusion and uncertainty.

In my view, the Caribbean cannot afford to make the same mistake. Psychiatry, Psychology and Social Work need to operate and be taught within the context of a multi-disciplinary team, within a single administrative and clinical framework. This is especially the case in the post-colonial context of this region, where perhaps the most important priority is the development of therapeutic programmes designed to transform and heal the psychological ravages of colonialism. Thus, the therapeutic agenda dictates programmes to correct personality disorders; identity crises; poor self-esteem and poorly developed emotional intelligence; impulse control and authority problems; as well as dependency of both a psychological and a sociological nature. These issues translate into problems of homicide and suicide; psychoses and neuroses; substance abuse and HIV/AIDS; childhood and adolescent problems; forensic issues; and the problems of old age. In my view, the University of the West Indies has a responsibility to the Caribbean community to set and implement a multi-disciplinary team approach to the management of these problems, and the training of professionals to address them.

## REFERENCES

Biddle, B. J. (1986) Recent Developments in Role Theory. *Annual Review of Sociology*. pp.1267-1292

Hunt, M. (1993). *The Story of Psychology*. New York: Random House.

Rathus, S. A. (1997). *Essentials of Psychology* (5th ed.). Orlando, FL: Harcourt Brace.

# 17  Reflections of a Psychologist in Jamaica

*Ruth Doorbar*

During the past 53 years I have lectured on, written about, and practised psychology. I spent 20 years in New York, and 33 years so far in Jamaica.

I had a penthouse at 930 Park Avenue, Manhattan, New York and simultaneously had an apartment at 79 West 12th Street (Greenwich Village). The patients were self-divided, with the upper class and upper-middle class attending at the Park Avenue office and the lower socio-economic class attending Greenwich Village. This led to interesting comparisons of similar problems at different socio-economic levels.

In Jamaica I worked for 29 years with the Ministry of Health and 10 years with the Ministry of Justice. This led to an interesting comparison of similar problems with upper-middle class compared to lower socio-economic groups. I saw the upper-middle class patients in private practice and the lower socio-economic patients in the government public hospitals, clinics, and in the prisons. Research is underway to analyse these comparisons.

The American and Jamaican comparisons are also being done in their respective classes. At first, the classical personality theories were clear in my mind and I sought out the persons who would support these theories. However, there were so many contradictions in the patients that the theories simply did not 'fit'. My first supervisor at my first job in psychology at the New Jersey State Diagnostic Center at Menlo Park, New Jersey was Dr Albert Ellis. I began to study his rational-emotive psychotherapy and found it refreshing and workable. And many of my later theories were developed from Dr Ellis's work. I believe that one should start by learning as much as possible about the persons being treated. One can develop a kind of pattern, a personality DNA that differs from everyone else's. Treatment plans specific to that person can then be introduced.

The Jamaican population has an overwhelming feeling of inadequacy, and of low self-esteem. This may have come in part from the history of slavery, knowing that one is a descendant of persons who would have been treated as less than human. Moreover, on a day-to-day basis there is a baffling bureaucracy. If one starts to do anything, there is either a law or a person to prevent one's progress. This leads to a feeling of inadequacy. When Jamaicans remove themselves and go to a country where everyone feels that they can succeed, they have proven themselves to be more than beautiful and talented. Indeed, they become industrious and goal-oriented. Therapy then is eclectic and grows out of analysing each individual person. Research has shown that treatment is successful, not because of the theory involved, but the transference and counter-transference between therapist and patient. This bond is a very useful tool in psychotherapy; for example, the therapist may suggest the meaning of a patient's behaviour to which the patient would normally be defensive. Now, under transference he will at least be thinking about it. From a perspective of positive thinking the therapist may make some strong positive statements which the patient may soon take up as his own. My advice to therapists is to listen to the patients, and learn.

## Working in Jamaica

Most mornings in Jamaica, with very few exceptions, are glorious, bright and sunshiny, and full of hope and encouragement. It was on just such a morning that I started out to report for my first job as a psychologist in Jamaica in July 1974. The Ministry of Health had assigned me to a north coast hospital as a consultant psychologist. The north coast had been my choice as I was living there. I followed the winding road up the hill to the hospital. I later learned that many folks said that if you can get up to the hospital, you really don't need to go there. Anyway, I proceeded, parked my vehicle, and went up the steep steps into the wide front entrance. I assumed that I should report to the Senior Medical Officer, so I went in search of his office. No nurse or secretary was in sight, so I knocked on his door.

A deep, kindly voice said, "Come in" and I complied. He was a middle-aged, rather tired looking man, whose desk was piled with dockets and papers. He seemed a little startled to see me, so I introduced myself, and added that I was the new psychologist. "Yes," he said. "I heard your name. You are a psychiatrist." "No," I explained, "I am a psychologist." "Well, welcome...just what does a psychologist do?" I proceeded to explain about psychological tests and diagnoses, and then about psychotherapy. "So, you don't prescribe drugs?" I explained that psychologists do not prescribe medication, but see patients, who may otherwise be on medication, for counselling. He seemed pleased with "counselling" so I proceeded to explain that psychotherapy was more than counseling, and involved methods of modifying thinking and changing behaviour. "Oh," he said. "Talk therapy". And he admitted he had heard of that, but had never met a practitioner.

He then telephoned the Mental Health Officer (MHO) who soon came – a short, sturdy young man whose very presence spelled/; "Helpful." That day began a 28-year relationship with one of the pillars of strength in the health system. He took me off to the out-patient clinic, and explained the process for handling new and repeat patients. He knew what a psychologist was – he had taken psychology in school, and had done some reading on his own.

Over the ensuing weeks, I began to see patients referred by the MHO, and each day we discussed our impressions of the patients' needs: medication – to be approved by the doctor-on-duty; psychotherapy on a bi-weekly basis. Word seems to have spread quickly – by "Jamaican telegraph", so called. Matrons of two nearby hospitals asked me to visit their hospitals to see referred patients. And finally, another hospital, in an adjacent parish asked for my services. So, quickly, I was very spread out – travelling one day per week to all four hospitals, with an extra day to return to my first hospital. By then I had acquired an apartment in Kingston, and I began spending weekends on the north coast, visiting those hospitals on Fridays, Mondays and Tuesdays, and adding a fifth hospital, in yet another parish, to my list– one near Kingston.

I often traveled to and from Kingston with a psychiatrist who was a consultant at the north coast hospitals. This was a most fortunate friendship for me, and we soon decided that we would open a private practice together in Kingston.

We found a four-room suite atop the NCR building in Kingston – one office for him, one for me, a waiting room, and an extra room with a bed and a fridge. The psychiatrist was an absolutely brilliant and inspired man, and we shared great mutual respect and trust. The practice went very well, for many months. Then he was offered a position as Senior Medical Officer at Bellevue Hospital. This meant that we separated, but only in terms of working space, and I proceeded to Oxford Medical Centre where I maintained an office from 1978 to the present [2007]. I continued to service the five hospitals for the Ministry of Health for a total of 28 years, conducting my private practice on the side and on weekends.

The following are the case histories of some of the many patients who consulted me. Of course, their names and particulars have been modified to protect their confidentiality.

## BERNARD AND SANDRA

Bernard had made the appointment, saying that he and his girlfriend had some problems. At first, I saw them together, and then suggested that individual appointments should be made, followed by a three-way conference after some of our work was done. This was agreed and he came for the individual appointment. "First you must know," he stated, "I am a Jehovah's Witness." He went on to explain that he felt this was at the root of their problems. He went on to explain that Sandra belonged to some church, "Anglican, Presbyterian or whatever", but that she and her family rarely attended. "As a Witnesses," he explained, "we go to Church very often, several times a week, and the Church is the center of our lives." But, he explained, the real problems come in relation to Christmas and birthdays. "We do not celebrate Christmas, as it is a pagan holiday," he explained. He then quoted passages from the Bible which state that serious consequences, indeed death, come to those who celebrate birthdays. He could not imagine changing any of those restrictions, and felt that Sandra should agree with him.

This couple had known each other since childhood, and Bernard professed his love for Sandra. They had been dating for about six months in an exclusive relationship – meaning each person kept his/her social and sexual activities confined exclusively to each other. Bernard was a bright, forthright man who had done well at his place of business – with several promotions within a year. He had also paid down on a house, several doors from his parent's house, and was paying off the mortgage. He hoped to move in, in a few months, and envisaged this to be "with a wife".

When Sandra came for her first individual appointment, she was obviously very unhappy. She cried, and said that she loved Bernard – and he was her best friend. They had experimented sexually, one weekend on the north coast. It was her first sexual experience. It would seem, however, that they found each other sexually compatible. The difficulties, she confirmed were related to Bernard's religion. Sandra, now 21, claimed that all of her life she and her family had celebrated birthdays, and certainly Christmas was a time of joyous activities – presents, parties, etc.

Sandra had a Master's degree in Business and was progressing well at her workplace. "What happens when we have the company Christmas party? Does this mean I could not go? And what about children?" They had both discussed wanting to have a family. "Do our children have to forgo birthday parties while other children – their friends – have them?" Sandra, of course, had her own demands. Bernard must have lunch with her every day, a request he found too taxing. Sometimes, he wanted just to have lunch with company friends. Interestingly, he had never told Sandra this. He just doggedly showed up at lunch.

Both these young people had their own vehicles, yet Sandra would call Bernard to pick this or that up at a shop for her. It was not a question of who paid for the things. She just wanted him to be her messenger. And this, he resented. Clearly, this resonated down to a power struggle. Who was going to demand how much of the other. The lunch and the messenger service were quickly resolved, but things finally boiled down to Christmas and birthday celebrations. Both parties were adamant about their lifestyles, yet each would give way on occasion to keep the relationship alive. Bernard actually went Christmas shopping with Sandra during the pre-holiday period. But he vowed, never again. When her birthday came around, he deliberately did not call her – and they had been in the habit of several phone calls a day. Eventually, they agreed to a period apart. There was great mutual sadness, because in so many ways, these two were compatible. Bernard met a Jehovah 's Witness young lady; Sandra learned of this and they both moved on. The pre-marital counselling had served its purpose and likely prevented years of unhappy experiences.

## ERNEST

Ernest was a tall, lanky 14-year-old, who looked as if he had become taller very recently, and had not yet filled out his body weight. He smiled pleasantly and made and sustained eye contact, somewhat unusual for a teenager. He was accompanied by his mother, a vivacious, attractive woman who presented a referral letter from a local doctor in Montego Bay. She also brought a bundle of report cards from grade 3 to grade 9, his present class placement. These report cards were a remarkable set of documents. Every year he received a straight row of F's with one or two C's interspersed in occasional years. These C's regularly occurred in the skill subjects taken in later grades. Also present was a maternal uncle who showed a great interest in Ernest and had taken an almost paternal role with him.

I soon learned that the mother had been present only two weeks in every six months. Since Ernest was three, she had been working overseas. The father, whom I later met, was a quiet, hard-working man, who worked on shifts. He was often absent at night, and when he was at home in the dark, he was sleeping. There were now three children in the household: Ernest and a brother, aged nine, and a sister of 12.

It turned out that Uncle Harry had really been looking after all three children, with the biological father giving financial aid only. "They think he is mentally retarded," said Uncle. "But I do not believe that. When he comes to help in my auto repair shop, he is really the brightest one there." The letter from the general practitioner in Montego Bay was most helpful. He reported that the boy had sustained three serious head injuries. The first as a toddler, when he fell off a verandah, and had required a number of stitches. As a young lad, at about seven, he was injured while playing football with some friends at school, again, deep lacerations and more stitches. On the third occasion, he was riding his bicycle, got into difficulties and had a serious blow to the head, necessitating stitches. The Montego Bay doctor had checked and found that Ernest had been hospitalized on all three occasions. Clearly, it was time for some psychological tests, and an evaluation of his cognitive functioning.

I began, as is my usual practice, with the House-Tree-Person drawings, quickly followed by the Wechsler Intelligence Scale for Children. Most remarkably, Ernest scored a Full Scale score of 120 that placed his intellectual functioning in the Superior Range.

More specific tests were required. The most revealing of these was the Wechsler Memory Scale. Here Ernest revealed a serious disability, scoring in the 20th percentile. Ernest himself told me that he did understand the schoolwork, the teacher's lectures etc., but that when it came to a test at the end of the time, he could not recall anything. He began to get failing grades and became progressively demotivated about schoolwork. However, he said he loved the Skills Training sessions, and had decided that he would become an auto mechanic when he was an adult. With his uncle being a mechanic and his pleasure in the work itself, I was willing to predict that he could not only become an excellent mechanic, but that he would eventually own the shop. Plans were made for Ernest to be referred for Special Education teaching, and fortunately, one lady in his deep rural school, had such training. Basic English and Mathematics would be emphasized, so that he could read better and do simple math. Ernest also said that he missed his mother tremendously, so some sessions were held with her, and she is now making plans to be resident at home for longer periods of time. I pointed out that her 12-year-old daughter, who was now approaching adolescence, really needed her now, and the mother agreed.

## ORLANDO AND DALE

Orlando called for an appointment and indicated that he and another person wanted to see me – together. He explained that they both had the same problem and to save time I could do "two in one". I pointed out that this was unusual and probably not possible, but that they should come in and we would take from there. Orlando led the way in, nicely dressed in business suit and tie. Dale followed, also nicely attired in tasteful sports clothes. Orlando explained that they had selected me as a therapist because they had heard a programme on RADIO MONA, on which I was interviewed on "Mind Set", a Psychology programme, on "Transsexuals". He felt, therefore, that I was knowledgeable on some of the less conventional types of sexual relationships, and that they would be in safe territory. They were right. Therapists are not judgemental. Orlando explained that he was the fifth of five children and that he had four older brothers. From the time of the third pregnancy, his parents had hoped for a little girl, but this was not forthcoming. He felt that his mother, in particular, kept him close to her – even when cooking, cleaning, and doing hand work (crocheting). As a little boy, he chose to dress up in his mother's clothes – high heels and all, and the family found it to be quite a humorous matter. But as he grew older, he kept choosing female activities. He did not want to go out and play football. In fact, gym class at school was traumatic for him. He would feign sickness, or a sore ankle – anything to avoid the rough and tumble of sports with other boys.

When he was nine years old, he attended church, as he had always done as a young lad. But this time, the minister asked him to stay after Sunday School to help him tidy up the place. Orlando complied only to find out that this man wanted to touch his genitals. He ran from the room, but later admitted to himself only, that it had felt pleasant. He began to masturbate and re-live the experience, sometimes substituting a male classmate as the perpetrator in his fantasies. Behaviour in the sexual area was very quiet except for masturbation, until he reached 12 years of age. He then began to feel an attraction to other boys and older men as well. One day when he was watching a movie in a theatre, the man next to him took up his hand and placed it on his genitals. "Put your mouth on it," the man requested. He then moved his head up and down until the man ejaculated. This upset Orlando and he left the seat for the washroom. The man followed him into the washroom and gave him $2.00. Orlando fled from the theatre. It was known around school that one of the boys, who was somewhat effeminate in his behaviour and who was subjected to a lot of teasing, was into unusual sexual games. Orlando sought him out, and soon experienced his own oral experience, with the boy performing fellatio on him. What he observed, also, was that the boy was also aroused. Orlando had a few fleeting experiences with girls – largely show, tell, and 'feel-up', but he never knew if the girls enjoyed any of it. How much more comforting it was to know your partner was aroused as well, as evidenced by an erect penis.

Dale's early days had been somewhat different. No father was available, and Dale grew up with his mother and two older sisters. He went along with all the family activities, and was quite naïve sexually until he reached puberty. He then began to feel close emotional ties to some of his male friends. They viewed him as a "hanger-on" mostly, until one boy told him, "You know, I love you". Things changed, and he began to do whatever this new "love" asked him, including indulging in oral relationships. Very soon, a pattern developed, and Dale found other loves as well.

When Orlando and Dale met in a lecture at university, there was an almost instant feeling of closeness. Dale admired Orlando's strong physique, and his ready sense of humor. They became study partners, and began seeing each other every evening. Sex soon entered the picture and a pattern of mutual fellatio became established. Both had heard of anal intercourse, but Dale was afraid to submit to this. Their basic pattern continued. Dale lived in a rented room in a large old Jamaican house. He had a bathroom, but shared the kitchen. The room had an outside door at the side of the house, so that one could enter and leave without going through the entire house. Orlando would visit. One day the owner of the house heard sounds he interpreted as sexual activity, and he planted a porch chair outside the door of the room, to see who came out. Unfortunately for Dale, it was not a girl, but Orlando. Dale was given immediate notice to leave. The man's wife protested that he was such a nice quiet man and always paid his rent on time – to no avail. Dale found another room to rent, but they began spending more time at Orlando's place, a fully contained apartment. They began cooking dinner together, studied, and made love. Neighbours began to talk, and one day a neighbour waited on the fire escape to see who left the apartment. Dale would leave at 3:00 a.m., go home to his room, and they would meet again at the university. Needless to say, this raised the stress level of their relationship, and sometimes they did not see each other for several days at a time. Orlando was employed in an electronics firm, part time, and he began to wonder if his supervisor suspected anything about him. He dated a few girls, to deflect his co-workers' suspicion, but it seemed to Orlando that they "had his number".

These two men, deeply in love, sharing each others' lifestyle, and showing much trust and respect for each other, were at an impasse. They had come to therapy to find out how to organize their lives more successfully. It was their respective last years at UWI, so the future needed planning. Dale wanted to attend law school. Orlando was more than willing to support him, and bring in the money to cover living expenses. Applications were made to law schools, and Dale was accepted in England. Visas were obtained, and they soon migrated. At last follow-up, Orlando was working in an IT firm, and Dale was in law school. They had obtained a council flat, as a sublet. Their partnership grew and at last communication, they were considering the Gay Marriage Law.

## MAX AND ABIGAIL

Abby made the appointment and came tearfully explaining that her marriage was over – she could no longer live as she was living. They had been married for five years. One afternoon at the Carib theatre, Abby and her girlfriend had gone to see a kung-fu flick. Her girlfriend was interested in martial arts. During the movie, Abby noticed a very nice looking man sitting a few rows away with two male friends. He glanced around and smiled, but she did not respond. After the movie Abby and the friend went outside to wait for a taxi that had promised to return. The three men came out as well, and the one who had smiled asked if they wanted a ride. They deferred, explaining that a taxi was coming. Max, as she later learned his name to be, hung around, and his two friends left in their vehicle. Max persisted, saying he would take them anywhere in Kingston. Abby and her girlfriend explained that they were staying at a hotel, and he agreed to take them there.

Once at the hotel, Abby's friend, realizing that Abby was admiring Max, excused herself and went into the hotel. Abby and Max sat for several hours in his car, exchanging information.

Abby was in Jamaica on a two-week vacation, and then it was back to France. Her family had invested in some vacation property in France, and she was in charge of renovating the premises, and making it suitable for guests. Only three days were left before departure from Jamaica, and Max insisted she must spend them with him. After explanations to her girlfriend, and promising to be back at the hotel on the day of their return flight, Abby went off with Max for two nights on the north coast. A passionate affair quickly developed, and it was with great reluctance that Abby returned on time for her flight. Once back in France, there were daily – sometimes five times daily – phone calls. Abby was, in a word, "swept off her feet".

She explained that she had had a brief affair in her 20s, and had one daughter, who was raised by her parents. Her only other relative was a much younger brother. At age 48, she had not expected to fall in love again. Then followed a series of trips to Jamaica, usually about every six months, and she would stay about a week. After the fourth trip, approximately two years after their meeting, Max and Abby were married. The plan was for Abby to move to Jamaica, but this was delayed by the work in France. Tearfully, Abby explained that in the first two years of marriage, they may have spent a total of six weeks together.

However, each of these one-week visits turned out to be a tempestu-ous period of love-making. There was little or no time for really consid-ering their respective lifestyles. Max, had been given by his mother at the age of two months, to a woman who soon passed him on to another keep-er. Max could not remember how many homes he had lived in before he began school at age five. He had no knowledge of where his mother, or father who had never been in the picture, lived. He vaguely thought they had probably migrated, since in the 1970s many people left Jamaica. Max began to work at age 12 – part-time jobs in the field. Then he got a job with a construction company at age 16, and had devoted himself to improving his situation. At this point, at age 37, he had become a partner in a firm that was developing townhouses and apartment complexes at six different locations. He was called upon to supervise masons, carpen-ters, and other labourers. His manner with these men was tough, rough, and filled with the usual Jamaica profanity. "We all talk like that," he explained.

Abby, on the other hand, had been raised in a middle-class home, where manners and decorum were the order of the day. She had high expectations of her new husband. He must sit at the table at dinner time; when his friends or workers came to the house, he must introduce them, not just "See my brethren here." Abby wanted names and surnames. "This is John Brown. This is my wife." If he was taking her shopping, he must open the car door for her, and above all, must speak in modulated polite tones. The harmony between Max and Abby began to deteriorate after they had lived together for about three years. She nagged and com-plained, he became resentful and resisted. Abby seemed to have no clue that she needed to accept Max as the man he was, and not the man she wanted him to be. Now, Abby became suspicious of extra-marital rela-tions. After a session of nagging and listing of the "house rules," Max would turn his back in bed, and sex became less and less frequent, which confirmed her suspicions. She began checking his wallet, his cell phone, his clothing. She found confirming evidence of extra-marital affairs, and she became more and more depressed. Much psychotherapy would be required to have these two very different persons accept each other and their respective cultural differences.

## MARK AND COLETTE

Mark made the appointment. He and his wife had some issues. Mark came in first, he was a man of medium build, well dressed in his business suit and tie. He produced a list of the issues he wished to discuss. History reveals that Mark was the youngest of four children. When he was age four, his father died suddenly of a heart attack. This put the family through a course of shock and grief, but his mother seemed to regroup, and soon began looking after the family business, a clothes manufacturing enterprise. All of the older children had their part to play in helping mother to succeed. As Mark recalled, mother became "different". No longer loving and attentive to small matters, but "strictly business" in all relationships. Mark recalls feeling resentful that his father had died, because as he saw it, he lost his father and a loving mother.

Mark grew up very withdrawn and studious. He did well in school, and by now had achieved a Masters Degree in Business. His social life was more or less negligible. A few passing girlfriends, and he wanted to, but did not have sexual relations with any of them. In fact, his sexual history prior to meeting Colette, consisted of only one girl who, he says, pushed herself on him.

When Colette came in she was a startlingly beautiful woman dressed in tasteful, but seductive clothing. She began her history with a series of romances, one of which (the last one) left her depressed and unhappy. He was an older, married man, who had been very assertive with her, and they had had a very passionate six months together. I could not help but think of "Rhett Butler" in Gone With The Wind. Even his picture, which she had in her wallet, looked a lot like Clarke Gable (the actor) in that movie. She said that two years before, when she and Mark got married, she was "already 27" and all her girlfriends, except one, had already married. A few had children already. She met Mark at a company function where she was employed as a Human Resource Consultant. Her friends were there, too, and seemed to think that he was "such a nice man, just for you." Well, he was nice, very polite and perhaps somewhat docile. Living with his mother had taught him how to behave with women.

Mark was a bit overwhelmed by her beauty and felt excited that she talked and danced with him. After a brief period of three months, the engagement was announced, and just as quickly came the marriage. The honeymoon as described by Mark, was wonderful. Colette was less enthusiastic. "He seems ashamed of having sex," she complained. "Could you believe," she said, "he actually used two condoms so as not to get me pregnant." Colette, of course, was on the birth control pill, told him so, but he insisted on condom use. Later, in conversation with me, he denied using the condoms to prevent any sexually transmitted disease, he just thought one should use a condom to prevent pregnancy and two condoms must be better than one. So, they set up house together. In two years, they bought a house and were paying the mortgage. They acquired a few investments – each of them seeking financial security. But Colette worked long hours and had evening company functions. He would wait for her alone at home, only to hear that she was tired. He would ask for sex, and she would say, "Not now," and that was the end of it. She turned her back in bed, and went to sleep.

I asked if he ever touched her afterwards in bed and he said, "No" – he claimed he respected her decision. Colette, for her part, said that he simply did not turn her on. She simply didn't see him as a sexual person. Everything else was very nice. Pleasant conversation, shared interests (tennis, for one), but the pattern continued. He asked, and she said "No".

I wondered if he ever considered other partners, but he quickly informed me that that was immoral. He had taken a vow. Moreover, his mother had never had another man, after Father died. One should be devoted to one's spouse (even after death). I began coaching him in methods of making himself more attractive to her, while at the same time pointing out to her that sex was an important part of marriage. She admitted that she did feel the need for sex sometimes, "but not with him". So, I wondered, "With whom?" And it did turn out that some of her business contacts, who I am sure made advances to her, were attractive to her. We discussed divorce, but each of these people wanted to hang on to the house, the investments, and the status of being "married". I did not feel that this relationship had much chance of continuing in its present form, I suggested a separation – each one to get an additional perspective on the marriage. This they agreed to, except that neither wanted to move out of the house.

Eventually, a man entered Colette's life from the business world and Mark learnt about it. As expected, he saw her outside interest as totally immoral. They divided up the assets and he moved back to his mother's house. Follow-up reports indicate that he found another lady, younger, more loving, and he has remarried.

## JEANNE

Jeanne was referred by the Women's Crisis Centre, after having been seriously physically abused by her husband. She had required hospitalization for three weeks as a result of a broken arm, broken and cracked ribs, and multiple cuts and bruises. Jeanne is a white, American girl who had come to Jamaica some 12 years ago. She was trained as an accountant, and held a CPA qualification. She had visited Jamaica several times previously, and was so impressed with the music, the magic and the vibes that she was considering living in Jamaica – away from Chicago's bitter cold winters. She met Alexander one night at Reggae Sunsplash. Alex had a business – three taxis – and was making payments on a house he had acquired through a National Housing Trust (NHT) loan. Alex was a very pleasant, polite young man and clearly attracted to Jeanne. After Sunsplash, they began dating. He would come to her rented apartment in Ocho Rios, and they spent time together travelling around Jamaica and on the beach. She was trying to get a work permit to start a business as a consultant accountant. He had friends in business who could use her services. So, she set up the two-room apartment using one room as an office.

Things went along very well. They were compatible sexually, and loved each other's company. Jeanne suggested marriage. Alex was more hesitant. His brother and sisters had children and lived with their respective partners; none were married. But Jeanne insisted, and soon got her way. They had a small ceremony at the minister's house, and life began to take form. Every Sunday, Jeanne would prepare a backyard barbecue at the house where they both now lived, and his family, i.e. his younger brother and his sisters, came over. Sometimes, Alex's mother would arrive Saturday night, and prepare and bake a cake or some dessert for the barbecue. The family seemed to fully accept the biracial marriage, and dearly loved Jeanne.

Jeanne pursued her work as an accountant. Clients increased. There was soon money to pay off some of the NHT loan, and Alex purchased a tractor. He had a contract to haul goods from Kingston to Montego Bay, and back. They took one-week vacations to Miami – which were mainly shopping trips. Alex wanted to have a child, but Jeanne thought they should wait until they were more financially stable. Sometimes, Jeanne would stay at her apartment at nights during the week, just for convenience and to cut down on travelling expenses. It was on one of these nights, that the tragedy occurred. Later analysis reveals that Raleigh, Alex's younger brother, had become extremely jealous of Alex's marriage. He had always wanted a "white girl" himself, and he became obsessed with disrupting Alex and Jeanne's really very happy marriage. Raleigh and two friends decided to get Alex (who hardly every drank) drunk. It didn't take much alcohol. Then they told him that Jeanne was over in Ocho Rios seeing other men.

Jeanne and her female secretary were there attending a concert, and had met lots of happy participants. Alex had not been able to make it because Raleigh had persuaded him that something very important had to be discussed. At about 6:00 a.m., a knock was heard at Jeanne's door. She opened the door, and was delighted to see Alex. He began by slugging her in the face, knocking her down. He then proceeded into the bedroom and found two men sleeping in the bed. Jeanne was sleeping alone on a convertible sofa-bed in the "office" part of the apartment. These two men had known Jeanne for a long time, and when they met her at the concert, explained that they had nowhere to stay, so she had offered them rest at her apartment. Jeanne tried to explain, but Alex was having none of it. He picked up a floor lamp and swung it at her. He proceeded to smash the glass in the bookcases along the wall. Jeanne retreated under the sofa bed, hanging onto the springs above her head. At some point, the guests seemed to have left, and Jeanne crawled out from under the bed. That was a mistake because the beating started again. Jeanne lost consciousness and did not come to until she saw several policemen in the room. They arrested Alex and called an ambulance for Jeanne.

Once in hospital, Jeanne was told about her various injuries. Then one doctor asked if she had a birth control device inside her abdomen. She did not. They removed the "device" which turned out to be the rubber tip of a cane Jeanne had used when she previously had a broken ankle from water skiing. It was horribly obvious that Alex had penetrated her vaginally with the cane. The doctor commented that it was a miracle some of her internal organs were not damaged.

Jeanne pressed charges: attempted murder, atrocious assault and battery, assault with a deadly weapon, and reckless abandonment of human life. Jeanne was not about to relent. Alex was held, tried, and was sentenced to 10 years at hard labour. Alex sent his sisters to see Jeanne to plead for him, but Jeanne could not forgive. Jeanne was referred for treatment to help her sort out her future. She was afraid to remain in Jamaica, fearing the wrath of Alex's brother. "She had sent Alex to prison," said Raleigh. In six weeks, a saddened Jeanne was back in Chicago and was referred to a psychologist there for follow-up treatment.

## CHRISTINA

Christina was a strong, sturdily built little girl, aged four years and five months. Her facial features would definitely qualify her as "very pretty". However, I was made aware of some unusual factors in her background, prior to seeing her. Her father, a well known criminal defence lawyer, said that he and Dawn, Christine's mother had been married for three years, and the marriage was not going well. Dawn had to work long hours as a nurse, and the two parents virtually never saw each other. A divorce had been agreed on, and was in its preliminary stages. Then Dawn contacted Bernard, her soon to be ex-husband, and complained that as a Catholic – and they had been married in a religious ceremony – she could never remarry and, therefore, could not have a child. She begged Bernard to impregnate her, as it was her wish to be a mother. Bernard complied, and after nine months, Christina was born just before the divorce became final.

Care and protection of the child was given to the mother, with the maternal grandmother much in the picture. Dawn came to see me, and explained that her life had become intolerable. She could not control Christina. Dawn explained that on weekends with the father, she was more controlled, but Bernard had remarried, and at this point had begun his own family. Dawn was jealous of the step-mother, and at every opportunity would visit the father's home on his weekends, cause a fuss, and take Christina back. I agreed to see Christina, who by now was making a lot of noise with grandma in the waiting room. As Christina came into the office, she rushed to the desk, upsetting a half-full glass of water. Before this could be mopped up, she had climbed into the couch and was extracting things from the nearby bookcase. Dawn asked her to sit down, on her lap, all to no avail.

There was a nice round table with small chairs in the office, with paper and crayons for the purpose of drawing. Christina sat in one of the small chairs – as do all the children- even those too old and big to fit – but this did not last for long. An attempt was made for her to draw a house, but she just proceeded to break up the crayons. She then discovered the wash-basin, hidden behind a small screen. At this point her mother took her hand, and turned off the water. Christina cried and began to scream, "I want water!". At one point she came beside my chair and I was able to put an arm around her and hug her. She liked that, but was soon off to tear up other things in the office.

My diagnosis was ADHD (Attention Deficit Hyperactivity Disorder), and it appeared that no further observation was really necessary. Dawn then called her mother, who, after much struggle, removed the girl from the office. Dawn's question to me was how would she get her into a basic school or kindergarten, as Christina had never been to school. Two schools had been tried, but within one day Christina was excluded. It was clear to me that she would have to be calmed down physically, before any school situation would be possible. Thank goodness for Dr. Robert Gray, retired Director of Child Services at University Hospital, who is still in private practice one day per week. Christina was referred. At a later date, Dawn came back to see me, wondering if Christina's problems were a result of how she had been conceived. I wondered if Dawn had hoped to have her marriage to Bernard re-united by having a child. At this point, Dawn's animosity toward Bernard was such that she could not even entertain that thought. However, she really just wanted to have Christina settled down, and to find a new partner for herself. Follow-up reveals that with medication and play therapy, Christina is now in school.

## THE 36 DEATH ROW INMATES

And it came to pass in the mid-1970s, that a decision was taken to study the condemned men and evaluate the St. Catherine District prison. The Hon. Carl Rattray was then Minister of Justice and National Security. (Justice and Security were then one ministry). A committee was appointed to head the study and they selected two psychiatrists and one psychologist to be the investigating team.

The psychiatrists were Dr. Frederick Hickling and Dr. Frank Knight. The psychologist was the writer of this chapter.

The selection of the psychologist was somewhat problematical. Having been chosen, I had three strikes against me. I was white, female, and not a Jamaican. I was told that the only females allowed inside the prison (aside from in the visitor's area) were Catholic nuns, who conducted a literacy rehabilitation program. I believe some influence by my co-workers had all to do with my being included in the study. We went to the prison every day (including Saturdays and Sundays) for approximately three months. The psychiatrists did clinical interviews individually with each inmate. I conducted psychological tests (intelligence and personality) and also did a clinical interview. The final result was a two-volume work – one volume dealing with analysis of, and suggestions for, solving problems found within the prison. The second volume consisted of individual case studies of each of the thirty-six men.

When we first arrived at the prison, we were taken on a tour by the Superintendent – a very pleasant, cooperative man. After an hour or so of viewing the dilapidated walls and crumbling structure, the Superintendent asked me what I thought about it. I commented that it resembled a 17th-century dungeon. He laughed and replied, "Sixteenth century."

It soon became evident that the men were especially anxious to be examined by me. They drew lots to see who would go first. I soon realized that most of these men's problems had been with black male figures – fathers, police, warders, etc. I became known as the 'White angel from the North,' who they perceived as someone who had come to help them out of their predicament. I rejected this concept and told them I had come to give them some tests, and we got down to business.

In retrospect, the men seemed to fall into three categories. They all claimed innocence, of course, but judging from the type of sometimes seemingly unjust legal and police procedures, at least a third of the men may well have been innocent (we had no access to police reports). A second third seemed to be cases for whom a defence of self-defence was applicable. In this third were cases of two men who got into a physical fight, and one succeeded in killing the other. The winner was then charged with murder. A third were chiefly men who had attempted a robbery, for example, at a gas station, and wantonly killed an attendant or a security guard who happened to be in the way. The personality tests showed this group of men to score very high as 'psychopathic personalities' or 'sociopathic personalities' and they were all quite obviously guilty of their crimes.

In the intelligence area, even more interesting results abounded. It turned out that a much higher percentage of these men scored I.Q.s of 120 or over – in the superior range – than is the case in the general population. Prison populations the world over usually score an average IQ in the 80s and are classified as Dull Normal. Our condemned men are clearly not an average prison population.

From reports from the men, it seemed that the most painful punishment was the waiting – endless waiting for their appeals to be considered. At a somewhat later time, this psychologist was asked to examine two inmates: Pratt and Morgan. These men had protested the long wait for their appeals, and finally the Privy Council considered their case. The outcome of this legal decision was that it was illegal to hold a man awaiting the death sentence for more than five years. His sentence must then be commuted to a life sentence.

After this duty was completed, the Department of Corrections in the Ministry of National Security and Justice offered this psychologist a position as a Consultant. Thereafter ensued ten years of steady work at the St. Catherine District Prison, examining men who were thought to be "unfit to plead" – many of whom were suffering from full blown schizophrenia. Medications were suggested, and approved by the medical doctor, and the men had psychotherapeutic sessions to help them plan their futures, should they return to court. These men were mostly housed in one section of the prison, and while I felt that my work was helpful, it was woefully inadequate for the magnitude of the job.

## RUDOLPH

Rudolph was self-referred. He said that he had been listening to my radio programme, "Lifeline" for almost two years. The programme was on KLAS, and was a call-in live programme in which I attempted to help the caller with his/her problem.

Rudolph, or Ruddy as he preferred to be called, was an employee of the US Embassy where he had one more year of a three-year stint at various administrative jobs. At the time of his coming to see me, he was employed interviewing Jamaican visa applicants, persons applying for U.S. visas. He hated the job and was trying to be transferred to another department. According to Ruddy, he had to interview 30 applicants every hour, which meant two minutes each. He claimed that he felt totally incompetent to decide which applicant would be likely to return to

Jamaica, which he said was the major criteria for granting a visa. There was not sufficient time to assess documents which the applicant might have brought. Just time to ask a few questions and form an "impression". During his time in therapy he was, unfortunately for him, never transferred. Rudy's presenting problem, according to him, was his uncontrollable temper. He cited numerous incidents in his life when, had he minded his own business and kept quiet, he would not have gotten into so many intense arguments, with various unfortunate outcomes.

Ruddy was a man of medium build, slightly obese, with long cut black hair and remarkable large green eyes. He admitted that his eyes were his "best quality" and he used them to accentuate many of his direct assertions. Immediately obvious was a rather sparkling sense of humor, as he cited experiences and then laughed, somewhat defensively, at himself. Ruddy was the oldest of four children for his parents, and when he was age 11, his father – an insurance agent – died of a heart attack very suddenly. His mother, who had always been a housewife, was overwhelmed with grief, and she and the four children retreated to the maternal grandmother's house where, fortunately, grandmother took charge. It was six months before the family returned home, and by this time mother had cast Ruddy in the role of 'man of the house.' He was not ready for this, and developed what seemed to be psychosomatic symptoms – sore throat, headache, upset stomach. But mother did not decrease her demands. He was to do chores, run errands, and assist his mother who claimed also to be 'sick,' and she held him responsible for the three younger children. Whatever went wrong in the house, no matter who was responsible, it was Ruddy's responsibility. Where Ruddy had been a more or less 'B' student, his grades in school declined. His interest in sports was thwarted, because he had to pick up a brother or sister from school and see that they got home. He was angry most of the time, and often slapped and abused the younger children. Mother did not disapprove of that – "Spare the rod and spoil the child" was her motto. This motto had also been held by the deceased father and Ruddy was regularly and soundly beaten as a child.

Ruddy's problems with the law began early. He stole a bicycle, as his mother said she did not have money to repair his and required many errands of him. He was caught and had to visit a Juvenile Detention Officer three times a week. His anger towards authority figures mounted.

When he finally obtained a driver's licence, at age 17, he would have daily arrests as he drove his mother's car too fast, down a one-way street the wrong way, broke a stoplight. One day, he passed an army recruiting centre. Here was the solution, he thought. He went in, was immediately welcomed warmly and before long he had taken his physical, been sworn in, and sent off to boot camp. But this same young man, who rebelled against authority, was soon in violation of various orders, and after six months was discharged as 'Unfit.' Next, he thought, he would try the U.S. Foreign Service. By then he had learned one or two lessons, and he was accepted and sent for training. Somehow the general atmosphere of men, together, serving the USA appealed to him, and the authorities did not hold his stint in the army against him. He decided he must control his urges to argue and lose his temper, and with a now somewhat grandiose idea of future political office he was marginally successful.

Now, he wished to understand why he had these character traits. "I need 'anger management' training," he said. He had been reading some psychology books, and understood the importance of analyzing his past, and particularly his early history. And this we did. His stay at the U.S. Embassy at Kingston was, however, a somewhat lonely affair for him. Social gatherings were not successful; in fact after a few alcoholic drinks, he usually ended in a fuss with his associates. He finally met a young lady, who was employed as a secretary in a sales office. They seemed to hit it off, but the meetings usually consisted of a visit to a supermarket, where Ruddy would buy all the things she wanted; and they would take them home to her parents, with whom she lived. The parents were warm and welcoming, and he spent his 'off' hours there. After about twelve months of weekly analysis, the anger periods were less frequent, and Ruddy went off to his next Embassy assignment a quieter and more mature man.

**NOTE**

*It is with great sadness that we report that our colleague, and friend, Dr Ruth Doorbar, passed away in 2007, during the compilation of this volume.*

# 18 The Application of Traditional Psychotherapy Models in the Caribbean

*Rosemarie Johnson, Peter Weller, Sharon Williams Brown, & Audrey Pottinger*

The question that practitioners in the Caribbean must contend with is: "Do we need our own theories, psychotherapeutic approaches, and assessment tools, or are the mainstream theories and techniques adequate and appropriate?" Some practitioners believe that traditional models of psychotherapy may have limited relevance for minority groups or across cultures (Castro-Blanco, 2005; Hickling & Gibson, 2005; Cushman, 1995; and Boyd, 1982). On the other hand, there are those who espouse, implicitly or explicitly. the universality of traditional psychology theory and psychotherapy (Wampold, 2001). These seemingly diametric viewpoints may make it difficult for the practitioner and student of psychology to approach the work of psychotherapy in a coherent and integrated manner. A chapter on the application of traditional psychotherapy, in a book on Caribbean Psychology, provides a platform for addressing this issue. Consequently, this chapter will explore how best to use these traditional approaches to psychotherapy with people in the Caribbean. It will not, however, focus on specific techniques because the decision to use specific techniques will emerge out of the practitioner's understanding of a patient's issues, dynamics, and his or her current situation.

This task of applying traditional psychotherapy can appear formidable because there are hundreds of models of psychotherapy (Norcross,

2002), as well as thousands of textbooks on the subject, as may be found on the website of Amazon, the major Internet bookseller. Moreover, it is even said that there are as many psychotherapeutic approaches as there are therapists (Korchin, 1976). Given this volume of information on psychotherapy, it is no wonder that many may suffer from information overload, and that the novice practitioner may be left confused and unsure about what to do. Even the more experienced therapist may stick to the tried and tested approaches without evaluating the efficacy of these techniques for different clients. Nevertheless, for the Caribbean practitioner to apply traditional psychotherapy in a coherent, integrated manner, clinically useful connections among the traditional approaches are needed, as well as the integration of these approaches within our cultural context. Moreover, an informal survey of Caribbean psychotherapists and counsellors revealed that many practitioners generally use an eclectic approach in treating patients seeking psychological relief. Additionally, while the psychotherapists were aware of differences between themselves and their clients, these differences were not usually addressed explicitly in treatment. Thus, part of the challenge of applying psychotherapy in the Caribbean is that it is difficult to know and appreciate which aspects of each of the traditional approaches apply and which do not.

However, before such integration can be achieved, a thorough and comprehensive knowledge of traditional psychotherapeutic models is needed (Corey, 2005). Many textbooks cover the basic tenets of the traditional psychotherapeutic models such as Psychodynamic, Behavioral, Cognitive, or Existential (Corey). While this is useful, the practitioner still needs to integrate the underlying assumptions of these models, especially as most Caribbean psychotherapists report that they use an eclectic approach. Additionally, these assumptions need to be understood within a cultural context. To begin the discussion, a definition of traditional psychotherapy is needed. Traditional psychotherapy has been defined as "an interpersonal process in which therapists explicitly communicate to their patients that they understand them, respect them, and want to be of help to them" (Weiner, 1998). In addition, the communication of this 'person-related understanding' constitutes the central feature of the method.

With regard to the issue of culture, La Roche's (2003; 2005) perspective may be used, where psychotherapy is "a dynamic process in which patient and therapist are mutually transformed and embedded within a consistently present specific cultural context." This broader definition also recognizes that the process of psychotherapy is more effective when patient, therapist, and the cultural context of the dyad are acknowledged and used coherently, rather than independently. Further, the aforementioned assumptions are consistent with the evolving field of psychotherapy where behaviours are understood as resulting from multiple factors and which sees psychotherapy as most effective when it integrates all these factors.

## Traditional Psychotherapy Models – Conceptualization

Traditional models of psychotherapy are associated with Psychodynamic, Existential, Cognitive, and Behavioural theories, to name a few (Corey, 2005). However, simply knowing these models does not provide practitioners with information on best practices in their application because of the challenge of integrating these seemingly distinct frameworks. La Roche's (2005) contextual framework for psychotherapy provides a useful solution to begin to understand what we do and how we do it. He proposes that one way of integrating the many psychotherapeutic approaches is to examine the assumptions that underlie them. Additionally, categorizing each model, based on focusing on subject, object, and context, makes conceptualization more manageable. Then, if this approach is taken, the therapeutic models can fit into the following three categories: Individualistic/Objective; Subjective/Relational; and Socioconstructive.

Psychotherapeutic models that use an Individualistic/Objective approach conceive of problems as residing within the patient. Many traditional models of psychotherapy understand patients in this way. Epistemologically, within this paradigm, since the problem resides within the patient, the patient becomes the focus of treatment, and the objectivity and neutral stance of the therapist are highlighted. Critics of this conceptualization argue that with the focus on individualism and objectivity, legitimate relational problems as well as the larger social/cultural context (e.g., poverty) may fade into the background, or are minimized (Pederson, 2002). Further, this way of understanding the patient falsely assumes an objective 'value free science' (Ponterotto, Casas, Suzuki, & Alexander, 2001); promotes the assumption of universality of psychotherapy (Wampold, 2001); and also minimizes issues related to the therapist, or the socio-cultural environment in which the patient lives (La Roche, 2005).

Given that a major assumption of the Individualistic/Objective model is that the problem lies within the patient, it is not inconceivable that a patient being treated using that understanding might be made to feel that he or she is to be blamed for his or her problems. This, no doubt, may also contribute to the stigma that is often associated with psychotherapy and the unwillingness of many Caribbean people to make psychotherapy a realistic option for sorting out problems of living. In Jamaica, for example, in many instances psychotherapy becomes an option only when there is a crisis, or someone is mandated to attend sessions. These realities have implications for patient motivation, how psychotherapy is conducted, and how it is used by patients.

Along with the broad epistemological understanding, a therapist also needs to focus on ontology; that is, understand at a deeper level the nature of what we know. In the psychotherapeutic process, this relates to what a therapist sees as critical for inclusion in the psychotherapeutic process. So, in order for a therapist to understand his or her ontological assumptions, La Roche (2005) recommends focusing on some of the following: which variables are consistently emphasized during a session, which variables are consistently omitted, and why? Are the issues that are highlighted objective, subjective, or contextual? Are formulations emphasizing or overlooking any of the areas? Thus, a therapist using an Individualistic Model is likely to focus primarily on childhood experiences and their impact on the current presenting problem. For example, in understanding and treating Caribbean battered women using the Individualistic/Objective paradigm, the therapist is likely to focus on the intrapsychic issues that would make a battered woman stay in an abusive relationship that endangers her not only physically but psychologically as well. The focus in therapy might therefore be on working through issues that relate to early attachments or self-esteem and empowering her internally so that she can have the courage to do something about her situation.

While the different levels of epistemology and ontology in the

Individualistic/Objective approach enhances the therapists conceptualization of a patient's issue, these still needs to be integrated within a cultural context. In some parts of the Caribbean, for example, there is a segment of the population that believes that if a woman is not beaten in her relationship, then she is not truly loved. This value system may have its roots in early child-rearing where children are told, "I'm beating you because I love you." Such a cultural context would then need to be integrated within the epistemological and ontological frame of understanding such a patient.

Another way of categorizing traditional models of psychotherapy is to look at what La Roche (2005) refers to as the Subjective/Relational Models. These subjective relational models epistemologically share the assumption that the process of therapy occurs between subjects rather than within individuals. As a result, it is the interactions among people (i.e., patient/others, patient/therapist) that ought to be the focus of attention. Furthermore, because of the relational focus within the psychotherapeutic process, the therapist's subjectivity is also included and used as an important tool for empathizing and connecting with the patient (Goldfield & Davila, 2005). Additionally, within this paradigm, the therapist's privileged standpoint is questioned and replaced by a more egalitarian relationship between patient and therapist (Hatcher, Favorite, Hardy Goode, Deshelter, & Thomas, 2005). It is presumed that the curative aspect of this paradigm is based on the assumption that if a patient is able to change his or her interpersonal dynamics, then he or she will be able to achieve significant psychotherapeutic change. The research in psychotherapy also supports this assumption in that consistently, the therapeutic relationship is shown to be a significant curative factor (Lambert, 1994).

While the subjective/relational approach adds richly to the psychotherapeutic process, many of the classic relational models – such as the Person-Centered model – with some exceptions, reduce culture to the interpersonal experience of the patient or therapist or common patterns of interaction of specific cultural groups. It may also de-emphasize or overlook external socioeconomic and political pressures such as poverty, race, and social class (La Roche, 2005). These assumptions of the Subjective/Relational models pose potential challenges for the Caribbean because people are used to a pedagogical stance in helping relationships (e.g., physician, pastor) where they expect answers and direction. Should these not be forthcoming, patients might perceive that they are not being helped and may terminate a process before it can even begin.

Notwithstanding, given the limitations of examining the categories of traditional theories along individualistic and subjective lines for the Caribbean, the broad consideration of culture now needs to be considered – the Socioconstructive Models. Practitioners need to be aware that in the application of traditional psychotherapy, culture is deeply embedded in the consciousness of all human beings and central in all psychological functioning (Hickling & Gibson, 2005; James, 2002; Hickling, 2001; and Colin, 1996). The importance of context is therefore central because patients are 'unknowable' without an understanding that locates them within a cultural and historical context (Cushman, 1995).

Culture influences the process of psychotherapy in several ways: through language, symbols, or narratives (Pedersen, 2002). Moreover, symbols also vary and have specific meanings, according to each cultural context (Sue & Lam, 2002). Thus, the therapist's job is that of understanding the meanings of specific symbols if therapy is to work. Practitioners also need to understand and recognize that culture also influences what is discussed or omitted. In the Caribbean, there is a common belief that one should not "wash their dirty linen in public." That is, people are supposed to sort out their personal problems and not involve outsiders (GoPaul-McNicol & Brice-Baker, 1998). The same censorship is not given to physical concerns. In fact, physical problems, with a few exceptions, are often not seen as the individual's fault or a sign of weakness, unlike the problems that require psychotherapy. Thus, in the Caribbean, a physician is generally the first line of entry for many people who end up receiving psychotherapy.

Understanding the impact of culture is not only a concern for Caribbean practitioners. Mainstream psychology also recognizes that encountering cultural differences in psychotherapy is inevitable (APA, 1993; Ponterotto, Casas, Suzuki, & Alexander, 2001; La Roche & Maxie, 2003). In fact, many cross-cultural psychotherapists think that those who work in a multicultural context must understand that cultural assumptions embedded within traditional psychotherapy practices may sometimes be discordant with various ethno-cultural world views (Stolle, Hutz, & Flanagan, 2005). This seems diametrically opposed to a common assumption that psychologists can achieve an objective, value-free universal knowledge of what might be happening with a patient (Smith, 2005).

In the Caribbean, while it is recognized that our people may be different culturally from those in the USA and Europe, the diversity within a country is often under-appreciated and its impact not fully addressed in the therapeutic process. For example, religion and the way it is handled by different social classes in the Caribbean highlight our heterogeneity. Thus, a belief in Obeah is common among many individuals who share a geographic space and socioeconomic background in Jamaica. These beliefs are also unlikely to be shared by the therapists who provide services. Consequently, Caribbean practitioners cannot make the assumption that sharing a nationality equates to unquestioned understanding (West, 2004). It is for this reason that the Caribbean practitioner needs to be even more vigilant because it is easy to not take differences into account; that is, they should be mindful that cultural differences exist between patient and therapist and that they are numerous, regardless of seeming surface similarities. Some of these cultural differences relate to gender, ethnicity, race, religion, sexual orientation, language, and geographic location and have implications for communication styles, power/control dynamics and expectations of outcomes. Lago and Thompson (1990) also speak of the additional complexity caused by the impact of a supervisor who may be from a cultural background different from that of the psychotherapy trainees.

The heterogeneity that exists among Caribbean people – especially in terms of ethnic identity, ethnic language proficiency, social class, and spiritual faith – is huge. Therefore, it is only through understanding the heterogeneity issues, and working them through on a personal level that therapists who practise in the Caribbean will provide the interpersonal climate for change in psychotherapy (O'Connor, 2005; Silverman, 2005; and Teyber, 2000). Training and in-service supervision must also reinforce this type of didactic instruction.

This cross-cultural perspective also recognizes that real and fundamental differences in values, role concepts, behavioural patterns, forms of expression, and cognitive styles must be acknowledged by practitioners before effective understanding of a patient can occur (Jones & Korchin, 1982). Moreover, without this understanding, change-oriented interventions are, at the very least, limited or even destined to fail (Sue & Lam, 2002). The debate on how to apply such a cross-cultural paradigm proposes two considerations. On one hand, there is the assumption that concepts, institutions, and practices developed by the mainstream mental health establishment are ill adapted to ethnic problems and needs. Furthermore, because of important cultural differences, traditional methods of psychotherapy are likely to be inadequate (Hickling & Gibson, 2005; Colin 1996).

This cross-cultural perspective also expands its conceptualization beyond the patient, to incorporate what happens socially and politically in the patient's life. The political perspective contends that the patient may not necessarily be sick. Instead, it could be the society in which that patient lives that is sick (James, 2002). There is no question that Caribbean people have to contend with the reality of social stress, economic disadvantage, and discrimination. The ethical and professional issues raised here speak to the issue of public education about the psychological impact of such environmental challenges, the resilience that emerges from successfully navigating such challenges, and the need to make care affordable for those most needy but who cannot afford it. Jamaica has attempted to address some of these social and political mental health issues through their child guidance and community mental health clinics and counselling centres. However, while these interventions may provide some relief, the environment in which many individuals live require larger macro solutions related to violence and poverty alleviation.

Unfortunately, the context in which mental health intervention occurs for some Caribbean people, particularly Jamaicans, is replete with violence and poverty thus creating great challenges for the practitioner. Thus, if an individual who successfully participated in a psychotherapeutic intervention is forced to return to a pathogenic environment of poverty, community disorganization, and violence, this is likely to erode the gains from the treatment. The therapist may also, unwittingly, be promoting acceptance of the status quo, especially if he/she adheres to the assumptions that problems lie within the patient, thereby preventing change at the sociological level. This paradigm emphasizes the psychological damage of economic deprivation and advocates broad social changes as the only ultimate prevention and cure for psychological problems (James, 2002).

To address the limitations of training programmes with respect to addressing the issue of cultural competence, there is a move in the field of psychotherapy for therapists to develop cultural expertise (APA, 2002). The framework put forth by Pedersen (2002) suggests that cultural competence on the part of the therapist begins with an awareness of culturally learned assumptions of which he or she is not necessarily aware. Once this awareness is present, the next step is to gather the facts, knowledge, and information required to comprehend the meaning behind the behaviour of self and the patient. La Roche and Maxie (2003) also suggest some considerations in addressing cultural differences in psychotherapy. They stress the importance of recognizing that cultural differences are subjective, complex and dynamic. Additionally, they recommend that the most salient cultural difference be addressed first; and emphasize the importance of understanding that if cultural differences are discussed in psychotherapy, they should be discussed as assets that can help in the therapeutic process.

Finally, they suggest that the patient's cultural history and the development of his or her racial identity are important factors in assessing how best to conceptualize presenting problems and facilitate therapeutic goals. Caribbean theorists such as Hickling (2005), in an attempt to address this issue therapeutically, also emphasize the tremendous creative genius of Caribbean people and the need to incorporate a mixture of local events, team-work, myth, religion, and cultural symbols to empower and transform patients.

While these are helpful considerations, multicultural and cross-cultural researchers and practitioners recognize that there are no simple answers to when and how cultural differences should be addressed. In spite of the richness that incorporation of culture brings to the psychotherapeutic process, it is not without its critics. Specifically, while it is recognized that such contextual models encourage empowerment in patients, there are some who think that it can also minimize individual responsibility and relational issues (Stolle, Hutz, & Sommers-Flanagan, 2005). Additionally, assuming general contextual characteristics about culturally diverse groups can minimize individual differences and promote cultural stereotypes (Jackson, 1999).

## Psychotherapy Research

Over the years, psychotherapy has expanded tremendously in its approach to the tasks of therapy, the psychotherapy theories, the range of people treated, the variety of professionals involved, and the amount of research devoted to its efficacy (Norcross, 2002). Today, there are more than 250 different psychotherapeutic systems guiding professional practice (Norcross, 2002). Because these various systems developed out of and borrow from each other, in practice, many therapists are more eclectic than purists (Korchin, 1976). Nevertheless, regardless of the approach, the fundamental issue is whether traditional psychotherapy works, and how it works. Moreover, does it work in the same way across cultures or for ethnic minority groups?

Research on the efficacy of psychotherapy consistently demonstrates that while there are many curative factors in the process (e.g., instilling and maintaining hope, a corrective emotional experience, increased self-awareness), the therapeutic relationship is the most important contributor to a positive outcome, regardless of demographics, theoretical orientation or pathology (Lambert & Barley, 2002; Lambert, 1994; Norcross, 2002; Jorgensen, 2004). It is also this therapeutic relationship that most traditional psychotherapy techniques have in common. Additionally, aspects of this relationship include empathy, warmth, acceptance, and the encouragement of risk-taking (Weiner, 1998).

There are also some implicit and explicit assumptions in traditional psychotherapy. A fundamental assumption is that human behaviour can be changed (Corey, 2005). Second, emotional relearning is central and a patient needs "an experience", not an explanation (Moursund, 1994). Further, therapeutic change occurs when the patient learns, for example, how not to be afraid, rather than only what and why he or she is afraid (Moursund, 1994). Additionally, because change depends on experiential and emotional learning, the psychotherapeutic process requires the patient's active participation. The therapist, in turn, provides the conditions that facilitate therapeutic relearning (such as a safe environment where there is unconditional acceptance), and this condition resides in the unique interpersonal relationship of therapy.

Given that the psychotherapeutic relationship is such a fundamental prerequisite for change, a therapist understanding a patient's personal meanings is therefore critical. This is achieved by the therapist listening, without responding in terms of his or her own needs and feelings, or the demands of social convention. It is the blending of these characteristics that gives the psychotherapeutic relationship its special ingredient – a setting within which emotional relearning can take place. However, clinical experience in this field suggests to the authors that the Caribbean psychotherapist may encounter certain barriers to the development of the psychotherapeutic relationship and should be prepared to address these relevant issues. That is, because of the familiarity within the Caribbean with pedagogical models, we find that there is an expectation of explanation, especially when one has paid money for some form of intervention. Additionally, perceptions of the change process may also be a barrier in the Caribbean, as there are many who believe that one is at the mercy of his or her 'nature' and/or that one is under the control of a higher power (e.g., it is God's will). As a result, some Caribbean people do not really believe that the power to change comes from within. For these people there is little or no sense of personal control. Thus, there is an acceptance of the existing behaviour or an expectation that some powerful 'other' should take charge. Frustration and recidivism, or dependency may be predicated as a result of this mindset.

Given that the passive patient is part of the health care tradition in the Caribbean – the expectation then is that the 'doctor' will decide and 'tell me' to do what is necessary. This mindset carries over into the counseling/psychotherapy setting, and patients are likely to feel that the 'doctor' should be able to tell what is happening because that is part of his/her job. This expectation of expecting a quick fix may cause the patient not to persevere long enough for the relationship to develop. Notwithstanding these challenges posed for the Caribbean therapist, once the aforementioned implicit and explicit assumptions are achieved, then the 'how' of the process needs to be understood. Part of understanding how requires the recognition that there is an external and internal structure to psychotherapy.

## Structure of Psychotherapy

While it is clearly important that a psychotherapist in training should have a deep appreciation for the structure of psychotherapy, it is also important to educate the patient about this structure in order to facilitate the therapeutic process. This is especially important in the Caribbean where the therapeutic structure is likely to be different from any other relationship that a patient has.

The external structure of psychotherapy starts with the very first contact between the clinician and the patient (Wampold, 2001). Once a fundamental commitment is made by the patient to seek help, a clear agreement (contract) that can be adhered to by the therapist and the patient needs to be reached (Korchin, 1976). Weiner (1998) suggests that the contract is generally over several sessions and may be negotiated and changed during the process of therapy. However, there are other practitioners who believe that the contract starts with the first telephone contact. For example, Talmon (1990) believes that "the moment a patient picks up the phone to call a therapist or clinic, the therapy has begun. The patient has recognized a problem and taken action." Once each individual in the therapeutic arrangement decides that treatment is needed, the first and easiest condition in this contract is the scheduling and fees. To honour his or her part of the contract, the therapist is then required to be available during the scheduled hours and to be accessible by telephone at other times if there is an emergency. The therapist also needs to arrange for uninterrupted privacy during the sessions and to protect the patient's confidences. With the exception of time-limited psychotherapy, how long the process will last is also left open.

In the Caribbean, the external structure does not always conform to these standards – as they might elsewhere. Therefore, psychotherapists must gently remind patients that the telephone is not the medium through which the process will occur. Additionally, patients have to be reminded that once they are given a time for their appointment, it does not mean that they will have to wait for several hours to be seen, as is often the experience with other healthcare providers. They also need to be reminded of the importance of punctuality for their scheduled appointments and that they do not have unlimited time in a session. This therapeutic structure can be difficult for some patients and even for the therapist to grasp, as Caribbean people generally are very relaxed and imprecise about time. In Jamaica, for example, "Mi soon come – I will be there soon" can mean 10 minutes as well as hours later.

Another aspect of the external structure includes the setting of goals and behavioural limits. The setting of goals generally emerges out of an open discussion that is mutually agreed upon by the therapist and the patient (Weiner, 1998). However, goal setting may be challenging in certain contexts as the supportive nature of some models of psychotherapy, coupled with developmental issues and psychosocial crises of lives lived in difficult circumstances, create new challenges that continually extend the scope of the work to be done. Notwithstanding the challenges to setting goals under certain circumstances, the behavioural limits of the process need to be made explicit. Generally, the boundaries of the therapeutic relationship are often characterized as permissive, but with certain limits. The specific limit is that the patient respects the person and property of the therapist. That is, while the patient is free to vent angry feelings, and is even encouraged to do so, he or she can only do so verbally. Similarly, feelings of admiration, affection, or love can be openly expressed by the patient, but sexual contact between patient and therapist is forbidden (APA, 1993). It should also be pointed out that while the patient is free to say what he or she wants, communication still needs to be directed toward exploration and understanding of the patient's experiences and feelings. Should the patient want to engage in "chit-chat", he or she should be reminded that such an activity is avoiding the therapeutic task (Moursund, 1993).

The authors have found that for some Caribbean people who seek psychotherapy, there is difficulty adjusting to this unique interpersonal structure. As such, many patients expect to have a traditional doctor/patient or teacher/preacher relationship. Thus, when they are engaged at the more affective level in the early stages of the therapeutic process, some may switch their mode of interacting to that of an intimate social relationship as this model is more familiar. As a result, chit-chat and expectations of friendship may make it difficult for clients to understand and respect the boundaries of this new professional therapeutic way of relating. It is at these times that the psychotherapist needs to be vigilant that certain interpersonal boundaries are not crossed. Moreover, the social context within which psychotherapy occurs in many Caribbean societies may also blur the boundaries of the professional relationship, as the patient may come in contact with the psychotherapist outside of the therapeutic relationship because of the small spaces in which Caribbean people operate. The reality of the Caribbean situations is that a therapist may have a patient who may later become a student, or the patient and therapist may end up on, say, the same committee in church. This creates challenges with dual relationships in our setting and requires practitioners to confront ethical dilemmas of confidentiality and social interactions. What is clear from these challenges is that Caribbean practitioners need to revisit the issues of dual relationships within the context in which we provide services. This revisiting may also involve modifying existing ethical guidelines. Syme (2003) provides a framework to balance the issues of dual relationships in an ethical manner and may be a point to begin dialogue among Caribbean practitioners.

Once the outer structure of psychotherapy is established, the focus turns to the inner structure. The inner structure of traditional psychotherapy contains three major phases: 1) establishing the therapeutic relationship; 2) seeking to understand the nature and sources of personality characteristics and defects; and 3) translating insights into actions and new life patterns (Weiner, 1998). Engagement in the therapeutic process suggests that the patient is implicitly making the commitment to communicate feelings and experiences openly and honestly, as best as he or she can, even if the process is painful (Goldfield & Davila, 2005). On the therapist's part, there is also an implicit agreement to provide the patient with undivided attention during each therapy session, as well as a commitment to avoid prejudgment – particularly of a moralistic nature. The therapist also commits to using his or her full knowledge as well as empathy on the patient's behalf. Beyond this, the therapist promises the patient privacy and confidentiality (Korchin 1976). While the therapist can commit to many things, he or she cannot assure a patient a particular outcome. The best he or she can offer in this regard is conjecture, "many people find after therapy . . ." (Wampold, 2001).

The Caribbean experience of the inner structure of psychotherapy is often through counselling. This is also primarily in the context of guidance counselling in the educational setting, and pastoral counselling where there are different rules of engagement. Thus, expectations of advice, recommendations, solutions, an emphasis on consequences, and following the rules of society are brought to the psychotherapy experience by both the patient and the less experienced therapist. Additionally, Caribbean patients may therefore not expect, want, nor deem it appropriate for the therapist to follow the inner structure of traditional psychotherapy. The result of not addressing these implicit expectations can lead to premature termination because the therapeutic relationship was not effectively established as the expectations of patient and therapist were so different. Additionally, the importance of appropriate training and supervision (Lago & Thompson, 1990; Hickling & Matthies, 2002), as well as requiring an initial focus on educating patients regarding the psychotherapeutic process and objectives, cannot be overemphasized.

The self-knowledge phase of therapy may also be painful and arduous (Lambert, 1994). It is also not a smooth ascending curve. Rather, it is important for the therapist and patient to understand that there will be setbacks as new problems arise, life conditions change, or the patient meets defeat in his or her efforts to change behaviour (Norcross, 2002). Consequently, patience on the part of each is critical during this phase. Therapists and patients also need to keep in mind that self-defeating patterns are not easily shed as a patient often moves back to the 'safer ground' of familiar behaviour after seeming to advance. Consequently, constant reexamination, reinterpretation, and re-analysis of emotional patterns need to be done to consolidate the gains of earlier therapeutic dialogues (Lambert, 1994).

As mentioned previously, models of helping relationships for Caribbean patients are generally pastors, village elders, guidance counsellors, and radio counselors. These groups of helpers are likely to be less theory bound, to be more didactic and to give advice in their focus and to reinforce the expectation of immediate relief of symptoms. Again, to address these potentially different expectations, it is critical for the Caribbean therapist to spend time initially in explaining the process and to anticipate those times in the process where difficulties may place the patient at risk for early termination. Additionally, use of therapeutic approaches such as Cognitive Behavioural, that match the mindsets of patients, at least initially, fit well because they are problem-focused, interventions can be early, there is often a pedagogical component, and it can be short-term. However, if a therapist is unable to switch theoretical stance, then referral to other professionals who can meet the client's expectations and needs is in order. While this might be what is best for the client, the therapist may feel that he/she is at the top of the chain/pyramid of providers and may not refer. However, in such a situation, the therapist needs to understand that he/she cannot be all things to all people.

In the third and last phase, therapeutic dialogue turns from consideration of self-defeating patterns to discussions of adaptive potentials. This phase, once successfully completed, naturally leads to termination. When should psychotherapy end? This question is often asked by beginning therapists and patients alike. In one sense, psychotherapy never ends because personal development and perfecting of behaviour is a lifelong process (Korchin, 1976; Talmon, 1990; and Weiner, 1998). Nonetheless, in the more usual and limited sense, psychotherapy should terminate when the stated goals are achieved (Weiner, 1998). It will be easier for the therapist to know when this has occurred, based on how precisely goals were stated in the beginning. However, as was noted previously, one problematic area for some therapists relates to the ongoing needs of patients in difficult circumstances or patients who are at a developmental stage where they continue to identify issues and feel the need for continued support. In these circumstances, termination may not be indicated at that particular time. However, termination is indicated when the patient is able to monitor and modify challenges that were once difficult. That is, the patient can now be his or her own therapist.

The termination phase begins with patient and therapist examining the patient's current status and future prospects (Goldfield & Davlia, 2005). However, agreement on termination does not abruptly stop the process of therapy, because there needs to be some working through on the part of the patient and the therapist about the ending of the relationship. Weiner (1998) suggests approximately six weeks for this working-through phase. In this phase, focus is on the meaning of discontinuing, as well as the patient's future plans. Emotions and reactions on the part of the therapist and the patient are also common during termination because of the emotions it evokes in both. For some patients, therapy can become a way of life rather than a proper means to an end. Moreover, just as there is resistance to beginning therapy in the first place, there can be resistance to leaving it in the end (Weiner, 1998).

Some common reactions of the patient may include the resurgence of earlier symptoms, a surge of dependency feelings, or generalized distress and anxiety (Korchin, 1976). The focus of the therapist during this phase is then to accentuate hope and the patient's growth, as well as minimize uncertainty and fear. It is also important to assure the patient that if there are setbacks in the future, follow-up is available. Talmon (1990) refers to this as an "open-door policy". With this open-door policy, the therapist is balancing therapeutic change with the patient's needs and pain. Working through the termination phase of psychotherapy cannot be overlooked or minimized, as to do so would erode the gains of the therapy (Jorgensen, 2004).

Problems with termination do not affect patients only; therapists can also experience difficulty with ending the therapeutic relationship. These difficulties could range from the reluctance to lose a steady source of income to re-awakening of the therapists' intrapsychic conflicts about attachment and abandonment. For the therapist, unresolved personal issues with endings may cause him or her to circumvent the working through process and may result in acting-out behaviours such as missing sessions, or abruptly stopping treatment.

In training environments, termination is also particularly challenging because trainees rotate briefly through practicum sites or firms. For many Caribbean psychotherapists-in-training, opportunities for supervised practicum and intern experiences may require that they work in a number of locations. In situations like these, special attention needs to be paid to the structure of these training programs to minimize the possible harmful impact of termination. Trainees also need to be adequately supervised as they navigate their way through this challenging aspect of the process. What then are the implications for the practice of traditional psychotherapy in the Caribbean?

## Caribbean Implications

As the debate on the application of traditional psychological theories and practice in psychotherapy continues, practitioners and students within the Caribbean need to understand that psychology and mental health is still stigmatized. There is no question that there have been tremendous gains in the field, and acceptance by a few of the benefits of psychotherapy, but the majority of the population still sees it as a last resort, and use it primarily for crisis management. Additionally, many disadvantaged individuals, especially the less educated, may need and want more direct interventions (explicit advice, financial counselling, vocational help) than is offered in traditional psychotherapy (Jones & Korchin, 1974). Given these realities, Caribbean therapists need to help clients make changes in an expeditious manner. Solution-Focused Psychotherapy (Miller, Hubble, & Duncan, 1996), Cognitive-Behaviour Therapy (Corey, 2005), and Single Session Psychotherapy (Talmon, 1990) offer promising alternatives for many patients. For example, Solution-Focused Therapy has some central assumptions that make it ideal for those individuals who need to experience change quickly. They include the following: people have strengths and resources to solve their own problems; change is constant; the therapist's job is to identify and amplify change; a small change is all that is needed; it is not necessary to know the cause or function of a complaint to resolve it; and the patient is the expert and knows what is best for him or her.

Cross-Cultural Psychology also needs to be an integral part of the process in that a therapist must assume a stance that allows him or her an empathetic grasp of how culture and social position influence a patient's phenomenology. Indeed, there is growing evidence that traditional psychotherapy, when practised within such a contextual framework, can be very successful with most patients (Lambert, 1994; Norcross 2002; Sue & Lam, 2002). However, the Caribbean therapist who enters into a therapeutic alliance with a patient should be mindful of the fact that he or she is entering a cultural system that is at least somewhat different from his or her own. Consequently, it is imperative that such a therapist become acquainted with the cultural values of the patient with whom he or she works. In this regard, understanding of spirituality and religion is important, particularly within the Caribbean context. In Jamaica for example, 83 per cent of the population consider themselves religious (PIOJ, 2000). It is also important that practitioners recognize that embedded within this religious and spiritual culture are beliefs about spirits and demons. Religion along with spirituality has long been recognized as an extremely important strength in the Caribbean. In fact, many people use it to survive and cope with life's challenges. It is therefore not surprising that religion is often brought into the treatment of our people. When this occurs, a therapist needs to be comfortable and respectful enough so as to use it to help the patient. Conversely, a therapist also needs to be aware that religion does not mean the same thing for every patient; and it is equally damaging to impose religion on a patient as it is to ignore it when it is introduced by the patient.

# Summary

It is clear that psychotherapists who use traditional psychotherapeutic approaches in the Caribbean context also need to integrate a contextual perspective. Extreme perspectives on the issue – rejection of traditional psychotherapy as irrelevant to Caribbean people, or rejection of the sociopolitical perspective – are not useful to the understanding of any patient. Each perspective has something unique to contribute to patient care. For example, the structure that is provided by traditional psychotherapy helps to curtail some of the potential acting-out behaviours of a therapist (time commitment, professional nature of the relationship). Psychotherapists should also avoid taking an overly rigid approach to psychotherapy, because psychotherapy is, at the fundamental level, an interpersonal process in which the therapist and the patient need to engage in a therapeutic relationship (Lambert & Bailey, 2002). Given the importance of the facilitative conditions and the therapeutic alliance for successful treatment, training in relationship skills is crucial for beginning therapists.

## REFERENCES

American Psychological Association (2002). *Guidelines on multicultural education, training, research, practice, and organizational change for psychologists.* Approved as APA Policy by the APA Council of Representatives, August 2002.

American Psychological Association Office of Minority Affairs (1993). Guidelines for providers of psychological services to ethnic, linguistic, and culturally diverse populations. *American Psychologist, 48,* 45-48.

Comas-Diaz, L., & Green, B. (Eds.). *Women of color: Integrating ethnic and gender identities in psychotherapy.* New York: The Guildford Press.

Boyd, N. (1982). Family therapy with black families. In E. E. Jones & S. J. Korchin (Eds.) *Minority mental health.* New York: Praeger Publishers.

Castro-Blanco, D. R. (2005). Cultural sensitivity in conventional psychotherapy: A comment on Martinez-Taboas. *Psychotherapy, Theory, Research, Practice, Training,* Vol. 42 (1), 14-16.

Colin, L. (1996). *Race, culture, and counselling.* Bristol, PA: Open University Press:

Corey, G. (2005). *Theory and practice of counseling and psychotherapy, 7th Ed.* New York: Thomson Learning, Inc.

Cushman, A. (1995). *Constructing the self, constructing America: Studies in cultural history of psychotherapy.* New York: Addison Wiley.

Goldfried, M. R., & Davila, J. (2005). *The role of relationship and technique in therapeutic change,* Vol. 42 (4), 421-430.

Gopaul-McNicol, S., & Brice-Baker, J. (1998). *Cross-cultural practice: Assessment, treatment and training*. New York: John Wiley & Sons.

Hatcher, S. L., Favorite, T. K., Hardy, E. A., Goode, R. L., Deshetler, L. A., & Thomas, R. M. (2005). An analogue study of therapist empathic process: Working with difference. *Psychotherapy, Theory, Research, Practice, Training*, Vol. 42 (2), 198-210.

Hickling, F. H., & Gibson, R. C. (2005). Philosophy and epistemology of Caribbean psychiatry. In F. W. Hickling & E. Sorel (Eds.), *Images of psychiatry: The Caribbean* (pp. 75-108). Kingston, Jamaica: Department of Community Health and Psychiatry, UWI.

Hickling, F. H., & Matthies, B. K. (2002). The establishment of a clinical psychological post-graduate programme at the University of the West Indies. *Caribbean Journal of Education*, Vol. 25(1), 25-36.

Jackson, M. (1999). Multicultural counseling: Historic perspectives. In J. Ponterotto, J. M. Casas, L. A. Suzuki, & C. M. Alexander (Eds.), *Handbook of multicultural counseling*. Newbury Park, CA: Sage.

James, J. M. (2002). Toward a cultural psychology of African Americans. In W. J. Lonner, D. L. Dinnel, S. A. Hayes, & D. N. Sattler (Eds.), *Online readings in psychology and culture* (Unit 3, Chapter 1), (http://www.wwu.edu/~culture), Center for Cross-Cultural Research, Western Washington University, Belligham, Washington, USA.

Jones, E. E., & Korchin, S. J. (1982). Minority mental health: Perspectives. In E. E. Jones and S. J. Korchin (Eds.), *Minority mental health*. New York: Praeger Publishers.

Jorgensen, C. R. (2004). Active ingredients in individual psychotherapy: Searching for common factors. *Psychoanalytic Psychotherapy*, Vol. 21 (4), 516-540.

La Roche, M. J. (2005). *The cultural context and the psychotherapeutic process: Toward a culturally sensitive psychotherapy*, Vol.15 (2). 169-185.

La Roche, M. J., & Maxie, A. (2003). *Ten considerations in addressing cultural differences in psychotherapy*, Vol. 34 (2), 180-186.

Lambert, M. J., & Barley, D. E. (2002). Research summary in therapeutic relationship and psychotherapy outcome. In J. C. Norcross (Ed.), *Psychotherapy relationships that work: Therapist contributions and responsiveness to patients*. New York: Oxford University Press.

Lambert, M. J. (1994). The effectiveness of psychotherapy. In A. E. Bergen & S. L. Garfield (Eds). *Handbook of psychotherapy and behavior change (4th Ed)*. New York: Wiley.

McLean, L. S. (2002). Overcoming obstacles: Therapeutic success despite external barriers. *Primary Care Companion Journal of Clinical Psychiatry*, 4 (1), 27-29.

Miller, S. D., Hubble, M., & Duncan, B. L. (1996). *Handbook of solution-focused/brief psychotherapy*. CA: Jossey-Bass Psychology.

Moodley, R., & West, W. (2005). *Integrating traditional healing practices into counselling and psychotherapy: Multicultural aspects of counselling and psychotherapy.* London: Sage Publications.

Moursund, J. (1993). *The process of counseling and psychotherapy* (3rd Ed.). New Jersey: Prentice Hall.

Norcross, J. C. (2002). *Psychotherapy relationships that work: Therapist contributions and responsiveness to patients.* New York: Oxford Press.

O'Connor, K. (2005). Addressing diversity issues in play therapy. *Professional Psychology, Research and Practice,* Vol. 36 (5), 566-573.

Pedersen, P. B. (2002). The making of a culturally competent counselor. In W. J. Lonner, D. L. Dinnel, S. A. Hayes, & D. N. Sattler (Eds.), *Online Readings in Psychology and Culture* (Unit 10, Chapter 2), (http://www.wwu.edu/~culture), Center for Cross-Cultural Research, Western Washington University, Belligham, Washington, USA.

PIOJ (2000). *Survey of Living Conditions.* Kingston, Jamaica: Planning Institute of Jamaica

Ponterotto, J. G., Casas, M. J., Suzuki, L., & Alexander, C. A. (2001). *Handbook of multicultural counselling.* London: Sage Publications.

Silverman, D. K. (2005). What works in psychotherapy and how do we know?: What evidence-based practice has to offer. *Psychoanalytic Psychology,* Vol. 22 (2), 306-312.

Smith, L. (2005). Psychotherapy, classism, and the poor: Conspicuous by their absence. *American Psychologist,* Vol. 60(7), 687-696.

Stolle, D., Hutz, A., & Sommers-Flanagan, J. (2005). The impracticalities of R. B. Stuart's practical multicultural competencies. *Professional Psychology, Research and Practice,* Vol. 36 (5), 574-578.

Sue, S., & Lam, A. G. (2002). Cultural and demographic diversity. In J.C. Norcross (Ed.), *Psychotherapy relationships that work: Therapist contributions and responsiveness to patients.* Oxford: Oxford University Press.

Syme, G. (2003). *Dual relationships in counselling and psychotherapy.* London: Sage Publications.

Talmon, M. (1990). *Single session therapy: Maximizing the effect of the first (and often only) therapeutic encounter.* CA: Jossey-Bass, Inc. Publishers.

Teyber, E. (2000). *Interpersonal process in psychotherapy: A relational approach* (4th Ed.). California: Wadsworth.

Wampold, B. E. (2001). *The great psychotherapy debate: Models, methods, and findings.* New Jersey: Lawrence, Erlbaum Associates Publishers.

Weiner, I. B. (1998). *Principles of psychotherapy (2nd Ed.).* New York: John Wiley & Sons Ltd.

West, W. (2004). *Spiritual issues in therapy: Relating experience to practice.* New York: Palgrave Macmillan.

# 19 Sport Psychology in the Caribbean

*Kai Morgan & Leapetswe Malete*

## Introduction

Sport psychology is a relatively young and evolving discipline world-wide and the concept is even more of a fledgling one in the Caribbean. The rapid growth of this discipline is a reflection of the realization among researchers and practitioners that there is more to sport performance than the physiological and biomechanical processes. While there has been rapid growth and popularity in sport psychology in industrialized nations, specifically those in Europe, North America and Asia, the discipline is yet to gain currency in the Caribbean and other developing regions of the world. In fact, the discipline is relatively unknown to most of the developing countries, particularly among those in Africa, South-East Asia, Latin America and the Caribbean. Consequently, very few professional sport psychologists are to be found in these regions. This explains the dearth of empirical research and sport psychology practice outside of the developed countries in Europe, Asia and North America. Much of this chapter is, therefore, focused on anecdotal and qualitative data garnered over a number of years by the authors, who have worked in the field of sport psychology – primarily in Jamaica, but also in a few other Caribbean countries. Examples of sport psychology practice will be drawn largely from popular sports in the Caribbean region, such as cricket, football, track and field, swimming and netball. References will also be made to other sports such as water polo and tennis. The chapter will provide a perspective on the nature, history and development of sport psychology as a discipline and its relevance within the Caribbean context. For the sake of brevity, the focus here will be solely on the English-speaking Caribbean. A brief overview of the theories, concepts, as well as current issues, trends and challenges of sport psychology practice across different sport contexts within the Caribbean will be presented.

As Morris and Summers (2004, p. 1) observed, "sport, in its many forms, is one of the most ubiquitous institutions in the world." For individuals within and across cultures, sport serves many functions, some of which are sociological and psychological, while others are economic (Malec, 1995). The sporting world encompasses individuals across their life-span, including those with physical or mental disabilities, as well as spectators. It is, therefore, not surprising that sport has attracted the interest of researchers across the academic spectrum. Previously, academic interest in sport focused mainly on the biomechanical and physiological aspects, which for obvious reasons were, and still are, perceived as central to athletic performance. However, as increasing evidence has emerged that there is more to participation and achievement in sport and physical activities than the apparent physical and biomechanical factors, interest in other possible determinants of athletic achievement such as the psychological dimensions of self-esteem, motivation, attention, concentration and so on, soared. The interest in researching this area grew alongside other emerging sub-disciplines devoted to understanding the sociological, cultural, economic, educational, political and philosophical aspects of sport.

A discussion of the development and practice of sport psychology in the Caribbean region will, therefore, be better served when placed within the context of the growth of sport as an academic field of study, as well as an aspect of sociocultural and economic development. It is also noteworthy that the emergent sub-disciplines of this relatively new field of study have been heavily influenced by the parent disciplines on which they are based. Consequently, any challenges facing the practice of sport psychology and its emergence as an academic discipline in the Caribbean would, in part, be a reflection of the challenges facing the growth and development of the parent discipline of psychology, as well as of sport and exercise sciences in the region. Similarly, the focus of sport psychology practice in the region is likely to be shaped by historical and cultural factors affecting the practice and development of psychology and sport and exercise sciences in the region.

## The Nature of Sport Psychology

In discussing the nature and development of sport psychology, it is fitting to first provide a definition of sport. Adapting Spears and Swanson's (1983) definition of sport, Wann (1997, p.3) defined sports as, "activities involving powers and skills, competition, strategy, and/or chance, and engagement for the enjoyment, satisfaction, and/or personal gain (such as income) of participant and/or others (e.g., spectators), including organized and recreational sports, as well as sport as entertainment." This definition gives a synopsis of the nature of sport and the motives for participation – all of which are issues in sport psychology.

Scholars have provided various definitions of sport psychology. Most of these definitions reflect their own backgrounds, as well as what they perceive as the role of a sport psychologist. However, using Cox's (2002, p. 5) observation, the various definitions of sport psychology share a common theme, which is "the interactive relationship between sport and exercise involvement and psychological and emotional factors." Cox (2002) defines sport psychology as, "the study of the effect of psychological and emotional factors on sport and exercise performance, and the effect of sport and exercise involvement on emotional and psychological factors." Another of the many definitions was provided by Wann (1997). He further defines it as "the primarily scientific study of the behavioural, affective, and cognitive reactions to sport settings, including the reactions of both participants and fans." Thus, sport psychology is concerned with the application of psychological principles to sport and exercise settings, as well as the reciprocal effect of sport and exercise activities on the psychological and emotional well-being of individuals. The definitions embrace sport psychology as it is applied in different contexts, such as elite competitive sports, leisure-type recreational physical activities and the health and well-being of both the general and clinical populations.

Sport psychology research and practice has focused largely on elite sport performance. For instance, as indicated in the literature, the relevance and application of various psychological concepts and theories to sport has been extensively examined among elite performers (Cox, 2002;

Horn, 2002; Singer, Hausenblas & Janelle, 2001). Some of the widely studied topics include: motivation and self-confidence; arousal, attention and concentration; personality, anxiety and mood; self-efficacy; attribution of success and failure; moral development; group dynamics; gender and socialization processes. Various intervention approaches have also been explored in the literature, such as imagery (Murphy & Martin, 2002), relaxation techniques (Nideffer, 1985; Orlick, 1986), goal setting (Weinberg & Gould, 1999), attention control training (Nideffer & Sagal, 1998) and the Carlstedt Protocol which utilizes the theory of critical moments in assessing and predicting sport performance (Carlstedt, 2004). For this reason there is a general perception that sport psychology is predominantly about elite sport performance with the goal of improving performance at critical times.

## Roles of Sport Psychologists

The role of a sport psychologist has also been the subject of much debate. Underlying this debate has always been the issue of how best to link theory with practice. Two general roles have been identified in the literature and these are: the sport psychologist as a researcher/academic; and the sport psychologist as a practitioner (Wann, 1997). Researchers or academic sports psychologists, sometimes referred to as experimental sport psychologists, have as their primary focus the generation of knowledge, often by developing and testing of psychological theory among athletes and other individuals such as coaches, officials, spectators and other populations (Wann, 1997). The practitioner or applied sport psychology area has been divided into two sub-areas: clinical sport psychologist and educational sport psychologist (Cox, 2002; Wann, 1997). Clinical sport psychologists are trained and licensed in clinical or counselling psychology and are able to deal with various emotional and personality disorders that affect athletes and other individuals (Cox, 2002). Cox explains that educational sport psychologists are trained in the principles of sport psychology and their role is "to help athletes develop psychological skills for performance enhancement." Their work also extends to helping individuals in other populations to enjoy sport and physical activities as vehicles for improving their quality of life.

Alongside the issue of linking theory and practice, or defining the roles of a sport psychologist, is the subject of training and accreditation. The general rule for service providers is to act within the boundaries of their training and/or accreditation and to adhere strictly to professional ethics governing the profession. The Caribbean situation offers challenges to this rhetoric as specialized training is unavailable in the area, yet the need is identified and often we find psychologists, psychiatrists and other mental health professionals, not specifically trained in the area, who provide consultation to athletes and teams. Ethical guidelines speak to the provision of services where there is no trained individual in the area and recommend that such individuals make every attempt to become minimally competent while functioning.

## History of Sport Psychology

> Cricket has always been more than a game in Trinidad. In a society, which demanded no skills and offered no rewards to merit, cricket was the only activity, which permitted a man to grow to his full stature and to be measured against international standards. Alone on a field, beyond obscuring intrigue, the cricketer's true worth could be seen by all. His race, education, wealth did not matter. We had no scientists, engineers, explorers, soldiers, or poets. The cricketer was our only hero figure.... The individual performance was what mattered. That was what we went to applaud; and unless the cricketer had heroic qualities we did not want to see him, however valuable he might be....
>
> V.S. Naipaul, *The Middle Passage*

As is articulated in this passage by the prolific Trinidadian author, V.S. Naipaul (cited in Yelvington, 1995), the psychological importance of cricket for both the player and the spectators in the Caribbean region can never be underestimated. Naipaul suggests that cricket plays a critical role in the development of a sense of identity (self and national), and self-worth among the West Indian people. Furthermore, he highlights the importance of identifying this individual as a saviour or a hero by the populace and spectators, and how very easily his value could be ignored if the spectators did not deem him worthy.

As long as there has been sport, there has been the psychology of sport, whether in a formal or an informal state. In any society, sport psychology begins informally, as an unscientific perusal of the way the people behave or perform in physical activity contexts and the factors that impact on this performance. The earliest attempts to implement formal, scientific research in sport psychology have been attributed to Norman Triplett, who in 1897 utilized field observations and secondary data to investigate the effect of social facilitation on the performance of cyclists (Davis, Huss & Becker, 1995). Tripplett concluded that the presence of other competitors facilitates better performance. In 1925 the first sport psychology laboratory was established at the University of Illinois by Coleman Roberts Griffith, who has been referred to as the "father of American sport psychology" (Gould & Pick, 1995). Over the years, with the alliance of the Physical Education department of the University, Griffith delved into the analysis of areas such as motor learning, personality and psychomotor skills, as well as physical performance. Other pioneers in the field included Franklin Henry, John Lawther and Arthur Slater-Hammel, who all developed research laboratories and implemented various graduate level courses in sport psychology (Cox, 2002). Sport psychology and applied sport psychology really began to become distinct from exercise physiology between the 1950s and 1980s, and during this time, became firmly established as an academic sub-discipline within psychology and physical education. Applied models, addressing practical applications of sport psychology, were developed by Bruce Oglivie who has been credited with the development of applied sport psychology in the USA (Cox, 2002).

## Sport Psychology in the Caribbean

While sport psychology has developed rapidly in Australia, Europe, North America and some parts of Asia, it has remained relatively unknown in the Caribbean. Anecdotal evidence suggests that individuals trained in psychiatry and clinical or counseling psychology have provided most of the psychological services for athletes. This is mainly due to the fact that psychiatry and clinical/counseling psychology services and training programmes are relatively well developed and widely available in the region, though none of these Caribbean graduates or programmes has nor offers specific training in sport psychology. Arguably, the provision of psychological interventions in the region is likely to be biased towards dealing with psychopathology or mental health issues affecting athletes, as opposed to performance enhancement or related areas.

The research component in sport psychology in the region is very sparse. One known study in the area examines correlates of Jamaican youths' involvement in sport and leisure-type recreational activities (Malete & Matthies, 2003). This is described later in the chapter. The relative absence of sport psychology practice in the Caribbean is somewhat surprising, considering the level of involvement and the achievements of elite professional athletes from the region in sports such as track and field, cricket and soccer, as well as the region's proximity to North America – a region that has led the development of the discipline. The Caribbean region has been able to send a team to the FIFA World Cup twice over the last decade, Jamaica in 1998 and Trinidad & Tobago in 2006. The region has a huge presence in track and field, boasting of several Olympic and Commonwealth games medalists in sprint events, including the current 100m and 200m world record-holder Usain Bolt, and Male Athlete of the Year 2006, Asafa Powell. It would seem that the limited sport psychology practice in the region is, therefore, due to a number of factors that are common to most of the developing world. These include: the absence of the academic programmes devoted to the study of sport and exercise sciences; the relative shortage of psychological services and professionals trained in the field of psychology; the lack of understanding of psychology and its role in society, together with a lack of understanding of the nature and benefits of sport psychology.

Notwithstanding the absence of academic programmes and trained sport psychology practitioners in the region, consulting services provided to athletes by professionals in mainstream psychology, suggest a general recognition of their value to athletes. Evidence of such services dates back to the 1960s when a Jamaican psychiatrist was consulted by coaches to address performance issues affecting their athletes. Similarly, in the 1990s, the West Indies cricket team sought the services of a psychologist to address the team's protracted decline in performance during their tours. Other evidence relates to the work of a trained sport psychologist with the Jamaica national junior swimming team during its preparations for the 2001 Central American and Caribbean Games and for a Runners' Club in Kingston. The Jamaican national netball (Sunshine Girls), football (Reggae Boyz) and water polo teams have all utilized the services of a psychologist in preparation for major international sporting events in the last few years. Additionally, management teams of tennis, golf and individual track and field athletes have recognized and sought such services. Within the last year, even high school football teams have sought psychological services. Although the approaches appear to suggest a one-time intervention (e.g. a presentation or lecture), indicating the lack of knowledge about the nature of sport psychology, these incidents still show that the overall understanding and knowledge of the discipline is growing.

## Theoretical Issues and their Application to the Caribbean

Many theoretical models have been put forward in this sub-discipline, however, one common criticism is that these models are all based on social psychological principles that have been 'manipulated' to fit sport psychology theory. This, of course, buttresses the inextricable link between sport psychology and social psychology, which formed the basis of most of the early sport psychology research and practice. Sport psychology theories have been espoused in areas such as motivation, attention and concentration, goal setting, self-confidence and self-efficacy, personality and attribution, to mention a few. While it would be inaccurate to espouse the differences in the meaning of psychological concepts and theories between regions or countries, it is important to acknowledge that perspectives may differ in terms of the application of concepts and theories across cultures. In acknowledging the influence of Europe and North America in the development of sport psychology as an academic and applied discipline, one also has to be cognizant of the limited diversity of the populations and cultures. As is the case with mainstream psychology, much of the research involved predominantly Caucasian, middle-class youth samples. Nevertheless, culture has become the focal point of researchers within the sport and performing arts studies (Fisher, Butryn, & Roper, 2003; Ryba & Wright, 2005). For example, Kontos and Breland-Noble (2002) have explored a cultural approach for African Americans, and in Australia, Hanrahan (2004) has sought a deeper understanding of aboriginal people. Most recently, cultural explorations have also utilized a community-based approach to understanding and shared ownership, leading to participant empowerment and refined service provision with Canadian aboriginal peoples (Gauthier, Schinke, Michel, Pickard, & Guay, 2005). Currently, these approaches add to the practical applications and research avenues, though much more is needed. It is hoped that these endeavours will secure culture as a basic tenet in the future of sport psychology (Schinke, Michel, Danielson, Gauthier, & Pickard, 2005).

As Biddle (1995) observed, despite the similarities among cultures, it is important for the development of the field that findings from different countries and cultures be communicated as much as possible. Consequently, the historical, cultural and socioeconomic factors that shaped the development of the Caribbean region must, of necessity, result in a different perspective on the development and application of sport psychology in the region. This chapter, therefore, attempts to incorporate a multicultural, Caribbean perspective in the discussion of selected topics in sport psychology.

## Motivation in Sport and Exercise

One of the most widely researched topics in sport psychology is motivation. Interest in this topic arises from the realization that an individual's decision to participate in sport and other physical activities, choice of activities and persistence or subsequent 'dropout' from activities are processes that are greatly influenced by a number of factors. Sometimes the factors are internal in nature, for instance, relating to the fun derived from the activity or the desire to succeed. This form of motivation is generally referred to as intrinsic motivation. At other times the motivational factors are external, such as the desire to receive rewards or incentives that come with participation (Cox, 2002). This form of motivation is referred to as extrinsic motivation.

Early research on motivation approached the subject from the perspective of innate drives and instincts, and was greatly influenced by the work of Hull (1943; 1951) and Spence (1956). Using drive theories for instance, the significant presence of West Indian athletes in world track events would be reduced to simple innate desires among individual athletes to become world or Olympic champions. The research has since evolved and recognizes the social cognitive aspects of motivation. In other words, there has been greater recognition among researchers and practitioners that individuals' emotions and cognitions in the sport and physical domain influence their motivational orientation within these domains. In line with this view point, the sport motivation framework has been used to investigate topics such as participant motivation (Gill, 2000), achievement goal orientation (Duda, 1989; Duda and Nicholls, 1992), competence motivation (Harter, 1978), self-confidence and self-efficacy in sport (Feltz & Lirgg, 2001; Vealey, 1986; 2001) and motivational climate and attribution (Duda & White, 1992).

## PARTICIPANT MOTIVATION

Much of the research on motivation in sport has examined the reason individuals give for participating. This topic, generally focusing on children and youth, tends to be examined alongside reasons for dropping out, as well as socialization into sport, the latter being an attempt to examine agents that influence individuals to engage in sport. Findings from the participant motivation literature show that the decision to participate in sport and physical activities is based on a variety of factors which are physical, social and psychological.

Age and gender differences have also been reported in the literature (Gill, Gross & Huddleston, 1983; Whitehead, 1995). In the case of young people, some of the commonly cited social-psychological factors include the desire to learn new skills, enjoyment, fitness benefits, the desire to be with others, skill improvement, self-esteem development, and the desire to show competence (Wann, 1997). These motives have been widely confirmed in research across cultures (Ashford, Biddle & Goudas, 1993; Malete, 2004a; Malete & Matthies, 2003). Although intrinsic factors have been found to be important for adults as well, most of their motives seem to reflect extrinsic factors such as weight management, stress release, and the need to get fit (Federick-Recascino & Morris, 2004). Rewards that go with participation are significant in elite sport contexts (Shepherd College People and Websites, 2000). While both males and females seem to be motivated by competition, fitness and health-related reasons, it would seem that men favour higher competition-related motives, while women tend to favour reasons related to social affiliation, tension release, and weight management or body-related factors (Biddle & Bailey, 1985; Frederick & Ryan, 1993).

## SOCIALIZATION INTO SPORT AND DISCONTINUATION

With regard to social influences for participation in sport, those that rank highly include parents, teachers, coaches and peers, as well as social environments, such as schools and communities. Parental and sibling encouragement, in the form of role modelling and direct support for the child's involvement in sporting activities, have been widely cited (Greendorfer, 1992; Gill, 2000; Malete, 2004b). Studies have found that parents' – mostly fathers' – past sporting experiences exerted a lot of influence on their children's decision to engage in sport. Additionally, material and emotional support also play a significant role in children's continued involvement.

Commonly cited reasons for ceasing participation are related to individual attitudes to sport or the value attributed to it, sport experiences and life transitions. For children and young people, interest in other activities and negative sporting experiences, such as limited play time and too much pressure from parents and coaches seem to rank highly among reasons for discontinuation. These normally stem from applying a commercial model to the organization of sporting activities for young people. Focus on winning and strict selection criteria also tend to deter youngsters who chose sports for affiliation, skill improvement, enjoyment and other intrinsic reasons.

## PARTICIPATION MOTIVATION IN THE CARIBBEAN CONTEXT

The only known participant motivation study within the Caribbean region involved high school youth in Jamaica (Malete & Matthies, 2003). This study found that Jamaican youth are motivated to participate in sport and leisure-time physical activities by similar social-psychological factors identified in the extensive participant motivation literature involving North American and European youth. Reasons related to skill improvement, athletic competence, enjoyment and being with others were rated highly by the youth in this study. An examination of the reasons the young people gave for discontinuing participation showed the most commonly cited reasons as health, academic pressure, loss of interest, doubt in their ability, and negative experiences in sports. A summary of the reasons comparing Jamaica with other countries is presented in Table 1.

Table 1a: _Ten most important reasons (in rank order) for participating in organized sports among boys in several different cultures._

| Mexican Boys 9-18 years[1] | Portuguese Boys 15-18 years[2] | Botswanan Boys 13-18 years[3] | American Boys 10-18 years[4] | Jamaican Boys 12-19 years[5] |
|---|---|---|---|---|
| 1. Fun | 1. Physical fit-ness | 1. Improving my skills | 1. Fun | 1. Improving my skills |
| 2. Physical fitness | 2. Fun | 2. Moving to a higher level | 2. Doing something I am good at | 2. Learning new skills |
| 3. Exercise | 3. Staying in shape | 3. Winning | 3. Improving my skills | 3. Doing something I am good at |
| 4. Getting rid of energy | 4. Exercise | 4. Learning new skills | 4. Excitement of competition | 4. Going to higher competition |
| 5. Improving my skills | 5. Team spirit | 5. Exercise | 5. Staying in shape | 5. Winning |
| 6. Doing something I am good at | 6. Improving my skills | 6. Doing something I am good at | 6. Challenge of competition | 6. Staying in shape |
| 7. Learning new skills | 7. Liking team-work | 7. Rewards and recognition | 7. Exercise | 7. Being part of my team |
| 8. Excitement of competition | 8. Meeting new friends | 8. Playing as part of a team | 8. Learning new skills | 8. For the challenge of competition |
| 9. Challenge of competition | 9. Moving to a higher level | 9. Popularity as a good athlete | 9. Playing as part of a team | 9. Getting exercise |
| 10. Moving to a higher level | 10. Being with friends | 10. Challenge of competition | 10. Moving to higher level | 10. Having fun |

1 Siegel et al. (2004)    2 Coelho e Silva and Malina (2004)

3 Malete (2004b)    4 Ewing and Seefeldt (1988)    5 Malete and Matthies (2003)

On the matter of socialization into sport, the Jamaican study (Malete & Matthies, 2003) revealed that teachers and coaches, parents, peers, and siblings in that order, were the most frequently cited social agents. This emphasized the role of the school and home environments in influencing youth's involvement in sport. At the community level, the Caribbean region lacks the elaborate sport and recreational programmes found in most of the developed world. The school, therefore, remains an important avenue for sport socialization. Although the media were not widely

*Table 1 b: Ten most important reasons (in rank order) for participating in organized sports among girls in several different cultures.*

| Mexican Girls 9-18 years[1] | Portuguese Girls 15-18 years[2] | Botswanan Girls 13-18 years[3] | American Girls 10-18 years[4] | Jamaican Girls 13-18 years[5] |
|---|---|---|---|---|
| 1. Fun | 1. Fun | 1. Exercise | 1. Fun | 1. Doing something I am good at |
| 2. Physical fitness | 2. Meeting new friends | 2. Improving my skills | 2. Staying in shape | 2. Learning new skills |
| 3. Exercise | 3. Physical fitness | 3. Learning new skills | 3. Exercise | 3. Improving my skills |
| 4. Getting rid of energy | 4. Being with friends | 4. Moving to higher level | 4. Improving my skills | 4. Getting exercise |
| 5. Improving skills | 5. Team spirit | 5. Doing something I am good at | 5. Doing something I am good at | 5. Having fun |
| 6. Doing something I am good at | 6. Exercise | 6. Winning | 6. Learning new skills | 6. Staying in shape |
| 7. Excitement of com-petition | 7. Staying in shape | 7. Rewards and recognition | 7. Excitement of competition | 7. Winning |
| 8. Learning new skills | 8. Team work | 8. Being popular as a good athlete | 8. Playing as part of a team | 8. Going to higher com-petition |
| 9. Having something to do | 9. Doing something I am good at | 9. Playing as part of team | 9. Making new friends | 9. For the chal-lenge of com-petition |
| 10. Being with friends | 10. Improving skills | 10. Challenge of competition | 10. Challenge of competition | 10. Meeting new friends |

1 Siegel et al. (2004)   2 Coelho e Silva and Malina (2004)
3 Malete (2004b)   4 Ewing and Seefeldt (1988)   5 Malete and Matthies (2003)

mentioned in this study, one cannot rule out their role in influencing the youth to take part in sport, as the Caribbean region is not short of role models in sport who have enjoyed media spotlight. As a consequence the impact of repeated exposure to the athletic achievements of these individuals, as well as their apparent economic success is bound to have profound effects on the desire of youth to take part in sport. Examples of these cricket, track and field and football legends are; Vivian Richards (Antigua), Gary Sobers (Barbados), Merlene Ottey-Page (formerly of Jamaica), Asafa Powell (Jamaica) and Veronica Campbell (Jamaica), Kim Collins (St Kitts and Nevis), Ato Boldon (Trinidad & Tobago), Dwight

York (Trinidad & Tobago), Brian Lara (Trinidad & Tobago) and the 2006 Olympic relay team from The Bahamas. In Jamaica, a school was even named after Merlene Ottey in recognition of her achievements. Many youths from difficult socioeconomic backgrounds within the region would, therefore, view sport as an avenue for escaping the economic circumstances into which they have been born.

Although the findings from the Jamaican study are not by any means representative of what obtains in the Caribbean region, they give an idea of the motivational factors that affect the youths' involvement in sport in the region. Much broader investigations on youth sport participatory patterns and psychological correlates for such participation in the region are needed. Similarly, an examination of participants' motivation across their life span is necessary, to determine appropriate interventions for health promotion and elite sport development. Cross-cultural comparisons are also important to investigate.

## Achievement Goal Orientations

The goal perspective theory of achievement motivation proposes that an individual uses task and/or ego goal-oriented criteria to evaluate success (Duda, 1993; Nicholls, 1989). This theory views personal goals as playing a critical role in an individual's investment and involvement in achievement-related contexts. An individual's goal orientation will be related to his or her cognitive and affective response in achievement-related contexts such as sport or schoolwork. The theory identifies two dispositional goals labeled task-goal orientation and ego-goal orientation. According to Nicholls (1989), individuals high in task orientation will use self-referenced criteria for success and competence, such as learning something new, personal improvement, and/or meeting the demands of the task. Individuals with high ego-goal orientation, on the other hand, tend to use normative or other-referenced criteria when making judgements about competence and adequacy. Such individuals tend to measure success and ability relative to outperforming others as opposed to self-improvement. As such, learning environments have been found to influence the development of dispositional goals (Amos, 1992; Nicholls, 1989; Williams, 1998).

The goal perspective theory has been widely used to explain behaviour in sport and exercise settings. This resulted in the development of various sport specific inventories, such as the Task and Ego Goal Orientations in Sport Questionnaire (TEOSQ) (Duda, 1989), the Sport Orientation Questionnaire (Gill, 1993; Gill & Deeter, 1988) and the Perception of Success Questionnaire (Roberts, 1993; Roberts & Treasure, 1995). As is the case with most of the sport psychology research, most of the studies on achievement goals were conducted in North America and Europe. However, a few studies have been conducted in other cultures, such as Zimbabwe and Korea (Biddle, Akande, Vlachopoulos, & Fox, 1996; Li, Harmer, Chi, & Vongjaturapat, 1996). The studies demonstrated that overall achievement goal orientation is significantly correlated with sport ability, effort and enjoyment. For instance, the Biddle et al. (1996) study showed that children who are high in task-goal orientation, but low in ego had significantly higher effort beliefs and reported greater enjoyment of sport, higher cooperation and less boredom than children who had high ego- and low task-orientation. These findings confirmed those of similar studies conducted among children in the UK and the USA. The results also confirmed the cross-cultural validity of the TEOSQ (Duda, 1993; Goudas, Biddle & Fox, 1994).

Within the Caribbean region, the study involving Jamaican youth confirmed the two-dimensional model of the TEOSQ proposed by Duda and Nicholls (1992). This study further revealed that participants in competitive sports had higher task-orientation than those involved in recreational physical activities (Malete & Matthies, 2003). Furthermore, the youths' goal orientation was related to their reasons for participating in sport. Task-orientation was associated with competition and skill improvement (challenge and personal improvement), while ego-orientation was associated with external reasons for participation (extrinsic motivation). As an extension of Chi's (2004) observation, achievement goal theory is a useful framework for explaining achievement-related cognitions, affects and behaviours in sport, not only in the widely studied cultures but also in the Caribbean region.

## Competence Motivation

Research on competence motivation in sport is based on Harter's (1978) Competence Motivation Theory. The theory proposes that individuals have an inherent desire to feel and express competence in the social, cognitive, and physical domains of achievement, and that expression of the motive towards competence is mediated by self-related cognitions, especially self-perceptions of competence and control. When applied to sport, the theory proposes that an individual's self-perception of success in the physical domain or sport contexts will promote high self-efficacy and feelings of personal competence in these areas which, in turn, will foster continued participation and further mastery attempts in sport (Cox, 2002). If mastery attempts result in failure or rejection, the result will be low competence motivation and negative affect. High competence motivation has been associated with task-goal-orientation and continued participation in sport even under challenging circumstances, while low competence motivation has been associated with ego-orientation and cessation of participation. These relationships have been confirmed in the sport psychology literature (Duda, 1993).

There is no known research testing the applicability of Harter's competence motivation theory within the Caribbean context. However, some extrapolations could be made from findings of a cultural extension of Fox's (1990) Physical Self-Perception Profile (PSPP) to patterns of youths' involvement in sport in Jamaica (Malete, Sullivan, & Matthies, 2008). Using Harter's competence motivation framework to develop the PSPP, Fox and colleagues (Fox, 1990; Fox & Corbin, 1989) argued that self-concept may be a factor predisposing people to be physically active. They found that in addition to perceptions of general physical self-worth, individuals engaging in sports hold meaningful perceptions of themselves in domains associated with sports competence, physical condition, physical strength and body attractiveness. A confirmatory factor analysis on the PSPP, using a sample of Jamaican youths, aged 12-18 years yielded a factor structure that closely resembled the original model, albeit with only three factors labeled Physical Self Worth, Sport Competence, and Body Attractiveness. The three factors were closely related to the youth's involvement in sport. While being specific to Jamaica, the findings show that studies testing the application of perceived competence and physical self-perception to sport behaviour in the Caribbean region are likely to yield interesting results. This further highlights the need for cross-cultural research in sport psychology.

## Self-confidence and Self-efficacy in Sport and Exercise

No concept has pervaded the achievement literature as much as self-confidence has. This is specifically because self-confidence is central to successful performance in various spheres of life, including sport and physical activities (Morris & Koehn, 2004). Some of the earliest work on self-confidence in sport was done by Vealey (1986). Vealey conceptualized a state-trait framework for studying self-confidence in sport which she referred to as "sport-confidence". She defined sport-confidence as "the belief or degree of certainty individuals possess about their ability to be successful in sport" (p. 222). Vealey's sport-specific model of sport-confidence is unique in that it does not borrow its theoretical principles from social psychology but is an attempt at an individual or separate theoretical perspective purely within the discipline of sport psychology. To any competitive situation, the athlete brings his or her own personality trait of sport confidence (SC-trait) and a particular competitive orientation. Together, these are predictive of the level of situational state-specific sport confidence (SC-state) that the athlete will exhibit during competition. SC-state is, therefore, predictive of performance or overt behavioural responses.

Using the sport confidence framework, several instruments were developed to measure confidence such as the Trait Sport-Confidence Inventory, the State Sport-Confidence Inventory and the Competitive Orientation Inventory (Vealey, 1986). The research served as a basis for examining the relationship between confidence and other factors such as competitive anxiety in sport. Studies examining sport-confidence within the competitive anxiety framework proposed that self-confidence plays a "central role in the cognitive processes that influence motivation and affect in athletes" (Morris & Koehn, 2004, p.178). Despite its contribution to understanding confidence and motivation in sport, Vealey's sport-confidence framework met with much criticism and was slow in growth.

A more successful approach to the study of self-confidence in sport is based on Bandura's (1977) self-efficacy theory. Self-efficacy has been defined as the belief individuals have about their ability to successfully execute a course of action under extenuating circumstances (Bandura, 1977). Compared to the more global concept of self-confidence, self-efficacy is a situation-specific or a task-specific form of self-confidence. It deals more with individuals' subjective judgment of their ability to meet the demands of a task, and not so much the ability itself. Efficacy beliefs have been found to be highly correlated with choice, effort and persistence in some activities and avoidance of others (Morris & Koehn, 2004). For instance, an individual who is highly efficacious about his or her running ability tends to choose track events and persists in these events even under challenging circumstances. If the same individual has low efficacy beliefs about his or her ability in ball sports, the individual will avoid sports and games where he or she might have to display ball skills. When applied to various techniques of the same skill, efficacy beliefs make the difference between "choking" under pressure and successful performance when confronted with a similar amount of pressure. Four major sources or antecedents of self-efficacy have been proposed by Bandura (1986):

1. *Performance Accomplishments* – Previous performance accomplishments are considered to be the most dependable source of efficacy. Efficacy beliefs are further strengthened when success is achieved in a difficult task, as compared to an easy one, and when such success is achieved with limited assistance from others. Early success in learning has also been found to enhance efficacy beliefs as opposed to failure. It is for this reason that coaches and teachers should be careful to reduce the complexity of a task early in the learning process so as to enhance efficacy, as failure in the early stages could lower efficacy.

2. *Vicarious experience* – Efficacy beliefs could also be enhanced vicariously through observation. This second most dependable source of efficacy can either be in vivo or represented in the persons of former athletes, more skilled teammates, or videos/DVDs of performances by other athletes. The process is likely to be more effective if the model is similar in skill and characteristics to the learner.

3. *Verbal persuasion* – Positive feedback and encouragement from individuals such as family members, coaches, friends and teammates is also believed to be another vital component in the development of self-efficacy. The effect is likely to be greater if

the persuasion is from a trustworthy or dependable source. Negative feedback should be carefully worded so as not to convey negativism which will hamper efficacy beliefs. This is considered to be one of the least dependable sources of efficacy.

4. *Emotional arousal* – Lastly, mental readiness and alertness are required in order to help an athlete master a particular skill and thus develop a sense of self-efficacy. An athlete's interpretation of his or her physiological state shortly before performance could be associated either with readiness for performance, which relates to high self-efficacy, or with performance and therefore be related to low efficacy beliefs.

The role of the four antecedents of self-efficacy in enhancing efficacy beliefs and athletic achievement has been well supported in the literature with results indicating that perceived self-efficacy is a significant and consistent predictor of individual and team performance (Feltz & Lirgg, 2001; Lowther, Lane & Lane, 2002; Moritz, Feltz, Fahrbach & Mack, 2000).

Although there is no known research on self-confidence and self-efficacy involving Caribbean athletes, anecdotal evidence from elite athletic performance suggests that athletes from this region hold efficacy beliefs similar to those found among athletes from elsewhere. The over-representation and success of sprinters from the Caribbean region demonstrate, among other things, the role of performance accomplishments and vicarious experiences in enhancing the athletes' efficacy beliefs in this domain of athletics. There is no doubt that the domination of male and female sprint events by athletes from The Bahamas and Jamaica with their comparatively small populations, owes much to the previous successes of their compatriots and of course, their own successes. The continued presence of these athletes in major meets has obviously enhanced the collective efficacy of people from the region. This could have reinforced the collective belief that people from the region can perform at those levels, as seen in the emergence of even more world-class sprinters from other islands such as Barbados, St. Kitts and Nevis, St. Vincent and the Grenadines and Trinidad and Tobago. The same could be said about cricket and now football, with Trinidad following Jamaica to the World Cup.

It is difficult to estimate the impact of history and culture on the development of the self-schema, especially the development and display of self-confidence among West Indian people. It is possible that prolonged periods of slavery and colonialism could have had an impact on the development of the self-belief system. There could also be a reciprocal relationship between the overall development of self-concept and the development of self-confidence in sport. However, this area needs further exploration within a research context.

## Attribution Theory

Attribution theory is significantly intertwined with the preceding construct of self-efficacy and it has consistently been linked to achievement motivation. This theory relates to the reasons that an individual devises to describe his or her failures and successes. Such cognitive appraisals or attributions are critical to establishing motivation and to the development of self-efficacy. Fritz Heider (1944; 1958) is considered to be the original proponent of Attribution theory, with Bernard Weiner (1972; 1985) making significant contributions to the theory's development. Attribution research within the context of sport has been used to examine beliefs about the causes of success or failure in competitive sports, as well as their relationship to achievement goals including motivational climate (Duda & White 1992; Kavussanu & Roberts, 1996).

Based on Heider's attributional model, "outcomes are attributed either internally to the person (personal force) or externally to the environment (environmental force)" (Cox, 2002, p. 51). The factors that make up the personal force are ability and effort, while the environmental factors are task difficulty and luck. Heider believes that the personal force of ability and the environmental force of task difficulty interact to form a separate dimension called 'can' (or 'cannot'). For example, if an athlete believes that a task is simple but he will be unable to accomplish it, then it must be due to his lack of ability. On the other hand, successful performance of a difficult task will be attributed to greater ability. Luck and effort are two unstable factors that also play a critical role in the attributional process. Combined with the more stable factors such as task difficulty and ability, they could have a profound impact on behavioural outcome. For instance an athlete's attribution of failure or success in a specific performance to luck or ability could make a difference between quitting and the amount of effort expended on the task.

Weiner (1972) added considerably to Attribution theory by restructuring the causal factors into three major dimensions: controllability, stability and locus of causality. Controllability refers to whether the outcome was perceived to be beyond the control of the actor or not. Controllable attributions are those under the control of the performer, such as the amount of effort an athlete expends in a competitive situation. Uncontrollable attributions relate to beliefs about behaviour that is beyond the control of the performer, such as inherited athletic ability in a sport or skill.   Locus of causality refers to whether an outcome was attributed to internal or external causes. Internal attributions or dispositional attribution relates to the belief that the behaviour was caused by the individual, such as a basketball player attributing his or her high free-throw percentage to skill or effort. External attribution or situation attributions reflect the belief that the behaviour was caused by the environment or sport setting. An example of this is if the same high free-throw percentage basketball player misses a critical free throw in a game that the team lost, he or she may attribute such failure to the hostile crowd or to the fact that it was simply not his or her day.

Stability attribution refers to either stable or unstable attributes within the person (personality traits) or environment. Examples of stable attributes are ability and task difficulty, as in cases where athletes attribute their success in a task to their ability (personality) and the ease of performing the task (environment). Examples of unstable attributes are effort and luck, for instance, where an athlete attributes his or her success to the amount of effort expended on the task or the athlete's mood on the day.

These dimensions of attribution are instrumental in the formation of future expectancies. Different combinations of the dimensions have enabled researchers and practitioners to predict the type of attributions associated with successful and unsuccessful performance in sport, as well as the type of goal orientation that accompanies attribution styles (Wann, 1997). Weiner has also factored in the emotion/affect, stating that both controllability and locus of causality would be the determinants of affective reactions in achievement contexts.

## ATTRIBUTION RESEARCH: IMPLICATIONS FOR THE CARIBBEAN CONTEXT

Considerations on the sociocultural issues and attribution in sport are very sparse but relevant to the Caribbean context. Cox (2002) alludes to the fact that there are conceptual problems in the development of causal attributions, such as failure to recognize that the kinds of attributions which people make are based on a socialization culture that may vary across cultures. To illustrate the influence of culture on attribution, Cox used two cultural contexts. In the Iranian context, children are said to view ability as an important attribution regardless of whether a child fails or succeeds, while in the American context children tend to value effort and intent regardless of innate ability (p. 55).

Although not researched extensively, race and ethnicity differences are also mentioned in the literature. For instance, Anglo athletes in the USA have been found to perceive success as internal and stable to a greater degree than African or Native American athletes (Morgan, Griffin & Heywood, 1996). Other findings are the controversial ones reported by Harris (1993) and Murrel and Curtis (1994), where Black athletes are said to hold "internal, unstable and uncontrollable attributions such as attributing success to natural ability while White athletes hold stable controllable attributions such as attributing their success to hard work, diligence and intelligence"(Wann, 1997, p. 197). The assumptions made from this limited research, which involved only six quarter-backs, was that the Black athletes displayed instinct and lack of thinking ability, while the abilities of White athletes were due to hard work, diligence and intelligence. However, the impact of methodological flaws on the outcome of this research could not be ruled out. Cox (2002) observed that attribution research is often plagued by bias, where the researcher biases a subject's perception of the outcome. He uses as an example the fact that in many cases of competitive sport, the subjects do not perceive themselves as failing or succeeding until they are asked a biasing question by the researcher.

Based on the foregoing, research on attribution in the Caribbean context should bring about the much deserved cross-cultural perspective on this subject. There is no doubt that Caribbean athletes make similar attributions about their successes or failures as do athletes elsewhere. However, it is probable that West Indian culture could be contributing some unique elements which have an influence on the way West Indian athletes structure their performance appraisal or causal attributions. Such unique elements are needed to broaden the multi-cultural debate on causal attributions and motivation. Surely it will be anomalous to reduce the significant successes of Caribbean and Black athletes overall, to a one-dimensional attribution style as suggested in the research cited above.

## ATTENTION AND CONCENTRATION

As the mental component most recognized and revered as integral to success by athletes and coaches, attention and concentration have attracted much interest among researchers in sport psychology. Attention is a multi-faceted construct, the definition of which incorporates at least three different psychological mechanisms: selectivity of perception, regulation of concurrent actions and maintenance of alertness (Moran, 1996). In other words, attention is viewed as the ability to selectively attend to stimuli, to utilize our mental capacities to effectively 'multi-task', or to maintain an optimal level of alertness to one's environment. Three major perspectives on attention have been put forth in the literature: informational processing, the social psychological, and the psychophysiological (Boutcher, 2002; Carlstedt, 2004).

The information-processing model refers to the involvement of mental operations in the stimulus-response set that occurs. In other words, pure behavioural theory (Skinner, 1938) states that all stimuli are followed by a particular response which can then be predicted. However, cognitive psychologists have adjusted this model to include the effect of thought and memory, which then mediates the particular response that emerges, thereby sparking an analysis of short and long-term memory, selective attention, attentional narrowing and attentional capacity (Cox, 2002). A study examining the extent to which visual search strategy, like selective attention, is mediated by the participant's level of task proficiency revealed that experts and novices often systematically fixate upon different areas of a given display (implying differences in cue usage), although the evidence relating to differences in search rate (as indicative of processing load) is equivocal (Abernethy,1988), This is a clear example of the mediating effects of selective attention on mental operations and thus performance.

The social psychological perspective relates to how an athlete focuses his or her attention on the appropriate stimuli in order to perform effectively. As such, there have evolved distraction theories which discuss the role of self-awareness, anxiety and pain. Social psychologists (Nideffer, 1976; Van Shoyck & Grasha, 1981) have also examined attentional style and the ability of the athlete to match the attentional demands of the sporting environment with the appropriate attentional style (which is proposed to be relatively stable). Nideffer's individual difference approach to attention proposes two independent dimensions along which athletes focus their attention, labelled width and direction. With regard to the width dimension, attention is believed to range on a continuum from broad focus to a narrow focus. Broad focus relates to focusing attention on a large number of stimuli, while narrow attentional focus relates to focusing attention on only one, or a few stimuli, or filtering out irrelevant information. The direction dimension refers to the target of one's attention, that is, whether the individual's attention is focused internally, as in his or her thoughts and emotions or externally on environmental stimuli. The different dimensions can be combined to elicit four attentional styles which are appropriate to demands of the performance.

The psychophysiological model is based on analyses of electroencephalograms (EEGs), evoked response potentials (ERPs) and heart rate, in order to assess attention and its concurrent relationship to performance. Based on cognitive neuroscience, this approach seeks to explain the neural processes that accompany the process of attention. Examples of the research using this approach are studies examining EEG activity in archery and rifle shooting (Boutcher, 2002; Hartfield & Hillman, 2001). Others have merged this model with personality theory (Carlstedt, 2004) in an attempt to evaluate and predict an athlete's performance during critical moments in competition.

The social psychological model has much wider application and probably has the greatest import to understanding attention and concentration among elite athletes in the Caribbean region. Broadly speaking, it relates to distraction theories. It is an oft mentioned and bemoaned fact that Caribbean teams and individual athletes normally manage to secure competitive advantage, only to lose it at the most critical moment. Many blame this on their inability to sustain attention. If this is the case, then what are the factors that distract our athletes? There are so many explanations. Some of the primary distractors have been group dynamics, self-efficacy and competitive anxiety. For instance, at the 2000 Sidney Olympic Games, the Jamaica 4x100 women's relay team, boasting some of the best 100m sprinters in the world, became embroiled in a disagreement about who was to be on the team a few days before the event. The upshot was that the entire Jamaican team picketed in protest of team officials' decision to include a highly experienced sprinter who had not trained with the team, at the expense of a younger and highly promising athlete. Ultimately, the team that went to the Olympics, highly ranked among the favourites to win the event, only managed to place fourth. This was a classic example of group dynamics interfering with attention and concentration prior to performance.

The above example suggests that examining attentional issues that affect athletes in the Caribbean region should yield interesting results. Issues related to leadership problems, respect for team officials by elite athletes and their impact on cohesion and team focus, as well as individual athletes, have been widely mentioned. Judging by the current success of our athletes on the world stage, it could be argued that self-efficacy, perceived competence and other psychosocial factors affecting the performance of Caribbean athletes have generally improved. There is also no doubt that the successes of the Caribbean athletes in big events in Europe and North America might have enhanced the efficacy beliefs of many athletes from the region. In addition, much credit is due to the pioneers from the region.

## Personality and Sport Performance

Personality may be defined as the distinctive and characteristic patterns of thought, emotion, and behaviour that define an individual's personal style and influence his or her interactions with the environment (Colman, 2003). Aidman and Schofield (2004) mention another important dimension to the understanding of personality, which is personality, from the point of view of how one sees oneself (actor's perspective) and personality from the point of view of how others view the self (observer's perspective). These perspectives are critical to understanding individuals' behaviour in sport. The critical issues of personality and sport performance relate to the relationship between personality and the athlete's performance, the impact of sport on personality development, and how personality profiles for athletes in one sport differ from those in another. The questions surrounding the issue of personality and sport are very intriguing, and warrant much exploration, however, they have been fraught with methodological difficulties.

For the issues to be fully examined, personality must be deemed measurable. Coming up with appropriate methodologies and instruments that accurately measure personality traits has been part of the challenge in personality research, not to mention the application to athletic performance. "No scientific study to date has shown a strong statistical relationship between personality variables and athletic ability" (Cox, 2002, p. 163). Despite this, there is a significant amount of assessment that is done in the realm of sport psychology with the use of some traditional personality instruments such as the Minnesota Multiphasic Personality Inventory – Second Edition (MMPI-II), Cattell's 16 Personality Factor Inventory (16PF), Eysenck Personality Inventory (EPI) and the more rarely used projective tests, such as the Rorschach Inkblot Test and The Thematic Apperception Test (TAT). However, many structured questionnaires have been designed particularly for athletes such as Vealey's Trait Sport-Confidence Inventory, the Task and Ego Orientation in Sport Questionnaire (TEOSQ), Nideffer's Test of Attentional and Interpersonal Style (TAIS), and the Profile of Mood States (POMS) (Cox, 2002; Nideffer & Sagal, 2001; Vanden Auweele, Nys, Rzewnicki & Van Mele, 2001).

Nevertheless, theories of personality (psychodynamic, social learning, humanistic, and trait) have been explored and used to explain how individuals learn skills, are motivated, develop self-efficacy, act aggressively and react to particular stimuli, to name a few (Cox, 2002). More recently, with the growing popularity of neuropsychology, more psychobiological orientations to personality assessment have been postulated and researched such as Carlstedt's critical moment theory (Carlstedt, 2004).

The rhetoric in the Caribbean with regard to personality and its impact on sport performance is one based on anecdotal evidence. Personality development of Caribbean people has been shaped by the legacy of slavery (Balutansky & Sourieau, 1998; Hickling & Hutchinson, 1999). Therefore, constructs of self-esteem and collectivism are merely two concepts which become critical components in the discussion.

The concept of self-esteem in Africans across the Diaspora is a widely debated issue (Cross, 1991) with proponents of the global low self-esteem model advocating this and others proposing that we are a resilient lot with normal to high self-esteem. Both groups maintain valid points which can be evidenced in the society, however, looking at the history of sports in the Caribbean, it can be said that this is an area where our people continuously shine. This success in the athletic world, as previously mentioned, is a tribute to great self-confidence and esteem. However, the argument is not this simplistic, as so many other factors impact on the individual or group's ability to perform successfully over time.

The relevance of motivation to performance can never be overemphasized, as is the influence of sociocultural factors on the development and refinement of motivational skill. Frame of reference inevitably also plays a role in what is regarded as meaningful. For instance, it has been recognized that not all cultures are inspired through self-determined and intrinsic motives (Baron, Byrne, & Watson, 2005). Some cultures are motivated through group process and shared achievement. The diverging values that belie individualism and collectivism are among myriad potential differences which result in shared perception or misunderstanding in life, as in sport. Collectivism, as opposed to individualism, is a concept and approach to life and family that is well-known amongst Africans and people of African descent. Eurocentric principles, which were inculcated in African people through slavery, advance the idea of the individual, which was in opposition to the natural collectivistic approach (Williams, 1987). This has left some element of confusion, one manifestation of which lies in performance in group/team sports. For example, the dialectic dilemma becomes apparent when evidence of the longevity of the success in Caribbean individual sports (e.g. track and field) is examined, as compared to team sports (e.g. football and cricket). One may then question how this relates to the success of West Indian cricket team in the 1970s and 1980s, the Reggae Boyz in 1998 and the Soca Warriors in 2006. However, these are but a few successes in a history of sport involvement. More importantly, the team dynamic is surely not the only causative factor. This, therefore, warrants further investigation and should be an area of extensive research in the realm of Caribbean sport psychology.

## DOES PERSONALITY AFFECT ATHLETIC PERFORMANCE?

Based on research conducted by Carlstedt (2004) on the relationship between personality and athletic performance, as measured by the Eysenck Personality Inventory and neurological processes during critical moments in competition, a mind-body model of critical moments was devised. Carlstedt provides a scientific explanation for why athletes fail or succeed in those critical moments of competition. He also presents a method by which the likelihood of success or failure during these critical moments can be predicted. Carlstedt's mind-body model has linked interactions among hypnotic ability, neuroticism and repressive coping with peak performance, task mastery and failure. These measures have been functionally isolated in various parts of the brain and facilitate or hinder performance, based on their constellation. For example, athletes who are high in hypnotic ability have the extraordinary capability to focus intensely on the task at hand (which facilitates performance), or the vulnerability to fixate on internal thoughts (which hinder performance), as a function of neuroticism and repressive coping.

The ideal constellation of high or low hypnotic ability, low neuroticism and high repressive coping is associated with zone-like performance; while athletes who are high in hypnotic ability, high in neuroticism and low in repressive coping are most likely to fail during critical moments, as a result of negative intrusive thoughts entering consciousness. Repressive coping has been found to block the transfer of negative intrusive thoughts between brain hemispheres, thereby helping to avert psychological breakdowns during crucial junctures of competition (Carlstedt, 2004). This provides one model, among many, of how personality can affect performance. Overall, there is evidence that personality characteristics such as emotional stability, self-concept, anxiety and self-discipline are predictive of athletic performance and persistence in sports, in addition to setting apart athletes from non-athletes. However, researchers generally agree that personality research in sport is sparse and lacks methodological and conceptual rigor (Aidman & Schofield, 2004).

## DOES SPORT INFLUENCE PERSONALITY DEVELOPMENT?

The impact of sport on personality development, especially character development and the development of adaptive behaviours, has been mentioned in the sport psychology literature. Most of the research has focused on youth. Theoretical models espoused by Piaget and Mead have emphasized the importance of 'play' as a critical medium for social development. For instance studies have shown that participation in constructive leisure activities facilitates positive development among youth (Morrissey & Werner-Wilson, 2005; Rhea & Lantz, 2004). Sport participation was found to be predictive of positive self-perceptions, good interpersonal relationships and pro-social behaviours. However, there is also evidence to suggest that an in-sport socialization process occurs, which tends to have negative effects on personality development, such as the use of legitimized illegal and extralegal aggression (Shields & Bredemeier, 1995). They suggest that some sports, especially contact sports, create the impression among youth that it is acceptable to use aggressive tactics to win. The involvement in sport, therefore, has both positive and negative effects. It can enhance social skills, build leadership qualities, prepare youth for the working world, and improve self-esteem. Nevertheless, sport can also promote aggressive and other antisocial behaviours and engender psychopathology by encouraging an overly competitive spirit.

Lever (1976) found that conflict resolution skills developed as a function of gender, evidenced by boys who played longer, more competitively and in larger age-heterogeneous groups, being able to resolve disputes more readily than girls who used termination of 'play' as the most common means of problem-solving. However, Anderson (1995) in a study conducted with 80 Jamaican men and women found contrary results which suggested that childhood sport socialization occurs regardless of gender, and that social class was more predictive of sport involvement, with middle to upper class parents being better able to provide opportunities for engaging in sporting activities.

## DO PERSONALITY PROFILES DIFFER ACROSS SPORTS?

Using pure logic, one should perceive that a football player would be more aggressive, tolerant of pain, and anxious than a golfer. Some of the earliest empirical attempts to answer the question of whether personality profiles differ across sports (Schurr, Ashley & Joy, 1977) found that there were personality differences among team, versus individual athletes, with the former being more anxious, dependent, extraverted and alert-objective, but less sensitive-imaginative, than the latter. However, such findings have not been substantiated in the literature. It is worth noting that there is much controversy surrounding the personality and sport research, which is in part due to the difficulty with accurately measuring personality profiles.

The role of personality in the choice of sport, that is, individual versus team sports, or direct versus parallel sports, remains a controversial topic. Direct sports are those in which contact is emphasized and player's positions are fluid (e.g. basketball and football), while parallel sports are those in which athletes tend to stay in particular positions and contact is not emphasized (e.g. volleyball and baseball). Comparisons of these two types of athletes suggested that there were clear differences, with direct athletes being more independent and having less ego strength than parallel athletes (Cox, 2002). Other studies (Schurr et al., 1977) have looked at the personality differences by athlete's playing position, by skill level and gender (Cox, 2002) but have found only inconclusive results establishing poor linkage between the variables.

## Psychopathology in Sport

Psychopathology is one of the most intriguing, yet seldom explored topics in the sport psychology literature. Drug abuse, eating disorders and depression are common among athletes (Brewer & Petrie, 1996). Narcissism and sociopathic personality disorders are also often diagnosed in athletes (Anderson, Denson, Brewer & Van Raalte, 1994). Yet, psychopathology among athletes is a generally under-reported and less explored area.

Sport has been espoused primarily as a mental enhancer, and a protective factor against psychopathology. In fact, exercise has been used prescriptively for depression and other disorders. A myth supported by Caribbean culture is that athletes are invincible. Real stories have shown that they are human too, and suffer from the same degree of stresses, if not more so. However, very little attention has been paid to the fact that psychopathology is just as prevalent in athletes as it is in the non-athletic population, thus deserving just as much consideration (Schienberg, 2003). Actually, some mental health problems are more prevalent in athletes of a particular sport (e.g. eating disorders), while others are less prevalent (e.g. schizophrenia) – all due to the nature of the sport. Among the most common mental disorders explored in the realm of sport include eating disorders, substance-related disorders, adjustment and personality disorders.

## EATING DISORDERS

In sports such as gymnastics, figure skating, dancing, synchronized swimming, running, and wrestling, where there is a great emphasis on being thin or on body image, there is greater vulnerability and higher rates of eating disorders, especially among female athletes (Thompson, 2004). Diagnostic rates of eating disorders as high as 62 per cent have been reported among female athletes in figure skating and gymnastics (Thompson, 2004). However, more conservative estimates have ranged from 4.1 per cent (bulimia nervosa) to 43 per cent of adolescent skaters (anorexia nervosa) (Petrie & Stoever, 1993). Depression also maintains a high co-morbidity, with eating disorders magnifying the problem and the risk of suicide.

There exists a general perception among Caribbean professionals that there is a low prevalence of eating disorders in the Caribbean population. It has been suggested that this is in part due to the difference in the perceived role of body image in self-esteem and the overall standard of beauty in the Caribbean, compared to North America and Western Europe. Inherent in the problem of eating disorders is a disturbance in the body image, which leads to behaviours instituted to control the perceived, unwanted image, which is usually that of being overweight. Traditional views of a 'sexy' body image for Caribbean people have included a figure for women that is curvaceous (small waists, wide hips, big bottoms). Hodes, Jones, and Davies (1996) found that when Caribbean mothers were presented with body shape drawings of children, they were more likely to choose plumper girl figures than their Caucasian, Asian, and Mediterranean counterparts.

The Caribbean region does not seem to feature prominently in those sporting activities which have high reported rates of eating disorders, such as gymnastics, wrestling and figure skating. However, the prevalence of eating disorders in the Caribbean region, both among athletes and the general population, is unknown as is the role of body image on general self-concept. The globalization of the ideal body image through repeated images from TV, magazines and other print media should certainly have an impact on the general body image of individuals from the region, especially the youth. This is bound to have an impact on the psychological well-being of the affected individuals, and possibly, that segment of the population suffering from eating disorders as a consequence. Preliminary studies conducted on a Jamaican sample (Minor, Harris, Darby, Rose & Burke, 2004) have shown that there is an increase in cases of eating disorders in the country, which may speak to the previously mentioned proliferation of Western ideals, and this increase may also be reflected in the sporting fraternity.

## SUBSTANCE-RELATED DISORDERS

Drug use is another serious concern among athletes and the International Athletic Association, as well as other athletic bodies, has been battling this issue ferociously with rigorous, random testing of athletes. In general, usage can be classified under three areas among this population (Levy, 1996): 1) therapeutic drugs (diuretics, opioids, OTCs, beta-blockers, etc.); 2) performance-enhancing drugs (amphetamines, caffeine, catecholamines, anabolic steroids, growth hormone, etc.); and 3) typical drugs of misuse (alcohol, marijuana, tobacco, cocaine, etc.)

Professional Caribbean athletes in their success (Asafa Powell, Veronica Campbell, Ato Boldon etc.) have come under scrutiny over the years and they have been routinely and randomly tested. Thus far, there has been no scandal associated with athletes from the region in relation to the use of performance-enhancing drugs, with the exception of Ben Johnson (Jamaican-born sprinter who competed for Canada). Nevertheless, Damm (1991) reports that the use of recreational drugs in athletes is typically the same as in the non-athletic population.

## PERSONALITY DISORDERS

The nature of the demands of sport, which maintains a sub-culture of its own with different behavioural norms, may play a role in the development of personality disorders in athletes (Brewer & Petrie, 1996). The arrogance and overconfidence that is encouraged for survival, and the excessive adulation experienced from fans may lead to narcissism – the aggressive, overly competitive spirit that may contribute to antisocial and other maladaptive behaviours. Elman and McKelvie (2003) conducted a two-part study on the level of narcissism in a group of university football players. The first segment explored whether university football players were perceived to be narcissistic. Thirty undergraduates completed the Narcissism Personality Inventory (NPI) as themselves, and as they thought a university football player would. Their scores were much higher when they responded as football players. In the second segment, a total of 112 university football players, other athletes, and non-athletes completed the NPI, but only as themselves. Scores were higher for football players than for non-athletes, and the scores for other athletes did not differ from either group. The researchers therefore concluded that part of the perceived difference in narcissism between football players and non-athletes is stereotypical, but that it was also real. The prevalence of personality disorders in the Caribbean has not been documented in the literature, however, anecdotal evidence suggests that it is equal, if not greater than North America.

## Current Issues in Professional Sport

Most professional and elite amateur athletes will agree that psychology has a large influence on their sports performance. Most will also concede that they could benefit from the services of a sport psychologist. Despite this, a significant majority underutilize these services (Carmen, Zerman & Blaine, 1968; Brewer & Petrie, 1996). In a descriptive study conducted by Ferraro and Rush (2000) on the reasons why professional and elite amateur athletes resisted utilizing sport psychology services, the results indicated that though all 20 athletes in the sample admitted to the integral role that psychology plays in their performance, only two had accessed these services. When the athletes were asked to articulate what they thought sport psychology involved, the majority mentioned some of the key words, "focus", "mental training", "concentration", "visualization", but none alluded to emotional management or feelings. Conscious reasons given for not accessing the services included: money; time; and the fact that sport was not important enough. The researchers, however, concluded that athletes have an underlying fear of recognizing and dealing with their affect, "… sports are about action and the discharge of emotion through movement rather than through words." (p. 4).

These findings are not far removed from the experiences of sport mental health professionals here in the Caribbean. As previously mentioned, the development of psychology in the Caribbean has been slower than in North America. Mechanisms of resistance to mental health professionals are, therefore, not exclusive to athletes and others in the sports fraternities but are part of the mentality of the wider population. The stigma of mental health is very much alive, and though this is improving as is evidenced by the increased accessing of mental health/clinical services, it does not escape the professional that this is a great consideration in the evaluation of mental health in general. Only recently in Jamaica, (November 2005), the Government established a post for a sport psychologist who would be responsible for the organization and development of psychology for the national teams. This also speaks to evidence of a changing mentality. More and more in the media (television, radio and newspaper), professional opinions are being sought on the nature and importance of sport psychology; and how an athlete prepares mentally. Homosexuality and psychopathology in sport are among many of the topics that have been explored only over the last two years in the Jamaican media. The sporting fraternities of netball, football, tennis, track and field, swimming, water polo, and cricket have all utilized the services of a sports psychologist at the national level in Jamaica. However, it is appropriate to mention that most of these services are voluntary, and have been requested by management or by coaches who are sadly unaware of the depth of the role of the sport psychologist. Unwittingly, the role of a sport psychologist is often relegated to one-off speeches/lectures about attention or concentration, or some such related topic. The role very rarely involves a detailed programme for teams or individuals. Additionally national teams have great difficulty in affording a sport psychology programme and this is part of the reason why "talking" with the athletes in seminar format is more acceptable.

The responses of the athletes have varied. Most would not have sought services on their own, however, they listen keenly and try to make the best of what is being offered. Others are plainly uninterested and do not engage in the process. For most coaches and management, the reasons for approaching the sport psychologist often relate to difficulties in sustaining attention and concentration/focus, anger management or to times when a team is experiencing a slump. The general perception among coaches is that a sport psychology consultant will provide a quick fix for the performance problems of their athletes, generally in preparation for an upcomoing game.

## Intervention Strategies

Intervention models used here in the Caribbean have largely been from either a North American or a European paradigm, which has been placed within a cross-cultural context in order for a 'best fit' with our athletes. To date, no formal scientific evaluation has been made of such intervention strategies. Components ususally include: relaxation techniques (the use of imagery to enhance concentration), team building (cohesiveness), psychological skills training (the effects of anxiety/distraction on performance, and self-esteem/confidence building).

## Sport Psychology and Youth Development

The growing recognition of the value of sport to children and the physical and psychosocial development of youth has led to the growing research in this area. In particular, many sport psychology researchers have come to realize the value of extending psychological constructs and theories, developed using mostly adult elite performers, to young people involved in sports. In developing countries, the research has for the most part, been conducted in schools and, to a limited extent, in communities. Because of its monumental importance to the wider society and the development of sport at the grassroots level, the role of the school environment would normally attract much attention. In Jamaica, for instance, it is the primary and secondary schools that have enhanced the growth of sport as an enterprise. Currently, girls' football, gymnastics, table tennis, lawn tennis and volleyball are burgeoning sports in schools and young people are participating in them at competitive levels nationally, regionally and internationally.

Most of the widely researched topics in the youth sport literature are participation motivation, social influences, achievement goal orientations, enjoyment, and dropping out of sport. Other topics include moral development (Shields and Bredemeier, 1995) and physical and mental health benefits, such as the impact of sport on the development of the self-concept. The roles of social environments on children and in youth development have also been widely explored, highlighting the positive and negative values transmitted by parents, teachers and coaches (discipline, cheating, aggression and violence) and the emphasis on winning. Psychological skills training for children is also an area that is growing in popularity. It focuses on optimal activation, concentration and attention, imagery, self-talk, time-management, self-confidence and other psychological variables for children involved in sport (Hanrahan, 2005).

In the Caribbean region, the findings on selected psychological correlates for the participation of Jamaican youths in sport showed promise in relation to the value of youth involvement in sport (Malete & Matthies, 2003). The study's findings suggest that intrinsic factors seem to override extrinsic factors on why youth participate in sport. The role of teachers, coaches and parents in socializing youth in sport also came out strongly. Overall, sport seems to be integral to the development of young minds. It is also possible that the success of the West Indian athletes serves as important inspiration for youth to engage in sport. Generally speaking, sport could be perceived as fundamental to the success of many individuals who might view it as an avenue to 'escape' from the banality of poverty which does not discriminate by talent. In the process, other potential benefits are likely to accrue, such as the development of leadership skills, self-esteem, emotional intelligence and self-discipline, as well as the reduction of social ills such as juvenile crime, delinquency, drug abuse and other mental disorders that are increasing in prevalence within the region.

## The Future of Sport and Exercise Psychology in The Caribbean

As stated at the outset, sport psychology is a relatively young discipline, yet to experience growth in the developing world. However, the rapid growth and application of the discipline in Europe, North America and Asia has definitely caught the attention of countries where it was never heard of before. The Caribbean is one such region that has developed interest in the discipline and as a significant player in major international sporting events, the region has no choice but to embrace this development. The psychological services that have been provided – for instance to the West Indies Cricket team and other athletes – show great potential for the growth and utilization of sport psychology services in the region. The role of the mental health professional in sport also presents another challenge in the Caribbean setting. As shown earlier, it has primarily been viewed as one which should provide a 'quick fix' to enhance mental toughness and to sustain concentration before an upcoming event – often two weeks or less before what are usually the biggest competitions (World Championships, World Cup etc.). Teams and their management are often not prepared to absorb the totality of the sport psychologist's role. However, while there is no doubt that there is an obvious role for mental health professionals in sport in the Caribbean and elsewhere in the world, there is need for a more structured approach to the development of the discipline. The development of academic programmes in sport psychology in the regional universities would be a good starting point. This would guide the development of research programmes in the discipline. The Caribbean region's most significant contribution to sport psychology is likely to be that of providing a multicultural perspective for existing theory and research. The importance of investigations into the cross-cultural dimensions to various psychological theories and constructs has been lauded by various researchers. Such approaches will guide the development of sport psychology interventions that are relevant to the cultural contexts within which they are applied. Considering the limited application of this discipline in the Caribbean region, it might be premature to narrow the focus of sport psychology research and interventions in the region to specific topics. However, the rapid growth and success of elite level sport in the region provides the basis for some preliminary, yet structured work in testing theories and models on topics such as motivation, self-confidence and self-efficacy, anxiety, attention and concentration, psychopathology, as well as on children and youth involvement in sports.

Another area that also has promise is exercise psychology. Researchers and practitioners in the region could contribute immensely to the growth of this discipline by examining cultural and ethic differences on such topics as exercise and mental health; exercise adherence; and exercise and eating disorders. Unique cultural aspects that the Caribbean region could contribute to the discipline relate to the social roles of sport, as well as sport and the development of identities. Caribbean culture has its own peculiar profile, given that it developed out of an infusion of rich

Afrocentric and Eurocentric elements, as well as from the influence of various indigenous cultures. Such a fusion is normally reflected in the music and works of art from the region. It would therefore be interesting to investigate the role of such a culture on the development of the Caribbean athlete or on Caribbean sport psychology.

## REFERENCES

Abernethy, B. (1988). Visual search in sport and ergonomics: Its relationship to selective attention and performer expertise. _Human performance_, 1, 205-235.

Aidman, E., & Schofield, G. (2004). Personality and individual differences in sport. In T. Morris and J. Summers (Eds.), _Sport psychology: Theory, applications and issues, second edition_ (pp.22-47). Sidney, Australia: John Wiley and Sons Australia.

Amos, C. (1992). Achievement goals, motivational climate, and motivational processes. In G. Roberts (Ed.), _Motivation in sport and exercise_ (pp.161-176). Champaign, IL: Human Kinetics.

Anderson, B. (1995). Gender, inequality, sport, and professional achievement in Jamaica. In M. A. Malec (Ed.), _The social roles of sport in Caribbean societies_ (pp.107-124). Amsterdam, Netherlands: Gordon and Breach Publishers.

Anderson, M. B., Denson,E. L., Brewer, B.W. & Van Raalte, J. L. (1994). Disorders of personality and mood in athletes: Recognition and referral. _Journal of Applied Sport Psychology_, 6, 168-184.

Ashford, B., Biddle, S. J. H., & Goudas, M. (1993). Participation in community sport centers: Motives, and predictors of enjoyment. _Journal of Sport Sciences_, 11, 249-256.

Balutansky, K. M., & Sourieau, M. (Eds.) (1998). _Caribbean Creolization: Reflections on the cultural dynamics of language, literature, and identity_. Tallahassee, FL: University Press of Florida.

Bandura, A. (1977). Self-efficacy: Towards a unifying theory of behaviour change. _Psychological Review_, 84, 191-215.

———. (1986). _Social foundation of thought and action_. Englewood Cliffs, NJ: Prentice Hall.

———. (1990). Perceived self-efficacy in the exercise of personal agency. _Journal of Applied Sport Psychology_, 2, 128-163.

———. (1997). _Self-efficacy: The exercise of control_. New York: Freeman

Baron, R.A., Byrne, D., & Watson, G. (2005). _Exploring social psychology (4th Canadian edition)_. Toronto, Canada: Pearson.

Biddle, S. J. H. (1995). Introduction. In S. J. H. Biddle (Ed.), _European perspectives on exercise and sport psychology_, (pp. xi-xviii). Leeds, UK: Human Kinetics Publishers.

Biddle, S., Akande, A., Fox, K., & Vlachopoulos, S. (1996). Towards an understanding of children's motivation for physical activity: Achievement goal orientations, beliefs about sport success, and sport emotion in Zimbabwean children. *Psychology and Health,* 12, 49-55.

Biddle, S. J. H., & Bailey, S. (1985). Motives for participation and attitudes toward physical activity of adult participants in fitness programmes. *Perceptual and Motor Skills,* 61, 831-834.

Boutcher, S. H. (2002). Attentional processes and sport performance. In T. Horn (Ed.), *Advances in sport psychology, second edition* (pp. 441-457). Champaign, IL: Human Kinetics Publishers.

Brewer, B. W., & Petrie, T. A. (1996). Psychopathology in sport and exercise. In J. L. van Raalte & B. W. Brewer (Eds.), *Exploring sport and exercise psychology* (pp.257-274). Washington, D. C.: American Psychological Association.

Carlstedt, R. A. (2004). *Critical moments during competition: A mind-body model of sport performance when it counts the most.* New York, NY: Psychology Press.

Carmen, L., Zerman, J., & Blaine, G. (1968), Use of Harvard psychiatric service by athletes and non-athletes. *Mental Hygiene,* 52, 134-137.

Chi, L. (2004). Achievement goal theory. In T. Morris and J. Summers (Eds.), *Sport psychology: Theory, applications and issues, second edition* (pp.153-174). Sidney, Australia: John Wiley and Sons Australia.

Chie-der, D., Chen, S., Hung-yu, C., & Li-Kang, C. (2003). *Male and female basketball players' goal orientation, perceived motivational climate, perceived ability and sources of sport confidence.* Retrieved May 31, 2006 from www.thesportjournal.org/2003Journal/Vol6-No3/confidence.asp

Coelho e Silva, M., & Malina, R.M. (2004). Biological and social relationships in participation motivation in youth sports. In M. Coelho e Silva & R. M. Malina (Eds.), *Children and youth in Organized sports* (pp. 54-69). Coimbra: Coimbra University Press.

Colman, A. M. (2003). *A dictionary of psychology.* New York: Oxford University Press.

Cox, R. H. (2002). *Sport psychology: concepts and applications, fifth edition.* New York: McGraw-Hill Publishers.

Damm, J. (1991). Drugs and the college student-athlete. In E. F. Etzel, A. P. Ferrante, & J. W. Pinkney (Eds.), *Counseling college student athletes: Issues and interventions* (pp.151-174). Morgantown, WV: Fitness Information Technology.

Davis, S. F., Huss, M. T., & Becker, A. H. (1995). Norman Triplett and the dawning of sport psychology. *The Sport Psychologist,* 9, 366-375.

Duda, J. L. (1989). The relationship between task and ego orientation and perceived purpose of sport among male and female high school athletes. *Journal of Sport and Exercise Psychology,* 11, 318-35.

———. (1993). Goals: A social cognitive approach to the study of motivation in sport. In R. N. Singer, M. Murphey & L. K. Tennant (Eds.), *Handbook on research in sport psychology* (pp.421-36). New York: MacMillan.

Duda, J. L., & Nicholls, J. G. (1992). Dimensions of achievement goal theory in school work and sport. *Journal of Educational Psychology*, 84, 1-10

Duda, J. L., & White, S. A. (1992). The relationship of goal perspectives to beliefs about success among elite skiers. *The Sport Psychologist*, 6, 334-43.

Elman, W. F., & McKelvie, S. J. (2003). *Narcissism in football players: Stereotype or reality?* Retrieved May 31st, 2006 from www.athleticinsight.com/Vol5Iss1/Narcissism.htm.

Ewing, M.E., & Seefeldt, V.D. (1988). *Participation and attrition patterns in American agency-sponsored and interscholastic sports: An executive summary.* East Lansing, MI: Michigan State University, Institute for the Study of Youth Sports.

Frederick, C. M., & Ryan, R. M. (1993). Differences in motivation for sport and exercise and their relations with participation and mental health. *Journal of Sport Behaviour*, 16, 124-46.

Federick-Recascino, C., & Morris, T. (2004). Intrinsic and extrinsic motivation in sport and exercise. In T. Morris and J. Summers (Eds.), *Sport psychology: Theory, applications and issues, second edition* (pp.120-151). Sidney, Australia: John Wiley and Sons Australia.

Feltz, D. L., & Lirgg, C. D. (2001). Self-efficacy beliefs of athletes, teams, and coaches. In R. N. Singer, H. A. Hausenblaus, & C. M. Janelle (Eds.), *Handbook of sport psychology, second edition* (pp. 340-361). New York, NY: John Wiley & Sons, Inc.

Ferraro, T., & Rush, S. (2000). *Why athletes resist sport psychology.* Retrieved May 17th, 2006 from www.athleticinsight.com/Vol2Iss3/Resistance.htm.

Fisher, L.A., Butryn, T.M., & Roper, E.A. (2003). Diversifying (and politicizing) sport psychology through cultural studies: A promising perspective. *The Sport Psychologist* 17(4), 391-405.

Fox, K.R. (1990). *The Physical Self perception Profile Manual: Development and Preliminary Validation.* Office of Health Promotion, Northern Illinois University.

Fox, K.R., & Corbin, C.B. (1989) The physical self perception profile: Development and preliminary validation. *Journal of Sport and Exercise Psychology*, 11, 408-420.

Gauthier, A., Schinke, R.J., Michel, G., Pickard, P., & Guay, M. (2005). Sport psychology research in Northern Ontario, Canada: Cultural and geographic challenges. Paper presented at the meeting of the Canadian Society for Sport Psychology and Motor Learning. Saint Catherines, Ontario, Canada.

Gill, D. L. (1993). Competitiveness and competitive orientation in sport. In R. N. Singer, M. Murphy, & L. K. Tennant (Eds.), *Handbook of research in sport psychology*, (pp.314-327). New York: Macmillan.

———. (2000). *Psychological dynamics of sport and exercise*, 2nd ed. Champagn, IL: Human Kinetics:.

Gill, D. L., & Deeter, T. E. (1988). Development of the SOQ. *Research Quarterly for Exercise and Sport*, 59, 191-202.

Gill, D., Gross, J.B., & Huddleston, S. (1983). Participation motivation in youth sports. *International Journal of Sport Psychology*, 14, 1-14.

Goudas, M., Biddle S. J. H., & Fox, K. R. (1994). Perceived locus of causality, goal orientations and perceived competence in school physical education classes. *British Journal of Educational Psychology, 64,* 453-463.

Gould, D., & Pick, S. (1995). Sport psychology: The Griffith era, 1920-1940. *The Sport Psychologist, 9,* 391-405.

Greendorfer, S. L. (1992). Sport socialization. In T. S. Horn (Ed.), *Advances in sport psychology* (pp. 201-218). Champaign, IL: Human Kinetics.

Hanrahan, S. J. (2004). Sport psychology and indigenous performing arts. *The Sport Psychologist, 18* (1), 60-74.

———. (2005). Using psychological skills training from sport psychology to enhance the life satisfaction of adolescent Mexican orphans. *Online Journal of Sport Psychology, 7* (3)

Harris, O. (1993). African-American predominance in college sports. In D. Brooks & R. Althouse (Eds.), *Racism in college athletics: The African-American athlete's experience* (pp.51-74). Morgantown, WV: Fitness Information Technology.

Harter, S. (1978). Effectance motivation reconsidered: Towards a developmental model. *Human Development, 21,* 34-64.

Hartfield, B. D., & Hillman, C. H. (2001). The psychophysiology of sport: a mechanistic understanding of the psychology of superior performance. In R. N. Singer, H. A. Hausenblaus, & C. M. Janelle (Eds.), *Handbook of sport psychology, second edition*(pp. 362-388). New York, NY: John Wiley & Sons, Inc.

Heider, F. (1944). Social perception and phenomenal causality. *Psychological Review, 3,* 58-374.

———. (1958). *The psychology of interpersonal relations.* New York: John Wiley & Sons.

Hickling, F. W., & Hutchinson, G. (1999). Roast breadfruit psychosis: Disturbed racial identification in African-Caribbeans. *Psychiatric Bulletin, 23,* 132-134.

Hodes, M., Jones, C., & Davies, H. (1996). Cross-cultural differences in maternal evaluation of children's body shapes. *International Journal of Eating Disorders, 19* (3), 257-263

Horn, T. (Ed.) (2002). *Advances in sport psychology, second edition.* Champaign, IL: Human Kinetics Publishers.

Hull, C. L. (1943). *Principles of behaviour.* New York: Appleton-Century-Crofts, Inc.

———. (1951). *Essentials of behaviour.* New Haven, CT: Yale University Press.

Kavussanu, M. & Roberts, G. C. (1996). Motivation in physical activity contexts : The relationship of perceived motivational climate to intrinsic motivation and self-efficacy. *Journal of Sport and Exercise Psychology, 18,* 254-80.

Kontos, A.P., & Breland-Noble, A.M. (2002). Racial / ethnic diversity in applied sport psychology: A multicultural introduction to working with athletes of colour. *The Sport Psychologist, 16*(3), 296-315.

Levy, W. (1996). *Substance use in athletes.* Retrieved May 17th, 2006 from www.alcoholmedicalscholars.org/athletes-out.htm.

Li, F., Harmer, P., Chi, L., & Vongjaturapat, N. (1996) Cross-cultural validation of the task and ego orientation in sport questionnaire. _Journal of Sport and Exercise Psychology,_ 18, 392-407.

Lowther, J, Lane, J., & Lane, A. (2002). _Self-efficacy & psychological skills during the amputee soccer World Cup._ Retrieved May 31st, 2006 from www.athleticinsight.com/Vol4Iss2/SoccerSelfEfficacy.htm

McAuley, E., & Blissmer, B. (2002). Self-efficacy and attributional processes in physical activity. In T. Horn (Ed.), _Advances in sport psychology, second edition_ (pp.185-191). Champaign, IL: Human Kinetics Publishers.

Malec, M. A. (Ed.) (1995). _The social roles of sport in Caribbean societies._ Amsterdam, Netherlands: Gordon and Breach Publishers.

Malete, L. (2004a). Perceived competence and physical activity among youths: An examination of Harter's competence motivation theory in Botswana. _South African Journal for Research in Sport, Physical Education and Recreation,_ 26, 91-103.

———. (2004b). Participant motivation, social influences, and patterns of physical activity involvement among Botswana youths. _PULA: Botswana Journal of African Studies,_ 18, 49-64.

Malete, L., & Matthies, B. (2003). Psychological determinants of the participation of Jamaican youths in sport and physical activity. Unpublished Manuscript: University of the West Indies, Mona, Kingston, Jamaica.

Malete, L., Sullivan, P., & Matthies B. K. (2008). Examining physical self perceptions and physical activity behaviors of youths: A cultural extension of the PSPP. _International Journal of Sport and Exercise Psychology,_ 6 (1).

Minor, S., Harris, J., Darby, S., Rose, G., & Burke, D. (unpublished manuscript). Prevalence of Eating Disorders in a Cohort of Jamaicans.

Moran, A.P. (1996). _The psychology of concentration in sport performers: A cognitive analysis._ East Sussex, United Kingdom: Psychology Press.

Morgan, L. K., Griffin, J., & Heyward, V. H. (1996). Ethnicity, gender, and experience effects on attributional dimensions. _The Sport Psychologist,_ 10, 4-16.

Morris, T., & Koehn, S. (2004). Self-confidence in sport and exercise. In T. Morris and J. Summers (Eds.), _Sport psychology: Theory, applications and issues, second edition_ (pp.175-209). Sidney, Australia: John Wiley and Sons Australia.

Morris, T. & Summers, J. (2004). Introduction. In T. Morris and J. Summers (Eds.), _Sport psychology: Theory, applications and issues, second edition_ (pp.1-19). Sidney, Australia: John Wiley and Sons Australia, .

Moritz, S.E., Feltz, D.L., Fahrbach, K.R., & Mack, D.E. (2000). The relation of self-efficacy measures to sports performance: A meta-analytic review. _Research Quarterly for Exercise and Sport,_ 71, 280-294.

Murrel, A. J., & Curtis, E. M. (1994). Causal attributions of performance for black and white quarterbacks in the NFL : A look at the sports pages. _Journal of Sport and Social Issues,_ 18, 224-233.

Murphy, S. M., & Martin, K A. (2002). The use of imagery in sport. In T. Horn (Ed.), *Advances in sport psychology, second edition* (pp. 405-439). Champaign, IL: Human Kinetics Publishers.

Nicholls, J. G. (1989). The general and the specific in the development and expression of achievement motivation. In G. Roberts (Ed.), *Motivation in sport and exercise* (pp.31-56). Champaign, IL : Human Kinetics.

Nideffer, R. (1976). Test of attentional and interpersonal style. *Journal of Personality and Social Psychology, 34*, 394-404

Nideffer, R. M. (1985). *Athlete's guide to mental training.* Champaign, IL: Human Kinetics Publishers.

Nideffer, R. M., & Sagal, M. (1998). Concentration and attention control training. In J. M. Williams (Ed.), *Applied sport psychology: Personal growth to peak performance* (pp. 296-315). Mountain View, CA: Mayfield Publishing Company.

Nideffer, R. M. & Sagal, M. (2001). *Assessment in sport psychology.* Morgantown, WV: Enhanced Performance Systems.

Orlick, T. (1986). *Psyching for sport: Mental training for athletes.* Champaign, IL: Leisure Press.

Petrie, T. A., & Stoever, S. (1993). The incidence of bulimia nervosa and pathogenic weight control behaviours in female collegiate gymnasts. *Research Quarterly for Exercise and Sport, 64*, 238-241.

Roberts, G. C. (1993). Motivation in sport: Understanding and enhancing the motivation and achievement of children. In R. N. Singer, M. Murphey & L. K. Tennant (Eds.), *Handbook on research in sport psychology* (pp.405-420). New York: MacMillan.

Roberts, G. C., & Treasure, D. C. (1995). Achievement goals, motivation climate and achievement strategies and behaviours in sport. *International Journal of Sport Psychology, 26*, 64-80.

Ryba, T., Kashope Wright, H. (2005). From mental game to cultural praxis: A cultural studies model's implications for the future of sport psychology. *Quest* 57, 192-212.

Schienberg, (2003). *Mental problems in sport & exercise.* Retrieved June 20, 2006 fromhttp://www.psychedonline.org/Articles/Vol3Iss2/MentalProblems.htm

Schinke, R. J., Michel, G., Danielson, R., Gauthier, A., & Pickard, P. (2005). Introduction to cultural sport psychology: special edition. *Athletic Insight: The Online Journal of Sport Psychology, 7*(3)

Schurr, K. T., Ashley, M. A., & Joy, K. L. (1977). A multivariate analysis of male athlete characteristics: Sport type and success. *Multivariate Experimental Clinical Research, 3*, 53-68.

Shepherd College People and Websites. (2000). "Professional Athletes Are Making Too Much Money." Retrieved on November 27, 2006 from http://webpages.shepherd.edu/mwidmy01/athhtm.htm)

Shields, D.L., & Bredemeier, B.J. (1995). *Character development and physical activity.* Champaign, IL: Human Kinetics.

Skinner, B. F. (1938). _The behaviour of organisms._ New York; Appleton Century-Crofts.

Siegel, S.R., Peña Reyes, M.E. Cardenas Barahona, E.E., & Malina, R.M. (2004). Organized sport among urban Mexican youth. In M. Coelho e Silva & R. M. Malina (Eds.), _Children and youth in organized sports_ (pp. 70-81). Coimbra: Coimbra University Press.

Singer, R. N., Hausenblaus, H. A., & Janelle, C. M. (Eds.) (2001). _Handbook of sport psychology, second edition._ New York: John Wiley & Sons, Inc.

Spears, B., & Swanson, R. (1983). _History of sport and physical activity in the United States_ (2nd Ed.). Dubuque, IA: Brown.

Spence, K. W. (1956). _Behaviour theory and conditioning._ New Haven, CT: Yale University Press.

Thompson, C. (2004). _Athletes and eating disorders._ Retrieved May 17th, 2006 from www.mirror-mirror.org/athletes.htm.

Vanden Auweele, Y., Nys, K., Rzewnicki, R., & Van Mele, V. (2001). Personality and the Athlete. In R. Singer, H. Hausenblas & C. Janelle (Eds.), _Handbook of sport psychology, second edition._ New York: John Wiley & Sons, Inc.

Van Schoyck, S. R., & Grasha, A. F. (1981). Attentional style variations and athletic ability: The advantage of a sports-specific test. _Journal of Sport Psychology, 3,_ 149-165.

Vealey, R. S. (1986). Conceptualization of sport-confidence and competitive orientation: Preliminary investigation and instrument development. _Journal of Sport Psychology, 8,_ 221-246.

———. (2001). Understanding and enhancing self-confidence in athletics. In R. N. Singer, H. A. Hausenblaus, & C. M. Janelle (Eds.), _Handbook of sport psychology, second edition_ (pp. 550-565). New York: John Wiley & Sons, Inc..

Wann, D. L. (1997). _Sport psychology._ New Jersey: Prentice-Hall.

Whitehead, J. (1995). Multiple achievement orientations and participation in youth sport: a cultural and developmental perspective. _International Journal of Sport Psychology, 26,_ 431-452.

Weinberg, R. S., & Gould, D. (1999). _Foundations of sport and exercise psychology._ Champaign, IL: Human Kinetics.

Weiner, B. (1972). _Theories of motivation: From mechanism to cognition._ Chicago: Rand McNally.

———. (1985). An attributional theory of achievement motivation and emotion. _Psychological Review, 92,_ 548-573.

Williams, C. (1987). _The destruction of black civilization: Great issues of a race from 4500 B.C. to 2000 A.D._ Chicago, IL: Third World Press.

Williams, L. (1998). Contextual influences and goal perspectives among female youth sport participants. _Research quarterly for Sport and Exercise, 69,_ 47-57.

Yelvington, K. A. (1995). Cricket, colonialism, and the culture of Caribbean politics. In M. A. Malec (Ed.), _The social roles of sport in Caribbean societies_ (p. 13). Amsterdam, Netherlands: Gordon and Breach Publishers.

# 20 Race, Language, and Self-concept in Caribbean Childhoods

*Karen Carpenter & Hubert Devonish*

## The Growth of Self-Concept in Young Children

### THEORETICAL APPROACHES

This chapter will examine research on the growth of self-concept in young children, with a special focus on research relevant to the Caribbean. Given the colonial past and current socio-political realities of the Caribbean, issues of racial identity, skin colour, language and national identity dominate popular and academic debate about self-concept. The research material to be examined covers issues of self-concept proper, as well as those involving the related and overlapping areas of self-esteem and self-image and spans the stages of development from early childhood to adolescence.

### SELF-CONCEPT

The self-concept refers to the ways in which we describe ourselves. Marsh and Shavelson (1985) have suggested that there are two major domains of the self-concept, which are further sub-divided into academic and non-academic self-concepts. Academic self-concept is further sub-divided into English, Mathematics and other subject areas; non-academic self-concept includes physical, social and emotional self-concepts. As the global self-concept is formed over time, it is also linked to the child's cognitive abilities at a given stage of development. As with other developmental gains, the growth in self-concept is a gradual process which entails adding both information and complexity to the child's understanding of self (Harter, 1999). Eder (1989; 1990) has discovered that by the age of three and a half years, children can already describe themselves and others, in terms of lasting internal states and qualities such as kindness, aggression and dominance. These skills are perfected in children generally by the age of seven and a half years.

## SELF-ESTEEM

The self-esteem is the aspect of the self-concept that includes both how we evaluate ourselves and how we see ourselves in relation to others (Byrne, 1996; Broderick & Blewitt, 2006). The evaluations of young children tend initially to be very egocentric, and can be appraisals that do not rely on any social comparisons. This preoperational egocentrism (Piaget, 1926) allows children to describe and evaluate themselves as good, bad or nice, without comparing that evaluation with other children. This is possible because, initially, they are unable to imagine a perspective other than their own. As children develop and expand their social network, they begin to compare their efforts, appearance and behaviours with others. It is this social comparison that contributes to the child's positive or negative evaluation of him or herself. However, during the pre-school and early school years, children tend to make favourable comparisons of themselves in relation to their friends and tend to make downward social comparisons with peers (Pyszczynski, Greenberg & La Prelle, 1985). That is, children only compare themselves with other children who they feel are less competent in a particular area or skill.

## SELF-IMAGE

How we see ourselves, as opposed to how others see us, is important in the formation of the overall self-concept. Through feedback from others and the internalization of our own self-appraisals, we develop a mental picture of ourselves, referred to as the perceived ideal self-image. This self-image that we internalize is continually challenged by contact with others. The effort to reconcile the perception others have of us, that is, our perceived actual self-image, with what we consider to be our true selves

– our perceived ideal self-image (Rogers, 1951), is part of the psychological struggle in which the child engages as his or her radius of significant others expands (Erikson, 1966; 1980; 1994). This radius begins with the close circle of primary caregivers in the home and gradually expands to include members of the school environment and wider society. School-aged children move from the restricted contact with people in the immediate family to interactions with peers and teachers. Contact with others outside the home helps children to adjust and refine their notions about themselves, as they encounter new criteria for evaluating their efforts, their physical appearance, as well as notions about their own identity.

## COMMUNICATING ABOUT THE SELF AND OTHERS IN CHILDREN

Getting children to cooperate with researchers can be challenging. Young children are particularly sensitive to changes in routine and the people with whom they interact, and are unlikely to be able to sit for the long periods sometimes required for conducting thorough research. Many people involved in child research resort to either very quick interview techniques or tracking methods which require that the researchers follow the children throughout long periods as they engage in their regular activities. Another issue in child research is how to elicit the target information from children whose conception of themselves and others is likely to differ greatly from those of the researchers. It is, therefore, important that researchers begin with some understanding of children's theory of mind, and the kinds of approaches that work best. Developmentally, the cognitive and expressive capabilities of a two-year-old are vastly different from those of a 10-year-old. The younger child's focus on the self creates a world in which the centre is the child. The ability to engage in projective and hypothetical thinking is not yet developed, and the child believes that everyone sees the world from his or her eyes.

False belief tasks with young children demonstrate their inability to engage in perspective taking (Wimmer & Permer, 1983; Wellman, 1990; Wellman, Cross & Watson, 2001). One such Snoopy experiment which tests children's cognitive development and which demonstrates the false belief task is described here. A kindergarten child is shown a crayon box which contains not crayons, but birthday candles. The child is asked, 'What do you think is in the box?' The child naturally answers, 'Crayons'. The researcher then reveals the birthday candles and the child now realizes his or her mistake. The box is closed once more, a Snoopy stuffed toy is introduced and the child is asked, 'What does Snoopy think is in the box?' The young child invariably answers 'Candles', thereby demonstrating no distinction between what they actually know and what another person might think. The same experiment repeated with older children results in their admitting both that they thought the box contained crayons and that later, Snoopy would also think the box contained crayons. Similar experiments with candies etc. have been conducted by Gopnik & Astington (1988). The ability to separate their own thinking from that of others is generally not well developed in children under five years old, as demonstrated by other false belief and transference tasks (Flavell & Miller cited in Damon, 1998; Mitchell & Neal, 2005). Developmental theories such as Erikson's psychosocial theory and Piaget's cognitive theory are also helpful in understanding other aspects of children's processes. A practical guide to questions which are useful in researching children can be found in texts such as Yussen's *Development of Reflection in Children* (1985).

## CROSS-CULTURAL CONCEPTIONS OF THE SELF

Increasingly, psychologists have looked towards non-Western societies in order to determine the extent to which psychological behaviours are universal. In the area of self-theory, researchers have discovered that not all societies have as clear a distinction between what is the descriptive component of the self (self-concept), the evaluative component (self-esteem) and the perceived component (self-image). We now know that cultures which are collectivist tend to have more integrated views of the self, while in more individualistic cultures people tend to have more defined, separate concepts of self. Another dimension on which individualistic, Western cultures and, for instance, East Asian cultures differ is the extent to which each culture experiences the self-concept as consistent or variable across contexts. Kashima, Kashima et al (2004) found that Western cultures such as Germany, the UK and Australia experience the self as invariant across different contexts and are, therefore, assumed to have a clear, defined sense of the self, while persons in Korea and Japan experience the self as context-variable, changing and adjusting to suit different situations resulting in more blurred conceptions of the self as context-free.

## REFLECTED APPRAISAL AND SOCIAL COMPARISON

Studies in racial identity and self-esteem have largely focused on comparisons between the self-esteem of minority groups and groups of Whites. The basic premise on which the bulk of these studies rest is that Blacks and other underprivileged minorities will experience poor self-esteem in comparison with Whites and other privileged majority groups (Cooley, 1902). That is, the reflected poor appraisal that Blacks internalize about themselves in the society would cause them to have poor self-esteem. Additionally, when they themselves make social comparisons between their status within the society, as opposed to that of Whites and other privileged groups, they would rate themselves unfavourably. The conclusions drawn about Blacks and their poor self-esteem in relation to the psychological concepts of reflected appraisal and social comparison, further assume that Blacks use between-group social comparisons with persons they do not see as being like themselves (i.e. Whites) and that this comparison is the basis for the poor self-evaluations. On the contrary, Rosenberg (1986) found in his review of studies conducted in the 1960s and up to the 1970s, that the majority reported high self-esteem among Blacks and that Blacks used other Blacks as a reference group – not Whites, as was previously believed. Recently, more and more studies showed Black Americans as having slightly higher self-esteem than White Americans (Gray-Little & Hafdahl, 2000). Other researchers have theorized that the reasons for the consistently higher self-esteem scores among Black Americans were threefold: (1) Black Americans and other minority groups largely view negative appraisals as a result of racial prejudice; (2) Blacks did not in fact use between-group social comparisons as their benchmarks for evaluating their own value or lack thereof, but rather that Blacks were more likely to make within-group comparisons with other Blacks; and (3) Blacks demonstrated greater ethnocentrism than Whites (Crocker Major, 1989). Judd, Park et al. (1995) also concluded that Black Americans were more likely to focus on the positive and distinctive achievements of their own race. Despite this, countless studies on race and self-esteem have been carried out based on Cooley's untested assumption.

# Effective Methodologies for the Study of Race, Language and Self-concept in Children

## CONCEPTS OF RACIAL IDENTITY

The concept of race is fluid and is essentially socially constructed (Derman-Sparks & Ramsey, 2005), differing in some aspects from community to community. Not only is race a culturally and politically-defined concept, it is one that continues to be re-defined, even within the same cultures. Under apartheid in South Africa, for instance, the racial classification assigned to an individual determined where he or she could live and work. In 1984 the South African Ministry of Home Affairs recorded 611 cases of reclassification of racial identity (BBC World Service, 2007) and in 1987 that number grew to just over 1,500 persons. The largest number among the 1987 reclassifications by race, was 666 Blacks who became Coloureds with the second largest being 506 Coloureds who became White. No Whites became Black, nor did any Blacks become White (*Time Magazine*, 1987; *New York Times*, 2007). In the USA the USDA, Economic Research Service (2003) listed seven racial categories for the American population: African/African-American; European/European-American; Jewish; Latin; American/Hispanic; Middle Eastern; Native American while the US Census Bureau lists seven slightly different categories: White; Black or African American; American Indian and Alaska Native; Asian; Native Hawaiian and Other Pacific Islander; Some other race; Two or more races. In the UK, the Commission for Racial Equality (2006) has identified six ethnic groups which subsume both race and ethnicity. These include: White Groups; Mixed Groups; Asian or Asian British Groups; Black or Black British Groups; Chinese Groups; and Other ethnic groups. All but the Mixed and Other groups are broken down into sub groups which also contain an additional category called 'Other'.

Increasingly, the trend appears to be towards categorizing racial groups not solely on the ground of genetic or hereditary characteristics, but on cultural, ethnic and geographic ones as well. Chacko (2003) notes that in the USA racial categorization has moved from, "...the rigid 'one-drop rule', which classified persons with even a trace of African blood as Black (Davis, 1991), to self-identification in multiple racial categories, which was allowed for the first time in the 2000 census" (p. 6). No definition or classification of a particular racial group can be sufficiently inclusive to reflect all the possible members of the particular geographic or cultural group, as the concept of race is both situational and subjective (Chacko, 2003; Kashima, Kashima, Farsides et al., 2004). For example, the photos in Figure 1 are all of the same young man.

*Figure 1:  Forming concepts of race*

One may have one's own ideas as to how to classify him racially, based on one's own experiences and knowledge of the racial groups encountered. In various parts of the world the same person may be classified quite differently. In Canada, he is often described as Ethiopian. Ethiopians living in Canada in turn, classify him as Eritrean; in the USA he may be seen as either Arab or Black; in Europe he may be seen as Black, Somali, Arab, or Ethiopian, and in his native West Indies, he is seen as either East Indian (Indian) or Dougla (a term used to describe an inter-racial descendant of African and Indian parents). The latter classification depends on the extent to which the population of the particular West Indian country is familiar with the phenotype characteristics of Indians and/or Douglas. In Guyana and Trinidad, where there are large numbers of Indians and a Dougla minority, our young man would most often be classified as Dougla. In Jamaica, and possibly Barbados, where there is a very small minority of Indians within the population, our young man would normally be classified as Indian. It appears that where there are large numbers of a particular racial group, that group will insist on more rigid criteria for inclusion in the group than when the racial group is small in number.

Some of the studies discussed here point to this culturally fluid definition of race. We have learned, through previous research that children in multi-racial environments become sensitive to physical and cultural traits that distinguish groups of people racially from as early as five years old. They can also identify themselves and others as members of a racial or cultural group (Katz, 1983; Cobb, 2001).

## TYPES OF STUDIES

Conducting research is seldom a perfect process. In most instances, researchers find themselves weighing up the relative benefits of one approach against the practicality of an alternative approach. The research methodology and overall design is invariably arrived at by deciding what approaches will yield the best results – given the objectives. We will explore some of the ways in which these approaches have been applied to psycholinguistic research contexts in the Caribbean and the world. In psycholinguistic studies we are concerned with the connection between psychological, neurological and biological factors associated with how humans acquire, use, and understand language. If you can think of an area of research that looks at some aspect of language and human thought or behaviour, you probably have uncovered a psycholinguistic issue. For psycholinguists, the chief interest is to uncover the ways in which humans process language and language-related information. This may be studied through intrusive measures such as brain scans as well as non-intrusive applied methods. The research topics in this field vary widely, and race, language and self-concept in children is one such area. The research approaches we will consider here are non-intrusive. They are longitudinal, experimental and single-engagement research. We will begin with a brief look at how these approaches are used in psycholinguistics, consider some data collection issues and techniques that are peculiar to the field, and examine some research findings from the Caribbean and the world.

## LONGITUDINAL RESEARCH

Longitudinal studies are carried out over extended periods of time, with the same or similar subjects, and are usually concerned with describing changes in the patterns of the subjects' behaviour. This can be either qualitative research (as in case studies) or quantitative (questionnaires, tests and measurements). The advantage of longitudinal research includes the possibility of studying the subject in a more natural environment, thereby increasing the possibility of capturing less artificial behaviour. Some longitudinal studies in the area of psycholinguistics include: how children acquire their first and second languages; the linguistic and psychological factors involved in attaining literacy; and children's conception of themselves as learners and speakers of particular language varieties.

## EXPERIMENTAL RESEARCH

When researchers employ experimental designs in psycholinguistics, they are usually interested in seeing how best they can isolate one or more variables and study the impact of those variables on a dependent variable. The objective is to control as many variables as possible. One way of achieving this is through large samples of people who share the same characteristics, so that statistical comparisons can be made across the data sets. Experimental designs require careful forward planning and allow for little adjustments during the data collection process. It is also important to ensure that the procedures used in the experiment are replicated accurately with all subjects, whether they are to receive the same or opposite stimuli. One advantage of an experimental design is the focus and accuracy it lends to the resulting data. Some of the research topics for which experimental designs have been used include children's early language and vocabulary acquisition, language and gender differences, and semantics and aphasias.

## SINGLE ENGAGEMENT RESEARCH

A single sampling of a set of data may, in some instances, be experimental research. What is important to this type of psycholinguistic 'snapshot' of language use and development, is that you have only one opportunity to get it right; there are no re-takes. Consider for a moment the collection of population data from large numbers of people, data that tell you in five minutes what their competence is in a particular language. Not only are the respondents strangers to you, but you must also collect the information without their knowing what your objective is. Psycholinguists have taken this kind of snapshot by conducting what is called a *rapid intercept interview* (Jamaican Language Unit, 2005; 2006). This involves literally approaching strangers in crowded areas, such as malls and markets, and asking their opinion on a topic. Generally, for the psychologist and the linguist the topic of conversation is unimportant. What is important is the language in which the respondent is approached and the language of response. This data can tell us a great deal about the language competence of the speakers, as well as signal to the psycholinguist what language behaviours respondents feel are most appropriate for formal conversations with strangers. Labov (1972) began his sociolinguistic research by using such interview techniques, but later rejected them as being too formal and therefore not capable of capturing naturalistic speech, or what he referred to as rapid anonymous observations. There are some other data collection techniques that are widely used in psycholinguistic research. These include matched guise tests, magic boxes, and stimuli.

## Data Collection Procedures

### MATCHED GUISE

Matched guise tests (Lambert, 1967) are designed to reveal what language varieties respondents associate with particular speakers or groups of people. They involve using taped recordings of the same speaker, saying the same rehearsed script in more than one language guise. The language guises are played individually as well as paired with stimulus cards of persons whom respondents would be likely to associate with each guise. Respondents are asked to choose from among the persons presented in the stimulus cards and to match the individual to the guise. Matched guise research is widely used for determining language attitudes and social stereotypes associated with speakers for different languages. In assessing children's language stereotypes researchers have combined matched guise tests with photo stimuli of persons dressed in clothing that identifies them with particular occupations and socio-economic groups (Carpenter, Devonish, unpublished manuscript, 2006). Two occupational pictures, one of an African Jamaican, female, doctor and one of an African Jamaican market vendor were presented individually to 76 children between the ages of 6 and 8 years, accompanied by two language guises (Standard Jamaican English and Jamaican Creole) of the same speaker. The children were asked to indicate which one of the two women was the speaker of each language guise. The researchers inserted a distraction between both guises, so as to interrupt the children's thinking about language before playing the second guise. The distraction was in the form of a colourful picture of children playing a ring game. After describing that picture, the children were played the second language guise and they were again asked to indicate who was the speaker, from the two occupational photos. To avoid the possibility of the children simply choosing each photo in turn, researchers switched the order of the cards from left to right and the Jamaican and English guises were played first for every other chid participant. The results showed that the majority of children (82%) saw the doctor as the speaker of English and the majority (81.8%) also saw the market vendor as the speaker of Jamaican Creole, thereby demonstrating that as early as 6-8 years old, Jamaican children have language stereotype views. In other instances, content-rich drawings have been used to test children's vocabulary development, language at interview, and general language competence. We will return to the other ways of combining some of these data gathering techniques as we look at specific research findings from studies on race and self-concept.

## MAGIC BOXES

In 1974 Rosenthal et al decided to test the attitudes of young children to people of different races. The researchers used tape recordings of an African American speaker and a Caucasian American speaker to test the perceptions of children with regard to different racial groups. The two taped recordings were placed in two separate boxes and children were asked, "Which person do you think would give the better present?" the children chose the box containing the recorded voice that they thought would be the better gift giver. By isolating all other stimuli except the guises, the researchers ensured that the children's choices were based only on their perception of the individual behind the voice. The majority of children chose the box with the Caucasian guise as the person they thought would give the best gift. Other useful stimuli include photographs, drawings and games. These are used in a number of ways to establish children's attitudes and perceptions to a variety of issues.

## ECOLOGICALLY SOUND TECHNIQUES

An additional consideration for any research project, particularly with children, is the issue of *ecological soundness*. In other words, how closely does the research design replicate ways in which humans normally interact, even if the research is conducted outside of the subjects' normal sphere of interaction? In the field of psycholinguistics, there are numerous ways of exploring the connection between the mind, speech, and language. The research methods chosen should employ the best approach to meet the objectives of the study, while striving for ecological soundness. Research that is sensitive to the particular environment and culture in which it is carried out, can expect to result in data that is trustworthy. We will talk more about such *naturalistic* techniques in a moment. First, we will concern ourselves with the ways in which longitudinal, experimental and single-sample research can best conform to the notions of being ecologically sound.

## NATURALISTIC RESEARCH

It is normal in linguistics to face what is known as the 'Observer's Paradox' (Labov, 1972). The problem is one of being able, as a linguist, to observe the natural language behaviour of people, the way they would speak when no strangers, notably linguists, are around. However, to observe this language behaviour, the linguist needs to be present in some shape or form. The problem, therefore, is how to observe language behaviour as it would be, if it were not under observation. The solution could hardly be to approach someone and ask, 'Speak naturally for me. Speak the way you would if I was not here observing or recording you'. The likely response is either no speech at all or very unnatural speech.

Richard (1958; 1963) managed, in the situation of the then British Guiana, to try to observe, by way of tape recording, language behaviours that he knew took place, but would not have been able to record. While he had carpenters working in his house, he left his recording machine at home and went out. By this means, he was able to overcome the Observer's Paradox by not actually being present but, via the tape recording, being able to observe the speech of the carpenters. Since this was in the early days of tape recorders, the carpenters did not realise that they were being recorded and spoke in a manner which was natural to them in the absence of strangers. His approach raises ethical issues within the research environment of the early 21st century but, at that time, his approach was not viewed as unethical or as an invasion of privacy.

The classic case of a linguist overcoming the paradox involves the Labov (1972) study of the use of /r/ in New York department stores. Labov, as the researcher approached store workers, asking them for a department which he knew was on the fourth floor. When they answered, he listened for the pronunciation or lack thereof of the post vocalic /r/ in each of the two words. He also pretended not to have heard, which forced a repetition with emphasis. The researcher then retired and made notes of what he had heard. He, therefore, overcame the paradox by participating in a real-life interaction.

## Researching Race, Language and Identity in Children

### RACE AND IDENTITY RESEARCH IN CHILDREN

One of the earliest pieces of research into children's racial perceptions was conducted by Clark and Clark (1939) in the USA. The research was actually carried out to determine whether African American children were adversely affected by segregation in the American school system. This research has come to be known as the 'Doll Studies' due to the stimuli used in the study. African American and Caucasian American children were shown one black doll and one white doll and asked to indicate "...the doll they would like to play with", "...the doll they would like to be", "...the doll that was pretty" and "...the doll that was rich". The results from these studies revealed that the majority (60%) of both African American and Caucasian American children preferred and identified with the white dolls as the one, "...they would like to be". Kenneth and Mamie Clark concluded from the response of the African American children that they suffered from poor self-esteem, as reflected by their choice of the white doll over the black one. The evidence presented by Clark and Clark in the landmark *Brown v. Board of Education* Supreme Court case, led to the racial desegregation of American primary schools. The Doll Studies have been replicated by several other researchers in the West Indies and North America with varied results. Some 30 years after the initial Doll Studies, Hraba and Grant (1970) replicated the study in Lincoln,

Nebraska in the now interracial schools and found that 60% of black children preferred the black doll. Fox and Jordan (1973) and Katz (1983) investigated self-concept among Black, Chinese and White children in integrated and segregated schools in New York and found that all children identified most closely with their own racial group. Criticisms of the methods used in the Doll Studies include the fact that the forced choice response did not in any way indicate the strength of the children's choices. Others have argued that the dolls are a limited measure of children's racial preferences. The differences between the pre-Civil Rights movement responses of the early studies, and those from 1969–1973 is sometimes attributed to the substantial progress made by racial minorities in the USA, greater racial diversity in schools and communities, and the positive impact of these advances on the views of all racial groups. Whatever the reasons for the change in responses over time, the results underscore the importance of interpreting findings with the historical, political and cultural context in mind.

## TRINIDAD AND JAMAICA

In the West Indies, Gopaul McNicol (1995) replicated Clark and Clark's doll studies with both Trinidadian and American children. Gopaul McNicol's findings mirrored those of Clark and Clark. The Afro-Trinidadian children and the Afro-American children selected the white doll as the one they preferred and would like to be. These findings appear to confirm the earlier conclusion that Black children have poor self-esteem. The studies in Trinidad and the USA are among the first to be documented in the Caribbean. In the last three decades, Miller (1975) Cramer and Anderson (2003) and Carpenter, Coore, and Devonish (2005) have conducted studies with adolescents and young children in Jamaica. Miller's study examined body image satisfaction among multiracial Jamaican adolescents between the ages of 11 and 15 years. The researchers asked the teens to say what parts of their bodies they were most satisfied with and most dissatisfied with. In addition, the teens were asked to describe their ideal male and female. The image that evolved of the 'handsome boy' and the 'beautiful girl' was one of an individual who was neither White nor Black, but who had the facial features of a White boy/girl with the body of a Black boy/girl. The research team also classified the participants into racial groups and arrived at a continuum of race and colour from Black, Dark, Brown, Indian, Chinese, Clear, Fair, White and hybrids. Like the Fox and Jordan studies, Miller's continuum moves the study of race and ethnicity from the two polarities of Black and White, and towards the kind of racial and skin colour diversity within groups that actually exists in the Caribbean. Cramer and Anderson's modified doll study involved Black and White interviewers examining skin colour and body size preferences of rural New England and rural Jamaican kindergarten children. The rural Jamaican children showed no bias for skin colour or body size, while White New England children showed reverse preferences for black skin colour and body size.

## CHILD LANGUAGE RESEARCH

Research into the language of children became significant in the period from 1960s onwards. In Europe and North America, as well as the Caribbean, this research took place against the background of a thrust towards social justice for the underprivileged in these societies. Perhaps the main source of social inequality was identified as a result of differences in access to the benefits of education. The research focused on the extent to which children from various social backgrounds had the linguistic and intellectual prerequisites to function successfully in the formal educational system. The work of Bernstein (1961; 1962) was one of the catalysts for this research. Bernstein found, within the context of Britain, that children of working-class and underprivileged backgrounds were predominantly users of what he called 'the restricted code'. By contrast, children of middle- and upper-class backgrounds tended to show themselves as users of what he called 'the elaborated code'. Users of restricted codes had less complex grammar and sentence structures, as well as more condensed vocabulary, while users of the elaborated code, as the name suggests, generally employed more complex grammatical structures, longer sentences and wider vocabularies. According to this early work, speakers of the restricted code tended to register lower measured intelligence and educational achievement than did users of the elaborated code. As a result, there developed a notion that there was a causal relationship between the habitual use of a particular language variety on one hand, and children's measured intelligence and educational performance on the other. This triggered a large body of research, notably that associated with William Labov (1972) in the USA, where evidence was presented that the speech of lower class, Black children was no less elaborated than that of middle class White ones.

In the context of the Caribbean, Craig (1986) pointed out that the linguistic features associated with Caribbean creole languages such as Jamaican, were also features thought to be typical of restricted codes. However, these vernacular languages functioned as full-fledged languages, with an equal level of creativity and linguistic resources. Craig (1986), therefore, through the study of groups of children across the social categories of 'Urban Lower Social Class', 'Rural Lower Social Class' and 'High Social Class', sought to investigate (1) whether there are any social class differences in natural language use amongst children across these social groupings, and (2) whether any of these represents features which can be regarded as more 'restricted' or 'elaborated' relative to the other.

## Race, Language and Identity – Belize

The results of research on language use of children 10-16 years in Belize point to the link between natural language and socio-economic status. The Le Page and Tabouret-Keller (1985) study involved the examination of five linguistic variables over five different speech styles of 280 children in the Cayo District of Belize. These data were subject to statistical cluster analysis, with each cluster being examined for a correlation with a particular non-linguistic feature, such as place of living, occupation of father, or socioeconomic status of family. The strongest calculated association between language behaviour and non-linguistic factors was 'place of living'. However, this only predicted about one-third of the information needed to explain clustering (Le Page & Tabouret-Keller 1985, p.131).

Cayo District, at the time of the research, represented a community previously zoned along ethnic and linguistic lines, and which was going through a transition to a more mixed kind of community (Le Page & Tabouret-Keller, 1985). The linkage observed between language and 'place of living', therefore, represented a hangover from the earlier situation of ethno-linguistic zoning. If we crudely reinterpret 'place of living' and language link as meaning 'language of home', the 'home language' factor seems to play only a limited role in predicting children's language behaviour, at least between the ages of 10 and 16 years. If children's language competence is in the process of development rather than static, we can view the children's language behaviour as the product, not just of family membership, but also membership of other social groups – the most influential being the school peer group. The official school language(s) is, therefore, involved in interaction with the 'home language', as well as with an emerging peer group school language, usually similar, but not identical, to that of the home language. Le Page and Tabouret-Keller note that "... languages do not do things; languages are abstractions from what people do" (p. 188). Language, because it is a medium for projecting social identities, is the subject of a substantial body of ideas, which form part of the belief systems of social groups.

## Race, Language and National Identity – The Jamaica Case

### JAMAICAN RACIAL CATEGORIES

Even more recent language, race, and national identity studies conducted by Carpenter, Coore and Devonish in Jamaica (2005) combined the use of Matched Guise Tests with a newly developed Racial Identity Instrument (RII) consisting of photographs of actual persons from the seven racial groups that make up the Jamaican society. Approximately 90 per cent of the population is of African descent, with a minority of approximately 6-10 per cent from other racial groups and mixtures. The research team decided to devise an instrument that would reflect the racial categories held by the children within the Jamaican society. This approach deviates from the traditional practice of assuming that children within a given society will reflect the thinking of adults from that society (Williams & Best, 1990). In developing the RII, the researchers focused on the phenotype characteristics that distinguished large groups of people from each other in Jamaica, such as skin colour, hair texture, eyes, and mouth (Henriques, 1953; Nettleford, 1970; Knight, 1990; Richardson, 1992; Alleyne, 2005). Thirty–six head shots of racially distinct young men and women representing African-Jamaicans, Indian-Jamaicans, Chinese-Jamaicans, Arab-Jamaicans, Jewish-Jamaicans, White/European-Jamaicans and Interracial-Jamaicans were reduced to nine photographs of each gender by conducting a standardization exercise with the grade six pupils in the target school. These 12-year-olds could, in this context, be considered 'key informants', having specialized knowledge about the social environment within the school and could, therefore, act as guides to the younger children's conceptions of race (Berg, 1995, p. 125). They would also be more articulate than the younger 6-10-year-olds in the target sample. The grade six pupils eliminated all photos of White/European-Jamaican men and women on the grounds that they were non-Jamaicans and, therefore, foreigners. Instead, they selected the photos that had been classified by the researchers as Interracial-Jamaicans and re-classified them as White-Jamaicans. The standardization participants also expanded the category African/Black-Jamaican by adding two new sub-categories: 'Dark-Brown-Jamaican', and 'Brown-Jamaican', thereby creating six Jamaican racial categories (Table 1).

*Table 1:  Comparison of racial categories*

| Traditional racial categories | Children's racial categories |
|---|---|
| 1. African-Jamaican | 1. African/Black-Jamaican |
|  | 2. Dark-brown-Jamaican |
|  | 3. Brown-Jamaican |
| 2. Indian-Jamaican | 4. Indian-Jamaican |
| 3. Chinese-Jamaican | 5. Chinese-Jamaican |
| 4. Interracial-Jamaican | 6. White-Jamaican |
| 5. European-Jamaican | White-American (Foreigner) |
| 6. Arab-Jamaican | White-American (Foreigner) |
| 7. Jewish-Jamaican | White-American (Foreigner) |

Additionally, the responses from the standardization exercise revealed that the grade six children perceived 'Jamaican' as a particular racial category, having a national identity which is defined by having a "dark brown, cool complexion, an oval-shaped face and cherry lips". This complexion was referred to by the younger children as 'Brown-dark'. The emergence of a national identity that appears to combine attributes of Black/African Jamaican and other racial groups is similar to that found in the case of the Belizean national identity discussed earlier.

## WHO LOOKS LIKE ME

One hundred and thirty eight boys and girls between the ages of 5 and 10 years were interviewed. The researchers used the language of the participants in all interviews, i.e., Standard Jamaican English or Jamaican Creole, and the children were matched by gender with the interviewers. The children were asked to select from the RII photo card the person who "...looks like you" and for Jamaican Creole speakers, "Pik di wan we fieva yu". This was accompanied by a Matched Guise Test, consisting of an array of photos of the six racial categories and two language guises (Standard Jamaican English or Jamaican Creole). Caricatures of the actual photographs are contained in Figure 2. The children were played each guise and asked to identify the person "...who said that?" or "Uu se dat?" from the photo array. The researchers were interested in uncovering which language variety the children associated with each of the six racial groups.

*Figure 2: Racial groups in Jamaica (Carpenter, Coore – Racial Identity Instrument)*

| Black/ African Jamaican | Dark-Brown Jamaican | Brown Jamaican | Indian Jamaican | Chinese Jamaican | White Jamaican |
|---|---|---|---|---|---|

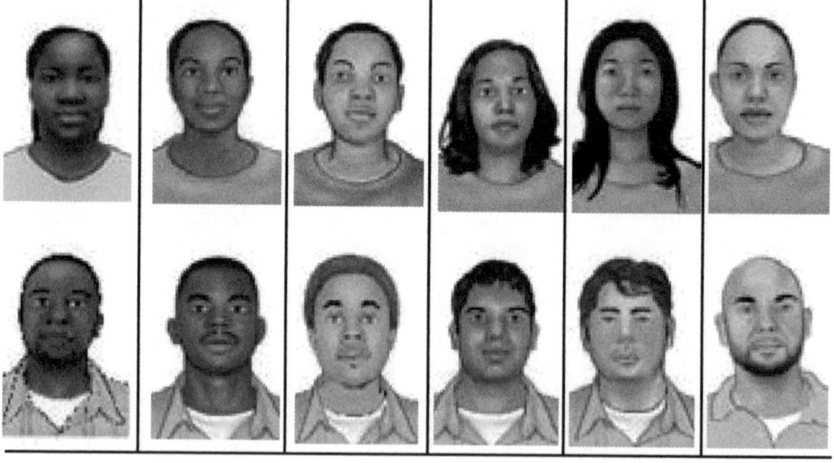

The Dark-Brown-Jamaicans were seen as the racial group that most "looks like me" by 60.9 per cent of the sample, followed by the

African/Black-Jamaican (41%) , Indian-Jamaican (32.1%), The children identified least with the Brown (24.6%), White (23.2%) and Chinese-Jamaicans (13.1%). Children who rejected the 'African/Black-Jamaican' cited reasons such as s/he is "too black", "I am more brown- black."

*Table 2: Overall responses by racial category*

| Racial category  N=138 | Like me | Not like me |
|---|---|---|
| 1  Dark-Brown-Jamaican | 60.9% | 39.1% |
| 2  African/Black-Jamaican | 41.3% | 58.0% |
| 3  Indian-Jamaican | 32.1% | 67.9% |
| 4  Brown-Jamaican | 24.6% | 75.4% |
| 5  White-Jamaican | 23.2% | 76.8% |
| 6  Chinese-Jamaican | 13.1% | 86.9% |

Further data analysis by gender showed that boys identified more with the Dark-Brown-Jamaican than did girls. Responses for the Brown-Jamaican category illustrated that boys were more likely than girls to see a Brown-Jamaican as someone who "looks like me" (37.1% and 11.6% respectively). Girls also had a slightly higher level of identification with the White-Jamaican persons (27.5%) than did boys (20%). Chi-square analyses of the children's level of identification by gender showed statistically significant results between the responses of boys and girls for the African/Black-Jamaican category, $\chi^2$ (2, N = 116) = 9.75, p = .008 and the Indian-Jamaican category, $\chi^2$ (2, N = 119) = 21.56, p = .000. Close to 47 per cent (46.6%) of the girls felt the Indian-Jamaican photo cards "looked like them" whereas only 16.6 per cent of the boys identified with the Indian-Jamaican.

Developmental differences in responses were analysed by dividing the responses into two age bands; 5-7-year-olds and 8-10-year-olds. In general, the younger children in the 5-7 age group identified more with the Dark-Brown-Jamaican (61.6%) and less with the Black/African-Jamaican photo cards (37%) than did the older children in the 8-10-year-old group (61.6%). Dark-Brown-Jamaicans were still seen by both age bands as being the Jamaican who most "looks like me", 61.6 per cent and

60 per cent, respectively. Statistically significant differences were seen in the Black-Jamaican ($\chi^2$ (2, N = 116) = 7.79, p = .020) and Brown-Jamaican ($\chi^2$(2, N = 118) = 6.15, p = .046) racial categories.

## WHO TALKS LIKE ME

Results from the Matched Guise test showed that the majority of the children identified the African/Black-Jamaican, Dark-Brown-Jamaican and the Chinese-Jamaicans as speakers of Jamaican Creole and the Brown-Jamaican, Indian- and White-Jamaicans as speakers of Standard Jamaican English. Forty-three per cent of the children felt they spoke most like the Black/African Jamaican, who was identified as a Jamaican Creole speaker, while 19 per cent identified with the Indian-Jamaican as a speaker of English.

A panel of six independent male and female judges was asked to verify the accuracy of the children's racial self-identification by indicating on a score sheet, the racial category from among the six they would classify each child as belonging to. The judges also classified the majority of the children (55.6%) as Dark-Brown-Jamaicans.

## DISCUSSION

What we have seen here, in terms of the accuracy of self-description and identification with a racial and linguistic group, and the labelling of self, has been documented elsewhere. Kowalski and Ya-Fen Lo (2001) discovered that as the ability of Taiwanese children – 3 to 11 years old – to identify their own racial group membership increased with age, they also expressed a bias towards persons who bore the same label as their racial group, even when the individual did not actually belong to that racial/ethnic group. Perhaps in the instance of the Jamaican children, as with the Taiwanese, there is this positive bias towards those RII photos that they believe to be representative of the labels they have accepted for themselves, as well as the image that they have come to see as the national Jamaican ideal.

Notwithstanding the implications of Jamaican children, and perhaps adults, seeing themselves as racially non-African, this study has moved the debate away from whether or not Black children see themselves as racially Black, towards the question of 'What kind of Black person do children see themselves as?' The issues of bi- and multi-racial identity and self-concept have not been explored here, except to the extent that children have classified what is generally considered to be one single racial group, African-Jamaican, into a variety of declensions: African/Black Jamaican, Dark-Brown-Jamaican, Brown-Jamaican and White-Jamaican. Additionally, the standardized instrument itself moved us further away from Clark and Clark's Black-White racial opposites and refined Miller's continuum, to reflect a wider variety of skin colour and phenotype characteristics.

## THE WAY FORWARD

For the most part, the studies we have discussed here have been carried out in urban areas with populations of children who have some exposure to multiracial social environments. What is of note is that studies conducted in the USA have been with African American children who are racially in the minority. In contrast, the Jamaican studies have been carried out with children who are part of a racial majority. We have yet to explore how being part of a racial majority affects the self-concept and self-esteem of non-White children, particularly in the context of developing nations. Most documented studies have sought to make between-group comparisons of Whites and a minority (usually Blacks). Clearly, there is room for much more research into the acquisition and expression of racial and linguistic self-concept among children, as well as other areas of the self-concept that pertain to culture. The relationship between the linguistic aspects, such as labelling, and expressed racial self-concept bears further investigation among children at different developmental stages in different cultures. Perhaps one of the most challenging future pieces of research would be to bring together the study of self-concept and developmental theories in a pan-cultural model.

# Summary – Key Concepts

## THE GROWTH OF SELF-CONCEPT IN YOUNG CHILDREN

1. The terms self-concept, self-esteem, and self-image are often used interchangeably. In this context, we understand self-concept to be the descriptive aspect, self-esteem to be the evaluative component and self-image to be the way we see ourselves.

2. The child's theory of mind is developed over time, to include conceptions of the self and others in ways that make it possible for the child to describe his or her own thoughts and feelings, as distinct from the thoughts and feelings of others. The growth of young children's taking perspective is critical to the child's appreciation of feedback from others and the incorporation of that feedback into the self-concept.

3. How we view the three aspects of the self (self-concept, self-esteem, self-image) and the relationships we assume among them is, in part, culturally mediated. Individualistic cultures tend to see the three as separate but interlinked concepts, while collectivist cultures tend to make little distinction between them. Additionally, in making sense of data from research carried out internationally, we must interpret the data in light of the cultural context.

## EFFECTIVE METHODOLOGIES FOR THE STUDY OF RACE, LANGUAGE & SELF-CONCEPT IN CHILDREN

1. There are many effective ways of studying race, language and self-concept in young children. The most effective method will most likely be the one which allows participants to engage with the researcher in ways that replicate their own natural behaviours. For children, this is doubly important because they are easily fatigued and generally more sensitive to external cues and changes in the environment.

2. Three of the most frequently used approaches in psycholinguistic studies have been longitudinal research, which takes place either over an extended period of time with the same participants or with samples of data from different participants within comparative age bands. Experimental research uses techniques that require lab settings and/or conditions, and often employs control groups of participants who have not been administered the treatment under study. These need to be carefully planned ahead of implementation, in order to control or match as many variables as possible, so as to increase the focus of the study. Single engagement research in psycholinguistics includes tech-

niques such as rapid anonymous interviews, matched guise tests and magic boxes, which are useful in sampling social behaviour.

3. Ecologically sound techniques for conducting research are those which allow the participants to feel, behave and respond as they would in their natural environment.

## RESEARCHING RACE, LANGUAGE AND IDENTITY IN CHILDREN

1. A number of studies have already been carried out in various parts of the world, which tell us something about how children see themselves as members of racial groups and speakers of particular languages. These studies help us to understand how race and language may interact with self-concept and self-esteem. We can further appreciate that race is a culturally bound phenomena and what distinguishes one racial group from the others varies across cultures.

2. Some studies have shown racial minorities to have poor self-esteem, others have contradicted these earlier findings among minorities. Still further studies among non-Whites as racial majorities, have shown that children in these environments have accurate self-concepts and do not show evidence of poor self-esteem on the basis of race, skin colour or other phenotype characteristics.

3. In the Caribbean, there is a growing body of literature and research in this area which needs to be brought together in order to make meaning of the ways in which we as a people view ourselves in a postcolonial dispensation. The racial and linguistic diversity of the region has been largely ignored by studies that report on the Caribbean. The studies included here are an attempt to address this omission.

## REFERENCES

Alleyne, M. C. (2002, 2005). *The construction and representation of race and ethnicity in the Caribbean and the world.* Barbados, Jamaica, Trinidad and Tobago: University of the West Indies Press.

Allsopp, R. (1958). Pronominal forms in the dialect of English used in Georgetown (British Guiana) and its environs by persons engaged in non-clerical occupations. Unpublished M. A. Thesis, London University, London.

———. (1962). Expressions of state and action in the dialect of English used in the Georgetown area of British Guiana. Ph. D Thesis, London University, London.

BBC World Service. Apartheid Law. http://www.bbc.co.uk/worldservice/africa/features/storyofafrica/12chapter7.shtml

Berg, B. (1995). *Qualitative research methods for the social sciences*. Boston: Allyn & Bacon.

Bernstein, B. (1961a). Social class and linguistic development: A theory of social learning. In A.H. Halsey, J. Floud & C. A. Anderson (Eds.), *Education, economy and society*. New York: Free Press, pp.288-314.

———. (1961b). Aspects of language and learning in the genesis of social process, *Journal of Child Psychology and Psychiatry*, 1, 313-24. Reprinted in D. Hymes, (Ed,). 1964. *Language in culture and society: A reader in Linguistics and Anthropology*. New York: Harper & Row, pp. 251-63.

Broderick, P. C., & Blewitt, P. (2006). *The life span: Human development for helping professionals* (2nd Ed.). Upper Saddle River, NJ: Prentice Hall.

Byrne, B. (1996). *Measuring self-concept across the life span: Issues and instrumentation*. (1st ed.). Washington, D. C.: American Psychological Association.

Carpenter, K., Coore, C., & Devonish, H. (2006). Language and self-concept in Jamaican elementary school children: Uu fieva mi, uu taak laik mi. (Unpublished manuscript).

Carpenter, K., & Devonish, H. (2006). Race, language and national identity in Jamaican elementary school children. Unpublished manuscript.

Chacko, E. (2003). Identity and assimilation among young Ethiopian immigrants in Metropolitan Washington. *Geographical Review*, 93(4), 491-506.

Clark, K. B., & Clark, M. P. (1939). The development of consciousness of self and the emergence of racial identification in Negro preschool children. Journal of Social Psychology, 10, 591-599.

Cobb, N. J. (2001). *The child*. Mountain View, CA: Mayfield Publishing Company.

Commission for Racial Equality. (2006). *A guide to ethnic groups in Britain*. (Retrieved January 1, 2007) http://www.cre.gov.uk/diversity/ethnicity/index.html.

Cooley, C. H. (1902). *Human nature and the social order*. New York: Scribner's.

Craig, D. (1986). Social class and the use of language. In M. Gorlach & J. A. Holm (Eds.), *Varieties of English around the world: Focus on the Caribbean*. (pp. 71-116). Amsterdam//Philadelphia: John Benjamins Publishing Company.

Cramer, P., & Anderson, G. (2003). Ethnic/racial attitudes and self-identification of Black Jamaican and White New England children. *Journal of Cross-cultural Psychology*. 34, (4), 395-416.

Crocker, J., & Major, B. (1989). Social stigma and self-esteem: *Psychological Review,* 96, 608-630.

Derman-Sparks, L., & Ramsey, P. (2005). What if all the children in my class are white? Historical & research background. *Journal of the National Association for the Education of Young Children.* http://www.journal.naeyc.org/btj/200511/DermanSparksBTJ1105.asp

Eder, R. A. 1989. The emergent personologist: The structure and content of 3 1/2-5 1/2, and 7 1/2-year-olds' concepts of themselves and other persons. *Child Development.* 60, 1218-1228.

————. 1990. Uncovering young children's psychological selves: Individual and developmental differences. *Child Development.* 1990. 61, 849-863. The Society for Research in Child Development, Inc.

Erikson, E. (1966, 1980, 1994). *Identity and the life cycle.* New York: W.W. Norton & Company.

Flavell, J. H., & Miller, P. H. (1998). Social cognition. In W. Damon (Series Ed.), D. Kuhn & R.S. Siegler (Vol. Eds.), *Handbook of child psychology: 2, Cognition, perception and language* (5th ed., pp. 851-888). New York: Wiley.

Fox, D.J., &. Jordan, V.B. (1973). Racial preference and identification of black, American, Chinese and White Children. *Genetic Psychology Monographs* 88:229-86.

Gopaul-McNicol, S. (1995). A cross-cultural examination of racial identity and racial preference of preschool children in the West Indies. *Journal of Cross-Cultural Psychology,* 26, 141-152.

Gopnik, A., & Astington, J. W. (1988). Children's understanding of representational change and its relation to the understanding of false belief and the appearance-reality distinction. *Child Development,* 59, 26-37.

Gray-Little, B., & Hafdahl, A. R. (2000). Factors influencing racial comparisons of self-esteem: A quantitative review. *Psychology Bulletin,* 126, 26-54.

Harter, S. (1999). *The construction of the self: A developmental perspective.* New York: Guilford Press.

Henriques, F. (1953). *Family and colour in Jamaica.* London: Eyre and Spottiswoode.

Hraba, J., & C. Grant. (1970). Black is beautiful. *Journal of Personality and Social Psychology.* 16, 398-402.

Jamaican Language Unit. (2005). *Language attitude survey of Jamaica.* University of the West Indies, Mona Campus. http://www.mona.uwi.edu/dllp/jlu/projects/Report%20for%20Language%20Attitude%20Survey%20of%20Jamaica.pdf

Jamaican Language Unit, (2006). *Language competence survey of Jamaica.* University of the West Indies, Mona Campus. http://www.mona.uwi.edu/ dllp/jlu/projects/Report%20for%20Language%20Attitude%20Survey%20of%20Jamaica.pdf

Judd, C., Park, B., Ryan, C. S., Bauer, M., & Kraus, S. (1995). Stereotypes and eth-nocentrism: Diverging interethnic perceptions of African American and White American youth. *Journal of Personality and Social Psychology.* 69, 460-481.

Kashima, Y., Kashima, E., Farsides, T., et al. (2004). Culture and context-sensitive self: The amount and meaning of context-sensitivity of phenomenal self differ across cultures. *Self and Identity.* 3, 125-141. Psychology Press. London: Taylor & Francis.

Katz, P. A. (1983). Developmental Foundations of Gender and Racial Attitudes. In R.L. Leahy (Ed.), *The child's construction of social inequality*, pp. 41-78. New York: Academic Press.

Knight, F. 1990. *The Caribbean: The genesis of a fragmented nationalism.* New York: Oxford University Press.

Kowalski, K., & Ya-Fen Lo. (2001). The influence of perceptual features, ethnic labels, and sociocultural information on the development of ethnic/racial/bias in young children. *Journal of Cross-Cultural Psychology*, 32(4), 444-445. Newbury, CA: Sage Publications.

Labov, W. (1966). *The social stratification of English in New York City.* Washington, D.C. Centre for Applied Linguistics.

———. (1972). *Language in the inner city: Studies in the Black English vernacular.* Oxford: Blackwell.

Lambert, W .E, Hodgson, R. C., et al. (1967). A social psychology of bilingualism. *Journal of Social Issues*, 23: 91-109.

Le Page, R. B., & Tabouret-Keller, A. (1985). *Acts of identity.* Cambridge: Cambridge University Press.

Marsh, H. W., & Shavelson, R. (1985). Self-concept: Its multifaceted, hierarchical structure. *Educational Psychologist*, 20, 107-123.

Meade, R. R. (2001). *Acquisition of Jamaican phonology.* Delft: De Systeem Dru.

Miller, E. (1975). Self evaluation among Jamaican high school girls. In C. Barrow & R. Reddock (Eds.), *Caribbean Sociology: Introductory readings.* 22, 407-426. Kingston: Ian Randle.

Mitchell, Robert W., & Neal, M. (2005). Children's understanding of their own and others' mental states. Part B. Understanding of others precedes self-understanding for some false beliefs. *British Journal of Developmental Psychology*, 23(2), 201-208.

Nettleford, R. M. (1970). *Mirror, mirror: Identity, race and protest in Jamaica.* Kingston: Collins & Sangster.

*New York Times.* (2007, January 4). Ma why did you make me black? (Retrieved January, 4, 2007). http://query.nytimes.com/gst/fullpage. html?res=9C0CE0DE163DF934A35752C0A966958260&sec=&spon=&page-wanted=1

Piaget, J. (1926). *The language and thought of the child.* New York: Harcourt Brace.

Pyszczynski, T. Greenberg, J., & La Prelle, J. (1985). Social comparisons after success and failure: Biased search for information consistent with a self-servicing conclusion. *Journal of Experimental Psychology.* 21,129-138.

Ramsey, P. (1987). Young children's thinking about ethnic differences. In J.S. Phinney & M.J. Rotheram (Eds.), *Children's ethnic socialization: Pluralism and development,* pp. 56-72. Newbury Park: Sage.

Richardson, M. F. (1992). *Identity in the Jamaican context.* Kingston: Faculty of Education University of the West Indies, Mona.

Rogers, C. R. (1951). *Client-centered therapy.* Boston: Houghton Mifflin.

Rosenberg, M. (1986). *Conceiving the self.* Malabar, FL: Robert E. Krieger Publishing Company.

Rosenthal, M. (1974). *The magic boxes: Pre-school children's attitudes toward black and standard English.* FL: Florida Reporter, Spring/Fall: 56ff.

Tannen, D. (1990, 2001). *You just don't understand.* NY: Harper Paperbacks

*Time Magazine Online.* (1987, Mar. 9). A crazy game of musical chairs. (Retrieved December 22, 2006). http://www.time.com/time/magazine/article/0,9171,963680,00.html

US Census Bureau. (2000). *Race.* (Retrieved January 1, 2007). http://quickfacts.census.gov/qfd/meta/long_68184.htm

USDA. Economic Research Service. (August 13, 2003). *Briefing Rooms. Race and ethnicity in rural America: Appendix.* (Retrieved January 1, 2007). http://www.ers.usda.gov/Briefing/RaceAndEthnic/appendix.htm

Williams, J. E., & Best, D. L. (1990). *Measuring sex stereotypes, A multination study.* CA: Newbury Park.

Wellman, H. M. (1990). *The child's theory of mind.* Cambridge, MA: MIT Press.

Wellman, H. M., Cross, D., & Watson, J. (2001). Meta-analysis of theory of mind development: The truth about false belief. *Child Development,* 72, 655-684.

Wimmer, H., & Permer, J., (1983). Beliefs about beliefs: Representation and constraining function of wrong beliefs in young children's understanding of deception. *Cognition,* 13, 103-128.

Yussen, S. (1985). (Ed.). *The growth of reflection in children.* Orlando: Orlando Academic Press.

# 21 Psychological Assessment

*Rosemarie Johnson & Tracey Coley*

## Introduction

Psychological assessment is the process by which a trained psychologist gains understanding of a patient so as to make informed decisions about that individual's life (Korchin, 1976). This understanding comes from the integration of data from many sources so that the patient can be understood in his or her context. The *Standards for Educational and Psychological Tests* (1999) provides guidelines for the scope of this context:

> Test scores ideally are interpreted in light of the available normative data, the psychometric properties of the test, the temporal stability of the constructs being measured, and the effect of moderator variables and demographic characteristics (e.g., gender, age, income, sexual orientation, sociocultural and language background, education, and other socio-economic variables) on test results.

Nevertheless, psychological assessment is sometimes confused with psychological testing. While psychological testing focuses on a score that is rarely used on its own, psychological assessment interprets scores in context (idiographic interpretation). Consequently, during an assessment, diagnosis in its broad application is both inevitable and necessary. However, nosological categories (DSM-IV-TR) are of limited value in a psychological assessment (Korchin, 1976). Instead, the task of the assessment practitioner is to describe a patient's intellectual, academic, and personality structure; his or her assets as well as failings; the demands on the patient; and his or her coping resources. This is, therefore, more a 'characterological diagnosis' rather than a 'symptomatic diagnosis' (Handler & Hilsenroth, 1998). Such a characterological diagnosis is critical from a psychologist's perspective because one needs to understand a patient before one can act on his or her behalf.

Psychological assessment in the Caribbean is also a major part of what psychologists do. However, it is also largely an 'imported' discipline that follows the Western tradition and paradigms in psychology (Cheung & Cheung, 2003; Hickling & Matthies, 2002). Additionally, most of the frequently used tests are developed and normed in the USA. This practice of applying 'foreign' assessment tools and constructs in the Caribbean culture assumes that these tests have cross-cultural validity and relevance with our population. Can this assumption be accepted? That is, are psychological tests measuring the same construct in our population as they do in the countries in which they were developed? Critics of testing in general are likely to say 'no' to their application, even when these tests are used in the countries in which they were developed. At the centre of this concern with the use of psychological tests is their application with ethnic minority groups (Sternberg, 2004; Johnson, 1992; Johnson, 1987).

In recent decades, ethnic minority groups in the USA have expressed strong dissatisfaction with the consequences of psychological testing (Marsella, 2003; Sam & Moreira, 2002). The major criticism has focused on two areas: greater denial of opportunity, and the underlying psychometric and clinical judgement issues that account for minority/non-minority test differences. Researchers and practitioners in the area of testing contend that to understand the meaning of test results, it is necessary to probe the theoretical, psychometric, and statistical underpinnings of the assessment procedure in question (Gopaul-McNicol & Brice-Baker, 1998; Groth-Marnat, 2003; Sattler, 2001). The central issue here is whether test scores reflect legitimate psychological differences or are a result of measurement error. Given the current equivocal results, there are researchers who believe that the jury is still out on what psychological tests really measure (Malgady, 1996). Consequently, it is still difficult to interpret what deficits are reflected in an individual's scores. Are they true deficits or are they an artefact resulting from the misapplication of inappropriate techniques? This uncertainty is not likely to disappear, because central to this position is the belief that many psychological tests developed and normed on samples of predominantly White subjects are of questionable validity for ethnic minorities (Malgady, 1996; Sattler, 2001)). Furthermore, because of distinctive Western values, beliefs, and expectations, at least some items and indicators on the tests must be interpreted differently for non-minority and non-Western individuals (Marsella, 2003). Given the above, it is no wonder then that the validity and reliability of assessment procedures have become the target of scrutiny. One way in which the profession of psychology has tried to address some of these ethnic minority and cultural issues, is to understand the impact of culture as a legitimate area of investigation. This has led to the development of Cross-Cultural Psychology as a discipline committed to exploring how cultural issues in training, research, and teaching should be addressed (APA, 1993).

As a result of these initiatives, there is increasing recognition of the fact that psychology cannot be understood outside of a cultural context (La Roche, 2005). This, in turn, has therefore focused attention on the impact of culture on how psychologists practise. The USA and the UK's psychological associations have instituted task forces to set out guidelines on multicultural issues in the practice of psychology. They have also broadened this to include research and training in psychology (APA, 2002). In addition, key ethical practices for addressing the non-Western application of tests are also provided by the International Testing Commission (ITC, 2001). These attempts to address the potential impact of culture on behaviour are critical because, since the inception of the discipline of psychology, there has been a need to understand human behaviour more fully. One major way through which this is done is through psychological assessment. Thus, the necessity of assessment to the practice of psychology is unquestionable.

Many disciplines in applied psychology utilize psychological testing and assessment, however, the focus of this chapter is on clinical and psycho-educational assessments, and not on organizational assessment. The goal of assessment is to understand an individual. Consequently, the focus ought not to be on a score; instead, a focus on what the score means in the context of what else is happening in a patient's life is critical. Moreover, when this approach is taken in assessment, some of the concerns about the appropriateness of 'foreign' tests are minimized. However, while trained psychologists understand this, individuals, agencies, and organizations outside of the discipline of psychology, sometimes insist on scores to make placement decisions. In such a situation, it is important that the assessment practitioner not go against what is considered and recommended as good practice in the cross-cultural application of tests. Moreover, a practitioner's ethical responsibility is to the patient, and any action that could be potentially harmful should be avoided. Consequently, it is necessary to educate such agencies, organizations, and individuals. As a compromise, some practitioners include scores as an appendix at the end of a report, once the test data have been interpreted in context.

## Psychological Assessment Data

There are several techniques available to the psychologist or psychometrician (a technician who administers and scores psychological tests) in the assessment process. The techniques, in turn, determine the way in which the information is gathered. There are four ways to gather data for a psychological assessment: ask the person; ask someone who knows the person; observe the person as he or she behaves naturally; and observe the person in the standardized testing situation (Sattler, 2001). When the individual is the source of the information, this requires an interview, which is the backbone of clinical assessment.

In the normal process of interviewing, the flow of statements and responses are relatively free, as the assessment practitioner follows the patient into areas that concern him or her. This mode of data gathering provides the practitioner with an opportunity to observe non-verbal behaviour and understand what is of most concern to the patient. In this way, any disparity between the patient's assertions and visible behaviour provides important information about personality trends. Notwithstanding this, there are still debates about the format that these interviews should take – structured versus semi-structured and unstructured (Aklin & Turner, 2006). Each format has its benefits and limitations and these need to be balanced with the other tests that are involved in the process.

Because the clinical interview is so critical in the diagnostic assessment process and cultural ethnic practices have been shown to influence the outcome, the practitioner needs to be vigilant. Specifically, the research on assessment interviews suggests that minority groups are consistently and disproportionately over-diagnosed with schizophrenia and under-diagnosed with affective disorders, compared to similar Caucasian patients (Sam & Moreira, 2002). In addition to over- and under-diagnos-ing, symptoms are also judged by clinicians to be more serious or more pathological with ethnic minority patients (Lopez, 1989). A similar phe-nomenon is observed with patients from disadvantaged backgrounds or in situations in which there are demographic differences between the practitioner and the patient. The influence of this diagnostic bias is also observed in the graduate psychology training programmes in the region. Often, students initially take extreme positions on issues of diagnosis. That is, they either over-diagnose or under-diagnose and this is often related to unexplored biases that can be difficult to address, as they are so entrenched.

In light of these trends, clinical interviewing therefore requires a com-plex set of skills. Included in this are a broad-based knowledge of psy-chopathology, proficiency in interpersonal communication, understand-ing of clinical phenomena and how these phenomena affect the person being interviewed, and the interview itself (Groth-Marnat, 2003). Additionally, cultural competence is a must, as ethnicity and culture play a role in how psychopathology is manifested or understood (Colin, 1996). Although there are considerable data to suggest that the 'core features' of major psychiatric disorders are universal (World Health Organization), ethnic and cultural groups sometimes experience and/or express psy-chopathology differently (Marsella, 2003), and may well exhibit many differences in secondary symptoms (Sam & Moreira, 2002). In the Caribbean, for example, one major challenge for practitioners is to sort out the nature of pathology when patients have strong cultural beliefs in spirits and demons. Confounding the issues even further is the coexis-tence of serious psychopathology and religiosity (Chambers, 2007).

It is also important for the psychologist to understand that barriers to accurate diagnosis of disadvantaged groups are created by communica-tion issues; social class; clinical judgement and bias; racism; and cultural mistrust, as well as paranoia (Hickling & Gibson, 2005; Jones & Korchin, 1982), While these issues are generally raised in the context of the USA, Caribbean practitioners cannot take it for granted that sharing a geo-graphic space with patients negates the concerns of culture or ethnicity.

Informants also provide data for an assessment. This individual should be a reasonably competent person and his or her role in the patient's life needs to be understood. While an informant provides added information, what is more critical is for the practitioner to understand the patient's problem from his or her vantage point. Additionally, there are issues with confidentiality that could arise, as well as the distortions that emerge from competing agendas.

Observation is yet another way that assessment information is obtained. While observing the patient as he behaves naturally is desirable, under most circumstances, this objective is unattainable. Notwithstanding this, observation is particularly important when assessing children. Finally, administering the standardized tests constitutes the next major aspect of psychological assessment. There are many and varied broad skills that are measured by these tests. They include, but are not limited to, cognitive/intellectual, behavioural, personality, neuropsychological, and organizational skills. In the standard testing situation, because of the uniformity of the administration and scoring procedures, there is the assumption that subjective bias is reduced.

## Orientations to Psychological Assessment

Psychological assessments are conducted for various reasons, which include the following: diagnosis; intervention, planning and outcome evaluation; informing legal and government decisions; and personal awareness, growth and action (Korchin, 1976). Given the many reasons for requesting assessments, the practitioner then needs to decide on what is to be assessed. This is guided by the referral question, that relates to one of the purposes for which psychological assessments are needed. Additionally, the assessment practitioner must initiate the process by clarifying the referral as much as possible because it guides the tests, inventories, and diagnostic procedures chosen.

While there is general agreement on the purpose of psychological assessment, there are conflicting orientations to the process. There are also debates that relate to the question: "Is behaviour better predicted by objective test scores that use predictive formulas, or is clinical judgement better able to integrate the data and better predict outcome?" The answers to these questions relate to the debates about clinical versus statistical prediction (Handler & Hilsenroth, 1998; Korchin, 1976; Malgady, 1996; Rushton & Jensen, 2005). Both approaches have served psychological assessment well. Statistical prediction, also referred to as the psychometric approach, focuses on differential, rather than personologic or dynamic psychology. In the psychometric tradition, the individual is compared with others along trait dimensions. Objectivity is sought, both in the acts required of the individual and those of the clinician. Interpretation of the test data also depends on comparisons between the individual's scores and well-developed norms. Judgement and inference are, therefore, minimized, both in test-taking and interpretation.

If the sole purpose of assessment were prediction, then the practitioner could be satisfied with the psychometric approach. However, a clinician's greater concern is describing and understanding the patient's character and problems (Korchin, 1976). Thus, in the clinical approach, the essential task of the practitioner is the synthesis of diverse, and sometimes fragmentary bits of information into a coherent picture of the individual. The psychologist has to fit the given facts together into a meaningful and useful conceptual scheme that accounts for the patient's thoughts, feelings and actions. In this multi-procedure, multi-level model of psychological assessment, the available raw data include the following: the clinician's first-hand observations, impressions, and empathic reactions; the reactions of others, as viewed by the patient and or reported to the clinician; the patient's self-description in interviews and tests, and the performance in test situations – both in terms of idiosyncratic responses and normative score or profile (Handler & Hilenroth, 1998). With all this information, the clinician must develop hypotheses that encompass and make sense of as much of the information as possible. This process is guided by formulated theory together with systematized knowledge and concepts, and arises inductively from the evidence in hand. Nevertheless, in spite of this multi-level approach, there are still sources for error in clinical interpretation that are worth mentioning. They include schematization, information overload, insufficient internal evidence for interpretation; over interpretation, insufficient external verification of interpretation, lack of individualization, lack of integration, over-pathologizing, and over- 'psychologizing' (James & Georgas, 2003; Sternberg, 2004; Sternberg & Kaufman, 1998). Additionally, another very important issue that needs to be considered as a psychologist contemplates an assessment is: who will have access to the test results and written reports? Other questions about how the results will be shared with the patient as with third parties also need to be considered.

# Interpreting Assessment Data

This process involves a continuous interplay of hypothesis-forming and hypothesis-testing acts, and goes toward formulating the best possible theory of the person. It proceeds by considering various, and sometimes conflicting, interpretive possibilities suggested by the data. Nevertheless, there is a general consensus regarding the process of interpreting psychological data (Korchin, 1976). That is, after the data are gathered and scored, preliminary hypotheses from careful review of the data are generated. This is the first stage in the interpretive process and involves generating initial hypotheses about the patient's functioning, based on a review of each discrete test score. The goal in this part of the process is to identify meaningful findings about the patient that are grounded in the results of the empirical literature, rather than developing a theoretically based explanation about the patient's presentation. At this stage of the process, all interpretive hypotheses should be entertained and none discarded, lest the practitioner dismiss a potentially meaningful finding. Additionally, in this initial stage of the interpretation, the process is data-driven rather than theory-driven (Sattler, 2001). Conceptually, it is also important to systematically review all interpretations because in that way it minimizes biased interpretation of the test data. That is, this approach of systematically reviewing all interpretations guards against confirmatory bias, which is a tendency for individuals to prematurely make decisions and then to maintain that conclusion without considering evidence contradicting one's initial impressions. When all possible hypotheses are reviewed, decisions are then made on which hypotheses to retain and which to discard. This is accomplished by systematically checking whether test data confirm or contradict initial impressions or other non-test data. Alternative interpretations also need to be deliberately formulated, even after initial hypotheses are formulated.

In the second stage of the interpretative process, the assessment practitioner identifies points of agreement and disagreement among initial interpretative findings in order to determine if preliminary hypotheses should be accepted, modified, or discarded. Generally speaking, a practitioner can have considerable confidence in the fact that a particular interpretation is correct, if it is confirmed by several pieces of data, especially if the same conclusion is suggested by each independent source.

Additionally, in the most ideal situation, all findings relate to specific hypotheses and mesh and agree. However, in practice, one should expect both agreement and disagreement among related test variables in nearly every case. As a result, it is not necessary to think that one must decide whether to discard the results of one test for another. Rather, test differences can be regarded as common occurrences to be resolved in a thoughtful, meaningful, and clinically useful manner.

At the integration stage of the interpretation, the assessment practitioner organizes, refines, and integrates hypotheses to describe psychological functioning as fully and completely as possible. It is important that discrete, independent signs and symptoms suggested by test scores should not be listed in a piecemeal manner. Instead, an in-depth, theoretically coherent description of the client's current psychological make-up, based on the integration of history, current clinical presentation, knowledge of psychopathology, human behaviour and development, as well as clinical theory, are needed so as to provide the context within which the data are analysed. Finally, even if the integration is achieved, awareness of one's mindset and biases still has important implications for this stage.

## Writing Psychological Assessment Reports

A report is the end product of the psychological assessment. It represents the clinician's efforts to integrate assessment data into a functional whole. It can be written in several ways, depending on the purpose for which the report is intended and the individual style and orientation of the practitioner. Nevertheless, regardless of the clinician's orientation and the purpose of the report, a general style to avoid is a 'shot-gun' report containing fragmented descriptions that are vague, stereotyped and over-inclusive (Korchin, 1976). Consequently, other approaches have been suggested when writing psychological reports. These include the *Case, Clinical,* and *Scientific* approaches (Groth-Marnat, 2003)

A *Case Approach* centres on the specific problems outlined by the referring person. It also reveals unique aspects of the patient and provides specific, accurate descriptions. These reports also use action oriented language rather than psychological abstractions. Such action oriented language links the person with specific behaviours and conveys a better understanding of the patient's active role in the testing situation. This approach also focuses on what differentiates one person from another. Consequently, it avoids discussions of what is average about the patient, but instead emphasizes what stands out and is unique. A *Clinical Approach* is another way of writing a report. This approach focuses on pathological dimensions or weaknesses of the person. Its strength is that it provides information about areas that require change, and alerts a potential practitioner to likely difficulties during the course of treatment. However, its weakness is that it is likely to give a distorted, unrealistic view of the patient – given its focus on pathology.

Yet another approach to writing reports is the *Scientific Approach*. This approach emphasizes normative comparisons and discusses the patient by addressing different, often isolated, segments of cognitive and personality functioning. Although claims of objectivity are made, this approach is criticized for violating the unity of personality. Notwithstanding this, regardless of the approach taken in writing the psychological report, it should be written with an awareness of the point of view of the intended reader. Furthermore, despite the approach, there is a current trend in psychological assessments to de-emphasize diagnosis and aetiology and emphasize current descriptions of persons that are tied to specific behaviour (Wierzbicki, 1999).

Another level to report writing is deciding how to present the interpretations that are made. There are several options that can be considered and they include using any of the following: the Hypothesis-Oriented Model; the Domain-Oriented Model; the Test Model; and the Topics Model (Groth-Marnat, 2003). With a Hypothesis-Oriented Model, the focus is primarily on answering specific questions asked by the referral source. This highly focused interpretative presentation is also well integrated and avoids extraneous variables. For example, with a referral question like "Does Marlon have brain damage?" all the interpretations based on the test data are directed toward answering whether this hypothesis is supported or not.

Domain-driven presentations, on the other hand, discuss patients in relation to specific topics, that is, cognitive abilities, interpersonal relationships, personality functioning. This approach is comprehensive and indicates a patient's strengths and weaknesses. While the referral question is still answered, it is addressed by responding to specific domains relating to it. In spite of its strengths, its weakness is its potential to provide too much information.

A report that presents test interpretations using the Test Model discusses each test separately. However, the emphasis on discrete tests can distract the reader, and tends to reduce the patient to a series of numbers. This approach has also been criticized as a reflection of a failure to integrate the test data and point to weaknesses in the practitioner's ability to understand what the test data mean (Groth-Marnat, 2003). Moreover, only half of all possible interpretations listed in an interpretative manual or computer narrative are actually true for a particular patient. Consequently, this approach can lead to misunderstanding of the patient. Furthermore, in practice, it is the clinician who determines which interpretation applies and which does not.

Finally, the Topics Model uses topics that serve as a conceptual tool to give the report form and direction. The three most common topics that are usually covered are cognitive functioning, emotional functioning, and interpersonal relations. Additional topics might also include interpersonal strengths, vocational attitude, suicidal potential, defences, areas of conflict, behaviours under stress, impulsiveness, or sexuality.

As mentioned previously, a practitioner still decides what to include in the report. The challenge, therefore, becomes what to include. The rule of thumb is that the report should provide information that will be most helpful in responding to the referral and that will meet the needs of the patient (Sattler, 2001). Thus, information should be included only if it serves to increase the understanding of the patient. Other things that should be considered when deciding what to include are: the needs of the referral setting; the background of the reader; the purpose of the testing; the relative usefulness of the information; and whether the information describes the unique characteristics of the person.

Another factor that needs to be considered is the terminology that is used. The most frequent readers of psychological reports include teachers, counsellors, administrators, judges, attorneys, psychiatrists, non-psychiatric physicians, and social workers. While these individuals are professionals in their own right, many do not have the necessary background in psychology to interpret technical psychological jargon accurately. Moreover, even psychologists with different theoretical persuasions may also misinterpret some of the terms. Therefore, the use of basic English allows the clinician, through the report, to communicate with and influence a wide audience. Moreover, clear basic English is more descriptive of the individual's uniqueness, whereas technical terms tend to deal with generalities. Furthermore, the clear basic use of language suggests that the examiner has more in-depth comprehension of the information and can communicate this comprehension in a precise, concrete manner.

In concluding the psychological report, focus should not only be on pathology, but it should also address psychological strengths compared with relative weaknesses. Additionally, in presenting the conclusions, it is essential that there is some indication of the relative degree of certainty that the clinician has. This is particularly pertinent when the clinician is attempting to predict a person's behaviour. Moreover, if a statement is speculation, it should be clear to the reader that this is so. Vague and ambiguously worded sentences that place incorrect or misleading emphasis on the patient's behaviour can also be problematic and lead to incorrect conclusions, for example, "The patient lacks social skills," versus "The patient's social skills are poorly developed." Thus, it is the responsibility of the clinician not to present misleading conclusions. Furthermore, this responsibility cannot be transferred to a test, because decisions made about a person should never be in the hands of a test (Standards, 1999). Neither should the clinician hide behind and transfer responsibility to the test (Groth-Marnat, 2003). For example, "test results indicate . . ."is commonly seen in many psychological reports.

## Assessment Practices in the Caribbean

Psychological assessments are routinely conducted in the Caribbean, especially in Jamaica, Trinidad and Tobago, and Barbados. These include intellectual, personality, behavioural, neuropsychological, and organizational assessments. An informal survey conducted among a group of assessment practitioners in Jamaica showed that their training ranged from the Certificate to the Doctoral level, with most of the practitioners having Master's level training in educational or clinical psychology. At the Doctoral level, most of the practitioners have PhDs in Clinical Psychology.

Because psychological assessment requires a psychometric approach, standardized test administration procedures are followed in the Caribbean. However, there may be instances when non-standard administration procedures are necessary (Edwards, 1990). While these are practical solutions to some of the challenges that arise with using tests developed outside the region, the issues of validity and reliability are still germane. Thus, in attempting to sort out these psychometric issues, it is not enough to ask the question: Are tests valid or reliable? A more useful approach to addressing this issue is questioning: "Valid for whom? Under what circumstances? In whose hands? To what end?" Moreover, attempts to answer these questions provide useful insights into the utility and limitations of any assessment tool, regardless of where it is applied. In contrast, generic questions about whether a test is valid or reliable contribute little, and encourage needless arguments.

What also helps to guide Caribbean test practitioners are the ethical guidelines (APA, 2002). Generally speaking, as a helping professional, the assessment practitioner's core ethical responsibility can be summed up as not causing harm to the patient (Foxcroft, 2002). It is, therefore, the responsibility of the practitioner to ensure that he or she uses tests appropriately and professionally. This involves the practitioner's ensuring that he or she has the necessary competencies spanning the entire process of testing, that is, a sound knowledge of psychometrics and testing; an understanding of the broader social, cultural, political, and legal context in which testing is used; and the manner in which such factors might affect test results, their interpretation, and the use to which the results are put (Camara, Nathan & Puente, 1998).

The foregoing speaks to issues of professional competence which are critical, as the professional bodies that regulate practice in countries like the USA and UK are not as functional in the region. The problem of professional competence in assessment and protection of the public is exacerbated in the Caribbean by the wide discrepancy in the assessment competence of practitioners. For instance, in Jamaica, it is common to hear complaints of confusion from individuals and organizations when they receive reports from some practitioners. Often, these reports simply focus on scores and utilize the 'shot-gun' style of report writing. One government organization in Jamaica that has expressed concerns is the Special Education Unit of the Ministry of Education Youth and Culture. They are concerned on two levels – the astronomical sums parents are charged for reports that provide limited information, and the inability to verify the competence of individuals performing such assessments.

It is also common to hear complaints from consumers about misdiagnosis and misapplication of psychometric tests. Take the case of John who was assessed when he was seven years old because of concerns that he was not learning as he should. He was assessed by a practitioner who informed John's parents that their son was mentally retarded, based on his scores on an intelligence test. Because of this, John's parents removed him from regular school and placed him at the School of Hope that teaches children with significant cognitive deficits. His mother also reportedly adjusted her expectations for her son and so did not require much from him. Intuitively, John's parents did not think that their son was mentally retarded, although they went along with the recommendation of the practitioner. Fours years later, at the suggestion of a teacher, John was re-evaluated by a different assessment practitioner. This assessment revealed that John was not mentally retarded but had a learning disability. Understandably, John's mother was most distressed and experienced many conflicting emotions about what had happened to her son, because she trusted a professional who was supposed to understand psychological assessment. This disservice to John and his family underscores the importance of practitioners having appropriate training and competence, and if they do not, they should seek consultation and collaboration with appropriately qualified professionals in the field. Moreover, the lack of regulation in the practice of psychology within the region puts the public more at risk, because there are often no consequences to these egregious violations.

The issues that involve cultural competence are also relevant for practitioners in the region. According to Foxcroft (2002),

> The provision of professional services to persons from diverse backgrounds by persons not competent in understanding and providing professional services shall be considered unethical . . . it shall equally be unethical to deny such persons professional services because the present staff is inadequately prepared . . . it shall be the obligation of all service agencies to employ competent persons to provide continuing education for the present staff to meet the service needs of the culturally diverse population it serves.

In order to perform an assessment in a valid, ethical, and fair way within a multicultural context, a practitioner needs to acquire knowledge of the test-taker in relation to his or her cultural, family, linguistic, educational and socio-economic background and heritage. In fact, Foxcroft (2002) cautions the assessment practitioner that such knowledge should be acquired before the decision is made to test, so that appropriate tests might be chosen. He goes further to say that "a practitioner should never presume he or she knows best how to assess some aspect of human or cognitive functioning, or how to interpret test performance without first having immersed self in the lived world of the test-taker." As with psychotherapy, the assessment practitioner also needs to be aware of his or her prejudices and preconceived ideas about certain community or cultural groups and ensure that these do not incorrectly colour the picture of the individual. For example, many children in inner-city communities are expected not to know certain types of information. So, if a client is initially unsuccessful with a test response, a practitioner might immediately assume that it is about a lack of knowledge and not seek to investigate other possible explanations.

Caribbean test practitioners also need to be mindful of the fact that a test is designed in a certain context (society, culture) for a specific purpose, and the way in which performance is interpreted is linked to behavioural criteria, norms, or cut-off scores formulated in the context where the test was developed. Additionally, test scores should be accurate and informative in the context in which the test is applied, especially when reporting scores to non-professional audiences. As such, when scores are reported, it is important for the psychologists to also include confounding factors, such as unequal educational opportunity, language difficulties, and poverty. As long as psychological tests continue to be applied routinely in the Caribbean without research to inform practice, the possibility of systematic bias in the interpretation and application of the results continues to be a challenge (Hart, 2006; Johnson, 2005; Minor & Alexander, 2004). Despite the limited research that exists on the validity of psychological tests used in the Caribbean, the results have so far been promising and point to some degree of cross-cultural applicability.

Another qualitative way to approach the issue of construct equivalence in relation to the psychological tests used in the Caribbean, is to examine the approach to a task or compare how an individual performs on certain tasks, as compared to others. Reports for Jamaican practitioners on the Wechsler Intelligence Scales reveal some interesting trends. It has been noted in one study that Jamaican children, across different social classes, do not generally perform as well on the Block Design subtest, as compared to other tests that assess perceptual organizational skills (Minor & Alexander, 2004). This apparent discrepancy in performance that is noted in the study and by practitioners, raises several questions. Is

WAIS - Ofent

this subtest measuring another skill? Or are there other cultural social explanations. Jamaican practitioners who have worked abroad often comment that, in general, Jamaican test-takers deal with issues of time in the testing situation differently from their overseas counterparts. Furthermore, many Jamaican patients who are assessed using Wechsler's Intelligence Tests achieve higher scores when time limits are removed than when one tests with the limits. This suggests that many test-takers may possess many of the skills assessed, and are able to improve their performance by up to 50 per cent, but they often do not demonstrate this because of the time restrictions. Similarly, many individuals do not change the pace at which they complete tasks, even with such instructions as "work as quickly as you can" are given. Additionally, in Jamaica, students in the public school system are encouraged to be methodical in the processing and solving of mathematical problems. This approach also uses a point system in which they are rewarded for having the correct strategy, even if the answer is wrong. This strategy encourages a mental approach where thoughtfulness and care are reinforced. It also implies a greater emphasis on understanding the inner complexities of a particular situation or problem. It is, therefore, not surprising that Jamaican students tend to methodically work through problems to find the solutions, even when they are advised that they must offer responses as quickly and accurately as possible. As a result, they are likely to lose bonus points on timed subtests such as Arithmetic and Symbol Search.

Other strategies for testing the limits would allow the examinee the opportunity to revisit particular areas within the tests on which the assessment practitioner feels the examinee could have performed better – given more flexible conditions. For example, in addition to receiving more time on a task, examinees can be provided with pen and paper to work through problems on the Arithmetic subtest. These allowances facilitate a greater understanding of the individual's capabilities and allow the assessment practitioner to note any changes or lack thereof in the examinee's performance as a result of this manipulation. Moreover, for examinees tested from areas where a dialect is the dominant language of expression and comprehension, using the flexibility offered by testing the limits to integrate the dialect into the instructions, has increased the Jamaican examinees' comfort and understanding of the test material and improved performance overall.

Because Standard English is not the first language of many Jamaican children, different responses often occur on verbal tasks on standardized tests. Additionally, even when there is not a language issue, cultural appropriateness of test items also need to be considered. For example, for an item that assesses verbal abstract reasoning, "How are rubber and paper alike?", many Jamaican children say, "Things you use in school." Within the Jamaican context, 'rubber' is another word for 'eraser'. Although this is just one example, the way in which words are used in different cultures affects interpretations to questions, and hence overall performance. Similarly, most Caribbean children who have not travelled to the USA would not know what a 'dime' is. Consider as an example the case of J.L., a 17-year-old male student attending a secondary school in Kingston, Jamaica. A psychological assessment was requested to determine J.L.'s level of cognitive functioning and areas of strength and weakness. In comparison to the standardization sample, J.L. appeared to perform particularly poorly on the Information subtest of the WAIS III. On close examination of the questions in this subtest, it was noted that J.L., like many other Jamaican students, especially those from the lower economic class, whose exposure to US history is limited to commercials and cartoons, was unable to answer questions that required knowledge of an American history curriculum. The Information subtest is intended to measure an individual's range and breadth of knowledge, as well as long-term memory. Given J.L.'s lack of exposure to the information being assessed, the testing of the limits technique was used at the end of the session to provide more information about his fund of knowledge and memory capabilities. He was asked questions such as: "Who was the first Prime Minister of Jamaica?" "When did slavery in the British Caribbean end?" and "Who is the Prime Minister of Barbados?" His performance on questions of this nature was much better than on the unaltered subtest.

Similarly, trying to administer a paper-based verbal written test could be inappropriate for members of a deep rural community who only know how to communicate orally. Relatedly, self -report questionnaires and self-reflection tasks are also routinely used in psychological assessments and research in the Caribbean. However, researchers and practitioners need to be mindful of the fact that Western and non-Western people differ in terms of how such tasks are interpreted (Sam & Moreira, 2002; Marsella, 2003). A consideration proposed in the literature is that Western

Individualism vs Collectivism

societies like the USA emphasize individualism, whereas in many non-Western societies collectivism is stressed (Colin, 1996). The implications of this are that the focus on individualism prepares Westerners to introspect (reflect), to be aware of personal needs, and to strive for personal growth and development. In contrast, the non-Westernised individual, because of the focus on collectivism, is less practised in self-focusing. Consequently, a self-report questionnaire or an introspection task will not necessarily reflect what is going on internally for individuals from collectively based societies (Boyd, 1982). Research using the Beck Depression Inventory with Jamaicans (Chambers, 2007; Hart & Johnson, 2006) and African Americans (Emory & Deiter, personal communication, September 10, 2005) indicates that, when completing the questionnaire, most respondents do not report symptoms that fit the criteria for clinical distress. However, when many of these people were spoken to one-on-one, they were more likely to mention symptoms that were consistent with depression.

While the research that examines issues of validity and reliability in testing using Caribbean samples is still too limited (Hart, 2006; Johnson, 2005; Minor & Alexander, 2004), it is important for assessment practitioners to know that the few studies that have been done support the validity of the tests with Jamaicans. Moreover, anecdotal reports from assessment practitioners also support the findings from the limited research. The implications of this is that assessment practitioners, when applying psychological tests cross-culturally, need to think beyond the standard administration, and understand those factors that may impact on a Caribbean individual's performance, and so make the necessary adjustments. That is, testing of the limits should be routine in cross-cultural assessment. Moreover, notwithstanding these cultural differences, the use of tests in the hands of a skilled and competently trained practitioner provides invaluable information that would not otherwise be available for making decisions about the examinee's life. Foxcroft (2002) also suggests that creativity, ingenuity, and knowledge of behavioural criteria associated with a construct in a specific culture are required when adapting test content or test items. Furthermore, the process of adapting test items should not be undertaken independently. Instead, it should be a collaborative effort, as local cultural experts, linguists, and anthropologists can provide valuable information to guide the process of modification. More importantly, the modified content, instructions, and items should be carefully piloted, and refined, if necessary, before the modified test is used.

Another approach in applying standardized tests cross-culturally is also recommended by the International Testing Commission. It involves comparing the factor structures of the test in the two cultures. If there is no evidence of factor structure equivalence and/or there is qualitative evidence from other sources (e.g., focus groups with psychologists) that the way the construct is defined or described in the two cultures differs in some ways, consideration could be given to modifying the test (International Test Commission Guidelines for Test Adaptation, 2003). Hart (2006) examined the factor structure of the Rorschach, using a sample of 450 Jamaicans. Her results suggested four factors: Processing Effort, Ideation, Interpersonal Behaviour, and Perceptual Accuracy that explained 66 percent of the variance. The Rorschach has been shown to have six factors when used with US samples, with the Affect and Self Perception factors not emerging for the Jamaican sample. Do these findings suggest that the Rorschach does not assess personality functioning in the Jamaican sample? That does not seem to be the case. In the Hart study, the variable selection process of including only those variables that were normally distributed contributed to the finding. Specifically, many of the variables that were excluded from the analysis (i.e. Sum T, AdjD, EB, Pure C, and M) traditionally cluster to form the two factors that did not emerge for this sample. Further, the fact that Pure C and Sum T had positively skewed distributions for the Jamaican sample was probably descriptive of what was taking place. That is, the findings suggested that the Jamaican population sample had difficulties modulating emotions (Pure C) and experienced high levels of emotional loss that had not been appropriately addressed (Sum T). These explanations seem plausible, given the degree of acting out and violence in the Jamaican society. Other findings supportive of the validity of the Rorschach with the population were also seen in the finding where individuals who reported sexual abuse in their history were more preoccupied with sexual content and had more morbid bodily concerns, as compared to those who did not report abuse in their history.

# Implications for the Teaching and Supervision of Prospective Caribbean Psychologists and Psychometricians

Because testing is going to be applied cross-culturally, it is important that Caribbean assessment practitioners understand mainstream psychometric issues, as well as the influence of culture on diagnosis and performance on standardized tests. This begins with the appropriate training, experience, and demonstrated competence. Given that the need for psychological assessment will only continue to increase because of the challenges that Caribbean people face, the demand for professionals with competencies in assessment will also increase. Those who develop training programmes thus have a responsibility not only to prepare individuals to meet this need, but also need to engage in the research to guide their practice. The developers could also benefit from looking at established programmes that have trained psychologists for decades with a view of adopting some of those strategies that have cross-cultural applicability, in particular, the educational requirements for independent practice.

## REFERENCES

Alexander, M., & Minor, S. C. (2003). Intelligence as a predictor of achievement. Unpublished Master's thesis, University of the West Indies, Kingston, Jamaica

American Educational Research Association, American Psychological Association & National Council of Measurement in Education. (1999). _Standards for Educational and Psychological Tests._

American Psychological Association (2002). _Guidelines on multicultural education, training, research, practice, and organizational change for psychologists. Approved as APA Policy by the APA Council of Representatives._

Chambers, S. (2007). The relationship between depression, religiosity, and irrational beliefs among a sample of Jamaican churchgoers. Unpublished master's thesis. University of the West Indies, Kingston, Jamaica.

Cheung, F. M., & Cheung, S. F. (2003). Measuring personality and values across cultures. Imported versus indigenous measures. In W. J. Lonner, D. L. Dinnel, S. A. Hayes, & D. N. Sattler, (Eds.), _Online readings in psychology and culture_ (Unit 6, Chapter 5), (http://www.wwu.edu/~culture), Centre for Cross-Cultural Research, Western Washington University, Belligham, Washington, USA.

Colin, L. (1996). _Race, culture, and counselling._ Bristol, PA: Open University Press.

Edwards, D. (1990). Developmental assessment for achievement in the school age population. *Proceedings of the 1990 Cross-Campus Conference on Education* (pp. 269-273). Kingston: Faculty of Education, University of the West Indies, Mona.

Foxcroft, C. D. (2002). Ethical issues related to psychological testing in Africa: What I have learned (so far). In W. J. Lonner, D. L. Dinnel, S. A. Hayes, & D. N. Sattler (Eds.), *Online readings in psychology and culture* (Unit 5, Chapter 4), (http://www.wwu.edu/~culture), Belligham, Washington, USA: Centre for Cross-Cultural Research, Western Washington University. Retrieved 10/30/2006.

Gopaul-McNicol, S. (1993). *Working with West Indian families.* New York: Guilford Press.

Gopaul-McNicol, S., & Brice-Baker, J. (1998). *Cross-cultural practice: Assessment, treatment and planning.* New York: John Wiley & Sons, Inc.

Groth-Marnat, G. (2003). *Handbook of psychological assessment (Fourth Ed).* New York: John Wiley & Son.

Handler, L., & Hilsenroth, M. J. (1998). *Teaching and learning personality assessment.* New Jersey: Lawrence Erlbaum Associates, Publishers.

Hart, J. (2006). Does the Rorschach Comprehensive System assess personality functioning in a sample of Jamaicans? Unpublished Master's thesis. University of the West Indies, Mona, Jamaica.

Hart, J., & Johnson, R. A. (2006). Degree of perfectionism and depression among a sample of undergraduate Jamaican students. Manuscript submitted for publication.

Hickling, F. H., & Gibson, R. C. (2005). Philosophy and epistemology of Caribbean psychiatry. In F. Hickling & E. Sorel (Eds.), *Images of psychiatry: The Caribbean* (pp. 75-108). Kingston: Department of Community Health and Psychiatry, University of the West Indies, Mona.

Hickling, F. H., & Matthies, B. K. (2002). The establishment of a clinical psychological post-graduate programme at the University of the West Indies. *Caribbean Journal of Education,* Vol 25 (1), 25-36.

International Test Commission Guidelines for Test Adaptation. http://www.intestcom.org/itc_projects.htm. Retrieved 11/6/2006.

Jacques, G. (2006). Some obstacles ahead for meeting the guidelines for test translation, and potential solutions. Keynote address at the 5th ITC Conference, July 6-8, 2006. Catholic University of Louvain, Belgium. www.interestcom.org/keynotesb.htm. Retrieved 6/11/06.

James, E., & Georgas, L. W. (2003). *Culture and children's intelligence: Cross-cultural analysis of the WISC-III.* New York: Elsevier.

Jang, K. L., McCrae, R. R., Angleitner, A., Riemann, R., & Livesley, W. J. (1998). Heritability of facet-level traits in a cross-cultural twin sample: Support for a hierarchical model of personality. *Journal of Personality and Social Psychology,* 74 (6), 1556-1565.

Johnson, R. A. (2004). Stimulus pull in Rorschach inkblots. *Caribbean Journal of Psychology.* 1 (1), 1-11.

———. (1992). Validity of Exner's Comprehensive System and Card Analysis as approaches to interpreting the Rorschach. PhD. Dissertation, Howard University, 1990. _Dissertation Abstracts International_, 52, P5055.

Johnson, R. A. (1987). The relationship between, intelligence, creativity, and academic achievement among a sample of black children. Unpublished master's thesis. Howard University, District of Columbia, USA.

Jones, E. E., & Thorne, A. (1987). Rediscovery of the subject: Intercultural approaches to clinical assessment. _Journal of Consulting and Clinical Psychology_, 35 (4), 488-495.

Korchin, S. J. (1976). _Modern clinical psychology: Principles of intervention in the clinic and community._ New York:.Basic Books.

La Roche, M. J. (2005). The cultural context and the psychotherapeutic process: Toward a culturally sensitive psychotherapy. _Journal of Psychotherapy Integration_, 15 (2), 169-185.

Malgrady, R. G. (1996). The question of cultural bias in assessment and diagnosis of ethnic minority clients: Lets reject the null hypothesis. _Professional Psychology, Research and Practice_, 27 (1), 73-77.

Marsella, A. J. (2003). Cultural aspects of depressive experience and disorders. In W. J. Lonner, D. L. Dinnel, S. A. Hayes, & D. N. Sattler, (Eds.), _Online readings in psychology and culture_ (Unit 9, Chapter 4), (http://www.wwu.edu/ ~culture), Belligham, Washington, USA: Centre for Cross-Cultural Research, Western Washington University.

Rushton, J. P., & Jensen, A. R. (2005). Thirty years of research on race differences in cognitive ability. _Psychology, Public Policy, and Law._ 11 (2), 235-294.

Saklofske, D. H., Gorsuch, R. L., Weiss, L. G., & Patterson, C. A. (2005). General ability index for the WAIS-III: Canadian norms. _Canadian Journal of Behavioural Science_, 37 (1), 44-48.

Sam, D. L., & Moreira, V. (2002). The mutual embeddedness of culture and mental illness. In W. J. Lonner, D. L. Dinnel, Hayes, S. A. & Sattler, D. N. (Eds.), _Online readings in psychology and culture_ (Unit 9, Chapter 1), (http://www.wwu.edu/~culture), Belligham, Washington, USA: Centre for Cross-Cultural Research, Western Washington University.

Sattler, J. (2001). _Assessment of children: Cognitive applications (Fourth Edition)._ La Mesa, California: Jerome Sattler Publishers, Inc.

Sternberg, R. J. (2004). Culture and intelligence. _American Psychologist_, 59 (5), 325-338.

Sternberg, R. J., & Kaufman. J. C. (1998). Human abilities. _Annual Review of Psychology_, 49, http://www.questia.com/PM.qst?a=o&se=gglsc&d=5001362792&cer=deny. Retrieved 11/6/2006.

Watkins, M. W. (2006). Orthogonal higher structure of the Wechsler Intelligence Scale for Children-Fourth Edition. _Psychological Assessment_, 18 (1), 123-125.

Wierzbicki, M. (1999). _Introduction to clinical psychology: Scientific foundations to clinical practice._ Boston: Allyn and Bacon.

# 22 Forensic Psychology in the Caribbean Context

## Lester O. Shields & Franklin Ottey

Forensic psychology is the application of psychological theories and methods to legal issues. It is the interaction of psychology with the law. Any request for a psychological appraisal of persons in any legal matter falls in the domain of forensic psychology. The judicial system requires the expert opinion of a psychologist on a person's capacity to make decisions, so the forensic psychologist appears as an expert witness in court to present such evaluation. The evaluation of a person by a psychologist in a legal procedure is not, however, limited to court trials. Persons already in the custody of the judicial system, such as those incarcerated or those who are wards of the state, may be evaluated for change of status in the system. Pure research on psychology and criminal matters, even by a psychologist who has no physical contact with the legal system, falls in the ambit of forensic psychology.

A study of forensic psychology in the Caribbean begins with a history of the development of mental health laws and procedures. The structure of the legal system, the court procedures governing expert witnesses, and knowledge of relevant legal terms are indispensable information for those involved in forensic psychology. A walk-through of the processing of a forensic patient will give the reader an understanding of the practice, bearing in mind that ethical considerations are critical. Finally, the format of a forensic report will be helpful for those getting started in the field. An umbrella term used for a person evaluated by a forensic psychologist for any legal proceedings is 'forensic patient' (Carroll, Lyall & Forrester, 2004).

## Brief History of the Development of Forensic Psychology in the Caribbean

Development of Caribbean laws pertaining to mental health pre-dated the independence of the countries of the region. Pre-independence laws were similar to the laws of European countries (Hickling & Maharajh, 2005).

In 19th-century European countries and their colonies, the accepted practice for persons who had mental illnesses that rendered them socially dysfunctional was compulsory detention (1873 Lunatic Asylum Law). In those of her colonies where precedent had been set to develop laws independent of Britain, efforts were made to humanize the Lunatic Law. Even those efforts by modern standards may seem callous. In Jamaica, in an attempt to modernize the treatment of the mentally disturbed, the Mental Hospital Law, enacted in 1930, gave the power of arrest "without a warrant" to the police of a "person . . . wandering at large . . . of unsound mind . . . [and] dangerous to continue wandering at large." The primary concern of the Law was to protect the public from the person. The second step of the new method of intervention was to detain the person at the police station to allow for an examination by a medical doctor as prescribed by Section 17 of the Law. This intervention was called Second Schedule. If the medical doctor deemed it prudent to hospitalize the individual, recognition of illness above the signature of a Justice of the Peace was required. The recognition, called a First Schedule was stating, in essence, that "it would be better for such a person [to be] detained in the Lunatic Asylum" (Hickling & Maharajh, 2005). There was no provision in the law for psychiatric assessment or treatment.

The UK's 1959 Mental Health Act targeted the inhumane treatment that had continued in mental institutions. Hickling and Maharajh (2005) described the situation at one Jamaican institution: loss of contact with the outside world; enforced idleness; bossiness of staff; loss of personal friends and possessions; poor ward atmosphere; withdrawal; and dependency. The 1959 Act retained the compulsory detention of the mentally disturbed (Hickling & Maharajh, 2005).

In the 1974 Amendment to the Mental Hospital Law, psychiatric personnel replaced the police as the first examiner of the mentally ill. The Amendment made provision for alternative placement other than a mental asylum, including community psychiatric centres. In the Amendment it became a punishable offence for a family member to resist the intervention of a mental health official (p. 56). Hickling and Maharajh reported that their informal research indicated that compulsory detention fell to 20 % of mentally ill persons examined (p. 57).

Mental health laws in the Caribbean can be divided into pre- and post-1960 (Moss, 1999). The countries with mental health laws older than 1960 are Grenada (1895), St. Lucia (1895), Guyana (1930), Belize (1953), Anguila (1956), Montserrat (1956), St. Kitts-Nevis (1956), Antigua and Barbuda (1957), and Turks and Caicos (1959). An equal number of Caribbean countries have enacted mental health laws since 1960: Bahamas (1969), Trinidad and Tobago (1975), The Cayman Islands (1979), British Virgin Islands (1985), Dominica (1987), St. Vincent and the Grenadines (1989), Barbados (1989) and Jamaica (1998).

Despite several changes in government over the past 30 years, continuity of public policy and fiscal support has allowed ongoing development of the islands' community mental health services (Hickling, 1994). There are indications from conversations with those in mental health work in the Caribbean that the Jamaican Act set a standard even where laws of the land do not pertain. The act broadens beyond the 1959 Amendment the locations that can be described as psychiatric facilities (II.4.1) to (a) the whole or any part of a building, house or other place, with any yard, garden, grounds or premises; (b) any part of a general hospital; (c) the whole or any part of a nursing home registered under the Nursing Homes Registration Act as a mental nursing home; (d) the whole or any part of a clinic; or (e) the whole or any part of a rehabilitation centre. The broadening of locations for psychiatric facilities opens the door for psychologists to interact further with the legal apparatus in providing aftercare service for persons found with an illness of the mind. "What happens to people diagnosed as having a psychopathic disorder may depend much more upon what services are available locally" (Carson, 2000).

The 1998 Act specified the actions of the officer of law. Section 15 of the Law, Power of Constable, makes a distinction between a person who is "wandering at large, in such manner or under such circumstances as to indicate that he is mentally disordered" (II.15.1) and a mentally disordered person who commits an offence (II.15.2). In the case of the former, "the constable may without warrant take such person in charge and forthwith accompany him to a psychiatric facility for treatment or forthwith arrange for him to be conveyed with all reasonable care and despatch to that facility. Where there is an offence, the constable may charge that person for the offence and bring him before a Resident Magistrate at the earliest opportunity."

The power to intervene under previous Acts was the sole right of an officer of the law. That legal power was extended to medical officers with special training; Mental Health Officers (II.16.1); or Prescribed Person (public health nurse or approved social worker (II.6.2.b). The 1998 Mental Health Act is not easily acceptable to a psychologist as there is no mention of a psychologist. A reading of Part I, 2(6) seems to indicate a provision for a psychologist to be registered as a mental health officer: "mental health officer" means: (a) a person registered as a nurse pursuant to section 9 of the Nurses and Midwives Act; and (6) any other person, who has successfully completed a course of study in mental health approved by the Minister responsible for health."

Ironically, it was an Act not specific to mental health that recognized the role of the forensic psychologist in the judicial system. With the Judicature (Rules of Court) Act 2002, the presence of the forensic psychologist in the legal system was formalized. As with previous relevant laws, no mention of the title psychologist is made. The psychologist appears in the legal system as an "expert witness." The law states: (a) "Expert witness" is a reference to an expert who has been instructed to prepare or give evidence for the purpose of court proceedings (2); (b) Expert evidence must be restricted to that which is reasonably required to resolve the proceedings justly (32.2); and (c) this duty overrides any obligations to the person by whom [the expert witness] is instructed or paid (32.3.2).

In summary, the provisions of the Mental Health Act are wider than what pertains to forensic psychology. It is important for the forensic psychologist operating within the bounds of the legal systems in the Caribbean to know the development of the laws pertaining to mental health, as this allows him or her to be conversant with officers of the law. Further, it permits the psychologist to engage clients in a more meaningful manner when matters of the law pertain.

## The Expert Witness

A forensic evaluation may be requested for any of the judicial branches. The Anglophone Caribbean has four levels of courts: The Resident Magistrate, the Supreme Court, the Court of Appeal, and the Judicial Committee of the Privy Council. After a criminal charge has been brought against a person, the director of Public Prosecutions may enter or direct nolle prosequi to be entered (The Criminal Justice –Administration- Act, 1973, 1.4). Most legal cases go first to the lowest court, the Resident Magistrate, where a determination is made whether there is enough evidence to go to trial. Serious crimes – those against the person – with enough evidence are sent to the next level. Figure 1 gives the levels of court system in one Caribbean country, Jamaica. With the exception of Guyana, the Judicial Council of the Privy Council is the final court of appeal (Dina, 2007).

*Figure 1: Structure of the Jamaican court system*

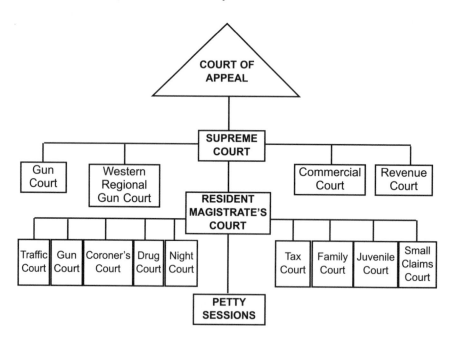

The forensic psychologist can give the evaluation, as expert witness, at the Resident Magistrate's (RM) Court, which has no jury. The role of the expert witness is to help the magistrate determine if, at the time of the crime, the accused had an illness of mind (mental disorder that is prone to recur) and so is not fit to plead. To be fit to plead, an accused must show that the charges are understood, that counsel (attorney-at-law) can be instructed, be able to challenge the witnesses (and jurors in some instances), and follow court proceedings. If the evidence is sufficient that the accused did commit the crime but that there is an illness of mind, the court judgment could be guilty, but insane ("a special verdict to the effect that the accused was guilty of the act or omission charged against him, but was insane as aforesaid at the time when he did the act or made the omission," Criminal Justice (Administration) Act, Jamaica, 1973, 25.2). Unfit to plead does not dismiss a case against an accused when the evidence is clear. The person is incarcerated until fit to plead ("the Court before whom the trial has taken place shall order the accused to be kept in custody as a criminal lunatic," (ibid.).

The law is specific in what is required of the forensic psychologist who gives expert witness (The Jamaican Judicature Rules of Court Act, 2002, Sec. 324):

1. Expert evidence presented to the court must be, and should be seen to be, the independent product of the expert witness uninfluenced as to form or content by the demands of the litigation;

2. An expert witness must provide independent assistance to the court by way of objective unbiased opinion in relation to matters within the expert witness' expertise;

3. An expert witness must state the facts or assumptions upon which his or her opinion is based. The expert witness must not omit to consider material facts which could detract from his or her concluded view;

4. An expert witness must state if a particular matter or issue falls outside his or her expertise;

5. Where the opinion of an expert witness is not properly researched, then this must be stated with an indication that the opinion is no more than a provisional one;

6. Where the expert witness cannot assert that his or her report contains the truth, the whole truth and nothing but the truth

without some qualification that qualification must be stated in the report;

7. Where after service or reports an expert witness changes his or her opinion on a material matter, such change of view must be communicated to all parties.

## RESIDENT MAGISTRATE'S COURTS

In Jamaica mentally disordered accused persons usually enter the justice system at the level of the Resident Magistrate's (RM) Court in the various parishes. When they appear before the Magistrate a decision is usually made as to whether they should be referred for mental health assessment. This decision is usually made because of the appearance and behaviour of the accused, e.g. looking very dishevelled or laughing and talking to himself, or the circumstances of the offence, e.g. stealing without making any effort to conceal the offence. The decision may also be made because the accused is reported to have been behaving in an odd fashion or is known to have a previous psychiatric history as reported by the local police, relatives, etc.

The accused is then taken by the police to the nearest psychiatric clinic for examination by a mental health professional, usually a psychiatrist. The decision to be made is whether or not the patient is suffering from a psychiatric disorder and if he is, whether or not he is fit to stand trial. Usually if he is suffering from a psychotic disorder (often Schizophrenia) he is started on treatment and a recommendation made for further treatment. If the offence is a minor one and the accused is not very disturbed and has family support a recommendation may also be made for him to be released from custody to continue out-patient treatment. Subsequent examinations would then be done to see whether his condition improves sufficiently for him to stand trial. Of course there will be instances when because he suffers from a severe, chronic psychosis or mental retardation, that he will remain unfit to stand trial and this will have to be indicated by the psychiatrist. The brief psychiatric report is given to the police to be taken to the Resident Magistrate's Court and the psychiatrist is not usually asked to appear.

When the offence is a minor one – e.g. simple or praedial larceny, simple assault or destruction of property – then the case will end at the level of the RM Court. For more serious offences, however, such as murder, manslaughter, arson and rape the RM Court is used as the venue for a preliminary enquiry where depositions are taken from various witnesses and a determination made as to whether a case has been sufficiently made for referral to the Supreme/Circuit Court.

## SUPREME/CIRCUIT COURTS

The Supreme Court of Jamaica is based in the capital city, Kingston, and its sittings in the various parishes are called Circuit Courts.

At the Supreme Court level the issue of fitness to plead arises. If there is any indication that the accused is suffering from a mental disorder (such indication usually arising from the depositions taken at the preliminary enquiry), then a psychiatric examination is requested. This may be done by the attorney-at-law but, in practice, is usually requested by the office of The Director of Public Prosecutions, as most accused persons cannot afford private representation. The mental health professional routinely then requests, and is given a copy of, the depositions from the preliminary enquiry before conducting the examination. Even if the accused person is suffering from a psychiatric disorder or some degree of mental retardation he would still be considered fit to plead if he is assessed as being capable of the following:

- understanding the nature of the charge
- understanding the difference between a plea of guilty or not guilty
- challenging jurors
- instructing counsel
- following the evidence in court.

If the accused is assessed as being unfit to plead, then a recommendation that he receives psychiatric treatment can be made and this is usually done at the institution where he is remanded in custody. Subsequent re-examinations are then usually requested.

# Issues Specific to Persons Accused of Murder

Murder is the only offence in which the issue of diminished responsibility arises. Therefore the request for mental health examination is both to determine the accused's fitness to plead and also what was likely to have been his mental state at the time the offence was allegedly committed. The information contained in the depositions together with any other available relevant information is useful in giving an opinion on the latter issue.

If the accused is unfit to plead and remains so after a period of treatment and subsequent re-examinations, then the Court may decide to have a trial at which the issue will be whether the accused is under disability and therefore unfit to plead. A jury is empanelled and usually the mental health professional is the only person called to give evidence as an expert witness. The opinion of the professional is invariably accepted and the accused judged to be unfit to plead. The Court then orders that he be detained at the Governor General's pleasure and a directive given that he receive psychiatric treatment. After subsequent re-examinations the case will be brought up again and he will be determined either still unfit to plead or fit to plead. In the past a number of these cases have got "lost in the system" and an effort is now being made to make sure that these accused be regularly re-examined by the psychologists and psychiatrists in the prisons.

If the murder accused is fit to plead but in the opinion of the mental health professional there was likely to have been substantial impairment of his mental state at the time that the offence was allegedly committed, then the accused has the option of pleading not guilty to murder but guilty to manslaughter on the grounds of diminished responsibility. This is the decision usually taken by the accused and his attorney if he did commit the offence. The mental health professional is called to give evidence as an expert witness and would indicate that in his opinion it is likely that the accused was suffering from a mental disorder (usually a psychotic disorder or significant mental subnormality) which would have substantially impaired his mental state at the time of the offence. The judge hears the evidence but a jury is not empanelled for this. The prosecuting attorney does not usually object to the plea, which is accepted, and the judge then passes an appropriate sentence usually with a direction that the accused receive psychiatric treatment, if this was recommended by the psychiatrist. Occasionally, the accused refuses to plead guilty to manslaughter and the case then goes to trial before a jury. If he is then found to be guilty, the judge may direct that the verdict be guilty but insane.

## Civil Matters

The psychiatrist or psychologist may be asked to do assessments in various civil matters such as divorce and child custody cases, testamentary capacity and guardianship. Child custody and divorce cases have been enhanced in the Caribbean by a reciprocal legal arrangement for foreign nationals who are in person liable to be ordered to maintain another (_see_ Appendix A). One of the main reasons for referral of clients, however, is where litigation has arisen following accidents or injuries to individuals from whatever cause. Here the attorney representing the injured party usually makes the referral for psychiatric or psychological examination of the client if it is felt that some impairment, such as brain injury, has arisen as a result of the injury. Often other medical specialists have also been consulted and their reports are usually made available to the psychiatrist or psychologist before the examination.

If some disability is found on examination, then an assessment of the severity of the disability is usually expected as this facilitates the settlement of these cases. Psychological assessment and testing is particularly useful where there has been some cognitive impairment and often both psychiatric examination and psychological assessment are requested. This report is directed to The Supreme Court of Jamaica although it is sent to the attorney who made the referral and it is done along guidelines outlined in the Civil Procedures Rules. Some of these cases are settled out of Court but if and when they do go to trial the psychiatrist or psychologist will be expected to appear as an expert witness.

## Ethical Considerations

The nature of the profession of forensic psychology and the reality of the forensic psychologist (being a part of the Caribbean culture) require that ethical guidelines be established and practised. This is especially relevant to countries in the Caribbean with high levels of crimes such as Jamaica (Harriott, 2003) and where they are mostly unsolved (National Crime Stop, 2004). In the evaluation of an accused who presents as a psychopath, the forensic psychologist has to be very professional but "tough-minded and exacting" (McWilliams, 1994). Forensic assessment is an exercise in minimizing uncertainty (Carroll, Lyall & Forrester, 2004). Assessment goes hand in hand with making recommendations.

Treatment options, even for psychopaths, are available (Davidson & Tyrer, 1996). That knowledge has to be balanced with a "duty to protect the wider community (overriding forensic patient) autonomy when necessary" (Carroll, Lyall & Forrester, 2004). The tension between the high ethical standards of psychologists to protect the well-being of their clients and the requirement of the legal system to have ownership of the information gathered by a psychologist will remain. It is the obligation of the forensic psychologist to inform the forensic patient of the limitations of confidentiality. Information that may be gathered, which is not related to the legal matter at hand – especially in light of the psychologist's skill in obtaining information – must be held in confidentiality.

All parties affected by a forensic assessment should be informed of the boundaries of the psychologist's competence. It is common procedure to inform the Court of one's education, length of experience, and qualifications for doing the assessment (Committee on Ethical Guidelines for Forensic Psychologists, 1991).

The experience of many expert witnesses, including psychologists, is that their testimony carries much weight in the determination of a case. There is a respect among professionals, in the legal and mental health arenas, for their expertise. It may weigh heavily on the forensic psychologist, knowing that his expert testimony impacts on a judge's decision to incarcerate or not. Further, 22 countries in the Caribbean (eleven English-speaking) fall in the top fifty of the list of Prison Population Rates per 100,000 of the national population (Prison Population Rates, 2006). Jamaica comes in at 67 (*see* Appendix B). The forensic psychologist has to apply the skills of assessment with maximum objectivity in order that justice be done.

## CAPITAL OFFENCES

One situation where ethics arise is in the matter of capital punishment. In the Commonwealth Caribbean, laws allow capital punishment. The forensic psychologist reserves the right to decline an evaluation of a client on a capital offence that may result in a death sentence. There is much evidence that many defendants in capital offence cases do not have adequate assistance of legal counsel (UN Human Rights System, 2000).

## PREVALENCE OF MENTAL DISORDERS

One's belief about the prevalence of a mental disorder can affect the diagnosis that is given after investigating a presenting problem. The forensic psychologist has to inform him or herself of the epidemiology of mental disorders in the Caribbean. It may be surprising to read, as reported by the World Health Organization (2001), that in Jamaica "mental health visits account for 2% of total public health centre visits, up from 1.4% in 1989. Of the 7,067 patients seen by the Community Mental Health Services, the most common diagnoses were schizophrenia (49.6%), depression (19.6%), substance abuse (9.6%), neurosis (7.0%), and organic psychosis (4.7%). Statistics inform the psychologist in making a diagnosis and recommendation.

## KNOWLEDGE OF LEGAL TERMS

Definitions of terms are critical. The forensic psychologist must acquire the legal meanings of terms used in psychology. At first glance, the definition of mental disorder as given in the Mental Health Act (1997) seems identical to how a psychologist may define it: (a) a substantial disorder of thought, perception, orientation or memory which grossly impairs a person's behaviour, judgement, capacity to recognise reality or ability to meet the demands of life which renders a person to be of unsound mind, or (b) mental retardation, where such a condition is associated with abnormally aggressive or seriously irresponsible behaviour. On closer examination it becomes obvious that legally, a mental disorder renders a person socially dysfunctional. For the psychologist, the use of 'mental disorder' is wider. Though many disorders in the DSM specify that a feature of the disorder must cause clinically significant distress in social or occupational functioning, this is not so for all mental disorders. Therefore, care must be taken in using the term when appearing as an expert witness. A distinction must be made between those psychological disorders that are more likely to produce social dysfunction and those less likely to do so.

Similarly, an essential legal term, _mens rea_ (guilty mind), is not one that is usually familiar to the psychologist. Law distinguishes between a criminal act or behaviour (_actus reus_) and criminal intent or attitude (_mens rea_). A person's _mens rea_ at the time of a crime is critical in determining criminal responsibility (Carson, 2000). A little knowledge of court proceedings quickly reveals that much of the debate that occurs is due to the difficulty in determining *mens rea*. This is the ideal juncture for a psychologist to be introduced to help the court. The psychologist must bear in mind that a forensic evaluation determines the mental status only at the time of the forensic interview and not at the time of the crime (Shapiro, 1991). It is the jurisdiction of the court to determine continuum in mental status. Without doubt, criminal attitude is an area that needs more research in psychology. "Psychological insights, and ways of conceptualizing 'mental attitudes' towards criminal conduct, need to be developed and offered to the legal system" (Carson, 2000). Until then, the expert opinion concerning an accused *mens rea* for the forensic psychologist is limited to the time of the forensic evaluation.

## The Forensic Report

A forensic evaluation helps the judicial system at many levels. The evaluation of a person in legal custody is to assist the court in determining the person's competency to receive a judgment concerning guilt, as well as the type of rehabilitation that is appropriate. Evaluation of non-custodial cases such as divorce or child protection helps in the determination of danger to others or with placement. The full scope of a forensic evaluation is under utilized; selection of juries, correctional officers, wardens in state homes, and police officers are just of few of the possible uses of a forensic evaluation. The evaluation considers the person's cognitive functioning, memory capacity and reasoning ability. The assessment can involve standardized psychological instruments and an extensive psychological interview. A multiaxial diagnosis may be given. The written and signed report of the expert witness may be submitted in court by the attorney without the appearance of the psychologist (Evidence Act of Jamaica, IV,50,1).

The format for a written forensic report is not uniform. The psychologist is advised to use a format that best represents the forensic evaluation. Standard psychological reports all include: Name; Date of Birth; Sex; Date of Report; and Name of Examiner. A forensic evaluation may also incorporate the person's medical history, previous psychological evaluations, information from the person's family members or friends, and criminal record (the Index). The reality in the Caribbean is that not all information pertinent to making an assessment may be available. The primary method of assessment is an extensive psychological interview, a process similar to that in the UK. In North America there is a preference for the inclusion of standardized instruments. That malingering may be more prevalent in a forensic population does not necessarily dictate the use of instruments to aid the forensic evaluation. There is evidence that the identification of malingering requires a battery of tests and 24-hour observation of the client (Heinze, 2003). In other words, no one instrument is robust. An interview by itself stands an equal chance of recognizing malingering as much as any one instrument.

The information gathered from a clinical interview may be apportioned in the following manner (Rogers, 1986):

**Referral source** The Referral Source in forensic psychology is most commonly an attorney-at-law.

**Description of Evaluation** The Description of Evaluation is of those instruments administered. Usually, the evaluation is an extensive interview.

**Defendant's behaviour at time of interview** The Defendant's Behaviour is a description at the time of the interview and an attempt to tie it into the history events surrounding the crime in question.

**Clinical Description** The Clinical Description is a psychological profile of the patient including a mental status examination.

**Consultations** The Consultation is a report of the findings of all other material provided by the attorney or the court.

**Clinical Conclusions** The Clinical Conclusions attempt a diagnosis of the patient with explanation.

**Opinion** The Opinion is an expert attempt to answer the referral question of the court.

Two formats have emerged from a survey of forensic reports generated in the Caribbean for an evaluation of a prisoner. The first has the following headings:

Last known address

Registration number

Institution

Charge

Reason for evaluation

Source information

Accounts of events

Family history

Psychiatric history

Medical history

Personal history

Mental status examination

Impression

Conclusion and recommendations

The second adds:
Referral source

Sources of information

Interview information

Progress while detained

Employment history

Relationship history

Events before offence

With no set standard for the report, the forensic psychologist in the Caribbean has the added burden of choosing a format for presentation in doing a forensic evaluation. It may be best to allow the format to be decided by the circumstances of the forensic patient and the volume of information gathered.

## Summary

A study of forensic psychology in North America and the U.K. may find many similarities with the Caribbean. The Caribbean presents circumstances that require specific knowledge of the region. Foremost are the laws of the Caribbean that pertain to mental health. Knowledge of these is indispensable. Further, criminal law in the Caribbean is specific as to what is a prosecutable crime. There will remain a tension between the ethical standards of the psychologist, especially pertaining to confidentiality and what information the courts deem privileged. The weight of giving an expert recommendation in legal matters is heavier for the forensic psychologist as treatment in the legal system is not the same as in psychotherapy.

## Appendix 1

Countries with Reciprocal Arrangements to Maintain Order
[Maintenance Orders (Facilities for Enforcement) Act 1987 (Act 8 of 1987)]

1. Antigua & Barbuda
2. The Bahamas
3. Belize
4. Cayman Islands
5. Cook Islands
6. Dominica
7. Grenada
8. Balwick of Guernsey
9. Guyana
10. Isles of Man
11. Jersey
12. Montserrat
13. New Zealand
14. Niue
15. St. Christopher (St. Kitts) & Nevis
16. St. Lucia
17. St. Vincent & the Grenadines
18. Trinidad & Tobago
19. United Kingdom
20. British Virgin Islands

## Appendix 2

Prison Population Rates per 100,000 of National Population

| | | |
|---|---|---|
| 1 | United States of America | 751 |
| 2 | Russian Federation | 627 |
| 3 | St. Kitts and Nevis | 588 |
| 4 | Virgin Islands (USA) | 549 |
| 5 | Cuba | c.531 |
| 6 | Turkmenistan | c.489 |
| 7 | Palau | 478 |

| 8  | Virgin Islands (United Kingdom)       | 464    |
|----|---------------------------------------|--------|
| 9  | Bahamas                               | 462    |
| 10 | Belize                                | 460    |
| 11 | Georgia                               | 428    |
| 12 | Belarus                               | 426    |
| 13 | Anguilla (United Kingdom)             | 401    |
| 14 | Bermuda (United Kingdom)              | 394    |
| 15 | Cayman Islands (United Kingdom)       | 391    |
| 16 | Barbados                              | 379    |
| 17 | Kazakhstan                            | 378    |
| 18 | Grenada                               | 372    |
| 19 | French Guiana/Guyane (France)         | 365    |
| 20 | American Samoa (USA)                  | 364    |
| 20 | Netherlands Antilles (Netherlands)    | 364    |
| 22 | Puerto Rico (USA)                     | 356    |
| 22 | Suriname                              | 356    |
| 24 | Dominica                              | 348    |
| 24 | South Africa                          | 348    |
| 26 | Maldives                              | 343    |
| 27 | Panama                                | 337    |
| 28 | Botswana                              | 329    |
| 29 | Ukraine                               | 328    |
| 30 | Aruba (Netherlands)                   | 324    |
| 31 | St. Vincent and the Grenadines        | 312    |
| 32 | Israel                                | 305    |
| 33 | St. Lucia                             | 303    |
| 34 | Antigua and Barbuda                   | 299    |
| 35 | Trinidad and Tobago                   | 288    |
| 35 | United Arab Emirates                  | 288    |
| 37 | Latvia                                | 287    |
| 38 | Guam (USA)                            | 286    |
| 39 | Chile                                 | 279    |
| 40 | Namibia                               | 267    |
| 41 | Singapore                             | 263    |
| 41 | Tunisia                               | c.263  |
| 43 | Guyana                                | 260    |
| 44 | Estonia                               | 259    |

| 45 | Thailand | 253 |
| 46 | Swaziland | 247 |
| 47 | Moldova (Republic of) | 246 |
| 48 | Mongolia | 244 |
| 49 | Lithuania | 239 |
| 50 | Poland | 233 |
| 51 | Taiwan | 228 |
| 52 | Iran | 222 |
| 53 | Brazil | 219 |
| 54 | Greenland (Denmark) | 216 |
| 55 | Azerbaijan | 210 |
| 56 | Libya | 209 |
| 57 | Jersey (United Kingdom) | 198 |
| 57 | Mexico | 198 |
| 59 | New Zealand | 197 |
| 60 | Gabon | 196 |
| 61 | Uruguay | 193 |
| 62 | Martinique (France) | 191 |
| 63 | Czech Republic | 186 |
| 64 | Uzbekistan | 184 |
| 65 | Costa Rica | 181 |
| 66 | Cape Verde (Cabo Verde) | 178 |
| 67 | El Salvador | 174 |
| 67 | Jamaica | |

## REFERENCES

Carroll, A., Lyall, M. & Forrester, A. (2004). Clinical hopes and public fears in forensic mental health. *Journal of Forensic Psychiatry & Psychology, 15* (3), 407-425.

Carson, D. (2000). The legal context: Obstacle or opportunity? In In J. McGuire, T. Mason & A. O'Kane (Eds.), *Behaviour, crime and legal processes: A guide for forensic practitioners*, (pp. 19-37). Wiley & Sons.

Committee on Ethical Guidelines for Forensic Psychologists. (1991). Specialty Guidelines for Forensic Psychologists. *Law and Human Behaviour, 15* (6), 655-665.

Davidson, K., & Tyrer, P. (1996). Cognitive therapy for antisocial and borderline personality disorders: Single case study series. *British Journal of Clinical Psychology. 35*(3), 413-429.

Dina, Y. (2007). _Guide to Caribbean Law Research_. Retrieved from http://www.nyu-lawglobal.org/globalex/caribbean1.htm.

Harriott, A. (2003). Editor's Overview. In A. Harriott (Ed.), _Understanding crime in Jamaica: New challenges for public policy_. Jamaica: UWI Press. ix-xx.

Heinze, M. (2003). Developing sensitivity to distortion: Utility of psychological tests in differentiating malingering and psychopathology in criminal defendants. _Journal of Forensic Psychiatry & Psychology_, 14 (1), 151–177.

Hickling, F. (1994). Community Psychiatry and Deinstitutionalization in Jamaica. _Hosp Community Psychiatry_. 45, 1122-1126.

Hickling, F., & Maharajh, H. (2005). Mental health legislation. In F. W. Hickling & E. Sorel (Eds.), _Images of psychiatry: The Caribbean_ (pp.43-74). Kingston: Department of Community Health and Psychiatry, University of the West Indies.

Jamaican Judicature Rules of Court Act, 2002, Sec. 324

McWilliams, N. (1994). _Psychoanalytic diagnosis: Understanding personality structure in clinical process_. New York: Guilford Press.

Mental Health Act of 1997, Jamaica. Part 1 Sec 2. (1999).

Moss, S. (1999). _Psychiatric Care and Mental Health Legislation in the English-speaking Caribbean Countries_. Technical Report Series. Public Policy and Health Program, Health and Human Development Division.

Prison Population Rates. (2006). International Centre for Prison Studies. King's College London. Retrieved on January 13, 2007 from http://www.prisonstudies.org/

Shapiro, D. (1991). _Forensic psychological assessment: An integrative approach_. Boston: Allyn & Bacon.

Supreme Court of Jamaica. (2002). _The judicature (Rules of court) act: The civil procedure rules_. Kingston, Jamaica: Caribbean Law Publ.

United Nations Human Rights System. (2000). _For the records: Jamaica: Special Rapporteur on Extrajudicial, summary or arbitrary executions_ (E/CN.4/ 2000/3). Retrieved February 6, 2006, from http://www.hri.ca/fortherecord2000/vol4/jamaicatr.htm#top.

# 23 Media Psychology in the Caribbean

*Frederick W. Hickling, Eulalee Thompson,*
*Sophia Chandler, & Brigitte K. Matthies*

The attraction media holds for psychology practitioners in the Caribbean, as in many other parts of the world, is inevitable. As with many other disciplines which promote education, the potential to reach a much larger audience, using cutting edge technology, together with media effects, has proved irresistible for psychology and psychiatry professionals. More than being simply an exotic location for weddings, the Caribbean offers a diversity and distinctiveness with which it stamps its peoples, cultures and products. As the media typically reflect the ideas, dreams, realities and concerns of their creators, it is no surprise that among these isles the internationally recognized association between media and psychology has given rise to a unique marriage, and the birth of a product that bears the stamp of distinctiveness associated with the Caribbean. Stuart Fischoff, in his seminal essay on the definition and purview of media psychology concludes: "To study media psychology is, in the final scene, to study how humans represent themselves to themselves through lenses, through harmonics and through spectra and how humans send these self-images across time and space in a fierce proclamation of existence" (Fischoff, 2005, p. 21).

## Definition of Media Psychology

Several definitions of media psychology have been suggested. Fischoff writes: "Media psychology employs the theories, concepts and methods of psychology to study the impact of the mass media on individuals, groups, and cultures" (p. 2). He, however, argues that this definition is too broad to be very useful, and that it ignores the very dynamic and reciprocal nature of media and people or consumers. More specifically, he suggests that media psychology is "concerned with the inter- and intra-personal psychological dimensions underlying the impact and use of any medium of communication, irrespective of the nature of the subject matter being communicated" (p. 2). Furthermore, he concludes that since media is a means of communication that allows us to circumvent traditional face-to-face interaction, media psychology attempts to examine the social and psychological parameters of communication between entities that is facilitated by a conduit other than simple air (Fischoff, 2005).

Practitioners in the field of media psychology are known to utilize their expertise in a variety of ways. They teach courses in the field, do research on media issues and appear in the print and electronic media as interviewees and columnists. In the Jamaican context, media psychologists are radio counsellors, commentators, talk-show hosts, co-hosts, expert guests, panelists, regular newspaper columnists and run advice columns in daily newspapers. Media psychologists also advise various media organizations (e.g. movie studios, independent filmmakers, television networks, screenwriters, producers and directors), on the nature of human behaviour and how such information might be most accurately portrayed in the media, with careful attention to the media's need to strike a balance between accuracy and values on the one hand and "entertainment" on the other.

## Historical Development

In the USA media psychology was formally recognized as a specialty field within professional psychology in the year 1986. It was at this time that the American Psychological Association (APA) created division 46, the media psychology division, in response to the burgeoning involvement of professional psychologists in media activity. The online journal, _Media Psychology_, was launched in January 1996.

Media psychology has its inspirational roots in social psychology, particularly the early work of psychologist Hugo Munsterberg more than 90 years ago. The British Psychological Society also demonstrated its recognition of media psychology as a specialized field by developing ethical guidelines for the operation of its members who were involved in media activity (Canter & Breakwell, 1986). Media Psychologists both appear via the mass media, and also research or write about the impact of the media on society. Those who appear on television or radio tend to be those who speak easily and succinctly and can explain complex social events and psychological issues without the use of professional jargon (Fischoff, 1995).

As in the case of the development of media psychology within North America (Boushoutsos et al., 1986), the roots of Caribbean media psychology can be traced to the culturally well-entrenched call-in programme. The phenomenon of the call-in programme is well rooted in the rich oral history of the Caribbean islands and the willingness of its people to articulate their views on political, religious and social issues, as well as on any other topic which may not be otherwise categorized. It was for this reason that the radio call-in programme became a kind of "catalyst for this burgeoning blend of media and psychology" (Boushoutsos et al., 1986). The use of radio in mental healthcare education and its influence on community mental health has become popular in recent years. Cave (1980), in an article in *Time* magazine, reported the establishment of the first radio psychiatry programme in the USA in California in 1976, while Rice (1981) commented on the growing popularity of these programmes in the USA and elsewhere. Ruben (1986) described the establishment of a similar programme on NBC Radio in New York in 1982. He outlined the role of a radio psychiatrist on such a programme; indicated the types of callers to his programme; the nature of their problems; and the ways in which he dealt with the issues which they raised. He concluded that his programme had served first to help to market psychiatry and enhance its stature in the public's consciousness. Second, he felt it served to engage the public in early primary prevention, and to initiate an approach to such primary prevention by using education to influence community mental health. Some authors have been critical of radio psychiatry talk-shows (Larson, 1981) and both the American Psychiatric Association (1977) and the American Psychological Association (1981) have published ethical guidelines for psychiatrists and psychologists working with the communications media. However, most will agree on the positive psycho-educational effect of such radio call-in programmes.

The establishment of the mass media as a daily staple in the lives of Caribbean people has provided a way in which the average individual can benefit from psychological help, even if it is not so termed. Although the radio call-in programmes were established primarily to provide a social voice to the working and middle classes, they soon began to address issues that were distinctly psychological in nature. In Barbados, Patrick 'P. G.' Gollop once hosted an on-air radio programme entitled _Heartbreak Hotel_. Participants called in to the programme to share relationship woes and in turn, expected a listening ear and to be given some sense of direction as they acknowledged their dilemmas. The host was able to assist his callers, and those who listened in, by helping them to deal, even if only superficially, with emotional and self-image issues. Although the host of that programme, and several others across the region, are not trained psychologists or counselors, they fill the apparent need for pseudo-psychological service. Clearly, however, there are many dangers involved in the provision of such a service by individuals not specifically trained to do so.

Much of the early relationship of mental health with the media involved psychiatry. Jamaican psychiatrist, Frederick Hickling, initiated a weekly 45-minute call-in radio programme in October 1975 that had a lifespan of ten years (Hickling, 1992) on the Jamaica Broadcasting Corporation. The radio psychiatrist received telephone calls from persons islandwide, and answered questions raised in letters by writers who did not have access to the telephone. The radio psychiatrist advised as to the possible causes of the callers' problems, discussed social, psychological and psychiatric themes raised by the callers, and referred these callers to agencies or therapists where they could obtain help. Since that time there have been a number of call-in programmes in Jamaica hosted by psychologists, psychiatrists and physicians, which have focused on the provision of mental health care to the general public. These have included programmes by psychologists Ruth Doorbar and Peter Weller, psychiatrists Earle Wright and Aggrey Irons, and physicians Mary Sloper and Anthony Vendryes, on the wide variety of radio stations in the country. In fact, the Jamaican radio public has been afforded a rich diet of health education and promotional programmes on topics ranging from condom use to stress management.

Television was another vehicle for the development of media

psychology in the Caribbean. The increasing popularity of talk shows like *Oprah* and *Dr. Phil* have paved the way for local talk-show programming. In recent years, such talk shows have included the thought- and opinion-provoking *Head On* in Barbados, which began in the early 1990s and covered topics like domestic abuse, sexual abuse and homosexuality. In addition to viewing the hosts and the various guests as they discussed topics, which in certain episodes had a heavy psychological tone, viewers also had the opportunity to call in and pose questions, make comments or even seek advice. On several occasions 'expert' guests were invited to participate in the discussions and these included psychologists who were often invited to provide a 'knowledgeable perspective'.

The concept of on-line psychotherapy or telemedicine within the Caribbean is yet to gain popularity, but it should be noted that on-line services could be a possible solution to one of the major concerns that Caribbean people have about such therapy. In large measure, because of the small size of many of our island communities, it is often challenging to source help from persons who are not friends or in some way connected to our families. This then affects the nature of the therapeutic relationship and leads to concerns about confidentiality and ethical violations related to Multiple Relationships and Conflict of Interests (APA, 2002). When the rich oral tradition and the common belief that our neighbor's business is our business is considered, we get a clear picture of why the issue of potential breaches of confidentiality are of such importance.

By using on-line therapy, face-to-face interaction can be avoided, thereby maintaining security and anonymity. Strictly confidential on-line environments with anonymous aliases can achieve this, with payments for services rendered using a platform that transmits over a secure connection like the Secure Sockets Layer protocol for credit card transmission.

Some of the difficulties with offering psychological services in the Caribbean through this medium would include the availability of computer access and credit facilities to the persons who may need such services. While the world-wide web expands and the global access by persons, including those in the Caribbean continues to grow, there is still the reality that not everyone has access to a computer, nor are credit cards dispensed freely to all those who may claim the need to acquire one. There are also important issues related to literacy, including computer literacy. Another consideration is that, to date, there is no known on-line psychological therapy service being offered by a Caribbean-based psychological team. What this means is that if on-line therapy were accessed, it would be provided by companies established outside of the Caribbean, in the USA and the UK. The provision of links such as cybercounseling.com by websites like that of the Berkeley Institute of Bermuda, demonstrates the budding awareness of internet psychological services. Provision of psychotherapy by non-Caribbean providers raises issues related to communication and language (many Caribbean islanders speak a local dialect), and the cultural relevance of the services provided.

With this seemingly new opportunity for service provision through the Internet also comes a great weight of responsibility, particularly within a field which is relatively new in the region and for which there are limited appropriately trained individuals. The gate keepers within 'helping' professions like psychology need to seek to ensure that the profession remains just that: a helping profession. While individual practitioners are expected to police themselves with the ethical code under which they trained, each island is encouraged to start a professional organization and draft codes of ethics – a process that has already begun in Jamaica and Trinidad.

Currently, most of the responsibility for finding qualified on-line help falls squarely on the consumer as there are numerous websites that purport to offer solutions to problems and answers to questions. However, it is difficult to verify the credentials of the individuals who offer these services. As such, there is limited control over any potential damage that might ensue as a result of receiving pseudo-psychological advice from an unqualified individual. The responsibility, therefore, lies with the individual who may be at his or her wits' end, to make a determination as to whether the site and its authors appear to be credible, licensed practitioners or pseudo-psychologists who may or may not offer 'good' advice. In fact, during the 2001 APA Convention, the Division 46 Telehealth Task Force addressed the issue of media hype related to the practice of psychotherapy on-line. The Task Force paid particular attention to the issue of non-empirically based claims for the efficacy of approaches, such as e-mail for psychotherapy, with unknown and unseen patients worldwide. The Task Force unanimously and resoundingly called for research before such services were offered to the public by psychologists. In addition, a model for practising psychotherapy within the standard of care for most communities, using the Internet and through videoconferencing was presented by Dr. Maheu, the Symposium chair (The Amplifier, 2001; Maheu, 2001). Interestingly, while the 90s saw a proliferation of new companies competing to provide psychological services through the Internet, almost all of these companies have ceased to exist, and no others have appeared to take their place (Benson, 2003). More recently, telemedicine has been focusing on the populations that need it most – those that otherwise lack access to health care – and developing technologies that will have a major impact on health care when the appropriate infrastructure is in place. In the USA, state and federal agencies, hospitals and other major health care providers, and not private companies, are taking the lead (Benson, 2003).

With regard to the print media, within the Caribbean psychology has been presented mainly through advice columns. These include the advice columns and even commentaries that may be found in daily papers or even those that appear in magazines like *SHE Caribbean*. In most instances the authors of these columns are not trained mental health practitioners but rather, are persons seeking to use a combination of common sense, experience and information gathered from their own reading and research to provide guidance for their distressed audience. Columns like 'Dear Christine' in the *Barbados Daily Nation*, and 'Dear Marguerite' in the Trinidadian *Sunday Express* are not written by trained psychologists, but often do have content that is heavily psychological.

In other islands like St. Lucia, the format of these columns is not question and answer but, rather, a simple commentary. The column, 'Women's World with Urleeza' in the *St. Lucia Star* provides opinions and, to some extent, advice on a wide range of issues. In the March 14, 2007 edition of the column the writer said "I am no expert, and I do not have a PhD in Relationship Sciences". Although it might be said that a clear disclaimer was made, in many instances such disclaimers are not given, and even when they are, many persons hold the unconscious belief that seeing something in a publication makes it fact.

Even when persons tout themselves as 'experts' it was discovered by a task force investigating media and new technology chaired by Luskin and Friedland (1998), that much of what is heard on television and radio and written in various self-help books and articles is 'pop psychology' and may, in fact, have little foundation in empirical research or a true understanding of psychological concepts.

## Media Psychology as a Change Agent

The media are constantly interfacing, perhaps unintentionally, with various disciplines in mental health. In all its forms, the media purvey images of mental illness, create stereotypes and define concepts of mental health and mental illness. Some research has shown that the general public's images of mentally ill persons derive from sources radically different from the images held by mental health professionals (Fischoff, 1996). As already mentioned, the media can enhance psychosocial well-being by giving information; and this can result in destigmatization, mental health promotion, stress reduction and behaviour modification.

Hickling conducted a detailed analysis of 150 recorded segments of his radio psychiatry programme aired between March 1980 and February 1983, including a total of 538 telephone calls and letters. The analysis indicated that a number of psychotherapeutic techniques were used with callers, including: mental status evaluation; contracting; ventilation; catharsis; confrontation; working through; and conflict resolution. The shattering of strongly held myths and belief systems was also a common technique used for providing insight for callers and listeners alike. The programme extensively explored religious, class, gender, political and racial conflicts within the Jamaican people who had lived through the historical conflicts of colonialism. The programme explored these conflicts of the callers, which were often revealed to be unconscious in nature. The programme openly encouraged individual and social change at the national level and advocated the psychotherapeutic model as the paradigm for praxis (_see_ Figure 1).

It was found that most of the calls and letters were from women. The radio psychiatrist spent an average of 12 minutes on each call, and the majority of the callers were single people, domestic helpers, unemployed persons or students. The majority of these callers belonged to the lower-middle to lower class (social class III-V). Based on the psychosocial issues raised by the callers, most were concerned about their own mental health, with symptoms ranging from worry (23%), nervousness and anxiety

(23%), headaches (17%), sadness (17%), and poor relationships or conflicts with spouse or other people (26%). From a diagnostic point of view,
33 per cent of the calls were about anxiety states and depression, 17 per
cent about physical disease, 13 per cent were about personality disorders,
six per cent about psychosexual disorders and six per cent about psychotic disorders. Almost 18 per cent of the callers reported experiencing
socioeconomic problems. The radio psychiatrist was able to make referrals; he referred 37 per cent of the callers to psychiatrists and 23 per cent
to general practitioners or other medical specialists. Nearly 30 per cent of
the calls were resolved on air. Over the four years of the study, certain
psychosocial themes became progressively more important to callers. For
example, emotional and self-image issues increasingly grew in importance, while discussion of religious and class issues became progressively less so (see Table 1).

Table 1: Analysis of the changing themes of the Hickling Radio call-in Programme in
Jamaica, 1980-1983.

|  | 1980 | | 1981 | | 1982 | | 1983 | | TOTAL | |
| --- | --- | --- | --- | --- | --- | --- | --- | --- | --- | --- |
|  | No. | % | No. | % | No. | % | No. | % | No. | % |
| Emotion/ Self-Image | 38 | 12 | 56 | 19 | 98 | 22 | 92 | 18 | 284 | 18 |
| Socio- economic | 45 | 14 | 29 | 10 | 62 | 14 | 78 | 15 | 214 | 13 |
| Self-therapy | 38 | 12 | 39 | 13 | 50 | 11 | 59 | 11 | 186 | 12 |
| Stress, conflict | 27 | 8 | 33 | 11 | 39 | 8 | 61 | 12 | 160 | 10 |
| Family, parenting | 40 | 13 | 31 | 10 | 36 | 8 | 53 | 10 | 160 | 10 |
| Physical problems | 28 | 9 | 22 | 7 | 33 | 7 | 62 | 12 | 145 | 9 |
| Mental illness | 38 | 12 | 28 | 9 | 40 | 8 | 31 | 6 | 137 | 9 |
| Sexual | 25 | 8 | 32 | 11 | 38 | 8 | 33 | 6 | 128 | 8 |
| Medical treatments | 14 | 4 | 15 | 5 | 20 | 4 | 31 | 6 | 80 | 5 |
| Class, religion | 24 | 8 | 9 | 3 |  |  |  |  |  |  |

Discussion of political issues such as racism, colonialism and slavery became progressively more frequent, while discussion of social and economic conditions remained at a consistently high level. It was concluded that radio psychiatry talk-shows of this nature create an approach to primary prevention which may be socially psychotherapeutic in nature. This is so especially if the programmes are aired over many years and the interventions with each caller are intensive and psychoanalytically based, and not restricted by commercial constraints of advertisements and network viability (Hickling, 1992).

_Figure 1: Psychodynamics of the Radio Psychiatry programme._

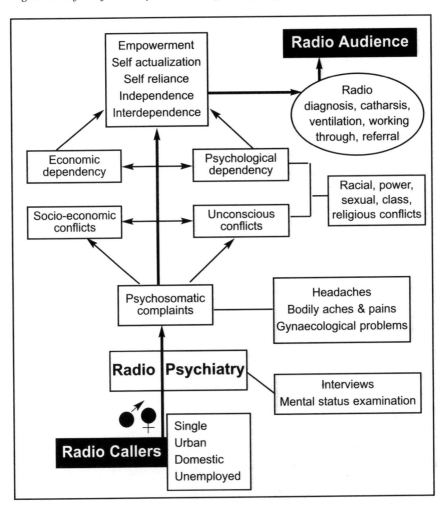

## The Development of Postcolonial Social Psychotherapy

The community work with media in Jamaica in the 1970s has led to the development of a relatively new body of knowledge that has been called *postcolonial social psychotherapy*. This construct arises within the context of European colonization of the New World, where institutions and laws of this colonization have catalyzed socially engineered forms of thinking, feeling and action. This legacy of European social engineering has left wide-ranging psychopathological attributes in the functioning of the colonized peoples. These problems include the breakdown of the family, distortion of psychosexual practices, development of personality disorders and a host of others that have been described in various chapters of this book. In the period of the 1970s in Jamaica, where the political leaders and institutions were struggling to undo this legacy of colonialism (Manley, 1982), fundamental changes were taking place in the island's mental health services (Hickling & Gibson, 2005a). These changes included the development of community mental health services, the deinstitutionalization of the Bellevue Mental Hospital and the psychological transformation of the Jamaican people.

In order to facilitate this psychological transformation, a number of social psychiatric community interventions were pioneered (*see* Figure 2). These included the Radio Psychiatry programme (described earlier), the Cultural Therapy Programme at the Bellevue Hospital (Hickling, 2005; 2007), and The Bellevue Mental Hospital Open-Week. This last was a week-long programme that was launched annually at the mental hospital, where the Jamaican public was invited on guided tours through the facility, and was allowed to view the wards where patients were housed, the vocational activities in which the patients were involved, and the cultural therapy programme in which the patients were participating. Every day, members of staff of the hospital escorted hundreds of Jamaican people in small groups, including scores of school children, to view the various activities and features of the mental hospital. In a society where the mental hospital was viewed as the 'Mad House' and was shrouded with vicious stigma and fantasized mystery, such a community 'soul searching' activity was startling and profound. The sight of clean, immaculately kept hospital wards, patients who were performing orderly and regular work and cultural activities confronted and disabused the stubbornly held myths of madness of the Jamaican people.

_Figure 2:  Jamaican Social Psychiatric Community Stimulators_

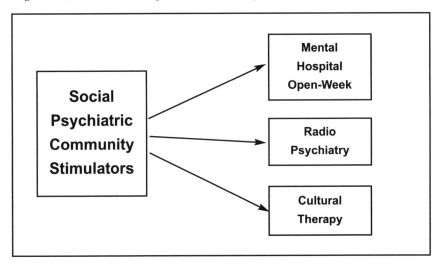

It was clear that the media in Jamaica responded quickly and significantly to such profound changes as were taking place in the mental hospital and in mental healthcare in Jamaica. In 1985, Hickling described the community and media response to these profound changes as _creative social psychotherapy_ (Figure 3). He further suggested that this had to be the new role of the media in the social reengineering process that was taking

_Figure 3:  Model for Creative Social Psychotherapy_

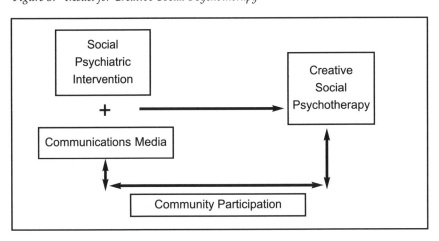

place to confront and challenge the social psychopathology, which was the legacy of European slavery and colonialism.

The graph (Figure 4) illustrates the response of the news media in Jamaica to the community social psychiatry stimulators, and illustrates the potential reader response of the Jamaican people to these events.

*Figure 4: Newspaper response to Community Social Psychiatric stimulators*

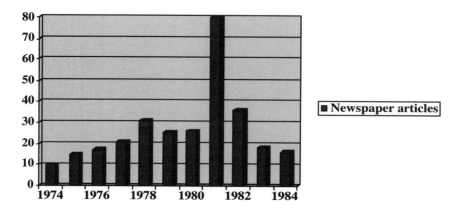

## The Psychological Analysis of Media Representations

A case study of the images and representations in the Jamaican media, specifically the leading daily newspaper, *The Gleaner*, Jamaica's oldest newspaper (established 1834), shows that these same processes have been used to transform individual perceptions of mental illness, the Bellevue Hospital (the country's only mental health hospital) and the process of de-institutionalization of the care of mentally ill persons. A content analysis of mental health-related stories published between January 2003 and March 2005 in *The Gleaner* promoting the de-institutionalization and reintegration of mentally ill persons into their communities, showed that mental health experts interacting with the media in Jamaica had significantly eroded the stigma, shame and inaccurate beliefs attached to the causation of mental illness, which had been hampering attempts by public officials to fully implement psychiatric de-institutionalization. This refers to the shift in the care of mentally ill patients from large psychiatric hospitals to smaller, community-based facilities (Whitley & Hickling, 2007).

Most of the articles acknowledged concerns among the general public regarding the closure of the country's only dedicated mental health hospital, Bellevue; and three arguments/rhetorical devices were frequently used, i.e. articles utilized expert knowledge by quoting the positive views of senior local medical officers; others 'appealed to reason' by quoting statistics and international trends on deinstitutionalization and some engaged in 'lay scientific education' using research findings to show how community treatment was already working in Jamaica and elsewhere. These strategies served to counter fears and to validate the planned closure of Bellevue, rooting the move in sound psychiatric practice with international precedent. The voices of those with expert knowledge in mental health also facilitated the shift in the conceptualization of mental illness held by the public and, therefore, allowed the physical process of deinstitutionalization to begin. The following are two excerpts from _The Gleaner._

> The last giant step in the ongoing policy shift in caring for mentally ill persons is to close down the Bellevue Hospital. But a shift must also take place in the national psyche...controversy is now brewing around the plan to shut down Bellevue...but Professor Hickling [Head of Psychiatry at the University of the West Indies] said that this is a critical step that must be taken to improve the country's mental healthcare and change the national attitude to madness. (February 5, 2003.)

> We have absolutely no intention of discharging anyone to the streets. There is no need to panic. We have never done so and we don't intend to do so. It will be done in an orderly and respectful manner' [said Dr. Irons-Morgan]. Various levels of supervised living arrangements will be made for those that are homeless and this will incorporate vocational and social rehabilitation...in other instances, shelters will be provided. (March 7, 2003.)

As mentioned earlier, the medium of radio in Jamaica was put to similar use in the 1970s – to assault the 'European delusion' (the belief that Europeans 'discovered' Jamaica and that Africans were sub-humans), shift post-colonial images of mentally ill persons and transform draconian European physical methods of treatment (Hickling & Gibson, 2005b).

In conclusion, social learning and priming (Bandura,1977), has been used by the Jamaican media in the establishment of an alliance with mental health experts, which has enabled significant erosion of the stigma, shame and inaccurate beliefs attached to the causation of mental illness and, by extension, the struggle experienced by public officials in their effort to implement psychiatric deinstitutionalization.

## Future of Media Psychology in the Caribbean

Media Psychology is a broad field, and many aspects of the discipline are still in their infancy in the region. The focus of this chapter has been the use and influence of the media on the provision of mental health services. However, the media also exert their presence and influence in entertainment, communication, and information technology. In the USA, for example, the media have come to be an integral part of a variety of social institutions such as schools, hospitals, churches and political and military systems, from both a real and a virtual point of view. According to Fischoff (2005), the media now shape the way news gathering and transmission, advertising, political processes and campaigns, wars, diplomacy, education, entertainment, and socialization are conducted. The effects the media have on these human enterprises are legitimate points of interest on the expanding scope of Media Psychology. Some examples include, first, the recent elevation of 'celebrities' as indicated by huge increases in the amount of time and space devoted to the coverage of their activities or their pop culture products. Another phenomenon related to this is the way in which national and local news programmes have changed so that viewers are less exposed to what directly affects their lives (e.g. global warming) and more and more to what has little or no consequence on their lives (e.g. Paris Hilton goes to jail). Media psychology looks at how "the networks' economic bottom-line directive to make news more entertaining has morphed into the directive to make entertainment more newsworthy." (Fischoff, 2005, p. 6)

Second, bibliotherapy, where patients are given books and other written materials to assist in the understanding of their psychological problems, is a well-known adjunct to therapy. More recently there has been the advent of 'cinema therapy' or 'film therapy', where patients are instructed to view specific movies to help manage their problems (*see* Hesley & Hesley, 2001).

Third, Media Psychology examines the recent tendency in the news towards hours or days of intense media coverage of what are determined to be great tragedies (e.g. the destruction of the World Trade Center in New York), and particularly, the possible adverse effects on viewers and on journalistic ethics. It then suggests ways to keep the public informed without causing additional psychological damage in the process.

Fourth, to combat the decrease in exposure to commercials (caused by the advent of the remote control, the videotape recorder and most recently, TiVo), savvy advertisers have switched to 'product placement', that is, placing a purchasable product conspicuously in a movie (or television programme), and this has proven to be a highly effective way to influence consumers. Finally, as mentioned above, the media transmit entertainment and related diversions (e.g. social bonding) and not just information. Most users of the Internet (both at work and outside) use it for e-mail, shopping, gambling, sex-related activities, games, chat rooms and other fora, and for some, these activities have simply become addictions. One wonders how Caribbean people are being influenced by, and are using the Internet; this is a valid new area of Media Psychology research.

Other areas of interest to Media Psychology that may be of particular relevance to the Caribbean, and that may already be influencing Caribbean people include the following:

1) How they are portrayed in film. Research has shown that people are often offended by how their groups are portrayed, and that different groups take offence at different portrayals and representations. Little research has been done on how Caribbean people feel about their stereotypic portrayal in film (e.g. Rastafarian drug dealers, or persons with 'many jobs'), or the impact of such portrayals on our self-perceptions, or the perception others have of us;

2) The negative effects on our young people of the glorification of violence and risky sexual behaviour, as inflicted by the media. Additionally, the media perpetuates stereotypes such as gender biases, racism, ageism, and so on;

3) The views of the people. Caribbean people hold strong opinions on a variety of issues (e.g. homosexuality, the need for corporal punishment), and have many entrenched behaviours (e.g. failure to use birth control). Campaigns to influence these attitudes and

behaviours have mainly been through 'informing' people about the issues in what are called Public Service Announcements (PSAs), often using local celebrities. However, research has shown that this is a far less effective means of education than bringing these issues into the storylines of fictional programmes like sitcoms, dramas, or soap operas. Many soap operas have begun to do just, that with storylines featuring the disabled, alternative sexual lifestyles, premarital sex and pornography, to name but a few. A pro-social message that is associated with the fate of a beloved character, say on "The Young and the Restless", has a greater chance of being internalized and to cause behaviour change than does an uninspired Public Service Announcement (Fischoff, 2005). Many of these programmes are now shown in the Caribbean, some in prime time, but the impact on attitudes and behaviour has yet to be examined. Moreover, the region has its own such programming that could attempt a more formalized effort at instilling pro-social behaviours;

4) Both the positive and negative aspects that television brings. Like the Internet, it is a window to a wider world, but it can also be an easy escape from learning necessary life skills. For example, research has shown that people who have poor reading skills fall further behind in school because they choose to watch television rather than read books. In the Caribbean, where literacy is already disadvantaged, this is a real problem, which has not been eased by the popularity of radio. Studies have consistently shown that information recall is greater for print media than for television. Is it that, as in the USA, the region's youth is turning away from its best source of information and analysis for understanding critical social issues and turning to a headline-depth source of information, i.e. television? Have the readership rates of local newspapers dropped? Or worse, has the amount of news on Caribbean television programmes dropped both absolutely and in proportion to the amount of time devoted to sport, entertainment and celebrity goings-on, as it has abroad? If so, this reliance on television or radio for transmitting most of our news should be a source of concern for the region. The implications of these changes on maintaining an educated elec-

torate and population are huge, and of major interest to media psychologists. In the USA, recent research has shown that young people between the ages of 14 and 35 are now spending more time surfing the Internet than watching television. Is this major shift in leisure-time activity also going to occur in the Caribbean? And if so, what impact will it have on our youth and the issues raised earlier?

5) The popularity of cellular phones in the Caribbean. With that comes instant messaging, the ability to take pictures and record film clips on the spot and widespread Internet access. What impact will this type of media penetration have, for instance, on crime fighting, word-of-mouth advertising, interpersonal relationships, reading skills, and so on? A big world awaits.

In conclusion, Caribbean adults and children need to become 'media savvy'. Knowing how the media can affect us cognitively, emotionally and behaviourally, and how to prevent the internalization of their message if we want to, is critical for an informed, free society. "Only by understanding how and why mass media influence our lives can we better cope with them and only by coping with them can we change them so that they serve us rather than control us" (Fischoff, 2005, p. 9).

## REFERENCES

American Psychiatric Association (1977). Joint Commission on Public Affairs: Guidelines for psychiatrists working with the communications media. _American Journal of Psychiatry_ 134, 609-611.

American Psychological Association (1981). Ethical principals of psychologists working with the communications media. _American Psychologist_, 36, 633-638.

———. (2002). Ethical principles of psychologists and code of conduct. _American Psychologist_, 57, 1060-1073.

Bandura, A. (1977). _Social learning theory_. London: Pearson Professional.

Benson, E. (2003). Telehealth gets back to basics. _Monitor on Psychology_, 34(6), 58.

Bouhoutsos, J. C. (1983). Media psychology. _The Clinical Psychologist_, 36(2), 32-35.

Bouhoutsos, J. C., Goodchilds, J. D., & Huddy, L. (1986). Media psychology: An empirical study of radio call-in psychology programs. _Professional Psychology: Research and Practice_, 17(5), 408-414.

Canter, D., & Breakwell, G. M. (1986). Psychologists and "the media". _Bulletin of the British Psychological Society_, 39, 281-286.

Cave, R. (1980). Dial Dr. Toni for Therapy. *Time*, 115(21), May 26, 1980.

Fischoff, S. (1995). Confessions of a TV Talk Show Shrink. *Psychology Today*, 28(5), 38-45.

————. (1996). Sources of stereotyped images of the mentally ill. *Journal of Media Psychology*, 1 (1), 4-11.

————. (2005). Media Psychology: A personal essay in definition and purview. *Journal of Media Psychology*, 10 (1), 1-21.

Hesley, J. W,. & Hesley, J. G. (2001). *Rent two films and let's talk in the morning: Using popular movies in psychotherapy*. Indianapolis, IN: Wiley Publishing Inc.

Hickling, F. W. (1985). The role of the communications media in the development of psychiatric services in Jamaica. *Black Psychiatrists of America Quarterly*, 14 (1), 4.

————. (1992). Radio psychiatry and community mental health. *Hospital and Community Psychiatry*, 43 (7), 739-741.

————. (2005). Catalyzing creativity: Psychohistoriography, sociodrama and cultural therapy. In F. W. Hickling & E. Sorel (Eds.), *Images of psychiatry: The Caribbean*. Kingston, Jamaica: Department of Community Health and Psychiatry, University of the West Indies.

————. (2007). *Dream a world: CARIMENSA and the development of cultural therapy in Jamaica*. Kingston, Jamaica: Carimensa.

Hickling, F. W., & Gibson, R. C. (2005a). The history of Caribbean psychiatry. In F. W. Hickling & E. Sorel (Eds.), *Images of psychiatry: The Caribbean*. Kingston, Jamaica: Department of Community Health and Psychiatry, University of the West Indies.

————. (2005b). Philosophy and epistemiology of Caribbean psychiatry. In F. W. Hickling & E. Sorel (Eds.), *Images of psychiatry: The Caribbean*. Kingston, Jamaica: Department of Community Health and Psychiatry, University of the West Indies.

Jamaica Information Service. www.jis.gov.jm/media/index.asp

Larson, C. (1981). Media psychology: New roles and new responsibilities. *APA Monitor*, 12 (12), 3, 7.

Luskin, B. J., & Friedland, L. (1998). *Task Force Report: Media psychology and new technologies*. Encino, CA: Media Analyst Publishing.

Maheu, M. (2001). *E-health, telehealth and telemedicine*. San Francisco: Jossey-Bass.

Manley, M. (1982). *Jamaica: Struggle in the periphery*. London: Third World Media for Writers and Readers.

Rice, B. (1981). Call-in therapy: reach out and shrink someone. *Psychology Today*, 39-41.

Ruben, H. L. (1986). Reflections of a radio psychiatrist. *Hospital and Community Psychiatry*, 37, 934-936.

The Amplifier (2001). *Ethics in telehealth.* Washington D.C.: American Psychological Association, Division 46, p.p. 3-4. Available online at www.apa.org/divisions/div46/images/ampfall01.pdf.

Whitley, R., & Hickling, F.W. (In Press). Open papers, open minds? Media representations of psychiatric deinstitutionalization in Jamaica. *Journal of Transcultural Psychiatry.*

# 24 The Application of Therapeutic Community Principles in Jamaica

*Frederick W. Hickling, Mylie McCallum,*
*Doreth Garvey, & Tracey Coley*

The anarchical rights of the doctor in the traditional hospital society had to be exchanged for the more sincere role of member in a real community, responsible not only to himself and his superiors, but to the community as a whole, privileged and restricted only in so far as the community allows or demands. The doctor no longer owns his patients, they are no longer captive children, obedient in nursery-like activities but have sincere adult roles to play.

*(Main, 1946 cited in Pines, 1999).*

The range of communal and societal responses to those labelled as mentally ill has evolved over time and almost come full circle. In the Caribbean, in the days before Spanish colonization, those considered strange were not separated from the community. They remained in their villages and were seen and treated as regular, though odd, members of the community (Las Casas, 1656). The advent of slavery and British colonial rule led to the institutionalization of those considered 'mad', and at this point in time the definition of 'madness' was often extended not only to those individuals who displayed abnormal behaviour, but also to those slaves who were resistant or difficult to manage.

692

# The Custodial Colonial Mental Hospital

Mental hospitals were established in the Caribbean by the colonial government in the 19th century (Hickling & Gibson, 2005). At that time treatment of the mentally ill was largely custodial. The general idea behind the institutions established at that time is reflected in the traditional psychiatric mental hospitals of today. The institution's stated primary aim was to protect society from the inmates and to enforce isolation. The 1950s brought a change in the perception of psychiatric hospitals. They came to be seen as cold, degrading, prison-like institutions that often led to the dehumanization of both staff and patient. Caudill et al. (1952) and Stanton and Schwartz (1954) in their detailed analysis of the mental hospital, Chestnut Lodge, in the USA, pointed out very clearly that all of the events that occurred in the life of the patient's 24-hour day influenced his mental state in one way or another. For example, if two staff members were in conflict about the treatment of a particular patient, the patient usually showed a worsening of psychotic symptoms. Stanton and Schwartz showed that there was a tendency for physicians to rationalize their day-to-day decisions about patients as being 'therapeutic', although in many cases these decisions were clearly made simply to suit the doctor's convenience, such as altering scheduled therapeutic programmes to suit the doctor's timetable. The features of such institutions, of which Bellevue Hospital in Jamaica or St. Ann's Mental Hospital in Trinidad are examples, are authoritarianism, custodialization and a deadening, desocializing environment. It seems then that the major function of these mental hospitals was to prevent a mentally ill individual from harming himself or others and to ensure that he could not escape. In fact, the original functions of mental hospitals aimed at the therapeutic treatments of the mentally ill, have become modified by the exploitative and manipulative aspects of social organization developed within the total institution – whereby the privileged staff have reorganized the initial agendas of treatment for the mentally ill. It appears that in a long stay custodial institution many patients who are admitted to these hospitals will remain there unnecessarily for many years, yet the outcome of patients who remain in such institutions for a period of several years is stark (Barton, 1959).

## Custodialization and Enforced Idleness

Barton's (1959) critical polemic suggests that features of the custodial institution such as loss of contact with the outside world, enforced idleness, bossiness of staff, loss of personal friends and possessions, poor ward atmosphere and loss of prospects outside the institution lead to a syndrome of 'institutional neurosis'. In a watershed study on institutionalization, Wing and Brown (1970) indicate that there are three factors that are likely to play a part in determining how a person will react to long incarceration in an institution. These include the social pressures that are brought to bear within that institution, the susceptibility or resistance of the individual to these pressures, and the length of time over which these pressures act. Their study was concerned with the adverse effects of a prolonged stay in three selected mental hospitals in the UK on patients with schizophrenia, and the ways in which these effects could be counteracted and prevented. They chose three hospitals with markedly different social conditions and administrative policies. They measured the clinical conditions of randomly selected patients with schizophrenia, the ward behaviour and attitude to discharge of these patients, and compared the social conditions experienced by these patients. The changes that they chronicled for these patients proved that the reduction of *enforced idleness* will reduce the tendency for institutionalism in the patients studied. They further identified that the syndrome of institutionalization is complicated by the fact that the symptoms of absence of emotional response and lack of motivation are common symptoms of schizophrenia, even when the patient has never been admitted to hospital. The authors concluded that a substantial portion of the morbidity shown by long-stay patients with schizophrenia in mental hospitals is a product of their environment. They showed that environmental poverty was very highly correlated with a 'clinical poverty syndrome' consisting of social withdrawal, flatness of affect and poverty of speech. Both environmental and clinical poverty became more intense with length of stay, and they concluded that patients with schizophrenia were vulnerable to an under-stimulating social environment and reacted by increased withdrawal even to such an environment which they had created themselves. The social pressures, which act to produce this extra morbidity they concluded, can to some extent be counteracted, but the process of reform may itself have a natural history and an end. They argued that an attempt could be made to reverse the process in such an environment by appropriate staff action. If the social milieu improved measurably there would be a corresponding decrease in clinical poverty.

## The Total Institution

Goffman's polemic (1961) demonstrated that the barrier to social intercourse with the outside world that exists within the custodial mental hospital symbolizes a social environment that he called the _total institution_. He described that the central features of the total institution reflected the breakdown of the barriers ordinarily separating the three major spheres of life, sleeping, playing and working. In the total institution, all aspects of life are conducted in the same place and under the same single authority. Each phase of the daily activity of the member of the institutional community is carried out in the immediate company of a large batch of other members, all of whom are treated alike, and are required to do the same things together. All phases of the day's activities are tightly scheduled with one activity leading automatically into the next, with a whole sequence of activities being imposed from above by a system of explicit formal rulings in a single rational plan, from a body of officials. Goffman emphasized that one of the key features of the total institution is the handling of large blocks of people by a small bureaucratic organization. The staff and the inmates tend to conceive of each other in narrow hostile stereotypes, while social mobility and communication between the groups are grossly restricted. The inmate reacts to this environment by withdrawal into an inner fantasy life; by rebelling against staff; by accepting humble status and menial roles; by becoming institutionalized, or by undergoing a type of conversion experience in which he or she becomes over-compliant and sycophantic to staff. Others may not commit to any of the above behaviours but devote their time to learning how to expedite their release or escape.

## The Therapeutic Community

The idea of the therapeutic community was born in May 1946 when the Bulletin of the Menninger Clinic published the first collection of papers from Northfield, England (Pines, 1999). Tom Main and Maxwell Jones pioneered and developed the therapeutic community independently of each other but with the same general guiding principles. Tom Main originally coined the concept and put it into practice while working in the Northfield Experiment with ex-prisoners of war during and after World War II (Thomstad, 1991). Maxwell Jones, however, popularized this idea in the 1950s. His enthusiasm and charisma were noted as the driving force of the movement (Rapoport, 1970).

The therapeutic community concept was developed soon after World War II, particularly in relation to the treatment of war neuroses, first in the Social Rehabilitation Unit which was later to become known as the Henderson Hospital in England, and later at Dingleton Hospital in Melrose, Scotland. The idea of the therapeutic community was to introduce what was missing in the psychiatric treatment formulation for the mentally ill. In the therapeutic community, the social structure of the ward is characteristically different from more traditional hospital ward units. Jones believed that altering the typical social structure of the psychiatric hospital and introducing a community environment – involving staff, patients and their relatives in treatment and administration – would create a long-lasting, positive effect on the patients' mental condition (Manning, 1991). There is emphasis on free communication within and between staff and patient groups and on permissive attitudes that encourage free expression of feelings. These factors imply a democratic egalitarian community rather than a traditional hierarchical social organization. In a therapeutic community, traditional mental hospital concepts and behaviour are abandoned, and staff and patient roles and role-relationships are the subject of frequent examination and discussion. The aim of this practice is to increase the effectiveness of roles and to sharpen the community's perception of them. This decentralization, or democratization of authoritarianism, creates an atmosphere, called a *therapeutic culture* by Jones, that emphasizes active rehabilitation, permissiveness and cooperation, and attempts to resocialize institutionalized people into the role of active normal human beings once more.

Jones described the main feature of the organization of a therapeutic community as being the *daily community meeting* whereby the entire patient and staff population of a particular unit would meet daily to work out problems of the day and to ventilate the tensions which, as a matter of course, exist in an organization of this nature. He also outlined an additional approach within the therapeutic community; namely that of the _patient government_ or the _patient council,_ which would be limited to the handling of practical ward details such as privileges, arrangements for ward cleanliness, rosters and so on. The essential principle of the therapeutic community, however, is the reliance on the group dynamic to break down dissension and hostility between staff and patients, in order to increase communication and engender resocialization for all concerned.

_Milieu therapy_ can be defined as the type of treatment in which the patient's social environment is manipulated to provide therapeutic benefit to him or her (Echternacht, 2001). The therapeutic community is one such type of therapeutic process. In the therapeutic community the patient resides in a residential facility or hospital and is exposed to structured activities designed to enhance their connection to the community and promote holistic wellness. This therapeutic modality represents a significant break from traditional modes of treatment of mental illness because of the conscious effort to create the effect of patients as participants in their own treatment rather than as captive inmates in a prison-like setting. There are two major components of the community therapeutic milieu: structured and unstructured (Peplau, 1982). The structured aspect of milieu therapy involves organized activities that in-patients participate in throughout the day – activities such as art therapy, occupational therapy, and drama therapy. The unstructured aspect of the therapeutic milieu entails the interactions among various stakeholders in the therapeutic community, including patients, mental health staff (especially nurses), and family members and friends of the patient (Peplau, 1982; 1989). This aspect of the community milieu therapy, although it rarely receives discussion in the literature (Echternacht, 2001), is of significant importance as these interactions allow the nurses and therapists to view patients in as natural a setting or activity as can be contrived and to observe how their difficulties are manifested. The information garnered from these observations can enhance the therapeutic value and effectiveness of the structured activities. The focus of community therapeutic milieu therapy is not only on the patient; the psychiatric nurses and other mental health workers who come into contact with the patients become apart of the process of initiating and maintaining positive change in the patients.

In summary, the rehabilitation of psychiatric patients involves their resocialization, the restoration of the individual integrity through honourable work, and the maximization of their personal and social self-respect. The key to the rehabilitation process is the recognition of the patient as a person. The essential principles of the process of rehabilitation have been expressed by the Russian psychiatrist, Kabanov (1973), as follows:

1. **The Principles of Partnership** This principle involves motivation and active participation of the patients and trust and cooperation between patients, the therapy team, and the patients' relatives.

2. **The Principle of the Variety of Efforts** This principle assumes the absolute understanding of rehabilitation as a complex process involving patients and therapist in widely different areas. These areas include psychological, occupational, familial and social spheres as well as the spheres associated with the patients' education and leisure time, the influence of hobbies, arts, games and other activities.

3. **The Principle of the Unity of Psychosocial and Biological Methods of Intervention** This is based on the understanding that rehabilitation is not merely a sociological process, but is a clinical process that requires the understanding of its essential physiological and pathophysioloical characteristics for its successful resolution. It is a question of activating and the regulation of restitution and compensation. Rehabilitation and therapy are a single process that can be divided analytically, though not practically, into (a) the individual as a whole (b) the therapy of the illness. Under these headings one must also consider the whole concept of the prevention of mental illness.

4. **The Principle of Stages** This principle can be restated by saying that any therapeutic effort, intervention or measure undertaken may be carried out step by step. Most failures in rehabilitation programmes result from different activities being undertaken simultaneously. For example, if the patient's acute illness is not controlled before attempts are made to place him in a job, then there is a marked likelihood of his failing in the job. Similarly, placement in a job and in new lodgings simultaneously can

result in the patient's inability to cope with either. One can see, therefore, that undertaking one aspect of a rehabilitation pro- gramme without another, dooms the programme to failure. Successful rehabilitation is an all-or-nothing phenomenon. It is a waste of time, effort and money to provide, for example, an industrial rehabilitation unit without an active therapeutic milieu or without an adequate follow-up service.

## The Influence of Psychoanalytic Theory and the Development of Group Psychotherapy

The establishment of the therapeutic community or milieu therapy was heavily influenced by psychoanalytic theory and practice and by changes in the prevailing social views. Psychoanalysis, commonly viewed as the parent of modern day psychotherapy, placed emphasis on an individual- istic assessment of behaviour. The theory minimized the importance of social or inter-relational issues in the manifestation of disordered behav- iour. Trigant Burrow, an American psychoanalyst, viewed this as a seri- ous shortcoming and introduced the study of human behaviour in the group setting (Pines, 1999). Group psychotherapy differs from other types of counselling in terms of its focus on severe emotional, debilitating problems and on long-term treatment (Gazda, 1989). Group psychother- apy is often touted as the most economical use of the professional's time and the patient's money. Mental illness is often a condition that is char- acterized by isolation, induced either by the individual or by society. As a result, these individuals often feel like outcasts in the society. These feel- ings are exacerbated by the often frightening changes that are taking place within the individual. Group psychotherapy offers the opportunity for these individuals to interact with others in an environment that is safe and supportive. Patients are given the opportunity to develop a sense of belonging, which often reduces their sense of isolation. The group also becomes a source of social support. Satisfaction with the system provides the main effect of engendering and increasing both an individual, as well as a collective, sense of well-being and a secondary stress-buffering effect through an increasing sense of value, mastery and problem solving capacity (Leszcz, 1987). The therapeutic community is also a group, and when the therapeutic community is effective it allows the individual's smoother reintegration into the family, community and society.

Particularly salient to group therapy are therapeutic factors such as group cohesion, universality, instillation of hope, interpersonal learning, imparting of information, development of socializing techniques and imitative behaviour. Yalom (1995) views cohesiveness as the culminating product of the energies of the group members and this compels individuals to participate in the group process. Group cohesion is an imperative group therapeutic mechanism, setting the stage for the utilization of all other therapeutic factors. Group members will feel inhibited and withdrawn if they do not feel a sense of unity and comfort with other group members, including the facilitators. The group setting provides the unique opportunity for in-patients to see that they are not alone in their suffering. They meet individuals with similar concerns and are given the opportunity to discuss common issues such as their perception of their illness and the side effects of medication.

Instillation of hope is also a very important therapeutic factor in working with this population. Patients with mental illnesses often fall prey to feelings of hopelessness and frustration because of the debilitating effects of various mental conditions on their mind, body and perception of self. The group experience, which offers exposure to different coping techniques and lifestyle methods, exposes the patients to the realms of possibility. The mentally ill experience social exclusion and stigmatization as no other population does. They are often seen as dangerous, dependent and incapable of making valuable contributions to the ideals that society prizes, such as industry and commerce. In a recent study in Jamaica by Abel et al. (2006) it was found that many people believed that mental illness was actually caused by the individuals and could somehow have been avoided. These stereotypes cripple the natural abilities of this group and lead them to question their own value as members of their family and of the larger society. Group participation allows them to create a world in which they form an integral part. Their contributions are valued and they are able to see themselves and evaluate their behaviour through the eyes of others. They give and receive the sort of constructive feedback that will allow them to change aspects of their behaviour that contribute to their feelings of worthlessness.

## The Open-door Policy

Psychiatric patients have not always been managed in closed systems. As early as the 13th century in Belgium, patients were managed in open wards in general hospitals (Baker et al., 1953). 'Moral treatment' was practised in many asylums in the USA and Europe in the 17th and 18th centuries. By the mid 18th century William Battie pioneered work on openness but this trend towards openness was practically abandoned between 1850 and 1940 (Rubin & Goldberg, 1963) only to be reintroduced at the beginning of the deinstitutionalization era in the 1940s by Stern (1950), Bell (1955), Rees (1957) and others. Various methods have been used in the conversion of closed to open wards, ranging from sudden to gradual approaches (Kim & Eaton 1959). The main conclusion has been that psychiatric ward openness could be achieved and is preferable to custodial environments. Openness varies from the process of unlocking a door without telling anyone about the fact, to a more elaborate procedure of developing a therapeutic community with free access for mental patients. The open-door policy is usually considered to be a vital aspect of a therapeutic community, affirming the milieu values of encouraging democratic participation, enhancing patient dignity and discouraging regression. Openness does not mean lack of controls on the wards or in hospitals but the presence of effective therapeutic measures to manage patients without infringing on their rights to freedom and dignity. While patients may not be physically locked up, in many cases in the current management of psychiatric patients, they are restricted by the use of other type of restraints. Restraints are any physical or pharmacological means used to restrict patients' movement, activity or access to their body (Wigder & Matthews, 2001). In this regard chemical restraints can be seen as restricting patients' movement, and if this is utilized as the least restrictive alternative in managing the psychiatric patient, it can be seen as more humane.

## The Management of Change

The management of the conversion of closed to open wards has been studied internationally in the early years of the implementation of the deinstitutionalization process. Kim and Eaton (1959) described a gradual conversion process and concluded that a closed ward in a general hospital can be opened without additional personnel and without modification of treatment methods or admission policies. In that study, the conversion was planned over a period of a year with staff members being sensitized to the concept and with a gradual opening of the doors eventually taking place. It was reported that the attitude of the patients was generally favourable to the changes, there was no increase in the number of patients leaving without permission and there was no increased use of sedation or other somatic treatments. In this study, also, no additional staff or changes in admission policy was needed. In another experience with openness, Rosenhan (1973) concluded that there was no ideal way of opening a closed ward and that the attitude of the staff was the most important component of its success. Rosenhan, reporting on a comparison of processes used in a locked ward that was converted, and a locked mental hospital that offered easy patient access, found that most people thought that an open hospital was synonymous with freedom, in addition to increased dignity of the patients, which was not a necessary consequence of the process. His study also indicated that there was a sharp difference in openness between large state hospitals and psychiatric units of general hospitals. In the case of the open wards of the mental hospitals, resocialization of chronic schizophrenic patients was greatly facilitated and was also associated with the therapeutic programmes. In the psychiatric units in general hospitals, the support for openness was not as remarkable. The main conclusion was that openness could be achieved only with difficulty, and was related to the development of a therapeutic community which facilitated hospital-to-outside transactions.

## Bellevue Mental Hospital in Jamaica

The Caribbean has applied open-door policies only in recent years and only to a limited extent. All the large Caribbean islands operate custodial mental hospitals, although custodial psychiatric units in general hospitals emerged in the latter half of the 20th century (Beaubrun, 1966). In Jamaica, custodial management was the *modus operandi* of the Bellevue Mental Hospital, as well as the psychiatric units in general hospitals – the University of the West Indies Hospital in Kingston, and the Cornwall Regional Hospital in Montego Bay. Hickling (1975) introduced the therapeutic community and an open-door policy at the Bellevue Mental

Hospital in the 1973, first as a pilot Rehabilitation Unit of 50 beds, then thereafter in the entire hospital. Within the first eight months of operation of the Rehabilitation Unit, 85 per cent of the 72 patients that had been admitted in the period had shown appreciable clinical improvement and 48 patients (67%) had been discharged. Of those discharged, 23 per cent were placed in jobs, and 7 per cent were readmitted within six months. Hickling and Gibson (2005) described the development of the rehabilitation/ deinstitutionalization process in the Bellevue Mental Hospital in the decade of the 1970s. Therapeutic community groups were established on all 24 wards of the mental hospital and were held daily between patients and staff. Vocational programmes and cultural therapy programmes offering arts, drama, dance and music therapy were offered to all patients in the hospital. The resident population fell from 2926 in 1970 to 1600 in 1980, and by 2005 the resident population had fallen to 850, 650 of whom were geriatric patients over the age of 65 who had no homes nor families to which they could be discharged. The therapeutic community policy had achieved a significant positive beneficial impact on the outcome of patient care as well as on the attitudes of staff and patients to psychiatric care.

## The University Hospital of the West Indies, Psychiatric Department

Psychiatry at the University of the West Indies started in 1966 under the leadership of Professor Michael H. Beaubrun with five in-patient beds in the Dermatology Unit of the University Hospital of the West Indies. The Psychiatric Unit at the University Hospital of the West Indies actually began with an open-door policy as the unit shared space with the Dermatology ward on the fourth floor of the specialist block. The common day and tutorial rooms were used as multipurpose areas – patients' sitting and television room, group and occupational therapy areas. There was mutual benefit to patients both for those with dermatological and those with psychiatric disorders. Patients were even managed on the other medical wards, given the limitation of five beds for psychiatric patients (Beaubrun, 1966). A separate, discrete unit of 20 beds was officially opened in 1972, and this provided clinical care for patients of the University Hospital of the West Indies and the teaching facilities for the

Department of Psychiatry of the University of the West Indies. After the new ward was built a closed-door system of custodial management replaced the open-door policy that had been in existence on the Dermatology Ward. This was the therapeutic modality that operated until 2000. Patients frequently complained of being imprisoned, disrespected, bored and treated as if they were children, and the absconder rate of patients escaping from the ward was extremely high. In October of 2000 an Open-door policy and Therapeutic Community was instituted. The Policy had 6 components:

**Component 1 – Opening the main gate of the psychiatric ward** The gate would open for approximately half of the day and this gradually increased to three-quarters of the day. It would be closed after visiting hours in the evenings. A security guard was assigned duties at the entrance of the ward. His duties did not involve any aspect of patient care but were concerned with preventing unwanted intrusion to the ward.

**Component 2 – Clinical grading of patients** Patients were assigned to clinical categories on a scale of 1-8 in which the highest category was ascribed to the most independent patient, while the lowest category was ascribed to the most disturbed patient. In Category 1 the patient was severely disturbed when awake, or heavily sedated, or unconscious, and requiring constant nursing assistance. Patients in Category 4 (mid point) were ambulatory, stabilizing, beginning to be insightful of their abnormal behaviour, and were self-caring.

Patients in Category 6 were discharged from the ward to the community, and were involved in vocational activities. Patients in Category 8 were fully recovered and discharged from the facility. Patients on the ward were assigned specific therapeutic activities based on their clinical status.

**Component 3 – Introduction of the Therapeutic Community Group** The implementation of daily Therapeutic Community Group (TCG) meetings followed in January 2001.The clinical psychologist facilitated these half-hour sessions. Patients and staff sat in a circular formation and patients were given an opportunity to discuss issues relating to their diagnoses and care. The patients were suffering mainly from acute psychotic illnesses and were at different stages of recovery. The group was allowed to 'free associate' with only few attempts being made to lead the discussion. A patient 'Chairperson' was selected at the start of each group meeting, and it was his/her responsibility to facilitate the orderly discussion of the group of patients. In this way, the patients were encouraged to exercise their own authority over the group process and over the maintenance of order and control in the group. The clinical psychologist and the nurses present helped to facilitate this process of leadership and control by the patient Chairperson. Specific topics were sometimes discussed and often the debates were lively and coherent. Because of the attempt to encourage 'peer' pressure by the group and patient leadership, this therapeutic community group often had a remarkable effect on the patients and their recovery. Patient discharge and medication treatment were often topics for discussion and often forced the staff members to operate with transparency and openness in the use of medication and the decisions for discharge. Religious issues were also a popular topic of discussion and often revealed the significant role played by religion in the culture of the Jamaican patients, and sometimes in their psychopathology.

**Component 4 – Art Therapy** The Art Therapy programme was also implemented in January, 2001.The Art tutor engaged patients from categories 4-7 in art related activities, such as simple use of colours, screen printing, tie and dye techniques and sewing. Patients would then discuss their feelings as they engaged in the activities. The completed pieces of patients' art were displayed on the walls of the Day area on the ward.

**Component 5 – Family meetings** Family meetings were implemented in May 2001 as a means of giving expression to relatives' concerns about several aspects of the patient's management. Meetings were conducted once weekly during visiting time and were facilitated by the resident and the nurse on duty. Clarification would be given on issues relating to the patient's diagnosis, treatment, improving compliance and outcome.

**Component 6 – Opening of the Occupational Therapy Centre**

The final component was the re-opening of the Occupational Therapy Centre in June, 2001.This allowed patients in categories 4–7 to take a short walk away from the ward to the Occupational Therapy Centre. The art sessions were transferred to this facility and additional activities such as embroidery and culinary skills were offered. Other activities introduced included music and drama activity and ward outings, which included walks in the 700-acre campus of the University of the West Indies and visits to the nearby Hope Botanical Gardens.

Garvey and Hickling (2001) reported on the attitudes to care and satisfaction with care of patients and staff of the psychiatric unit. Individual unstructured interviews and focus group sessions were conducted with patients and members of staff, both those on the psychiatric ward as well as from other areas of the hospital, about the newly implemented open-door policy and therapeutic community programme. Patients' responses to the Open-door Policy were sampled using the Verona Service Satisfaction Scale (Ruggeri et al., 1994; 1996), which was given first at eight months, and again at 16 months after the implementation of the Policy. The initial response of staff members to the opening of the main gate was one of anger and hostility with acts of passive resistance. Patient response was cautious but favourable, and they soon took advantage of being allowed to leave the ward unaccompanied. Demarcation of the patients into groups of clinical severity soon allowed the staff to rationalize therapeutic activities for the patients. Both staff and patients were cooperative to this change. Implementation of the therapeutic community group meetings had a profound resocializing effect on patients and staff. Finally, the implementation of the art and activity therapy was warmly received by the patients, and proudly acclaimed by the staff. Analysis of the Verona Satisfaction Scores indicated a general acceptance and appreciation by the patients. The general consensus was that the ward atmosphere was positively transformed by the Open-door Policy and the Therapeutic Community Programme, with patients being more satisfied with their care and being less hostile in their interactions with staff. Staff cooperated with the changes, and expressed appreciation of the benefits derived from the process.

A quantitative prospective study of patients admitted after the initiation of the Open-door Policy and the Therapeutic Community Programme between the period October 1, 2000 and August 31, 2002 was carried out and reported by Lowe and Hickling (2003). Patients admitted from October 2000 to September 2001 were followed prospectively for one year. Demographic, clinical and outcome variables were collected and analyzed. Retrospective data from patients who absconded from the unit for the period October 1999 to September 2000 was also collected. The total number of patients studied in the period was N = 277. Of these, 51.3% (N=142) were female and 48.7% (N = 134) male. The mean age was 33.03 ± 13.96 years. Of the cohort, 74% (N = 205) were single and 74.7% (N = 207), were diagnosed as having an acute psychotic illness. The mean length of stay was 11.923 ± 10.326 days. Marijuana was the substance of abuse in 23.5% (N = 65) of the patients. There was no significant difference in the rate of absconding during the period of admission during the Open-Door period (F = 1.76, df =20, p = 0.0926 n.s.) as compared to the period of admission when the doors were kept closed. Two hundred and sixteen (78%) were discharged to the hospital out-patient clinics. On discharge, 96% (N = 267) were placed on oral maintenance pharmacological therapy, with 15.6%, (N= 43) on long-acting intramuscular antipsychotic therapy. Thirty-five (12.7%) of the cohort had relapsed during the one-year period following discharge, while 26 (9.4%) had been readmitted. The Open-Door model of managing acute psychiatric patients was efficient and effective.

## Combating the Locked Ward (Custodialization) in Jamaica

Openness may not have the same meaning everywhere. As mentioned previously, in psychiatric hospitals openness varies from the process of unlocking a door without telling anyone about the fact to a more elaborate procedure of developing a therapeutic community with free access for mental patients. An editorial report in the *Lancet* (1954) suggested that in some mental hospitals when opening of the doors was attempted, severe mentally ill patients were transferred to closed wards, or areas of the ward would be left closed to be used for more disturbed patients. Others, including violent patients were not admitted to some facilities, implying that although psychiatric management had changed from custodial care, openness ranged from a partial to an absolute state. The open-door policy is usually considered to be a vital aspect of a therapeutic community, affirming the milieu values of encouraging democratic participation, enhancing patient dignity and discouraging regression. What needs to be emphasized is that openness does not mean lack of controls on the wards or in hospitals but the presence of effective therapeutic measures to manage patients without infringing on their rights to freedom and dignity. Although a closed-door policy is seen as anti-therapeutic, promoting regression and breeding patients' mistrust, some authors in the earlier stages of the discourse suggested that there was no evidence that maintaining either open or closed doors has any significant impact on treatment outcome (Abroms, 1973). The evidence that has emerged in recent years indicate quite unequivocally that open doors in a mental health unit have significant beneficial therapeutic effect, and that the closed system was a crude, impersonal and undifferentiated therapeutic technique which had an undesirable human impact.

At a Caribbean Psychiatric Association (CARPA) meeting held in Ocho Rios, Jamaica in October 2000, the Keynote lecture was delivered by Professor Ezra Griffith, Barbadian psychiatrist from Yale University, on the topic of seclusion and restraint in the USA. He emphasized the right of patients to be free of restraints, that restraints should be used in emergency context only, and to prevent injury to self or others. He also highlighted the fact that restraints impinged on the dignity and autonomy of the patient; that restraints and seclusion should never be used as punishment or for the convenience of the staff, and that use of restraints involves potential medical and psychological risks both to patient and staff (Griffith, 2000). The lively debate that ensued reviewed the use of seclusion and restraint in the Caribbean. It emerged that the mental hospitals in Barbados and Jamaica still used seclusion rooms. It was noted that the use of seclusion rooms at the Bellevue Hospital disappeared in the 1970s during the period of the implementation of the therapeutic community, and then returned in the 1980s on the return to custodialization. There was a constant battle with the nurses to open up the wards at the Bellevue Hospital. It was an ideological struggle to change the policy in the ward from maximum seclusion being offered by the walls to that offered by staff-patient interaction.

Hickling and Gibson (2005) described the development of the general hospital psychiatric unit programme at Cornwall Regional Hospital in Montego Bay, and at the University Hospital of the West Indies in Kingston, both of which began with a custodial policy of care. They described the simultaneous development of the treatment of patients with acute psychoses in the open medical wards of general hospitals across Jamaica, which accounted for more than one-half of all acute psychiatric admissions in the country. This extraordinary public policy situation in Jamaica presented a unique opportunity to evaluate the benefits of open care versus custodial care. Hickling et al. (2000), comparing the admissions and outcomes of first contact patients who were suffering from schizophrenia on the open general medical wards in Jamaica, with those admitted to the custodial psychiatric units in the general hospitals or to the custodial wards of the mental hospital had a superior clinical outcome one year after discharge relative to length of stay, absconding, relapse rate, and clinical status. The patients treated in the open medical wards of the general hospitals had shorter hospital stay, greater outpatient compliance with appointments and greater potential for gainful employment after discharge. These patients were also much less stigmatized and were more openly received by their families and communities after discharge. Hickling, Abel and Garner (2003) in *A Systematic Review for the Cochrane Schizophrenia Library* noted:

> ...As international healthcare policy has moved away from treating people with severe mental illness in large inpatient psychiatric institutions, beds for people with acute psychiatric disorders are being established in specialised psychiatric units in general hospitals. In developing countries, however, limited resources mean that it is not always possible to provide discrete psychiatric units, either in general hospitals or in the community. An alternative model of admission, used in the Caribbean, is to treat the person with acute psychosis in a general hospital ward. The Caribbean practice of treating people with severe mental illness on general medical wards has been influenced by socio-economic factors rather than evidence from randomised trials. This practice affords an opportunity for a well designed, well conducted and reported randomised trial, now impossible in many other settings...

## Resistance to Change

The problems of resistance to change associated with individual and group psycho-sociological processes have been well documented as a major and significant part of these processes (Yalom, 1995). The resistance to the implementation of the therapeutic community programmes in psychiatric treatment institutions has been described (Hickling 1989; 1995) but not studied empirically until recently. In the case of the Bellevue Mental Hospital, the process of resistance was triggered by the labour relation dispute of the nursing staff in 1978 described by Hickling (1989). The labour dispute of 1978 led to a legal Commission of Enquiry that ruled that the therapeutic community change processes being implemented at the mental hospital were legal and appropriate, and the striking nurses were reprimanded and ordered back to work. This forced the resistance underground, only for it to re-emerge through the national political processes that were heralded by the change of Government in Jamaica following the General Election in 1980 (Hickling & Gibson, 2005). Within two years of the change of Government, the administrative leadership of the Bellevue Mental Hospital was removed and replaced with the nurses who had led the dispute a few years previously in 1978. This change in nursing and medical leadership led to an immediate cessation of the therapeutic community processes, and a return to the custodial processes instituted in the colonial period. Twenty-five years later, the custodial processes still remain entrenched in the Bellevue Mental Hospital with little traces of the therapeutic community principles that had been instituted in the 1970s.

The experience in the transformation process in the 20-bed Psychiatric Unit of the University Hospital of the West Indies twenty years later replicated elements of the resistance process seen in the Bellevue Mental Hospital two decades previously. The implementation of the therapeutic community meetings and principles, and the open-door policy were seriously challenged and undermined by the staff of the Unit, and would have completely disappeared had a murder of one of the patients not occurred on the Ward in 2003. As a result, the nursing leadership and administration were completely restructured and revamped by the hospital administration, and the therapeutic community principles integrated into the operational nursing principles and guidelines of the hospital. As mentioned above, therapeutic groups were organized and institutionalized in the psychiatric ward around targeted issues that had therapeutic benefit for the inpatients. The groups were designed to help patients make sense of and cope with the experience of being in an inpatient facility and being separated from all that was familiar and therefore comforting. One of the principal techniques was to build on the sense of shared community between inmates and encourage cohesion. Various types of group experiences were offered on the ward, experiences that sought to achieve and enhance particular skill sets that have been found to be deficient in inpatients on an acute psychiatric unit. Clinical and staffing responsibilities were redefined, and under restructured strong leadership the therapeutic community principles were re-instituted. In spite of continued but diminishing resistance to the programme the policies have taken root and have become firmly established in the ward culture and remain effective at the present, in spite of significant political changes that have occurred in the hospital and in the country. Unlike the previous initiative in 2001 and 2002 to evaluate the clinical outcome of patients treated in this therapeutic community programme, the present process implemented in 2004 has not yet been clinically evaluated and the survival of this process remains to be seen.

## REFERENCES

Abel, W. H., Porter, S. K. Hamil, H. K. White, S. A., & Hickling, F. W. (2006). Knowledge of traditional and non-traditional treatment of mental disorders. *West Indian Medical Journal*, 55 (4), 32.

Abroms, G. M. (1973). The open-door policy: A rational use of controls. *Hospital and Community Psychiatry*. 24 (2), 81-84.

Anderson, J., & Kayner, D. (1995). Milieu issues in the treatment of a person with chronic fatigue syndrome on an inpatient psychiatric unit. *Journal of the American Psychiatric Nurses Association*, 1, 12.

Beaubrun, M. H. (1966) (Unpublished). A Community Mental Health Pilot Project for the West Indies. Department of Psychiatry, University College Hospital, Mona, Jamaica.

Baker, A. A, Jones, M., & Merry, J. (1953). A community method of psychotherapy. *British Journal of Medical Psychology*. 26, 222-244.

Barton, R. (1959). *Institutional neurosis*. Bristol: Wright.

Battie, W. A. (1963). Treatise on Madness, London, 1758. In B. Rubin & A. Goldberg (Eds.), An investigation of openness in the psychiatric hospital. *Archives of General Psychiatry*, 8, 269-276.

Bell, G. M. (1955). A mental hospital with open doors. *International Journal of Social Psychiatry*, 1, 42- 48.

Caudill, W., Redlich, F. C., Gilmore, H. R., et al. (1952). Social structure and interaction processes in a psychiatric ward. *American Journal of Orthopsychiatry*, 22, 314-318.

Crouch, W. (1998). The therapeutic milieu and treatment of emotionally disturbed children: Clinical application. *Clinical Child Psychology and Psychiatry*, 3, 115-129.

Echternacht, M. (2001). Fluid group: Concept and clinical application in the therapeutic milieu. *Journal of the American Psychiatric Nurses Association, 7*, 39.

Garvey, D. M., & Hickling, F. W. (2001). Attitudes of patients and staff to the implementation of an open door policy in a psychiatric unit of a general hospital [Abstract]. *West Indian Medical Journal*, 50 (Suppl 5), 20.

Gazda, G. (1989). *Group counseling: A developmental approach* (4th Ed.). Boston: Allyn and Bacon.

Griffith, E. (2000). Lecture: Seclusion and restraints in the USA. Caribbean Psychiatric Association Symposium. Unpublished.

Goffman, E. (1961). *Asylums: Essays on the social situation of mental patients and other inmates*. New York: Anchor.

Hickling, F. W. (1975). The establishment of rehabilitation service at Bellevue Mental Hospital, Jamaica and an analysis of the first six months of that service. Ph. D. Diss, Department of Psychiatry, University of the West Indies.

———. (1995). Community psychiatry and deinstitutionalization in Jamaica. *Hospital and Community Psychiatry* 159, 817-821.

Hickling, F. W., McCallum, M., Nooks, L., & Rodgers-Johnson, P. (2000). Treatment of acute schizophrenia in open general medical wards in Jamaica. *Psychiatric Services*, 51, 659-663.

Hickling, F. W, Abel, W., & Garner, P. (2003). Open general medical wards versus specialist psychiatric units for acute psychoses. Cochrane Database of Systematic Reviews, 1, Art. No.: CD003290. DOI: 10.1002/14651858. CD003290.

Hickling, F., & Gibson, R. (2005). The history of Caribbean psychiatry. In F. Hickling & E. Sorel (Eds.), *Images of psychiatry: The Caribbean*. Kingston: Dept. of Community Health and Psychiatry, University of the West Indies.

Kabanov, M. M. (1973). *The principles of psychiatric rehabilitation*. New York: National Academy of Neurological Science.

Kim, K., & Eaton, M.T. (1959). Experiences in the conversion of a closed to an open psychiatric ward in a general hospital. *American Journal of Psychiatry*, 116, 74-76.

*Lancet*, 1954. Freedom in mental health. Nov. 6: 964 – 966.

*Lancet*, 1954. The unlocked door. Nov. 6: 953 –954.

Las Casas (1656) History of the Indies 1559. Madrid 1875. Historia de las Indies (Edición de Augustin Millares y estudio preliminario de Lewis Hanke). Mexico City: Fondo de Cultura Economica (1951).

Leszcz, M. (1987). Group psychotherapy with the elderly. In J. Sadavoy & M. Leszcz (Eds.), _Treating the elderly with psychotherapy: The scope for change in later life_. Madison, CT: International University Press.

Lowe, G. A., & Hickling, F. W. (2002). Evaluation of the effects of an open-door-policy on the clinical outcome of patients treated in a psychiatric ward of a general hospital. _West Indian Medical Journal_, 51 (Suppl. 2), 30.

Manning, N. (1991). Maxwell Jones and the therapeutic movement: A sociological view. _The Journal of the Association of Therapeutic Communities_, 12 (2), 83-97.

Peplau, H. E. (1982, October). Some ideas about nursing in the psychiatric milieu. Paper presented to nursing staff at Boulder Psychiatric Institute.

———. (1989). The history of milieu as a treatment modality. In A. O'Toole & S. Welt (Eds.), _Interpersonal theory in nursing practice – Selected works of Hildegard E. Peplau_. New York: Springer.

Pines, M. (1999). Forgotten pioneers: The unwritten history of the therapeutic community movement. _The Journal of the Association of Therapeutic Communities_, 20, 1.

Rapoport, R. (1970). A new era in psychiatry. _Social Science and Medicine_, 3, 407-12.

Rees, T. P. (1957). Back to moral treatment and community care. _Journal of Mental Science_,103, 303-313.

Rosenhan, D. L. (1973). On being sane in insane places. _Science_, 179, 250-258.

Rubin B., & Goldberg A. (1963). An investigation of openness in the psychiatry hospital. _Archives of General Psychiatry_, 8, 269-276.

Ruggeri, M., Dall 'Angola, R., Agostini, C., & Bisoffi, G. (1994) Acceptability, sensitivity and content validity of the VECS and VSSS in measuring expectations and satisfaction in psychiatric patients and their relatives. _Social Psychiatry and Psychiatric Epidemiology_, 29 (6), 265-76.

Ruggeri, M., Dall' Agnola, R., et al. (1996). Factor analysis of the Verona Service Satisfaction Scale – 82 and development of reduced versions. _International Journal of Methods in Psychiatry Research_, 6 (1), 23-38.

Stern, E. S. (1950). Operation sesame. _Lancet_, 1, 577-578.

Stanton, A. & Schwartz, M. (1954). _The mental hospital_. New York: Basic Books.

Thomstad H. (1991). Møte med det terapeutiske samfunn og dets skapere. (A meeting with the Therapeutic Community and its creators. A personal retrospect.) _Tidsskr Nor Lægeforen_, 111, 1019–22.

Wigder, H. N., & Matthews, M. S. (2001). Restraints. E-medicine website. Http://www.emedicine.com/emerg/topic776.htm.

Wing, J. K., & Brown, G. W. (1970). _Institutionalism and schizophrenia. A comparative study of three mental hospitals, 1960-1968_. London: Cambridge University Press.

Yalom, I. (1995). _The theory and practice of group psychotherapy_ (4th Ed.). New York: Basic Books.

# Index

and, 8, 9; schizophrenia in adolescent, 56-57
Black Power Movement, 21-22, 38
Black women. *See* Women.
Blacks: and paranoia, 27; and self-hatred, 37, 38
Black Child Rearing Practices Report, 190
Block Design subtest: use of the, 644
Brain development: in the early years, 175-177
Britain. *See* United Kingdom.
British colonisation: sexuality and, 365
British Psychological Association: role of the, 500
British Virgin Islands: domestic violence in, 413
Bobo Shanti, 20
Boundaries: concept of, 103
Boys: sexual abuse of, 426
Buggery law: in Jamaica, 371-372

Capital offences: forensic psychology and, 662
Caregivers: coping strategies of, 122
Caribbean: adoption opportunities in the, 170-171; anal and oral sex in the, 380-381; child abuse in the, 418-430; court system, 656-663; culture, 28-29; culture and psychotherapy in the, 542-545; development psychology in infants in the, 163-197; domestic violence in the, 413-430; evolution of sexual behaviour in the, 360-388; fertility rates in the, 170-171; forensic psychology in the, 653-670; and homosexuality, 370-376; language research among children in the, 616-617; measurement of psychopathology in the, 224-245; media psychology in the, 675-689; mental health laws in the, 653-664; participation motivation in the, 568-572; psychotherapy structure in the, 547-555; psychological abuse of children in the, 427-428; psychology, 498-515; psychology and HIV and AIDS in the, 289-332; race in the, 13-16; sickle cell in the, 172; suicide in the, 431; swinging in the, 382; violence in the, 393-450
Caribbean athletes: and the attribution theory, 579-580
Caribbean children: motor development in, 176

Caribbean family structure, 94-96, 185-189; assessment of the, 107-108; slavery and, 7-9
Caribbean father: and the parenting role, 187
Caribbean identity: features of, 3, 28-29; psychocultural challenges and the, 26-27, 50-52
Caribbean Network of Seropositives (CRN+), 319, 324
Caribbean Symptom Checklist: development of the, 227, 229, 231, 233-245; factor loadings for behavioural and emotional problems, 246-253
CARICOM: and homosexuality, 373-374; and creation of a psychosocial network, 322-324; violence in 398-399
Carnival: and Caribbean identity, 28; and sexuality, 376-378
Carnival mentality: in Trinidad and Tobago culture, 135, 140, 142, 145-146, 149, 150
Carrington, Vernon: and the Twelve Tribes sect, 20
Cartesian dualism: concept of, 6; race and, 10-11
Case: neo-Piagetian theory, 179
Case approach: in psychological assessment reports, 638-639
Case study: on Afro-Chinese male, 62-63; on 32-year-old Afro-Chinese woman, 44; on Bernard and Sandra, 519-520; on 16-year-old Black girl, 41; 38-year-old Black farm labourer, 43; on 32-year-old Black female, 60; on 30-year-old Black man, 47-48; on 30-year-old Black woman, 49; on brown-skinned woman, 38; on Christina, 531-532; on 534; death row inmates, 532; on Ernest, 521-522; on 25-year-old middle class female, 45; on Jeanne, 529-531; on Max and Abby, 525-526; on mark and Colette, 527-529; on Orlando and Dale, 522-525; on 41-year-old professional brown-skinned male, 59; on risk and resilience, 80-81; on Rudolph, 534-536; on secrets of success, 75-76, 81-82; on 23-year-old social class III Black male, 56-57; on white female, 34; on white male, 33-34
Centre for HIV/AIDS Research Education and Service (CHARES), 319, 321
Centre for International Education: and the CASS scholarship programme, 72-74

# Contributors

**Wendel D. Abel,** MBBS, Dip (Psych), MPH, DM, is currently the Head of the Section of Psychiatry in the Department of Community Health and Psychiatry at the University of the West Indies, Mona. His special areas of research include community mental health and mental health policy and programme development within the Caribbean region.

**Carlotta Arthur,** PhD, Program Officer, The Andrew W. Mellon Foundation, USA, is a clinical psychologist who has interests in psychological stress and health and the stigma of mental illness in the African Diaspora.

**Jacqueline Benn,** BSc, MSc, is a clinical psychologist at the Psychiatric Hospital in Black Rock, St Michael in Barbados. Her interests include forensic psychology, interpersonal relationships, and male-female relationships.

**Stacey N. Brodie-Walker,** PhD, is a lecturer in the Department of Sociology, Psychology and Social Work at the University of the West Indies, Mona. Her areas of interest consist of adolescent development, juvenile delinquency and conduct disorder.

**Orlean Brown Earle,** PhD, is a child psychologist and family therapist. She is also an Associate Professor at the Northern Caribbean University. Her research interests include child abuse prevention and children with special needs.

**Karen Carpenter,** PhD, is a psychologist and Florida Board Certified clinical sexologist. She currently conducts psycholinguistic research at the University of the West Indies, Mona.

**Sophia Chandler,** BSc, MEd, MSc, is a clinical psychologist who currently works as an educational psychologist in the Department of Education Services with the Cayman Islands Government. Her research interests include media psychology, child protection, child abuse prevention, and risk reduction.

**Tracey Coley,** MA, MS Ed, is a final year PhD candidate in the Clinical Psychology programme at the University of the West Indies, Mona.

**Claudette Crawford-Brown,** BSc, MSW, PhD, has been a lecturer in social work at the University of the West Indies, Mona for the past 26 years. Her interests have mainly been in the area of child welfare and child advocacy, including issues such as street and working children, child abuse, children of migration, in particular those left behind, and the impact of violence on children.

**Avril Daley,** MS, PhD, is a lecturer at the Mico University College and the University of the West Indies, Mona, lecturing in special education and child health, respectively. Her special areas of interest include behavioural disorders and violence.

**Barrington Davidson,** PhD, is the co-founder and Chief Executive Officer of Family Life Ministries. He is currently a part-time lecturer in the Department of Sociology, Psychology and Social Work at the University of the West Indies, Mona. Since 1981, Dr. Davidson has counselled many couples, adults, adolescents, and families, and has assisted them in resolving personal and relational problems.

**Hubert Devonish,** PhD, is a Professor of Linguistics at the University of the West Indies, Mona. He has researched and published in the areas of creole linguistics and language policy in the Caribbean.

**Ruth Doorbar,** PhD, was a clinical psychologist who relocated her clinical practice from Park Lane, New York USA, to Port Antonio Jamaica in 1974. She worked for 32 years in Jamaica in private practice, as well as with the Ministry of Health and with the Ministry of Justice before her passing in 2006.

**Kena Douglas,** BSc, MSc, is the Dean of the Faculty of Education at the College of Agriculture, Science and Education (CASE). Her special interests include child development and educational administration.

**Doreth Garvey,** BSc, MBBS, DM, is the Regional Psychiatrist in the Southern Regional Health Authority in Jamaica. Her research interests are in the areas of community health, and child and adolescent mental health.

**Roger C. Gibson,** MBBS, MPH, DM, is a lecturer and consultant psychiatrist in the Department of Community Health and Psychiatry at the University of the West Indies, Mona. He has a special interest in social issues and how these impact on mental health and illness.

**Sharon-Ann Gopaul-McNicol,** BSc, MA, MSc, MEd, PhD, is a psychologist and for-mer Professor of Howard University whose research interests include all areas in assessment and treatment with Caribbean populations.

**Elaine Gordon** is currently working towards her doctorate in clinical psychology. She has practised in this area in both the UK and Jamaica and is especially interested in substance abuse rehabilitation and mental health issues affecting youth.

**Allison Harrisingh-Dewar,** Bsc, Msc, is a clinical psychologist currently pursuing studies towards a doctorate in education. Her areas of interest include personality disorders and test anxiety in students.

**Tamika Haynes-Robinson,** PhD, is a clinical psychologist and is currently the Clinical Director of the Mico CARE Centre in Kingston Jamaica. Her research interests include neuropsychology with emphasis on traumatic brain injuries, sexuality, and cognitive rehabilitation.

**Frederick W. Hickling,** DM, MRCPsych (UK), FRSM, is a Professor of Psychiatry in the Department of Community Health and Psychiatry at the University of the West Indies, Mona. He helped to establish a unique community psychiatric service in Jamaica and to pioneer the original cultural therapy technique of psychohistoriog-raphy in the 1970s. His research interests include African-Caribbean mental health, political psychology, schizophrenia, community psychiatry and psychotherapy.

**Caryl James,** BSc, MSc, is currently a PhD candidate in clinical psychology at the University of the West Indies, Mona. Her research interests include traditional medicine and Western medicine, phenomenology of psychiatric patients' lived experiences, sexuality and body image, eating disorders and culture and self.

**Rosemarie Johnson,** PhD, is a clinical psychologist and lecturer in the Department of Sociology, Psychology and Social Work at the University of the West Indies, Mona. She is a certified master practitioner and trainer of neuro-linguistic programming, time empowerment techniques and hypnosis. Her interests include the validation of clinical assessment tools and intervention strategies, burnout and stress.

**Akleema Kalpoo,** BSc, is currently a Guidance Officer in the Student Support Services Division of the Ministry of Education in Trinidad. Her research interests includ suicide, depression, self-esteem and mental health.

**Katija Khan,** BSc, MSc, is a PhD candidate and Teaching Fellow in the Clinical Neuroscience Centre at the University of Hull in England. Her research interests include cross-cultural assessment, HIV/AIDS, Alzheimer's disease and dementia.

**Clement T. M. Lambert,** BA, PhD, is a lecturer in the Institute of Education at the University of the West Indies, Mona. His areas of interest include violence in schools and violence prevention, media literacy, Jamaican literary initiatives and curriculum development.

**Michael C. Lambert,** PhD, is a licensed psychologist with 3-C Family Services and a Senior Researcher with the 3-C Institute for Social Development based in North Carolina, USA.

**Hari D. Maharajh,** BSc, MBBS, MRC Psych, Dip. Neuro, LLB, CMT, FRC Psych, is a senior lecturer in Psychology, Psychiatry and Neurology at the University of the West Indies, St Augustine Campus, Trinidad. His research interests include adolescent problems, transcultural psychiatry, substance abuse, depression and psychotherapy.

**Leapetswe Malete,** PhD, is a senior lecturer and the Deputy Director in the Office of International Education and Partnerships at the University of Botswana.

**Jacqueline Martin,** BSc, MBBS, DM, is the Senior Registrar in the Department of Psychiatry at the University Hospital of the West Indies. Her special areas of research include personality disorders, depression and suicide.

**Brigitte K. Matthies,** PhD, is a licensed clinical psychologist with over 15 years experience in teaching, conducting research and practising both in Jamaica and the USA. She is currently an assistant professor of Psychology at California State University, Los Angeles, where she coordinates the Marriage and Family Therapy Program, and is the Director of the Psychology Clinic.

**Mylie McCallum,** RN, RMN, MScN, is the Mental Health Programme Director at the University Hospital of the West Indies and an associate lecturer at the University of the West Indies, Mona. Her research interests include community mental health, adolescent schizophrenia and policy and programme development.

**Julie Meeks Gardner,** BSc, Dip (Nutr), PhD, is the head of the Child Development Centre, and Director of the Consortium for Social Development and Research for the University of the West Indies Open Campus. Her special areas of interest include issues of child development in the developing world, including nutritional deficiencies, the development of aggressive behaviour and the effects of violence.

**Kai Morgan,** BS, MS, PsyD, is currently a lecturer in the Department of Community Health and Psychiatry at the University of the West Indies, Mona. She is also a consultant at the Department of Psychiatry, University Hospital of the West Indies. Her research interests include sports psychology, cross-cultural psychology, personality disorders and sexuality.

**Keisha-Gaye N. O'Garo,** PsyD, is a clinical psychologist based at the Womack Army Medical Center in North Carolina. Her interests include body image disturbance, chronic pain, weight management, and multicultural education.

**Franklin Ottey,** MBBS, DPM, DM, is a consultant psychiatrist and a part-time lecturer in the Department of Community Health and Psychiatry at the University of the West Indies, Mona. His main research interest is in community mental health.

**Audrey Pottinger,** PhD, is a senior lecturer and consultant psychologist at the University Hospital of the West Indies. Her research interests include loss, trauma and reproductive health psychology.

**Marina Ramkissoon,** MSc, is currently a lecturer and the Undergraduate Coordinator of psychology at the University of the West Indies, Mona. She is currently pursuing her PhD in the area of barriers to organizational learning and is also an editor of the *Caribbean Journal of Psychology*. Ms. Ramkissoon is interested in a wide range of research areas including child shifting, organizational learning, work motivation, self efficacy, wellness, race and ethnicity

**Hilary Robertson-Hickling,** PhD, is a lecturer in Human Resources Management, in the Department of Management Studies at the University of the West Indies, Mona. Her research interests include migration and mental health and other health systems management, migration of the health workforce, and cultural therapy.

**Maureen Samms-Vaughan,** MBBS, DM, PhD, is a Professor of Child Health, Child Development and Behaviour at the University of the West Indies, Mona, as well as a developmental and behavioural paediatrician with the University Hospital of the West Indies. Her research interests have focused on the comprehensive identification of factors influencing children's development through childhood.

**Lester O. Shields,** PhD, is a counsellor at the University of the West Indies, Mona Health Centre and also the President of the Jamaica Psychological Society. His main research interest is in psychopathy.

**Eulalee Thompson,** MSc, PG Dip, is a media psychologist as well as the editor of the weekly Health feature in the *Daily Gleaner* newspaper. She is also a group facilitator with the community mental health residential facilities in Kingston. Her special areas of research and interest include psychotraumatology; psychotherapy in seriously mentally ill clients and media as a behaviour change agent in mental health.

**Tony Ward,** BSc, PGDip, MSc, PhD, is the Head of Psychology and Counselling at the Newman University College. His research interests include psychotherapy with neurological populations, psychological approaches to myalgic encephalopathy.

**Peter D. Weller,** BSc, MSc, PhD, is a psychologist/counsellor with the University of the West Indies, Mona Health Centre Counselling Unit. He is also the Convenor of the Caribbean Male Action Network (CariMAN) Initiative. His research interests consist of behaviour change targeted interventions, HIV/AIDS prevention and care, sexual behaviour, and health promotion, masculinity/gender, gender-based violence and parenting.

**Rob Whitley, PhD,** is a research sociologist and anthropologist. He is currently Associate Professor in the Department of Psychiatry at Dartmouth Medical School in New Hampshire, USA. His areas of interest include transcultural psychiatry, community mental health and substance abuse.

**Sharon Williams Brown,** BSc, Dip Ed, MA, is a counselling psychologist and is currently a counsellor at the University Health Centre at the University of the West Indies, Mona. Her areas of interest include anxiety disorders, peer counsellor training, and academic difficulties at the tertiary level.